AMERICAN GOVERNMENT

★

Freedom and Power

BRIEF FIFTH EDITION

THEODORE J. LOWI

CORNELL UNIVERSITY

BENJAMIN GINSBERG

THE JOHNS HOPKINS UNIVERSITY

W · W · NORTON & COMPANY NEW YORK · LONDON

The text of this book is composed in Palatino
with the display set in Caslon.
Composition by TSI Graphics
Manufacturing by Maple-Vail Book Manufacturing
Book design by Jack Meserole
Cover photograph © Joel Gordon 1998

Library of Congress Cataloging-in-Publication Data
Lowi, Theodore J.
American government: freedom and power / Theodore J. Lowi,
Benjamin Ginsberg. — Brief 5th ed.
p.   cm.
Includes bibliographical references and index.
ISBN 0-393-97190-2 (pbk.)
1. United States—Politics and government.   I. Ginsberg,
Benjamin.   II. Title.
JK271.L68   1998b
320.473—dc21   97-38518

W. W. Norton & Company, Inc.
500 Fifth Avenue, New York, N.Y. 10110

W. W. Norton & Company Ltd.
10 Coptic Street, London WC1A 1PU
www.wwnorton.com
2 3 4 5 6 7 8 9 0

Contents

PART 2

INSTITUTIONS

5 Congress: The First Branch 103

Preface to the Brief Edition

In the years since the original publication of *American Government: Freedom and Power,* the world has changed in a number of surprising ways. Symbolized by the destruction of the Berlin Wall, the Soviet Union has collapsed, Russia has been compelled to seek economic aid from the West, and the cold war that once seemed to threaten the survival of civilization has come to an end. In the Middle East, the United States fought a short but decisive war against Iraq and is now leading a diplomatic initiative that may, after fifty years of violence, bring about some solution to the problems of the Middle East. In South Africa, the hated system of apartheid has disintegrated in the face of domestic opposition and international pressure. The nations of western Europe have taken giant steps toward economic and political integration.

American domestic politics also seems to be undergoing dramatic change. After years of Democratic control, both the House and the Senate were captured by the Republicans in the 1994 elections. With the once solidly Democratic South becoming solidly Republican, we may be witnessing a major electoral realignment that will leave the GOP in control of the nation's government. Of course, some elements of American politics never seem to change. Political participation in the United States is as low as ever, while the federal government's budget deficit seems to be unconquerable.

But in a changing world it is more important than ever to understand the politics of the United States. More than at any other time since the Second World War, the world is looking to America for leadership and for an example of popular government in action. Throughout the world, America—despite its problems and faults—symbolizes the combination of freedom and power to which so many now aspire. This makes the task of our book all the more important.

This Brief Edition of *American Government: Freedom and Power* is designed specifically for use in courses whose length or format requires a more concise text. We preserved as much as possible of the narrative style and historic and comparative analysis of the larger text. Though this is a Brief Edition, we have sought to provide a full and detailed discussion of every topic that, in our view, is central to understanding American government and politics. We hope that we have written a book that is physically brief but is not intellectually sketchy.

The collaboration on this book began nearly ten years before its publication, and the book is in every way a product of collaboration in teaching, research, and writing. Each author has taught other courses—for thirty-nine and twenty-five years, respectively—and has written other books; but we agree that no course has been more challenging than the introductory course, and no book has been more difficult to write. Someone once asked if it is difficult for scholars to "write down" to introductory students. No. It is difficult to "write up" to them. Introductory students, of whatever age or reading level, need more, require more, and expect more of a book.

A good teaching book, like a good novel or play, is written on two levels. One is the level of the narrative, the story line, the characters in action. The second is the level of character development, of the argument of the book or play. We would not be the first to assert that there is much of the theatrical about politics today, but our book may be unusual to the extent that we took that assertion as a guide. We have packed it full of narrative—with characters and with the facts about the complex situations in which they find themselves. We have at the same time been determined not to lose sight of the second level, yet we have tried to avoid making the second level so prominent as to define us as preachers rather than teachers.

The book is only one product of our collaboration. The other important product is about 5,000 Cornell and Johns Hopkins students who took the course out of which this book grew. There is no way to convey adequately our appreciation to those students. Their raw intelligence was not satisfied until the second level could provide a logic linking the disparate parts of what we were asserting was a single system of government. And these linkages had to be made in ordinary language. We hope we brought this to the book.

We hope also that we brought over from our teaching experience a full measure of sympathy for all who teach the introductory course, most particularly those who are obliged to teach the course from departmental necessity rather than voluntarily as a desired part of their career. And we hope our book will help them appreciate the course as we do—as an opportunity to make sense of a whole political system. Much can be learned about the system from a re-examination of the innumerable familiar facts, under the still more challenging condition that the facts be somehow interesting, significant, and, above all, linked.

This points to what must be the most troublesome, sometimes the most embarrassing, problem for this course, for this book, and for political science in general: All Americans are to a great extent familiar with the politics and government of their own country. No fact is intrinsically difficult to grasp, and in such an open society, facts abound. In America, many facts are commonplace that are suppressed elsewhere. The ubiquity of political commonplaces is indeed a problem, but it can be turned into a virtue. These very commonplaces give us a vocabulary that is widely shared, and such a vocabulary enables us to communicate effectively at the first level of the book, avoiding abstract concepts and professional language (jargon). Reaching beyond the commonplaces to the second level also identifies what is to us the single most important task of the teacher of political science—to confront the million facts and to choose from among them the small number of really significant ones.

We have tried to provide a framework to help the teacher make choices among facts and to help the students make some of the choices for themselves. This is good political science, and it is good citizenship, which means more than mere obedience and voting; it means participation through constructive criticism, being able to pierce through the information explosion to the core of enduring political reality.

Our framework is freedom and power. To most Americans that means freedom *versus* governmental power, because Americans have been raised to believe that every expansion of the government's power involves a contraction of personal freedom. Up to a point we agree with this traditional view. The institutions of American government are in fact built on a contradiction: Popular freedom and governmental power *are* contradictory, and it is the purpose of our Constitution to build a means of coping with that contradiction. But as Supreme Court justices sometimes say to their colleagues, "We concur, dissenting in part." For in truth, freedom and power are related to each other as husband and wife—each with some conflicting requirements, but neither able to produce, as a family, without the other.

Just as freedom and power are in conflict, so are they complementary. *There can be little freedom, if any, without governmental power.* Freedom of any one individual depends fundamentally on the restraints of everyone else in his or her vicinity. Most of these restraints are self-imposed. We call that *civility,* respect for others born of our awareness that it is a condition of their respect for us. Other restraints vital to personal freedom are imposed spontaneously by society. Europeans call those restraints *civil society;* sociologists call them *institutions.* Institutions exist as society's means of maintaining order and predictability through routines, customs, shared values. But even in the most stable society, the restraints of civility and of civil society are incomplete and insufficient; there remains a sphere of deliberate restraint that calls for the exercise of public control (public power). Where society falls down, or where new events and new technologies produce new stresses, or where even the most civil of human beings find their basic needs in conflict with others, there will be an exercise of public control, or public power. Private property, that great bastion of personal freedom in the Western world, would disappear without elaborate government controls.

If freedom were only a matter of the absence of control, there would be no need for a book like ours. In fact, there would be little need for political science at all. But politics, however far away in the national or the state capital, is a matter of life and death. It can be as fascinating as any good novel or adventure film if the key political question is one's own survival or the survival of one's society. We have tried to write each chapter of this book in such a way that the reader is tempted to ask what that government institution, that agency, this committee or that election, this group or that amendment has to do with *me* and *us,* and how has it come to be that way? That's what freedom and power are all about—my freedom and your restraint, my restraint and your freedom.

Having chosen a framework for the book there was also a need for a method. The method must be loyal to the framework; it must facilitate the effort to choose which facts are essential, and it must assist in evaluating those facts in ways that not only enlighten students but enable them to engage in analysis and evaluation for themselves. Although we are not bound exclusively to a single method in any scientific or philosophic sense, the method most consistently employed is one of history, or history as development. First, we present the state of affairs, describing the legislature, the party, the agency, or policy, with as many of the facts as are necessary to tell the story and to enable us to reach the broader question of freedom versus governmental power. Next, we ask how we have gotten to where we are. By what series of steps, and when by choice, and when by accident? To what extent was the history of Congress or of the parties or the presidency a fulfillment of constitutional principle, and when were the developments a series of dogged responses to economic necessity? History is our method because it helps choose which facts are significant. History also helps those who would like to try to explain why we are where we are. But more important even than explanation, history helps us make judgments. In other words, we look less to causes and more to consequences. Political science cannot be satisfied with objective description, analysis, and explanation. Political science would be a failure if it did not have a vision about the ideal as well as the real. What is a good and proper balance between freedom and governmental power? What can a constitution do about it? What can enlightened people do about it?

Evaluation makes political science worth doing but also more difficult to do. Academics make a distinction between the hard sciences and the soft sciences, implying that hard science is the only real science: laboratory, people in white coats, precision instruments making measurements to several decimal points, testing hypotheses with "hard data." But as medical scientist Jared Diamond observes, that is a recent and narrow view, considering that science in Latin means knowledge and careful observation. Diamond suggests, and we agree, that a better distinction is between hard (i.e., difficult) science and easy science, with political science fitting into the hard category, precisely because many of the most significant phenomena in the world cannot be put in a test tube and measured to several decimal points. We must nevertheless be scientific about them. And more: unlike physical scientists, social scientists have an obligation to judge whether the reality could be better. In trying to meet that obligation, we hope to demonstrate how interesting and challenging political science can be.

The Design of the Book

The objective we have taken upon ourselves in writing this book is thus to advance our understanding of freedom and power by exploring in the fullest possible detail the way Americans have tried to balance the two through careful crafting of the rules, through constructing balanced institutions, and by maintaining moderate forms of organized politics. The book is divided into four parts, reflecting the historical process by which freedom and governmental power are (or are not) kept in balance. Part I, "Foundations," comprises the chapters concerned with the writing of the rules of the contract. The founding of 1787–1789

put it all together, but that was actually a second effort after a first failure. The original contract, the Articles of Confederation, did not achieve an acceptable balance—too much freedom, and not enough power. The second founding, the Constitution ratified in 1789, was itself an imperfect effort to establish the rules, and within two years new terms were added—the first ten amendments, called the Bill of Rights. And for the next century and a half following their ratification in 1791, the courts played umpire and translator in the struggle to interpret those terms. Chapter 1 introduces our theme. Chapter 2 concentrates on the founding itself. Chapters 3 and 4 chronicle the long struggle to establish what was meant by the three great principles of limited government: *federalism, separation of powers,* and *individual liberties and rights.*

Part II, "Institutions," includes the chapters sometimes referred to as the "nuts and bolts." But none of these particles of government mean anything except in the larger context of the goals governments must meet and the limits that have been imposed upon them. Chapter 5 is an introduction to the fundamental problem of *representative government* as this has been institutionalized in Congress. Congress, with all its problems, is the most creative legislative body in the world. But how well does Congress provide a meeting ground between consent and governing? How are society's demands taken into account in debates on the floor of Congress and deliberations by its committees? What interests turn out to be most effectively "represented" in Congress? What is the modern Congress's constituency?

Chapter 6 explores the same questions for the presidency and the government bureaucracy. Although Article II of the Constitution provides that the president should see that the laws made by Congress are "faithfully executed," the presidency was always part of our theory of representative government, and the modern presidency has increasingly become a law *maker* rather than merely a law implementor. What, then, does a strong presidency with a large executive branch do to the conduct and the consequences of representative government?

Chapter 7 on the judiciary should not be lost in the shuffle. Referred to by Hamilton as "the least dangerous branch," the judiciary truly has become a co-equal branch, to such an extent that if Hamilton were alive today he would probably eat his words.

Part III we entitle "Politics and Policy." Politics encompasses all the efforts by any and all individuals and groups inside as well as outside the government to determine what government will do and on whose behalf it will be done. Our chapters take the order of our conception of how politics developed since the Revolution and how politics works today: Chapter 8, "Public Opinion and the Media"; Chapter 9, "Elections"; Chapter 10, "Political Parties"; and Chapter 11, "Groups and Interests." But we recognize that, although there may be a pattern to American politics, it is not readily predictable.

The last chapters are primarily about public policies, which are the most deliberate and goal-oriented aspects of the still-larger phenomenon of "government in action." Chapter 12 is virtually a handbook of public policy. Since most Americans know far less about policies than they do about institutions and politics, we felt it was necessary to provide a usable, common vocabulary of public policy. Since public policies are most often defined by the goals that the government establishes in broad rhetorical terms and since there can be an uncountable number of goals, we have tried to get beyond and behind goals by looking at the "techniques of control" that any public policy goal must embody if the goal is even partially to be fulfilled. Chapter 13, "Foreign Policy and World Politics," turns to the international realm and America's place in it. Our concern here is to understand American foreign policies and why we have adopted the policies that we have. Given the traditional American fear of "the state" and the genuine danger of international involvements

to domestic democracy, a chapter on foreign policies is essential to a book on American government and also reveals a great deal about America as a culture.

Chapter 14 is our analysis of the state of American politics today. Much has been said and written about the state of American politics, but we believe that to fully understand the transformations occurring in American politics, one must assess the historical roots of these changes. However, we recognize that, although there may be a pattern to American politics, it is not readily predictable. One need only contemplate the year-long nomination of presidential candidates to recognize how much confusion and downright disorder there is in what we political scientists blithely call "political process." Chapter 14 is an evaluation of that process. We ask whether our contemporary political process is consistent with good government. Unfortunately, the answer is not entirely positive.

With this new Fifth Edition, we have moved many steps forward into the electronic age. A brief version of the Lowi and Ginsberg web*BOOK*, an interactive study guide supporting the text, provides students with a thorough and in-depth review of the "nuts and bolts" material included in each chapter, a "click and drag" exercise that helps students learn key concepts and terms, and an interactive practice quiz for each chapter that immediately grades students' responses and directs them to the portions of the text they need to review.

We hope that students find the material on the Lowi and Ginsberg web*BOOK* useful to their review of American Government. Visit the site at: **http:/www.wwnorton.com/lowibr**

Acknowledgments

Our students at Cornell and Johns Hopkins have already been identified as an essential factor in the writing of this book. They have been our most immediate intellectual community, a hospitable one indeed. Another part of our community, perhaps a large suburb, is the discipline of political science itself. Our debt to the scholarship of our colleagues is scientifically measurable, probably to several decimal points, in the footnotes of each chapter. Despite many complaints that the field is too scientific or not scientific enough, political science is alive and well in the United States. It is an aspect of democracy itself, and it has grown and changed in response to the developments in government and politics that we have chronicled in our book. If we did a "time line" on the history of political science, as we have done in each chapter of the book, it would show a close association with developments in "the American state." Sometimes the discipline has been out of phase and critical; at other times, it has been in phase and perhaps apologetic. But political science has never been at a loss for relevant literature, and without it, our job would have been impossible.

There have, of course, been individuals on whom we have relied in particular. Of all writers, living and dead, we find ourselves most in debt to the writing of two—James Madison and Alexis de Tocqueville. Many other great authors have shaped us as they have shaped all political scientists. But Madison and Tocqueville have stood for us not only as the bridge to all timeless political problems; they represent the ideal of political science itself—that political science must be steadfastly scientific in the search for what is, yet must keep alive a strong sense of what ought to be, recognizing that democracy is neither natural nor invariably good, and must be fiercely dedicated to constant critical analysis of all political institutions in order to contribute to the maintenance of a favorable balance between individual freedom and public power.

We are pleased to acknowledge our debt to the many colleagues who had a direct and active role in criticism and preparation of the manuscript. The first edition was read and reviewed by Gary Bryner, Brigham Young University; James F. Herndon, Virginia Polytechnic Institute and State University; James W. Riddlesperger, Jr., Texas Christian University; John Schwarz, University of Arizona; Toni-Michelle Travis, George Mason University; and Lois Vietri, University of Maryland. Their comments were enormously helpful.

For subsequent editions, we relied heavily on the thoughtful manuscript reviews we received from David Canon, University of Wisconsin; Russell Hanson, University of Indiana; William Keech, University of North Carolina; Donald Kettl, University of Wisconsin; Anne Khademian, University of Wisconsin; William McLauchlan, Purdue University; J. Roger Baker, Wittenburg University; James Lennertz, Lafayette College; Allan McBride, Grambling State University and Joseph Peek, Jr., Georgia State University. The advice we received from these colleagues was especially welcome because all had used the book in their own classrooms. Other colleagues who offered helpful comments based upon their own experience with the text include Douglas Costain, University of Colorado; Robert Hoffert, Colorado State University; David Marcum, University of Wyoming; Mark Silverstein, Boston University; and Norman Thomas, University of Cincinnati.

We also want to reiterate our thanks to the four colleagues who allowed us the privilege of testing a trial edition of our book by using it as the major text in their introductory American Government courses. Their reactions, and those of their students, played an important role in our first edition. We are grateful to Gary Bryner, Brigham Young University; Allan J. Cigler, University of Kansas; Burnet V. Davis, Albion College; and Erwin A. Jaffe, California State University–Stanislaus.

We are also extremely grateful to a number of colleagues who were kind enough to loan us their classrooms. During the past two years, we had the opportunity to lecture at a number of colleges and universities around the country and to benefit from discussing our book with those who know it best—colleagues and students who used it. We appreciate the gracious welcome we received at Austin Community

College, Cal State-Fullerton, University of Central Oklahoma, Emory University, Gainesville College, Georgia Southern University, Georgia State University, Golden West College, Grambling State, University of Houston–University Park, University of Illinois–Chicago, University of Illinois–Urbana-Champaign, University of Maryland–College Park, University of Massachusetts–Amherst, Morgan State University, University of North Carolina–Chapel Hill, University of North Texas, University of Oklahoma, Oklahoma State University, Pasadena City College, University of Richmond, Sam Houston State, San Bernadino Valley College, Santa Barbara City College, Santa Monica College, University of Southern California, Temple University, University of Texas–Austin, Texas Tech University, Virginia Commonwealth University, and University of Wisconsin–Madison.

We owe a special debt to Robert J. Spitzer, State University of New York–College at Cortland, for preparing most of the essays profiling important individuals that appear throughout the book. By linking concepts and events to real people, these essays help to make this a more lively and interesting book and thus one that students will be more likely to read and remember. Professor Spitzer also helped develop the "Debating the Issues" boxes, in which core concepts are debated by political thinkers.

One novel feature is a series of "Process Boxes" that illustrate the actual operation of a major political institution or procedure. Several individuals, all leading figures in their own fields, were generous enough to contribute their time and expertise to helping us develop these useful pedagogic tools. Our thanks to Thomas Edsall, the *Washington Post;* Kathleen Francovic, CBS News; Benjamin L. Ginsberg, Republican National Committee; and Ray Rist, U.S. General Accounting Office. Another novel feature of the text is the inclusion of "Concept Maps," which are new to this edition. As a result of our own teaching, we realized that students benefit from *seeing* how ab-

stract concepts work in practice. We have sought to visualize a number of concepts that we deemed both central to the study of American government and potentially difficult to understand. One or more Concept Maps are included in most of the chapters of this book.

We also are grateful for the talents and hard work of several research assistants, whose contribution can never be adequately compensated: Douglas Dow, John Forren, Michael Harvey, Doug Harris, Brenda Holzinger, Steve McGovern, Melody Butler, Nancy Johnson, Noah Silverman, Rebecca Fisher, David Lytell, Dennis Merryfield, Rachel Reiss, Nandini Sathe, Rob Speel, Jennifer Waterston, and David Wirls. For the Fifth Edition, Mingus Mapps devoted a great deal of time and energy.

Jacqueline Discenza not only typed several drafts of the manuscript, but also helped to hold the project together. We thank her for her hard work and dedication.

Theodore Lowi would like to express his gratitude to the French-American Foundation and the Gannett Foundation, whose timely invitations helped him prepare for his part of this enterprise.

Perhaps above all, we wish to thank those who kept the production and all the loose ends of the book coherent and in focus. Steve Dunn has been an extremely talented editor, continuing to offer numerous suggestions for each new edition. Sarah Caldwell and Scott McCord helped keep track of the many details. Margaret Farley has been a superb manuscript and project editor, following the great tradition of her predecessors. Through all our editions, Ruth Dworkin has been an efficient production manager. Neil Ryder Hoos located the photos illustrating the book. John Darger contributed many good ideas to the book and a great deal of time to its success. Steve Hoge brought a vision to the website and spent countless hours, assisted by Kirsten Miller and Yash Holbrook, making it a reality. For their work on previous editions of the book, we want to thank Traci Nagle, Margie Brassil, Stephanie Larson,

Nancy Yanchus, Jean Yelovich, Sandra Smith, Sandy Lifland, Amy Cherry, and especially Roby Harrington.

We are more than happy, however, to absolve all these contributors from any flaws, errors, and misjudgments that will inevitably be discovered. We wish the book could be free of all production errors, grammatical errors, misspellings, misquotes, missed citations, etc. From that standpoint, a book ought to try to be perfect. But substantively we have not tried to write a flawless book; we have not tried to write a book to please everyone. We have again tried to write an effective book, a book that cannot be taken lightly. Our goal was not to make every reader a political scientist. Our goal was to restore politics as a subject matter of vigorous and enjoyable discourse, re-capturing it from the bondage of the thirty-second sound bite and the thirty-page technical briefing. Every person can be knowledgeable because everything about politics is accessible. One does not have to be a television anchor to profit from political events. One does not have to be a philosopher to argue about the requisites of democracy, a lawyer to dispute constitutional interpretations, an economist to debate a public policy. We would be very proud if our book contributes in a small way to the restoration of the ancient art of political controversy.

Theodore J. Lowi
Benjamin Ginsberg
July 1997

PART 1

FOUNDATIONS

CHAPTER 1

Freedom and Power:
An Introduction to the Problem

A STORY often told by politicians concerns a voter from the Midwest who, upon returning home from military service in Korea, took advantage of his federal educational benefits under the G.I. Bill to complete college. After graduation, this individual was able to obtain a government loan from the Small Business Administration (SBA) to help him start a business and a mortgage subsidized by the Federal Housing Administration (FHA) to purchase a home. Subsequently, he received medical care in a Veterans Administration Hospital, including treatment with drugs developed by the National Institutes of Health. This voter drove to work every day on a four-lane highway built under the federal interstate highway program, frequently used Amtrak to travel to a nearby city, and, though he was somewhat nervous about air travel, relied on the Federal Aviation Administration (FAA) to make certain that the aircraft he depended on for business and vacation trips were safe. When this voter's children reached college age, they obtained federal student loans to help pay their expenses. At the same time, his aging parents were happy to be receiving monthly Social Security checks, and, when his father unexpectedly required major surgery, financial ruin

was averted because the federal government's Medicare program paid the bulk of the cost.

What was our midwestern friend's response to all of this? Well, in both 1980 and 1984, he strongly supported Ronald Reagan's presidential candidacy because of Reagan's promise to get the federal government off people's backs. In 1988, our friend voted for George Bush because he believed that Bush would continue Reagan's efforts to hold the line on federal domestic spending. In 1992, disgruntled by Bush's failure to adhere to

CORE OF THE ARGUMENT

- Government has become a powerful and pervasive force in the United States.
- American government is based on democratic electoral institutions and popular representative bodies.
- Once citizens perceive that government can respond to their demands, they become increasingly willing to support its expansion.
- The growth of governmental power can pose a threat because it reduces popular influence over policy making and diminishes the need for citizen cooperation.

his pledge not to raise taxes, this midwesterner supported Ross Perot. In 1996, our midwestern friend voted for the re-election of Bill Clinton, though without much enthusiasm, because the economy was strong, his stock investments were performing extremely well, and he did not think Bob Dole was up to the job of running the country. Just to be on the safe side, however, he voted for the Republican's House and Senate candidates, calculating that as long as control of the government was divided, neither party would be able to get the country into too much trouble. In previous elections our friend had always voted for the re-election of his congressman, a staunch Democrat, who steadfastly opposed any cuts in the government's domestic programs. This is an example of the love-hate relationship between Americans and their government.

Government has become a powerful and pervasive force in the United States. In 1789, 1889, and even in 1929, America's national government was limited in size, scope, and influence, while states provided most of the important functions of government. By 1933, however, the influence of the government expanded to meet the crises created by the stock market crash of 1929, the ensuing Great Depression, and the run on banks of 1933. Congress passed legislation that brought the government into the business of home mortgages, farm mortgages, credit, and relief of personal distress. Today, the national government is an enormous institution with programs and policies reaching into every corner of American life. It oversees the nation's economy; it is the nation's largest employer; it provides citizens with a host of services; it controls a formidable military establishment; and it regulates a wide range of social and commercial activities. The past few years have seen attempts to establish a national health care system, which would give the federal government a substantial measure of control over another enormous segment of the country's economy. America's founders never dreamed the government could take on such obligations; we today

can hardly dream of a time when the government was not such an important part of our lives.

The growth of government in the United States has been accompanied by a change in the way Americans look at government. In the nineteenth century, Americans generally were wary of government, especially the remote national government. Government meant control, and control meant fewer individual liberties. The best government, as Thomas Jefferson put it, was the one that governed least. Many Americans today continue to pay lip service to this early view, but a new theory of democratic government has gradually come to dominate political thought. This new theory states that if government could be made less of a threat and less remote by the development of elections and other forms of popular control, then a more powerful government would be one with a greater capacity to serve the people. In other words, government control of the people would be more acceptable if people, in turn, controlled the government.[1]

Today, a broad concensus favors a large and active government. In his first inaugural address, Ronald Reagan, our most conservative president in more than half a century, pledged to curb the growth of the federal establishment but at the same time declared, "Now so there will be no misunderstanding, it is not my intention to do away with government. It is, rather, to make it work."[2] Reagan repeated this sentiment in his 1985 inaugural address. In 1992, in his speech accepting the Democratic presidential nomination, Bill Clinton noted correctly that "the Republicans have campaigned against big government for a generation. . . . But have you noticed? They've run this big government for a generation and they haven't changed a thing."[3]

---

[1]For examples, see Richard Wollheim, "A Paradox of the Theory of Democracy," in *Philosophy, Politics, and Society*, ed. Peter Laslett and W. G. Runciman (Oxford: Blackwell, 1962).

[2]"President Reagan's Inaugural Address," *New York Times*, 21 January 1981, p. B1.

[3]E. J. Dionne, "Beneath the Rhetoric, an Old Question," *Washington Post*, 31 August 1992, p. 1.

TABLE 1.1

Some Activities of the U.S. Government in 1996

BENEFICIARY AND PROGRAM	COST (IN $)	BENEFICIARY AND PROGRAM	COST (IN $)
Business		**Farmers**	
Department of Energy, *Energy Supply, Research & Development Activities*	3,200,000,000	USDA, *Farm Income Stabilization*	5,000,000,000
Export-Import Bank of U.S.	3,200,000,000	USDA, *Research*	2,700,000,000
Needy Children		**Homeowners**	
Department of Agriculture, Food & Nutrition Science, *Child Nutrition Program*	6,200,000,000	HUD, *Federal Housing Administration Fund*	2,300,000,000
Department of Health & Human Services, *Health Resources & Human Services*	2,100,000,000	**Labor**	
		Department of Labor, *Unemployment Compensation*	26,000,000,000
College and University Students		**The Sick and Disabled**	
Department of Education, Office of Postsecondary Education, *Grants and Loans*	11,400,000,000	Department of Health, *Consumer and Occupational Health*	2,900,000,000
		HHS, *Health Research*	11,500,000,000
The Elderly		HHS, Social Security, *Federal Disability Insurance*	63,000,000,000
HHS, *Medicare*	177,600,000,000	**Veterans**	
HHS, *Federal Old-Age and Survivors Insurance*	350,900,000,000	Veterans Administration, *Compensation*	18,100,000,000
		VA, *Education & Rehabilitation*	1,100,000,000
Law Enforcement		VA, *Medical Care*	17,100,000,000
Federal Agencies	13,800,000,000		
Federal Prisons	3,000,000,000		

SOURCE: Executive Office of the President, Office of Management and Budget, *Budget of the United States, Fiscal Year 1996* (Washington, DC: Government Printing Office, 1997).

Americans want to keep the political and economic benefits they believe they derive from government *(see Table 1.1)*. A recent survey by the *Washington Post*, for example, revealed that nearly 75 percent of all Americans opposed making any cuts in Social Security and Medicare, although, in theory, most also favor the idea of balancing the federal budget.[4] Social Security and Medicare programs are, of course, major components of the federal government's domestic spending. According to the 1994 University of Michigan National Election Study, over half of all voters believe that it is important for the government to provide more services, even if it requires more spending.[5] How did government come to play such an important role in our lives? How did Americans come to lose some of their fear of remote government and to look at government as a valuable servant rather than a threat to freedom?

[4]Eric Pianin and Mario Brossard, "Social Security and Medicare: Sacred Cows," *Washington Post National Weekly Edition*, 7 April 1997, p. 35.

[5]1994 American National Election Study conducted by the Center for Political Studies at the University of Michigan. Data is provided by the Inter-University Consortium for Political and Social Research in Ann Arbor, Michigan.

CONCEPT MAP 1.1

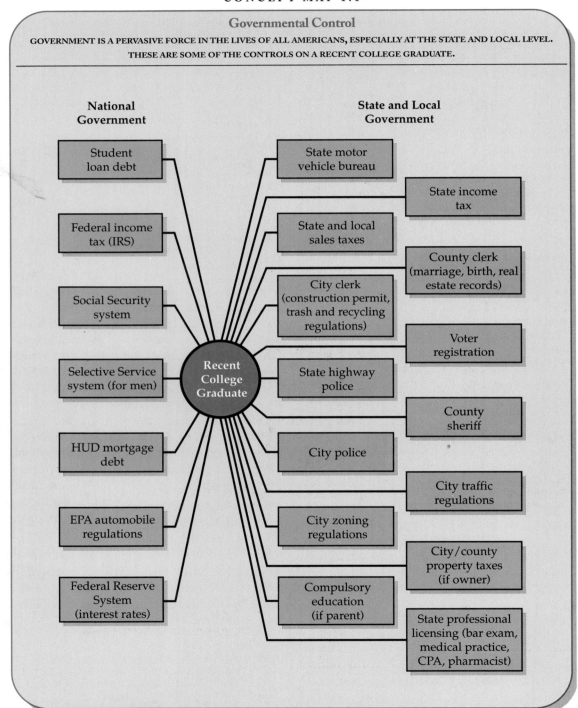

Governmental Control

GOVERNMENT IS A PERVASIVE FORCE IN THE LIVES OF ALL AMERICANS, ESPECIALLY AT THE STATE AND LOCAL LEVEL. THESE ARE SOME OF THE CONTROLS ON A RECENT COLLEGE GRADUATE.

National Government

- Student loan debt
- Federal income tax (IRS)
- Social Security system
- Selective Service system (for men)
- HUD mortgage debt
- EPA automobile regulations
- Federal Reserve System (interest rates)

Recent College Graduate

State and Local Government

- State motor vehicle bureau
- State income tax
- State and local sales taxes
- County clerk (marriage, birth, real estate records)
- City clerk (construction permit, trash and recycling regulations)
- Voter registration
- State highway police
- County sheriff
- City police
- City traffic regulations
- City zoning regulations
- City/county property taxes (if owner)
- Compulsory education (if parent)
- State professional licensing (bar exam, medical practice, CPA, pharmacist)

FOUNDATIONS OF GOVERNMENT

Governments must have a means to maintain order and to fend off rivals, and they must raise funds in order to accomplish these tasks.

Means of Coercion	Means of Collecting Revenue
conscription	individual income taxes
jury duty	corporate income taxes
forced appearance before a tribunal	social insurance taxes
filing of income tax returns	excise taxes
requirement to attend school	miscellaneous revenue

To answer these questions, this chapter will first assess the meaning and character of government in general, describing some of the alternative forms government can take and the major differences among them. Second, we will examine the factors that led to one particular form of government—*representative democracy*—in western Europe and the United States. Representative government is a system of government that provides the populace with the opportunity to make the government responsive through the selection of representatives. Finally, we will begin to address the question central not only to this book but also to the most fundamental and enduring problem of democratic politics—the relationship between government and freedom.

GOVERNMENT AND CONTROL

Government is the term generally used to describe the formal institutions through which a land and its people are ruled. To govern is to rule. *Government is composed of institutions and processes that rulers establish to strengthen and perpetuate their power or control over a territory and its inhabitants.* A government may be as simple as a tribal council that meets occasionally to advise the chief, or as complex as our own vast establishment with its forms, rules, and bureaucracies.

Foundations of Government

Groups aspire to govern for a variety of reasons. Some have the most high-minded aims, while others are little more than ambitious robbers. But whatever their motives and character, those who aspire to rule must be able to secure obedience and fend off rivals as well as collect the revenues needed to accomplish these tasks.[6] That is why, whatever their makeup, governments historically have included two basic components: a means of coercion, such as an army or police force, and a means of collecting revenue. Some governments, including many in the less developed nations today, have consisted of little more than an army and a tax-collecting agency. Other governments, especially those in the developed nations such as the United States, attempt to provide services as well as to collect taxes in order to secure popular consent for control. For some, power is an end in itself. For most, power is necessary to maintain public order.

[6]For an excellent discussion, see Charles Tilly, "Reflections on the History of European State-Making," in *The Formation of National States in Western Europe,* ed. Charles Tilly (Princeton, Princeton University Press, 1975), pp. 3–83. See also Charles Tilly, "War Making and State Making as Organized Crime," in *Bringing the State Back In,* ed. Peter Evans, Dietrich Rueschemeyer, and Theda Skocpol (New York: Cambridge University Press, 1895), pp. 169–91.

SCOPE AND LIMITS OF POWER IN CONSTITUTIONAL, AUTHORITARIAN, AND TOTALITARIAN GOVERNMENTS

Constitutional Governments
Scope: power prescribed by a constitution
Limits: society can challenge government when it oversteps constitutional boundaries
Examples: United States, France, Canada

Authoritarian Governments
Scope: answer only to a small number of powerful groups
Limits: recognize no obligations to limit actions, whether or not such obligations exist
Examples: Spain (under General Francisco Franco) and Portugal (under Prime Minister Antonio Salazar)

Totalitarian Governments
Scope: government encompasses all important social institutions
Limits: rivals for power are not tolerated
Examples: Germany's Third Reich in the 1930s and 1940s (under Adolf Hitler) and the Soviet Union from the 1930s through the 1950s (under Joseph Stalin)

THE MEANS OF COERCION Government must have the power to order people around, to get people to obey its laws, and to punish them if they do not. *Coercion* takes many different forms, and each year millions of Americans are subject to one form of government coercion or another. One aspect of coercion is *conscription*, whereby the government requires certain involuntary services of citizens. The best-known example of conscription is military conscription, which is called "the draft." Although there has been no draft since 1974, there were drafts during the Civil War, World War I, World War II, and the postwar period, and the wars in Korea and Vietnam. With these drafts, the American government compelled millions of men to serve in the armed forces; one-half million of these soldiers made the ultimate contribution by giving their lives in their nation's service. If the need arose, military conscription would undoubtedly be reinstituted. Eighteen-year-old males are required to register today, just in case. American citizens can also, by law, be compelled to serve on juries, to appear before legal tribunals when summoned, to file a great variety of official reports, including income tax returns, and to attend school or to send their children to school.

THE MEANS OF COLLECTING REVENUE Each year American governments on every level collect enormous sums from their citizens to support their institutions and programs. Taxation has grown steadily over the years. In 1989, the national government alone collected $516 billion in individual income taxes, $117 billion in corporate income taxes, $341 billion in social insurance taxes, $26 billion in excise taxes, and another $18 billion in miscellaneous revenue. The grand total amounted to more than one trillion dollars, or more than $4,000 from every living soul in the United States. But not everyone benefits equally from programs paid for by their tax dollars. One of the perennial issues in American politics is the distribution of tax burdens versus the distribution of program benefits. Every group would like more of the benefits while passing more of the burdens of taxation onto others.

Forms of Government

Governments vary in their institutional structure, in their size, and in the way they operate. Two questions are of special importance in determining how governments differ from one another: Who governs? How much government control is permitted?

In some nations, a single individual—a king or dictator—governs. This is called *autocracy*. Where a small group of landowners, military officers, or wealthy merchants control most of the governing decisions, that government is an *oligarchy*. If many people participate, and if the populace is deemed to have some influence over the leaders' actions, that government is tending toward *democracy*.

Governments also vary considerably in how they govern. In the United States and a small number of other nations, governments are severely limited by law as to *what* they are permitted to control (substantive limits), as well as *how* they go about it (procedural limits). Governments that are so limited are called *constitutional*, or liberal, governments. In other nations, including many in Europe, South America, Asia, and Africa, political and social institutions that the government is unable to control—such as an organized church, organized business groups, or organized labor unions—may help keep the government in check, but the law imposes few real limits. Such governments are called *authoritarian*. In a third group of nations, including the Soviet Union under Joseph Stalin, governments not only are free of legal limits but seek to eliminate those organized social groupings or institutions that might challenge or limit their authority. Because these governments typically attempt to dominate every sphere of political, economic, and social life, they are called *totalitarian*.

Influencing the Government: Politics

In its broadest sense, the term *"politics"* refers to conflicts over the character, membership, and policies of any organizations to which people belong. As Harold Lasswell, a famous political scientist, once put it, politics is the struggle over "who gets what, when, how."[7] Although politics is a phenomenon that can be found in any organization, our concern in this book is more narrow. Here, politics will refer only to conflicts and struggles over the leadership, structure, and policies of *governments*. The goal of politics, as we define it, is to have a share or a say in the composition of the government's leadership, how the government is organized, and what its policies are going to be. Having such a share is called *power* or *influence*. Most people are eager to have some "say" in matters affecting them, witness the willingness of so many individuals over the past two centuries to risk their lives for voting rights and representation. In recent years, of course, Americans have become more skeptical about their actual "say" in government, and many do not bother to vote. This increased skepticism, however, does not mean that Americans no longer want to have a share in the governmental process. Rising levels of skepticism mean, rather, that many Americans doubt the capacity of the political system to provide them with influence.

As we shall see throughout the book, not only does politics influence government, but the character and actions of government also influence a nation's politics. A constitutional government tries to gain more popular consent by opening channels for political expression. People accept these channels in the hope that they can make the government more responsive to their demands.

FROM COERCION TO CONSENT

Americans have the good fortune to live in a constitutional democracy, with legal limits on what government can do and how it does it. But such

---

[7]Harold Lasswell, *Politics: Who Gets What, When, How* (New York: Meridian Books, 1958).

democracies are relatively rare in today's world— it is estimated that only twenty or so of the world's nearly two hundred governments could be included in this category. And constitutional democracies were unheard of before the modern era. Prior to the eighteenth and nineteenth centuries, governments seldom sought—and rarely received—the support of their ordinary subjects. History strongly suggests that the ordinary people had little love for the government or for the social order. After all, they had no stake in it. They equated government with the police officer, the bailiff, and the tax collector.[8]

Beginning in the seventeenth century, in a handful of Western nations, two important changes began to take place in the character and conduct of government. First, governments began to acknowledge formal limits on their power. Second, a small number of governments began to provide the ordinary citizen with a formal voice in public affairs through the vote.

Limits and Democratization

Obviously, the desirability of limits on government and the expansion of popular influence on government were at the heart of the American Revolution of 1776. "No taxation without representation," as we shall see in Chapter 2, was hotly debated, beginning with the American Revolution and continuing through the founding in 1789. But even before the American Revolution, there was a tradition of limiting government and expanding participation in the political process all over western Europe. Thus, to understand how the relationship between rulers and the ruled was transformed, we must broaden our focus to take into account events in Europe as well as those in America. We will divide the transformation into two separate parts. The first is the effort to put limits on government. The second is the effort to expand the influence of the people through politics.

LIMITING GOVERNMENT   The key force behind the imposition of limits on government power was a new social class, the "bourgeoisie." *Bourgeois* is French for freeman of the city, or bourg. Being part of the bourgeoisie later became associated with being "middle class" and with being in commerce or industry. In order to gain a share of control of government—to join the kings, aristocrats, and gentry who had dominated governments for centuries—the bourgeoisie sought to change existing institutions—especially parliaments—into instruments of real political participation. Parliaments had existed for hundreds of years, controlling from the top and not allowing influence from below. The bourgeoisie embraced parliament as the means by which they could use their greater numbers and growing economic advantage against their aristocratic rivals.

Although motivated primarily by self-interest, the bourgeoisie advanced many of the principles that became the central underpinnings of individual freedom for *all* citizens—freedom of speech, of assembly, of conscience, and freedom from arbitrary search and seizure. It is important to note here that the bourgeoisie generally did not favor democracy as such. They were advocates of electoral and representative institutions, but they favored property requirements and other restrictions so as to limit participation to the middle classes. Yet, once the right to engage in politics was established, it was difficult to limit it just to the bourgeoisie. We will see time after time that principles first stated to justify a selfish interest can take on a life of their own, extending beyond those for whom the principles were designed.

THE EXPANSION OF DEMOCRATIC POLITICS   Along with limits on government came an expansion of democratic government. Three factors explain why rulers were forced to give ordinary citizens a greater voice in public affairs: internal conflict, external threat, and the promotion of national unity and development.

First, during the eighteenth and nineteenth centuries, every nation was faced with intense

---

[8]See Eugen Weber, *Peasants into Frenchmen* (Stanford, CA: Stanford University Press, 1976), Chapter 5.

IN BRIEF BOX

THE EXPANSION OF DEMOCRATIC POLITICS

Causes of Expansion

Internal conflict: To quell conflicts between different social groups and economic classes; rulers have found it useful to extend the rights of political participation—to give the masses a bigger stake in the system so that they will be more inclined to support that system.

External conflict: In order to maintain a permanent army as a defense against other nation-states, governments needed popular support for military endeavors. The expansion of participation in government helped ensure enthusiasm for cause and country.

Promotion of national unity: Governments sometimes see local or regional loyalties as an obstacle to national unity and by expanding participation, they hope to tie people more strongly to the central government.

Consequences of expansion

Citizens might use government for their own benefit (rather than watch it being used for the benefit of others).

The public believes it can control the government and therefore supports the continued expansion of government.

---

conflict among the landed gentry, the bourgeoisie, lower-middle-class shopkeepers and artisans, the urban working class, and farmers. Many governments came to the conclusion that if they did not deal with basic class conflicts in some constructive way, disorder and revolution would result. One of the best ways of dealing with such conflict was to extend the rights of political participation, especially voting, to each new group as it grew more powerful. Such a liberalization was sometimes followed by suppression, as rulers began to fear that their calculated risk was not paying off.

This was true even in the United States. The Federalists, who were securely in control of the government after 1787, began to fear the emergence of a vulgar and dangerous democratic party led by Thomas Jefferson. The Federalist majority in Congress adopted an infamous law, the Alien and Sedition Acts of 1798, which, among other things, declared any opposition to or criticism of the government to be a crime. Alexander Hamilton and other Federalist leaders went so far as to urge that the opposition be eliminated by force, if necessary. The Federalists failed to suppress their Republican opposition, however, in large measure because they lacked the military

and political means of doing so. Their inability to crush the opposition eventually led to acceptance of the principle of the "Loyal Opposition."[9]

Another form of internal threat is social disorder. Thanks to the Industrial Revolution, societies had become much more interdependent and therefore much more vulnerable to disorder. As that occurred, and as more people moved from rural areas to cities, disorder had to be managed, and one important approach to that management was to give the masses a bigger stake in the system itself. As one supporter of electoral reform put it, the alternative to voting was "the spoliation of property and the dissolution of social order."[10] In the modern world, social disorder helped to compel East European regimes and the republics of the former Soviet Union to take steps toward democratic reform.

The second factor that helped expand democratic government was external threat. The main external threat to governments' power is the

---

[9]See Richard Hofstadter, *The Idea of a Party System* (Berkeley: University of California Press, 1969).

[10]Quoted in John Cannon, *Parliamentary Reform, 1640–1832* (Cambridge, England: Cambridge University Press, 1973), p. 216.

DEBATING THE ISSUES

Freedom and Power: The Enduring Debate

*S*TRIKING *the right balance between freedom and power is the essential paradox of governing. One could select any point in American history and find a vigorous debate between those who want a stronger government and those who believe that individual freedom is endangered by an encroaching state. This debate was a central feature of the early struggle to establish a permanent, stable, yet limited national government in America.*

Thomas Jefferson was an eloquent spokesman for a government of sharply limited powers. He laid his trust in majority will and personal freedom. In fact, he considered regular revolts by the people to be healthy for a democracy, not unlike the way the physicians of his time viewed bloodletting. "The tree of liberty must be refreshed from time to time, with the blood of patriots and tyrants."

Opposing him was Alexander Hamilton, an avowed elitist, who recognized the failings of weak government (such as the country had experienced under the Articles of Confederation). Hamilton argued that the national government had to possess the power to enforce its decisions in order to ensure the political and economic well-being of its citizenry.

JEFFERSON

I own, I am not a friend to a very energetic government. It is always oppressive. It places the governors indeed more at their ease, at the expense of the people. The late rebellion in Massachusetts [Shays's Rebellion] has given more alarm, than I think it should have done. Calculate that one rebellion in thirteen States in the course of eleven years, is but one for each State in a century and a half. No country should be so long without one. Nor will any degree of power in the hands of government, prevent insurrections. . . . And say . . . whether peace is best preserved by giving energy to the government, or information to the people. This last

existence of other nation-states. During the past three centuries, more and more tribes and nations—people tied together by a common culture and language—have formed into separate principalities, or *nation-states*, in order to defend their populations more effectively. But as more nation-states formed, the more likely it was that external conflicts would arise. War and preparation for war became constant rather than intermittent facts of national life, and the size and expense of military forces increased dramatically with the size of the nation-state and the size and number of its adversaries.

The cost of defense forced rulers to seek popular support to maintain military power. It was easier to raise huge permanent armies of citizen-soldiers and induce them to fight more vigorously and to make greater sacrifices if they were im-

bued with enthusiasm for cause and country. The turning point was the French Revolution in 1789. The unprecedented size and commitment and the military success of the French citizen-army convinced the rulers of all European nations that military power was forevermore closely linked with mass support. The expansion of participation and representation in government were key tactics used by the European regimes to raise that support. Throughout the nineteenth century, war and the expansion of the suffrage went hand in hand.

The third factor often associated with the expansion of democratic politics was the promotion of national unity and development. In some instances, governments seek to subvert local or regional loyalties by linking citizens directly to the central government via the ballot box. America's

is the most certain, and the most legitimate engine of government. Educate and inform the whole mass of the people. Enable them to see that it is their interest to preserve peace and order, and they will preserve them. And it requires no very high degree of education to convince them of this. They are the only sure reliance for the preservation of our liberty. After all, it is my principle that the will of the majority should prevail.[1]

Hamilton

If it be possible at any rate to construct a federal government capable of regulating the common concerns, and preserving the general tranquillity, it must be founded . . . upon the reverse of the principle contended for by the opponents of the proposed Constitution [that is, a confederacy]. It must carry its agency to the persons of the citizens. It must stand in need of no intermediate legislations, but must itself be empowered to employ the arm of the ordinary magistrate to execute its own resolutions. The majesty of the national authority must be manifested through the medium of the courts of justice. The government of the Union, like that of each state, must be able to address itself immediately to the hopes and fears of individuals; and to attract to its support those passions which have the strongest influence upon the human heart. It must, in short, possess all the means, and have a right to resort to all the methods, of executing the powers with which it is entrusted, that are possessed and exercised by the governments of the particular States.[2]

[1] Thomas Jefferson to James Madison, 20 December 1787, in *Jefferson's Letters,* arr. Willson Whitman (Eau Claire, WI: E. M. Hale, 1950), p. 85.
[2] Clinton Rossiter, ed., *The Federalist Papers*, no. 16, (New York: New American Library, 1961), p. 116.

founders saw direct popular election of members of the House of Representatives as a means through which the new federal government could compete with the states for popular allegiance.

The Great Transformation: Tying Democracy to Strong Government

The expansion of democratic politics had two historic consequences. First, democracies opened up the possibility that citizens might use government for their own benefit rather than simply watching it being used for the benefit of others. This consequence is widely understood. But the second is not so well understood: Once citizens perceived that governments could operate in response to their demands, they *became increasingly willing to support the expansion of government.* The public's belief in its

capacity to control the government's action is only one of the many factors responsible for the growth of government. But at the very least, this linkage of democracy and strong government set into motion a wave of governmental growth in the West that began in the middle of the nineteenth century and has continued to the present day.

FREEDOM AND POWER: THE PROBLEM

Ultimately, the growth of governmental power poses the most fundamental threat to the liberties that Americans have so long enjoyed. Because ours is a limited government subject to democratic control, we often see government as simply a powerful servant. But the growth of governmental power continues to raise profound questions about the future.

First, expansion of governmental power can reduce popular influence over policy making. On the one hand, expanding the role of government has the effect of removing decisions from the private to the public sphere. This means that questions that might have been decided by, say, a small number of business executives can become issues to be decided by a popularly elected legislature or even the electorate itself. Environmental policy is an example. Questions about who is responsible for cleaning up pollution are, for better or worse, regulated by the U.S. Congress and are thus matters for public discussion rather than private decision-making alone.

At the same time, however, the enormous scope of national programs in the twentieth century has required an elaborate bureaucracy and the transfer of considerable decision-making power from politically responsive bodies like Congress to administrative agencies. As a result, today's public policies are increasingly dominated by bureaucratic institutions, rules, and procedures that voters cannot easily affect. Can citizens use the power of the bureaucracies we have created, or are we doomed simply to become their subjects?

Second, as government has grown in size and power, the need for citizen cooperation has diminished. In the eighteenth and nineteenth centuries, rulers became responsive to mass opinion because their power was so fragile. Without popular support, rulers lacked the means to curb disorder, collect taxes, and maintain their military power. In an important sense, the eighteenth and nineteenth centuries in the West represented a "window of opportunity" for popular opinion. A conjunction of political and social circumstances compelled those in power to respond to public opinion to shore up their power. Westerners tend to assume that this commitment on the part of eighteenth- and nineteenth-century rulers forever binds their successors to serve public opinion.

It is true that the links between government and opinion—elections, representative bodies, and so on—that were developed during the eighteenth and nineteenth centuries have flourished for nearly 200 years. What has generally gone unnoticed is that the underlying conditions—the windows of opportunity—that produced these institutions have, in many respects, disappeared. Many Western states today may now have sufficiently powerful administrative, military, and police agencies that they *could* curb disorder, collect taxes, and keep their foes in check without necessarily depending upon popular support and approval. Will government continue to bow to the will of the people even though favorable public opinion may not be as crucial as it once was?

Finally, because Americans view government as a servant, they believe that they can have both the blessings of freedom and the benefits of a strong government. Even the most self-proclaimed conservatives have learned to live with Big Brother. In today's America, agencies of the government have considerable control over who may enter occupations, what may be eaten, what may be seen and heard over the airwaves, which forms of education are socially desirable, what types of philanthropy serve the public interest, what sorts of business practices are acceptable, as well as citizens' marital plans, vacation plans, child-rearing practices, and medical care. Is this government still a servant?

Of course, we continue to exert our influence through elections, representation, and, occasionally, direct popular referenda. But do even these processes mean that we can *control* the government? One hundred fifty years ago, Alexis de Tocqueville predicted that Americans would eventually permit their government to become so powerful that elections, representative processes, and so on would come to be ironic interludes providing citizens little more than the opportunity to wave the chains by which the government had bound them. Can we have both freedom and government? To what extent can we continue to depend upon and benefit from government's power while still retaining our liberties? These are questions every generation of Americans must ask.

KEY TERMS

authoritarian government A system of rule in which the government recognizes no formal limits but may, nevertheless, be restrained by the power of other social institutions.

autocracy A form of government in which a single individual—a king, queen, or dictator—rules.

coercion Forcing a person to do something by threats or pressure.

conscription An aspect of coercion whereby the government requires certain involuntary services of citizens, such as compulsory military service, known as "the draft."

constitutional government A system of rule in which formal and effective limits are placed on the powers of the government.

democracy A system of rule that permits citizens to play a significant part in the governmental process, usually through the election of key public officials.

government Institutions and procedures through which a territory and its people are ruled.

nation-state A political entity consisting of a people with some common cultural experience (nation), who also share a common political authority (state), recognized by other sovereignties (nation-states).

oligarchy A form of government in which a small group—landowners, military officers, or wealthy merchants—controls most of the governing decisions

politics Conflicts over the character, membership, and policies of any organizations to which people belong.

representative democracy A system of government that provides the populace with the opportunity to make the government responsive to its views through the selection of representatives, who, in turn, play a significant role in governmental decision making.

totalitarian government A system of rule in which the government recognizes no formal limits on its power and seeks to absorb or eliminate other social institutions that might challenge it.

FOR FURTHER READING

Bendix, Reinhard. *Kings or People: Power and the Mandate to Rule.* Berkeley: University of California Press, 1978.

Bendix, Reinhard. *Nation-Building and Citizenship.* New York: Wiley, 1964.

Dahl, Robert A. *Polyarchy: Participation and Opposition.* New Haven: Yale University Press, 1971.

Grant, Ruth W. *John Locke's Liberalism.* Chicago: University of Chicago Press, 1987.

Hartz, Louis, *The Liberal Tradition in America.* New York: Harcourt, Brace, 1955.

Higgs, Robert. *Crisis and Leviathan: Critical Episodes in the Growth of American Government.* New York: Oxford University Press, 1987.

Huntington, Samuel P. *American Politics: The Promise of Disharmony.* Cambridge: Harvard University Press, 1981.

Keller, Morton. *Affairs of State: Public Life in Late Nineteenth Century America.* Cambridge: Harvard University Press, 1977.

Moore, Barrington. *Social Origins of Dictatorship and Democracy.* Boston: Beacon Press, 1966.

Putnam, Robert. *Making Democracy Work: Civic Traditions in Modern Italy.* Princeton: Princeton University Press, 1993.

Schumpeter, Joseph A. *Capitalism, Socialism, and Democracy.* New York: Harper, 1942.

Skocpol, Theda. *States and Social Revolutions.* New York: Cambridge University Press, 1979.

Strayer, Joseph R. *On the Medieval Origins of the Modern State.* Princeton: Princeton University Press, 1970.

Tilly, Charles, ed. *The Formation of National States in Western Europe.* Princeton: Princeton University Press, 1975.

Tocqueville, Alexis de. *Democracy in America.* Translated by Phillips Bradley. New York: Knopf, Vintage Books, 1945; orig. published 1835.

Weber, Max. *The Theory of Social and Economic Organization.* Translated by Talcott Parsons. New York: Oxford University Press, 1947.

CHAPTER 2

Constructing a Government:
The Founding and the Constitution

"*No* taxation without representation" were words that stirred a generation of Americans long before they even dreamed of calling themselves Americans rather than Englishmen. Among the new English attempts to extract tax revenues to pay for the troops that were being sent to defend the colonial frontier was the infamous Stamp Act of 1765. This act created revenue stamps and required that they be affixed to all printed and legal documents, including newspapers, pamphlets, advertisements, notes and bonds, leases, deeds, and licenses. Protests erupted throughout the colonies against the act. The colonists conducted mass meetings, parades, bonfires, and other demonstrations throughout the spring and summer of 1765. In Boston, for example, a stamp agent was hanged and burned in effigy. Later, the home of the lieutenant governor was sacked, leading to his resignation and that of all of his colonial commission and stamp agents. By November 1765, business proceeded and newspapers were published without the stamp; in March 1766, Parliament repealed the detested law. Through their protest, the colonists took the first steps that ultimately would lead to war and a new nation.

To most contemporary Americans, the revolutionary period represents a heroic struggle by a determined and united group of colonists against

CORE OF THE ARGUMENT

- Both the American Revolution and the Constitution were expressions of competing interests.
- The Constitution laid the groundwork for a government sufficiently powerful to promote commerce and to protect private property.
- The framers sought to prevent the threat posed by "excessive democracy" through internal checks and balances, the indirect selection of the president, and lifetime judicial appointments.
- To secure popular consent for the government, the Constitution provides for the direct popular election of representatives and includes the Bill of Rights.
- To prevent the government from abusing its power, the Constitution incorporates principles such as the separation of powers and federalism.

British oppression. The Boston Tea Party, the battles of Lexington and Concord, the winter at Valley Forge—these are the events that are emphasized in American history. Similarly, the American Constitution—the document establishing the system of government that ultimately emerged from this struggle—is often seen as an inspired, if not divine, work, expressing timeless principles of democratic government.

To understand the character of the American founding and the meaning of the American Constitution, however, it is essential to look beyond the myths and rhetoric and explore the conflicting interests and forces at work during the revolutionary and constitutional periods. Thus, we will first assess the political backdrop of the American Revolution, and then we will examine the Constitution that ultimately emerged as the basis for America's government.

THE FIRST FOUNDING: INTERESTS AND CONFLICTS

Competing ideals and principles often reflect competing interests, and so it was in revolutionary America. The American Revolution and the American Constitution were outgrowths of a struggle among economic and political forces within the colonies. Five sectors of society had interests that were important in colonial politics: (1) the New England merchants; (2) the Southern planters; (3) the "royalists"—holders of royal lands, offices, and patents (licenses to engage in a profession or business activity); (4) shopkeepers, artisans, and laborers; and (5) small farmers. Throughout the eighteenth century, these groups were in conflict over issues of taxation, trade, and commerce. For the most part, however, the Southern planters, the New England merchants, and the royal office and patent holders—groups that together made up the colonial elite—were able to maintain a political alliance that held in check the more radical forces representing shopkeepers, laborers, and small farmers. After 1750, however, British tax and trade policies split the colonial elite, permitting radical forces to expand their political influence and setting into motion a chain of events that culminated in the American Revolution (see Box 2.1).[1]

Political Strife and the Radicalizing of the Colonists

The political strife within the colonies was the background for the events of 1773–1774. In 1773, the British government granted the politically powerful East India Company a monopoly on the export of tea from Britain, eliminating a lucrative form of trade for colonial merchants. Together with their Southern allies, the merchants called upon their radical adversaries—shopkeepers, artisans, laborers, and small farmers—for support. The most dramatic result was the Boston Tea Party of 1773, led by Samuel Adams.

This event was of decisive importance in American history. The merchants had hoped to force the British government to rescind the Tea Act, but they did not support any demands beyond this one. They certainly did not seek independence from Britain. Samuel Adams and the other radicals, however, hoped to provoke the British government to take actions that would alienate its colonial supporters and pave the way for a rebellion. This was precisely the purpose of the Boston Tea Party, and it succeeded. By dumping the East India Company's tea into Boston Harbor, Adams and his followers goaded the British into enacting a number of harsh reprisals. The House of Commons closed the port of Boston to commerce, changed the provincial government of Massachusetts, provided for the removal of accused persons to England for trial, and, most important, restricted movement to the West—fur-

[1]The social makeup of colonial America and some of the social conflicts that divided colonial society are discussed in Jackson Turner Main, *The Social Structure of Revolutionary America* (Princeton: Princeton University Press, 1965).

BOX 2.1

The Road to Revolution

THE ROAD that led the American colonies to break with England was long, indirect, and by no means inevitable. Most rebel leaders hoped for reform; few spoke openly of revolution. Yet dissatisfaction, misunderstanding, and violence spread, yielding what in many ways was an eighteenth-century American guerrilla war against the world's superpower of the day.

The first American casualties of the Revolution came on a frosty March day in 1770. Massachusetts had been a hotbed of dissent against various British actions, including impressment (forced military conscription) and various economic measures. Boston was the center of colonial smuggling that proliferated as Americans sought to avoid what they considered unfair and oppressive levies and taxes. Among the many repugnant economic measures were the Townshend Acts, enacted in 1767, which levied duties on colonial imports and created a Board of Customs Commission in Boston to oversee the collection of revenue.

In 1769, the British stationed 2,000 soldiers in Boston to quell the rising tide of disturbances. The presence of the troops, however, merely provided a focal point for local discontent. Moreover, the British soldiers began to take the jobs of local people at a time when jobs were scarce, driving up unemployment.

On March 5, 1770, a crowd that included ropemakers who had lost their jobs to British soldiers gathered in front of the Boston Customhouse (where the hated customs commissioners did their work). At the head of the crowd was a runaway slave named Crispus Attucks, who had worked for several years on ships out of Boston. The crowd taunted the sentry on duty, who called for help. Nine other soldiers appeared, and they soon found themselves being taunted and pelted with snowballs, clamshells, and sticks by the growing crowd. In the fear and confusion of the moment, one soldier was knocked to the ground. He rose and fired. The other soldiers then fired into the belligerent but unarmed crowd. When the smoke cleared, five were dead and eight wounded. The first to be shot and mortally wounded was Attucks. Thus it was that the first casualty of the Revolutionary War was a black man.

The resistance cause had its first real martyrs, and resistance leaders lost no time in capitalizing on the propaganda value of the incident. After the "Boston Massacre," as it was dubbed by pamphleteers, the Massachusetts governor ordered the troops withdrawn from Boston to avoid further incidents. Six British soldiers were tried for murder. Four were acquitted, and two were punished by having their thumbs branded and being discharged from the army.

Despite a subsequent lull in direct confrontations, anti-British sentiment escalated, as did the cycle of violence. As with many revolutions to follow, few anticipated where the cycle of repression and violence would lead. But leaders were quick to seize as symbols those actions deemed unjust and pernicious. Indeed, the facts of the day were in a real sense less important than the symbols they generated.

SOURCE: Robert A. Divine, et al., *American Past and Present* (Glenview, IL: Scott, Foresman, 1984).

ther alienating the Southern planters who depended upon access to new western lands. These acts of retaliation confirmed the worst criticisms of England and helped radicalize the American colonists.

Thus, the Boston Tea Party set into motion a cycle of provocation and retaliation that in 1774 resulted in the convening of the First Continental Congress—an assembly consisting of delegates from all parts of the country—that called for a total boycott of British goods and, under the prodding of the radicals, began to consider the possibility of independence from British rule. The result was the Declaration of Independence.

The Declaration of Independence

In 1776, the Second Continental Congress appointed a committee consisting of Thomas Jefferson of Virginia, Benjamin Franklin of Pennsylvania, Roger Sherman of Connecticut, John Adams of Massachusetts, and Robert Livingston of New York to draft a statement of American independence from British rule. The Declaration of Independence, written by Jefferson and adopted by the Second Continental Congress, was an extraordinary document in both philosophical and political terms. Philosophically, the Declaration was remarkable for its assertion that certain rights, which it called "unalienable rights"—including life, liberty, and the pursuit of happiness—could not be abridged by governments. In the world of 1776, a world in which some kings still claimed to rule by divine right, this was a dramatic statement. The Declaration was remarkable as a political document because it identified and focused on problems, grievances, aspirations, and principles that might unify the various colonial groups. The Declaration was an attempt to identify and articulate a history and set of principles that might help to forge national unity.[2]

The Articles of Confederation

Having declared independence, the colonies needed to establish a government. In November 1777, the Continental Congress adopted the Articles of Confederation and Perpetual Union—the first written constitution of the United States. Although it was not ratified by all the states until 1781, it served as the country's constitution for almost twelve years, until March 1789.

The *Articles of Confederation* was concerned primarily with limiting the powers of the central government. It created no executive branch. Congress constituted the central government, but it had little power. Execution of its laws was to be left to the individual states. Its members were not much more than messengers from the state legislatures. They were chosen by the state legislatures, their salaries were paid out of the state treasuries, and they were subject to immediate recall by state authorities. In addition, each state, regardless of its size, had only a single vote.

Congress was given the power to declare war and make peace, to make treaties and alliances, to coin or borrow money, and to regulate trade with the Native Americans. It could also appoint the senior officers of the United States Army. But it could not levy taxes or regulate commerce among the states. Moreover, the army officers it appointed had no army to serve in because the nation's armed forces were composed of the state militias. Probably the most unfortunate part of the Articles of Confederation was that the central government could not prevent one state from discriminating against other states in the quest for foreign commerce.

In brief, the relationship between Congress and the states under the Articles of Confederation was much like the contemporary relationship between the United Nations and its member states, a relationship in which virtually all governmental powers are retained by the states. It was called a "confederation" because, as provided under Article II, "each state retains its sovereignty, freedom and independence, and every Power, Jurisdiction and right, which is not by this confederation expressly delegated to the United States, in Congress assembled." Not only was there no executive, there was also no judicial authority and no other means of enforcing Congress's will. If there was to be any enforcement at all, it would have to be done for Congress by the states.[3]

---

[2]See Carl Becker, *The Declaration of Independence* (New York: Vintage, 1942).

[3]See Merrill Jensen, *The Articles of Confederation* (Madison: University of Wisconsin Press, 1963).

THE SECOND FOUNDING: FROM COMPROMISE TO CONSTITUTION

The Declaration of Independence and the Articles of Confederation were not sufficient to hold the nation together as an independent and effective nation-state. From almost the moment of armistice with the British in 1783, moves were afoot to reform and strengthen the Articles.

International Standing and Balance of Power

There was a special concern for the country's international position. Competition among the states for foreign commerce allowed the European powers to play the states off against one another, which created confusion on both sides of the Atlantic. At one point during the winter of 1786–1787, John Adams, a leader in the independence struggle, was sent to negotiate a new treaty with the British, one that would cover disputes left over from the war. The British government responded that, since the United States under the Articles of Confederation was unable to enforce existing treaties, it would negotiate with each of the thirteen states separately.

At the same time, well-to-do Americans—in particular the New England merchants and Southern planters—were troubled by the influ-

---

DEBATING THE ISSUES

The Constitution: Property versus Pragmatism

*T*HROUGHOUT *the second half of the nineteenth century, the prevailing attitude toward the country's founders was increasingly that of veneration, even worship. Like Moses receiving the Ten Commandments, the founders came to be viewed as messengers from God who had received the Constitution intact and whole rather than creating it through a messy political process. Historian Charles Beard helped shatter this myth in the early twentieth century when he argued that the founders were members of the social and economic elite, little interested in democracy and more motivated by a desire to protect their property and wealth, and that the Constitution was their instrument to achieve this end.*

Many have examined Beard's work and found fault with his arguments and facts. Notably, political scientist John P. Roche, writing in the 1960s, argued that the founders, even if they were elite, were excellent politicians who were simply trying to forge a government that would be more effective than the Articles of Confederation. Still, Beard's impact was great, in that he helped move constitutional analysis away from uncritical worship and much closer to viewing the political realities of the late eighteenth century.

BEARD

The Constitution was essentially an economic document based upon the concept that the fundamental private rights of property are anterior to government and morally beyond the reach of popular majorities.

The major portion of the members of the [Constitutional] Convention are on record as recognizing the claim of property to a special and defensive position in the Constitution.

In the ratification of the Constitution, about three-fourths of the adult males failed to vote on the question, having abstained from the elections at which delegates to the state conventions were chosen, either on account of their indifference or their disfranchisment by property qualifications.

ence that "radical" forces exercised in the Continental Congress and in the governments of several of the states. The colonists' victory in the Revolutionary War had not only meant the end of British rule, but it had also significantly changed the balance of political power within the new states. As a result of the Revolution, one key segment of the colonial elite—the royal land, office, and patent holders—was stripped of its economic and political privileges. In fact, many of these individuals, along with tens of thousands of other colonists who considered themselves loyal British subjects, left for Canada after the British surrender. And while the elite was weakened, the radicals were now better organized than ever before.

They controlled such states as Pennsylvania and Rhode Island, where they pursued economic and political policies that struck terror into the hearts of the pre-revolutionary political establishment. The central government under the Articles of Confederation was powerless to intervene.

The new nation's weak international position and domestic turmoil led many Americans to consider whether a new version of the Articles might be necessary. In the fall of 1786, delegates from five states met in Annapolis, Maryland, and called on Congress to send commissioners to Philadelphia at a later time to devise adjustments to the Constitution. Their resolution took on force as a result of an event that occurred the

The Constitution was ratified by a vote of probably not more than one-sixth of the adult males.

It is questionable whether a majority of the voters participating in the elections for the state [ratifying] conventions in New York, Massachusetts, New Hampshire, Virginia, and South Carolina actually approved the ratification of the Constitution. . . .

In the ratification, it became manifest that the line of cleavage for and against the Constitution was between substantial personalty interests on the one hand and the small farming and debtor interests on the other.

The Constitution was not created by "the whole people" as the jurists have said; neither was it created by "the states" as Southern nullifiers long contended; but it was the work of a consolidated group whose interests knew no state boundaries and were truly national in their scope.[1]

ROCHE

The Constitution . . . was not an apotheosis of "constitutionalism," a triumph of architectonic genius; it was a patch-work sewn together under the pressure of both time and events by a group of extremely talented democratic politicians. They refused to attempt the establishment of a strong, centralized sovereignty on the principle of legislative supremacy for the excellent reason that the people would not accept it. They risked their political fortunes by opposing the established doctrines of state sovereignty because they were convinced that the existing system was leading to national impotence and probably foreign domination. For two years, they worked to get a convention established. For over three months, in what must have seemed to the faithful participants an endless process of give-and-take, they reasoned, cajoled, threatened, and bargained amongst themselves. The result was a Constitution which the people, in fact, by democratic processes, did accept, and a new and far better national government was established.[2]

[1]Charles Beard, *An Economic Interpretation of the Constitution of the United States* (New York: Macmillan, 1913), pp. 324–25.
[2]John P. Roche, "The Founding Fathers: A Reform Caucus in Action," *American Political Science Review* 55 (December 1961), pp. 816–16.

following winter in Massachusetts: Shays's Rebellion. Daniel Shays led a mob of farmers, who were protesting foreclosures on their land, in a rebellion against the state government. The state militia dispersed the mob within a few days, but the threat posed by the rebels scared Congress into action. The states were asked to send delegates to Philadelphia to discuss constitutional revision, and eventually delegates were sent from every state but Rhode Island.

The Constitutional Convention

Twenty-nine of a total of 73 delegates selected by the state governments convened in Philadelphia in May 1787, with political strife, international embarrassment, national weakness, and local rebellion fixed in their minds. Recognizing that these issues were symptoms of fundamental flaws in the Articles of Confederation, the delegates soon abandoned the plan to revise the Articles and committed themselves to a second founding—a second, and ultimately successful, attempt to create a legitimate and effective national system. This effort occupied the convention for the next five months.

THE GREAT COMPROMISE   The proponents of a new government fired their opening shot on May 29, 1787, when Edmund Randolph of Virginia offered a resolution that proposed corrections and enlargements in the Articles of Confederation. His proposal was not a simple motion. It provided for virtually every aspect of a new government. Randolph later admitted it was intended to be an alternative draft constitution, and it did in fact serve as the framework for what ultimately became the Constitution. (There is no verbatim record of the debates, but James Madison, a Virginia delegate, was present during nearly all of the deliberations and kept full notes on them.)[4]

[4]Madison's notes are included in Max Farrand, ed., *The Records of the Federal Convention of 1787*, 4 vols., rev. ed. (New Haven: Yale University Press, 1966).

The portion of Randolph's motion that became most controversial was the *"Virginia Plan."* This plan provided for a system of representation in the national legislature based upon the population of each state or the proportion of each state's revenue contribution, or both. (Randolph also proposed a second branch of the legislature, but it was to be elected by the members of the first branch.) Since the states varied enormously in size and wealth, the Virginia Plan was thought by many to be heavily biased in favor of the large states.

While the convention was debating the Virginia Plan, additional delegates were arriving in Philadelphia and were beginning to mount opposition to it. In particular, delegates from the less populous states, which included Delaware, New Jersey, Connecticut, and New York, asserted that the more populous states, such as Virginia, Pennsylvania, North Carolina, Massachusetts, and Georgia, would dominate the new government if representation were to be determined by population. The smaller states argued that each state should be equally represented in the new regime regardless of its population. The proposal, called the *"New Jersey Plan"* (it was introduced by William Paterson of New Jersey), focused on revising the Articles rather than replacing them. Their opposition to the Virginia Plan's system of representation was sufficient to send the proposals back to committee for reworking into a common document.

The outcome was the Connecticut Compromise, also known as the *Great Compromise*. Under the terms of this compromise, in the first branch of Congress—the House of Representatives—the representatives would be apportioned according to the number of inhabitants in each state. This, of course, was what delegates from the large states had sought. But in the second branch—the Senate—each state would have an equal vote regardless of its size; this was to deal with the concerns of the small states. This compromise was not immediately satisfactory to all the delegates. In the end, however, both sets of forces preferred compromise to the breakup of the union, and the plan was accepted.

THE QUESTION OF SLAVERY: THE "THREE-FIFTHS" COMPROMISE   The story so far is too neat, too easy, and too anticlimactic. After all, the notion of a bicameral (two-chambered) legislature was very much in the air in 1787. Some of the states had had this for years. The Philadelphia delegates might well have gone straight to the adoption of two chambers based on two different principles of representation even without the dramatic interplay of conflict and compromise. But a far more fundamental issue had to be confronted before the Great Compromise could take place: the issue of slavery.

Many of the conflicts that emerged during the Constitutional Convention were reflections of the fundamental differences between the slave and the nonslave states—differences that pitted the Southern planters and the New England merchants against one another. This was the first premonition of a conflict that was almost to destroy the Republic in later years. In the midst of debate over large versus small states, Madison observed, "The great danger to our general government is the great southern and northern interests of the continent, being opposed to each other. Look to the votes in Congress, and most of them stand divided by the geography of the country, not according to the size of the states."[5]

Over 90 percent of all slaves resided in five states—Georgia, Maryland, North Carolina, South Carolina, and Virginia—where they accounted for 30 percent of the total population. In some places, slaves outnumbered nonslaves by as much as ten to one. Were they to be counted in determining how many congressional seats a state should have? Northerners and Southerners eventually reached agreement through the *Three-fifths Compromise*. The seats in the House of Representa-

tatives would be apportioned according to a "population" in which five slaves would count as three persons. The slaves would not be allowed to vote, of course, but the number of representatives would be apportioned accordingly. This arrangement was supported by the slave states, which included some of the biggest and some of the smallest states at that time. It was also accepted by delegates from nonslave states who strongly supported the principle of property representation, whether that property was expressed in slaves or in land, money, or stocks.

The concern exhibited by most delegates was over how much slaves would count toward a state's representation rather than whether the institution of slavery would continue. The Three-fifths Compromise, in the words of political scientist Donald Robinson, "gave Constitutional sanction to the fact that the United States was composed of some persons who were 'free' and others who were not, and it established the principle, new in republican theory, that a man who lives among slaves had a greater share in the election of representatives than the man who did not. Although the Three-fifths Compromise acknowledged slavery and rewarded slave owners, nonetheless, it probably kept the South from unanimously rejecting the Constitution."[6]

THE CONSTITUTION

The political significance of the Great Compromise and Three-fifths Compromise was to reinforce the unity of those who sought the creation of a new government. The Great Compromise reassured those who feared that the importance of their own local or regional influence would be reduced by the new governmental framework. The Three-fifths Compromise temporarily defused

[5]Ibid., vol. 1, p. 476.

[6]Donald Robinson, *Slavery in the Structure of American Politics, 1765–1820* (New York: Harcourt Brace Jovanovich, 1971), p. 201.

the rivalry between the merchants and planters. Their unity secured, members of the alliance supporting the establishment of a new government moved to fashion a constitutional framework for this government that would be congruent with their economic and political interests.

In particular, the framers sought a new government that, first, would be strong enough to promote commerce and protect property from radical state legislatures such as Rhode Island's. This became the basis for the establishment in the Constitution of national control over commerce and finance, as well as the establishment of national judicial supremacy and a strong presidency. Second, the framers sought to prevent what they saw as the threat posed by the "excessive democracy" of the state and national governments under the Articles of Confederation (see Concept Map 2.1, page 26). This led to such constitutional principles as *bicameralism* (division of the Congress into two chambers), checks and balances, staggered terms in office, and indirect election (selection of the president by an electoral college rather than by voters directly).

Third, hoping to secure support from the states or the public-at-large for the new form of government they proposed, the framers provided for direct popular election of representatives and, subsequently, for the addition of the Bill of Rights. Finally, to prevent the new government from abusing its power, the framers incorporated principles such as the separation of powers and federalism into the Constitution. Let us now assess the major provisions of the Constitution's seven articles to see how each relates to these objectives.

The Legislative Branch

The Constitution provided in the first seven sections of Article I for a Congress consisting of two chambers—a House of Representatives and a Senate. Members of the House of Representatives were given two-year terms in office and were to be subject to direct popular election—though generally only white males had the right to vote. State legislatures were to appoint members of the Senate (this was changed in 1913 by the Seventeenth Amendment, providing for direct election of senators) for six-year terms. These terms, moreover, were staggered so that the appointments of one-third of the senators would expire every two years. The Constitution assigned somewhat different tasks to the House and Senate. Though the approval of each body was required for the enactment of a law, the Senate alone was given the power to ratify treaties and approve presidential appointments. The House, on the other hand, was given the sole power to originate revenue bills.

The character of the legislative branch was directly related to the framers' major goals. The House of Representatives was designed to be directly responsible to the people in order to encourage popular consent for the new Constitution and, as we saw in Chapter 1, to help enhance the power of the new government. At the same time, to guard against "excessive democracy," the power of the House of Representatives was checked by the Senate, whose members were to be appointed for long terms rather than elected directly by the people for short terms.

Staggered terms of service in the Senate were intended to make that body even more resistant to popular pressure. Since only one-third of the senators would be selected at any given time, the composition of the institution would be protected from changes in popular preferences transmitted by the state legislatures. Thus, the structure of the legislative branch was designed to contribute to governmental power, to promote popular consent for the new government, and at the same time to place limits on the popular political currents that many of the framers saw as a radical threat to the economic and social order.

THE POWERS OF CONGRESS AND THE STATES   The issues of power and consent were important throughout the Constitution. Section 8 of Article I specifically listed the powers of Congress, which

THE SEVEN ARTICLES OF THE CONSTITUTION

1. The Legislative Branch

House: two-year terms, elected directly by the people.

Senate: six-year terms (staggered so that only one-third of the Senate changes in any given election), appointed by state legislature (changed in 1913 to direct election).

Expressed powers of the national government: collecting taxes, borrowing money, regulating commerce, declaring war, and maintaining an army and a navy; all other power belongs to the states, unless deemed otherwise by the elastic ("necessary and proper") clause.

Exclusive powers of the national government: states are expressly forbidden to issue their own paper money, tax imports and exports, regulate trade outside their own borders, and impair the obligation of contracts; these powers are the exclusive domain of the national government.

2. The Executive Branch

Presidency: four-year terms (limited in 1951 to a maximum of two terms), elected indirectly by the electoral college.

Powers: can recognize other countries, negotiate treaties, grant reprieves and pardons, convene Congress in special sessions, and veto congressional enactments.

3. The Judicial Branch

Supreme Court: lifetime terms, appointed by the president with the approval of the Senate.

Powers: include resolving conflicts between federal and state laws, determining whether power belongs to national government or the states, and settling controversies between citizens of different states.

4. National Unity and Power

Reciprocity among states: establishes that each state must give "full faith and credit" to official acts of other states, and guarantees citizens of any state the "privileges and immunities" of every other state.

5. Amending the Constitution

Procedures: requires two-thirds approval in Congress and three-fourths adoption by the states.

6. National Supremacy

The Constitution and national law are the supreme law of the land and cannot be overruled by state law.

7. Ratification

The Constitution became effective when approved by nine states.

include the authority to collect taxes, to borrow money, to regulate commerce, to declare war, and to maintain an army and navy. By granting it these powers, the framers indicated very clearly that they intended the new government to be far more influential than its predecessor. At the same time, by giving these important powers to Congress, the framers sought to reassure citizens that their views would be fully represented whenever the government exercised its new powers.

As a further guarantee to the people that the new government would pose no threat to them, the Constitution implied that any powers *not* listed were not granted at all. This is the doctrine of

CONCEPT MAP 2.1

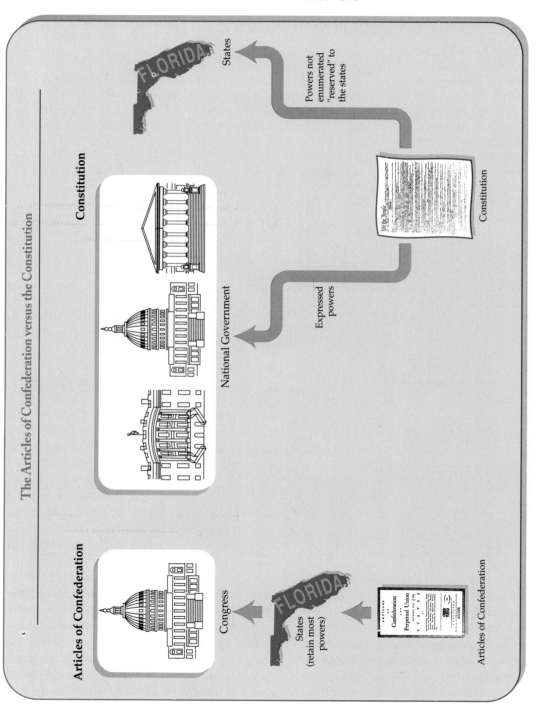

The Articles of Confederation versus the Constitution

Constitution

Constitution

States

FLORIDA

Powers not enumerated "reserved" to the states

National Government

Expressed powers

Articles of Confederation

Congress

States (retain most powers)

FLORIDA

Articles of Confederation

Articles of Confederation

expressed power. The Constitution grants only those powers specifically *expressed* in its text. But the framers intended to create an active and powerful government, and so they included the *necessary and proper clause*, sometimes known as the *elastic clause*, which signified that the enumerated powers were meant to be a source of strength to the national government, not a limitation on it. Each power could be used with the utmost vigor, but no new powers could be seized upon by the national government without a constitutional amendment. Any power not enumerated was conceived to be "reserved" to the states (or the people).

If there had been any doubt at all about the scope of the necessary and proper clause, it was settled by Chief Justice John Marshall in one of the most important constitutional cases in American history, *McCulloch v. Maryland,* which dealt with the question of whether states could tax the federally chartered Bank of the United States.[7] This bank was largely under the control of the Federalist party and was extremely unpopular in the West and South. A number of states, including Maryland, imposed stiff taxes on the bank's operations, hoping to weaken or destroy it. When the bank's Baltimore branch refused to pay state taxes, the state brought a suit that was eventually heard by the U.S. Supreme Court (see also Chapter 3).

Writing for the Court, Chief Justice John Marshall ruled that states had no power to tax national agencies. Moreover, Marshall took the opportunity to give an expansive interpretation of the necessary and proper clause of the Constitution by asserting that Congress clearly possessed the power to charter a bank even though this was not explicitly mentioned in the Constitution. Marshall argued that so long as Congress was passing acts pursuant to one of the enumerated powers, then any of the means convenient to such an end were also legitimate. As he put it, any government "entrusted with such ample powers . . . must also be entrusted with ample means for

[7]McCulloch v. Maryland, 4 Wheaton 316 (1819).

their execution." It was through this avenue that the national government could grow in power without necessarily taking on any powers that were not already enumerated.

LIMITS ON THE NATIONAL GOVERNMENT AND THE STATES The Constitution listed in Section 9 a number of important limitations on the national government, which are in the nature of a mini bill of rights. These included the right of *habeas corpus*, which means, in effect, that the government cannot deprive a person of liberty without explaining the reason to a court. These limitations are part of the reason that most delegates at the Constitutional Convention felt no urgent need to add a full-scale bill of rights to the Constitution. Some provisions were clearly designed to prevent the national government from threatening important property interests. For example, Congress was prohibited from giving preference to the ports of one state over those of another. Furthermore, neither Congress nor the state legislatures could require American vessels to pay duty as they entered the ports of any state, thereby preventing the states from charging tribute. All this was part of the delegates' effort to clear away major obstructions to national commerce.

The framers also included restrictions on the states because of their fear of the capacity of the state legislatures to engage in radical action against property and creditors. There are few absolutes in the Constitution, and most of them are found in Article I, Section 10, among the limitations on state powers in matters of commerce. The states were explicitly and absolutely denied the power to tax imports and exports and to place any regulations or other burdens on commerce outside their own borders. They were also explicitly prohibited from issuing paper money or providing for the payment of debts in any form except gold and silver coin.

Finally, and of greatest importance, the states were not allowed to impair the obligation of contracts. This was almost sufficient by itself to reassure commercial interests because it meant that state legislatures would not be able to cancel their contracts to purchase goods and services. Nor would they be able to pass any laws that would seriously alter the terms of contracts between private parties. All the powers that the states were in effect forbidden to exercise came to be known as the *exclusive powers* of the national government.

The Executive Branch

The Constitution provided for the establishment of the presidency in Article II. As Alexander Hamilton put it, the presidential article sought "energy in the Executive." It did so in an effort to overcome the natural stalemate that was built into the bicameral legislature as well as into the separation of powers among the legislative, executive, and judicial branches. The Constitution afforded the president a measure of independence from the people and from the other branches of government—particularly the Congress.

In line with the framers' goal of increased power to the national government, the president was granted the unconditional power to accept ambassadors from other countries; this amounted to the power to "recognize" other countries. He was also given the power to negotiate treaties, although their acceptance required the approval of the Senate. The president was given the unconditional right to grant reprieves and pardons, except in cases of impeachment. And he was provided with the power to appoint major departmental personnel, to convene Congress in special session, and to veto congressional enactments. (The veto power is formidable, but it is not absolute, since Congress can override it by a two-thirds vote.)

At the same time, the framers sought to help the president withstand (excessively) democratic pressures by making him subject to indirect rather than direct election (through his selection by a separate electoral college). The extent to which the framers' hopes were actually realized will be the topic of Chapter 6.

The Judicial Branch

Article III establishes the judicial branch. This provision reflects the framers' concern with giving more power to the national government and checking radical democratic impulses, while guarding against abuse of liberty and property by the new national government itself.

The framers created a court that was to be literally a supreme court of the United States, and not merely the highest court of the national government. The Supreme Court was given the power to resolve any conflicts that might emerge between federal and state laws and to determine to which level of government a power belonged. In addition, the Supreme Court was assigned jurisdiction over controversies between citizens of different states. The long-term significance of this was that as the country developed a national economy, it came to rely increasingly on the federal judiciary, rather than on the state courts, for resolution of disputes.

Judges were given lifetime appointments in order to protect them from popular politics and from interference by the other branches. But they would not be totally immune to politics or to the other branches, for the president was to appoint the judges and the Senate to approve the appointments. Congress would also have the power to create inferior (lower) courts, to change the jurisdiction of the federal courts, to add or subtract federal judges, even to change the size of the Supreme Court.

No direct mention is made in the Constitution of *judicial review*—the power of the courts to render the final decision when there is a conflict of interpretation of the Constitution or of laws. This conflict could be between the courts and Congress, the courts and the executive branch, or the courts and the states. Scholars generally feel that judicial review is implicit in the very existence of a written Constitution and in the power given directly to the federal courts over "all Cases . . . arising under this Constitution, the Laws of the United States and Treaties made, or which shall be made, under their Authority" (Article III, Section 2). The Supreme Court eventually assumed the power of judicial review. Its assumption of this power, as we shall see in Chapter 7, was based not on the Constitution itself but on the politics of later decades and the membership of the Court.

National Unity and Power

Various provisions in the Constitution addressed the framers' concern with national unity and power. Article IV's provisions for comity (reciprocity) among states and among citizens of all states were extremely important, for without them there would have been little prospect of unobstructed national movement of persons and goods. Both "comity clauses," the *full faith and credit clause* and the *privileges and immunities clause*, were taken directly from the Articles of Confederation. The first clause provided that each state had to give "full faith and credit" to the official acts of all other states. The second provided that the citizens of any state were guaranteed the "privileges and immunities" of every other state, as though they were citizens of that state. Each state was also prohibited from discriminating against the citizens of other states in favor of its own citizens, with the Supreme Court being the arbiter in each case.

The Constitution also contained the infamous provision that obliged persons living in free states to capture escaped slaves and return them to their owners. This provision, repealed in 1865 by the Thirteenth Amendment, was a promise to the South that it would not have to consider itself an economy isolated from the rest of the country.

The Constitution provided for the admission of new states to the union and guaranteed existing states that no territory would be taken from any of them without their consent. The Constitution provided that the United States "shall guarantee to every State . . . a Republican Form of Government." But this is not an open invitation to the national government to intervene in the affairs of any of the states. A clause states that the federal government can intervene in matters of domestic violence only when invited to by a state legislature or the state executive when the legislature is not in session or when necessary to enforce a federal court order. This has left the question of national intervention in local disorders almost completely to the discretion of local and state officials.

The framers' concern with national supremacy was also expressed in Article VI, in the *supremacy clause*, which provided that national laws and treaties "shall be the supreme law of the land." This meant that all laws made under the "authority of the United States" would be superior to all laws adopted by any state or any other subdivision, and that the states would be expected to respect all treaties made under that authority. This was a direct effort to keep the states from dealing separately with foreign nations or businesses. The supremacy clause also bound the officials of all state and local as well as federal governments to take an oath of office to support the national Constitution. This meant that every action taken by the United States Congress would have to be applied within each state as though the action were in fact state law.

To found the nation on a solid economic base, the Constitution also provided that all debts entered into under the Articles of Confederation were to be continued as valid debts under the new Constitution. The first Congress acted to assume all debts incurred by the states during the Revolution. This action secured the allegiance of the mercantile class within the country, because most of the debts incurred by the national and state governments during and after the Revolution were held by wealthy Americans concerned about the dependability of their government. It was one of the most important assurances to the commercial interests that the Constitution favored commerce. It also assured foreign countries, especially France and England, that the United States could be trusted in matters of trade, treaties, defense, and credit. Repudiation of debts at the very outset would have endangered the

COMPARING THE ARTICLES OF CONFEDERATION AND THE CONSTITUTION

	Articles of Confederation	Constitution
legislative branch	*power to:* declare war and make peace, make treaties and alliances, coin or borrow money, regulate trade with Native Americans, appoint senior officers of the United States Army *limits on power:* No power to levy taxes or regulate commerce among the states, create national armed forces	*power to:* collect taxes, borrow money, regulate commerce, declare war, and maintain an army and navy *limits on power:* all other powers belong to the states
executive branch	no executive branch was created	*power to:* recognize other countries, negotiate treaties, grant reprieves and pardons, appoint major departmental personnel, convene special sessions of Congress, veto congressional actions *limits on power:* Senate must approve treaties and Congress can override a veto by a two-thirds vote
judicial branch	no judiciary was created	*power to:* resolve conflicts between state and federal laws, determine to which level of government a power belongs, decide conflicts between citizens of different states *limits on power:* judicial appointments made by the President and approved by the Senate; Congress creates lower courts and can change the jurisdiction of the federal courts; Congress can add or subtract federal judges and can change the size of the Supreme Court

country's sovereignty, since sovereignty depends on the credibility a nation enjoys in the eyes of other nations.

Amending the Constitution

The Constitution established procedures for its own revision in Article V. Its provisions are so difficult that Americans have succeeded in the amending process only seventeen times since 1791, when the first ten amendments were adopted. Many other amendments have been proposed in Congress, but fewer than forty of them have even come close to fulfilling the Constitution's requirement of a two-thirds vote in Congress, and only a fraction have gotten anywhere near adoption by three-fourths of the states. (A breakdown of these figures and further discussion of amending the Constitution appear in Chapter 3.) The Constitution could also be amended by a constitutional convention. Occasionally, proponents of particular measures, such as a balanced-budget amendment, have called for a constitutional convention to consider their proposals. Whatever the purpose for which it was called, however, such a convention would presumably have the authority to revise America's entire system of government.

Ratifying the Constitution

The rules for the ratification of the Constitution of 1787 made up Article VII of the Constitution. This provision actually violated the lawful procedure for constitutional change incorporated in the Articles of Confederation. For one thing, it adopted a nine-state rule in place of the unanimity among the states required by the Articles of Confederation. For another, it provided that ratification would occur in special state conventions called for that purpose rather than in the state legislatures. All the states except Rhode Island eventually did set up state conventions to ratify the Constitution, and none seemed to protest very loudly the extralegal character of the procedure.

Constitutional Limits on the National Government's Power

As we have indicated, though the framers sought to create a powerful national government, they also wanted to guard against possible misuse of that power. To that end, the framers incorporated two key principles into the Constitution—the *separation of powers* and *federalism* (see also Chapter 3). A third set of limitations, in the form of the *Bill of Rights*, was added to the Constitution to help secure its ratification when opponents of the document charged that it paid insufficient attention to citizens' rights.

THE SEPARATION OF POWERS   No principle of politics was more widely shared at the time of the 1787 founding than the principle that power must be used to balance power. The French political theorist Montesquieu (1689–1755) believed that this balance was an indispensable defense against tyranny, and his writings, especially his major work, *The Spirit of the Laws*, "were taken as political gospel" at the Philadelphia Convention.[8] This principle is not stated explicitly in the Constitution, but it is clearly built on Articles I, II, and III, which provide for

1. Three separate branches of government (see Concept Map 2.2).
2. Different methods of selecting the top personnel, so that each branch is responsible to a different constituency. This is supposed to produce a "mixed regime," in which the personnel of each department will develop very different interests and outlooks on how to govern, and different groups in society will be assured some access to governmental decision making.
3. *Checks and balances*, a system under which each of the branches is given some power over the others. Familiar examples are the presidential veto power over legislation and the power of the Senate to approve high-level presidential appointments (see Concept Map 2.3, page 33).

[8]Max Farrand, *The Framing of the Constitution of the United States* (New Haven: Yale University Press, 1962), p. 49.

CONCEPT MAP 2.2

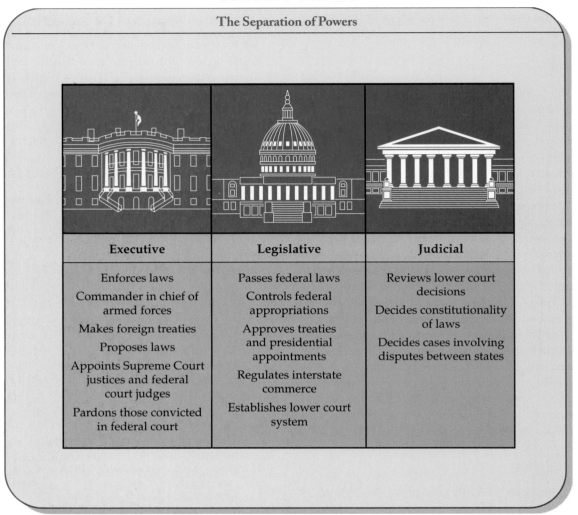

The Separation of Powers

Executive	Legislative	Judicial
Enforces laws	Passes federal laws	Reviews lower court decisions
Commander in chief of armed forces	Controls federal appropriations	Decides constitutionality of laws
Makes foreign treaties	Approves treaties and presidential appointments	Decides cases involving disputes between states
Proposes laws	Regulates interstate commerce	
Appoints Supreme Court justices and federal court judges	Establishes lower court system	
Pardons those convicted in federal court		

One clever formulation conceives of this system not as separated powers but as "separated institutions sharing power,"[9] thus diminishing the chance that power will be misused.

[9]Richard E. Neustadt, *Presidential Power* (New York: Wiley, 1960), p. 33.

FEDERALISM Federalism was actually a step toward greater centralization of power. The delegates agreed that they needed to place more power at the national governmental level, without completely undermining the power of the state governments. Thus, they devised a system of two sovereigns—the states and the nation—with the hope that competition between the two would be an effective limitation on the power of both.

THE BILL OF RIGHTS Late in the Philadelphia Convention, a motion was made to include a bill of rights in the Constitution. After a brief debate in which hardly a word was said in its favor and only one speech was made against it, the motion to include it was almost unanimously turned down. Most delegates sincerely believed that since the federal government was already limited to its expressed powers, further protection of citizens was not needed. The delegates argued that the states should adopt bills of rights because their powers needed more limitations than those of the federal government. But almost immediately after the Constitution was ratified, there was a movement to adopt a national bill of rights. This is why the Bill of Rights, adopted in 1791, comprises the first ten amendments to the Constitution rather than being part of the body of it. We will have a good deal more to say about the Bill of Rights in Chapter 3.

THE FIGHT FOR RATIFICATION

The first hurdle faced by the new Constitution was ratification by state conventions of delegates elected by white, propertied males of each state. This struggle for ratification was carried out in thirteen separate campaigns. Each involved different individuals, moved at a different pace, and was influenced by local as well as national considerations. Two sides faced off throughout all the states, however, taking the names of Federalists and Antifederalists. The *Federalists* supported the Constitution and preferred a strong national government. The *Antifederalists* opposed the Constitution and preferred a more decentralized federal system of government; they took on their name by default, in reaction to their better-organized opponents. The Federalists were united in their support of the Constitution. The Antifederalists, although opposing this plan, were divided as to what they believed the alternative should be.

Under the name of "Publius," Alexander Hamilton, James Madison, and John Jay wrote 85 articles in the New York newspapers supporting ratification of the Constitution. These *Federalist Papers,* as they are collectively known today, defended the principles of the Constitution and sought to dispel the fears of a national authority. The Antifederalists, however, such as Richard Henry Lee and Patrick Henry of Virginia, and George Clinton of New York, argued that the new Constitution betrayed the Revolution and was a step toward monarchy. They accused the Philadelphia Convention of being a "Dark Conclave," which had worked under a "thick veil of secrecy" to overthrow the law and spirit of the Articles of Confederation.

By the end of 1787 and the beginning of 1788, five states had ratified the Constitution. Delaware, New Jersey, and Georgia ratified it unanimously; Connecticut and Pennsylvania ratified by wide margins. Opposition was overcome in Massachusetts by the inclusion of nine recommended amendments to the Constitution to protect human rights. Ratification by Maryland and South Carolina followed. In June 1788, New Hampshire became the ninth state to ratify. That put the Constitution into effect, but for the new national government to have real power, the approval of both Virginia and New York would be needed. After impassioned debate and a great number of recommendations for future amendment of the Constitution, especially for a bill of rights, the Federalists mustered enough votes for approval of the Constitution in June (Virginia) and July (New York) of 1788. North Carolina joined the new government in 1789, after a bill of rights actually was submitted to the states by Congress, and Rhode Island held out until 1790 before finally voting to become part of the new union.

CONCEPT MAP 2.3

Checks and Balances

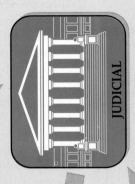
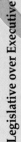
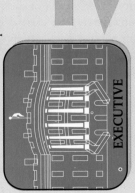
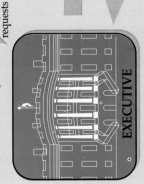

JUDICIAL

LEGISLATIVE

EXECUTIVE

Legislative over Judicial
Can change size of federal court system and the number of Supreme Court justices
Can propose constitutional amendments
Can reject Supreme Court nominees
Can impeach and remove federal judges

Judicial over Legislative
Can declare laws unconstitutional
Chief justice presides over Senate during hearing to impeach the president

Judicial over Executive
Can declare executive actions unconstitutional
Power to issue warrants
Chief justice presides over impeachment of president

Executive over Judicial
Nominates Supreme Court justices
Nominates federal judges
Can pardon those convicted in federal court
Can refuse to enforce Court decisions

Executive over Legislative
Can veto acts of Congress
Can call Congress into a special session
Carries out, and thereby interprets, laws passed by Congress
Vice president casts tie-breaking vote in the Senate

Legislative over Executive
Can override presidential veto
Can impeach and remove president
Can reject president's appointments and refuse to ratify treaties
Can conduct investigations into president's actions
Can refuse to pass laws or to provide funding that president requests

FEDERALISTS VERSUS ANTIFEDERALISTS

	Federalists	Antifederalists
Who were they?	Property owners, creditors, merchants	Small farmers, frontiersmen, debtors, shopkeepers
What did they believe?	Believed that elites were best fit to govern; feared "excessive democracy"	Believed that government should be closer to the people; feared concentration of power in hands of the elites
What system of government did they favor?	Favored strong national government; believed in "filtration" so that only elites would obtain governmental power	Favored retention of power by state governments and protection of individual rights
Who were their leaders?	Alexander Hamilton James Madison George Washington	Patrick Henry George Mason Elbridge Gerry George Clinton

REFLECTIONS ON THE FOUNDING: PRINCIPLES OR INTERESTS?

The final product of the Constitutional Convention would have to be considered an extraordinary victory for those who wanted a new system of government to replace the Articles of Confederation. The new Constitution laid the groundwork for a government that would be sufficiently powerful to promote trade, to protect property, and to check the activities of radical state legislatures. Moreover, this new government was so constructed through internal checks and balances, indirect selection of officeholders, lifetime judicial appointments, and other similar provisions to preclude the "excessive democracy" feared by many of the founders. Some of the framers favored going even further in limiting popular influence, but the general consensus at the convention was that a thoroughly undemocratic docu-

ment would never receive the popular approval needed to be ratified by the states.[10]

Though the Constitution was the product of a particular set of political forces, the principles of government it established have a significance that goes far beyond the interests of its authors. Two of these principles, federalism and civil liberties, will be discussed in Chapters 3 and 4. A third important constitutional principle that has affected America's government for the past two hundred years is the principle of checks and balances. As we saw earlier, the framers gave each of the three branches of government a means of intervening in and blocking the actions of the others. Often, checks and balances have seemed to prevent the government from getting much done. During the 1960s, for example, liberals were often infuriated as they watched Congress stall presidential initiatives in the area of civil rights. More recently,

[10]See Farrand, *The Records of the Federal Convention*, vol. 1, p. 132.

JAMES MADISON AND GEORGE CLINTON
A Federalist and an Antifederalist Who Built a Nation

JAMES MADISON is best known as the man who, more than any other, shaped the U.S. Constitution, forged in Philadelphia in 1787. George Clinton, who served as a popular New York governor from 1777 to 1795 and again from 1801 to 1804, is little remembered by history except for his opposition to the Constitution. Yet Clinton's contribution as an Antifederalist was nearly as significant in the formation of the new government as Madison's.

As a member of Congress under the Articles of Confederation, Madison was convinced that a new system of government was necessary. At the Constitutional Convention, he was the primary architect of the Virginia Plan, the original constitutional blueprint, and even though some of Madison's most cherished ideas were defeated by the convention (such as the idea that Congress should have an absolute veto over all state laws), he is credited with being the "father" of the Constitution. After the convention, Madison worked tirelessly for the document's ratification; with Alexander Hamilton and John Jay, he wrote *The Federalist* essays, which were published in newspapers around the country to persuade the nation to accept the Constitution.

George Clinton was among the prominent figures who opposed Madison's efforts. Like many Antifederalists, Clinton was suspicious of the enhanced powers of this new central government, fearing that a single government ruling a large population would be too quick to deprive the people of their liberties. Unlike Madison, who opposed too

JAMES MADISON

conservatives were outraged when President Clinton thwarted congressional efforts to enact legislation promised in the Republican "Contract With America." At various times, all sides have vilified the judiciary for invalidating legislation enacted by Congress and signed by the president.

Over time, checks and balances have acted as brakes on the governmental process. Groups hoping to bring about changes in policy or governmental institutions seldom have been able to bring about decisive and dramatic transformations in a short period of time. Instead, checks and balances have slowed the pace of change and increased the need for compromise and accommodation.

Groups able to take control of the White House, for example, must negotiate with their rivals who remain entrenched on Capitol Hill. New forces in Congress must reckon with the influence of other forces in the executive branch and in the courts. Checks and balances inevitably frustrate those who desire change, but they also function as a safeguard against rash action. During the 1950s,

much government by the people, Clinton believed that government should be founded on the consent of the governed. His opinions on direct representation based on geographically small districts buttressed arguments on behalf of retaining a "popular house" in Congress—that is, the House of Representatives.

When the new Constitution was sent to the states for ratification, it met a chilly reception in New York, a hotbed of Antifederalist sentiment. When the state's ratification convention met in the summer of 1788, Antifederalists outnumbered Federalists 2 to 1. The convention selected Governor Clinton to preside, but in doing so, silenced his eloquent voice (since he had to concern himself with conducting the meetings). Led by Alexander Hamilton, the Federalists decided to stall the proceedings in the hope that other key states would ratify the new document in the meantime, thereby increasing the pressure on New York. News of Virginia's ratification—the tenth state to do so—forced the collapse of Antifederalist resistance, and New York ratified by the closest vote of any state, 30 to 27.

Despite Clinton's silence at the state convention, once the Constitution was approved, his was a leading voice on behalf of the addition of a Bill of Rights to safeguard individual liberties against governmental encroachment. In 1791, the first ten amendments were added to the Constitution, thanks in part to the key guidance of Congressman James Madison. Despite enduring personal animosities, when Madison became president in 1808, he chose George Clinton for his vice president.

GEORGE CLINTON

SOURCE: Stephen L. Schechter, ed., *The Reluctant Pillar* (Troy, NY: Russell Sage College, 1985).

for example, Congress was caught up in a quasi-hysterical effort to unmask subversive activities in the United States, which might have led to a serious erosion of American liberties if not for the checks and balances provided by the executive and the courts. Thus, a governmental principle that serves as a frustrating limitation one day may become a vitally important safeguard the next.

Yet, while the Constitution sought to lay the groundwork for a powerful government, the framers struggled to reconcile government power with freedom. The framers surrounded the powerful institutions of the new regime with a variety of safeguards—a continual array of checks and balances—designed to make certain that the power of the national government could not be used to undermine the states' power and their citizens' freedoms. Thus, the framers were the first Americans to confront head-on the dilemma of freedom and power. Whether their solutions to this dilemma were successful is, of course, the topic of the remainder of our story.

CHAPTER REVIEW

Political conflicts between the colonies and England, and among competing groups within the colonies, led to the first founding as expressed by the Declaration of Independence. The first constitution, the Articles of Confederation, was adopted one year later (1777). Under this document, the states retained their sovereignty. The central government, composed solely of Congress, had few powers and no means of enforcing its will. The national government's weakness soon led to the second founding as expressed by the Constitution of 1787.

In this second founding, the framers sought, first, to fashion a new government sufficiently powerful to promote commerce and protect property from radical state legislatures. Second, they sought to bring an end to the "excessive democracy" of the state and national governments under the Articles of Confederation. Third, they sought to introduce mechanisms that would secure popular consent for the new government. Finally, the framers sought to make certain that their new government would not itself pose a threat to liberty and property.

The Constitution consists of seven articles. Article I provides for a Congress of two chambers (Sections 1–7), defines the powers of the national government (Section 8), interprets the national government's powers as a source of strength rather than a limitation (necessary and proper clause), places specific restrictions on the national government (Section 9), and limits state powers (Section 10). Article II describes the presidency and establishes it as a separate branch of government. Article III is the judiciary article. While there is no direct mention of judicial review in this article, the Supreme Court eventually assumed that power. The main provisions of Article IV, the full faith and credit clause and the privileges and immunities clause, provide for reciprocity among the states. Article V describes the procedures for amending the Constitution. Article VI establishes that national laws and treaties are "the supreme law of the land." And finally, Article VII specifies the procedure for ratifying the Constitution of 1787.

Events		Institutional Developments
TIME LINE ON THE FOUNDING		
Events		**Institutional Developments**
	1750	
		Albany Congress calls for colonial unity (1754)
French defeated in North America (1760)		
Stamp Act enacted (1765)		Stamp Act Congress attended by delegates from all colonies (1765)
Townshend duties enacted (1767)		
Boston Massacre (1770)	1770	
Tea Act; Boston Tea Party (1773)		
British adopt Coercive Acts to punish colonies (1774)		First Continental Congress adopts Declaration of American Rights (1774)

Events	Institutional Developments
Battles of Lexington and Concord (1775)	Second Continental Congress assumes role of revolutionary government (1775); adopts Declaration of Independence (1776)
	New state constitutions adopted (1776–1784)
	Second Continental Congress adopts Articles of Confederation (1777)
1780	
British surrender at Yorktown (1787)	
Shays's Rebellion (1787)	Annapolis Convention calls for consideration of government revision (1786)
	Constitutional Convention drafts blueprint for new government (1787)
Federalist Papers (1788)	Constitution ratified by states (1788–1790)

KEY TERMS

Antifederalists Those who favored strong state governments and a weak national government and who were opponents of the constitution proposed at the American Constitutional Convention of 1787.

Articles of Confederation America's first written constitution. Adopted by the Continental Congress in 1777, the Articles of Confederation and Perpetual Union were the formal basis for America's national government until 1789, when they were supplanted by the Constitution.

bicameralism Division of a legislative body into two houses, chambers, or branches.

Bill of Rights The first ten amendments to the U.S. Constitution, ratified in 1791. They ensure certain rights and liberties to the people.

checks and balances Mechanisms through which each branch of government is able to participate in and influence the activities of the other branches. Major examples include the presidential veto power over congressional legislation, the power of the Senate to approve presidential appointments, and judicial review of congressional enactments.

elastic clause Article I, Section 8, of the Constitution (also known as the necessary and proper clause). It enumerates the powers of Congress and provides Congress with the authority to make all laws "necessary and proper" to carry them out.

exclusive powers All the powers that the states are in effect forbidden to exercise by the Constitution rest exclusively with the national government.

expressed power The notion that the Constitution grants to the federal government only those powers specifically named in its text.

federalism System of government in which power is divided by a constitution between a central government and regional governments.

Federalists Those who favored a strong national government and supported the constitution proposed at the American Constitutional Convention of 1787.

full faith and credit clause Article IV, Section 1, of the Constitution provides that each state must accord the same respect to the laws and judicial decisions of other states that it accords to its own.

Great Compromise Agreement reached at the Constitutional Convention of 1787 that gave each state an equal number of senators regardless of its population, but linked representation in the House of Representatives to population.

habeas corpus   A court order demanding that an individual in custody be brought into court and shown the cause for detention. *Habeas corpus* is guaranteed by the Constitution and can be suspended only in cases of rebellion or invasion.

judicial review   Power of the courts to declare actions of the legislative and executive branches invalid or unconstitutional. The Supreme Court asserted this power in *Marbury v. Madison.*

necessary and proper clause   Article I, Section 8, of the Constitution, which enumerates the powers of Congress and provides Congress with the authority to make all laws "necessary and proper" to carry them out; also referred to as the "elastic clause."

New Jersey Plan   A framework for the Constitution, introduced by William Paterson, which called for equal representation in the national legislature regardless of a state's population.

privileges and immunities clause   Article IV of the Constitution, which provides that the citizens of any one state are guaranteed the "privileges and immunities" of every other state, as though they were citizens of that state.

separation of powers   The division of governmental power among several institutions that must cooperate in decision making.

supremacy clause   Article VI of the Constitution, which states that laws passed by the national government and all treaties are the supreme laws of the land and superior to all laws adopted by any state or any subdivision.

Three-fifths Compromise   Agreement reached at the Constitutional Convention of 1787 that stipulated that for purposes of the appointment of congressional seats, every slave would be counted as three-fifths of a person.

Virginia Plan   A framework for the Constitution, introduced by Edmund Randolph, which called for representation in the national legislature based upon the population of each state.

FOR FURTHER READING

Bailyn, Bernard. *The Ideological Origins of the American Revolution.* Cambridge: Harvard University Press, 1967.

Beard, Charles. *An Economic Interpretation of the Constitution of the United States.* New York: Macmillan, 1913.

Becker, Carl L. *The Declaration of Independence.* New York: Vintage, 1942.

Cohler, Anne M. *Montesquieu's Comparative Politics and the Spirit of American Constitutionalism.* Lawrence: University Press of Kansas, 1988.

Farrand, Max, ed. *The Records of the Federal Convention of 1787,* 4 vols., rev. ed. New Haven: Yale University Press, 1966.

McDonald, Forrest. *The Formation of the American Republic.* New York: Penguin, 1967.

Palmer, R. R. *The Age of the Democratic Revolution.* Princeton: Princeton University Press, 1964.

Storing, Herbert, ed. *The Complete Anti-Federalist,* 7 vols. Chicago: University of Chicago Press, 1981.

Walker, Samuel. *In Defense of American Liberties—A History of the ACLU.* New York: Oxford University Press, 1990.

Wills, Garry. *Explaining America.* New York: Penguin, 1982.

Wood, Gordon S. *The Creation of the American Republic.* New York: W. W. Norton, 1982.

CHAPTER 3

The Constitutional Framework: Federalism and the Separation of Powers

*T*HE FAILINGS of the Articles of Confederation frustrated the newly emerging economic interests in the United States seeking larger national and international markets. Their frustration fueled a movement to reform the Articles. This "reform movement" was powerful enough to create a revolutionary new constitution that gave the national government far more authority (see Chapter 2).

But the political power of the new economic interests alone would never have been sufficient to push through an entirely new constitution. These interests had to be translated into higher *principles* in order to gain loyalty and support from other powerful interests as well as from the American people. In fact, loyal support for any government depends on the powerful and the powerless alike accepting the principles of government as *legitimate.*

Legitimacy can be defined as *the next best thing to being good.* Legitimacy is not synonymous with popularity. A government can be considered legitimate when its actions appear to be consistent with the highest principles that people already hold. In most countries, governments have attempted to derive their legitimacy from *religion* or from a common past of shared experiences and sacrifices that are called *tradition.* Some governments, or their rulers, have tried to derive their legitimacy from the *need for defense against a common enemy.* The American approach to legitimacy con-

CORE OF THE ARGUMENT

- Federalism limits national power by creating two sovereigns—the national government and the state governments.
- Under "dual federalism," which lasted from 1789–1937, the national government limited itself primarily to promoting commerce, while the state governments directly coerced citizens.
- After 1937, the national government exerted more influence, yet the states maintained most of their traditional powers.
- Checks and balances ensure the sharing of power among separate institutions of government. Within the system of separated powers, the framers of the Constitution provided for legislative supremacy.
- The Constitution and its amendments establish a framework within which government and lawmaking can take place.

tained parts of all of these factors but with a unique addition: *contract.* A contract is an exchange, a deal. The contract we call the American Constitution was simply this: *the people would give their consent to a strong national government if that government would in turn accept certain strict limitations on its powers.* In other words, power in return for limits.

Three fundamental limitations were the principles involved in the contract between the American people and the framers of the Constitution: *federalism,* the *separation of powers,* and *individual rights.* Nowhere in the Constitution are these mentioned by name, but we know from the debates and writings that they were to be the primary framework within which constitutional power would be exercised.

The principle of *federalism* sought to limit the national government by recognizing a second layer of state governments in opposition to it. American federalism recognized two sovereigns in the original Constitution and reinforced the principle in the Bill of Rights by granting a few "expressed powers" to the national government and reserving all the rest to the states.

The principle of the *separation of powers* sought to limit the power of the national government by dividing government against itself—by giving the legislative, executive, and judicial branches separate functions, thus forcing them to share power.

The principle of *individual rights* sought to limit government by defining the people as separate from it—granting to each individual an identity in opposition to the government itself. Individuals are given rights, which are claims to identity, to property, and to personal satisfaction or "the pursuit of happiness," that cannot be denied except by extraordinary procedures that demonstrate beyond doubt that the need of the government or the "public interest" is more compelling than the claim of the citizen. The principle of individual rights implies also the principle of *representation.* If there is to be a separate private sphere,

there must be a set of procedures, separate from judicial review of individual rights, that somehow takes into account the preferences of citizens before the government acts.

This chapter will be concerned with the first two principles—federalism and the separation of powers. The purpose here is to look at the evolution of each principle in order to understand how we got to where we are and what the significance of each principle in operation is. After that we will look briefly at how and why the constitutional framework can be changed through the process of constitutional amendment. The third key principle, individual rights, will be the topic of the next chapter. But all of this is for introductory purposes only. All three principles form the background and the context for every other chapter in this book.

THE FIRST PRINCIPLE:
FEDERALISM

The Constitution has had its most fundamental influence on American life through federalism. *Federalism* can be defined with misleading ease and simplicity as the division of powers and functions between the national government and the state governments. Tracing out the influence of federalism is not so simple, but we can make the task easier by breaking it down into three distinctive forms.

First, federalism sought to limit national power by creating two sovereigns—the national government and the state governments. It was called *"dual federalism."* At the time of our nation's founding, the states already existed as former colonies and, for nearly thirteen years, as virtually autonomous units under the Articles of Confederation. The Constitution imposed a stronger national government upon the states. But even after the ratification of the Constitution, the states continued to be more important than the national government. For nearly a century and a half, virtually all of the fundamental policies governing the lives of American citizens were made by the state legislatures, not by Congress.

The novelty of this arrangement can be appreciated by noting that each of the major European countries at that time had a *unitary* government: a single national government with national ministries; a national police force; and a single, national code of laws for crimes, commerce, public works, education, and all other areas.

Second, that same federalism specifically restrained the power of the national government over the economy. The Supreme Court's definition of "interstate commerce" was so restrictive that Congress could only legislate as to the actual flow of goods across state lines; local conditions were protected from Congress by the contrary doctrine called "intrastate" commerce. As we shall see later in this chapter and again in Chapter 13, the federalism of strong states and weak national government reigned until 1937, when the Supreme Court redefined "interstate commerce" to permit the national government to regulate local economic conditions.

Third, since federalism freed the states to make so many important policies according to the wishes of their own citizens, states were therefore also free to be different from one another. Federalism allowed a great deal of variation from state to state in the rights enjoyed by citizens, in the roles played by governments, and in definitions of crime and its punishment. During the past half-century, we have moved toward greater national uniformity in state laws and in the rights enjoyed by citizens. Nevertheless, as we shall see, federalism continues even today to permit significant differences among the states.

Each of these consequences of federalism will be considered in its turn. The first two—the creating of two sovereigns and the restraining of the economic power of the national government—will be treated in this chapter, along with an assessment of their continuing influence. The third,

even though it is an aspect of federalism, will be an important part of the next chapter, because it relates to the framework of individual rights and liberties.

Restraining National Power with Dual Federalism, 1789–1937

As we have noted, the Constitution created two layers of government: the national government and the state governments. This two-layer system is called dual federalism or dual sovereignty. The consequences of this dual sovereignty are fundamental to the American system of government in theory and in practice; they have meant that states have done most of the fundamental governing in this country. For evidence, look at Table 3.1. It lists the major types of public policies by which Americans were governed for the first century and a half under the Constitution. We call it the "traditional system" because it prevailed for three-quarters of our history and because it closely approximates the intentions of the framers of the Constitution.

Under the traditional system, the national government was quite small by comparison both to the state governments and to the governments of other Western nations. Not only was it smaller than most governments of that time, it was actually very narrowly specialized in the functions it performed. Our national government built or sponsored the construction of roads, canals, and bridges ("internal improvements"). It provided cash subsidies to shippers and ship builders and free or low-priced public land to encourage western settlement and business ventures. It placed relatively heavy taxes on imported goods (tariffs), not only to raise revenues but to protect "infant industries" from competition from the more advanced European enterprises. It protected patents and provided for a common currency, also to encourage and facilitate enterprises and to expand markets.

TABLE 3.1

The Federal System: Specialization of Governmental Functions in the Traditional System (1800–1933)

NATIONAL GOVERNMENT POLICIES (DOMESTIC)	STATE GOVERNMENT POLICIES	LOCAL GOVERNMENT POLICIES
Internal improvements Subsidies Tariffs Public lands disposal Patents Currency	Property laws (including slavery) Estate and inheritance laws Commerce laws Banking and credit laws Corporate laws Insurance laws Family laws Morality laws Public health laws Education laws General penal laws Eminent domain laws Construction codes Land-use laws Water and mineral laws Criminal procedure laws Electoral and political parties laws Local government laws Civil service laws Occupations and professions laws	Adaptation of state laws to local conditions ("variances") Public works Contracts for public works Licensing of public accommodations Assessible improvements Basic public services

What do these functions of the national government reveal? First, virtually all its functions were aimed at assisting commerce. It is quite appropriate to refer to the traditional American system as a "commercial republic." Second, virtually none of the national government's policies directly coerced citizens. The emphasis of governmental programs was on assistance, promotion, and encouragement—the allocation of land or capital where they were insufficiently available for economic development.

Meanwhile, state legislatures were actively involved in economic regulation during the nineteenth century. In the United States, then and now, private property exists only in state laws and state court decisions regarding property, trespass, and real estate. American capitalism as we know it took its form from state property and trespass laws, as well as state laws and court decisions regarding contracts, markets, credit, banking, incorporation, and insurance. Laws concerning slavery were a subdivision of property law in states where slavery existed. The practice of important professions such as law and medicine was and is illegal, except as provided for by state law. The birth or adoption of a child, marriage, and divorce have always been regulated by state law. To educate or not to educate a child has been a decision governed more by state laws than by parents, and not at all by national law. It is important to note also that virtually all the criminal laws—regarding everything from trespass to murder—have been state laws. Most of the criminal laws adopted by Congress are concerned with the District of Columbia and other federal territories.

All this (and more, as shown in column 2 of Table 3.1) demonstrates without any question that most of the fundamental governing in this country was done by the states. The contrast between national and state policies, as shown by the table, demonstrates the difference in the power vested in each. The list of items in column 2 could actually have been made longer. Moreover, each item on the list is a category of law that fills many volumes of statutes and court decisions.

This contrast between national and state governments is all the more impressive because it is basically what the framers of the Constitution intended. There is probably no better example in world history of consistency between formal intentions and political reality. Since the 1930s, the national government has expanded into local and intrastate matters, far beyond what anyone would have foreseen in 1790, 1890, or even in the 1920s. But this significant expansion of the national government did not alter the basic framework. The national government has become much larger, but the states have continued to be central to the American system of government.

Here lies probably the most important point of all: The fundamental impact of federalism on the way the United States is governed comes not from any particular provision of the Constitution but from the framework itself, which has determined the flow of government functions and, through that, the political developments of the country. By allowing state governments to do most of the fundamental governing, the Constitution saved the national government from many policy decisions that might have proven too divisive for this large and very young country. There is no doubt that if the Constitution had provided for a unitary rather than a federal system, the war over slavery would have come in 1789 or 1809 rather than 1860; and if it had come that early, the South might very well have seceded and established a separate and permanent slaveholding nation.

In helping the national government remain small and aloof from the most divisive issues of the day, federalism contributed significantly to the political stability of the nation, even as the social, economic, and political systems of many of the states and regions of the country were undergoing tremendous and profound, and sometimes violent, change.[1] As we shall see, some important aspects of federalism have changed, but the federal framework has survived two centuries and a devastating civil war.

Federalism as a Limitation on the National Government's Power

Having created the national government, and recognizing the potential for abuse of power, the states sought through federalism to constrain the national government. The "traditional system" of a weak national government prevailed for over a century despite economic forces favoring its expansion and despite Supreme Court cases giving a pro-national interpretation to Article I, Section 8, of the Constitution.

That article delegates to Congress the power "to regulate commerce with foreign nations, and among the several States and with the Indian tribes," and this clause was consistently interpreted *in favor* of national power by the Supreme Court for most of the nineteenth century. The first and most important case favoring national power over the economy was *McCulloch v. Maryland* (1819).[2] The case involved the question of

---

[1]For a good treatment of the contrast between national political stability and social instability, see Samuel P. Huntington, *Political Order in Changing Societies* (New Haven: Yale University Press, 1968), Chapter 2.
[2]McCulloch v. Maryland, 4 Wheaton 316 (1819).

PROCESS BOX 3.1

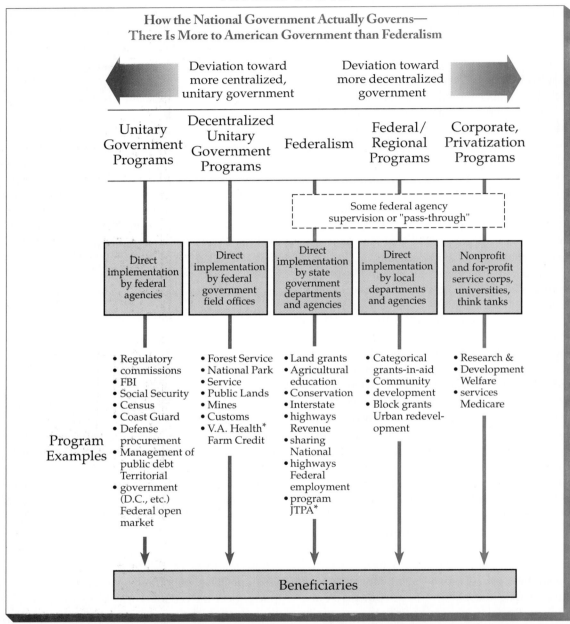

**How the National Government Actually Governs—
There Is More to American Government than Federalism**

Deviation toward more centralized, unitary government ←

Deviation toward more decentralized government →

Unitary Government Programs	Decentralized Unitary Government Programs	Federalism	Federal/ Regional Programs	Corporate, Privatization Programs
		Some federal agency supervision or "pass-through"		
Direct implementation by federal agencies	Direct implementation by federal government field offices	Direct implementation by state government departments and agencies	Direct implementation by local departments and agencies	Nonprofit and for-profit service corps, universities, think tanks
• Regulatory • commissions • FBI • Social Security • Census • Coast Guard • Defense procurement • Management of public debt Territorial • government (D.C., etc.) Federal open market	• Forest Service • National Park Service • Public Lands • Mines • Customs • V.A. Health* Farm Credit	• Land grants • Agricultural education • Conservation • Interstate • highways Revenue • sharing National • highways Federal employment • program JTPA*	• Categorical grants-in-aid • Community • development • Block grants Urban redevelopment	• Research & • Development Welfare • services Medicare

Program Examples

Beneficiaries

whether Congress had the power to charter a national bank, since such an explicit grant of power was nowhere to be found in Article I, Section 8. Chief Justice John Marshall answered that the power could be "implied" from other powers that were expressly delegated to Congress, such as the "powers to lay and collect taxes; to borrow money; to regulate commerce; and to declare and conduct a war."

The constitutional authority for the implied powers doctrine is a clause in Article I, Section 8, which enables Congress "to make all laws which shall be necessary and proper for carrying into Execution the foregoing powers." By allowing Congress to use the "necessary and proper" clause to interpret its delegated powers expansively, the Supreme Court created the potential for an unprecedented increase in national government power. Marshall also concluded that whenever a state law conflicted with a federal law (as in the case of *McCulloch v. Maryland*), the state law would be deemed invalid since the Constitution states that "the laws of the United States . . . 'shall be the supreme law of the land.'" Both parts of this great case are "pro-national," yet Congress did not immediately seek to expand the policies of the national government.

Another major case, *Gibbons v. Ogden* in 1824, reinforced this nationalistic interpretation of the Constitution. The important but relatively narrow issue was whether the state of New York could grant a monopoly to Robert Fulton's steamboat company to operate an exclusive service between New York and New Jersey. Chief Justice Marshall argued that the state of New York did not have the power to grant this particular monopoly. In order to reach this decision, it was necessary for Marshall to define what Article I, Section 8, meant by "commerce among the several states." He insisted that the definition was "comprehensive," extending to "every species of commercial intercourse." He did say that this comprehensiveness was limited "to that commerce which concerns more states than one," giving rise to what later came to be called "interstate commerce." *Gibbons*

is important because it established the supremacy of the national government in all matters affecting interstate commerce.[3] But what would remain uncertain during several decades of constitutional discourse was the precise meaning of interstate commerce.

Article I, Section 8, backed by the "implied powers" decision in *McCulloch* and by the broad definition of "interstate commerce" in *Gibbons*, was a source of power for the national government as long as Congress sought to facilitate commerce through subsidies, services, and land grants. But later in the nineteenth century, when the national government sought to use those powers to *regulate* the economy rather than merely to promote economic development, federalism and the concept of interstate commerce began to operate as restraints on, rather than sources of, national power.

Any effort of the national government to regulate commerce in such areas as fraud, the production of impure goods, the use of child labor, or the existence of dangerous working conditions or long hours was declared unconstitutional by the Supreme Court as a violation of the concept of interstate commerce. Such legislation meant that the federal government was entering the factory and workplace—local areas—and was attempting to regulate goods that had not passed into commerce. To enter these local workplaces was to exercise **police power**—the power reserved to the states for the protection of the health, safety, and morals of their citizens. No one questioned the power of the national government to regulate businesses that intrinsically involved interstate commerce, such as railroads, gas pipelines, and waterway transportation. But well into the twentieth century, the Supreme Court used the concept of interstate commerce as a barrier against most efforts by Congress to regulate local conditions.

This aspect of federalism was alive and well during an epoch of tremendous economic development, the period between the Civil War and the

[3]Gibbons v. Ogden, 9 Wheaton 1 (1824).

1930s. It gave the American economy a freedom from federal government control that closely approximated the ideal of "free enterprise." The economy was, of course, never entirely free; in fact, entrepreneurs themselves did not want complete freedom from government. They needed law and order. They needed a stable currency. They needed courts and police to enforce contracts and prevent trespass. They needed roads, canals, and railroads. But federalism, as interpreted by the Supreme Court for seventy years after the Civil War, made it possible for business to have its cake and eat it, too. Entrepreneurs enjoyed the benefits of national policies facilitating commerce and were protected by the courts from policies regulating commerce.[4]

All this changed after 1937, when the Supreme Court threw out the old distinction between interstate and intrastate commerce, converting the commerce clause from a source of limitations to a source of power. The Court began to refuse to review appeals challenging acts of Congress protecting the rights of employees to organize and engage in collective bargaining, regulating the amount of farmland in cultivation, extending low-interest credit to small businesses and farmers, and restricting the activities of corporations dealing in the stock market, and many other laws that contributed to the construction of the "welfare state." This has been referred to as the First Constitutional Revolution.[5] (A Second Constitutional Revolution will be discussed in Chapter 4.)

The Continuing Influence of Federalism: State and Local Government Today

STATE GOVERNMENT   Expansion of the power of the national government has not left the states powerless. We cannot repeat too often that the state governments continue to make most of the fundamental laws and that the national government did not expand at the expense of the states. Growth of the national government has been an addition, not a redistribution, of power from the states. No better demonstration of the continuing influence of the federal framework can be offered than the fact that column 2 of Table 3.1 is still a fairly accurate characterization of state government today. State governments have actually increased in power during the last decade because *Congress has been choosing to delegate and devolve some of its recognized powers to the states.* Congress has frequently chosen to delegate important responsibilities to state governments to implement federal programs. For example, a very large portion of the important programs that comprise welfare and public assistance in the United States are federally financed and federally authorized programs that are implemented in large part at the discretion of the states.

LOCAL GOVERNMENT AND THE CONSTITUTION Local government occupies a peculiar but very important place in the American system. In fact, the status of American local government is probably unique in world experience. First, it must be pointed out that local government has no status in

---

[4]The Sherman Antitrust Act, adopted in 1890, for example, was enacted not to restrict commerce, but rather to protect it from monopolies, or trusts, so as to prevent unfair trade practices, and to enable the market again to become *self-regulating*. Moreover, the Supreme Court sought to uphold liberty of contract to protect businesses. For example, in Lochner v. New York, 198 U.S. 45 (1905), the Court invalidated a New York law regulating the sanitary conditions and hours of labor of bakers on the grounds that the law interfered with liberty of contract.
[5]The key case in the First Constitutional Revolution is generally considered to be NLRB v. Jones & Laughlin Steel Corporation, 301 U.S. 1 (1937), in which the Supreme Court approved federal regulation of the workplace and thereby virtually eliminated interstate commerce as a limit on national government power. Since at least the 1960s, "interstate commerce" has become a source of congressional power rather than restraint, es-

pecially in national efforts to improve the status of blacks and other minorities. In April 1995, however, the Supreme Court, by a bare 5-to-4 majority, struck down the 1990 federal Gun-Free School Zones Act, on the grounds that possession of a gun near a school was not sufficiently related to interstate commerce (United States v. Lopez, 115 S.Ct. 1624 [1995]). Although this decision opened up the possibility of a historic change in the Court's interpretation of the commerce clause, only one week later the Court unanimously upheld the use of a federal racketeering law against a local business that had only incidental ties to interstate commerce, but that was involved in money laundering (United States v. Robertson, 94-251 [1995]). These two cases left the Court just about where it had been for the previous sixty years.

the American Constitution. The policies listed in column 3 of Table 3.1 are there because state legislatures created local governments, and state constitutions and laws permitted local governments to take on some of the responsibilities of the state governments. Most states amended their own constitutions to give their larger cities *home rule*—a guarantee of noninterference in various areas of local affairs. But local governments enjoy no such recognition in the U.S. Constitution. Local governments have always been mere conveniences of the states.[6]

Local governments became administratively important in the early years of the Republic because the states possessed little administrative capability. They relied on local governments—cities and counties—to implement the laws of the state. Local government was an alternative to a statewide bureaucracy (see Table 3.2).

UPDATING FEDERALISM   Paradoxically, as the national government has expanded, state and local governments have become stronger, not weaker. Since 1937, the national government has exerted more and more influence over the states and localities; but, thanks to American federalism, the form of some of that influence has contributed to state and local power. One type of federal influence is direct, imposed by law and administrative control—for example, in occupational health and safety regulations, air pollution control laws, and voting rights. Most of the influence of the national government, however, is through two forms: *grants-in-aid* and *mandates.* Mandates are national laws directing state or local governments to comply with federal regulations. A grant-in-aid is really a kind of bribe—Congress gives money to

TABLE 3.2

85,006 Governments in the United States

TYPE	NUMBER
National	1
State	50
County	3,043
Municipal	19,279
Townships	16,656
School districts	14,422
Other special districts	33,555

SOURCE: *Statistical Abstract of the United States,* 1996 (Washington, DC: Government Printing Office, 1996).

state and local governments, but with the condition that the money will be spent for a particular purpose as designed by Congress. Thus, Congress uses grants-in-aid because it recognizes that it does not usually have the political or constitutional power to command the cities to do its bidding directly.

The principle of grants-in-aid goes back to the nineteenth-century land grants to states for the improvement of agriculture and farm-related education. Since farms were not in "interstate commerce," it was unclear whether the Constitution would permit the national government to provide direct assistance to agriculture. Grants-in-aid to the states, earmarked to go to the farmers, presented a way of avoiding the constitutional problem while pursuing what was recognized in Congress as a national goal.

This same approach was applied to cities beginning in the late 1930s. Congress set national goals such as public housing and assistance to the unemployed and provided grants-in-aid to meet these goals. The value of these *categorical grants-in-aid* increased from $2.3 billion in 1950 to roughly $245 billion in 1997 (see Table 3.3). Sometimes Congress requires the state or local government to match the national contribution dollar for dollar; but for some programs, such as the interstate highway system, the congressional grant-in-aid provides 90 percent of the cost of the program.

---

[6]A good discussion of the constitutional position of local governments is in York Willbern, *The Withering Away of the City* (Bloomington: Indiana University Press, 1971). For more on the structure and theory of federalism, see Thomas R. Dye, *American Federalism: Competition among Governments* (Lexington, MA: Lexington Books, 1990), Chapter 1; and Martha Derthick, "Up-to-Date in Kansas City: Reflections on American Federalism" (the 1992 John Gaus Lecture), *PS: Political Science & Politics* 25 (December 1992), pp. 671–75.

On more than one occasion, the number of grants-in-aid and the amount of money involved have come under criticism, by Democrats as well as Republicans, liberals as well as conservatives. But there is general agreement that grants-in-aid help to reduce disparities of wealth between rich states and poor states. And although some critics have asserted that grants encourage state and local governments to initiate programs merely because "free money from Washington" is available, the fact is that when federal grants were reduced by the Reagan administration, most states and localities continued funding the same programs with their own revenues.

Federalism has not stood still. If the traditional system of two separate sovereigns performing highly different functions (as shown in Table 3.1) could be called dual federalism, historians of federalism suggest that the system since the New Deal era could be called *cooperative federalism,* through which grants-in-aid have been used strategically to encourage states and localities (without commanding them) to pursue nationally defined goals. The most important student of the history of federalism, Morton Grodzins, characterized this as a move from "layer cake federalism" to "marble cake federalism" in which intergovernmental cooperation and sharing have

TABLE 3.3

Historical Trend of Federal Grants-in-Aid

		GRANTS-IN-AID AS A PERCENTAGE OF			
FISCAL YEAR	AMOUNT OF GRANTS-IN-AID (IN BILLIONS)	TOTAL	DOMESTIC PROGRAMS[†]	STATE AND LOCAL EXPENDITURES	GROSS DOMESTIC PRODUCT
Five-year intervals					
1950	$2.3	5.3%	11.6%	8.2%	0.8%
1955	3.2	4.7	17.2	9.7	0.8
1960	7.0	8.0	18.0	19.0	1.0
1965	10.9	9.0	18.0	20.0	2.0
1970	24.1	12.0	23.0	24.0	2.0
1975	49.8	15.0	22.0	27.0	3.0
1980	91.4	15.0	22.0	31.0	3.0
1985	105.9	11.0	18.0	25.0	3.0
1990	135.3	11.0	17.0	21.0	2.0
Annually					
1995	225.0	15.0	22.0	25.0	3.0
1996	227.8	15.0	21.0	24.0	3.0
1997 (estimate)	244.8	15.0	21.0	NA	3.0

[†]Excludes outlays for national defense, international affairs, and net interest.
NA = Not available.
SOURCE: Office of Management and Budget, *Budget of the United States Government, Fiscal Year 1998, Analytical Perspectives* (Washington, DC: Government Printing Office, 1997), Table 9-2, p. 196.

FIGURE 3.1

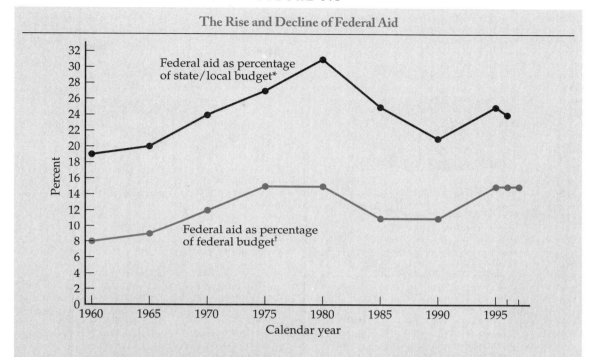

The Rise and Decline of Federal Aid

Federal aid as percentage of state/local budget*

Federal aid as percentage of federal budget†

Percent

Calendar year

*Federal aid as a percentage of state/local expenditures after transfers.
†Federal aid as a percentage of federal expenditures from own funds.
SOURCE: Office of Management and Budget, *Budget of the United States Government, Fiscal Year 1998,* Analytical Perspectives (Washington, DC: Government Printing Office, 1997), Table 9-2, p. 196.

blurred the line between where the national government ends and the state and local governments begin.[7] Figure 3.1 demonstrates the financial basis of the marble cake idea. At the high point of grant-in-aid policies, in 1977–1978, federal aid contributed an average of 25 percent of the operating budgets of all the state and local governments in the country.

Developments in the past twenty-five years have moved well beyond marble cake federalism to what might be called *"regulated federalism."*[8] In some areas the national government actually regulates the states by threatening to withhold

[7]Morton Grodzins, "The Federal System," in *Goals for Americans,* President's Commission on National Goals (Englewood Cliffs, NJ: Prentice-Hall, 1960), p. 265. In a marble cake, the white cake is distinguishable from the chocolate cake, but the two are streaked rather than in distinct layers.

[8]The concept and the best discussion of this modern phenomenon will be found in Donald F. Kettl, *The Regulation of American Federalism* (Baltimore: Johns Hopkins University Press, 1983 and 1987), especially pp. 33–41.

CONCEPT MAP 3.1

Evolving Federalism

Dual Federalism

National Government

State Governments

"Layer Cake"

Cooperative Federalism

Cooperate on some policies {

National Government

State Governments

"Marble Cake"

Regulated Federalism

State governments mandated to provide the "ingredients"

National government mandates the "recipe"

NATIONAL STANDARDS
CONDITIONAL GRANTS
UNFUNDED MANDATES
PREEMPTION

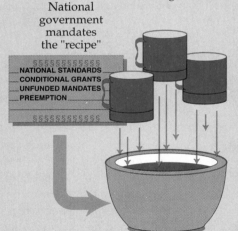

National government determines policies; state governments pay for and administer

New Federalism

National government provides "ingredients"

State governments provide the "recipe"

Block grants

Revenue sharing

Devolution of power

LAWS AND POLICIES

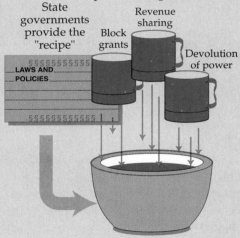

State governments have more flexibility to make policy and administer programs

BOX 3.1

Other Federal Systems

IN CONTRAST to unitary systems, the key feature of federal systems of government is that their powers are constitutionally divided between a central government and regional governments. Each of these levels of government typically has constitutionally allocated legislative, executive, and judicial powers, and each level has sovereignty within its sphere of responsibility.

The United States, which owes its federalism largely to the fact that separate states existed as politically distinct entities long before any unitary national government, is by no means unique in possessing a federal system. Switzerland, for instance, has a history of federalism that goes back as far as the thirteenth century. If one defines federalism broadly to mean any system that permits some degree of regional internal autonomy from a central government, nearly two dozen countries, possessing in total about half of the world's territory and a third of its population, may be seen as having federal systems. Even if one defines federalism more narrowly to mean those in which neither the central nor the regional governments have constitutional or political supremacy, the list includes Switzerland, Australia, Brazil, India, and Canada.

The "marble cake" image of American federalism derives in part from the incorporation of the principle of the separation of powers into both levels of government in the United States. With power and authority widely diffused at both the national and the state levels of government, there are many points of contact between the two levels. In federal systems that have not incorporated the principle of the separation of powers to such a great degree, the two levels of government have far fewer points of contact, and most of the interactions and relations between levels occur at the parliamentary or cabinet level. Such a pattern of "parliamentary" or "executive" federalism typifies states like Canada and Australia.

grant money unless state and local governments conform to national standards. The most notable instances of this regulation are in the areas of civil rights, poverty programs, and environment laws. In these instances, the national government provides grant-in-aid financing but sets conditions the states must meet in order to keep the grants. In other instances, the national government imposes obligations on the states without providing any funding at all. The national government refers to these policies as "setting national standards." Important cases of such efforts are in interstates highway use, in social services, and in education. The net effect of these national standards is that state and local policies are more uniform from coast to coast. An increasing number of states and their representatives in Con-

gress, however, refer to these policies as *"unfunded mandates."*[9]

There have been countertrends, attempts to reverse this nationalization and reestablish traditional policy making and implementation. Presidents Nixon and Reagan called their efforts the *"new federalism,"* by which national policies attempted to return more discretion to the states. This was the purpose of Nixon's revenue sharing and the goal of Reagan's block grants, which

[9]John DiIulio and Don Kettl report that in 1980 there were 36 laws that could be categorized as unfunded mandates. And despite the concerted opposition of the Reagan and Bush administrations, another 27 laws qualifying as unfunded mandates were adopted between 1982 and 1991. See John DiIulio, Jr., and Donald F. Kettl, *Fine Print: The Contract with America, Devolution, and the Administrative Realities of American Federalism* (Washington, DC: The Brookings Institution, 1995), p. 41.

TOMMY THOMPSON AND LAWTON CHILES
Revitalizing State Politics

THE SHIFT of governance burdens and responsibilities to the states has put the national spotlight on many of the states' governors. Wisconsin's Tommy Thompson and Florida's Lawton Chiles have each garnered national praise and criticism for their innovative approaches.

A Wisconsin native, Tommy Thompson was born in 1941 and raised in a family where work was highly valued. When four-year-old Tommy asked for a tricycle, his father put him to work in the family grocery store to earn the necessary money. After earning undergraduate and law degrees at the University of Wisconsin, where he also embraced the conservatism of 1964 Republican presidential candidate Barry Goldwater, he ran for the state assembly in 1966 where he served for twenty years. In 1986, Thompson ran for governor on a platform of criticizing the Democratic incumbent for turning Wisconsin into a magnet for welfare recipients. The anti-welfare mood of the voters propelled him into office. Among his first acts was a six-percent cut in welfare benefits.

Since then, Thompson has experimented with a variety of programs to curb welfare spending and encourage alternate programs. The popularity of his get-tough approach earned him re-election in 1990 and 1994. In 1994, Thompson enacted the nation's first "work not welfare" program, putting a two-year limit on welfare benefits. Thompson also buttressed job training and day-care programs in order to make the work option more viable. He has also experimented with a "Learnfare" program, which withdraws welfare payments when recipients' children skip school; a "Child First" program, which threatens to jail fathers who fail to pay child support; and a "Family Cap," which calls for an end to added payments for welfare mothers who bear additional children. As the Republican National Committee's chair observed about Thompson's experimental programs, "He's the leader of the country and the Republican pathfinder on welfare reform."[1]

Wisconsin welfare rolls have indeed dropped by almost twenty percent, and the state has generated nearly 400,000 new jobs. But critics charge that these changes occurred mostly because of an improved state economy, and that Thompson is cultivating class warfare for political gain. Yet Thompson's programs have stimulated national debate and experimentation with welfare contraction, culminating in national legislation passed in 1996 that mimicked many of Thompson's ideas.

TOMMY THOMPSON

consolidated a number of categorical grants into one larger category, leaving the state (or local) government to decide how to use the grant. Presidents Nixon and Reagan, as well as President Bush, were sincere in wanting to return somewhat to a traditional notion of freedom of action for the states. They called it new federalism, but their concept and their goal were really much closer to the older, traditional federalism that predated Franklin Roosevelt (see Concept Map 3.1).

Florida's popular governor, Lawton Chiles, has taken state policy experimentation in a different direction. Born in 1930, the Florida native earned undergraduate and law degrees at the University of Florida. After practicing law for a time, Chiles ran for the state legislature on a literal shoestring budget. Running for office on his own, Chiles walked the length of the district to meet voters and grab attention. The tactic worked, and Chiles served in the state legislature until 1970, when he decided to run for the U.S. Senate. Relying on the same campaign tactic, Chiles walked the length of Florida, logging over a thousand miles in three months. The successful tactic earned him the nickname "Walkin' Lawton."

After serving eighteen years in the Senate, Chiles mounted a successful campaign for governor in 1990, where he continued his "progressive conservative" approach to governance. For example, Chiles has championed "reinventing government" in Florida, calling for the elimination of thousands of state regulations and rules. He also spearheaded the effort to turn the promotion of state tourism and travel over to private tourism industry professionals, and away from the state Department of Commerce. Such ideas have found wide favor among the state's business community, whom Chiles has carefully courted.

Yet Chiles has also spearheaded stronger government in other areas. He insists on maintaining government rules and protections for such areas as child nutrition and environmental protection. In 1994, he pushed through the state legislature the Medicaid Third Party Recovery Act, which allowed the state of Florida to sue the tobacco industry to recover billions of dollars spent to treat people suffering from tobacco-related illnesses, such as cancer. Chiles also sponsored an ambitious overhaul of state health-care policy,

meeting with more success than was achieved at the national level. In addition, Chiles has pushed the national government on foreign policy issues, because of the impact of Cuban and Haitian immigration in Florida. Chiles has also blocked such popular conservative initiatives as a charter school program and student-led public school prayer.

Chiles's mixed political approach continues to earn him favor with Florida voters. In his 1994 re-election bid, Democrat Chiles won his race when other prominent Democrats around the country were turned out of office in the Republican landslide of that year. Chiles's progressive conservatism continues to find favor with Floridians, and to garner him national attention.

SOURCE: David C. Nice, *Federalism: The Politics on Intergovernmental Relations* (New York: St. Martin's Press, 1987).
[1]Norman Atkins, "Tommy Thompson," *New York Times Magazine,* 15 January 1995, p. 24.

LAWTON CHILES

Although President Reagan succeeded in reducing national appropriations for grants-in-aid during his first term, he could not prevent increases during his second term. Both he and Bush were able to hold the line only enough to keep these outlays from increasing faster than the overall increase in the national budget. Note that in Figure 3.1, federal aid as a percentage of total federal outlays has been close to constant since 1984—the beginning of Reagan's second term.

DEBATING THE ISSUES

Can the States Do It Better?

*F*OR THE LAST *two decades, the hallowed principle of federalism has come under intense focus, as a rising chorus of critics have argued on behalf of turning over more powers and responsibilities to the states. Few have defended a stronger role for the federal government; rather, arguments have centered on how far this process of "devolution" of powers to the states should go. In 1994, Republican governors issued the "Williamsburg Resolves," constituting a blueprint for devolution of powers to the states. Clinton administration official Alice Rivlin argues for a more cautious approach, urging a "dividing the job" approach between the federal government and the states.*

REPUBLICAN GOVERNORS' CONFERENCE

Concerns about the condition of federal-state relations have been voiced throughout our nation's history. But, today, there is a unique need—and a unique opportunity—for reform.

Never has there been a broader consensus among the states—and among the elected officials and voters in the states, regardless of party—that the federal government has pervasively exceeded its constitutional bounds and must be restrained. . . .

Recognizing the urgency of the need and the uniqueness of the opportunity for reform, we declare our common resolve to restore balance to the federal-state relationship and renew the framers' vision. An agreed agenda for concerted action to achieve this objective is essential. Among the principal elements of this common agenda of reform are these:

I. Mobilizing the People to Reclaim Their Freedom. . . .

Too few of our citizens appreciate the central role that the erosion of state and local prerogatives, and the emergence of the federal bureaucratic, judicial and legislative leviathan, have played in their loss of political liberty.

We are resolved to bring these developments and consequences urgently to the attention of the people of our states, and all Americans. Only when our citizens fully appreciate the practical and pervasive impact on their daily lives of federalism's decline will they demand change.

II. Litigation to Enforce the Tenth Amendment. . . .

We are . . . resolved to pursue energetically in the federal courts Tenth Amendment challenges to federal encroachments in the domain of the states.

III. Restriction on Federal Mandates and Other Legislative Initiatives

Across the country, governors, mayors, county officials, and state legislators of both parties are working together to obtain relief from burdensome federal mandates. . . . we are resolved to promote prompt and dramatic mandate relief during the next Congress.

IV. A Conference of the States to Forge Consensus on Structural Reforms. . . .

Grants-in-aid began to grow slowly toward the end of the Bush administration and through Clinton's first term; however, the growth has been modest and almost entirely through *block grants* that give states and localities considerable flexibil-ity. In effect, President Clinton has adopted the "new federalism" of Nixon and Reagan even while expanding federal grant activity. Clinton also signed the Unfunded Mandates Reform Act of 1995. And, although he signed it with misgiv-

A Conference of the States would enable state representatives to consider, refine, and adopt proposals for structural change in our federal system. The proposals so adopted would comprise the States' Petition, which would be a powerful instrument for arousing popular support and promoting change in Congress and state legislatures. . . ."[1]

RIVLIN:

"Dividing the job" would involve five major changes in policy. First, the federal government would take charge of reforming the nation's health care financing system to accomplish two objectives: firm control of medical costs and universal health insurance. . . . Second, the states, not the federal government, would take charge of accomplishing a "productivity agenda" of reforms designed to revitalize the economy and raise incomes. These reforms would address needs such as education and skills training, child care, housing, infrastructure, and economic development. . . .

Third, the following federal programs would be devolved to the states or gradually wither away: elementary and secondary education, job training, economic and community development, housing, most highways and other transportation, social services, and some pollution control programs. Some specific programs where federal action is needed would be retained, even expanded; for example, higher education scholarships for low-income students and federal support for scientific research. . . .

Fourth, the federal government would bring its budget from deficit into surplus (including social security). . . . Fifth, the states, with the blessing or the assistance of the federal government, would strengthen their tax systems and increase revenue by adopting one or more common taxes (same base, same rate) and sharing proceeds. . . .

Despite its name, the "dividing the job" scenario does not involve a return to dual federalism. There are important areas in which cooperative federalism is necessary and desirable. One of those is environmental protection. Many hazards to the environment cross state lines and cannot be satisfactorily dealt with by the states and localities acting alone. Others are of largely local concern.

Welfare for families with children (AFDC) also remains a shared state and federal responsibility in this scenario. Some would argue for making AFDC federal or at least for a basic federal program that the state could supplement. Joint responsibility, however, would give both levels of government incentives to try hard to reduce welfare dependency. To this end, the states should improve education, training, and child care for welfare mothers, and the federal government should adjust the income tax to increase the after-tax rewards for low-wage work.[2]

[1]"The Williamsburg Resolves," *Rockefeller Institute Bulletin 1996: The Devolution Revolution* (Albany, NY: The Rockefeller Institute, 1996), pp. 17–19.
[2]Alice M. Rivlin, "Rethinking Federalism," in *Readings in State and Local Government,* ed. by David C. Saffell and Harry Basehart (New York: McGraw-Hill, 1994), pp. 27–36.

ings and promises to "fix it" in 1997, President Clinton signed into law the Personal Responsibility and Work Opportunity Reconciliation Act of 1996, which goes farther than any other act of Congress in the past 60 years to relieve the states from national mandates, funded or unfunded. The new law replaces the 61-year-old program of *Aid to Families with Dependent Children (AFDC)* and its education, work, and training program, with block grants to states for Temporary

IN BRIEF BOX

FEDERALISM

Consequences of Federalism as Established in the Constitution

Existence of two sovereigns—the national government and the state governments, with state governments wielding more power for the first 150 years after the writing of the Constitution.

Particular restraint on the power of the national government to affect economic policy.

Great variations from state to state in terms of citizens' rights, role of government, and judicial activity.

Evolution of the Federal System

1789–1834   *Nationalization:* The Marshall Court interprets the Constitution broadly so as to expand and consolidate national power.

1835–1930s *Dual federalism:* The functions of the national government are very specifically enumerated. States do much of the fundamental governing that affects citizens' day-to-day life. There is tension between the two levels of government and the power of the national government begins to increase.

1930s–1970s *Cooperative federalism:* Grants-in-aid used by the national government to encourage states and localities to pursue nationally defined goals.

1970s–   *Regulated federalism:* The national government sets conditions that states and localities must meet in order to keep certain grants. The national government also sets national standards in ares without providing funding to meet them.

New federalism: Some effort made by the national government to return more power to the states through block grants to the states.

Assistance to Needy Families (TANF). Although some national standards remain (see Chapter 11), the place of the states in the national welfare system has been virtually revolutionized through **devolution,** the strategy of granting the states more authority over a range of policies currently under national government authority.

The decision to terminate national poverty entitlements under the most important welfare program, Aid to Families with Dependent Children (AFDC), and to turn over virtually all of the discretion for the implementation of these welfare activities to state governments is indicative of the present and future of federalism in the United States. The national government under Democrats as well as Republicans has tentatively preferred to leave a great deal of discretion to the states in the implementation of national policies, *except* *where there is an extremely strong majority in Congress that is opposed to a great deal of variability in the implementation of a national program.* For example, many of the programs under the Social Security system are national programs because states differ greatly in their wealth, which would create a disparity in the security of retired persons. President Richard Nixon, a partisan Republican president, successfully sought the passage of Supplemental Security Income (SSI) in 1974 to reduce still further the variations in Social Security benefits between a poor state like Mississippi and a wealthier state like New York or California. But in so many other instances, where a variation from state to state and region to region was either desirable or tolerable, Congress has regularly entrusted a great deal of discretion to each state to implement federal programs according to that state's discretion.[10] Republicans have made more of the desirability of a general principle of a smaller national government as well as the devolution of a number of national government programs to state discretion. But this is not exclusively a Republican position. It is a bipartisan tradition and a testimonial to the continuing strength of federalism, regardless of whether the national government is in an expanding or a contracting phase of its own cycle.

Federalism remains a vital part of the American system of government, even as the national government grows larger. States and cities clamor (and lobby) for a larger share of the national budget, but they hold on jealously to their freedom of action.

THE SECOND PRINCIPLE: THE SEPARATION OF POWERS

James Madison is best qualified to speak to Americans about the *separation of powers:*

> There can be no liberty where the legislative and executive powers are united in the same person . . . [or] if the power of judging be not separated from the legislative and executive powers.[11]

Using this same reasoning, many of Madison's contemporaries argued that there was not *enough* separation among the three branches, and Madison had to do some backtracking to insist that the principle did not require complete separation:

> . . . unless these departments [branches] be so far connected and blended as to give each a constitutional control over the others, the degree of separation which the maxim requires, as essential to a free government, can never in practice be duly maintained.[12]

This is the secret of how we have made the separation of powers effective: We made the principle self-enforcing by giving each branch of government the means to participate in and partially or temporarily to obstruct the workings of the other branches.

Checks and Balances

The means by which each branch of government interacts with each other branch is known informally as **checks and balances.** The best-known examples are shown in the In Brief Box on page 00. The framers sought to guarantee that the three branches would in fact use these checks and balances as weapons against one another by giving each branch a different political constituency and therefore a different perspective on what the government ought to do: direct, popular election for the members of the House; indirect election of senators (until the Seventeenth Amendment, adopted in 1913); indirect election of the president through the electoral college; and appointment of federal judges for life. All things considered, the best characterization of the separation of powers principle in action is "separated institutions sharing power."[13]

Legislative Supremacy

Although each branch was to be given adequate means to compete with the other branches, it is also clear that within the system of separated

---

[10]For example, at the beginning of 1996, the maximum monthly payment for a family of three from welfare, including both Aid to Families with Dependent Children and Food Stamps, was $424 in Mississippi and $1,223 in Alaska. Such extreme variations are not likely to disappear in 1997 and beyond, after full implementation of the 1996 welfare reform, the Personal Responsibility and Work Opportunity Reconciliation Act, which not only eliminates automatic entitlement for anyone who passes a means test but provides maximum discretion to the states in the implementation of a whole variety of welfare programs. For a thorough comparison of the old with the new welfare provisions, see Vee Burke, "New Welfare Law: Comparison of the New Block Grant Program with Aid to Families with Dependent Children," (Congressional Research Service, The Library of Congress, August 26, 1996).

[11]Clinton Rossiter, ed., *The Federalist Papers* (New York: New American Library, 1961), No. 47, p. 302.

[12]*The Federalist Papers,* No. 48, p. 308.

[13]Richard E. Neustadt, *Presidential Power* (New York: Wiley, 1960), p. 33.

CHECKS AND BALANCES

Legislative Branch

Checks executive:

Controls appropriations. (Neither the executive branch nor the judicial branch can spend any money without an act of Congress appropriating it. Includes salaries, except Congress cannot reduce compensation of president or judges during their term.)

Controls by statute. (Except for a narrow sphere of national security and emergency operations under executive order of the president, no agency in the executive branch has any authority to act except as provided by statutes delegating such authority to the agency or to the department in which the agency is housed.)

Checks judicial:

Controls appropriations (see above).

Can create inferior courts. (All federal district courts and courts of appeal were created by Congress; so were the tax court, the court of claims, and the U.S. customs court.)

Can add new judges. (Congress can add new judges by expanding the number of judgeships for existing courts, including the Supreme Court, and it can add judges whenever it creates a new court.)

Executive Branch

Checks legislative:

Can call a special session. (The president may call Congress into special session "on extraordinary occasions" to take care of unfinished or new legislative business—e.g., to pass a law without which the president feels he cannot carry out his promises or responsibilities.)

Power to veto legislation.

Checks judicial:

Appoints federal judges.

Judicial Branch

Checks legislative:

Judicial review of legislation. (Any and all legislation can come before the federal courts when there is a dispute over the interpretation of a law or over its constitutionality. It is rare, however, that courts will declare a law unconstitutional, although that is always a possibility.)

Checks executive:

Can issue or refuse to issue warrants. (The police or any other executive officers cannot engage in any searches or arrests without a warrant from a judge showing "probable cause" and specifying the place to be searched and the persons or things to be seized.)

powers the framers provided for *legislative supremacy* by making Congress the preeminent branch. Legislative supremacy made the provision of checks and balances in the other two branches all the more important.

The most important indications of the intentions of the framers were the provisions in Article I, the legislative article, to treat the powers of the national government as powers of Congress and

their decision to give Congress the sole power over appropriations.

Legislative supremacy became a fact and not just theory soon after the founding decade. National politics centered on Congress. Undistinguished presidents followed one another in a dreary succession. Even Madison—so brilliant as a constitutional theorist, so loyal as a constitutional record keeper, and so effective in the struggle for the founding—was a weak president. Jackson and Lincoln are the only two who stand out in the entire nineteenth century, and their successors dropped back out of sight; except for these two, the other presidents operated within the accepted framework of legislative supremacy (see also Chapter 6).

The development of political parties, and in particular the emergence in 1832 of the national party convention as a way of nominating presidential candidates, saved the presidency from complete absorption into the orbit of legislative power by giving the president a base of power independent of Congress. But although this development preserved the presidency and salvaged the separation of powers, it did so only in a negative sense. That is to say, presidents were more likely after 1832 to veto congressional enactments than before. They were also more likely to engage in a military action. But they were not more likely to present programs for positive legislation or to attempt to lead Congress in the enactment of legislation.[14] Given the extent to which we are today confronting *presidential* supremacy, it is difficult to grasp at first the extent of legislative supremacy in the nineteenth century.

The role of the judicial branch in the separation of powers has depended upon the power of judicial review, a power not provided for in the Constitution but asserted by Chief Justice Marshall in 1803:

> If a law be in opposition to the Constitution; if both the law and the Constitution apply to a particular case, so that the Court must either decide that case conformable to the law, disregarding the Constitution, or conformable to the Constitution, disregarding the law; the Court must determine which of these conflicting rules governs the case: This is of the very essence of judicial duty.[15]

The Supreme Court has exercised the power of judicial review with caution, as though to protect its power by using it sparingly. For example, in the fifty years since the rise of big government and strong presidents, no important congressional enactment has been invalidated on constitutional grounds. During the same period, there have been only two important judicial confrontations with the president.[16]

All in all, the separation of powers has had an uneven history. Although "presidential government" seemed to supplant legislative supremacy after 1937, the relative power position of the three branches has varied. The power play between the president and Congress is especially intense when one party controls the White House and another controls Capitol Hill, as has been the case almost continuously since 1969.

CHANGING THE FRAMEWORK: CONSTITUTIONAL AMENDMENT

The Constitution has endured for two centuries as the framework of government. But it has not endured without change. Without change, the Constitution might have become merely a sacred text, stored under glass.

Amendments: Many Are Called, Few Are Chosen

The framers of the Constitution recognized the need for change. The provisions for amendment incorporated into Article V were thought to be "an easy, regular and Constitutional way" to make changes, which would occasionally be necessary because members of Congress "may abuse their power and refuse their consent on that very account . . . to admit to amendments to correct the source of the abuse."[17] James Madison, again writing in *The Federalist*, made a more balanced

---

[14]For a good review of the uses of the veto, see Raymond Tatalovich and Byron Daynes, *Presidential Power in the United States* (Monterey, CA: Brooks/Cole, 1984), pp. 148–51.

[15]Marbury v. Madison, 1 Cranch 137 (1803).

[16]Youngstown Sheet & Tube Co. v. Sawyer, 343 U.S. 579 (1952); and U.S. v. Nixon, 418 U.S. 683 (1974).

[17]Observation by Colonel George Mason, delegate from Virginia, early during the convention period. Quoted in Max Farrand, *The Records of the Federal Convention of 1787*, vol. 1, rev. ed. (New Haven: Yale University Press, 1966), pp. 202–3.

defense of the amendment procedures: "It guards equally against that extreme facility, which would render the Constitution too mutable; and that extreme difficulty, which might perpetuate its discovered faults."[18]

Experience since 1789 raises questions even about Madison's more modest claim. The Constitution has proven to be extremely difficult to amend. In the history of efforts to amend the Constitution, the most appropriate characterization is "many are called, few are chosen." Between 1789 and 1993, 9,746 amendments were formally offered in Congress. Of these, Congress officially proposed only twenty-nine, and only twenty-seven of these were eventually ratified by the states. But the record is even more severe than that. Since 1791, when the first ten amendments,

[18]*The Federalist*, No. 43, p. 278, in Rossiter edition.

the Bill of Rights, were added, only seventeen amendments have been adopted. And two of them—prohibition of alcohol (Eighteenth) and its repealer (Twenty-first)—cancel each other out, so that for all practical purposes, only fifteen amendments have been added to the Constitution since 1791. Despite vast changes in American society and its economy, only twelve amendments have been adopted since the Civil War amendments (Thirteenth, Fourteenth, and Fifteenth) in 1868.

As Process Box 3.2 illustrates, four methods of amendment are provided for in Article V:

1. Passage in House and Senate by two-thirds vote; then ratification by majority vote of the legislatures of three-fourths (thirty-eight) of the states.
2. Passage in House and Senate by two-thirds vote; then ratification by conventions called for the purpose in three-fourths of the states.

PROCESS BOX 3.2

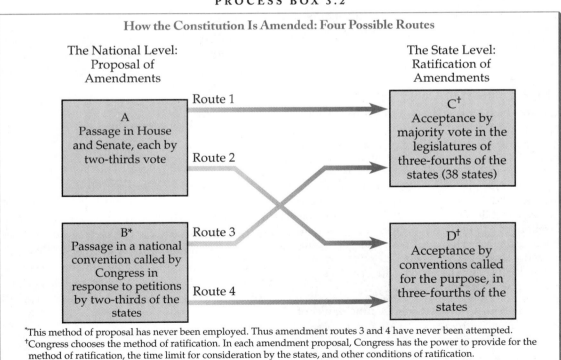

How the Constitution Is Amended: Four Possible Routes

The National Level: Proposal of Amendments

The State Level: Ratification of Amendments

Route 1

Route 2

Route 3

Route 4

A
Passage in House and Senate, each by two-thirds vote

B*
Passage in a national convention called by Congress in response to petitions by two-thirds of the states

C†
Acceptance by majority vote in the legislatures of three-fourths of the states (38 states)

D†
Acceptance by conventions called for the purpose, in three-fourths of the states

*This method of proposal has never been employed. Thus amendment routes 3 and 4 have never been attempted.
†Congress chooses the method of ratification. In each amendment proposal, Congress has the power to provide for the method of ratification, the time limit for consideration by the states, and other conditions of ratification.

3. Passage in a national convention called by Congress in response to petitions by two-thirds of the states; ratification by majority vote of the legislatures of three-fourths of the states.
4. Passage in a national convention, as in (3); then ratification by conventions called for the purpose in three-fourths of the states.

Since no amendment has ever been proposed by national convention, however, methods 3 and 4 have never been employed. And method 2 has only been employed once (the Twenty-first Amendment, which repealed the Eighteenth, or Prohibition, Amendment). Thus, method 1 has been used for all the others.

It is now clear why it has been so difficult to amend the Constitution. The main reason is the requirement of a two-thirds vote in the House and the Senate, which means that any proposal for an amendment in Congress can be killed by only 34 senators *or* 136 members of the House. The amendment can also be killed by the refusal or inability of only thirteen state legislatures to ratify it. Since each state has an equal vote regardless of its population, the thirteen holdout states may represent a small fraction of the total American population. In the 1970s, the Equal Rights Amendment (ERA), granting protection from denial of rights on account of sex, got the necessary two-thirds vote in Congress but failed by three states to get the necessary three-fourths votes of the states, even after a three-year extension for its ratification.[19]

If the ERA was a defeat for liberal forces, conservatives have done no better. Constitutional amendments were high on the agenda of the Republican party from the beginning of their presidential victories in the 1980s, and had the blessings of Presidents Reagan and Bush. The school

prayer amendment sought to restore power to the states to require selected religious observances, thereby reversing a whole series of earlier Supreme Court decisions.[20] The pro-life amendment sought to reverse *Roe v. Wade* in order to restore to the states the power to outlaw abortions. And President Bush made an effort in 1989 to get Congress to adopt an amendment outlawing the burning or other desecration of the American flag. A gesture to his party's dispirited right wing in the 1988 campaign, it got nowhere in Congress.

Which Were Chosen? An Analysis of the Twenty-seven

There is more to the amending difficulties than the politics of getting votes. It would appear that only a limited number of changes needed by society can actually be made through the Constitution. Most efforts to amend the Constitution fail because they are simply attempts to use the Constitution as an alternative to legislation for dealing directly with a public problem. The school prayer amendment is an example. A review of the successful amendments will provide two insights: First, it will give us some understanding of the condition underlying successful amendments; and second, it will reveal a great deal about what constitutionalism means.

The purpose of the ten amendments in the Bill of Rights was basically *to give each of the three branches clearer and more restricted boundaries* (see Table 3.4). The First Amendment clarified Congress's turf. Although the powers of Congress under Article I, Section 8, would not have justified laws regulating religion, speech, and the like, the First Amendment made this limitation explicit: "Congress shall make no law. . . . " The Second,

[19]Marcia Lee, "The Equal Rights Amendment—Public Policy by Means of a Constitutional Amendment," in *The Politics of Policy Making in America,* ed. David Caputo (San Francisco: W. H. Freeman, 1977); Gilbert Steiner, *Constitutional Inequality: The Political Fortunes of ERA* (Washington, DC: Brookings Institution, 1985); and Jane Mansbridge, *Why We Lost the ERA* (Chicago: University of Chicago Press, 1986).

[20]For judicial action, see Engel v. Vitale, 370 U.S. 421 (1926). For the efforts of states to get around the Supreme Court requirement that public schools be secular, see John A. Murley, "School Prayer: Free Exercise of Religion or Establishment of Religion?" in *Social Regulatory Policy,* ed. Raymond Tatalovich and Byron Daynes (Boulder, CO: Westview Press, 1988), pp. 5–40.

TABLE 3.4

The Bill of Rights: An Analysis of Its Provisions

AMENDMENT	PURPOSE
I	*Limits on Congress:* Congress is not to make any law establishing a religion or abridging speech, press, assembly, or petition freedoms.
II, III, IV	*Limits on Executive:* The executive branch is not to infringe on the right of people to keep arms (II), is not to arbitrarily take houses for a militia (III), and is not to engage in the search or seizure of evidence without a court warrant swearing to belief in the probable existence of a crime (IV).
V, VI, VII, VIII	*Limits on Courts:* The courts are not to hold trials for serious offenses without provision for a grand jury (V), a petit (trial) jury (VII), a speedy trial (VI), presentation of charges, confrontation of hostile witnesses (VI), immunity from testimony against oneself (V), and immunity from trial more than once for the same offense (V). Neither bail nor punishment can be excessive (VIII), and no property can be taken without just compensation (V).
IX, X	*Limits on National Government:* All rights not enumerated are reserved to the states or the people.

Third, and Fourth Amendments similarly spelled out limits on the executive branch, a necessity given the abuses of executive power Americans had endured under British rule.

The Fifth, Sixth, Seventh, and Eighth Amendments contain some of the most important safeguards for individual citizens against the arbitrary exercise of government power. And these amendments sought to accomplish their goal by defining the judicial branch more concretely and clearly than had been done in Article III of the Constitution.

Five amendments adopted since 1791 are directly concerned with expansion of the electorate (see Table 3.5). The founders were unable to establish a national electorate with uniform voting qualifications. They decided to evade the issue by providing in the final draft of Article I, Section 2, that eligibility to vote in a national election would be the same as "the Qualification requisite for

TABLE 3.5

Amending the Constitution to Expand the Electorate

AMENDMENT	PURPOSE	YEAR PROPOSED	YEAR ADOPTED
XV	Extended voting rights to all races	1869	1870
XIX	Extended voting rights to women	1919	1920
XXIII	Extended voting rights to residents of the District of Columbia	1960	1961
XXIV	Extended voting rights to all classes by abolition of poll taxes	1962	1964
XXVI	Extended voting rights to citizens aged 18 and over	1971	1971[*]

[*]The Twenty-sixth Amendment holds the record for speed of adoption. It was proposed on March 23, 1971, and adopted on July 5, 1971. The only other adoption time that comes close is the Prohibition repealer (XXI), proposed February 20, 1933, and adopted December 5, 1933.

TABLE 3.6

Amending the Constitution to Change the Relationship between Elected Offices and the Electorate

AMENDMENT	PURPOSE	YEAR PROPOSED	YEAR ADOPTED
XII	Created separate ballot for vice president in the electoral college	1803	1804
XIV	(Part 1) Provided a national definition of citizenship*	1866	1868
XVII	Provided direct election of senators	1912	1913
XX	Eliminated "lame duck" session of Congress	1932	1933
XXII	Limited presidential term	1947	1951
XXV	Provided presidential succession in case of disability	1965	1967

*In defining *citizenship*, the Fourteenth Amendment actually provided the constitutional basis for expanding the electorate to include all races, women, and residents of the District of Columbia. Only the "eighteen-year-olds' amendment" should have been necessary, since it changed the definition of citizenship. The fact that additional amendments were required following the Fourteenth suggests that voting is not considered an inherent right of U.S. citizenship. Instead it is viewed as a privilege.

Elector of the most numerous branch of the state Legislature." Article I, Section 4, added that Congress could alter state regulations as to the "Times, Places and Manner of holding Elections for Senators and Representatives," but this meant that any important *expansion* of the American electorate would almost certainly require a constitutional amendment.

Six more are also electoral in nature, although not concerned directly with voting rights and the expansion of the electorate. These six amendments are concerned with the elective offices themselves or with the relationship between elective offices and the electorate (see Table 3.6).

Another five have sought to expand or to delimit the powers of the national and state governments (see Table 3.7).[21] The Eleventh Amendment protected the states from suits by private

[21]The Fourteenth Amendment is included in this table as well as in Table 3.6 because it seeks not only to define citizenship but seems to intend also that this definition of citizenship included, along with the right to vote, all the rights of the Bill of Rights, regardless of the state in which the citizen resided. A great deal more will be said about this in the next chapter.

TABLE 3.7

Amending the Constitution to Expand or Limit the Power of Government

AMENDMENT	PURPOSE	YEAR PROPOSED	YEAR ADOPTED
XI	Limited jurisdiction of federal courts over suits involving the states	1794	1798
XIII	Eliminated slavery and eliminated the right of states to allow property in persons	1865*	1865
XIV	(Part 2) Applied due process of Bill of Rights to the states	1866	1868
XVI	Established national power to tax incomes	1909	1913
XXVII	Limited Congress's power to raise its own salary	1789	1992

*The Thirteenth Amendment was proposed January 31, 1865, and adopted less than a year later, on December 18, 1865.

individuals and took away from the federal courts any power to take suits by private individuals of one state (or a foreign country) against another state. The other three amendments in Table 3.7 are obviously designed to reduce state power (Thirteenth), to reduce state power and expand national power (Fourteenth), and to expand national power (Sixteenth). The Twenty-seventh put a moderate limit on Congress's ability to raise its own salary.

The one missing amendment underscores the meaning of the rest: the Eighteenth, or Prohibition, Amendment. This is the only amendment that the country used to try to *legislate*. In other words, it is the only amendment that was designed to deal directly with some substantive social problem. And it was the only amendment ever to have been repealed. Two other amendments—the Thirteenth, which abolished slavery, and the Sixteenth, which established the power to levy an income tax—can be said to have had the effect of legislation. But the purpose of the Thirteenth was to restrict the power of the states by forever forbidding them to treat any human being as property. As for the Sixteenth, it is certainly true that income tax legislation followed immediately; nevertheless, the amendment concerns itself strictly with establishing the power of Congress to enact such legislation. The legislation came later; and if down the line a majority in Congress had wanted to abolish the income tax, they could also have done this by legislation rather than through the arduous path of a constitutional amendment repealing the income tax.

All of this points to the principle underlying the twenty-five amendments in force: All are concerned with the structure or composition of the government. This is consistent with the concept of a constitution as "higher law," because the whole point and purpose of a higher law is to establish *a framework within which government and the process of making ordinary law can take place*. Even those who would have preferred more changes in the Constitution would have to agree that there is

great wisdom in this principle. A constitution ought to *enable* legislation and public policies to take place, but it should not attempt to *determine* what that legislation or those policies ought to be.

THE CONSTITUTION AND LIMITED GOVERNMENT

Federalism and the separation of powers are two of the three most important constitutional principles upon which the United States' system of limited government is based (the third is the principle of individual rights). As we have seen, federalism limits the power of the national government in numerous ways. By its very existence, federalism recognizes the principle of two sovereigns, the national government and the state government (hence the term "dual federalism"). In addition, the Constitution specifically restrained the power of the national government to regulate the economy. As a result, the states were free to do most of the fundamental governing for the first century and a half of American government. This began to change during and following the New Deal, as the national government began to exert more influence over the states through grants-in-aid and mandates. But even as the powers of the national government grew, so did the powers of the states. In the last decade, as well, we have noticed a countertrend to the growth of national power as Congress has opted to devolve some of its powers to the states. The most recent notable instance of devolution was the welfare reform plan of 1996. Federalism has also been strengthened by a revival of state governments over the last two decades. When all is said and done, one can confidently conclude that federalism remains a vital part of American government.

The second principle of limited government, separation of powers, is manifested in our system of checks and balances, whereby separate institutions of government share power with each other. Even though the Constitution clearly provided for legislative supremacy, checks and balances have functioned well. Some would say it has worked too well. The last fifty years has witnessed long periods of *divided government,* when one party has controlled the White House and the other party controlled Congress. During these periods, the level of conflict between the executive and legislative branches has been particularly divisive, resulting in what some analysts derisively call *gridlock.* Nevertheless, this is a genuine separation of powers, not so far removed from the intent of the framers. With the rise of political parties, Americans developed a parliamentary theory that "responsible party government" requires that the same party control both branches, including both chambers of the legislature. But that kind of parliamentary/party government is a "fusion of powers," not a separation of powers. Although it may not make for good government, having an opposition party in majority control of the legislature reinforces the separation and the competition that was built into the Constitution. We can complain at length about the inability of divided government to make decisions, and we can criticize it as stalemate or gridlock.[22] But even that is in accord with the theory of the framers that good public policy should be difficult to make.

The purpose of a constitution is to provide a framework. A constitution is good if it produces the *cause of action* that leads to good legislation, good case law, and appropriate police behavior. A constitution cannot eliminate power. But its principles can be a citizen's dependable defense against the abuse of power.

CHAPTER REVIEW

In this chapter we have had two objectives. The first was to trace the development of two of the three basic principles of the U.S. Constitution—federalism and the separation of powers. Federalism involves a division between two layers of government, national and state. The separation of powers involves the division of the national government into three branches. These principles are limitations on the powers of government; Americans specified these principles as a condition of giving their consent to be governed. And these principles became the framework within which the government operates. The persistence of local government and of reliance of the national government on grants-in-aid to coerce local governments into following national goals demonstrates the continuing vitality of the federal framework. The intense competition among the president, Congress, and the courts dramatizes the continuing vitality of the separation of powers.

The second goal was to gain an appreciation of constitutionalism itself. In addition to describing how the Constitution is formally amended, we analyzed the twenty-seven amendments in order to determine what they had in common, in contrast to the hundreds of amendments that were offered but never adopted. With the exception of the Prohibition Amendment, the amendments were oriented toward some change in the framework or structure of government. The Prohibition Amendment was the only adopted amendment that sought to legislate by constitutional means.

Our conclusion was that the purpose of a constitution is to organize the makeup or the composition of the government, the *framework within which* government and politics, including actual legislation, can take place. A country does not require federalism and the separation of powers to

---

[22]Not everybody will agree that divided government is all that less productive than government in which both branches are controlled by the same party. See David Mayhew, *Divided We Govern: Party Control, Law Making and Investigations, 1946–1990* (New Haven: Yale University Press, 1991). For another good evaluation of divided government, see Charles O. Jones, *Separate But Equal Branches—Congress and the Presidency* (Chatham, NJ: Chatham House, 1995).

have a real constitutional government. And the country does not have to approach individual rights in the same manner as the American Constitution. But to be a true constitutional government, a government must have some kind of framework, which consists of a few principles that cannot be manipulated by people in power merely for their own convenience. This is the essence of constitutionalism—principles that are above the reach of everyday legislatures, executives, bureaucrats, and politicians, yet that are not so far above their reach that they cannot sometimes be adapted to changing conditions.

TIME LINE ON FEDERALISM

Events		Institutional Developments
		Congress establishes national economic power, power to tax, power over foreign policy (1791–1795)
		Bill of Rights ratified (1791)
Territorial expansion; slaves taken into territories (1800s)	**1800**	Epoch of dual federalism: Congress promotes commerce; states possess unchallenged police power (1800–1937)
Hartford Convention—New England states threaten secession from Union (1814)		*McCulloch v. Maryland* (1819) and *Gibbons v. Ogden* (1824) reaffirm national supremacy
Attempt to use U.S. Bill of Rights to restrict state power (1830s)		
President Andrew Jackson decisively deals with South Carolina's threat to secede (1833)		*Barron v. Baltimore*—State power not subject to the U.S. Bill of Rights (1833)
		Dred Scott v. Sandford—Congress may not regulate slavery in the territories (1857)
Secession of Southern states (1860–1861); Civil War (1861–1865)	**1860**	Union destroyed (1860–1861)
		Union restored (1865)
Reconstruction of South (1867–1877)		Constitution amended: XIII (1865), XIV (1868), XV (1870) Amendments
Compromise of 1877—self-government restored to former Confederate states (1877)	**1870**	Reestablishment of South's full place in the Union (1877)
Consolidation of great national industrial corporations (U.S. Steel, AT&T, Standard Oil) (1880s and 1890s)		Interstate Commerce Act (1887) and Sherman Antitrust Act (1890) provide first national regulation of monopoly practices
Franklin D. Roosevelt's first New Deal programs for national economic recovery enacted by Congress (1933)	**1930**	Supreme Court upholds expanded powers of president in *U.S. v. Curtiss-Wright* (1936), and of Congress in *Stewart Machine v. Davis* (1937) and *NLRB v. Jones & Laughlin Steel* (1937)

Events	Institutional Developments
Blacks reject segregation after World War II (1950s)	**1950** Supreme Court holds that segregation is "inherently unequal" in *Brown v. Board of Ed.* (1954)
Black protests against segregation in South (1950s and 1960s)	National power expanded to reach discrimination, poverty, education, and poor health (1960s)
Drive to register Southern blacks to vote (1965)	Voting Rights Act (1965)
Republicans take control of the White House (1968)	Entire Bill of Rights effectively "nationalized" (1969)
	1970 Revenue sharing under Nixon to strengthen state governments (1972)
Election of Ronald Reagan (1980)	States' rights reaffirmed by Reagan and Bush administrations (1980–1990s)
Election of George Bush (1988)	
	1990 Americans with Disabilities Act (1990)
Election of Bill Clinton; Democrats control Congress and Executive (1992)	Civil Rights Act (1991)
Republicans take control of both houses of Congress (1994)	Republicans in 104th Congress move to devolve more powers back to the states (1994–1996)

KEY TERMS

Aid to Families with Dependent Children (AFDC) Federal funds, administered by the states, for children living with parents or relatives who fall below state standards of need.

block grants Federal grants-in-aid that allow states considerable discretion in how the funds should be spent.

categorical grants-in-aid Grants by Congress to states and localities, given with the condition that expenditures be limited to a problem or group specified by the national government.

checks and balances Mechanisms through which each branch of government is able to participate in and influence the activities of the other branches. Major examples include the presidential veto power over congressional legislation, the power of the Senate to approve presidential appointments, and judicial review of congressional enactments.

cooperative federalism A type of federalism existing since the New Deal era in which grants-in-aid have been used strategically to encourage states and localities (without commanding them) to pursue nationally defined goals. Also known as *intergovernmental cooperation.*

devolution A strategy in which the national government would grant the states more authority over a range of policies currently under national government authority.

divided government The condition in American government wherein the presidency is controlled by one party while the opposing party controls one or both houses of Congress.

dual federalism The system of government that prevailed in the United States from 1789 to 1937 in which most fundamental governmental powers were shared between the federal and state governments.

federalism   System of government in which power is divided by a constitution between a central government and regional governments (in the United States, between the national government and state governments).

grants-in-aid   A general term for funds given by Congress to state and local governments.

gridlock   Term used to describe the state of affairs when the executive and legislative branches cannot agree on major legislation and neither side will compromise.

home rule   Power delegated by the state to a local unit of government to manage its own affairs.

legislative supremacy   The preeminence of Congress among the three branches of government, as established by the Constitution.

mandates   National laws directing state or local governments to comply with federal regulations.

new federalism   Attempts by Presidents Nixon and Reagan to return power to the states through block grants.

police power   Power reserved to the state to regulate the health, safety, and morals of its citizens.

regulated federalism   A form of federalism in which Congress imposes legislation on the states and localities requiring them to meet national standards.

separation of powers   The division of governmental power among several institutions that must cooperate in decision making.

unfunded mandates   Regulations or conditions for receiving grants that impose costs on state and local governments for which they are not reimbursed by the federal government.

FOR FURTHER READING

Anton, Thomas. *American Federalism and Public Policy.* Philadelphia: Temple University Press, 1989.

Bensel, Richard. *Sectionalism and American Political Development: 1880–1980.* Madison: University of Wisconsin Press, 1984.

Berger, Raoul. *Executive Privilege: A Constitutional Myth.* Cambridge: Harvard University Press, 1974.

Bowman, Ann O'M., and Richard Kearny. *The Resurgence of the States.* Englewood Cliffs, NJ: Prentice-Hall, 1986.

Corwin, Edward, and J. W. Peltason. *Corwin & Peltason's Understanding the Constitution,* 13th ed. Fort Worth: Harcourt Brace, 1994.

Crovitz, L. Gordon, and Jeremy Rabkin, eds. *The Fettered Presidency: Legal Constraints on the Executive Branch.* Washington, DC: American Enterprise Institute, 1989.

Dye, Thomas R. *American Federalism: Competition among Governments.* Lexington, MA: Lexington Books, 1990.

Elazar, Daniel. *American Federalism: A View from the States.* New York: Harper & Row, 1984.

Ginsberg, Benjamin, and Martin Shefter. *Politics by Other Means: Institutional Conflict and the Declining Significance of Elections in America.* New York: Basic Books, 1990.

Grodzins, Morton. *The American System.* Chicago: Rand McNally, 1974.

Kelley, E. Wood. *Policy and Politics in the United States: The Limits of Localism.* Philadelphia: Temple University Press, 1987.

Kettl, Donald. *The Regulation of American Federalism.* Baltimore: Johns Hopkins University Press, 1987.

Palley, Marian Lief, and Howard Palley. *Urban America and Public Policies.* Lexington, MA: D.C. Heath, 1981.

Peterson, Paul, Barry Rabe, and Kenneth K. Wong. *When Federalism Works.* Washington, DC: Brookings Institution, 1986.

Robinson, Donald L. *To the Best of My Ability.* New York: W. W. Norton, 1986.

Wright, Deil S. *Understanding Intergovernmental Relations.* Monterey, CA: Brooks/Cole, 1982.

CHAPTER 4

The Constitution and the Individual: The Bill of Rights, Civil Liberties, and Civil Rights

WHEN AMERICANS think of liberties and rights, they think of written guarantees, like the Bill of Rights—the first ten amendments to the Constitution, adopted in 1791 to provide a framework for the defense and protection of the individual. The words of those first ten amendments have remained unchanged for 200 years, and they have inspired people of all nations. But they have also generated controversy. The Bill of Rights is as lively a topic today as it was two centuries ago.

The Bill of Rights—its history and the controversy of interpretation surrounding it—can be usefully subdivided into two categories: civil liberties and civil rights. This chapter will be divided accordingly. *Civil liberties* are defined as protections of citizens from improper government action. When adopted in 1791, the Bill of Rights was seen as marking out a private sphere of personal liberty or freedom from governmental restrictions.[1] As Jefferson had put it, a bill of rights "is

[1]Lest there be confusion in our interchangeable use of the words "liberty" and "freedom," treat them as synonymous. "Freedom" is from the German, *Freiheit.* "Liberty" is from the French, *liberté.* Both have to do with the absence of restraints on individual choices of action.

THE BILL OF RIGHTS

Amendment I: Limits on Congress
Congress cannot make any law establishing a religion or abridging freedoms of religious exercise, speech, assembly, or petition.

Amendments II, III, IV: Limits on the Executive
The executive branch cannot infringe on the right of people to keep arms (II), cannot arbitrarily take houses for militia (III), and cannot search for or seize evidence without a court warrant swearing to the probable existence of a crime (IV).

Amendments V, VI, VII, VIII: Limits on the Judiciary
The courts cannot hold trials for serious offenses without provision for a grand jury (V), a trial jury (VII), a speedy trial (VI), presentation of charges and confrontation by the accused of hostile witnesses (VI), immunity from testimony against oneself and immunity from trial more than once for the same offense (V). Furthermore, neither bail nor punishment can be excessive (VIII), and no property can be taken without "just compensation"(V).

Amendments IX, X: Limits on the National Government
Any rights not enumerated are reserved to the states or the people (X), but the enumeration of certain rights in the Constitution should not be interpreted to mean that those are the only rights the people have (IX).

---

what people are entitled to *against every government on earth*." Note the emphasis—citizen *against* government. In this sense, we could call the Bill of Rights a "bill of liberties" because the amendments focus on what government must *not* do. For example (with emphasis added):

1. "Congress shall make *no* law. . . ." (I)
2. "The right to . . . bear Arms, shall *not* be infringed." (II)
3. "No soldier shall . . . be quartered. . . ." (III)
4. "*No* warrants shall issue, but upon probable cause . . ." (IV)
5. "*No* person shall be held to answer . . . unless on presentment or indictment of a Grand Jury. . . ." (V)
6. "Excessive bail shall *not* be required . . . *nor* cruel and unusual punishments inflicted." (VIII)

Thus, the Bill of Rights is a series of "thou shalt nots"—restraints addressed to government. Some of these restraints are substantive, putting limits on *what* the government shall and shall not have power to do—such as establishing a religion, quartering troops in private homes without consent, or seizing private property without just compensation. Other restraints are procedural, dealing with *how* the government is supposed to act. For instance, the Sixth Amendment requires the government to provide the accused with a "speedy and public trial, by an impartial jury."

While civil liberties are phrased as negatives, *civil rights* are obligations imposed on government to take *positive (or affirmative) action to protect citizens from the illegal actions of other private citizens and other government agencies*. Civil rights did not become part of the Constitution until 1868 with the adoption of the Fourteenth Amendment, which addressed the issue of who was a citizen and provided for each citizen "the equal protection of the laws." From that point on, we can see more clearly the distinction between civil liberties and civil rights, because civil liberties issues arise under the "due process of law" clause, and civil rights issues arise under the "equal protection of the laws" clause.[2]

CIVIL LIBERTIES: NATIONALIZING THE BILL OF RIGHTS

The First Amendment provides that "Congress shall make no law respecting an establishment of religion . . . or abridging freedom of speech, or of the press; or the right of [assembly and petition]." But this is the only amendment in the Bill of Rights that addresses itself exclusively to the national government. For example, the Second Amendment provides that "the right of the people to keep and bear Arms shall not be infringed." The Fifth Amendment says, among other things, that *"no person* shall . . . be twice put in jeopardy of life or limb" for the same crime; that *no person* "shall be compelled in any Criminal Case to be a witness against himself"; that *no person* shall "be deprived of life, liberty, or property, without due process of law"; and that private property cannot be taken "without just compensation."[3]

Dual Citizenship

Since the First Amendment is the only part of the Bill of Rights that is explicit in its intention to put limits on the national government, a fundamental question inevitably arises: *Do the remaining amend-ments of the Bill of Rights put limits on state governments or only on the national government?* This question was settled in 1833 in a way that seems odd to Americans today. The case was *Barron v. Baltimore,* and the facts were simple. In paving its streets, the city of Baltimore had disposed of so much sand and gravel in the water near Barron's wharf that the value of the wharf for commercial purposes was virtually destroyed. Barron brought the city into court on the grounds that it had, under the Fifth Amendment, unconstitutionally deprived him of his property without just compensation. Barron had to take his case all the way to the Supreme Court. There Chief Justice Marshall, in one of the most significant Supreme Court decisions ever handed down, disagreed with Barron:

> The Constitution was ordained and established by the people of the United States for themselves, for their own government, and not for the government of the individual States. Each State established a constitution for itself, and in that constitution provided such limitations and restrictions on the powers of its particular government as its judgment dictated. . . . If these propositions be correct, *the fifth amendment must be understood as restraining the power of the general government, not as applicable to the States.*[4]

In other words, if an agency of the *national* government had deprived Barron of his property, there would have been little doubt about Barron's winning his case. But if the constitution of the state of Maryland contained no such provision protecting citizens of Maryland from such action, then Barron had no legal leg to stand on against Baltimore, an agency of the state of Maryland.

Barron v. Baltimore confirmed "dual citizenship"—that is, that each American was a citizen of the national government and *separately* a citizen of one of the states. This meant that the Bill of Rights did not apply to decisions or procedures of

---

[2]For recent scholarship on the Bill of Rights and its development, see Geoffrey Stone, Richard Epstein, and Cass Sunstein, eds., *The Bill of Rights and the Modern State* (Chicago: University of Chicago Press, 1992); and Michael J. Meyer and William A. Parent, eds., *The Constitution of Rights* (Ithaca: Cornell University Press, 1992).

[3]It would be useful at this point to review all the provisions of the Bill of Rights (in the Appendix) to confirm this distinction between the wording of the First Amendment and the rest. Emphasis in the example quotations was not in the original. For a spirited and enlightening essay on the extent to which the entire Bill of Rights was about equality, see Martha Minow, "Equality and the Bill of Rights," in Meyer and Parent, *The Constitution of Rights,* pp. 118–28.

[4]Barron v. Baltimore, 7 Peters 243 (1833). [Emphasis added.]

CONCEPT MAP 4.1

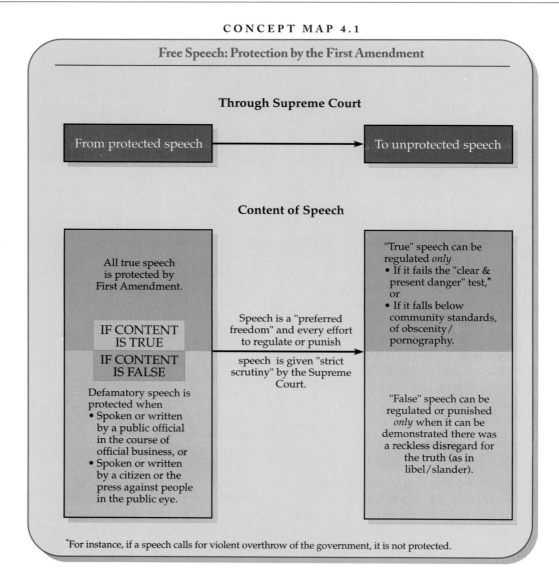

Free Speech: Protection by the First Amendment

Through Supreme Court

From protected speech → To unprotected speech

Content of Speech

All true speech is protected by First Amendment.

IF CONTENT IS TRUE

IF CONTENT IS FALSE

Defamatory speech is protected when
• Spoken or written by a public official in the course of official business, or
• Spoken or written by a citizen or the press against people in the public eye.

Speech is a "preferred freedom" and every effort to regulate or punish speech is given "strict scrutiny" by the Supreme Court.

"True" speech can be regulated *only*
• If it fails the "clear & present danger" test,* or
• If it falls below community standards, of obscenity/ pornography.

"False" speech can be regulated or punished *only* when it can be demonstrated there was a reckless disregard for the truth (as in libel/slander).

*For instance, if a speech calls for violent overthrow of the government, it is not protected.

state (or local) governments. Even slavery could continue, because the Bill of Rights could not protect anyone from state laws treating people as property. In fact, the Bill of Rights did not become a vital instrument for the extension of civil liberties for anyone until after a bloody Civil War and a revolutionary Fourteenth Amendment intervened. And even so, as we shall see, nearly a second century would pass before the Bill of Rights would truly come into its own.

The Fourteenth Amendment

From a constitutional standpoint, the defeat of the South in the Civil War settled one question and raised another. It probably settled forever the question of whether secession was an option for any state. After 1865, there was more "united" than "states" to the United States. But this left unanswered just how much the states were obliged to obey the Constitution, in particular, the Bill of Rights. Just reading the words of the Fourteenth Amendment, anyone might think it was almost perfectly designed to impose the Bill of Rights on the states and thereby to reverse *Barron v. Baltimore*. The very first words of the Fourteenth Amendment point in that direction.

All persons born or naturalized in the United States, and subject to the jurisdiction thereof, are citizens of the United States and of the State wherein they reside.

This provides for a *single national citizenship,* and at a minimum that means that civil liberties should not vary drastically from state to state. That would seem to be the spirit of the Fourteenth Amendment: *to nationalize the Bill of Rights by nationalizing the definition of citizenship.*

This interpretation of the Fourteenth Amendment is reinforced by the next clause of the Amendment:

No state shall make or enforce any law which shall abridge the privileges or immunities of citizens of the United States; nor shall any state deprive any person of life, liberty, or property, without due process of law. [Emphasis added.]

All of this sounds like an effort to extend the Bill of Rights in its *entirety* to citizens *wherever* they might reside.[5] But this was not to be the Supreme Court's interpretation for nearly a hundred years. Within five years of ratification of the Fourteenth Amendment, the Court was making decisions as though it had never been adopted.[6] The shadow of *Barron* grew longer and longer. Table 4.1 outlines the major developments in the history of the Fourteenth Amendment against the backdrop of *Barron,* citing the particular provisions of the Bill of Rights as they were incorporated by Supreme Court decisions into the Fourteenth Amendment as limitations on all the states. This is a measure of the degree of "nationalization" of civil liberties.

The only change in civil liberties during the first sixty years after the adoption of the Fourteenth Amendment came in 1897, when the Supreme Court held that the due process clause of the Fourteenth Amendment did in fact prohibit states from taking property for a public use without just compensation.[7] This effectively overruled the specific holding in *Barron;* henceforth a citizen of Maryland or any state was protected from a "public taking" of property (eminent domain) even if the state constitution did not provide such protection. But in a broader sense, *Barron* still cast a shadow, because the Supreme Court had "incorporated" into the Fourteenth Amendment *only* the property protection provision of the Fifth Amendment, despite the fact that the **due process** clause applied to the taking of life and liberty as well as property.

No further expansion of civil liberties through incorporation occurred until 1925, when the

---

[5]The Fourteenth Amendment also seems designed to introduce civil rights. The final clause of the all-important Section 1 provides that no state can "deny to any person within its jurisdiction the equal protection of the laws." It is not unreasonable to conclude that the purpose of this provision was to obligate the state governments as well as the national government to take *positive* actions to protect citizens from arbitrary and discriminatory actions, at least those based on race. This will be explored in the second half of the chapter.
[6]The Slaughter-House Cases, 16 Wallace 36 (1873); The Civil Rights Cases, 109 U.S. 3 (1883).
[7]Chicago, Burlington and Quincy Railroad Company v. Chicago, 166 U.S. 266 (1897).

TABLE 4.1

Incorporation of the Bill of Rights into the Fourteenth Amendment

SELECTED PROVISIONS AND AMENDMENTS	YEAR "INCORPORATED"	KEY CASE
Eminent domain (V)	1897	Chicago, Burlington and Quincy Railroad v. Chicago
Freedom of speech (I)	1925	Gitlow v. New York
Freedom of press (I)	1931	Near v. Minnesota
Freedom of assembly (I)	1939	Hague v. CIO
Freedom from warrantless search and seizure (IV) ("exclusionary rule")	1961	Mapp v. Ohio
Right to counsel in any criminal trial (VI)	1963	Gideon v. Wainwright
Right against self-incrimination and forced confessions (V)	1964	Malloy v. Hogan Escobedo v. Illinois
Right to counsel and to remain silent (VI)	1966	Miranda v. Arizona
Right against double jeopardy (V)	1969	Benton v. Maryland
Right to privacy (III, IV, & V)	1973	Roe v. Wade Doe v. Bolton

Supreme Court held that freedom of speech is "among the fundamental personal rights and 'liberties' protected by the due process clause of the Fourteenth Amendment from impairment by the states."[8] In 1931, the Supreme Court added freedom of the press to that short list of civil rights protected by the Bill of Rights from state action; in 1939, it added freedom of assembly.[9] But that was as far as the Court was willing to go for the next two decades.

The shadow of *Barron* extended into its second century, despite adoption of the Fourteenth Amendment. At the time of World War II, the Constitution, as interpreted by the Supreme Court, left standing the framework in which the states had the power to determine their own law on a number of fundamental issues. It left states with the power to pass laws segregating the races. It also left states with the power to engage in searches and seizures without a warrant, to indict

accused persons without benefit of a grand jury, to deprive persons of trial by jury, to force persons to testify against themselves, to deprive accused persons of their right to confront adverse witnesses, and to prosecute accused persons more than once for the same crime.[10] Few states exercised these powers, but the power was there for any state whose legislative majority chose to use it.

The Second Constitutional Revolution

Signs of change in the constitutional framework could be detected beginning after World War II, and virtually everyone could see the writing on the wall after 1954, in *Brown v. Board of Education*, when the Court found state segregation laws for schools unconstitutional. Even though *Brown* was not a civil liberties case, it indicated rather clearly that the Supreme Court was going to be expansive about civil liberties, because with *Brown* the

---

[8]Gitlow v. New York, 268 U.S. 652 (1925).
[9]Near v. Minnesota, 283 U.S. 697 (1931); Hague v. C.I.O., 307 U.S. 496 (1939).

[10]All of these were implicitly identified in Palko v. Connecticut, 302 U.S. 319 (1937), as "not incorporated" into the Fourteenth Amendment as limitations on the powers of the states.

Court had effectively promised that it was going to *actively* subject the states and all actions affecting civil rights and civil liberties to **strict scrutiny.** In retrospect, one could say that the Second Constitutional Revolution began with or soon after *Brown v. Board of Education* (1954). This can be seen in Table 4.1 by the number of civil liberties incorporated after 1954.

NATIONALIZING THE BILL OF RIGHTS   The First Constitutional Revolution, as we saw in Chapter 3, began when the Supreme Court in 1937 interpreted "interstate commerce" in favor of federal government regulation.[11] Both revolutions, then, were movements toward nationalization, but they required opposite motions on the part of the Supreme Court. In the area of commerce (the first revolution), the Court had to decide to assume a *passive* role by not interfering as Congress expanded the meaning of the commerce clause of Article I, Section 8. This expansion has been so extensive that the national government can now constitutionally reach a single farmer growing twenty acres of wheat or a small neighborhood restaurant selling barbecues to local "whites only" without being anywhere near interstate commerce routes. In the second revolution—involving the Bill of Rights and particularly the Fourteenth Amendment—the Court had to assume an *active* role. It required close review of the laws of state legislatures and decisions of state courts, in order to apply a single national Fourteenth Amendment standard to the rights and liberties of all citizens.

Table 4.1 shows that until 1961, only the First Amendment and one clause of the Fifth Amendment had been clearly incorporated into the Fourteenth Amendment.[12] After 1961, several other

important provisions of the Bill of Rights were incorporated. Of the cases that expanded the Fourteenth Amendment's reach, the most famous was *Gideon v. Wainwright,* which established the right to counsel in a criminal trial, because it became the subject of a best-selling book and a popular movie.[13] In *Mapp,* the Court held that evidence obtained in violation of the Fourth Amendment ban on unreasonable searches and seizures would be excluded from trial.[14] This *"exclusionary rule"* was particularly irksome to the police and prosecutors because it meant that patently guilty defendants sometimes go free because the evidence that clearly damned them could not be used. In *Miranda,* the Court's ruling required that arrested persons be informed of the right to remain silent and to have counsel present during interrogation.[15] This is the basis of the **Miranda rule** of reading persons their rights.

By 1969, the Supreme Court had come full circle regarding the rights of the criminally accused, explicitly reversing a 1937 ruling and thereby incorporating double jeopardy. During the 1960s and early 1970s, the Court also expanded another important area of civil liberties: rights to privacy. When the Court began to take a more activist role in the mid-1950s and 1960s, the idea of a "right to privacy" was revived. In 1958, the Supreme Court recognized "privacy in one's association" in its decision to prevent the state of Alabama from using the membership list of the National Association for the Advancement of Colored People in the state's investigations.[16]

The sphere of privacy was drawn in earnest in 1965, when the Court ruled that a Connecticut statute forbidding the use of contraceptives violated the right of marital privacy. Estelle Griswold, the executive director of the Planned Parenthood League of Connecticut, was arrested by

---

[11]NLRB v. Jones & Laughlin Steel Corp. (1937).
[12]The one exception was the right to public trial (Sixth Amendment), but a 1948 case (In re Oliver, 33 U.S. 257) did not actually mention the right to public trial as such; it was cited in a 1968 case (Duncan v. Louisiana, 391 U.S. 145) as a precedent establishing the right to public trial as part of the Fourteenth Amendment.

[13]Gideon v. Wainwright, 372 U.S. 335 (1963); Anthony Lewis, *Gideon's Trumpet* (New York: Random House, 1964).
[14]Mapp v. Ohio, 367 U.S. 643 (1961).
[15]Miranda v. Arizona, 384 U.S. 436 (1966).
[16]NAACP v. Alabama ex rel. Patterson, 357 U.S. 449 (1958).

the state of Connecticut for providing information, instruction, and medical advice about contraception to married couples. She and her associates were found guilty as accessories to the crime and fined $100 each. The Supreme Court reversed the lower court decisions and declared the Connecticut law unconstitutional because it violated "a right of privacy older than the Bill of Rights— older than our political parties, older than our school system.[17] Justice William O. Douglas, author of the majority decision in the *Griswold* case, argued that this right of privacy is also grounded in the Constitution, because it fits into a "zone of privacy" created by a combination of the Third, Fourth, and Fifth Amendments. A concurring opinion, written by Justice Arthur Goldberg, attempted to strengthen Douglas's argument by adding that "the concept of liberty . . . embraces the right of marital privacy though that right is not mentioned explicitly in the Constitution [and] is supported by numerous decisions of this Court . . . and *by the language and history of the Ninth Amendment* [emphasis added]"[18]

The right to privacy was confirmed—and extended—in 1973 in the most important of all privacy decisions, and one of the most important Supreme Court decisions in American history: *Roe v. Wade*.[19] This decision established a woman's right to have an abortion and prohibited states from making abortion a criminal act. The basis for the Supreme Court's decision in *Roe* was the evolving right to privacy. But it is important to realize that the preference for privacy rights and for their extension to include the rights of women to control their own bodies was not something invented by the Supreme Court in a political vacuum. Most states did not begin to regulate abortions in any fashion until the 1840s (by 1839 only

six of the twenty-six existing states had any regulations governing abortion). In addition, many states began to ease their abortion restrictions well before the 1973 Supreme Court decision. In recent years, however, a number of states have reinstated restrictions on abortion, testing the limits of *Roe*.

Like any important principle, once privacy was established as an aspect of civil liberties that was protected by the Bill of Rights through the Fourteenth Amendment, it took on a life all its own. In a number of important decisions, the Supreme Court and the lower federal courts sought to protect rights that could not be found in the text of the Constitution but could be discovered through the study of the philosophic sources of fundamental rights. Through this line of reasoning, the federal courts ruled to protect sexual autonomy, lifestyle choices, sexual preferences, procreational choice, and various forms of intimate association.

Criticism mounted with every extension of this line of reasoning. The federal courts were accused of creating an uncontrollable expansion of rights demands. The Supreme Court, the critics argued, had displaced the judgments of legislatures and state courts with its own judgment of what is reasonable, without regard to public preferences and without regard to specific constitutional provisions. This is virtually the definition of what came to be called "judicial activism" in the 1980s, and it was the basis for a more critical label, "the imperial judiciary."[20]

REHNQUIST: A DE-NATIONALIZING TREND? Controversy over judicial power has not diminished. In fact, it is intensifying under Chief Justice William Rehnquist, an avowed critic of "judicial activism" as it bears on privacy and other new

---

[17]Griswold v. Connecticut, 381 U.S. 479 (1965).

[18]Griswold v. Connecticut, concurring opinion. In 1972, the Court extended the privacy right to unmarried women: Eisenstadt v. Baird, 405 U.S. 438 (1972).

[19]Roe v. Wade, 410 U.S. 113 (1973).

[20]A good discussion will be found in Paul Brest and Sanford Levinson, *Processes of Constitutional Decisionmaking: Cases and Materials*, 2nd ed. (Boston: Little, Brown, 1983), p. 660. See also Chapter 7.

rights, such as the right to be represented in districts of numerically equal size[21] and the right not to be required to participate in prayers in school.[22]

Although it is difficult to determine just how much influence Rehnquist has had as Chief Justice, the Court has in fact been moving in a less activist and more conservative, de-nationalizing direction.

The best measure of the decline of activism is the decline in the Court's annual case load from 150 to 75, which Court watchers call the "incredible shrinking docket."[23] One of the most eminent Court watchers agrees that this is a momentous trend, which must be attributed in large part to Rehnquist's personal influence. Granted, there was a diminishing supply of new statutory activity during the 1980s and early 1990s, and granted also, there was far less civil rights litigation than there had been. As Justice Souter observed in a very frank appraisal of the recent history of the Supreme Court, "There hasn't been an awful lot for us to take."[24] However, this did not "just happen." An activist court can virtually always find cases if it is seeking them. Meanwhile, year by year during the Rehnquist tenure, the case load shrank from the average of 150 cases during the years prior to his appointment in 1986 to 132 cases in 1988–1989, to 129 in 1989–1990, to 112 in 1990–1991, to 108 in 1991–1992, to 107 in 1992–1993. There was a sharp drop to 84 in 1993–1994, to 82 in 1994–1995 and finally to 75 in the most recently completed term of 1995–1996.[25]

A good measure of the Court's growing conservatism is the following comparison made by constitutional scholar David M. O'Brien: Between 1961 and 1969, more than 76 percent of the Warren Court's rulings from term to term tended to be liberal—that is, tending toward nationalizing the Bill of Rights to protect individuals and minorities mainly against the actions of state government. During the Burger years, 1969–1986, the liberal tendency dropped on the average below 50 percent. During the first four years of the Rehnquist Court (the extent of O'Brien's research), the average liberal "score" dropped to less than 35 percent.[26] For example, O'Brien reports that in the 1990 term, the Court ruled against prisoners' claims in twenty-three out of thirty-one cases, leaving more power over prisoners in state and local hands.

Deference to state power over prisoners was extended most significantly in one particular area, capital punishment. In 1991, Rehnquist achieved his first victory in a 6-to-3 ruling severely limiting repeated prisoner *habeas corpus* petitions, stressing in the 1991 opinion that "perpetual disrespect for the finality of convictions disparages the entire criminal justice system."[27] But he achieved closer to complete victory in 1996 in *Felker v. Turpin*. Writing for a *unanimous* Court, Rehnquist upheld provisions of the Antiterrorism and Effective Death Penalty Act of 1996 that sought to limit state prisoners' filing second or successive applications for writs of *habeas corpus* if no new claim is presented.[28]

The conservative trend has also extended to the burning question of abortion rights. In *Webster v. Reproductive Health Services*, the Court narrowly upheld by a 5-to-4 majority the constitutionality of restrictions on the use of public medical facili-

[21]Baker v. Carr, 369 U.S. 186 (1962).

[22]Engel v. Vitale, 370 U.S. 421 (1962), in which the Court struck down a state-composed prayer for recitation in the schools. Of course, a whole line of cases followed *Engel*, as states and cities tried various means of getting around the Court's principle that any organized prayer in the public schools violates the First Amendment.

[23]Quoted in David Garrow, "The Rehnquist Reins," *New York Times Magazine*, 6 October 1996, p. 82.

[24]Quoted in *ibid.*, p. 71.

[25]Quoted in *ibid.*, p. 71.

[26]David M. O'Brien, *Supreme Court Watch—1991*, Annual Supplement to *Constitutional Law and Politics* (New York: W. W. Norton, 1991), p. 6 and Chapter 4.

[27]McCleskey v. Zant, 111 S.Ct. 1454 (1991).

[28]Op cit.

NORMA McCORVEY AND RANDALL TERRY
From Roe v. Wade *to "Operation Rescue"*

ABORTION is perhaps the most potent and explosive issue of the last two decades. Norma McCorvey (known to most as Jane Roe) and Randall Terry demonstrate the power of this issue to bring average people into the political fray in a highly personal way. In their own way, McCorvey and Terry have sought to redefine the constitutional interpretation surrounding abortion.

In 1969, Norma McCorvey was a twenty-one-year-old carnival worker, divorced, with a five-year-old daughter, and living on the edge of poverty. She was in Texas with the carnival when she discovered she was pregnant. Seeking an abortion, McCorvey found she was in a state that allowed abortions only to save the life of the mother. In her words, "I found one doctor who offered to abort me for $500. Only he didn't have a license, and I was scared to turn my body over to him. So there I was—pregnant, . . . alone and stuck."

McCorvey bore her child and gave it up for adoption, but in the process, she met two recent law school graduates, Sarah Weddington and Linda Coffey. These three women decided to challenge the Texas abortion law in court. In order to avoid personal stigma, McCorvey's name was changed to Jane Roe. The defendant was Henry Wade, a district attorney for Dallas County, Texas. The result of the challenge was the controversial landmark Supreme Court case *Roe v. Wade* (1973), in which a seven-member majority of the Court affirmed a constitutional right to abortion under most circumstances.

The case stunned and mobilized abortion opponents, including Randall Terry, a used-car salesman. A native of upstate New York, Terry settled with his wife in Binghamton, where they began to stand in front of abortion clinics to try to talk women out of getting abortions. By 1988, Terry quit his job and devoted his energies full time to his organization, Operation Rescue. Led by Terry, the group has sought to close down doctors' offices, clinics, and other places where

NORMA McCORVEY

ties for abortion.[29] And in 1992, in the most recent major decision on abortion, *Planned Parenthood v. Casey,* another 5-to-4 majority of the Court barely upheld Roe but narrowed its scope, refusing to invalidate a Pennsylvania law that significantly restricts freedom of choice. The decision defined

[29]In Webster v. Reproductive Health Services, 109 S.Ct. 3040 (1989), Chief Justice Rehnquist's decision upheld a Missouri law that restricted the use of public medical facilities for abortion. The decision opened the way for other states to limit the availability of abortion. The first to act was the Pennsylvania legislature, which adopted in late 1989 a law banning all abortions after pregnancy had passed twenty-four weeks, except to save the life of the pregnant woman or to prevent irreversible impairment of her health. In 1990, the pace of state legislative action increased, with new statutes being passed in South Carolina, Ohio, Minnesota, and Guam. In 1991, the Louisiana legislature adopted, over the governor's veto, the strictest law yet. The Louisiana law prohibits all abortions except when the mother's life is threatened or when rape or incest victims report these crimes immediately.

abortion is discussed or practiced. His means have been highly controversial. At the Southern Tier Women's Services office near Binghamton, for example, Terry was arrested for the first of many times for spreading nails in the office's parking lot and for gluing the office doors shut.

Terry has led large-scale protests in such cities as Wichita, Kansas, and Buffalo, New York, where his followers have attempted to forcibly block clinic entrances, harass physicians as well as clients, and otherwise disrupt abortion-related activities. Terry has been repeatedly cited and tried for trespass, destruction of property, harassment, and other violations. During the Democratic National Convention in 1992, an associate of Terry's attempted to present Democratic presidential nominee Bill Clinton with an aborted fetus. Terry's motivation for the action was his belief that "to vote for Bill Clinton is to sin against God." He also accused Clinton of "actively promoting rebellion against the Ten Commandments."

To members of Operation Rescue, such illegal activities are justifiable as a means to discourage abortions. Yet the extreme tactics of Operation Rescue, while receiving much publicity, have served to alienate many Americans.

In 1994, the Supreme Court ruled in *Madsen v. Women's Health Center* that restrictions on how close anti-abortion protesters could come to abortion clinics were constitutional; in the same year, the Access to Clinics Act defined local interference with a woman's right to an abortion as a federal crime. *Roe v. Wade*'s guarantee of a woman's right to an abortion remains the law of the land, reaffirmed by the most recent major Supreme Court decision on the issue, *Planned Parenthood v. Casey* (1992). But for a tiny number of Americans, no laws or Supreme Court decisions will lessen their determination to stop abortions by any means, as evidenced by the murders of clinic workers in 1993 and 1994 by anti-abortion militants at abortion clinics in Pensacola, Florida, and Brookline, Massachusetts.

RANDALL TERRY   SOURCE: Marian Faux, *Roe v. Wade* (New York: Dutton, 1989).

the right to an abortion as a "limited or qualified" right subject to regulation by the states as long as the regulation does not impose an "undue burden."[30] As one constitutional authority concluded from the decision in *Casey*, "Until there is a Freedom of Choice Act, and/or a U.S. Supreme Court able to wean *Roe* from its respirator, state legisla-

tures will have significant discretion over the access women will have to legalized abortions."[31]

One area in which Chief Justice Rehnquist seems determined to expand rather than shrink the Court's protection of privacy rights is in the constitutional protection of property rights. But

[30]Planned Parenthood of Southeastern Pennsylvania v. Casey, 112 S.Ct. 2791 (1992).

[31]Gayle Binion, "Undue Burden? Government Now Has Wide Latitude to Restrict Abortions," *Santa Barbara News-Press*, 5 July 1992, p. A13.

DENATIONALIZATION OF THE BILL OF RIGHTS

Provision/amendment	Year	Case
abortion rights	1989	*Webster v. Reproductive Health Services,* 5-to-4 ruling that restrictions on the use of public medical facilities for abortion are constitutional
writ of habeas corpus	1991	*McCleskey v. Zant,* 6-to-3 ruling severely limiting repeated prisoner *habeas corpus* petitions
abortion rights	1992	*Planned Parenthood v. Casey,* 5-to-4 ruling upheld but narrowed the scope of *Roe v. Wade*
writ of habeas corpus	1996	*Felker v. Turpin,* Court unanimously upheld legislation that limits state prisoners' right to file second or successive applications for writs of *habeas corpus* if no new claim is presented

this is itself a conservative direction and the Court's conservative justices, led by Chief Justice Rehnquist, have pushed for a broader interpretation of the Fifth Amendment's takings clause to put limits on the degree to which local, state, and federal governments can impose restrictions on land use. In an important case from 1994, the Court overturned a Tigard, Oregon, law that had required any person seeking a building permit to give the city 10 percent of his or her property. In a 5-to-4 decision, the Court ruled that such a requirement fell into the Fifth Amendment's prohibition against taking of property "without just compensation." In his opinion, Chief Justice Rehnquist wrote, "We see no reason why the takings clause of the Fifth Amendment, as much a part of the Bill of Rights as the First Amendment or Fourth Amendment, should be relegated to the status of a poor relation in those comparable circumstances."[32]

Still the question remains: Will a Supreme Court, even with a majority of conservatives, reverse the nationalization of the Bill of Rights? Possibly, but not necessarily. First of all, the Rehn-

quist Court has not actually reversed any of the decisions made by the Warren or Burger courts during the 1960s nationalizing most of the clauses of the Bill of Rights. As we have seen, the Rehnquist Court has given narrower and more restrictive interpretations of some earlier decisions, but it has not literally reversed any, not even *Roe v. Wade.* Second, President Clinton's appointments to the Court, Ruth Bader Ginsburg and Stephen Breyer, have helped form a centrist majority that seems unwilling, for the time being, at least, to sanction any major steps to turn back the nationalization of the Bill of Rights. But with any future Clinton nominations to the Court now having to be approved by a Republican-controlled Senate, the question of the expansion or contraction of the Bill of Rights and the Fourteenth Amendment is certain to be in the forefront of political debate for a long time to come.

Thus we end about where we began. The spirit of *Barron v. Baltimore* has not been entirely put to rest, and its shadow over the Bill of Rights still hovers. We hear less of the plea for the Supreme Court to take the final step they didn't quite take in the 1960s, to declare as a matter of constitutional law that the *entire* Bill of Rights is incorpo-

[32]Dolan v. City of Tigard, 93-518 (1994).

rated into the Fourteenth Amendment. If that more liberal Court was not willing to do so, the more conservative Court of today is all the less willing. We are thus still in suspense, because a Court with the power to expand the Bill of Rights also has the power to contract it.[33]

CIVIL RIGHTS

The very simplicity of the civil rights clause of the Fourteenth Amendment left its meaning open to interpretation:

> No State shall make or enforce any law which shall . . . deny to any person within its jurisdiction the equal protection of the laws.

But in the very first Fourteenth Amendment case to come before the Supreme Court, in 1873, the majority gave it a distinct meaning:

> . . . it is not difficult to give a meaning to this clause ["the equal protection of the laws"]. The existence of laws in the States . . . which discriminated with gross injustice and hardship against [Negroes] as a class, was the evil to be remedied by this clause, and by it such laws are forbidden.[34]

The Court at the time understood well that private persons offering accommodations or places of amusement to the public had an obligation to offer them to one and all.[35] That obligated the government to take positive actions extending to each citizen the opportunities and resources necessary to the enjoyment of his or her freedom.

Discrimination is the use of unreasonable and unjust exclusion. Of course, all laws discriminate, including some people while excluding others; but some discrimination is considered unreasonable. Now, for example, it is considered reasonable to enforce twenty-one as the legal drinking age; thus the age criterion is considered reasonable discrimination. But is age a reasonable distinction when seventy (or sixty-five or sixty) is selected as the age for compulsory retirement? In the mid-1970s, Congress answered this question by making old age a new civil right; compulsory retirement at seventy is now an unlawful, unreasonable discriminatory use of age.[36]

Plessy v. Ferguson: *"Separate but Equal"*

Following its initial decision making ***"equal protection"*** a right, the Supreme Court turned conservative, no more ready to enforce the civil rights aspects of the Fourteenth Amendment than it was to enforce the civil liberties provisions. The Court declared the Civil Rights Act of 1875 unconstitutional on the ground that the act sought to protect blacks against discrimination by *private* businesses, while the Fourteenth Amendment, according to the Court's interpretation, was intended to protect individuals only against discrimination by *public* officials of state and local governments.

In 1896, the Court went still further, in the infamous case of *Plessy v. Ferguson,* by upholding a Louisiana statute that *required* segregation of the races on trolleys and other public carriers (and by implication in all public facilities, including schools). The Supreme Court held that the Fourteenth Amendment's "equal protection of the laws" was not violated by racial distinction as long as the facilities were equal.[37] People generally

---

[33]For a lively and readable treatment of the possibilities of restricting provisions of the Bill of Rights, without actually reversing Warren Court decisions, see David G. Savage, *Turning Right: The Making of the Rehnquist Supreme Court* (New York: Wiley, 1992).

[34]The Slaughter-House Cases, 16 Wallace 36 (1873).

[35]See Civil Rights Cases, 109 U.S. 3 (1883), where the Supreme Court affirmed this position even as it was holding against the black plaintiffs by declaring the Civil Rights Act of 1875 unconstitutional.

[36]A superb discussion of age discrimination is found in Lawrence Friedman, *Your Time Will Come—The Law of Age Discrimination and Mandatory Retirement* (New York: Russell Sage, 1984).

[37]Plessy v. Ferguson, 163 U.S. 537 (1896).

pretended they were equal as long as some accommodation existed. What the Court was saying, in effect, was that it was not unreasonable to use race as a basis of exclusion in public matters. This was the origin of the "separate but equal" doctrine that was not reversed until 1954.

Racial Discrimination after World War II

The shame of discrimination against black military personnel during World War II, plus revelation of Nazi racial atrocities, moved President Harry S. Truman finally to bring the problem to the White House and national attention, with the appointment in 1946 of a President's Commission on Civil Rights. In 1948, the committee submitted its report, *To Secure These Rights,* which laid bare the extent of the problem of racial discrimination and its consequences.

The Supreme Court had begun to change its position regarding racial discrimination just before World War II by being stricter about what the states would have to do to provide equal facilities under the "separate but equal" rule. In 1938, the Court rejected Missouri's policy of paying the tuition of qualified blacks to out-of-state law schools rather than admitting them to the University of Missouri Law School.[38] After the war, modest progress resumed. In 1950, the Court rejected Texas's claim that its new "law school for Negroes" afforded education equal to that of the all-white University of Texas Law School; without confronting the "separate but equal" principle itself, the Court's decision anticipated *Brown v. Board* by opening the question of whether *any* segregated facility could be truly equal.[39]

As the Supreme Court was ordering the admission of blacks to all-white state law schools, it was also striking down the Southern practice of "white primaries," which legally excluded blacks from participation in the nominating process.[40]

The most important pre-1954 decision was probably *Shelley v. Kraemer,*[41] in which the Court ruled against the practice of "restrictive convenants," whereby the seller of a home added a clause to the sales contract requiring the buyer to agree not to resell the home to a non-Caucasian, non-Christian, etc.

Although none of those cases confronted "separate but equal" and the principle of racial discrimination as such, they were extremely significant to black leaders, and gave them encouragement enough to believe that there was at last an opportunity and enough legal precedent to change the constitutional framework itself. By the fall of 1952, the Court had on its docket cases from Kansas, South Carolina, Virginia, Delaware, and the District of Columbia challenging the constitutionality of school segregation. Of these, the Kansas case became the chosen one. It seemed to be ahead of the pack in its district court, and it had the special advantage of being located in a state outside the Deep South.[42]

Oliver Brown, the father of three girls, lived "across the tracks" in a low-income, racially mixed Topeka neighborhood. Every school-day morning, Linda Brown took the school bus to the Monroe School for black children about a mile away. In September 1950, Oliver Brown took Linda to the all-white Sumner School, which was actually closer to home, to enter her into the third grade in defiance of state law and local segregation rules. When they were refused, Brown took his case to the NAACP, and soon thereafter *Brown v. Board of Education* was born.

In deciding the case, the Court, to the surprise of many, rejected as inconclusive all the learned

---

[38]Missouri ex. rel. Gaines v. Canada, 305 U.S. 337 (1938).
[39]Sweatt v. Painter, 339 U.S. 629 (1950).
[40]Smith v. Allwright, 321 U.S. 649 (1944).

[41]Shelley v. Kraemer, 334 U.S. 1 (1948).
[42]The District of Columbia case came up too, but since the District of Columbia is not a state, it did not directly involve the Fourteenth Amendment and its equal protection clause. It confronted the Court on the same grounds, however—that segregation is inherently unequal. Its victory in effect was "incorporation in reverse," with equal protection moving from the Fourteenth Amendment to become part of the Bill of Rights. See Bolling v. Sharpe, 347 U.S. 497 (1954).

arguments about the intent of the Fourteenth Amendment and committed itself to considering only the consequences of segregation:

> Does segregation of children in public schools solely on the basis of race, even though the physical facilities and other "tangible" factors may be equal, deprive the children of the minority group of equal educational opportunities? We believe that it does. . . . We conclude that in the field of public education the doctrine of "separate but equal" has no place. Separate educational facilities are inherently unequal.[43]

The *Brown* decision altered the constitutional framework in two fundamental respects. First, after *Brown*, the states would no longer have the power to use race as a basis of discrimination in law. Second, the national government would from then on have the power (and eventually the obligation) to intervene with strict regulatory policies against the discriminatory actions of state or local governments, school boards, employers, and others in the private sector (see Chapter 13).

Simple Justice: *The Courts, the Constitution, and Civil Rights after* Brown v. Board of Education

Although *Brown v. Board of Education* withdrew all constitutional authority to use race as a criterion of exclusion, this historic decision was merely a small opening move.[44] First, most states refused to cooperate until sued, and many ingenious schemes were employed to delay obedience (such as paying the tuition for white students to attend newly created "private" academies). Second, even as Southern school boards began to cooperate by eliminating their legally enforced (*de jure*) school segregation, there remained extensive actual (*de facto*) school segregation in the

North as well as the South. *Brown* could not affect *de facto* segregation, which was not legislated but happened as a result of racially segregated housing. Third, *Brown* did not directly touch discrimination in employment, public accommodations, juries, voting, and other areas of social and economic activity.

A decade of frustration following *Brown* made it fairly obvious to all that the goal of "equal protection" required positive, or affirmative, action by Congress and by administrative agencies. And given massive Southern resistance and a generally negative national public opinion toward racial integration, progress would not be made through courts, Congress, *or* agencies without intense, well-organized support.

SCHOOL DESEGREGATION Although the District of Columbia and some of the school districts in the border states began to respond almost immediately to court-ordered desegregation, the states of the Deep South responded with a well-planned delaying tactic. Southern legislatures passed laws ordering school districts to maintain segregated schools and state superintendents to withhold state funding from racially mixed classrooms. Some Southern states centralized public school authority in order to give them power to close the schools that might tend to obey the Court and to provide alternative private schooling.

Most of these plans of "massive resistance" were tested in the federal courts and were struck down as unconstitutional.[45] But Southern resistance was not confined to legislation. For example, in Arkansas in 1957, Governor Orval Faubus ordered the National Guard to prevent enforcement of a federal court order to integrate Central High School of Little Rock. President Eisenhower was forced to deploy U.S. troops and literally place the

---

[43]Brown v. Board of Education of Topeka, Kansas, 347 U.S. 483 (1954).

[44]The heading for this section is drawn from the title of Richard Kluger's important book, *Simple Justice* (New York: Vintage, 1975).

[45]The two most important cases were Cooper v. Aaron, 358 U.S. 1 (1958), which required Little Rock, Arkansas, to desegregate; and Griffin v. Prince Edward County School Board, 337 U.S. 218 (1964), which forced all the schools of that Virginia county to reopen after five years of closing to avoid desegregation.

MARTIN LUTHER KING, JR., AND MALCOLM X
Civil Rights, Nonviolence, and Separatism

ALTHOUGH VERY DIFFERENT in background, approach, and style, Martin Luther King, Jr., and Malcolm X were both motivated by the centuries of injustice and maltreatment that typified the African American experience.

An educated, charismatic minister from Georgia, Martin Luther King, Jr., received his Ph.D. in theology from Boston University in 1955. His studies of philosophy and religion shaped his approach to the struggle for civil rights: "From my Christian background I gained my ideals, and from [Mohandas K.] Gandhi my operational technique."

King first received national attention for his leadership of the Montgomery Improvement Association, an organization formed in 1955 to integrate that Alabama city's segregated bus system. During a 382-day bus boycott, King's home was firebombed, and he was arrested for the first of many times. Yet he urged positive, nonviolent action, a strategy borrowed from Gandhi's successful effort to free India from British rule, and Christian forgiveness of one's enemies. The strategy worked in Montgomery and throughout the South.

In 1957, King co-founded the Southern Christian Leadership Conference, becoming its president and leader of its efforts to eliminate racial discrimination in transportation facilities, public accommodations, hiring practices, and voting rights. In 1957 alone, King traveled 780,000 miles and delivered 208 speeches. Repeatedly beaten, arrested, and threatened with death, King and his followers continued to employ the tactics of civil disobedience and passive resistance in the face of guns, fire hoses, and police dogs.

King galvanized national opinion as a leader of the famous March on Washington in August 1963. Addressing the more than 250,000 participants from the steps of the Lincoln Memorial, he delivered his prophetic and moving "I Have a Dream" speech. The following year, King was awarded the Nobel Peace Prize, becoming at thirty-five the youngest recipient of that honor. This and other efforts stirred the nation's conscience, contributing directly to the enactment of landmark civil rights legislation in the 1960s.

Despite rising violence in the mid-1960s, King continued to urge nonviolence. Eventually the Georgia preacher was killed by an assassin's bullet outside a Memphis, Tennessee, motel on April 4, 1968.

MARTIN LUTHER KING, JR.

city under martial law. The Supreme Court handed down a unanimous decision requiring desegregation in Little Rock.[46] The end of massive resistance, however, became simply the beginning of still another Southern strategy. "Pupil placement" laws authorized school districts to place each pupil in a school according to a whole variety of academic, personal, and psychological consid-

---

[46]In Cooper v. Aaron, the Supreme Court ordered immediate compliance with the lower court's desegregation order and went beyond that with a stern warning that it is "emphatically the province and duty of the judicial department to say what the law is." The justices also took the unprecedented action of personally signing the decisions.

Malcolm X was born in 1925 as Malcolm Little, the son of a midwestern Baptist preacher. After tragically losing both of his parents, Malcolm left school after eighth grade and moved to New York City. There, he worked as a waiter for a time, but soon fell into a life of crime, becoming a drug pusher and user, as well as a burglar. Malcolm was arrested, convicted, and sentenced to a ten-year prison term in 1946.

In prison, Malcolm became a convert to the Black Muslim faith, also known as the Nation of Islam, or simply the Nation. After his parole in 1952, Malcolm became the Nation's most outspoken leader. Known for its emphasis on social conservatism (it bars alcohol, tobacco, gambling, dancing, movies, and abortion) and economic self-help, the Black Muslim faith also incorporates a separatist ideology that is sometimes accompanied by overt hostility toward whites or others outside the movement. Malcolm emphasized all of these themes in the 1950s as he rose in the ranks of the Nation's leadership and helped swell its membership to 100,000. But his emphasis on what he saw as the evil "white man's Christian world" and his characterization of whites as "devils" both fanned white resentment and won adherents among those who had grown weary of white racism. Many blacks welcomed Malcolm's "eye-for-an-eye" message.

After a power struggle with Nation leader Elijah Muhammad, Malcolm lost his position as minister of Harlem's Black Muslim Mosque, and he split from Muhammad's leadership by announcing the formation of a more political black nationalist party. After the split, Malcolm made a pilgrimage to Mecca, the holy center of the Islamic faith. On his return, Malcolm began to articulate a more moderate and humanistic view, emphasizing "life, liberty, and the pursuit of happiness for all people." Yet his troubles escalated; his house was firebombed, and his family was nearly killed. On February 21, 1965, Malcolm was assassinated as he spoke to a crowd. The murderers were followers of his rival, Elijah Muhammad.

Malcolm's tumultuous life, and the contrast between his earlier, more angry views and his later, more humanistic expressions left a dual legacy—he is demonized by some, deified by others. Unquestionably, though, Malcolm's influence today far exceeds that during his lifetime.

MALCOLM X

SOURCES: Juan Williams, *Eyes on the Prize* (New York: Penguin, 1988); Alex Haley, *The Autobiography of Malcolm X* (New York: Ballantine Books, 1965).

erations, never mentioning race at all. This put the burden of transferring to an all-white school on the nonwhite children and their parents.[47] It was

thus almost impossible for a single court order to cover a whole district, let alone a whole state. This delayed desegregation a while longer.

[47]Shuttlesworth v. Birmingham Board of Education, 358 U.S. 101 (1958). This decision upheld a "pupil placement" plan purporting to assign pupils on various bases, with no mention of race. This case interpreted Brown v. Board of Educa-

tion to mean that school districts must stop explicit racial discrimination but were under no obligation to take positive steps to desegregate. For a while, black parents were doomed to case-by-case approaches.

As new devices were invented by the Southern states to avoid desegregation, it was becoming unmistakably clear that the federal courts could not do the job alone.[48] The first modern effort to legislate in the field of civil rights was made in 1957, but the law contained only a federal guarantee of voting rights, without any powers of enforcement, although it did create the Civil Rights Commission to study abuses. Much more important legislation for civil rights followed during the 1960s, especially the Civil Rights Act of 1964. These acts will be discussed in Chapter 12.

Further progress in the desegregation of schools came in the form of busing[49] and redistricting, but it was slow and is likely to continue to be slow unless the Supreme Court decides to permit federal action against *de facto* segregation and against the varieties of private schools and academies that have sprung up for the purpose of avoiding integration.[50] A Supreme Court decision handed down in 1995, in which the Court signaled to the lower courts to "disengage from desegregation efforts," dimmed the prospects for further school integration. This is a direct and explicit threat to the main basis of the holding in the original *Brown v. Board* case.

The Rise of the Politics of Rights

OUTLAWING DISCRIMINATION IN EMPLOYMENT
Despite the agonizingly slow progress of school desegregation, there was some progress in other areas of civil rights during the 1960s and 1970s.

Voting rights were established and fairly quickly began to revolutionize Southern politics. Service on juries was no longer denied to minorities. But progress in the right to participate in politics and government dramatized the relative lack of economic progress, and it was in this area that battles over civil rights were increasingly fought.

The federal courts and the Justice Department entered this area through Title VII of the Civil Rights Act of 1964. Title VII outlawed job discrimination by all private and public employers, including governmental agencies (such as fire and police departments), that employed more than fifteen workers. We have already seen that the Supreme Court gave "interstate commerce" such a broad definition that Congress had the constitutional authority to outlaw discrimination by virtually any local employer.[51] Title VII made it unlawful to discriminate in employment on the basis of color, religion, sex, or national origin, as well as race.

One problem with Title VII was that the complaining party had to show that deliberate discrimination was the cause of the failure to get a job or a training opportunity. Rarely does an employer explicitly admit discrimination on the basis of race, sex, or any other illegal reason. For a time, courts allowed the complaining parties to make their case if they could show that an employer's hiring practices, whether intentional or

---

[48]For good treatments of that long stretch of the struggle of the federal courts to integrate the schools, see Brest and Levinson, *Processes of Constitutional Decisionmaking*, pp. 471–80; and Kelly et al., *The American Constitution*, pp. 610–16.

[49]Swann v. Charlotte-Mecklenburg Board of Education, 402 U.S. 1 (1971). See also Bernard Schwartz, *Swann's Way: The School Busing Case and the Supreme Court* (New York: Oxford University Press, 1986).

[50]For a good evaluation, see Gary Orfield, *Must We Bus? Segregated Schools and National Policy* (Washington, DC: Brookings Institution, 1978), pp. 144–46. See also Bob Woodward and Scott Armstrong, *The Brethren: Inside the Supreme Court* (New York: Simon and Schuster, 1979), pp. 426–27; and J. Anthony Lukas, *Common Ground* (New York: Random House, 1986).

[51]See especially Katzenbach v. McClung, 379 U.S. 294 (1964). Almost immediately after passage of the Civil Rights Act of 1964, a case was brought challenging the validity of Title II, which covered discrimination in public accommodations. Ollie's Barbecue was a neighborhood restaurant in Birmingham, Alabama. It was located eleven blocks away from an interstate highway and even farther from railroad and bus stations. Its table service was for whites only; there was only a take-out service for blacks. The Supreme Court agreed that Ollie's was strictly an intrastate restaurant, but since a substantial proportion of its food and other supplies were bought from companies outside the state of Alabama, there was sufficient connection to interstate commerce; therefore, racial discrimination at such restaurants would "impose commercial burdens of national magnitude upon interstate commerce." Although this case involved Title II, it had direct bearing on the constitutionality of Title VII.

PROCESS BOX 4.1

Cause and Effect in the Civil Rights Movement:
Which Came First—Government Action or Political Action?

Judicial and Legal Action	Political Action
1954 *Brown v. Board of Education*	
1955 *Brown* II—Implementation of *Brown* I	**1955** Montgomery bus boycott
1956 Federal courts order school integration, especially one ordering Autherine Lucy admitted to University of Alabama, with Governor Wallace officially protesting	
1957 Civil Rights Act creating Civil Rights Commission; President Eisenhower sends paratroops to Little Rock, Arkansas, to enforce integration of Central High School	**1957** Southern Christian Leadership Conference (SCLC) formed, with King as president
1960 First substantive Civil Rights Act, primarily voting rights	**1960** Student Nonviolent Coordinating Committee formed to organize protests, sit-ins, freedom rides
1961 Interstate Commerce Commission orders desegregation on all buses, trains, and in terminals	
1961 JFK favors executive action over civil rights legislation	
1963 JFK shifts, supports strong civil rights law; assassination; LBJ asserts strong support for civil rights	**1963** Nonviolent demonstrations in Birmingham, Alabama, lead to King's arrest and his "Letter from the Birmingham Jail"
	1963 March on Washington
1964 Congress passes historic Civil Rights Act covering voting, employment, public accommodations, education	
1965 Voting Rights Act	**1965** King announces drive to register 3 million blacks in the South
1966 War on Poverty in full swing	**1966** Movement dissipates: part toward litigation, part toward Community Action Programs, part toward war protest, part toward more militant "Black Power" actions

not, had the *effect* of exclusion. Employers, in effect, had to justify their actions.[52]

GENDER DISCRIMINATION   Even before equal employment laws began to have a positive effect on the economic situation of blacks, something far more dramatic began happening—the universalization of civil rights. The right not to be discriminated against was being successfully claimed by the other groups listed in Title VII—those defined by sex, religion, or national origin—and eventually by still other groups defined by age or sexual preference. This *universalization of rights* has become the new frontier of the civil rights struggle, and women have emerged with the greatest prominence in this new struggle. The effort to define and end gender discrimination in employment has led to the historic joining of women's rights to the civil rights cause.

Despite its interest in fighting discrimination, the Supreme Court in the 1950s and 1960s paid little attention to gender discrimination. Ironically, it was left to the more conservative Burger Court (1969–1986) to establish gender discrimination as a major and highly visible civil rights issue. In recent years, the Court has furthered the civil rights of women by making it easier for individuals to prove sexual harassment and by ruling in favor of the integration of the formerly all-male Virginia Military Institute. The future direction of the Court on gender discrimination may quite possibly be toward an even broader definition and application of civil rights with regard to women.

The development of gender discrimination as an important part of the civil rights struggle has coincided with the rise of women's politics as a discrete movement in American politics. As with the struggle for racial equality, the relationship between government policies and changes in political action suggests that changes in government policies to a great degree produce political action. Today, the existence of a powerful women's movement derives in large measure from the enactment of Title VII of the Civil Rights Act of 1964 and from the Supreme Court's vital steps in applying that law to protect women. The recognition of women's civil rights has become an issue that in many ways transcends the usual distinctions of American political debate. In the heavily partisan debate over the federal crime bill enacted in 1994, for instance, the section of the bill that enjoyed the widest support was the Violence Against Women Act, whose most important feature is that it defines gender-biased violent crimes as a matter of civil rights and creates a civil rights remedy for women who have been the victims of such crimes. Women may now file civil as well as criminal suits against their assailants, which means that they are no longer solely dependent on prosecutors to defend them against violent crime.

DISCRIMINATION AGAINST OTHER GROUPS   As gender discrimination began to be seen as an important civil rights issue, other groups arose demanding recognition and active protection of their civil rights. Under Title VII of the 1964 Civil Rights Act, any group or individual can try, and in fact is encouraged to try, to convert his or her goals and grievances into questions of rights and the deprivation of those rights. A plaintiff must only establish that his or her membership in a group is an unreasonable basis for discrimination unless it can be proven to be a "job-related" or otherwise clearly reasonable and relevant decision. In America today, the list of individuals and groups claiming illegal discrimination is lengthy. The disabled, for instance, increasingly press their claim to equal treatment as a civil rights matter, a stance encouraged by the Americans with Disabilities Act of 1990.[53] Deaf Americans increasingly demand social and legal recognition of deafness as a separate

---

[52]Griggs v. Duke Power Company, 401 U.S. 24 (1971).

[53]In 1994, for instance, after pressure from the Justice Department under the terms of the Americans with Disabilities Act, one of the nation's largest rental-car companies agreed to make special hand-controls available to any customer requesting them. See "Avis Agrees to Equip Cars for Disabled," *Los Angeles Times*, 2 September 1994, p. D1.

culture, not simply as a disability.[54] One of the most familiar of these "new" groups has been the gay and lesbian movement, which in less than thirty years has emerged from invisibility to become one of the largest civil rights movements in contemporary America. The place of gays and lesbians in American society is now the subject of a highly charged debate, but it is a debate that was not even heard before the rise of the politics of rights in the last thirty years. Signs of legal progress became apparent in the Supreme Court's decision in *Romer v. Evans* (1996). In November 1992, a Colorado referendum approved an amendment to the state constitution forbidding localities from enacting any ordinance that outlaws discrimination against homosexuals. The amendment denied to any municipality the power to adopt a law that gives homosexuals "minority status" that protects them from discrimination. In a 6-to-3 decision, the Court held that the Colorado Amendment actually classifies homosexuality not as a status equal to everyone else but as a status that "make[s] them unequal to everyone else. This Colorado cannot do. A State cannot so deem a class of persons a stranger to its laws. Amendment 2 violated the Equal Protection Clause. . . ."[55]

AFFIRMATIVE ACTION   The relatively narrow goal of equalizing opportunity by eliminating discriminatory barriers had been developing toward the far broader goal of *affirmative action*—compensatory action to overcome the consequences of past discrimination. An affirmative action policy tends to involve two novel approaches: (1) positive or benign discrimination in which race or some other status is actually taken into account, but for compensatory action rather than mistreatment; and (2) compensatory action to favor members of the disadvantaged group who themselves

may never have been the victims of discrimination. Quotas may be, but are not necessarily, involved in affirmative action policies.

President Johnson inaugurated affirmative action by ordering a policy of minority employment in the federal civil service and in companies doing business with the national government. As the movement spread in the 1970s, it also began to divide civil rights activists and their supporters. Must more highly qualified white candidates have to give way to less qualified minority candidates? Wasn't this a case of "reverse discrimination"? The whole issue was addressed formally in the case of Allan Bakke. Bakke, a white male with no minority affiliation, brought suit against the University of California at Davis Medical School on the grounds that in denying him admission the school had discriminated against him on the basis of his race (that year the school had reserved 16 of 100 available seats for minority applicants). He argued that his grades and test scores had ranked him well above many black or Hispanic students who had been accepted.

In 1978, Bakke won his case before the Supreme Court and was admitted to the medical school, but he did not succeed in getting affirmative action declared unconstitutional. The Court rejected the procedures at the University of California because its medical school had used both a quota *and* a separate admissions system for minorities. The Court held that the method of a rigid quota of student slots assigned on the basis of race was incompatible with the equal protection clause. Thus, the Court permitted universities (and presumably other schools, training programs, and hiring authorities) to continue to take minority status into consideration, but restricted the use of quotas to situations in which (1) previous discrimination had been shown, and (2) it was used more as a *guideline* for social diversity than as a mathematically defined ratio.[56]

---

[54]Thus a distinction has come to be made between "deaf," the pathology, and "Deaf," the culture. See Andrew Solomon, "Defiantly Deaf," *New York Times Sunday Magazine,* 28 August 1994, pp. 40ff.

[55]Romer v. Evans, 116 S.Ct. 1620 (1996).

[56]Regents of the University of California v. Bakke, 438 U.S. 265 (1978).

DEBATING THE ISSUES

Affirmative Action

THE PRINCIPLE of equality has long been a bedrock value of the American political system. Yet the devotion to equality has contrasted sharply with the fact that Americans have not all been treated equally. Women, African Americans, Latinos, Native Americans, and other groups rightly claim that they have suffered historical patterns of discrimination that have deprived them of basic rights. Many African Americans in particular believe that hundreds of years of slavery and savage treatment cannot simply be wiped away by the proclamation that all are now equal.

This belief has prompted the government to promote affirmative action programs designed to provide an added advantage for minorities in areas such as college admissions and employment, based on the principle that past discrimination against African Americans and others can be rectified only by tilting the scales more in their favor now. Advocates of affirmative action, such as Supreme Court Justice Thurgood Marshall, have argued that equal treatment of unequals merely perpetuates inequality. Opponents of such programs, such as law professor Stephen L. Carter, contend that such preferential treatment is inconsistent with American values and may actually harm those it tries to help.

MARSHALL

Three hundred and fifty years ago, the Negro was dragged to this country in chains to be sold into slavery. Uprooted from his homeland and thrust into bondage for forced labor, the slave was deprived of all legal rights. It was unlawful to teach him to read; he could be sold away from his family and friends at the whim of his master; and killing or maiming him was not a crime. The system of slavery brutalized and dehumanized both master and slave.

The denial of human rights was etched into the American colonies' first attempts at establishing self-government. . . . The self-evident truths and the unalienable rights were intended . . . only to apply to white men. . . . The implicit protection of slavery embodied in the Declaration of Independence was made explicit in the Constitution. . . . The status of the Negro as property was officially erased by his emancipation at the end of the Civil War. But the long awaited emancipation, while freeing the Negro from slavery, did not bring him citizenship or equality in any meaningful way. Despite the passage of the Thirteenth, Fourteenth, and

---

For nearly a decade after *Bakke*, the Supreme Court was tentative and permissive about efforts by corporations and governments to experiment with affirmative action programs in employment.[57] But in 1989, the Court returned to the *Bakke* position that any "rigid numerical quota" is suspect. In *Wards Cove v. Atonio*, the Court further weakened affirmative action by easing the way for employers to prefer white males, holding that the burden of proof of unlawful discrimination should be shifted from the defendant (the employer) to the plaintiff (the person claiming to be the victim of discrimination).[58] This decision virtually overruled the Court's prior holding. That

---

[57]United Steelworkers v. Weber, 443 U.S. 193 (1979); and Fullilove v. Klutznick, 100 S.Ct. 2758 (1980).

[58]City of Richmond v. J. A. Croson Co., 109 S.Ct. 706 (1989); Wards Cove v. Atonio, 109 S.Ct. 2115 (1989).

Fifteenth Amendments, the Negro was systematically denied the rights those amendments were supposed to secure. . . . In light of the sorry history of discrimination and its devastating impact on the lives of Negroes, bringing the Negro into the mainstream of American life should be a state interest of the highest order. To fail to do so is to ensure that America will forever remain a divided society. . . . We now must permit the institutions of this society to give consideration to race in making decisions about who will hold the positions of influence, affluence and prestige in America. For far too long, the doors to those positions have been shut to Negroes.[1]

CARTER

If we as a people were not defeated by slavery and Jim Crow, we will not be defeated by the demise of affirmative action. Before there were any racial preferences, before there was a federal antidiscrimination law with any teeth, our achievements were already on the rise: our middle class was growing, as was our rate of college matriculation—both of them at higher rates than in the years since. Black professionals, in short, should not do much worse without affirmative action than we are doing with it, and thrown on our own resources and knowing that we have no choice but to meet the same tests as everybody else, we may do better.

We must be about the business of defining a future in which we can be fair to ourselves and demand opportunities without falling into the trap of letting others tell us that our horizons are limited, that we cannot make it without assistance. . . . The likely demise, or severe restriction, of racial preferences will also present for us a new stage of struggle, and we should treat it as an opportunity, not a burden. It is our chance to make ourselves free of the assumptions that too often underlie affirmative action, assumptions about our intellectual incapacity and other competitive deficiencies. It is our chance to prove to a doubting, indifferent world that our future as a people is in our hands.[2]

[1]Regents of the University of California v. Bakke, 438 U.S. 265, 387 (1978).
[2]Stephen L. Carter, *Reflections on an Affirmative Action Baby* (New York: Basic Books, 1991), as excerpted in George McKenna and Stanley Feingold, eds., *Taking Sides: Clashing Views on Controversial Political Issues*, 8th ed. (Guilford, CT: Dushkin, 1993), pp. 192–93.

same year, the Court ruled that any affirmative action program already approved by federal courts could be subsequently challenged by white males who alleged that the program discriminated against them.[59]

[59]Martin v. Wilks, 109 S.Ct. 2180 (1989). In this case, Chief Justice Rehnquist held that white firefighters in Birmingham could challenge the legality of a consent decree mandating goals for hiring and promoting blacks, even though they had not been parties to the original litigation.

In 1991, Congress strengthened affirmative action with the Civil Rights Act of 1991, which put the burden of proof back on the employer to show that educational and other standards for employment that favored whites or males were "essential to the job." Despite Congress's actions, however, the federal judiciary will have the last word when cases under the new law reach the courts. In fact, in a 5-to-4 decision in 1993, the Court ruled that employees had to prove their employers intended

IN BRIEF BOX

DEVELOPMENT OF AFFIRMATIVE ACTION

Regents of the University of California v. Bakke (1978)	Court permitted minority status to be considered in hiring/selection processes, but restricted the use of quotas.
Wards Cove v. Atonio (1989)	Court ruled that the burden of proof for unlawful discrimination should be shifted from the defendant (employer) to the plaintiff (person claiming to be a victim of discrimination).
Martin v. Wilks (1989)	Any affirmative action program already approved by federal courts could be subsequently challenged by white males who alleged that the program discriminated against them.
Civil Rights Act of 1991	Congress put the burden of proof back on the employer to show that standards for employment that favored whites or males were "essential to the job."
St. Mary's Honor Center v. Hicks (1993)	Employees must prove that their employers intended discrimination, once again placing the burden of proof on employees.
Adarand Constructors, Inc. v. Pena (1995)	"Benign" federal racial classifications could be used, like those of the state, but a federal set-aside program violated the "equal protection" clause of the Fourteenth Amendment.

discrimination, once again placing the burden of proof on employees.[60]

Meanwhile, even as the Court was still restricting any effort by state and local governments to engage in affirmative action on employment, the Clinton administration was trying to go the opposite way by liberalizing and reinvigorating federal affirmative action policies. But this was also brought to an abrupt halt in 1995 with the *Adarand* case.[61] The facts are as follows. Adarand Constructors submitted the low bid for a federal contract from the Department of Transportation, but Gonzales Construction Company, a Hispanic-American-owned company, was selected instead because the Small Business Act had established the federal policy of encouraging such contracting to "small business concerns owned and controlled by socially and economically disadvantaged individuals." A goal was set such that 5 percent of the total value of all such contracts should go to companies whose owners have been subject to racial or ethnic prejudice. Justice O'Connor held for the Court that such federal set-aside programs violated the "equal protection" clause in the Fourteenth Amendment. The Court did go on in *Adarand* to recognize that "benign" federal racial classifications could still be used, like those of the state, as long as they are "narrowly tailored to further . . . a compelling governmental interest. . . .

[60]St. Mary's Honor Center v. Hicks 113 S.Ct. 2742 (1993).
[61]Adarand Constructors, Inc. v. Pena, 115 S.Ct. 2097 (1995). [Emphasis added.]

CONSERVATIVE AND LIBERAL ATTITUDES TOWARD AFFIRMATIVE ACTION

Conservatives	Liberals
rights are individual and affirmative action concerns itself with group rights	discrimination affects an entire group or classification of individuals, thus it must be remedied on a group basis
any discrimination, even positive or benign discrimination, violates the equal protection clause	

The conservatives' argument against affirmative action can be reduced to two major points. The first is that rights in the American tradition are innately individual, and affirmative action violates this concept by concerning itself with "group rights," an idea said to be alien to the American tradition. The second point has to do with quotas. Conservatives would argue that the Constitution is "color-blind" and that any discrimination, even if it is called positive or benign discrimination, ultimately violates the equal protection clause and the American way.

The liberal side agrees that rights ultimately come down to individuals, but argues that the essence of discrimination is the use of unreasonable and unjust exclusion to deprive *an entire group* access to something valuable in society. Thus, discrimination itself has to be attacked on a group basis. Liberals can also use Court history to support their side. The first definitive interpretation of the Fourteenth Amendment by the Supreme Court in 1873 stated explicitly that

> The existence of laws in the state where the newly emancipated Negroes resided, which discriminated with gross injustice the hardship against them *as a class,* was the evil to be remedied by this clause.[62]

Although the problems of rights in America are agonizing, they can be looked at optimistically. The United States has a long way to go before it constructs a truly just, "equally protected" society. But it also has come very far in a relatively short time. All explicit *de jure* barriers to minorities have been dismantled. Many *de facto* barriers have also been dismantled, and thousands upon thousands of new opportunities have been opened.

CHAPTER REVIEW

Civil liberties and *civil rights* are two quite different phenomena and have to be treated legally and constitutionally in two quite different ways. We have defined civil liberties as that sphere of individual freedom of choice created by restraints on governmental power. The Bill of Rights explicitly placed an entire series of restraints on government. Some of these restraints were *substantive,* regarding *what* government could do; other restraints were *procedural,* regarding *how* the government was permitted to act. We call the rights listed in the Bill of Rights civil liberties because they are the rights of citizens to be free from arbitrary government interference.

[62]Slaughter-House Cases, 16 Wallace 36 (1873). [Emphasis added.]

But *which* government? This was settled in the *Barron v. Baltimore* case in 1833 when the Supreme Court held that the restraints in the Bill of Rights were applicable only to the national government and not to the states. The Court was recognizing "dual citizenship." At the time of its adoption in 1868, the Fourteenth Amendment was considered by many observers as a deliberate effort to reverse *Barron*, to put an end to the standard of dual citizenship, and to nationalize the Bill of Rights, applying its restrictions to state governments as well as to the national government. But the post–Civil War Supreme Court interpreted the Fourteenth Amendment otherwise. Dual citizenship remained almost as it had been before the Civil War, and the shadow of *Barron* extended across the rest of the nineteenth century and well into the twentieth century.

The slow process of nationalizing the Bill of Rights began in the 1920s, when the Supreme Court recognized that at least the restraints of the First Amendment had been "incorporated" into the Fourteenth Amendment as restraints on the state governments. But it was not until the 1960s that most of the civil liberties in the Bill of Rights were also incorporated into the Fourteenth Amendment.

The second aspect of protection of the individual, *civil rights*, stresses the expansion of governmental power rather than restraints upon it. If the constitutional base of civil liberties is the due process clause of the Fourteenth Amendment, the constitutional base of civil rights is the equal protection clause. This clause imposes a positive obligation on government to advance civil rights, and its original motivation seems to have been to eliminate the gross injustices suffered by "the newly emancipated Negroes . . . as a class." But as with civil liberties, there was little advancement in the interpretation or application of the equal protection clause until after World War II. The major breakthrough came in 1954 with the case of *Brown v. Board of Education*, and advancements came in fits and starts during the succeeding ten years.

After 1964, Congress finally supported the federal courts with effective civil rights legislation. From that point, civil rights developed in two ways. First, the definition of civil rights was expanded to include victims of discrimination other than blacks. Second, the definition of civil rights became increasingly positive through affirmative action policies. Judicial decisions, congressional statutes, and administrative agency actions all have moved beyond the original goal of eliminating discrimination toward creating new opportunities for minorities and, in some areas, compensating present minority individuals for the consequences of discriminatory actions against members of their group in the past. This kind of compensatory civil rights action has sometimes relied upon quotas. The use of quotas, in turn, has given rise to intense debate over the constitutionality as well as the desirability of affirmative action.

The story has not ended and is not likely to end. The politics of rights will remain an important part of American political discourse.

TIME LINE ON CIVIL LIBERTIES AND CIVIL RIGHTS

Events	Institutional Developments
Bill of Rights sent to states for ratification (1789)	States ratify U.S. Bill of Rights (1791)
Undeclared naval war with France (1798–1800); passage of Alien and Sedition Acts (1798)	

1800

Events	Institutional Developments
Slaves taken into territories (1800s)	Alien and Sedition Acts, limiting free speech, press, and aliens disregarded and not renewed (1801)
Maine admitted to Union as free state (1820); Missouri admitted as slave state (1821)	Missouri Compromise regulates expansion of slavery into territories (1820)
	Barron v. Baltimore confirms dual citizenship (1833)
	Dred Scott v. Sandford invalidates Missouri Compromise, perpetuates slavery (1857)

1860

Events	Institutional Developments
Civil War (1861–1865)	Emancipation Proclamation (1863); Thirteenth Amendment prohibits slavery in the U.S. (1865)
Southern blacks now vote but Black Codes in South impose special restraints (1865)	Civil Rights Act (1866)
Reconstruction (1867–1877)	Fourteenth Amendment ratified (1868)
"Jim Crow" laws spread throughout the South (1890s)	*Plessy v. Ferguson* upholds doctrine of "separate but equal" (1896)
World War I (1914–1918)	

1920

Events	Institutional Developments
Postwar pacifist and anarchist agitation and suppression (1920s and 1930s)	*Gitlow v. N.Y.* (1925) and *Near v. Minnesota* (1931) apply First Amendment to states
U.S. in World War II (1941–1945); pressures to desegregate in the Army; revelations of Nazi genocide	President's commission on civil rights (1946)

1950

Events	Institutional Developments
Civil rights movement: Montgomery bus boycott (1955); lunch counter sit-ins (1960); freedom riders (1961)	*Brown v. Board of Education* overturns *Plessy,* invalidates segregation (1954); federal use of troops to enforce court order to integrate schools (1957)
March on Washington—largest civil rights demonstration in American history (1963)	
	Civil Rights Act outlaws segregation (1964)
	Katzenbach v. McClung upholds use of commerce clause to bar segregation (1964)

Events	Institutional Developments
Spread of movement politics—students, women, environment, right to life (1970s)	**1970** *Roe v. Wade* prohibits states from outlawing abortion (1973)
Affirmative action plans enacted in universities and corporations (1970s and 1980s)	Court orders to end malapportionment and segregation (1970s and 1980s)
Challenges to affirmative action plans (1980s–1990s)	Georgia law upheld in *Bowers v. Hardwick* allowing states to regulate homosexual activity (1986)
	Court accepts affirmative action on a limited basis—*Regents of Univ. of Calif. v. Bakke* (1978), *Wards Cove v. Atonio* (1989), *Martin, v. Wilks* (1989)
	Missouri law restricting abortion upheld in *Webster v. Reproductive Health Services* (1989)
1990	
States adopt restrictive abortion laws (1990–1991)	
Bush signs civil rights bill favoring suits against employment discrimination (1991)	Court permits school boards to terminate busing (1991)
	Roe upheld (1992)
	Clinton's positions on abortion and gay rights revive civil rights activity and controversy (1993)
Clinton elected president (1992); Republicans win majority in Congress (1994)	Clinton and Republican Congress agree to devolve more power back to the states (1994–1996)

KEY TERMS

affirmative action   A policy or program designed to redress historic injustices against specified groups by actively promoting equal access to educational and employment opportunities.

civil liberties   Areas of personal freedom with which governments are constrained from interfering.

civil rights   Legal or moral claims that citizens are entitled to make upon the government to protect them from the illegal actions of other citizens and government agencies.

de facto segregation   Racial segregation that is not a direct result of law or government policy but is, instead, a reflection of residential patterns, income distributions, or other social factors.

de jure segregation   Racial segregation that is a direct result of law or official policy.

due process   To proceed according to law and with adequate protection for individual rights.

equal protection clause   A clause in the Fourteenth Amendment that requires that states provide citizens "equal protection of the laws."

exclusionary rule   The ability of the court to exclude evidence obtained in violation of the Fourth Amendment.

Miranda rule   Principles developed by the Supreme Court in the 1966 case of *Miranda v. Arizona* requiring that persons under arrest be informed of their legal rights, including their right to counsel, prior to police interrogation.

strict scrutiny   Higher standard of judicial protection for speech cases and other civil liberties and civil rights cases, in which the burden of proof shifts from the complainant to the government.

universalization of rights   The recognition that any group—whether defined by sex, religion, race, ethnicity, or gender—has the right not to be discriminated against.

FOR FURTHER READING

Abraham, Henry. *Freedom and the Court: Civil Rights and Liberties in the United States,* 5th ed. New York: Oxford University Press, 1994.

Baer, Judith A. *Equality under the Constitution: Reclaiming the Fourteenth Amendment.* Ithaca, NY: Cornell University Press, 1983.

Brigham, John. *Civil Liberties and American Democracy.* Washington, DC: Congressional Quarterly Press, 1984.

Eisenstein, Zillah. *The Female Body and the Law.* Berkeley: University of California Press, 1988.

Forer, Lois G. *A Chilling Effect: The Mounting Threat of Libel and Invasion of Privacy Actions to the First Amendment.* New York: W. W. Norton, 1987.

Friendly, Fred W. *Minnesota Rag: The Dramatic Story of the Landmark Supreme Court Case That Gave New Meaning to Freedom of the Press.* New York: Vintage, 1982.

Garrow, David J. *Bearing the Cross: Martin Luther King and the Southern Christian Leadership Conference: A Personal Portrait.* New York: William Morrow, 1986.

Hentoff, Nat. *The First Freedom: The Tumultuous History of Free Speech in America.* New York: Delacorte, 1980.

Kelly, Alfred, Winfred A. Harbison, and Herman Beltz. *The American Constitution: Its Origins and Development,* 7th ed. New York: W. W. Norton, 1991.

Levy, Leonard. *Freedom of Speech and Press in Early America: Legacy of Suppression.* New York: Harper & Row, 1963.

Lewis, Anthony. *Gideon's Trumpet.* New York: Random House, 1964.

Minow, Martha. *Making All the Difference—Inclusion, Exclusion, and American Law* (Ithaca, NY: Cornell University Press, 1990).

Randall, Richard S. *Censorship of the Movies.* Madison: University of Wisconsin Press, 1970.

Silberman, Charles. *Criminal Violence, Criminal Justice.* New York: Random House, 1978.

Silverstein, Mark. *Constitutional Faiths.* Ithaca, NY: Cornell University Press, 1984.

Thernstorm, Abigail M. *Whose Votes Count? Affirmative Action and Minority Voting Rights.* Cambridge: Harvard University Press, 1987.

PART 2

INSTITUTIONS

CHAPTER 5

Congress: The First Branch

*T*HE U.S. CONGRESS is the "first branch" of government under Article I of our Constitution. Prior to the twentieth century, the Congress, not the executive, was the central policy-making institution in the United States. Congressional leaders were the dominant political figures of their time and often treated mere presidents with disdain. But during the twentieth century, congressional influence waned relative to that of the executive branch. The presidency became the central institution of American government. Members of Congress may support or oppose, but they are seldom free to ignore presidential leadership. Moreover, the bureaucracies of the executive branch have—often with the encouragement of Congress—seized a good deal of legislative power.

Congress has not taken the diminution of its influence lightly. From time to time it stands up to the White House and flexes its legislative muscles. And we may well be seeing a resurgence of congressional influence, as we will discuss in the last section of this chapter. First, however, we will examine closely how Congress exercises its most important power—making laws. Then we will take a look at some congressional powers that go beyond legislation.

MAKING LAW

In 1996, Americans elected eighty-nine new senators and representatives to the most diverse Congress ever. Thirty-nine African Americans now serve in the House and one in the Senate. At the same time, fifty-three women serve in the House and nine in the Senate. This was a substantial increase over only six years earlier, when

CORE OF THE ARGUMENT

- Before a bill can become law, it must pass through the legislative process, a complex set of procedures in Congress.
- The legislative process is driven by six sets of political forces: political parties, committees, staffs, caucuses, rules of lawmaking, and the president.
- From the New Deal through the 1960s, the presidency seemed to be the dominant institution in American government; since the 1960s, Congress has sought to reassert its power by effectively representing important new groups and forces in society.

twenty-nine women had served in the House and only two in the Senate. In 1994, California became the first state to be represented by two women in the Senate when it elected Diane Feinstein and Barbara Boxer.

Many observers hailed the emergence of a more representative Congress and expressed confidence that this Congress would rapidly enact important new programs and policies. Others were more cautious about predicting any sort of quick action on its part.

It is extraordinarily difficult for a large, representative assembly to formulate, enact, and implement laws. The internal complexities of conducting business within Congress—the legislative process—are daunting. In addition, many individuals and institutions have the capacity to influence the legislative process. For example, legislation to raise the salaries of members of the House of Representatives received input from congressional leaders of both parties, special legislative task forces, the president, the national chairs of the two major parties, public interest lobbyists, the news media, and the mass public before it became law in 1989. Since successful legislation requires the confluence of so many distinct factors, it is little wonder that most of the thousands of bills considered by Congress each year are defeated long before they reach the president.

Before an idea or proposal can become a law, it must pass through a complex set of organizations and procedures in Congress. Collectively, these are called the policy-making process, or the legislative process. Understanding this process is central to understanding why some ideas and proposals eventually become the law of the land while most do not. Although the supporters of legislative proposals often feel that the formal rules of the congressional process are deliberately designed to prevent their own deserving proposals from ever seeing the light of day, these rules allow Congress to play an important role in lawmaking. If it wants to be more than simply a rubber stamp for the executive branch, like so many other representative assemblies around the world, a national legislature like the Congress must develop a division of labor, set an agenda, maintain order through rules and procedures, and place limits on discussion. Equality among the members of Congress must give way to hierarchy—ranking people according to their function within the institution.

To exercise its power to make the law, Congress must first bring about something close to an organizational miracle. In this chapter, we will examine the organization of Congress and the legislative process. In particular, we will be concerned with the basic building blocks of congressional organization: bicameralism, political parties, the committee system, congressional staff, the caucuses, and the parliamentary rules of the House and Senate. Each of these factors plays a key role in the organization of Congress and in the process through which Congress formulates and enacts laws. We will also look at other powers Congress has in addition to lawmaking, and we will explore the future role of Congress in relation to the powers of the executive.

Bicameralism: House and Senate

The framers of the Constitution provided for *bicameralism*—that is, a legislative body consisting of two chambers. As we saw in Chapter 2, the framers intended each of these chambers, the House and Senate, to serve a different constituency. Members of the Senate, appointed by state legislatures for six-year terms, were to represent the elite members of society and to be more attuned to the interests of property than to those of population. Today, members of the House and Senate are elected directly by the people. The 435 members of the House are elected from districts apportioned according to population; the 100 members of the Senate are elected by state, with two senators from each. Senators continue to have much longer terms in office and usually represent much larger and more diverse constituencies than do their counterparts in the House (see In Brief Box on page 105).

MAJOR DIFFERENCES BETWEEN THE HOUSE AND THE SENATE

House	Senate
Larger (435 members)	Smaller (100 members)
Shorter term of office (two years)	Longer term of office (six years)
Less flexible rules	More flexible rules
Narrower constituency	Broader, more varied constituencies
Policy specialists	Policy generalists
Less press and media coverage	More press and media coverage
Power less evenly distributed	Power more evenly distributed
Less prestige	More prestige
More expeditious in floor debate	Less expeditious in floor debate
Less reliance on staffs	More reliance on staffs
Initiate all money bills	Confirms Supreme Court justices, ambassadors, and heads of executive departments
	Confirms treaties

SOURCE: Walter J. Oleszek, *Congressional Procedures and the Policy Process* (Washington, DC: Congressional Quarterly Press, 1978), p. 24.

The House and Senate play different roles in the legislative process. In essence, the Senate is the more deliberative of the two bodies—the forum in which any and all ideas can receive a thorough public airing. The House is the more centralized and organized of the two bodies—better equipped to play a routine role in the governmental process. In part, this difference stems from the different rules governing the two bodies. These rules give House leaders more control over the legislative process and provide for House members to specialize in certain legislative areas. The rules of the much-smaller Senate give its leadership relatively little power and discourage specialization.

Both formal and informal factors contribute to differences between the two chambers of Congress. Differences in the length of terms and requirements for holding office specified by the Constitution in turn generate differences in how members of each body develop their constituencies and exercise their powers of office. The result is that members of the House most effectively and frequently serve as the agents of well-organized

local interests with specific legislative agendas—used car dealers seeking relief from regulation, labor unions seeking more favorable legislation, or farmers looking for higher subsidies. The small size and relative homogeneity of their constituencies and the frequency with which they must seek re-election make House members more attuned to the legislative needs of local interest groups.

Senators, on the other hand, serve larger and more heterogeneous constituencies. As a result, they are somewhat better able than members of the House to serve as the agents for groups and interests organized on a statewide or national basis. Moreover, with longer terms in office, senators have the luxury of considering "new ideas" or seeking to bring together new coalitions of interests, rather than simply serving existing ones.

In recent years, the House has exhibited considerably more intense partisanship and ideological division than the Senate. Because of their diverse constituencies, senators are more inclined to seek compromise positions that will offend as few voters and interest groups as possible. Members of the House, in contrast, typically represent more homogeneous districts in which their own party is dominant. This situation has tended to make House members less inclined to seek compromises and more willing to stick to partisan and ideological guns than their Senate counterparts during the policy debates of the past several decades.

Political Parties: Congress's Oldest Hierarchy

The Constitution makes only one provision for the organization of business in Congress. In Article I, it gives each chamber a presiding officer. In the Senate, this officer is known as the president, and the office is held ex officio by the vice president of the United States. The Constitution also allows the Senate to elect a president pro tempore—a temporary president—to serve in the absence of the vice president. In the House of Representatives, the presiding officer is known as the Speaker and is elected by the entire membership of the House.

Article I of the Constitution gives little guidance for how to conduct congressional business. Even during the first Congress (1789–1791), it was the political parties that provided the organization needed by the House and Senate. For the first century or more of the Republic, America had literally a party government in Congress.[1]

PARTY LEADERSHIP IN THE HOUSE AND THE SENATE
Every two years, at the beginning of a new Congress, the members of each party gather to elect their House leaders. This gathering is traditionally called the *caucus,* or conference (by the Republicans).

The elected leader of the majority party is later proposed to the whole House and is automatically elected to the position of *Speaker of the House,* with voting along straight party lines. The House majority caucus (or conference) then also

elects a *majority leader.* The minority party goes through the same process and selects the *minority leader.* Both parties also elect whips to line up party members on important votes and relay voting information to the leaders.

In December 1996, prior to the opening of the 105th Congress, House Republicans re-elected Newt Gingrich of Georgia to serve as Speaker. Richard Armey of Texas, a close Gingrich ally, was re-elected majority leader, and Tom DeLay, also of Texas, was re-elected Republican whip.

House Democrats re-elected Richard Gephardt of Missouri to the post of minority leader. David Bonior of Michigan was re-elected Democratic whip.

Next in order of importance for each party after the Speaker and majority or minority leader are the majority and minority whip, followed by the caucus (Democrats) or conference (Republicans) chairs. Next comes the Committee on Committees (called the Steering and Policy Committee by the Democrats), whose tasks are to assign new legislators to committees and to deal with the requests of incumbent members for transfers from one committee to another. The Speaker serves as chair of the Republican Committee on Committees, while the minority leader chairs the Democratic Steering and Policy Committee. (The Republicans have a separate Policy Committee.) At one time, party leaders strictly controlled committee assignments, using them to enforce party discipline. Today, representatives expect to receive the assignments they want and resent leadership efforts to control committee assignments. For example, during the 104th Congress the chairman of the powerful Appropriations Committee, Robert Livingston (R-La.), sought to remove freshman Mark Neumann (R-Wisc.) from the committee because of his lack of party loyalty. The entire Republican freshman class angrily opposed this move and forced the leadership to back down. Not only did Neumann keep his seat on the Appropriations Committee, but he was given a seat on the Budget Committee, as well, to placate

[1]*Origins and Development of Congress* (Washington, DC: Congressional Quarterly Press, 1982).

the freshmen. The leadership's best opportunities to use committee assignments as rewards and punishments come when a seat on the same committee is sought by more than one member.

Generally, representatives seek assignments that will allow them to influence decisions of special importance to their districts. Representatives from farm districts, for example, may request seats on the Agriculture Committee.[2] Seats on powerful committees such as Ways and Means, which is responsible for tax legislation, and Appropriations are especially popular.

[2]Richard Fenno, Jr., *Home Style: House Members in Their Districts* (Boston: Little, Brown, 1978).

Within the Senate, the president pro tempore exercises mainly ceremonial leadership. Usually, the majority party designates a member with the greatest seniority to serve in this capacity. Real power is in the hands of the majority leader and minority leader, each elected by party caucus. Currently, Trent Lott of Mississippi is majority leader and Tom Daschle of South Dakota is minority leader. Together they control the Senate's calendar or agenda for legislation. In addition, the senators from each party elect a whip. Each party also selects a Policy Committee, which advises the leadership on legislative priorities. The majority party structures for the House and Senate are shown in Figures 5.1 and 5.2 (page 110).

FIGURE 5.1

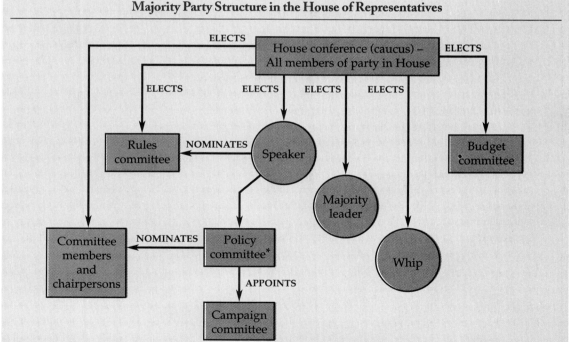

Majority Party Structure in the House of Representatives

*Includes Speaker (chair), majority leader, chief and deputy whips, caucus chair, four members appointed by the Speaker, and twelve members elected by regional caucuses.

ADAM CLAYTON POWELL, JR., AND J. C. WATTS

From "Keep the Faith, Baby" to the New Conservatism

THE CAREERS of Adam Clayton Powell, Jr., and J. C. Watts reflect sharply divergent political philosophies. They also underscore the impact of a representative's constituency base in shaping the representative's behavior.

Arrogant, irreverent, and outspoken, Adam Clayton Powell, Jr., was the first African American to wield real power in Congress. Idolized by his Harlem constituents, he was returned to Congress for 22 years until scandal and failing health finally ended his career.

Born in 1908 to the son of a minister, Powell grew up in Harlem at a time when this predominantly black section of New York City was a cultural, social, and political mecca for black talent and aspirations. Powell earned a bachelor's degree from Colgate University in 1930 and a master's degree from Columbia University. During the Depression, Powell's charisma, eloquence, and style propelled him to the forefront of the still-embryonic civil rights movement. Through his father's Abyssinian Baptist Church, he organized relief efforts to help Harlem's poor (Powell later inherited his father's ministry). Powell led successful demonstrations to force area businesses to hire blacks, often for the first time. In 1941, Powell was elected to a seat on the New York City Council. Four years later, he took a seat in Congress. Powell began immediately to fight discrimination in racially segregated Washington, D.C., by personally using facilities formerly barred to blacks and insisting on the admission of black reporters to congressional galleries.

Powell had little patience with segregationist Southerners of his own party, and his dissatisfaction with the Democratic party's conservative wing drove him to endorse Republican President Dwight D. Eisenhower in 1956. Powell's outspokenness won him few friends in Congress, but his seniority landed him a position of real power in 1960—the chairmanship of the House Committee on Education and Labor. From that vantage, Powell oversaw the enactment of 48 major pieces of legislation, including such areas as unemployment benefits, minimum wage increases, anti-poverty legislation, and an array of education bills. Powell's support proved vital to the legislative goals of Presidents Kennedy and Johnson.

Powell's personal excesses caught up with him. He was sharply criticized for taking a six-week junket to Europe, at taxpayer expense, with two young women. He was frequently absent from Congress, and was found guilty of both civil and criminal contempt because he refused to pay damages in a civil suit. Instead, he took up residence on the Caribbean island of Bimini, even though he continued to serve in Congress. In 1967, the House voted to exclude Powell from his seat, a decision the Supreme Court eventually overturned. Two years later,

ADAM CLAYTON POWELL, JR.

In addition to these tasks of organization, congressional party leaders may also seek to establish a legislative agenda. Since the New Deal, presidents have taken the lead in creating legislative agendas (this trend will be discussed in the next chapter). But in recent years congressional leaders, facing a White House controlled by the opposing party, have attempted to devise their own

Harlem again returned Powell to Congress. This time, Congress voted to seat him, but he was fined and stripped of his seniority; by this time, he was spending nearly all his time in Bimini. In 1970, the cancer-stricken Powell was narrowly defeated in a Democratic primary by Charles Rangel. He died in 1972. To the end, Powell was known for his invocation to friends and allies: "Keep the faith, baby."

Oklahoma Representative Julius Caesar Watts took a very different path to the House of Representatives. Born in 1957 in Oklahoma, Watts attended the University of Oklahoma, where he gained widespread fame as the university's star quarterback. Among other football accolades, J. C. Watts was named most valuable player in the Orange Bowl for two consecutive years. After playing professional football in Canada for six years, Watts returned to Oklahoma, where he worked in petroleum sales and real estate. In 1990, after switching from the Democratic to Republican party, Watts won election to the state Corporation Commission, an energy-regulating arm of state government. In doing so, he became the first African American elected to statewide office since the post–Civil War era.

In 1994, Watts won election to the House, despite his district's two-to-one Democratic edge in voter registration. Although popular from his football days, Watts also benefited from the Republican landslide of 1994, which saw the Republicans win control of both houses of Congress for the first time since 1952. The primary economic base of Watts's district—agriculture, energy, and three large military installations—became a primary focus of Watts's attentions. In the face of numerous military base closings at the end of the Cold War, Watts made protection of Tinker Air Force Base a top priority. To that end, he won a seat on the House National Security Committee (formerly known as the Armed Services Committee). Watts also gained a seat on the Banking and Financial Services Committee.

Aside from service to his district, the conservative Watts identified closely with the policy agenda of Republican House Speaker Newt Gingrich. Watts campaigned for a ban on gays in the military, and also stressed his opposition to abortion. He supported curtailing welfare benefits, calling them "anti-family, anti-investment, anti-savings," saying that welfare "encourages irresponsibility."[1] As one of only two African American Republicans in Congress (the other, Gary Franks of Connecticut, was defeated in his re-election bid in 1996), Watts believes that the Democratic party has taken black support for granted and has ignored their needs. At the same time, he also criticized the Republican party for writing off blacks entirely. "I want to change all that," he said.[2]

J. C. WATTS

[1]Philip D. Duncan and Christine C. Lawrence, *Politics in America 1996* (Washington, D.C.: Congressional Quarterly, Inc., 1995), p. 1080.
[2]Ibid.

SOURCE: Joel Silbey, ed., *Encyclopedia of the American Legislative System*, 3 vols. (New York: Charles Scribner's Sons, 1994).

agendas. Democratic leaders of Congress sought to create a common Democratic perspective in 1981 when Ronald Reagan became president. The Republican Congress elected in 1994 expanded on this idea with its Contract with America. In both cases, the majority party leadership has sought to create a consensus among its congressional members around an overall vision to guide legislative

FIGURE 5.2

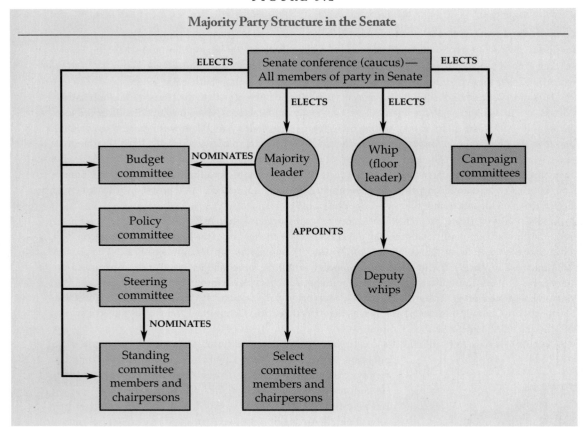

Majority Party Structure in the Senate

activity and to make individual pieces of legislation part of a bigger picture that is distinct from the agenda of the president.

The Committee System: The Core of Congress

The committee system provides Congress with its second organizational structure, but it is more a division of labor than a hierarchy of power. Committee and subcommittee chairs have a number of important powers, but their capacity to discipline committee members is limited. Ultimately, committee members are hired and fired by the voters, not by the leadership. Committee chairs just have to put up with members whose views they might find distasteful.

Six fundamental characteristics define the congressional committee system:

1. *Each **standing committee** is given a permanent status by the official rules, with a fixed membership, officers, rules, staff, offices, and, above all, a jurisdiction that is recognized by all other committees and usually the leadership as well (see Table 5.1).

2. *The jurisdiction of each standing committee is defined according to the subject matter of basic legislation.* Except for the House Rules Committee, all the important committees are organized to receive proposals for legislation and to process them into official bills. The House Rules Committee decides the order in which bills come up for a vote and determines the specific rules that govern the length of debate and the opportunity for amendments. Rules can be used to help or hinder particular proposals.

3. *Standing committees' jurisdictions usually parallel those of the major departments or agencies in the executive branch.* There are important exceptions— Appropriations (House and Senate) and Rules (House), for example—but by and large, the division of labor is self-consciously designed to parallel executive branch organization.

4. *Bills are assigned to standing committees on the basis of subject matter, but the Speaker of the House and the Senate's presiding officer have some discretion in the allocation of bills to committees.* Most bills "die in committee"—that is, they are not reported out favorably. Ordinarily this ends a bill's life. There is only one way for a legislative proposal to escape committee processing: A bill passed in one chamber may be permitted to go directly on to the calendar of the other chamber. Even here, however, the bill has received the full committee treatment before passage in the first chamber.

5. *Each standing committee is unique.* No effort is made to compose the membership of any committee to be representative of the total House or Senate membership. Members with a special interest in the subject matter of a committee are expected to seek membership on it. In both the

TABLE 5.1

Permanent Committees of Congress

HOUSE COMMITTEES

Agriculture	National Security
Appropriations	Resources
Banking and Financial Services	Rules
Budget	Science
Commerce	Small Business
Economic and Educational Opportunities	Standards of Official Conduct
Government Reform and Oversight	Transportation and Infrastructure
House Oversight	Veterans Affairs
International Relations	Ways and Means
Judiciary	

SENATE COMMITTEES

Agriculture, Nutrition, and Forestry	Finance
Appropriations	Foreign Relations
Armed Services	Governmental Affairs
Banking, Housing, and Urban Affairs	Judiciary
Budget	Labor and Human Resources
Commerce, Science, and Transportation	Rules and Administration
Energy and Natural Resources	Small Business
Environment and Public Works	Veterans Affairs

House and the Senate, each party has established a Committee on Committees, which determines the committee assignments of new members and of established members who wish to change committees. Ordinarily, members can keep their committee assignments as long as they like.

6. *Each standing committee's hierarchy is based on seniority.* **Seniority** is determined by years of continuous service on a particular committee, not by years of service in the House or Senate. In general, each committee is chaired by the most senior member of the majority party. Although the power of committee chairs is limited, they play an important role in scheduling hearings, selecting subcommittee members, and appointing committee staff. Because Congress has a large number of subcommittees and has given each representative a larger staff, the power of the committee chairs has been diluted.

The Staff System: Staffers and Agencies

A congressional institution second in importance only to the committee system is the staff system. Every member of Congress employs a large number of staff members, whose tasks include handling constituency requests and, to a large and growing extent, dealing with legislative details and overseeing the activities of administrative agencies. Increasingly, staffers bear the primary responsibility for formulating and drafting proposals, organizing hearings, dealing with administrative agencies, and negotiating with lobbyists. Indeed, legislators typically deal with one another through staff, rather than through direct, personal contact. Representatives and senators together employ nearly eleven thousand staffers in their Washington and home offices. Today, staffers even develop policy ideas, draft legislation, and, in some instances, have a good deal of influence over the legislative process.

In addition to the personal staffs of individual senators and representatives, Congress also employs roughly two thousand committee staffers. These individuals are the permanent staff, who

stay regardless of turnover in Congress, attached to every House and Senate committee, and who are responsible for organizing and administering the committee's work, including research, scheduling, organizing hearings, and drafting legislation. Congressional staffers can come to play key roles in the legislative process. One example of the importance of congressional staffers is the so-called Gephardt health care reform bill, introduced in August 1994. Although the bill bore Representative Richard Gephardt's name, it was actually crafted by a small group of staff members of the House Ways and Means Committee. These aides, under the direction of David Abernathy, the staff's leading health care specialist, debated methods of cost control, service delivery, the role of the insurance industry, and the needs of patients, and listened to hundreds of lobbyists before drafting the complex Gephardt bill.[3]

The number of congressional staff members grew rapidly during the 1960s and 1970s, leveled off in the 1980s, and decreased dramatically in 1995. This sudden drop fulfilled the Republican congressional candidates' 1994 campaign promise to reduce the size of committee staffs.

Not only does Congress employ personal and committe staff, but it has also established three *staff agencies* designed to provide the legislative branch with resources and expertise independent of the executive branch. These agencies enhance Congress's capacity to oversee administrative agencies and to evaluate presidential programs and proposals. They are the Congressional Research Service, which performs research for legislators who wish to know the facts and competing arguments relevant to policy proposals or other legislative business; the General Accounting Office, through which Congress can investigate the financial and administrative affairs of any government agency or program; and the Congressional Budget Office, which assesses the economic

---

[3]Robert Pear, "With Long Hours and Little Fanfare, Staff Members Crafted a Health Bill," *New York Times,* 6 August 1994, p. 7.

implications and likely costs of proposed federal programs, such as health care reform proposals.

Informal Organization: The Caucuses

In addition to the official organization of Congress, there also exists an unofficial organizational structure—the caucuses, formally known as *legislative service organizations (LSOs)*. Caucuses are groups of senators or representatives who share certain opinions, interests, or social characteristics. They include ideological caucuses such as the liberal Democratic Study Group, the conservative Democratic Forum (popularly known as the "boll weevils"), and the moderate Republican Wednesday Group. At the same time, there are a large number of caucuses composed of legislators representing particular economic or policy interests, such as the Travel and Tourism Caucus, the Steel Caucus, the Mushroom Caucus, and the Concerned Senators for the Arts. Legislators who share common backgrounds or social characteristics have organized caucuses such as the Congressional Black Caucus, the Congressional Caucus for Women's Issues, and the Hispanic Caucus.

All these caucuses seek to advance the interests of the groups they represent by promoting legislation, encouraging Congress to hold hearings, and pressing administrative agencies for favorable treatment.

RULES OF LAWMAKING: HOW A BILL BECOMES A LAW

The institutional structure of Congress is one key factor that helps to shape the legislative process. A second and equally important factor is the rules of congressional procedures. These rules govern everything from the introduction of a bill through its submission to the president for signing. Not only do these regulations influence the fate of each and every bill, they also help to determine the distribution of power in the Congress.

Committee Deliberation

Even if a member of Congress, the White House, or a federal agency has spent months developing and drafting a piece of legislation, it does not become a bill until it is submitted officially by a senator or representative to the clerk of the House or Senate and referred to the appropriate committee for deliberation. No floor action on any bill can take place until the committee with jurisdiction over it has taken all the time it needs to deliberate. During the course of its deliberations, the committee typically refers the bill to one of its subcommittees, which may hold hearings, listen to expert testimony, and amend the proposed legislation before referring it to the full committee for its consideration. The full committee may accept the recommendation of the subcommittee or hold its own hearings and prepare its own amendments. Or, even more frequently, the committee and subcommittee may do little or nothing with a bill that has been submitted to them. Many bills are simply allowed to "die in committee" with little or no serious consideration ever given to them. Often, members of Congress introduce legislation that they neither expect nor desire to see enacted into law, merely to please a constituency group. These bills die a quick and painless death. Other pieces of legislation have ardent supporters and die in committee only after a long battle. But in either case, most bills are never reported out of the committees to which they are assigned. In a typical congressional session, 95 percent of the roughly eight thousand bills introduced die in committee—an indication of the power of the congressional committee system.

The relative handful of bills that are reported out of the committee to which they were originally referred must, in the House, pass one additional hurdle within the committee system— the Rules Committee. This powerful committee determines the rules that will govern action on the bill on the House floor. In particular, the Rules Committee allots the time for debate and

PROCESS BOX 5.1

How a Bill Becomes a Law

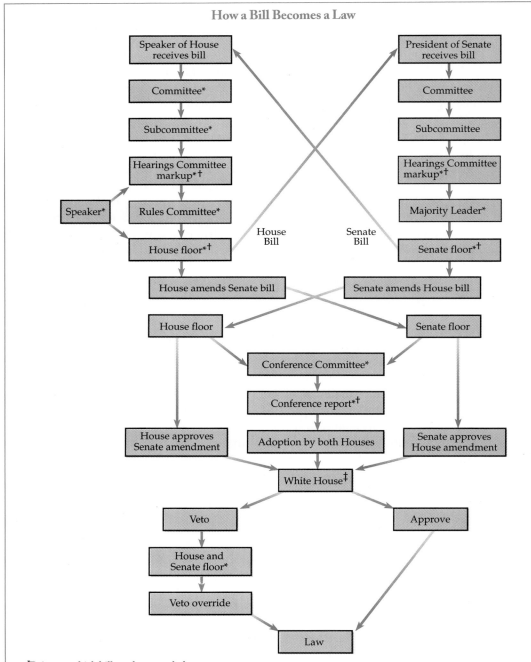

*Points at which bill can be amended.

†Points at which bill can die.

‡If the president neither signs nor vetoes the bill within ten days, it automatically becomes law.

decides to what extent amendments to the bill can be proposed from the floor. A bill's supporters generally prefer what is called a *closed rule,* which puts severe limits on floor debate and amendments. Opponents of a bill usually prefer an "open rule," which permits potentially damaging floor debate and makes it easier to add amendments that may cripple the bill or weaken its chances for passage. Thus, the outcome of the Rules Committee's deliberations can be extremely important and the committee's hearings can be an occasion for sharp conflicts.

Debate

Party control of the agenda is reinforced by the rule giving the Speaker of the House and the president of the Senate the power of recognition during debate on a bill. Usually the chair knows the purpose for which a member intends to speak well in advance of the occasion. Spontaneous efforts to gain recognition are often foiled. For example, the Speaker may ask, "For what purpose does the member rise?" before deciding whether to grant recognition.

In the House, virtually all of the time allotted by the Rules Committee for debate on a given bill is controlled by the bill's sponsor and by its leading opponent. In almost every case, these two people are the committee chair and the ranking minority member of the committee that processed the bill—or those they designate. These two participants are, by rule and tradition, granted the power to allocate most of the debate time in small amounts to members who are seeking to speak for or against the measure. Preference in the allocation of time goes to the members of the committee whose jurisdiction covers the bill.

In the Senate, the leadership has much less control over the floor debate. Indeed, the Senate is unique among the world's legislative bodies for its commitment to unlimited debate. Once given the floor, a senator may speak as long as he or she wishes. On a number of memorable occasions, senators have used this right to prevent

action on legislation that they opposed. Through this tactic, called the *filibuster,* small minorities or even one individual in the Senate can force the majority to give in to their demands. During the 1950s and 1960s, for example, opponents of civil rights legislation often sought to block its passage by adopting the tactic of filibuster. The votes of three-fifths of the Senate, or sixty votes, are needed to end a filibuster. This procedure is called *cloture.*

Whereas the filibuster was once an extraordinary tactic used only on rare occasions, in recent years it has been used increasingly often (see Figure 5.3, page 116).

Conference Committee: Reconciling House and Senate Versions of a Bill

Getting a bill out of committee and through one of the houses of Congress is no guarantee that a bill will be enacted into law. Frequently, bills that began with similar provisions in both chambers emerge with little resemblance to each other. Alternatively, a bill may be passed by one chamber but undergo substantial revision in the other chamber. In such cases, a *conference committee* composed of the senior members of the committees or subcommittees that initiated the bills may be required to iron out differences between the two pieces of legislation. Sometimes members or leaders will let objectionable provisions pass on the floor with the idea that they will get the change they want in conference. Usually, conference committees meet behind closed doors. Agreement requires a majority of each of the two delegations. Legislation that emerges from a conference committee is more often a compromise than a clear victory of one set of political forces over another.

When a bill comes out of conference, it faces one more hurdle. Before a bill can be sent to the president for signing, the House-Senate conference report must be approved on the floor of each chamber. Usually, such approval is given quickly. Occasionally, however, a bill's

FIGURE 5.3

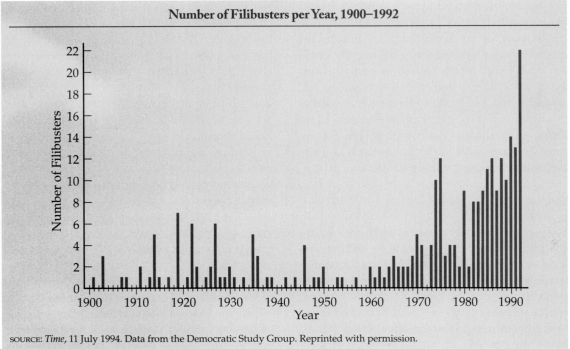

Number of Filibusters per Year, 1900–1992

SOURCE: *Time*, 11 July 1994. Data from the Democratic Study Group. Reprinted with permission.

opponents use approval as one last opportunity to defeat a piece of legislation.

Presidential Action

Once adopted by the House and Senate, a bill goes to the president, who may choose to sign the bill into law or veto it. The *veto* is the president's constitutional power to reject a piece of legislation. To veto a bill, the president returns it within ten days to the house of Congress in which it originated, along with his objections to the bill. If Congress adjourns during the ten-day period, and the president has taken no action, the bill is also considered to be vetoed. This latter method is known as the *pocket veto.* The possibility of a presidential veto affects how willing members of Congress are to push for different pieces of legislation at different times. If they think a proposal is likely to

be vetoed by the president, they might shelve it for a later time.

A presidential veto may be overridden by a two-thirds vote in both the House and the Senate. A veto override says much about the support that a president can expect from Congress, and it can deliver a stinging blow to the executive branch. Bush used his veto power on forty-six occasions during his four years in office and, in all but one instance, was able to defeat or avoid a congressional override of his action. Bush's frequent resort to the veto power was one indicator of the struggle between the White House and the Congress over domestic and foreign policy that took place during his term. Similarly, President Clinton used the veto to block Republican programs in 1995 and 1996.

The president's veto power is provided in Article I, Section 7, of the Constitution. In 1996, this constitutional veto power was augmented by the congressional enactment of a line-item veto. This is a provision allowing the president to strike out specific portions of a bill passed by Congress without vetoing the entire bill. Many state governors have the line-item veto power, and presidents have long sought it, arguing that it would allow them to eliminate unnecessary spending provisions from otherwise desirable pieces of legislation. The line-item veto power granted to the president in 1996, however, is very limited. The president is given five days after the passage of a bill to strike out any spending figure or any tax break affecting fewer than 100 individuals. The president does not have the authority to strike any actual provisions of a spending bill—only the dollar amounts to be spent. Any expenditure vetoed by the president is canceled unless Congress votes to restore it. The new veto does not apply to entitlement spending, such as Social Security or Medicare, or to major tax cuts. Congress, moreover, may insert language in a bill exempting any or all of its provisions from the line-item veto. The president's line-item veto authority will expire in seven years unless it is renewed by Congress at that time.[4]

How Congress Decides

What determines the kinds of legislation that Congress ultimately produces? According to the most simple theories of representation, members of Congress would respond to the views of their **constituents**—the members of the district from which they are elected. In fact, the process of creating a legislative agenda, drawing up a list of possible measures, and deciding among them is very complex, and a variety of influences from inside and outside government play

important roles. External influences include a legislator's constituency and various interest groups. Influences from inside government include party leadership, congressional colleagues, and the president. Let us examine each of these influences individually and then consider how they interact to produce congressional policy decisions.

Constituency

Because members of Congress, for the most part, want to be re-elected, we would expect the views of their constituents to have a key influence on the decisions that legislators make. Yet constituency influence is not so straight-forward. In fact, most constituents do not even know what policies their representatives support. The number of citizens who *do* pay attention to such matters—the attentive public—is usually very small. Nonetheless, members of Congress spend a lot of time worrying about what their constituents think, because these representatives realize that the choices they make may be scrutinized in a future election and used as ammunition by an opposing candidate. Because of this possibility, members of Congress try to anticipate their constituents' policy views.[5] Legislators are more likely to act in accordance with those views if they think that voters will take them into account during elections. In this way, constituents may affect congressional policy choices even when there is little direct evidence of their influence.

Interest Groups

Interest groups are another important external influence on the policies that Congress produces. When members of Congress are making voting decisions, those interest groups that have some

---

[4]David Rosenbaum, "Line-Item Veto Power: Less Than Meets the Eye," *New York Times,* 25 March 1996, p. B11.

[5]See John W. Kingdon, *Congressmen's Voting Decisions* (New York: Harper and Row, 1973), Chapter 3; and R. Douglas Arnold, *The Logic of Congressional Action* (New Haven, CT: Yale University Press, 1990).

connection to constituents in particular members' districts are most likely to be influential. For this reason, interest groups with the ability to mobilize followers in many congressional districts may be especially influential in Congress. The small-business lobby, for example, played an important role in defeating President Clinton's proposal for comprehensive health care reform in 1993–1994. The mobilization of networks of small businesses across the country meant that virtually every member of Congress had to take their views into account. In recent years, Washington-based interest groups with little grassroots strength have recognized the importance of such locally generated activity. They have, accordingly, sought to simulate grassroots pressure, using a strategy that has been nicknamed "Astroturf lobbying." Such campaigns encourage constituents to sign form letters or postcards, which are then sent to congressional representatives. Sophisticated "grassroots" campaigns set up toll-free telephone numbers for a system in which simply reporting your name and address to the listening computer will generate a letter to your congressional representative. One Senate office estimated that such organized campaigns to demonstrate "grassroots" support account for two-thirds of the mail the office received. As such campaigns increase, however, they may become less influential, because members of Congress are aware of how rare actual constituent interest actually is. [6]

Interest groups also have substantial influence in setting the legislative agenda and in helping to craft specific language in legislation. Today, sophisticated lobbyists win influence by providing information about policies to busy members of Congress. As one lobbyist noted, "You can't get access without knowledge. . . . I can go in to see [former Energy and Commerce Committee chair] John Dingell, but if I have nothing to offer or

nothing to say, he's not going to want to see me."[7] In recent years, interest groups have also begun to build broader coalitions and comprehensive campaigns around particular policy issues. These coalitions do not rise from the grass roots, but instead are put together by Washington lobbyists who launch comprehensive lobbying campaigns that combine simulated grassroots activity with information and campaign funding for members of Congress. In the 104th Congress, the Republican leadership worked so closely with lobbyists that critics charged that the boundaries between lobbyists and legislators had been erased, and that lobbyists had become "adjunct staff to the Republican leadership."[8]

Party Discipline

In both the House and the Senate, party leaders have a good deal of influence over the behavior of their party members. This influence, sometimes called "party discipline," was once so powerful that it dominated the lawmaking process. At the turn of the century, because of their control of patronage and the nominating process, party leaders could often command the allegiance of more than 90 percent of their members. A vote on which 50 percent or more of the members of one party take a particular position while at least 50 percent of the members of the other party take the opposing position is called a **party vote**. At the beginning of the twentieth century, most **roll-call votes** in the House of Representatives were party votes. Today, primary elections have deprived party leaders of the power to decide who receives the party's official nomination. The patronage resources available to the leadership, moreover, have become quite limited. As a result, party-line voting happens less often. It is, however, fairly common to

---

[6]Jane Fritsch, "The Grass Roots, Just a Free Phone Call Away," *New York Times,* 23 June 1995, p. A1.

[7]Daniel Franklin, "Tommy Boggs and the Death of Health Care Reform," *Washington Monthly,* April 1995, p. 36.
[8]Peter H. Stone, "Follow the Leaders," *National Journal,* 24 June 1995, p. 1641.

find at least a majority of Democrats opposing a majority of Republicans on any given issue.

Typically, party unity is greater in the House than in the Senate. House rules grant greater procedural control of business to the majority party leaders, which gives them more influence over their members. In the Senate, however, the leadership has few sanctions over its members. Senate Minority Leader Tom Daschle once observed that a Senate leader seeking to influence other senators has as incentives "a bushel full of carrots and a few twigs."[9] Party unity has increased in recent sessions of Congress as a consequence of the in-

[9]Holly Idelson, "Signs Point to Greater Loyalty on Both Sides of the Aisle," *Congressional Quarterly Weekly Report,* 19 December 1992, p. 3849.

tense partisan struggles during the 1980s and 1990s (see Figure 5.4). On the whole, there was more party unity in the House during 1995 than in any year since 1954 (see Figure 5.4). By 1996, the level of party unity was back to average. In 1997, party unity diminished as House Republicans divided over budget and tax cut negotiations with President Clinton, leading to an unsuccessful attempt to oust Gingrich as speaker. Though Gingrich survived the battle, the Republican party was damaged by the affair.

To some extent, party unity is based on ideology and background. Republican members of Congress are more likely than Democrats to be drawn from rural or suburban areas. Democrats are likely to be more liberal on economic and social questions than their Republican colleagues.

FIGURE 5.4

Party Unity Scores by Chamber*

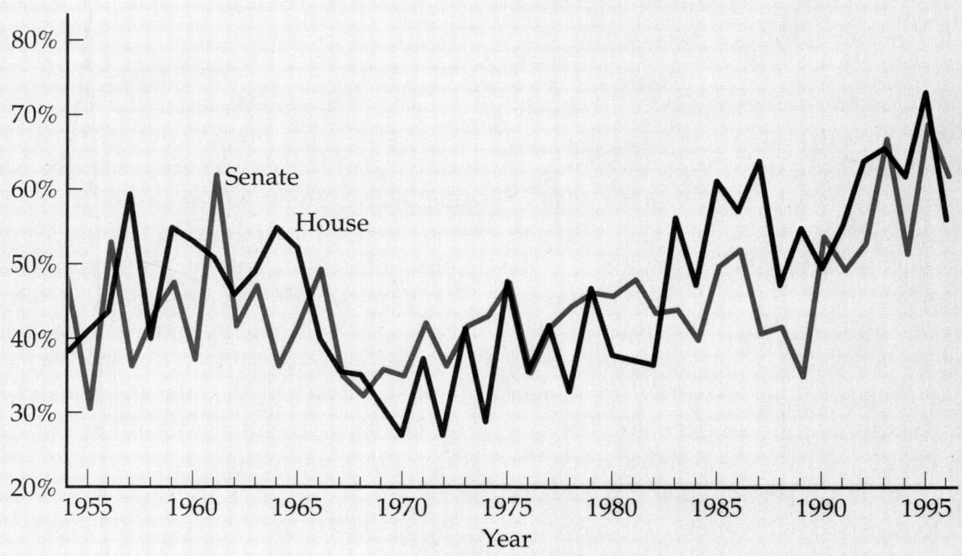

*The percentage of times that members voted with the majority of their party, based on recorded votes on which a majority of one party voted against the majority of the other party.
SOURCE: *Congressional Quarterly Weekly Report,* 31 December 1994, p. 3849. Used by permission.

These differences certainly help to explain roll-call divisions between the two parties. Ideology and background, however, are only part of the explanation of party unity. The other part has to do with organization and leadership.

Although party organization has weakened since the turn of the century, today's party leaders still have some resources at their disposal: (1) committee assignments, (2) access to the floor, (3) the whip system, (4) logrolling, and (5) the presidency. These resources are regularly used and are often effective in securing the support of party members.

COMMITTEE ASSIGNMENTS   Leaders can create debts among members by helping them get favorable committee assignments. These assignments are made early in the congressional careers of most members and cannot be taken from them if they later balk at party discipline. Nevertheless, if the leadership goes out of its way to get the right assignment for a member, this effort is likely to create a bond of obligation that can be called upon without any other payments or favors.

ACCESS TO THE FLOOR   The most important everyday resource available to the parties is control over access to the floor. With thousands of bills awaiting passage and most members clamoring for access in order to influence a bill or to publicize themselves, floor time is precious. In the Senate, the leadership allows ranking committee members to influence the allocation of floor time—who will speak for how long; in the House, the Speaker, as head of the majority party (in consultation with the minority leader), allocates large blocks of floor time. Thus, floor time is controlled in both houses of Congress by the majority and minority leaders. More important, the Speaker of the House and the majority leader in the Senate possess the power of recognition. Although this power may not appear to be substantial, it is a formidable authority and can be used to block a piece of legislation completely or to frustrate a member's attempts to speak on a particular issue.

Because the power is significant, members of Congress usually attempt to stay on good terms with the Speaker and the majority leader in order to ensure that they will continue to be recognized.

THE WHIP SYSTEM   Some influence accrues to party leaders through the *whip system,* which is primarily a communications network. Between twelve and twenty assistant and regional whips are selected by zones to operate at the direction of the majority or minority leader and the whip. They take polls of all the members in order to learn their intentions on specific bills. This enables the leaders to know if they have enough support to allow a vote, as well as whether the vote is so close that they need to put pressure on a few swing votes. Leaders also use the whip system to convey their wishes and plans to the members, but only in very close votes do they actually exert pressure on a member. In those instances, the Speaker or a lieutenant will go to a few party members who have indicated they will switch if their vote is essential. The whip system helps the leaders limit pressuring members to a few times per session.

The whip system helps maintain party unity in both houses of Congress, but it is particularly critical in the House of Representatives because of the large number of legislators whose positions and votes must be accounted for. The majority and minority whips and their assistants must be adept at inducing compromise among legislators who hold widely differing viewpoints. The whips' personal styles and their perception of their function significantly affect the development of legislative coalitions and influence the compromises that emerge.

LOGROLLING   An agreement between two or more members of Congress who have nothing in common except the need for support is called *logrolling.* The agreement states, in effect, "You support me on bill X and I'll support you on another bill of your choice." Since party leaders are the center of the communications networks in the two chambers, they can help members create large logrolling coalitions. Hundreds of logrolling deals are made each year, and while there are no official record-keeping books, it would be a poor party leader whose whips did not know who owed what to whom.

In some instances, logrolling produces strange alliances. In August 1994, for example, an unlikely coalition of Republicans, conservative Democrats, and members of the Congressional Black Caucus temporarily blocked President Clinton's crime bill in the House of Representatives. The Republicans were interested in undermining Clinton. Conservative Democrats had been mobilized by the National Rifle Association (NRA) to oppose the bill's ban on the sale of several types of assault weapons. Some members of the Congressional Black Caucus were opposed to the bill because it expanded the potential use of the death penalty in federal cases. A "racial justice" provision, designed to ensure that blacks convicted of capital offenses could not be sentenced to death with greater frequency than whites, had been demanded by many African American representatives as a condition for supporting the president's anti-crime initiative. This provision, however, had

been defeated several weeks earlier by the same Republicans and conservative Democrats who now joined with disgruntled members of the Black Caucus to block the entire bill. Eventually Clinton was able to secure passage of the legislation by making concessions to the Republicans.

THE PRESIDENCY   Of all the influences that maintain the clarity of party lines in Congress, the influence of the presidency is probably the most important. Indeed, it is a touchstone of party discipline in Congress. Since the late 1940s, under President Truman, presidents each year have identified a number of bills to be considered part of the administration's program. By the mid-1950s, both parties in Congress began to look to the president for these proposals, which became the most significant part of Congress's agenda. The president's support is a criterion for party loyalty, and party leaders in Congress are able to use it to rally some members.

Weighing Diverse Influences

Clearly, many different factors affect congressional decisions. But at various points in the

IN BRIEF BOX

PARTY DISCIPLINE

Party discipline—the influence party leaders have over the behavior of their party members—is maintained through a number of sources.

committee assignments—by giving favorable committee assignments to members, party leaders create a sense of debt.

access to the floor—ranking committee members in the Senate and the Speaker of the House control the allocation of floor time, so House and Senate members want to stay on good terms with these party leaders in order that their bills get time on the floor.

whip system—allows party leaders to keep track of how many votes they have for a given piece of legislation; if the vote is close, they can try to influence members to switch sides.

logrolling—members who have nothing in common agree to support one another's legislation because each needs the vote.

presidency—The president's legislative proposals are often the most important part of Congress's agenda. Party leaders use the president's support to rally members.

decision-making process, some factors are likely to be more influential than others. For example, interest groups may be more effective at the committee stage, when their expertise is especially valued and their visibility is less obvious. Because committees play a key role in deciding what legislation actually reaches the floor of the House or Senate, interest groups can often put a halt to bills they dislike, or they can ensure that the options that do reach the floor are those that the group's members support.

Once legislation reaches the floor, and members of Congress are deciding among alternatives, constituent opinion will become more important. Legislators are also influenced very much by other legislators: many of their assessments about the substance and politics of legislation come from fellow members of Congress.

The influence of the external and internal forces described in the preceding section also varies according to the kind of issue being considered. On policies of great importance to powerful interest groups—farm subsidies, for example—those groups are likely to have considerable influence. On other issues, members of Congress may be less attentive to narrow interest groups and more willing to consider what they see as the general interest.

Finally, the mix of influences varies according to the historical moment. The 1994 electoral victory of Republicans allowed their party to control both houses of Congress for the first time in forty years. That fact, combined with an unusually assertive Republican leadership, meant that party leaders became especially important in decision making. The willingness of moderate Republicans to support measures they had once opposed indicated the unusual importance of party leadership in this period. As House Minority Leader Richard Gephardt put it, "When you've been in the desert 40 years, your instinct is to help Moses."[10]

---

[10]David Broder, "At 6 Months, House GOP Juggernaut still Cohesive," *Washington Post*, 17 July 1995, p. A1.

BEYOND LEGISLATION: ADDITIONAL CONGRESSIONAL POWERS

In addition to the power to make the law, Congress has at its disposal an array of other instruments through which to influence the process of government. The Constitution gives the Senate the power to approve treaties and appointments. And Congress has drawn to itself a number of other powers through which it can share with the other branches the capacity to administer the laws. The powers of Congress can be called "weapons of control" to emphasize the fact of Congress's power to govern and to call attention to what governmental power means. The In Brief Box on page 123 is an outline of Congress's weapons of control.

Oversight

Oversight, as applied to Congress, refers not to something neglected but to the effort to oversee or to supervise how legislation is carried out by the executive branch. Individual senators and members of the House can engage in a form of oversight simply by calling or visiting administrators, sending out questionnaires, or talking to constituents about programs. But in a more formal sense, oversight is carried out by committees or subcommittees of the Senate or House, which conduct hearings and investigations in order to analyze and evaluate bureaucratic agencies and the effectiveness of their programs. The purpose may be to locate inefficiencies or abuses of power, to explore the relationship between what an agency does and what a law intended, or to change or abolish a program. Most programs and agencies are subject to some oversight every year during the course of hearings on *appropriations,* that is, the funding of agencies and government programs. Committees or subcommittees have the power to subpoena witnesses, take oaths, cross-examine, compel testimony, and bring crim-

IN BRIEF BOX

CONGRESSIONAL WEAPONS OF CONTROL

Power	Means of Exercising Power
Statutes	Public laws: Authorization acts Public laws: Revenue acts Public laws: Appropriations acts Private legislation
Oversight of administration	Hearings Investigation Supervision (congressional lobbying)
Oversight of citizens (committee as grand jury)	Hearings Investigation
Advice and consent (Senate)	
Debate	
Direct committee government (public works)	
Legislative veto	

inal charges for contempt (refusing to cooperate) and perjury (lying).

Hearings and investigations resemble each other in many ways, but they differ on one fundamental point. A hearing is usually held on a specific bill, and the questions asked there are usually intended to build a record with regard to that bill. In an investigation, the committee or subcommittee does not begin with a particular bill, but examines a broad area or problem and then concludes its investigation with one or more proposed bills. One example of an investigation is the congressional inquiry into the Reagan administration's shipment of arms to the government of Iran.

Advice and Consent: Special Senate Powers

The Constitution has given the Senate a special power, one that is not based on lawmaking. The president has the power to make treaties and to appoint top executive officers, ambassadors, and federal judges—but only "with the Advice and Consent of the Senate" (Article II, Section 2). For treaties, two-thirds of those present must concur; for appointments, a majority is required.

The power to approve or reject presidential requests also involves the power to set conditions. The Senate only occasionally exercises its power to reject treaties and appointments, and usually that is when opposite parties control the Senate and the White House. During the final two years of President Reagan's term, Senate Democrats rejected Judge Robert Bork's Supreme Court nomination and gave clear indications that they would reject a second Reagan nominee, Judge Douglas Ginsburg, who withdrew his nomination before the Senate could act. Such instances, however, actually underscore the restraint with which the Senate usually uses its consent power. For example, only nine judicial nominees have been rejected by the Senate during the past century, while hundreds have been approved.

More common than Senate rejection of presidential appointees is a senatorial "hold" on an appointment. By Senate tradition, any member may place an indefinite hold on the confirmation of a mid- or lower-level presidential appointment. The hold is typically used by senators trying to wring concessions from the White House on matters having nothing to do with the appointment in question. In 1994, for example, Senator Max Baucus (D-Mont.) placed a hold on the confirmation of Mary Shapiro, President Clinton's choice to head the Commodity Futures Trading Commission, as well as those of four other Clinton nominees for federal regulatory posts, in order to win concessions for farmers in his state.

Most presidents make every effort to take potential Senate opposition into account in treaty negotiations and will frequently resort to *executive agreements* with foreign powers instead of treaties. The Supreme Court has held that such agreements are equivalent to treaties, but they do not need Senate approval.[11] In the past, presidents sometimes concluded secret agreements without informing Congress of the agreements' contents, or even their existence. American involvement in the Vietnam War grew in part out of a series of secret arrangements made between American presidents and the South Vietnamese during the 1950s and 1960s. Congress did not even learn of these agreements until 1969.

In 1972, Congress passed the Case Act, which requires that the president inform Congress of any executive agreement within sixty days of its having been reached. This provides Congress with the opportunity to cancel agreements that it opposes. In addition, Congress can limit the president's ability to conduct foreign policy through executive agreement by refusing to appropriate the funds needed to implement an agreement. In this way, for example, executive agreements to provide American economic or military assistance to foreign governments can be modified or even canceled by Congress.

Direct Patronage

Another instrument of congressional power is direct *patronage.* Members of Congress often have an opportunity to provide direct benefits for their constituents. The most important of these opportunities for direct patronage is in legislation that has been described half-jokingly as the *"pork barrel."* This type of legislation specifies the projects or other authorizations and the location within a particular district. Many observers of Congress argue that pork-barrel bills are the only ones that some members take seriously because they boost the members' re-election prospects. Often, congressional leaders will use pork-barrel projects in exchange for votes on other matters, and other members seek immortality through pork. The Mark Hatfield Marine Science Center in Oregon was built with funds obtained by Oregon's Senator Mark Hatfield. The Mildred and Claude Pepper fountain is the centerpiece of a Miami park project that had been strongly supported by the late Representative Claude Pepper. Federal dollars secured by Pennsylvania Representative Bud Shuster helped to build the Bud Shuster Byway, a four-lane highway serving Everett, Pennsylvania. The most important rule of pork-barreling is that any member of Congress whose district receives a project as part of a bill must support all the other projects on the bill. This cuts across party and ideological lines.

A common form of pork-barreling is the "earmark," the practice through which members of Congress insert into otherwise "pork-free" public laws language that provides special benefits for their own constituents. The military budget currently contains about $4 billion in earmarks. For example, in 1991, Representative Paul Kanjorski (D-Pa.) was able to insert into a section of the Pentagon's budget two paragraphs earmarking $20 million to create "an advanced technology demonstration facility for environmental technology" and stipulating further that "these funds are to be provided only to the organization known as 'Earth Conservancy' in Hanover Township, Penn-

---

[11]U.S. v. Pink, 315 U.S. 203 (1942). For a good discussion of the problem, see James W. Davis, *The American Presidency* (New York: Harper & Row, 1987), Chapter 8.

sylvania." This organization not only was in Mr. Kanjorski's district, but was also headed by his brother.[12]

The pork-barrel tradition in Congress is so strong that some members insist on providing their districts with special benefits for which they can claim credit whether their constituents want them or not. In 1994, for example, members of the House Public Works Committee managed to channel millions of dollars in federal highway funds to their own states and districts. California, which has eight representatives on the Public Works Committee, received fifty-one special federal highway projects worth nearly $300 million. The problem is that under federal law, these special funds are charged against the state's annual grant from the Highway Trust Fund. States rely heavily upon their Highway Trust Fund grants to fund high-priority road construction and repairs. One exasperated state official declared, "For years our members have tried to explain that to the members of Congress . . . 'No, you did not bring me any new money. All you did was reprogram money from here to there.'"[13]

Another form of direct patronage is intervening with federal administrative agencies on behalf of constituents and supporters. Members of the House and Senate spend a great deal of time on the telephone and in administrative offices seeking to get favorable treatment for a constituent. A small but related form of patronage is getting an appointment to one of the military academies for the child of a constituent. Traditionally, these appointments are allocated one to a district.

A different form of patronage is the **private bill**—a proposal to grant some kind of relief, special privilege, or exemption to the person named in the bill. The private bill is a type of legislation, but it is distinguished from a public bill, which is supposed to deal with general rules and categories of behavior, people, and institutions.

As many as 75 percent of all private bills introduced (and one-third of the ones that pass) are concerned with providing relief for foreign nationals who cannot get permanent visas to the United States because the immigration quota for their country is filled or because of something unusual about their situation. Most of the other private bills are introduced to give money to individual citizens for injuries allegedly received from a public action or for a good deed that would have otherwise gone unrewarded. About 20 percent of those bills become law.[14]

Private legislation is a congressional privilege that is often abused, but it is impossible to imagine members of Congress giving it up completely. It is one of the easiest, cheapest, and most effective forms of patronage available to each member.

THE FALL AND RISE OF CONGRESSIONAL POWER

Because they feared both executive and legislative tyranny, the framers of the Constitution pitted Congress and the president against one another. But for more than one hundred years, the contest was unequal. During the first century of American government, Congress was the dominant institution. American foreign and domestic policy was formulated and implemented by Congress and generally, the most powerful figures in American government were the Speaker of the House and the leaders of the Senate—not the president. The War of 1812 was planned and fought by Congress. The great sectional compromises prior to the Civil War were formulated in Congress, without much intervention from the executive branch. Even during the Civil War, a period of extraordinary presidential leadership, a joint congressional committee on the conduct of the war played a role in formulating war plans

[12]Tim Weiner, "Sending Money to Home District: Earmarking and the Pork Barrel," *New York Times*, 13 July 1994, p. 1

[13]Jon Healy, "The Unspoken Expense of the Highway Bill," *Congressional Quarterly Weekly Report*, 28 May 1994, p. 1375.

[14]Congressional Quarterly, *Guide to the Congress of the United States*, 2nd ed. (Washington, DC: Congressional Quarterly Press, 1976), pp. 229–310.

CONCEPT MAP 5.1

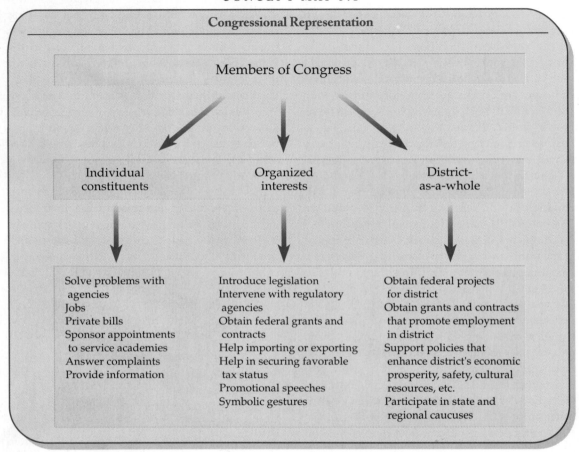

Congressional Representation

Members of Congress

Individual constituents	Organized interests	District-as-a-whole
Solve problems with agencies Jobs Private bills Sponsor appointments to service academies Answer complaints Provide information	Introduce legislation Intervene with regulatory agencies Obtain federal grants and contracts Help importing or exporting Help in securing favorable tax status Promotional speeches Symbolic gestures	Obtain federal projects for district Obtain grants and contracts that promote employment in district Support policies that enhance district's economic prosperity, safety, cultural resources, etc. Participate in state and regional caucuses

and campaign tactics, and even had a hand in the promotion of officers. After the Civil War, when President Andrew Johnson sought to interfere with congressional plans for Reconstruction, he was summarily impeached, saved from conviction by only one vote. Subsequent presidents understood the moral and did not attempt to thwart Congress.

This congressional preeminence began to diminish after the turn of the century, so that by the 1960s, the executive had become, at least temporarily, the dominant branch of American government. The major domestic policy initiatives of the twentieth century—Franklin Roosevelt's "New Deal," Harry Truman's "Fair Deal," John F. Kennedy's "New Frontier," and Lyndon Johnson's "Great Society"—all included some congressional involvement but were essentially developed, introduced, and implemented by the executive. In the area of foreign policy, though Congress continued to be influential during the twentieth century, the focus of decision-making power clearly moved into the executive branch. The War 1812 may have been a congressional war, but in the twentieth century, American entry into World War I, World War II, Korea, Vietnam, and a host of lesser conflicts was essentially a presidential—not a congressional—decision. What accounts for this decline of congressional power?

A key factor in understanding the power of any political institution, be it Congress, the executive, or the judiciary, is its representative character. If a political institution is able to link itself to important groups and forces in the society by serving their interests and meeting their needs, then these forces can generally be expected, in turn, to support that institution in its struggles with other agencies or against any public opposition to its programs. On the other hand, if a political institution is unable to link itself to a political constituency, then it may find itself without defenses if it comes under attack. During the nineteenth century, Congress—particularly the House of Representatives—was the most accessible and permeable institution of American government. Turnover in the House was rapid, and new groups and forces in American society generally found it easy to obtain access to the House and to find members of Congress to support their aims and interests. In other words, Congress was the most representative governmental institution. This led various groups in society to support Congress in its battles with the executive branch and the courts. For example, during the 1830s, many merchants and bankers found Congress very receptive to their interests and became s strong constituency for congressional power vis-à-vis what they called the "usurpations" of the executive branch under President Andrew Jackson, in particular his attack on the Bank of the United States, an institution that business interests saw as essential to their well-being.

During the twentieth century, the executive branch became far more accessible than Congress[15] and important national political forces began more and more to turn to the executive with their problems. To the extent that they found the executive to be hospitable to them, these forces began to support executive or presidential rather than congressional power. The critical juncture in the congressional-executive balance was the period of the New Deal. In the 1930s, President Franklin Delano Roosevelt succeeded, through major innovations in programs and policies, in linking a number of important social and political forces—organized labor, urban political machines, farmers, blacks, key sectors of American industry—to the executive branch. These forces were the beneficiaries of the programs developed by the Roosevelt administration and its successors. In turn, these forces formed a constituency for executive power.[16] The upshot was that during the Roosevelt era, powerful groups, forces, and interests in American society came to see the executive branch as more representative—as the agency most likely to be open to their demands. This perception helped greatly to enhance executive power at the expense of congressional power.

Thus, power and representation have been closely linked in congressional history. Congress was most powerful when it was most representative, least powerful when it was least accessible to important groups in society. In the last thirty years, there has been a good deal of resurgence of congressional power vis-à-vis the executive. This has occurred mainly because Congress has sought to represent many important political forces, such as the civil rights, feminist, environmental, consumer, and peace movements, which in turn became constituencies for congressional power. During the mid-1990s, Congress became more receptive to a variety of new conservative political forces, including groups on the social and religious right as well as more traditional economic conservatives. After Republicans won

[15]See Samuel Huntington, "Congressional Responses to the Twentieth Century," in *Congress and America's Future*, ed. David Truman (Englewood Cliffs, NJ: Prentice-Hall, 1965), Chapter 1.

[16]See Thomas Ferguson, "From Normalcy to New Deal: Industrial Structure, Party Competition and American Public Policy in the Great Depression," *International Organization* 38 (Winter 1984), pp. 42–94.

DEBATING THE ISSUES

The Republican Congress:
Revolution or Business as Usual?

*W*HEN THE *Republicans swept into power in 1994, winning control of both houses of Congress for the first time since 1952, House Speaker Newt Gingrich was seen as the leader of a bold new Republican conservatism that promised to decisively change the direction of national policy. Two years later, the Republicans retained control of both houses; yet the experience of nearly two years of confrontation with a Democratic president, and negative public reaction to much of Speaker Gingrich's agenda, encouraged a more moderate and conciliatory tone on the part of the Speaker. Below are excerpts from Gingrich's comments after the 1994 and 1996 elections. They suggest very different approaches to governance and the role of Congress.*

GINGRICH, NOVEMBER 11, 1994

[We] have the most explicitly ideologically committed House Republican Party in modern history. That we held an event [the September 27 unveiling of the Republican "Contract With America"] on the Capitol steps that 330 members signed or candidates signed up for. That we told the country in a full-page ad in *TV Guide* where we were going and the direction we would take. . . . That the president personally attacked the contract virtually everywhere he went. And that in the end, there was the most shatteringly one-sided Republican victory since 1946. . . .

I would argue [that] this was clearly a historic election, which clearly had a mandate. . . . I am very prepared to cooperate with the Clinton administration. I am not prepared to compromise. . . . On those things that are at the core of our contract, those things which are at the core of our philosophy, and on those things where we believe we represent the vast majority of Americans, there will be no compromise. . . . [W]e simply need to reach out and erase the slate and start over. . . .

If this just degenerates after an historic election back into the usual baloney of politics in Washington and the pettiness of Washington, then the American people I believe will move towards a third party in a massive way. I think they are fed up with this city; they are fed up with its games; they are fed up with petty partisanship.[1]

control of both houses in the 1994 elections, Congress took the lead in developing programs and policies supported by these groups. These efforts won Congress the support of conservative forces in its battles for power against a Democratic White House.

To herald the new accessibility of Congress, Republican leaders instituted a number of reforms designed to eliminate many of the practices they had criticized as examples of Democratic arrogance during their long years in opposition. Republican leaders imposed term limits on committee chairmen, eliminated the

practice of proxy voting, reduced committee staffs by one-third, ended Congress's exemption from the labor, health, and civil rights laws it imposed on the rest of the nation, and prohibited members from receiving most gifts. The Republicans also introduced a budget resolution that would lead to a balanced budget within seven years. Fearing that he would be marginalized in the legislative process, President Clinton announced his own proposals for cuts in taxes and spending under the rubric of a "middle-class bill of rights." In June 1995, Clinton introduced his own balanced budget plan. Congressional Re-

GINGRICH, NOVEMBER 20, 1996

For my part personally, I am going to report that in some ways it was a very difficult two years. . . . The last Congress was, legitimately, the confrontation Congress. We entered at a point where our friends on the left were talking about government-run health care, massive tax increases, liberal social values, and we had, frankly, a fairly big fight. Some of it we did well, some of it we did badly. . . . We made some mistakes. As the first Republican Congress in 40 years, I think some of those mistakes were probably unavoidable; and had we been clever enough to avoid one set, we might have made others. I made a few big errors. I was both the speaker of the House and our leading advocate, and some days I didn't do it very well. . . .

The American people also chose William Jefferson Clinton to serve as president. This is our system. The Founding Fathers consciously designed a Constitution that divides power. It was their intent to design a governing machine so inefficient that no dictator could force it to work. The corollary, of course, is that as volunteers, we can barely get it to work. . . . And so we find ourselves here with a Democratic president and a Republican Congress, and we have an absolute moral obligation to make this system work. . . . And so we bear the unusual burden of reaching out to a Democratic president and saying, together we are in fact going to find common ground.

Fortunately, this campaign did create a lot of common ground. President Clinton, as candidate, was for a balanced budget, for smaller government, for tax cuts, for welfare reform, and for an all-out effort to stop drugs. That's a ground it seems to me we can do a lot of work together because we share the common direction. We won't always agree on details, but I want to suggest to you that if the last Congress was the "Confrontation Congress," this Congress will be the "Implementation Congress," and we will be very pleased two years from now at how much we have implemented, working together and placing the nation first.[2]

[1]"New House Speaker Envisions Cooperation, Cuts, Hard Work," *Congressional Quarterly Weekly Report*, 12 November 1994, pp. 3295–97.
[2]"Remarks by House Speaker Newt Gingrich (R-Ga.) to the House Republican Party Caucus Following His Election as Speaker for the 105th Congress," 20 November 1996.

publicans dismissed the president's proposals as a crass effort to copy the GOP's successful campaign pledges. Even many Democrats felt that the president was in no position to compete with Gingrich and his resurgent party. Instead they hoped that Gingrich and congressional Republicans would make damaging errors. The Democrats' hopes were realized in 1995 and 1996 when the GOP's congressional leadership suffered a crushing defeat in the battle with President Clinton over the federal budget. In early 1997, despite promises to work together, congressional Republicans and President Clinton once again fought over the budget. Congress and the White House both appeared ready for at least two more years of struggle.

CONGRESS: FREEDOM AND POWER

The struggle between Congress and the White House is one more illustration of the dilemma that lies at the heart of the American system of government. The framers of the Constitution checked and balanced a powerful Congress with a powerful executive. This was seen as a way of limiting the potential for abuse of governmental power and protecting freedom. No doubt, it has this effect. Certainly, a vigilant Congress was able to curb presidential abuse of power during the Nixon era. Similarly, the executive branch under the leadership of President Eisenhower played a role in curbing the congressional witch hunts, ostensibly aimed at uncovering communist agents in the federal government, that were conducted by Senator Joseph McCarthy (R-Wisc.) during the 1950s.

At the same time, however, the constant struggle between Congress and the president can hinder stable and effective governance. Over the past quarter-century, in particular, presidents and Congresses have often seemed to be more interested in undermining one another than in promoting the larger public interest. On issues of social policy, economic policy, and foreign policy, Congress and the president have often been at each other's throats while the nation suffered. As noted earlier in this chapter, for example, this struggle between the White House and Capitol Hill is one reason that the United States presently faces a deficit crisis of unprecedented magnitude.

Thus, we face a fundamental dilemma. A political arrangement designed to preserve freedom can undermine the government's power. Indeed, it can undermine the government's very capacity to govern. Must we always choose between freedom and power? Can we not have both? Let us turn now to the second branch of American government, the presidency, to view this dilemma from a somewhat different angle.

Chapter Review

The legislative process must provide the order necessary for legislation to take place amid competing interests. It is dependent on a hierarchical organizational structure within Congress. Six basic dimensions of Congress affect the legislative process: (1) the parties, (2) the committees, (3) the staff, (4) the caucuses (or conferences), (5) the rules, and (6) the presidency.

Since the Constitution provides only for a presiding officer in each house, some method had to be devised for conducting business. Parties quickly assumed the responsibility for this. In the House, the majority party elects a leader every two years. This individual becomes Speaker. In addition, a majority leader and a minority leader (from the minority party) and party whips are elected. Each party has a committee whose job it is to make committee assignments. Party structure in the Senate is similar, except that the vice president of the United States is the president of the Senate.

The committee system surpasses the party system in its importance in Congress. In the early nineteenth century, standing committees became a fundamental aspect of Congress. They have, for the most part, evolved to correspond to executive branch departments or programs and thus reflect and maintain the separation of powers.

The Senate has a tradition of unlimited debate, on which the various cloture rules it has passed have had little effect. Filibusters still occur. The rules of the House restrict talk and support committees; deliberation is recognized as committee business. The House Rules Committee has the power to control debate and floor amendments. The rules prescribe the formal procedure through which bills become law. Generally, the parties control scheduling and agenda, but the committees determine action on the floor. Committees, seniority, and rules all limit the ability of members to represent their constituents. Yet, these factors enable Congress to maintain its role as a major participant in government.

While party voting regularity remains strong, party discipline has declined. Still, parties do have several means of maintaining discipline:

(1) Favorable committee assignments create obligations; (2) Floor time in the debate on one bill can be allocated in exchange for a specific vote on another; (3) The whip system allows party leaders to assess support for a bill and convey their wishes to members; (4) Party leaders can help members create large logrolling coalitions; and (5) Presidents, by identifying pieces of legislation as their own, can muster support along party lines. In most cases, party leaders accept constituency obligations as a valid reason for voting against the party position.

This power of the post–New Deal presidency does not necessarily signify the decline of Congress and representative government. During the 1970s, Congress again became the "first branch" of government. During the early years of the Reagan administration, some of the congressional gains of the previous decade were diminished, but in the last two years of Reagan's second term, and in President Bush's term, Congress reasserted its role. At the start of the Clinton administration, congressional leaders promised to cooperate with the White House, rather than confront it. But only two years later, confrontation was once again the order of the day.

TIME LINE ON CONGRESS

Events	Institutional Developments
New Congress of U.S. meets for first time (1789)	Creation of House Ways and Means Committee (1789)
Jeffersonian party born in Congress (1792)	House committees develop. First procedural rules adopted—Jefferson's Rules (1790s)

1800

	Congressional party caucuses control presidential nominations (1804–1828)
	Congressional committees take control of legislative process. Rise of congressional government (1820s)
Andrew Jackson renominated for president by Democratic party convention (1832)	Presidential nominating conventions replace caucuses (1831–1832)
Whigs and Democrats struggle for power (1840s)	

1850

Abraham Lincoln elected president (1860)	
South secedes. Its delegation leaves Washington (1860–1861); period of Republican leadership (1860s)	No longer blocked by Southerners, Congress adopts protective tariff, transcontinental railroad, Homestead Act, National Banking Act, Contract Labor Act (1861–1864)
Congress impeaches but does not convict Andrew Johnson (1868)	
	Filibuster develops as a tactic in the Senate (1880s)
Era of Republican ascendancy begins (1897)	

Events	Institutional Developments
1900	
Theodore Roosevelt makes U.S. a world power (1901–1909)	House revolt against power of Speaker; rise of seniority system in House (1910)
Democratic interlude with election of Woodrow Wilson (1912)	Seventeenth Amendment ratified; authorizes direct election of senators (1913)
Democrats take charge: Franklin Delano Roosevelt elected president (1932)	Rise of presidential government as Congress passes legislation putting into effect FDR's New Deal (1930s)
	Legislative Reorganization Act (1946)
	Regulation of lobbyists (1949)
1950	
McCarthy hearings (1950s)	Democratic Congresses expand Social Security and federal expenditures for public health (1954–1959)
	Use of legislative investigations as congressional weapon against executive (1950–1980s)
	Growing importance of incumbency (1960s–1980s)
1970	
	Code of ethics adopted (1971)
Watergate hearings (1973–1974)	Campaign Finance Act (1974)
Richard Nixon resigns presidency (1974)	Congress given more power through Budget and Impoundment Act (1974)
	Filibuster reform (1975)
	Enactment of statutory limits on presidential power—War Powers Resolution (1973); Budget and Impoundment Control Act (1974); amendments to Freedom of Information Act (1974); Ethics in Government Act (1978)
	Revival of party caucus and weakening of seniority rules (1970s–1980s)
1980	
Ronald Reagan elected president; begins conflict with Congress (1980)	
Republicans control Senate (1980–1986)	Deficits impose budgetary limits on Congress (1980s and 1990s)
Iran-Contra hearings damage Reagan administration (1987)	Intense conflict between president and Congress resulting from divided government (1980s and 1990s)
George Bush elected president (1988)	

Events	Institutional Developments
1990	
Congress defeats Bush in budget crisis (1990)	
Congress authorizes military action against Iraq (1991)	
Democrats control Congress and White House for first time in 12 years; Republicans use Senate filibuster threat to influence Clinton program (1993)	Congress enacts new tax and deficit reduction programs (1993)
Republicans win control of Congress (1994)	
Clinton defeats Republicans in budget battle (1995)	Republicans in Congress fight to enact "Contract with America" (1995)
Republicans retain control of Congress (1996)	

KEY TERMS

appropriations The amounts of money approved by Congress in statutes (bills) that each unit or agency of government can spend.

bicameralism Division of a legislative body into two houses, chambers, or branches.

caucus (congressional) An association of members of Congress based on party, interest, or social group such as gender or race.

closed rule Provision by the House Rules Committee limiting or prohibiting the introduction of amendments during debate.

cloture Rule allowing a majority or two-thirds or three-fifths of the members in a legislative body to set a time limit on debate over a given bill.

conference committee A joint committee created to work out a compromise on House and Senate versions of a piece of legislation.

constituents Members of the district from which an official is elected.

executive agreement Agreement between the president and another country, which has the force of a treaty but does not require the Senate's "advice and consent."

filibuster A tactic used by members of the Senate to prevent action on legislation they oppose by continuously holding the floor and speaking until the majority backs down. Once given the floor, senators have unlimited time to speak, and it requires a vote of three-fifths of the Senate to end the filibuster.

logrolling A legislative practice wherein reciprocal agreements are made between legislators, usually in voting for or against a bill. In contrast to bargaining, parties to logrolling have nothing in common but their desire to exchange support.

majority leader The elected leader of the party holding a majority of the seats in the House of Representatives or in the Senate. In the House, the majority leader is subordinate in the party hierarchy to the Speaker.

minority leader The elected leader of the party holding less than a majority of the seats in the House or Senate.

oversight The effort by Congress, through hearings, investigations, and other techniques, to exercise control over the activities of executive agencies.

party vote A roll-call vote in the House or Senate in which at least 50 percent of the members of one party take a particular position and are opposed by at least 50 percent of the members of the other party. Party votes are rare today, although they were fairly common in the nineteenth century.

patronage The resources available to higher officials, usually opportunities to make partisan appointments to offices and to confer grants, licenses, or special favors to supporters.

pocket veto A presidential veto of legislation wherein the president takes no formal action on a bill. If Congress adjourns within ten days of passing a bill, and the president does not sign it, the bill is considered to be vetoed.

pork barrel Appropriations made by legislative bodies for local projects that are often not needed but that are created so that local representatives can win re-election in their home district.

private bill   A proposal in Congress to provide a specific person with some kind of relief, such as a special exemption from immigration quotas.

roll-call vote   A vote in which each legislator's yes or no vote is recorded as the clerk calls the names of the members alphabetically.

seniority   Priority or status ranking given to an individual on the basis of length of continuous service in a committee in Congress.

Speaker of the House   The chief presiding officer of the House of Representatives. The Speaker is elected at the beginning of every Congress on a straight party vote. The Speaker is the most important party and House leader, and can influence the legislative agenda, the fate of individual pieces of legislation, and members' positions within the House.

standing committee   A permanent committee with the power to propose and write legislation that covers a particular subject such as finance or appropriations.

veto   The president's constitutional power to turn down acts of Congress. A presidential veto may be overridden by a two-thirds vote of each house of Congress.

whip system   Primarily a communications network in each house of Congress, whips take polls of the membership in order to learn their intentions on specific legislative issues and to assist the majority and minority leaders in various tasks.

FOR FURTHER READING

Arnold, R. Douglas. *The Logic of Congressional Action*, New Haven: Yale University Press, 1990.

Baker, Ross K. *House and Senate*, 2nd ed. New York: W. W. Norton, 1995.

Burnham, James. *Congress and the American Tradition*. Chicago: Henry Regnery, 1965.

Congressional Quarterly. *Origins and Development of Congress*, 2nd ed. Washington, DC: Congressional Quarterly Press, 1982.

Davidson, Roger, ed. *The Postreform Congress*. New York: St. Martin's Press, 1991.

Dodd, Lawrence, and Bruce I. Oppenheimer, eds. *Congress Reconsidered*, 5th ed. Washington, DC: Congressional Quarterly Press, 1993.

Fenno, Richard F. *Congressmen in Committees*. Boston: Little, Brown, 1973.

Fenno, Richard. *Home Style: House Members in Their Districts*. Boston: Little, Brown, 1978.

Fiorina, Morris. *Congress: Keystone of the Washington Establishment*, 2nd ed. New Haven: Yale University Press, 1989.

Fisher, Louis. *The Politics of Shared Power: Congress and the Executive*, 3rd ed. Washington, DC: Congressional Quarterly Press, 1993.

Foreman, Christopher. *Signals from the Hill: Congressional Oversight and the Challenge of Social Regulation*. New Haven: Yale University Press, 1988.

Fowler, Linda, and Robert McClure. *Political Ambition: Who Decides to Run for Congress?* New Haven: Yale University Press, 1989.

Leloup, Lance, T. *Budgetary Politics*. Brunswick, OH: King's Court, 1986.

Light, Paul. *Forging Legislation*. New York: W. W. Norton, 1991.

Malbin, Michael. *Unelected Representatives: Congressional Staff and the Future of Representative Government*. New York: Basic Books, 1980.

Mayhew, David R. *Congress: The Electoral Connection*. New Haven: Yale University Press, 1974.

Oleszek, Walter J. *Congressional Procedures and the Policy Process*, 3rd ed. Washington, DC: Congressional Quarterly Press, 1989.

Rieselbach, Leroy. *Congressional Reform*. Washington, DC: Congressional Quarterly Press, 1986.

Ripley, Randall. *Congress: Process and Policy*, 4th ed. New York: W. W. Norton, 1988.

Schroedel, Jean Reith. *Congress, the President, and Policymaking: A Historical Analysis*. Armonk, NY: M. E. Sharp, 1994.

Sinclair, Barbara. *The Transformation of the U.S. Senate*. Baltimore: Johns Hopkins University Press, 1989.

Smith, Steven S., and Christopher Deering. *Committees in Congress*, 2nd ed. Washington, DC: Congressional Quarterly Press, 1990.

Strahan, Randall. *New Ways and Means: Reform and Change in a Congressional Committee*. Chapel Hill: University of North Carolina Press, 1990.

Sundquist, James L. *The Decline and Resurgence of Congress*. Washington, DC: Brookings Institution, 1981.

CHAPTER 6

The President and the Executive Branch

THE ELECTIONS of 1994, which gave Republicans control of both houses of Congress for the first time in forty years, left President Bill Clinton in perhaps the weakest position of any modern president. Clinton had never had a strong power base; he was elected with only 43 percent of the popular vote. (Given a voter turnout rate of 61 percent, that means only one in four Americans eligible to vote did in fact vote for him.) Even with Democratic majorities in Congress during the first two years of his administration, Clinton had suffered setbacks in what he had hoped to accomplish, including a crushing defeat on health care reform. Now he faced two years during which he would be opposed by a Congress led by Republicans, who warned him to either adopt their issues or lose his ability to lead.

But the modern presidency is too powerful to be negated even by an upheaval like the elections of 1994. By 1996, President Clinton was back, at least at the center of attention if not at the center of power. He had vetoed the appropriations bills that provided for the budget for the 1996 fiscal year, which included the raising of the congressionally set limit on the federal debt; but the Republican Congress got most of the blame for shut-ting down the government. In August 1996, he signed the enormous welfare reform bill, virtually making it his own; but the Republicans got most of the blame from the elderly for endangering Medicare (which was never in danger). President Clinton has many other considerable powers on which he can draw. A strong presidency no longer depends on the person who holds the office, or even on enormous popularity; the strength of the presidency has become institutionalized.

CORE OF THE ARGUMENT

- Since the 1930s, the presidency has been the dominant branch of American government.
- Most of the real power of the modern presidency comes from the powers granted by the Constitution and the laws made by Congress. Mass public opinion, however, is the president's most potent resource of power.
- Both the president and the Congress attempt to make the bureaucracy accountable to the people—the president through management control, the Congress through legislative oversight.

Presidential supremacy, or "presidential government," dates only from the late 1930s. How presidential supremacy developed, its sources, and its problems will be the focus of this chapter. We will divide the discussion into four sections. First, we will review the constitutional origins of the presidency, especially the constitutional basis for the president's foreign and domestic roles. Second, we will review the history of the American presidency to see how the office has evolved from its original status under the Constitution. We will look particularly at the way in which Congress has added to the president's constitutional powers by deliberately delegating to the presidency some of its own responsibilities. Third, we will assess both the formal and the informal means by which presidents seek to enhance their own ability to govern, including their efforts to build popular support. Finally, we will close the chapter with a look at how the presidency and the American system of government have tried to adapt the vast apparatus of the national government to the requirements of a representative democracy.

THE CONSTITUTIONAL BASIS OF THE PRESIDENCY

Although Article II of the Constitution, which establishes the presidency, has been called "the most loosely drawn chapter of the Constitution,"[1] the framers were neither indecisive nor confused. They held profoundly conflicting views of the executive branch, and Article II was probably the best compromise they could make. The formulation the framers agreed upon is magnificent in its ambiguity: "The executive power shall be vested in a President of the United States of America" (Article II, Section 1, first sentence). The meaning of "executive power," however, is defined only in-

directly in the very last sentence of Section 3, which provides that the president "shall take Care that the Laws be faithfully executed."[2]

One very important conclusion can be drawn from these two provisions: The office of the president was to be an office of **delegated powers**. Since, as we have already seen, the Constitution defines all of the powers of the national government as powers of Congress, then "executive power" must be understood as the power to execute faithfully the laws *as they are adopted by Congress*. This does not doom the presidency to weakness. Presumably, Congress can pass laws delegating almost any of its powers to the president. But presidents are not free to discover sources of executive power completely independent of the laws passed by Congress. In the 1890 case of *In re Neagle*, the Supreme Court did hold that presidents could be bold and expansive in their views of the Constitution as to "the rights, duties and obligations" of the presidency; but the powers of the president would have to come from the Constitution and laws and not from some independent or absolute idea of executive power.[3]

Immediately following the first sentence of Section 1, Article II defines the manner in which the president is to be chosen. This is a very odd sequence, but it does say something about the struggle the delegates were having over how to give power to the executive and at the same time to balance that power with limitations. The struggle was between those delegates who wanted the president to be selected by Congress, and thus re-

---

[1]Edward S. Corwin, *The President: Office and Powers*, 3rd rev. ed. (New York: New York University Press, 1957), p. 2.

[2]There is a Section 4, but all it does is to define impeachment.

[3]In re Neagle, 135 U.S. 1 (1890). Neagle, a deputy U.S. marshal, had been authorized by the president to protect a Supreme Court justice whose life had been threatened by an angry litigant. When the litigant attempted to carry out his threat, Neagle shot and killed him. Neagle was then arrested by the local authorities and tried for murder. His defense was that his act was "done in pursuance of a law of the United States." Although the law was not an act of Congress, the Supreme Court declared that it was an executive order of the president and that the protection of a federal judge was a reasonable extension of the president's power to "take care that the laws be faithfully executed."

sponsible to it, and those delegates who preferred that the president be elected directly by the people. Direct popular elections would create a more independent and more powerful presidency. The framers finally agreed on a scheme of indirect election through an *electoral college* in which the electors would be selected by the state legislatures (and close elections would be resolved in the House of Representatives). In this way, the framers hoped to achieve a "republican" solution: a strong president who would be responsible to state and national legislators rather than directly to the electorate.

The heart of presidential power as defined by the Constitution is found in Sections 2 and 3, where several clauses define the presidency in two dimensions: the president as head of state and the president as head of government. Although these will be given separate treatment here, the presidency can be understood only by the combination of the two.

The President as Head of State: Some Imperial Qualities

The position of the president as head of state is defined by three constitutional provisions, which are the source of some of the most important powers on which presidents can draw. The areas covered by these provisions can be classified as

1. *Military.* Article II, Section 2, provides for the power as "Commander in Chief of the Army and Navy of the United States, and of the Militia of the several states, when called in to the actual Service of the United States."
2. *Judicial.* Article II, Section 2, also provides the power to "grant reprieves and pardons for Offenses against the United States, except in Cases of impeachment."
3. *Diplomatic.* Article II, Section 3, provides the power to "receive Ambassadors and other public ministers."

MILITARY   The position of commander in chief makes the president the highest military officer in the United States, with control of the entire military establishment. The preference for civilian control of the military is so strong in America, however, that no president would dare put on a military uniform for a state function—not even a former general like Eisenhower. The president is also the head of the secret intelligence hierarchy, which includes not only the Central Intelligence Agency (CIA) but also the National Security Council (NSC), the National Security Agency (NSA), the Federal Bureau of Investigation (FBI), and a host of less well-known but very powerful international and domestic security agencies.

JUDICIAL   The presidential power to grant reprieves, pardons, and amnesties involves the power of life and death over all individuals who may be a threat to the security of the United States. Presidents may use this power on behalf of a particular individual, as did Gerald Ford when he pardoned Richard Nixon in 1974 "for all offenses against the United States which he . . . has committed or may have committed." Or they may use it on a large scale, as did President Andrew Johnson in 1868, when he gave full amnesty to all Southerners who had participated in the "Late Rebellion," and President Carter in 1977, when he declared an amnesty for all the draft evaders of the Vietnam War. President Bush used this power before his retirement in mid-December 1992, when he pardoned former Secretary of Defense Caspar Weinberger and five other participants in the Iran-Contra affair. This power of life and death over others has helped elevate the president to the level of earlier conquerors and kings by establishing the president as the person before whom supplicants might come to make their pleas for mercy.

DIPLOMATIC   When President George Washington received Edmond Genêt ("Citizen Genêt") as the formal emissary of the revolutionary government of France in 1793, he transformed the power to "receive Ambassadors and other public ministers" into the power to "recognize" other

DEBATING THE ISSUES

Presidential Power: Broad or Narrow?

*P*RESIDENTS AND PUNDITS *have debated the proper scope of presidential power since the founding of the Republic. Some have argued that the Constitution provides broad latitude for presidents to act as they think best; others have asserted that presidents must be mindful of constitutional and political limitations in a three-branch system of government. In the twentieth century, the argument for a strong presidency has carried more weight. Yet in the face of such abuses of presidential power as Watergate and Iran-Contra, some have argued for a return to a more limited view of the presidency.*

The first elected president of this century, Theodore Roosevelt, described in his autobiography his support for expansive presidential authority. Roosevelt's successor, William Howard Taft, summarized the arguments for presidential restraint. Their views are as timely today as a century ago.

ROOSEVELT

My view was that every executive officer, and above all every executive officer in high position, was a steward of the people bound actively and affirmatively to do all he could for the people, and not to content himself with the negative merit of keeping his talents undamaged in a napkin. I declined to adopt the view that what was imperatively necessary for the nation could not be done by the president unless he could find some specific authorization to do it. My belief was that it was not only his right but his duty to do anything that the needs of the nation demanded unless such action was forbidden by the Constitution or by the laws.

---

countries. That power gives the president the almost unconditional authority to review the claims of any new ruling groups to determine if they indeed control the territory and population of their country, so that they can commit it to treaties and other agreements. Critics questioned the wisdom of President Franklin Roosevelt's exchange of ambassadors with the Soviet Union fifteen years after the Russian Revolution in 1917.

They also questioned the wisdom of President Nixon's recognition of the People's Republic of China and of President Carter's recognition of the Sandinista government in Nicaragua. But they did not question the president's authority to make such decisions. Because the breakup of the Soviet bloc was generally perceived as a positive event, no one criticized President Bush for his quick recognition of the several former Soviet and Yugoslav republics as soon as they declared themselves independent states. And few would not approve of President Clinton's recognition of the two new republics that came into being in January 1993 when Czechoslovakia was split into the Czech Republic and Slovakia.

THE IMPERIAL PRESIDENCY?   Have presidents used these three constitutional powers—military, judicial, and diplomatic—to make the presidency too powerful, indeed "imperial"?[4] Debate over the answer to this question has produced an unusual lineup, with presidents and the Supreme Court on one side and Congress on the other. The Supreme Court supported the expansive view of the presidency in three historically significant cases. The first was *In re Neagle,* discussed above. The second was the 1936 *Curtiss-Wright* case, in

[4]Arthur M. Schlesinger, Jr., *The Imperial Presidency* (Boston: Houghton Mifflin, 1973).

Under this interpretation of executive power I did and caused to be done many things not previously done by the president and the heads of the departments. I did not usurp power, but I did greatly broaden the use of executive power. In other words, I acted for the public welfare, I acted for the common well-being of all our people, whenever and in whatever manner was necessary, unless prevented by direct constitutional or legislative prohibition.[1]

TAFT

The true view of the executive functions is, as I conceive it, that the president can exercise no power which cannot be fairly and reasonably traced to some specific grant of power or justly implied and included within such express grant as proper and necessary to its exercise. Such specific grant must be either in the federal Constitution or in an act of Congress passed in pursuance thereof. There is no undefined residuum of power which he can exercise because it seems to him to be in the public interest, and there is nothing in the . . . law of the United States, or in other precedents, warranting such an inference. The grants of executive power are necessarily in general terms in order not to embarrass the executive within the field of action plainly marked for him, but his jurisdiction must be justified and vindicated by affirmative constitutional or statutory provision, or it does not exist.[2]

[1]*The Autobiography of Theodore Roosevelt* (New York: Scribners, 1958), pp. 197–200.
[2]William Howard Taft, *Our Chief Magistrate and His Powers* (New York: Columbia University Press, 1916), pp. 138–45.

which the Court held that Congress may delegate a degree of discretion to the president in foreign affairs.[5] In the third case, *U.S. v. Pink*, the Supreme Court upheld the president's power to use executive agreements to conduct foreign policy.[6] An *executive agreement* is exactly like a treaty because it is a contract between two countries, but an executive agreement does not require a two-thirds vote of approval by the Senate. Ordinarily, executive agreements are used to carry out commitments already made in treaties, or to arrange for matters well below the level of policy. But when presidents have found it expedient to use an executive agreement in place of a treaty, the Court has gone along. This verges on an imperial power.

The Domestic Presidency: The President as Head of Government

The constitutional basis of the domestic presidency also has three parts. Here again, although real power grows out of the combination of the

[5]U.S. v. Curtiss-Wright Export Corp., 299 U.S. 304 (1936). In 1934, Congress passed a joint resolution authorizing the president to prohibit the sale of military supplies to Bolivia and Paraguay, who were at war, if the president determined that the prohibition would contribute to peace between the two countries. When prosecuted for violating the embargo order by President Roosevelt, the defendants argued that Congress could not constitutionally delegate such broad discretion to the president. The Supreme Court disagreed. Previously, however, the Court had rejected the National Industrial Recovery Act precisely because Congress had delegated too much discretion to the president in a domestic policy. See Schechter Poultry Corp. v. U.S., 295 U.S. 495 (1936).
[6]In U.S. v. Pink, 315 U.S. 203 (1942), the Supreme Court confirmed that an executive agreement is the legal equivalent of a treaty, despite the absence of Senate approval. This case approved the executive agreement that was used to establish diplomatic relations with the Soviet Union in 1933.

parts, the analysis is greatly aided by examining the parts separately:

1. *Executive.* The "executive power" is vested in the president by Article II, Section 1, to see that all the laws are faithfully executed (Section 3), and under Article II, Section 2, to appoint and supervise all executive officers and to appoint all federal judges.
2. *Military.* This power is derived from Article IV, Section 4, which stipulates that the president has the power to protect every state "against Invasion . . . and against domestic Violence."
3. *Legislative.* The president is given the power under various provisions to participate effectively and authoritatively in the legislative process.

EXECUTIVE POWER   The most important basis of the president's power as chief executive is to be found in the sections of Article II, which stipulate that the president must see that all the laws are faithfully executed and which provide that the president will appoint all executive officers and all federal judges. In this manner, the Constitution focuses executive power and legal responsibility upon the president. The famous sign on President Truman's desk, "The buck stops here," was not merely an assertion of Truman's personal sense of responsibility. It acknowledged his acceptance of the constitutional imposition of that responsibility upon the president. The president is subject to some limitations, because the appointment of all the top officers, including ambassadors and ministers and federal judges, is subject to a majority approval by the Senate. But these appointments are at the discretion of the president. Although the Constitution is silent on the power of the president to remove such officers, the federal courts have filled this silence with a series of decisions that grant the president this power.[7]

MILITARY SOURCES OF DOMESTIC PRESIDENTIAL POWER   Although Article IV, Section 4, provides that the "United States shall protect every State . . . against Invasion and . . . domestic Violence," Congress has made this an explicit presidential power through statutes directing the president as commander in chief to discharge these obligations.[8] The Constitution restrains the president's use of domestic force by providing that a state legislature (or governor when the legislature is not in session) must request federal troops before the president can send them into the state to provide public order. Yet, this proviso is not absolute. First, presidents are not obligated to deploy national troops merely because the state legislature or governor makes such a request. And more important, presidents may deploy troops in a state or city without a specific request if they consider it necessary to maintain an essential national service, to enforce a federal judicial order, or to protect federally guaranteed civil rights.

A famous example of the unilateral use of presidential power to protect the states against domestic disorder occurred in 1957 under President Eisenhower. He decided to send troops into Little Rock, Arkansas, literally against the wishes of the state of Arkansas, to enforce court orders to integrate Little Rock's Central High School. Arkansas Governor Orval Faubus had actually posted the Arkansas National Guard at the entrance of the school to prevent the court-ordered admission of nine black students. After an effort to negotiate with Governor Faubus failed, President Eisenhower reluctantly sent a thousand paratroopers to Little Rock, who stood watch while the black students took their places in the all-white classrooms. This case makes quite clear that the president does not have to wait for a request by a state legislature or governor before acting as domestic commander in chief.[9] However, in most instances

---

[7]Myers, v. U.S., 272 U.S. 52 (1926); modified by Humphrey's Executor v. U.S., 295 U.S. 602 (1935), Wiener v. U.S., 357 U.S. 349 (1958), Bowsher v. Synar, 478 U.S. 714 (1986), and Morrison v. Olson, 108 S.Ct. 2597 (1988). See also Michael Nelson, ed., "The Removal Power," in *Congressional Quarterly's Guide to the Presidency* (Washington, DC: Congressional Quarterly Press, 1989), pp. 414–15.

[8]These statutes are contained mainly in Title 10 of the United States Code, Sections 331, 332, and 333.
[9]The best study covering all aspects of the domestic use of the military is that of Adam Yarmolinsky, *The Military Establishment* (New York: Harper & Row, 1971).

of domestic disorder—whether from human or from natural causes—presidents tend to exercise unilateral power justified by declaring a "state of emergency," thereby making available federal grants, insurance, and direct assistance as well as troops. In 1992, in the aftermath of the riots in Los Angeles and the devastating storms in Florida, American troops were very much in evidence, sent in by the president, but in the role more of Good Samaritan than of military police.

THE PRESIDENT'S LEGISLATIVE POWER   The president plays a role not only in the administration of government but also in the legislative process. Two constitutional provisions are the primary sources of the president's power in the legislative arena. Article II, Section 3, provides that the president "shall from time to time give to the Congress Information of the State of the Union, and recommend to their consideration such measures as he shall judge necessary and expedient." The second of the president's legislative powers is the "veto power" assigned by Article I, Section 7.[10]

The first of these powers has been important only since Franklin Delano Roosevelt began to use the provision to initiate proposals for legislative action in Congress. Roosevelt established the presidency as the primary initiator of legislation.

The second, the *veto* power, is the president's constitutional power to turn down acts of Congress. This power alone makes the president the most important single legislative leader. No bill vetoed by the president can become law unless both the House and the Senate override the veto by a two-thirds vote. In the case of a *pocket veto*, Congress does not even have the option of overriding the veto, but must reintroduce the bill in the next session. A pocket veto can occur when the president is presented with a bill during the last ten days of a legislative session. Usually, if a president does not sign a bill within ten days, it automatically becomes law. But this is true only while Congress is in session. If a president chooses not to sign a bill within the last ten days that Congress is in session, then the ten-day limit does not expire until Congress is out of session, and instead of becoming law, the bill is vetoed. Process Box 6.1 illustrates the president's veto option. In 1996 a new power was added—the *line-item veto*—giving the president power to strike specific spending items from appropriations bills passed by Congress, unless re-enacted by a two-thirds vote of both House and Senate. The line-item veto was challenged by several members of Congress who argued that it was an unconstitutional violation of the separation of powers; their reasoning was that "the power to 'make' the laws of the nation is the exclusive, nondelegable power of Congress." The Supreme Court ruled, however, that the challengers lacked standing to bring the suit.[11] In August 1997, Clinton used the line-item veto to strike three items from the federal budget.

When one considers these two sources of legislative power—the president's constitutional duty to address Congress on the state of the union and recommend action and the president's veto power—together, it is remarkable that it took so long (well over a century) for the presidency to develop into a strong institution. Let us see how this happened as well as why it took so long.

---

[10]There is a third source of presidential power implied from the provision for "faithful execution of the laws." This is the president's power to impound funds—that is, to refuse to spend money Congress has appropriated for certain purposes. One author referred to this as a "retroactive veto power" (Robert E. Goosetree, "The Power of the President to Impound Appropriated Funds," *American University Law Review,* January 1962). This impoundment power was used freely and to considerable effect by many modern presidents, and Congress occasionally delegated such power to the president by statute. But in reaction to the Watergate scandal, Congress adopted the Budget and Impoundment Control Act of 1974 and designed this act to circumscribe the president's ability to impound funds requiring that the president must spend all appropriated funds unless both houses of Congress consent to an impoundment within forty-five days of a presidential request. Therefore, since 1974, the use of impoundment has declined significantly. Presidents have either had to bite their tongues and accept unwanted appropriations or had to revert to the older and more dependable but politically limited method of vetoing the entire bill.

[11]Raines v. Byrd, S.Ct. 117 (1997).

PROCESS BOX 6.1

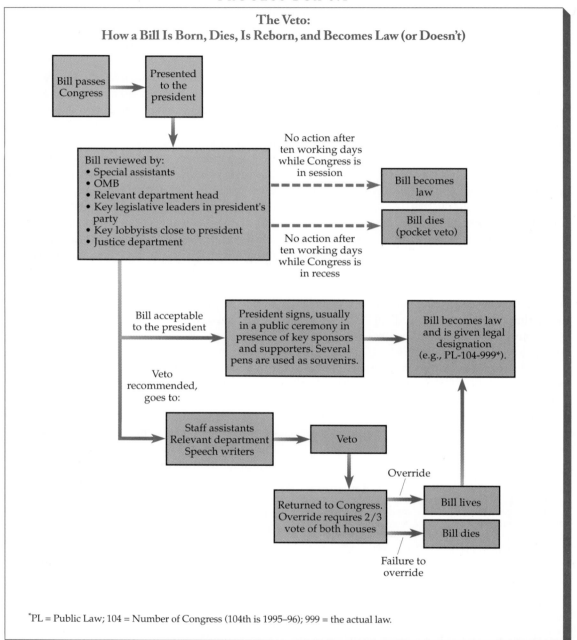

The Veto:
How a Bill Is Born, Dies, Is Reborn, and Becomes Law (or Doesn't)

Bill passes Congress

Presented to the president

Bill reviewed by:
• Special assistants
• OMB
• Relevant department head
• Key legislative leaders in president's party
• Key lobbyists close to president
• Justice department

No action after ten working days while Congress is in session

Bill becomes law

No action after ten working days while Congress is in recess

Bill dies (pocket veto)

Bill acceptable to the president

President signs, usually in a public ceremony in presence of key sponsors and supporters. Several pens are used as souvenirs.

Bill becomes law and is given legal designation (e.g., PL-104-999*).

Veto recommended, goes to:

Staff assistants
Relevant department
Speech writers

Veto

Override

Returned to Congress. Override requires 2/3 vote of both houses

Bill lives

Bill dies

Failure to override

*PL = Public Law; 104 = Number of Congress (104th is 1995–96); 999 = the actual law.

THE RISE OF PRESIDENTIAL GOVERNMENT

Most of the real power of the modern presidency comes from the powers granted by the Constitution and the laws made by Congress.[12] Thus, any person properly elected and sworn in as president will possess all of the power held by the strongest presidents in American history. That is true regardless of how large or small a margin of victory a president has. *The popular base of the presidency is important less because it gives the president power than because it gives him consent to use all the powers already granted by the Constitution.* Anyone installed in the office could exercise most of its powers.

The presidency is a democratic institution. Although the office is not free from the influence of powerful interests in society, neither is it a product or a captive of any one set of interests. Its broad popular base is a great resource for presidential power. *But resources are not power.* They must be converted to power, and as in physics, energy is expended in the conversion. It took more than a century, perhaps as much as a century and a half, before presidential government came to replace congressional government. A bit of historical review will be helpful in understanding how presidential government arose.

The Legislative Epoch, 1800–1933

In 1885, an obscure political science professor named Woodrow Wilson entitled his general textbook *Congressional Government* because American government was just that, "congressional government." This characterization seemed to fly in the face of the separation of powers principle that the three separate branches were and ought to be equal. Nevertheless, the clear intent of the framers of the Constitution was for *legislative supremacy*. As we saw in Chapter 3, the strongest evidence of this original intent is the fact that the powers of the national government were listed in Article I, the legislative article. Madison had laid it out explicitly in *The Federalist*, No. 51: "In republican government, the legislative authority necessarily predominates."

The first decade of America's government was unique precisely because it was first; everything was precedent making, and nothing was secure. It was a state-building decade in which relations between president and Congress were more cooperative than they would be at any time thereafter. Before the Republic was a decade old, Congress began to develop a strong organization, including its own elected leadership, the first standing committees, and the party hierarchies. Consequently, by the second term of President Jefferson (1805), the executive branch was beginning to play the secondary role anticipated by the Constitution. The quality of presidential performance and then of presidential personality and character declined accordingly. The president was seen by some observers as little more than America's "chief clerk." Of President James Madison, who had been the principal author of the Constitution, it was said that he knew everything about government except how to govern. Indeed, after Jefferson and until the beginning of this century, most historians agree that Presidents Jackson and Lincoln were the only exceptions to what was the rule of weak presidents; and those two exceptions can be explained, since one was a war hero and founder of the Democratic party and the other was a wartime president and the first leader of the newly founded Republican party.

One reason that so few great men became presidents in the nineteenth century is that there was only occasional room for greatness in such a weak

---

[12]This very useful distinction between *power* and *powers* is inspired by Richard E. Neustadt, *Presidential Power* (New York: Wiley, 1960), p. 28.

office.[13] As Chapter 3 indicated, the national government of that period was not particularly powerful. Another reason is that during this period, the presidency was not closely linked to major national political and social forces. Federalism had taken very good care of this by fragmenting political interests and diverting the energies of interest groups toward state and local governments, where most key decisions were being made.

The presidency was strengthened somewhat in the 1830s with the introduction of the national convention system of nominating presidential candidates. Until then, presidential candidates had been nominated by their party's congressional delegates. This was the caucus system of nominating candidates, and it was derisively called "King Caucus" because any candidate for president had to defer to the party's leaders in Congress in order to get the party's nomination and the support of the party's congressional delegation in the election. The national nominating convention arose outside Congress in order to provide some representation for a party's voters who lived in districts where they weren't numerous enough to elect a member of Congress. The political party in each state made its own provisions for selecting delegates to attend the presidential nominating convention, and in virtually all states, the selection was dominated by the party leaders (called "bosses" by the opposition party). Only in recent decades have state laws intervened to regularize the selection process and provide (in all but a few instances) for open election of delegates.

In the nineteenth century, the national nominating convention was seen as a victory for democracy against the congressional elite. And the national convention gave the presidency a base of power independent of Congress. Eventually, though more slowly, the presidential selection process began to be further democratized, with the adoption of primary elections through which millions of ordinary citizens were given an opportunity to take part in the presidential nominating process by popular selection of convention delegates.

This independence did not immediately transform the presidency into the office we recognize today, because Congress was able to keep tight reins on the president's power. The real turning point came during the administration of Franklin Delano Roosevelt. The New Deal was a response to political forces that had been gathering national strength and focus for fifty years. What is remarkable is not that they gathered but that they were so long gaining influence in Washington.

The New Deal and the Presidency

The "First Hundred Days" of the Roosevelt administration in 1933 have no parallel in U.S. history. But this period was only the beginning. The policies proposed by President Roosevelt and adopted by Congress during the first thousand days of his administration so changed the size and character of the national government that they constitute a moment in American history equivalent to the founding or to the Civil War. The president's constitutional obligation to see "that the laws be faithfully executed" became, during Roosevelt's presidency, virtually a responsibility to *shape* the laws before executing them.

NEW PROGRAMS EXPAND THE ROLE OF NATIONAL GOVERNMENT   Many of the New Deal programs were extensions of the traditional national government approach, which was described in Chapter 3 (see especially Table 3.1, p. 44). But the New Deal also adopted policies never before tried on a large scale by the national government. It began intervening into economic life in ways that had hitherto

[13]For related appraisals, see Jeffrey Tulis, *The Rhetorical Presidency* (Princeton: Princeton University Press, 1988); Stephen Skowronek, *The Politics Presidents Make: Presidential Leadership from John Adams to George Bush* (Cambridge, MA: Harvard University Press, 1993); and Robert Spitzer, *President and Congress: Executive Hegemony at the Crossroads of American Government* (New York: McGraw-Hill, 1993).

been reserved to the states. In other words, the national government discovered that it, too, had "police power" and could directly regulate individuals as well as provide roads and other services.

The new programs were such dramatic departures from the traditional polices of the national government that their constitutionality was in doubt. The turning point came in 1937 with *National Labor Relations Board v. Jones & Laughlin Steel Corporation*. At issue was the National Labor Relations Act, or Wagner Act, which prohibited corporations from interfering with the efforts of employees to engage in union activities. The newly formed National Labor Relations Board (NLRB) had ordered Jones & Laughlin to reinstate workers fired because of their union activities. The appeal reached the Supreme Court because Jones & Laughlin had made a constitutional issue over the fact that its manufacturing activities were local and therefore beyond the national government's reach. The Supreme Court rejected this argument with the response that a big company with subsidiaries and suppliers in many states was innately in interstate commerce.[14] Since the end of the New Deal, the Supreme Court has never again questioned the constitutionality of an important act of Congress authorizing the executive branch to intervene into the economy or society.[15]

DELEGATION OF POWER   The most important constitutional effect of Congress's actions and the Supreme Court's approval of those actions during the New Deal was the enhancement of *presidential power*. Most major acts of Congress in this period involved significant exercises of control over the economy. But few programs specified the actual controls to be used. Instead, Congress authorized the president or, in some cases, a new agency to determine what the controls would be. Some of the new agencies were independent commissions responsible to Congress. But most of the new agencies and programs of the New Deal were placed in the executive branch directly under presidential authority.

This form of congressional act is called the "delegation of power." In theory, the delegation of power works as follows: (1) Congress recognizes a problem; (2) Congress acknowledges that it has neither the time nor the expertise to deal with the problem; and (3) Congress therefore sets the basic policies and then delegates to an agency the power to "fill in the details." But in practice, Congress was delegating not merely the power to "fill in the details," but actual and real *policy-making powers*, that is, real legislative powers, to the executive branch.

No modern government can avoid the delegation of significant legislative powers to the executive branch. But the fact remains that these delegations of power cumulatively produced a fundamental shift in the American constitutional framework. *During the 1930s, the growth of the national government through acts delegating legislative power tilted the American national structure away from a Congress-centered government toward a president-centered government.* Congress continues to be the constitutional source of policy, and Congress can rescind these delegations of power or restrict them with later amendments, committee

---

[14]NLRB v. Jones & Laughlin Steel Corporation, 301 U.S. 1 (1937). Congress had attempted to regulate the economy before 1933, as with the Interstate Commerce Act and Sherman Antitrust Act of the late nineteenth century and with the Federal Trade Act and the Federal Reserve in the Wilson period. But these were rare attempts, and each was restricted very carefully to a narrow and acceptable definition of "interstate commerce." The big break did not come until after 1933.

[15]Some will argue that there are at least two exceptions to this statement. One was the 1976 case declaring unconstitutional Congress's effort to supply national minimum wage stan-

dards to state and local government employees (National League of Cities v. Usery, 426 U.S. 833 [1976]). But the Court reversed itself on this nine years later, in 1985 (Garcia v. San Antonio Metropolitan Transit Authority, 469 U.S. 528 [1985]). The second exception was the 1986 case declaring unconstitutional the part of the Gramm-Rudman law authorizing the comptroller general to make "across the board" budget cuts when total appropriations exceeded legally established ceilings (Bowsher v. Synar, 478 U.S. 714 [1986]). But cases such as these are few and far between, and they only touch on part of a law, not the constitutionality of an entire program.

ELEANOR ROOSEVELT AND HILLARY RODHAM CLINTON
Going Beyond What Is Expected

THE CONSTITUTION provides for a president, but not for a first lady. Yet throughout history, presidential wives have played an important, even decisive role in the administrations of their spouses. Two of the most active and controversial first ladies are also among the most accomplished.

Eleanor Roosevelt was born in 1884 into a socially prominent New York family; she was the niece of future president Theodore Roosevelt. At the age of 19, she married her fifth cousin, Franklin Roosevelt. As Franklin rose in the ranks of New York state and national politics, Eleanor was drawn reluctantly into political life; such involvement was expected of a politician's wife. In 1921, Franklin was stricken with polio, which paralyzed him for the rest of his life. Over her objections, but in an effort to keep Franklin's political ambitions alive, Eleanor was thrust alone into the political world during her husband's long recuperation. By the time Franklin was elected governor of New York in 1928, Eleanor was one of her husband's most important political advisers.

Franklin Roosevelt's election to the presidency in 1932 ushered in a new political era, as well as a first lady who broke with more conventions than any of her predecessors had. Eleanor became the first first lady to hold regular press conferences. Because her husband's paralysis limited his travel, Eleanor toured the country and world on his behalf. She wrote a daily newspaper column and delivered countless lectures and talks. She was a tireless advocate for the poor, the working class, blacks, and other disadvantaged groups, and she advised her husband daily on policy issues. In addition, she was the first first lady to hold a formal governmental post: assistant director of the Office of Civilian Defense. Yet despite her accomplishments, she was widely ridiculed in print and on the radio for her pivotal role in the administration; these "Eleanor jokes" continued throughout her husband's administration.

Hillary Rodham Clinton is the product of a very different political and social world, one in which women are no longer obliged to stand in the shadows of their husbands. Hillary Rodham was born in 1947 and was raised in the Chicago area, where she demonstrated acade-

ELEANOR ROOSEVELT

---

oversight, or budget costs. But since Congress has continued to enact large new programs involving very broad delegations of legislative power to the executive branch, and since the Court has gone along with such actions,[16] we can say that presi-

dential government has become an established fact of American life.

---

[16]The Supreme Court did in fact *dis*approve broad delegations of legislative power by declaring the National Industrial Recovery Act of 1933 unconstitutional on the grounds that Congress did not accompany the broad delegations with

sufficient standards or guidelines for presidential discretion (Panama Refining Co. v. Ryan, 293 U.S. 388 [1935], and Schechter Poultry Corp. v. U.S., 295 U.S. 495 [1935]). The Supreme Court has never reversed those two decisions, but it has also never really followed them. Thus, broad delegations of legislative power from Congress to the executive branch can be presumed to be constitutional.

mic excellence and leadership early on. While a student at Yale Law School, she met her future husband, Bill Clinton, whom she married in 1975. In the years before her marriage, she worked for Marian Wright Edelman's Washington Research Project (which later became the Children's Defense Fund), providing legal aid to children and the poor. She also served as one of only three women lawyers working on the impeachment investigation of Richard Nixon being conducted by the House Judiciary Committee.

Hillary joined Bill in Arkansas in 1974, teaching part-time at the University of Arkansas law school while assisting her husband's rising career. During Clinton's tenure as Arkansas governor, Hillary worked full-time as a partner in the state's biggest law firm. She also headed the governor's Rural Health Advisory Committee and directed a successful effort to improve the state public-education system.

Hillary played a similarly prominent role in Bill's 1992 presidential campaign; she is credited, in fact, with persuading him to run that year. Yet even during the campaign, she encountered criticism from many who found her influence too great. In an effort to soften her image, campaign handlers tried to emphasize her commitment to children and family issues, areas where the first lady's influence is traditionally more widely accepted.

After the election, Hillary became active in White House policy making, most notably being designated by the president to head the Task Force on National Health Care Reform, one of the primary policy priorities of the Clinton administration. Of course, some complained about the prominent role of the first lady, and many blamed her for the failure to pass health care reform during the 103rd Congress (1993–94). Nevertheless, she won respect for her intelligence and political toughness.

During the 1992 campaign, Bill Clinton boasted that Americans who voted for him were getting added value at no extra cost, saying that voters could "buy one, get one free," referring to himself and Hillary. But Hillary Clinton was by no means the first such package deal in the history of the presidency.

HILLARY RODHAM CLINTON

SOURCE: Betty Boyd Caroli, *First Ladies* (New York: Oxford University Press, 1987).

PRESIDENTIAL GOVERNMENT

There was no great mystery in the shift from Congress-centered government to president-centered government. Congress simply delegated its own powers to the executive branch. Congressional delegations of power, however, are not the only resources available to the president. Presidents have at their disposal a variety of other formal and informal resources that enable them to govern. Indeed, without these other resources, presidents would lack the tools needed to make much use of the power and responsibility given to them by Congress. Let us first consider the president's formal or official resources. Then, in the section following, we will turn to the more informal resources that affect a president's capacity to govern, in particular the president's popular support.

FIGURE 6.1

The Institutional Presidency*

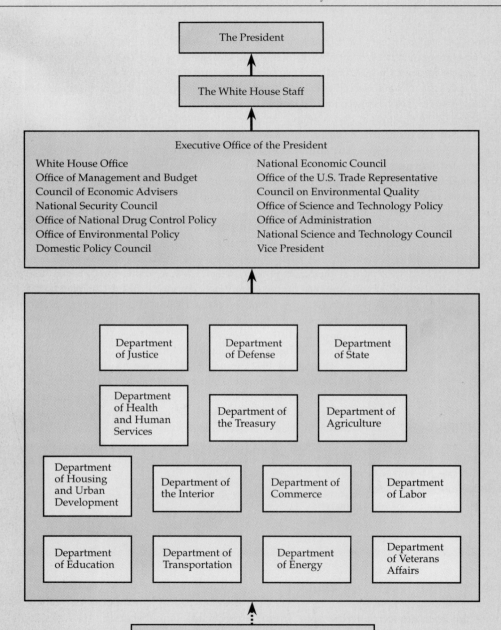

The President

The White House Staff

Executive Office of the President

White House Office
Office of Management and Budget
Council of Economic Advisers
National Security Council
Office of National Drug Control Policy
Office of Environmental Policy
Domestic Policy Council

National Economic Council
Office of the U.S. Trade Representative
Council on Environmental Quality
Office of Science and Technology Policy
Office of Administration
National Science and Technology Council
Vice President

Department of Justice

Department of Defense

Department of State

Department of Health and Human Services

Department of the Treasury

Department of Agriculture

Department of Housing and Urban Development

Department of the Interior

Department of Commerce

Department of Labor

Department of Education

Department of Transportation

Department of Energy

Department of Veterans Affairs

Independent Commissions, Establishments, and Government Corporations†

*Note: Arrows are used to indicate lines of legal responsibility.
†There are fifty-six independent regulatory commissions in the executive branch, but they are legally responsible to Congress, not directly to the president.

SOURCE: *Congressional Quarterly's Washington Information Directory, 1994–1995* (Washington, DC: Congressional Quarterly Press, 1994), p. 4.

Formal Resources of Presidential Power

PATRONAGE AS A TOOL OF MANAGEMENT The first tool of management available to most presidents is a form of *patronage*—the choice of high-level political appointees. These appointments allow presidents to fill top management positions with individuals committed to their agendas and, at the same time, to build links to powerful political and economic interests by giving them representation in the administration.

When President Clinton took office, he had about 4,000 appointments he could make "at the pleasure of the president." At the top are roughly 700 cabinet and high-level White House positions. Next are about 800 Senior Executive Service (SES) positions that can be appointed from outside the career service.[17] Although 4,000 plums were far too many appointments for President Clinton to make personally, as a person committed to being a "strong president," he did supervise a large percentage of these appointments.

THE CABINET In the American system of government, the *cabinet* is the traditional but informal designation for the heads of all the major federal government departments. The cabinet has no constitutional status. Unlike that of England and many other parliamentary countries, where the cabinet *is* the government, the American cabinet is not a collective body. It meets but makes no decisions as a group. Each appointment must be approved by the Senate, but the person appointed is not responsible to the Senate or to Congress at large. Cabinet appointments help build party and popular support, but the cabinet is not a party organ. The cabinet is made up of directors but is not a board of directors.

Why can't a president have a real cabinet that serves as a board of directors and as a collective lightning rod to share political responsibilities? The explanation lies deep in the American system of national politics, which catches the cabinet and each member of it in a web of three basic interacting forces:

1. Each presidential candidate must build a winning electoral coalition, state by state. Expectations come to focus *personally* on the candidate, who is under too much personal pressure, once nominated, to stop and create a viable cabinet. In fact, by the time a president is inaugurated, it is already too late to create a cabinet government. Presidents don't even know personally some of their appointees, and many of them don't know each other.
2. Cabinet members have their own constituencies and are usually selected by the president because of the support they can bring with them. But these constituencies do not automatically transfer to the president, and they may be at odds with the president's wishes. For the same reason, it is extremely difficult to remove a cabinet member or other high-level official.
3. Each cabinet member heads a department that is composed of a large bureaucracy with a momentum of its own. Cabinet members often face a choice between giving loyalty to the president or gaining the loyalty of their department.

Aware of this web of forces, presidents tend to develop a burning impatience with and a mild distrust of cabinet members. Presidents seek to make the cabinet a rubber stamp for actions already decided on, demanding results, or the appearance of results, more immediately and more frequently than most department heads can provide. Since cabinet appointees generally come from differing careers, the formation of an effective, governing group out of this motley collection of appointments is very unlikely.

President Clinton's insistence on a cabinet diverse enough to resemble American society could be considered an act of political wisdom. On the other hand, it virtually guaranteed that few of his appointees would ever have spent any time working together or would know the policy positions or beliefs of the other appointees.

[17]For a complete directory of these exempt positions, see Committee on Post Office and Civil Service, House of Representatives, *United States Government, Policy and Supporting Positions* (Washington, DC: Government Printing Office, 1992).

Some presidents have relied heavily on an "inner cabinet," the **National Security Council (NSC)**. The NSC, established by law in 1947, is composed of the president, the vice president, the secretaries of state, defense, and the treasury, the attorney general, and other officials invited by the president. It has its own staff of foreign-policy specialists run by the special assistant to the president for national security affairs. A counterpart, the Domestic Council, was created by law in 1970, but no specific members were designated for it. President Clinton hit upon his own version of the Domestic Council, called the National Economic Council, which shares competing functions with the Council of Economic Advisers.

Presidents have obviously been uneven and unpredictable in their reliance on the NSC and other subcabinet bodies, because executive management is inherently a personal matter. However, despite all the personal variations, one generalization can be made: Presidents have increasingly preferred the White House staff to the cabinet as their means of managing the gigantic executive branch.

THE WHITE HOUSE STAFF   The White House staff is composed mainly of analysts and advisers. Although many of the top White House staffers are given the title "special assistant" for a particular task or sector, the types of judgments they are expected to make and the kinds of advice they are supposed to give are a good deal broader and more generally political than those that come from the cabinet departments or the Executive Office of the President. For example, the special assistant to the president for intergovernmental affairs will advise the president on the functioning of the various branches of government.

From an informal group of fewer than a dozen people (popularly called the **Kitchen Cabinet**), and no more than four dozen at the height of the domestic Roosevelt presidency in 1937, the White House staff has grown substantially (see Table 6.1).[18] Richard Nixon employed 550 people in

[18]All the figures since 1967, and probably 1957, are understated; additional White House staff members who were on "detailed" service from the military and other departments are not counted here because they were not on the White House payroll.

TABLE 6.1

The Expanding White House Staff

Year	President	Full-time Employees	Year	President	Full-time Employees*
1937	Franklin D. Roosevelt	45	1975	Gerald R. Ford	533
1947	Harry S. Truman	190	1980	Jimmy Carter	488
1957	Dwight D. Eisenhower	364	1984	Ronald Reagan	575
1967	Lyndon B. Johnson	251	1992	George Bush	605**
1972	Richard M. Nixon	550	1996	Bill Clinton	514**

*The vice president employs over 20 staffers, and there are at least 100 on the staff of the National Security Council. These people work in and around the White House and Executive Office but are not included in the above totals.

**These figures include the staffs of the Office of the President, the Executive Residence, and the Office of the Vice President, according to OMB. They don't include the 50 to 75 employees temporarily detailed to the White House from outside agencies. While not precisely comparable to previous years, these figures convey a sense of scale.

SOURCES: Thomas E. Cronin, "The Swelling of the Presidency: Can Anyone Reverse the Tide?" in *American Government: Readings and Cases*, 8th ed., ed. Peter Woll (Boston: Little, Brown, 1984), p. 347. Copyright © 1984 by Thomas E. Cronin. Reproduced with the permission of the author. For 1990: U.S. Office of Personnel Management, *Federal Civilian Workforce Statistics, Employment and Trends as of January 1990* (Washington, DC: Government Printing Office, 1990), p. 29. For 1992 and 1996: Office of Management and Budget and the White House.

1972. President Carter, who found so many of the requirements of presidential power distasteful, and who publicly vowed to keep his staff small and decentralized, built an even larger and more centralized staff.

President Clinton promised during the 1992 campaign to reduce the White House staff by 25 percent, and by 1996 had trimmed it by 15 percent. Nevertheless, a large White House staff has become essential.

The biggest variation among presidential management practices lies not in the size of the White House staff but in its organization. President Reagan went to the extreme in delegating important management powers to his chief of staff, and he elevated his budget director to an unprecedented level of power in *policy* making rather than merely *budget* making. President Bush centralized his staff even more under his chief of staff, John Sununu. At the same time, Bush continued to deal directly with his cabinet heads, the press, and key members of Congress. President Clinton showed a definite preference for competition among equals in his cabinet and among senior White House officials, obviously liking competition and conflict among staff members, for which FDR's staff was also famous. But the troubles Clinton has had in turning this conflict and competition into coherent policies and clear messages suggests that he might have done better to emulate his immediate predecessors in their preference for hierarchy and centralization.[19]

THE EXECUTIVE OFFICE OF THE PRESIDENT   The development of the White House staff can be appreciated only in its relation to the still larger Executive Office of the President (EOP). Created in 1939, the EOP is what is often called the "institutional presidency"—the permanent agencies that perform defined management tasks for the presi-

dent (see Figure 6.2 on page 152). Somewhere between fifteen hundred and two thousand highly specialized people work for EOP agencies.[20]

The numbers in parentheses in Figure 6.2 are the official numbers of employees in each EOP agency. The importance of each agency varies according to the personal orientations of each president. For example, the NSC staff was of immense importance under President Nixon, especially because it served essentially as the personal staff of presidential assistant Henry Kissinger. But it was of less importance to President Bush, who looked outside the EOP altogether for military policy matters, much more to the Joint Chiefs of Staff and its chair, General Colin Powell.

The status and power of the Office of Management and Budget (OMB) within the EOP has grown in importance from president to president. Under President Reagan, the budget director was granted cabinet status. Presidents Bush and Clinton continued to increase the director's role, but even if they had not chosen to make the budget director a virtual prime minister, circumstances would have imposed the choice upon them. In 1974, Congress passed the Budget and Impoundment Act, to impose upon itself a more rational approach to the budget. Up until 1974, congressional budget decisions were decentralized, with budget decisions made by the appropriations committees and subcommittees in the House and Senate, and with revenue decisions made independently by the House Ways and Means Committee and by the Senate Finance Committee. The primary purpose of the 1974 act was to impose enough discipline on congressional budget decision making to enable Congress as a whole to confront the presidency more effectively. This centralization of Congress's budget process also centralized the executive budget process, concentrating it more than ever in the OMB.

[19]See Donna K. H. Walters, "The Disarray at the White House Proves Clinton Wouldn't Last as a Fortune 500 CEO," *The Plain Dealer*, 10 July 1994, p. 1C; and Paul Richter, "The Battle for Washington: Leon Panetta's Burden," *Los Angeles Times Sunday Magazine*, 8 January 1995, p. 16.

[20]The actual number is difficult to estimate because some EOP personnel, especially in national security work, are detailed to EOP from outside agencies.

FIGURE 6.2

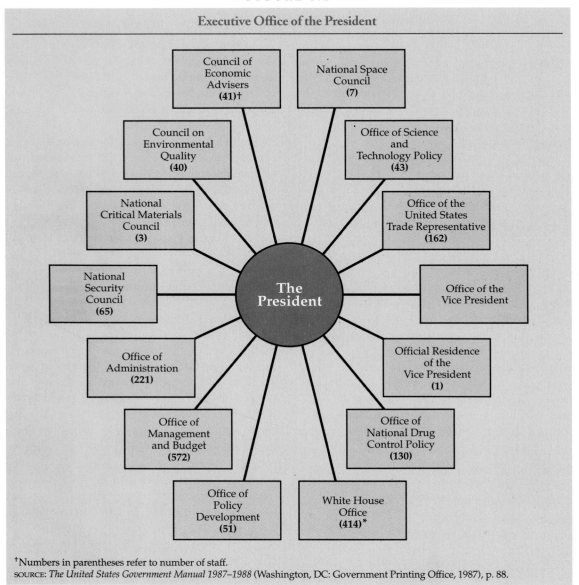

Executive Office of the President

Council of Economic Advisers (41)†

National Space Council (7)

Council on Environmental Quality (40)

Office of Science and Technology Policy (43)

National Critical Materials Council (3)

Office of the United States Trade Representative (162)

National Security Council (65)

The President

Office of the Vice President

Office of Administration (221)

Official Residence of the Vice President (1)

Office of Management and Budget (572)

Office of National Drug Control Policy (130)

Office of Policy Development (51)

White House Office (414)*

†Numbers in parentheses refer to number of staff.
SOURCE: *The United States Government Manual 1987–1988* (Washington, DC: Government Printing Office, 1987), p. 88.

Budgeting is no longer "bottom up," with expenditure and program requests passing from the lowest bureaus through the departments to "clearance" in OMB and hence to Congress, where each agency could be called in to reveal what its "original request" had been before OMB got hold of it. The process became one of "top down," with OMB setting the budget guidelines for agencies as well as for Congress.

THE VICE PRESIDENCY   The vice presidency was created along with the presidency by the

PROCESS BOX 6.2

The Budget and Deficit Process Set by Law for 1992–1996

Schedule for the Budget

First Monday in February (Budget Day): President's budget is sent to Congress.

February 25: House and Senate authorizing committees submit their estimates to the budget committees.

April 1–15: Budget resolutions from budget committees are submitted for passage; integrated appropriations tied to revenue estimates.

June 10–15: Appropriations Committee reports out all appropriations bills; Congress passes single budget reconciliation bill.

June 30: All appropriations bills are adopted.

October 1: Fiscal year begins—or is postponed by continuing resolutions until budget agreement is worked out.

Schedule for Deficit and Sequestration

January 21: President must notify Congress if he will exercise his discretion to adjust the maximum allowable deficit amounts for the next fiscal year.

Budget Day minus 5: Congressional Budget Office (CBO) makes its sequestration review report.

Budget Day: OMB must send its sequestration review report with the budget.

August 10: President must notify Congress if he intends to exempt military personnel from sequestration or to sequester at lower rate.

August 20: OMB sequestration update report.

End of Session + 15 days: OMB files final sequestration report; President/OMB decide if sequestration is needed.

End of Session + 30 days: General Accounting Office (GAO) files compliance report.

Constitution and exists for two purposes only: to succeed the president in the case of a vacancy[21] and to preside over the Senate, casting the tie-breaking vote when necessary.[22] The main value of the vice presidency as a political resource for the president is electoral. Traditionally, a presidential candidate's most important rule for the choice of a running mate is that he or she bring the support of at least one state (preferably a large one) not otherwise likely to support the ticket. Another rule holds that the vice presidential nominee should come from a region and, where possible, from an ideological or ethnic subsection of the party differing from the presidential nominee's. It is very doubtful that John Kennedy would have won in 1960 without his vice presidential candidate, Lyndon Johnson, and the contribution Johnson made to carrying Texas. The emphasis has recently shifted away from geographical to ideological balance. Bill Clinton combined considerations of a region and ideology in his selection of a vice presidential running mate. The choice of Al Gore signaled that Bill Clinton was solidly in the right wing of the Democratic party and would remain steadfastly a Southerner. Democratic strategists had become convinced that Clinton could not win without carrying a substantial number of Southern states.

Presidents have constantly promised to give their vice presidents more responsibility, but they almost always break their promise. No one can explain exactly why. Perhaps it is just too much trouble to share responsibility. But management

style is certainly a key factor. President Clinton has relied greatly on his vice president, Al Gore, and Gore has emerged as one of the most trusted and effective figures in the Clinton White House. Vice President Gore's relatively enhanced status was signalled early on, when President Clinton kept him ostentatiously present in all public appearances during the transition and during the vital public and private efforts to present and campaign for the president's program early in 1993. Since then, he has remained one of the consistently praised members of the administration. Gore's most important task in the Clinton White House has been to oversee the National Performance Review (NPR), an ambitious program to "reinvent" the way the federal government conducts its affairs. The NPR was initially dismissed as show rather than substance, but even the administration's toughest critics have had to admit that Gore has led the drive to streamline the federal government with energy and effectiveness. With President Clinton's re-election, Gore's stature and role have increased as a key advisor on new cabinet appointments. This takes on all the greater significance because it gives Gore an ideal opportunity to build his Washington base and his national reputation toward a run for the presidency in 2000.

Informal Resources of Presidential Power

ELECTIONS AS A RESOURCE   Although we emphasized earlier that even an ordinary citizen, legitimately placed in office, would be a very powerful president, there is no denying that a decisive presidential election translates into a more effective presidency. Some presidents claim that a landslide election gives them a *"mandate,"* by which they mean that the electorate approved the programs offered in the campaign and that Congress ought to therefore go along. And Congress is not unmoved by such an appeal. The Johnson and Reagan landslides of 1964 and 1980 gave them real strength during their honeymoon year. In

---

[21]This provision was clarified by the Twenty-fifth Amendment (1967), which provides that the president (with majority confirmation of House and Senate) must appoint someone to fill the office of vice president if the vice president should die or should fill a vacancy in the presidency. This procedure has been invoked twice—once in 1973 when President Nixon nominated Gerald Ford, and the second time in 1974 when President Ford, having automatically succeeded the resigned President Nixon, filled the vice presidential vacancy with Nelson Rockefeller.

[22]Article I, Section 3, provides that the vice president "shall be President of the Senate, but shall have no Vote, unless they be equally divided."

RESOURCES OF PRESIDENTIAL POWER

Formal Resources of Presidential Power

patronage—presidents fills top management positions with persons committed to their agendas and with individuals who represent powerful political and economic interests.

cabinet—another venue where presidents may appoint individuals with important political and economic interests. Presidents want the cabinet to rubber stamp actions already decided on.

National Security Council (NSC)—some presidents rely heavily on this "inner cabinet" comprised of the president, the vice president, the secretaries of state, defense, and the treasury, and the attorney general.

White House staff—presidents have increasingly preferred to rely on the White House Staff, which consists of analysts and advisers, to manage the executive branch.

Executive Office of the President (EOP)—permanent agencies that perform defined tasks for the president. The agencies vary in importance from president to president, but the Office of Management and Budget (OMB) has been relied upon increasingly by the chief executive.

vice presidency—the main value of the vice presidency is electoral. Presidential candidates select a running mate who will bring the support of a state whose votes they might not win otherwise.

Informal Resources of Presidential Power

elections—Some presidents who have won elections by a large percentage feel they have been given a mandate, meaning that the electorate has approved their programs and Congress should therefore go along.

initiative—presidents are better able to initiate decisive action than is Congress because the legislative body must get a majority of its members to agree on something before it can move forward.

media—Press conferences have been the primary avenue for media access to the chief executive, but other forums, such as direct television addresses, radio broadcasts, and now television talk shows, are used.

party—party can be a resource in passing legislation because legislators of the president's party will often support legislation put forward by the chief executive.

groups—groups organized by regional or ethnic interests, by labor concerns, by big business concerns, or by religious belief can provide core bases of support for presidents.

mass popularity—decisive presidential actions, particularly in foreign policy, often increase a president's popularity, but usually only briefly, and the trend is for presidential popularity to decrease throughout a president's term in office.

contrast, the close elections of Kennedy in 1960, Nixon in 1968, and Carter in 1976 seriously hampered their effectiveness.

President Clinton, an action-oriented president, was seriously hampered by having been elected in 1992 by a minority of the popular vote, a mere 43 percent. Clinton was re-elected in 1996 with 49 percent of the vote, a larger percentage of the electorate but still a minority. His appeals to

bipartisanship in early 1997 reflected his lack of a mandate.

INITIATIVE AS A RESOURCE   "To initiate" means to originate, and in government that can mean power. The president as an individual is able to initiate decisive action, while Congress as a relatively large assembly must deliberate and debate before it can act.

Over the years, Congress has sometimes deliberately and sometimes inadvertently enhanced the president's power to seize the initiative. Curiously, the most important congressional gift to the president seems the most mundane, namely, the Office of Management and Budget (OMB), known until 1974 as the Bureau of the Budget.

In 1921, Congress provided for an "executive budget" and turned over to a new Bureau of the Budget in the executive branch the responsibility for maintaining the nation's accounts. In 1939, this bureau was moved from the Treasury Department to the newly created Executive Office of the President. The purpose of this move was to enable the president to make better use of the budgeting process as a management tool. In addition, Congress provided for a process called *legislative clearance*, which enables the president to require all agencies of the executive branch to submit through the budget director all requests for new legislation along with estimates of their budgetary needs.[23] Thus, heads of agencies must submit budget requests to the White House so that the requests of all the competing agencies can be balanced. Although there are many violations of this rule, it is usually observed.

At first, legislative clearance was a defensive weapon, used mainly to allow presidents to avoid the embarrassment of having to oppose or veto legislation originating in their own administrations. But eventually, legislative clearance became far more important. It became the starting point for the development of comprehensive presidential programs.[24] As noted earlier, recent presidents have also used the budget process as a method of gaining tighter "top down" management control. Professed anti-government Republicans, such as Reagan and Bush, as well as allegedly pro-government Democrats, such as Clinton, are alike in their commitment to central management control and program planning. This is precisely why all three recent presidents have given the budget directorship cabinet status.

PRESIDENTIAL USE OF THE MEDIA   The president is able to take full advantage of access to the communications media mainly because of the legal and constitutional bases of initiative. Virtually all the media look to the White House as the chief source of news, and they tend to assign their most skillful reporters to the White House "beat." Since news is money, they need the president as much as the president needs them to meet their mutual need to make news. Presidents have successfully gotten from Congress significant additions to their staff to take care of press releases and other forms of communications.

Presidential personalities affect how the media are used by each president. Although Franklin Roosevelt gave several press conferences a month, they were not recorded or broadcast live; direct quotes were not permitted. The model we know today got its start with Eisenhower and was put into final form by Kennedy. Since 1961, the presidential press conference has been a distinctive institution, available whenever the president wants to dominate the news. About 400 reporters attend and file their accounts within minutes of the concluding words, "Thank you, Mr. President."

But despite the importance of the press conference, its value to each president has varied. Its use declines notably when presidents are in political trouble. Although the average from Kennedy through Carter was about two press conferences a month, Johnson dropped virtually out of sight for almost half of 1965 when Vietnam was warming up, and so did Nixon for over five months in 1973 during the Watergate hearings. President Reagan

---

[23]Sometimes in appropriations hearings before committees, a member of Congress will attempt to reverse the OMB effort to hold down requests by asking an executive branch witness to reveal "what was your original request." But generally the rule of clearance through OMB and the White House has been observed. The clearance function was formalized in 1940.

[24]Although dated in some respects, the best description and evaluation of budgeting as a management tool and as a tool of program planning is still found in Richard E. Neustadt's two classic articles, "Presidency and Legislation: Planning the President's Program" and "Presidency and Legislation: The Growth of Central Clearance," in *American Political Science Review,* September 1954 and December 1955.

was not comfortable with the give and take of press conferences. He single-handedly brought the average down by holding only seven press conferences during his first year in office and only sporadically thereafter.

In great contrast, President Bush held more news conferences during his first seventeen months than Reagan did in eight years. Moreover, Bush shifted them from elaborate prime-time affairs in the ornate East Room to less formal gatherings in the White House briefing room. Fewer reporters and more time for follow-up questions permitted media representatives to "concentrate on information for their stories, rather than getting attention for themselves."[25]

President Clinton has tended to take both Reagan's and Bush's approaches, combining Reagan's high profile—elaborate press conferences and prime-time broadcasts—with the more personal one-on-one approach generally preferred by Bush. But thanks to Ross Perot, there is now a third approach, for which President Clinton has shown a certain aptitude—the informal and basically nonpolitical talk shows, such as those of Larry King, MTV, and Oprah Winfrey. Such an informal approach has its risks, however: President Clinton is widely perceived as lacking the gravity a president is expected to possess. It is hard to argue with this conclusion when one considers that he is the first president to answer a question (on MTV) about what kind of underwear he wears.

Of course, in addition to the presidential press conference there are other routes from the White House to news prominence.[26] For example, President Nixon preferred direct television addresses, and President Carter tried to make his initiatives more homey with a television adaptation of

President Roosevelt's "fireside chats." President Reagan made unusually good use of prime-time television addresses and also instituted more informal but regular Saturday afternoon radio broadcasts, a tradition that President Clinton has continued.

PARTY AS A PRESIDENTIAL RESOURCE   Although on the decline, the president's party is far from insignificant as a political resource, as Figure 6.3 dramatically demonstrates. The figure gives a forty-three-year history of the "presidential batting average" in Congress—the percentage of winning roll-call votes in Congress on bills publicly supported by the president. Note, for example, that President Eisenhower's "batting average" started out with a very impressive .900 but declined to .700 by the end of his first term and to little more than half his starting point by the end of his administration. The single most important explanation of this decline was Eisenhower's loss of a Republican party majority in Congress after 1954, the recapture of some seats in 1956, and then a significant loss of seats to the Democrats after the election of 1958.

The presidential batting average went back up and stayed consistently higher through the Kennedy and Johnson years, mainly because these two presidents enjoyed Democratic party majorities in the Senate and in the House. Even so, Johnson's batting average in the House dropped significantly during his last two years, following a very large loss of Democratic seats in the 1966 election. Note how much higher Carter's success rate was than that of Ford or Nixon during their last two years in office; this was clearly attributable to the *party* factor—the substantial Democratic party majorities in the two chambers of Congress.

At the same time, party has its limitations as a resource. The more unified the president's party is behind the president's legislative requests, the more unified the opposition party is also likely to be. Unless the president's party majority is very large, the White House must

[25]David Broder, "Some Newsworthy Presidential CPR," *Washington Post National Weekly Edition*, 4–10 June 1990, p. 4.

[26]See George Edwards III, *At the Margins—Presidential Leadership of Congress* (New Haven: Yale University Press, 1989), Chapter 7; and Robert Locander, "The President and the News Media," in *Dimensions of the Modern Presidency*, ed. Edward Kearny (St. Louis: Forum Press, 1981), pp. 49–52.

FIGURE 6.3

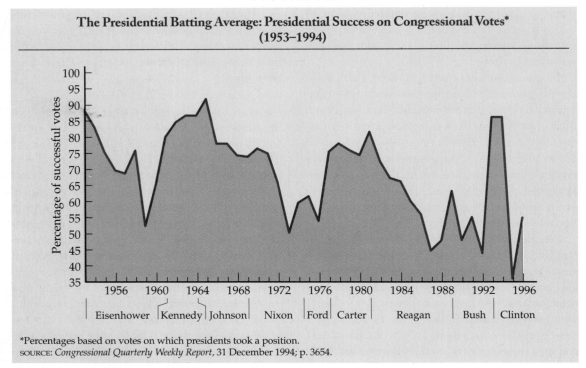

The Presidential Batting Average: Presidential Success on Congressional Votes*
(1953–1994)

*Percentages based on votes on which presidents took a position.
SOURCE: *Congressional Quarterly Weekly Report*, 31 December 1994; p. 3654.

also appeal to the opposition to make up for the inevitable defectors within the ranks of the president's own party. Consequently, the president often poses as being above partisanship in order to win "bipartisan" support in Congress. Thus, even though President Clinton enjoyed Democratic majorities in the House and the Senate during the first two years of his presidency, he had to be cautious with Republicans because the defection of just four or five Democrats in a close Senate vote could have endangered important but controversial legislation. To the extent that presidents pursue a bipartisan strategy, they cannot afford to throw themselves fully into building their own party discipline, and vice versa.

GROUPS AS A PRESIDENTIAL RESOURCE   The classic case in modern times of groups as a resource for the presidency is the New Deal coalition that supported President Franklin Roosevelt (see also

Chapter 14).[27] The New Deal coalition was composed of an inconsistent, indeed contradictory, set of interests. Some of these interests were not organized interest groups, but were regional or ethnic interests, such as Southern whites, or residents of large cities in the industrial Northeast and Midwest, or blacks who later succeeded in organizing as an interest group. In addition, there were several large, self-consciously organized interest groups, including organized labor, agriculture, and the financial community[28] All of

[27]A wider range of group phenomena will be covered in Chapter 11. In that chapter the focus is on the influence of groups *upon* the government and its policy-making processes. Here our concern is more with the relationship of groups to the presidency and the extent to which groups and coalitions become a dependable resource for presidential government.

[28]For updates on the group basis of presidential politics, see Thomas Ferguson, "Money and Politics," in *Handbooks to the Modern World—The United States*, vol. 2, ed. Godfrey Hodgson (New York: Facts on File, 1992), pp. 1060–84; and Lucius J. Barker, ed., "Black Electoral Politics," *National Political Science Review*, vol. 2 (New Brunswick, NJ: Transaction Publishers, 1990).

the parts were held together by a judicious use of patronage—not merely in jobs but also in policies. Many of the groups were permitted virtually to write their own legislation. In exchange, the groups supported President Roosevelt and his Democratic successors in their battles with opposing politicians.

Republicans have had their group coalition base, too, including not only their traditional segments of organized business, upper-income groups, and certain ethnic groups but also a very large share of traditionally Democratic Southern whites and Northern blue-collar workers. When the Reagan/Republican coalition began to loosen in the late 1980s, toward the end of the Bush administration, the Democrats were quick to sense it, especially the astute Bill Clinton, whose nomination chances were certainly improved by the fact that he was a Democrat from the New South—with emphasis on South. But try as he might, he did not succeed in bringing back together one more time the original elements of the New Deal coalition. He captured only 5 of the 13 Deep South states in 1992 (Georgia, Louisiana, Arkansas, Tennessee, and Kentucky) and a slightly different set of 5 in 1996 (Florida, Louisiana, Arkansas, Tennessee, and Kentucky). It would seem that the Republican party had finally incorporated the South into its national coalition—and it was reinforced by the heavily Southern concentration of the Christian Right. But Clinton seemed able to compensate for this by keeping the vast northeast, middle west, and far west states within the Democratic column. And he was able to make advances among corporate interests, despite the revival of Democratic support from the trade unions.[29]

MASS POPULARITY AS A RESOURCE (AND A LIABILITY)   As presidential government grew, a presidency developed whose power is linked directly to the people.[30] Successful presidents have to be able to mobilize mass opinion. But presidents tend to *use up* their mass resources as they *use* them. Virtually everyone is aware that presidents constantly make appeals to the public over the heads of Congress and the Washington community. But the mass public is not made up of fools. Americans generally react to presidential *actions* rather than mere speeches or other image-making devices.

The public's sensitivity to presidential actions can be seen in the tendency of all presidents since Kennedy to *lose* popular support over the course of their time in office (Figure 6.4). The general downward tendency is to be expected if the American voters are rational, since almost any action taken by the president is bound to please some voters and displease others. Public disapproval of specific actions has a cumulative effect on the president's overall performance rating.

All presidents are faced with the problem of keeping up their approval rating. And the public generally reacts favorably to presidential actions in foreign policy or, more precisely, to international events associated with the president. Analysts call this the *"rallying effect."* However, the rallying effect turns out be a momentary reversal of the more general tendency of presidents to lose popular support.

Because the public rallies behind the president when there is an international crisis, presidents are under pressure to use foreign events as a means of shoring up domestic political support. But Clinton enjoyed almost no rallying effect during his first term despite a number of front-page international events. The overall picture is presented on Figure 6.5 on page 161, so that only a few examples need to be provided here. Take Clinton's first front-page international event, the failure of his initial Bosnia peace effort, following a bombing attack on a Bosnian Serb airstrip, May 7, 1993. His approval rating actually dropped, from 55 percent approval

[29]For more up-to-date figures on the corporate members of the Clinton coalition, see Thomas Ferguson, *Golden Rule—The Investment Theory of Party Competition and the Logic of Money-Driven Political Systems* (Chicago: University of Chicago Press, 1995).

[30]For a book-length treatment of this shift, see Lowi, *The Personal President.* For an analysis of the character of mass democracy, see Benjamin Ginsberg, *The Captive Public* (New York: Basic Books, 1986).

FIGURE 6.4

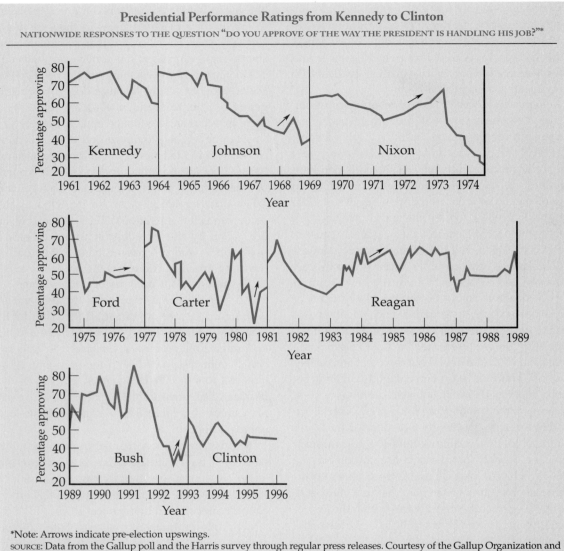

Presidential Performance Ratings from Kennedy to Clinton

NATIONWIDE RESPONSES TO THE QUESTION "DO YOU APPROVE OF THE WAY THE PRESIDENT IS HANDLING HIS JOB?"*

*Note: Arrows indicate pre-election upswings.
SOURCE: Data from the Gallup poll and the Harris survey through regular press releases. Courtesy of the Gallup Organization and Louis Harris & Associates.

in the April 24th poll to 44 percent approval in the post-event poll of May 21st. Take the spectacularly important Israel-Palestine peace accord of September 13: Clinton could only realize a modest 2 percent increase, from 44 percent in the late August poll to 46 percent in the mid-September poll.

In another case, the Somalia disaster, where 18 U.S. Marines were killed and their bodies dragged through the streets of Mogadishu—a type of event that had always produced a strong rallying effect in the past—Clinton's ratings went from 50 percent approval in early October to 47 percent ap-

FIGURE 6.5

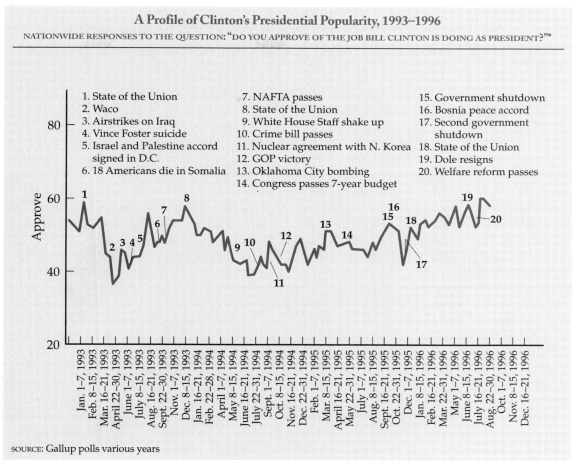

A Profile of Clinton's Presidential Popularity, 1993–1996

NATIONWIDE RESPONSES TO THE QUESTION: "DO YOU APPROVE OF THE JOB BILL CLINTON IS DOING AS PRESIDENT?"*

1. State of the Union
2. Waco
3. Airstrikes on Iraq
4. Vince Foster suicide
5. Israel and Palestine accord signed in D.C.
6. 18 Americans die in Somalia

7. NAFTA passes
8. State of the Union
9. White House Staff shake up
10. Crime bill passes
11. Nuclear agreement with N. Korea
12. GOP victory
13. Oklahoma City bombing
14. Congress passes 7-year budget

15. Government shutdown
16. Bosnia peace accord
17. Second government shutdown
18. State of the Union
19. Dole resigns
20. Welfare reform passes

SOURCE: Gallup polls various years

proval in mid-October to 48 percent approval for the end of October. And his ratings remained absolutely flat following his greatest 1993 victory, passage of NAFTA. There were fewer international events in 1994, but only on one of those was there a rallying effect: the sending of troops to occupy Haiti in mid-September. Approval ratings jumped 5 points, from 39 percent before the event to 44 percent afterward. Clinton's approval ratings moved upward all during 1995, but no thanks to a rallying effect. *Not one single international event produced a positive approval effect.* Presidential election years tend to distort the polls, but it may be worth reporting that the two major events of March 10

(ships sent to China) and June 18 (China yields on trade restrictions) produced absolute zero in rallying energy. Thus, "the force" of international events seems no longer to be with post–Cold War presidents. The days of "the foreign policy fix" may be over.

There is a dark side and a bright side to the end of the Cold War. The dark side is that America seems to have lost a lot of its capacity to think and act as a nation. The "rallying effect" was a consistent tendency to think and act as a people with a common interest. That is Americanism at its best. It could be manipulated, and that possibility did not go unnoticed. There is a story, probably true, that not long before his assassination, President Kennedy, in a depressed mood over his declining approval ratings, told a visiting journalist that he was going to write a letter to his successor, with instructions that it be opened only when that president was in an equally depressed mood. All that letter would say is "Go to Berlin." One of the largest rallying effects ever followed Kennedy's speech at the Berlin Wall: "Ich bin ein Berliner."

The bright side for foreign policy in the post–Cold War era is that the one constant crisis of nuclear annihilation has been replaced by many crises that may be of historic importance to one or two countries but are not cumulative toward world war. Each problem must be confronted by American policy, but virtually all such challenges allow some time for deliberation. This gives us an opportunity to parliamentarize the presidency in foreign policy. The model may well be the January 1991 debate in Congress over the actions President Bush proposed to take against Iraq. The president lost nothing and gained a tremendous amount of stature by that debate, while the American people gained in civic education. If we no longer have the emotional resource of the rallying effect, we may very well be able to give the president something better in an *informed* rallying effect. That is another kind of power. It was never a healthy situation for a president in a democracy to have to decide *between* popularity and diplomacy.

BUREAUCRACY IN A DEMOCRACY

Despite widespread and consistent complaints about how bureaucracy is out of control and how difficult it is to supervise over five million civilian and military personnel working for the executive branch, most Americans ultimately recognize that maintaining order in a large society is impossible without a large governmental apparatus of some sort.[31] When we approve of what government is

doing, we tend to give the phenomenon a positive name, *administration;* when we disapprove of what government is doing, we call the same phenomenon *bureaucracy.*

The In Brief Box on page 163 defines bureaucracy by identifying its six basic characteristics. These characteristics enable us to look more clearly at the bureaucratic phenomenon. The size of the federal service is less imposing when placed against the context of the total workforce and the number of state and local government employees. The ratio of federal service employment to the total workforce has been relatively steady since 1950; in fact, the ratio has actually declined slightly in the past twenty-five years. Moreover, between 1950 and 1995, during which the federal civil service employment remained at around 3 percent of the total workforce, public employment in state and local governments moved from about 6.5 percent of the country's workforce to nearly 15 percent. All in all, we can say that the growth of the national government bureaucracy has merely kept pace with the growth of the national economy. The national government is indeed very large, but so are the American economy and society.

Although the federal executive branch is large and complex, everything about it is commonplace. Bureaucracies are commonplace because they touch so many aspects of daily life. Government bureaucracies implement the decisions made by the political process. Bureaucracies are full of routine because that assures the regular delivery of the services and ensures that each agency fulfills its mandate. Public bureaucracies are powerful because legislatures and chief executives, and indeed the people, delegate to them vast power to make sure a particular job is done—enabling citizens to be more free to pursue their private ends. And for the same reason, bureaucracies are a threat to freedom, because their size, their momentum, and the interests of the civil servants themselves in keep-

---

[31]The title of this section was inspired by an important book by

Charles Hyneman, *Bureaucracy in a Democracy* (New York: Harper, 1950).

SIX PRIMARY CHARACTERISTICS OF BUREAUCRACY

Division of Labor
    In order to increase productivity, workers are specialized.
    Each develops a skill in a particular job and then performs that job routinely.

Allocation of Functions
    Each worker depends on the output of other workers.
    No worker makes an entire product alone.

Allocation of Responsibility
    A task becomes a personal and contractual responsibility.

Supervision
    An unbroken chain of command ties superiors to subordinates from top to bottom to ensure
        orderly communication between workers and levels of the organization.
    Each superior is assigned a limited number of subordinates to supervise—this is the span of
        control.

Purchase of Full-time Employment
    The organization controls all the time the worker is on the job, so each worker can be assigned
        and held to a task.

Identification of Career within Organization
    Paths of seniority along with pension rights and promotions are all designed to encourage
        workers to identify with an organization.

ing their jobs impel bureaucracies and bureaucrats to resist any change of direction.

Bureaucrats

"Government by offices and desks" conveys to most people a picture of hundreds of office workers shuffling millions of pieces of paper. There is a lot of truth in that image, but we have to look more closely at what papers are being shuffled and why. More than seventy years ago, an astute observer defined bureaucracy as "continuous routine business."[32] Almost any organization succeeds by reducing its work to routines, with each routine being given to a different specialist. But specialization separates people from each other; one

worker's output becomes another worker's input. The timing of such relationships is essential, and this requires that these workers stay in communication with each other. Communication is the key. In fact, bureaucracy was the first information network. Routine came first; voluminous routine came as bureaucracies grew and specialized.

WHAT DO BUREAUCRATS DO? Bureaucrats, whether in public or in private organizations, first communicate with each other in order to coordinate all the specializations within their organization. All the shuffling of paper we associate with bureaucracy is a product of the second task of bureaucrats: the need to maintain a *"paper trail,"* which is a routinized means of ensuring that individuals' responsibilities are met. If a process breaks down, if there is a failure, if there is a loss of profit in a private company or a rising dissatisfaction among clients of public agencies, the

---

[32]Arnold Brecht and Comstock Glaser, *The Art and Techniques of Administration in German Ministries* (Cambridge, MA: Harvard University Press, 1940), p. 6.

paper trail provides a means of determining who was responsible, who was at fault, and where routines ought to be improved.

One of the major reasons why there may be more paper shuffling in public agencies than in private agencies is the need to establish *accountability.* As long as Americans want the agencies in the government bureaucracy to be maximally responsible to the people—directly and through Congress and the chief executive—there must be dependable and thorough means of determining responsibility and blame. "Red tape" is the almost universal cry of citizens against all the numbered forms and required signatures that bureaucracies generate.[33] Yet many of the same people who complain about red tape are the first to demand subpoenas requiring delivery of every conceivable document that may have some bearing on an alleged error of an agency or of individuals in an agency. What if the issue is the tragic explosion of the *Challenger* space shuttle or a gigantic overrun of expenditures for a new missile system for the Air Force? The bureaucrats in the National Aeronautics and Space Administration (NASA) or in the Air Force are required to create the record by which their own performances will later be judged.[34] And since Americans are more fearful of public bureaucracies and are therefore more likely to demand their accountability, public bureaucracies are likely to produce a great deal more paper than private bureaucracies.

Those first two activities of bureaucrats—communicating with each other and keeping copies of all those communications to maintain a paper trail—add up to a third: *implementation,* that is, implementing the objectives of the organization as laid down by its board of directors (if a private company) or by law (if a public agency). In government, the "bosses" are ultimately the legislature and the elected chief executive.

When the bosses—Congress, in particular, when it is making the law—are clear in their instructions to bureaucrats, implementation is a fairly straightforward process. Bureaucrats translate the law into specific routines for each of the employees of an agency. But what happens to routine administrative implementation when there are several bosses who disagree as to what the instructions ought to be? This requires yet a fourth job for bureaucrats: *interpretation.* Interpretation is a form of implementation, in that the bureaucrats still have to carry out what they believe to be the intentions of their superiors. But when bureaucrats have to interpret a law before implementing it, they are in effect engaging in *lawmaking.*

In sum, government bureaucrats do essentially the same things that bureaucrats in large private organizations do, and neither type deserves the disrespect embodied in the term "bureaucrat." But because of the authoritative, coercive nature of government, far more constraints are imposed on public bureaucrats than on private bureaucrats, even when their jobs are the same. Public bureaucrats are required to maintain a far more thorough paper trail. Public bureaucrats are also subject to a great deal more access from the public. Newspaper reporters, for example, have access to public bureaucrats that they could never hope to get with private bureaucrats. Public access has been vastly facilitated in the past thirty years; the adoption of the Freedom of Information Act (FOIA) in 1966 gave ordinary citizens the right of access to agency files and agency data to determine whether derogatory information exists in the file about the citizens themselves and to learn about what the agency is doing in general.

---

[33]"Red tape" actually refers to the traditional practice of tying up bundles of bureaucratic records before storing them.

[34]The presidential commission that investigated the *Challenger* tragedy was able to pinpoint a single technical failure on the basis of the evidence—the paper trail—assembled. Analysts of the tragedy concluded that "the decision to launch the *Challenger* was flawed. Those who made the decision were unaware of the recent history of [technical] problems. . . . If the decision-makers had known all the facts it is highly unlikely that they would have decided to launch [the shuttle] on January 28, 1986." See Barbara S. Romzek and Melvin Dubnick, "Accountability in the Public Sector: Lessons from the *Challenger* Tragedy," in *Current Issues in Public Administration,* 5th ed., ed. Frederick S. Lane (New York: St. Martin's, 1994), pp. 158–59.

And finally, citizens are given far more opportunities to participate in the decision-making processes of public agencies. There are limits of time, money, and expertise to this kind of access, but it does exist, and it occupies a great deal of the time of mid-level and senior public bureaucrats. This public exposure and access serves a purpose, but it also cuts down significantly on the efficiency of public bureaucrats. Thus, much of the lower efficiency of public agencies can be attributed to the political, judicial, legal, and publicity restraints put on public bureaucrats.

In studying bureaucracy, the important question is not one of size or efficiency, but whether government and society relate to each other in a productive way.

In the balance of this chapter, we explore how the American system of government has tried to adapt the vast apparatus of the national government to the requirements of representative democracy. The title of this section, "Bureaucracy in a Democracy," conveys the sense that the two are contradictory. We cannot live without bureaucracy, because bureaucracy is the most efficient way to organize people and technology to get a large collective job done. But we can't live comfortably with bureaucracy either, because hierarchy, appointed authority, and professional expertise make bureaucracy the natural enemy of representation, discussion, reciprocity, and individualism. Our task is neither to retreat nor to attack but to try constantly to take advantage of the strengths of bureaucracy while trying to make it more accountable to democratic processes. We look first to the role of the president in the struggle for accountability, and then to Congress (see Concept Map 6.1 on p. 166).

The President as Chief Executive

In 1939, President Roosevelt, through his President's Committee on Administrative Management, made the plea that "the president needs help." This is the story of the modern presidency. It can be told largely as a series of responses to the rise of big government: *Each expansion of the national government in the twentieth century has been accompanied by a parallel expansion of presidential management authority.* The In Brief Box on pages 168-169 provides a sketch of this pattern over most of this century.

FROM CABINET TO WHITE HOUSE STAFF   We have already observed that the president's cabinet does not perform as a board of directors. The cabinet is not a constitutionally or historically recognized, collective decision-making body, and only a minority of the members of the cabinet are sufficiently in command of their own respective departments to be able to contribute much to the president's need to be an actual chief executive officer. The vacuum created by the absence of cabinet management has been filled to a certain extent by the White House staff.

Within the White House staff, in the past thirty years, the "special assistants to the president" have been given specialized jurisdictions over one or more executive departments. These staffers have additional power and credibility beyond their access to the president because they also have access to the CIA for international intelligence and to the FBI and the Treasury for knowledge about the agencies themselves. With this information they can go beyond what the agencies themselves report and gain a great deal of leverage over the departments.

OMB AS A MANAGEMENT AGENCY   It was not accidental that the Bureau of the Budget, established in 1921 and brought into the EOP in 1939, was reorganized and given a new name (OMB) in 1970. President Nixon was deeply committed to making the existing bureaucracy, a product of eight years of growth and commitment under the Democrats, more responsive to Republican programs. The Office of Management and Budget was his instrument of choice, and the management power

CONCEPT MAP 6.1

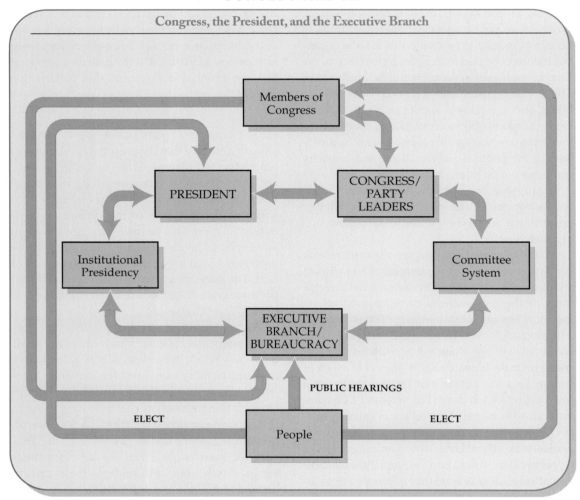

Congress, the President, and the Executive Branch

Members of Congress

PRESIDENT

CONGRESS/ PARTY LEADERS

Institutional Presidency

Committee System

EXECUTIVE BRANCH/ BUREAUCRACY

PUBLIC HEARINGS

ELECT

People

ELECT

of the director of OMB seems to have increased with each president since Nixon. Some management authority had always been lodged with the director of the budget, but greater emphasis was placed on planning and budgetary allocations. From President Nixon onward, questions of management became central to the operation of the executive branch, but the need for executive management control goes far beyond what even the boldest of OMB directors can do.

REINVENTING GOVERNMENT President Clinton has engaged in the most systematic and probably the most successful effort to "change the way the government does business," to borrow a phrase he has often used to describe the goal of his National Performance Review (NPR). The NPR is one of the more important administrative reforms of the twentieth century. All recent American presidents have decried the size and unmanageability of the federal bureaucracy, but Clinton has actually managed to turn proposals for change into real reform. In September 1993, he launched the NPR, based on a set of 384 proposals drafted by a panel headed by Vice President Gore. The avowed goal of the NPR is to "reinvent government"—to make the federal bureaucracy more efficient, accountable, and effective. Its goals include saving more than $100 billion over five years, in large part by cutting the federal workforce by 12 percent, or more than 270,000 jobs, by the end of fiscal year 1999. The NPR is also focused on cutting red tape, streamlining the way the government purchases goods and services, improving the coordination of federal management, and simplifying federal rules. Virtually all observers agree that the NPR has made substantial progress. For instance, the government's Office of Personnel Management has abolished the notorious 10,000-page Federal Personnel Manual and Standard Form 171, the government's arduous job application. Another example illustrates the nature of the NPR's work: The Defense Department's method for reimbursing its employees' travel expenses used to take seventeen steps and two months; an employee-designed reform encouraged by the NPR streamlined this to a four-step computer-based procedure that takes less than fifteen minutes, with anticipated savings of $1 billion over five years.

One potential weakness of the NPR noted by its critics is that it has no strategy for dealing with congressional opposition to bureaucratic reform. Donald Kettl, a respected reform advocate, warns that "virtually no reform that really matters can be achieved without at least implicit congressional support. The NPR has not yet developed a full strategy for winning that support."[35]

Responsible bureaucracy will never come sim-

ply from more presidential power, more administrative staff, more management control, or simpler procedures. All this was inadequate to the task of keeping the national security staff from running its own policies toward Iran and Nicaragua for at least two years (1985–1986) after Congress had explicitly restricted activities with Nicaragua and the president had formally forbidden negotiations with Iran. These incidents underscore the fact that each White House management innovation, from one president to the next, reveals plainly the inadequacy of previous innovations. As the White House staff grows, and the Executive Office of the President grows, the management bureaucracy itself becomes a management problem. Congress may be part of the solution, but Congress is also part of the problem.

Congress and Responsible Bureaucracy

Congress is constitutionally essential to responsible bureaucracy because, in "a government of laws," legislation is the key to government responsibility. When a law is passed and its intent is clear, the president knows what to "faithfully execute," and the agency understands its guidelines. But when Congress enacts vague legislation, everybody, from president to agency to courts to interest groups, gets involved in the interpretation of legislation. In that event, to whom is the agency responsible?

Congress's answer has not been to clarify its legislative intent but to try to supervise agency actions and interpretations through *oversight* (see also Chapter 5). The more legislative power Congress delegates to the executive, the more it seeks to get back into the game of government through committee and subcommittee oversight of the agencies. The standing committee system of Congress is well-suited for oversight, inasmuch as most congressional committees and subcommittees have jurisdictions roughly parallel to one or

[35]Quoted in Stephen Barr, "Midterm Exam for 'Reinvention'; Study Cites 'Impressive Results' but Calls for Strategy to Win Congressional Support," *Washington Post,* 19 August 1994, p. A25.

IN BRIEF BOX

GOVERNMENT: EXPANSION AND RESPONSE

Period of Government Expansion	Response of Presidency to Expansion
Wilson (1914–18): World War I; budget rises from $800 million to over $18 billion in 1919; agencies expanded	Budget and Accounting Act, 1921; executive branch forms Bureau of the Budget; General Accounting Office (GAO) becomes agent of Congress
Roosevelt (1933–36): New Deal period; budget growth; new agencies formed resulting in the "alphabetocracy"	Reorganization of powers including Budget Bureau as part of Executive Office of the President in 1939
Roosevelt (1940–44); World War II; total mobilization	Council of Economic Advisers formed, 1946; Secretary of Defense, National Security Council; Joint Chiefs of Staff in 1947
Truman (1947–51); post–World War II: Korean War mobilization	Emergence of "president's program," 1948–; White House Staff, 1950–
Eisenhower (1953–60): cold war; reaction against domestic government	Formalizing of White House staff; enhancement of National Security Council; effort to control social agencies; Hoover Commission
Kennedy (1961–63): Increased taxing power; direct pressure to control wages and prices	Specialized White House staff; applied central budgeting to Defense Department (Planning Programming Budgeting System, PPBS); upgraded Council of Economic Advisers
Johnson (1964–66): Expansion of domestic and social programs like Medicare and Medicaid and civil rights agencies; expansion of war powers	Applied PPBS to domestic agencies; created Organization for Economic Opportunity (OEO) to coordinate welfare programs; established HUD and Department of Transportation

more executive departments or agencies. Appropriations committees and authorization committees have oversight powers—and delegate their respective oversight powers to their subcommittees. In addition, there is a committee on government operations both in the House and in the Senate, and these committees have oversight powers not limited by departmental jurisdiction.

Committees and subcommittees oversee agencies through public hearings. Representatives from each agency, the White House, major interest groups, and other concerned citizens are called as witnesses to present testimony at these hearings. These are printed in large volumes and are widely circulated. Detailed records of the recent activities and expenditures of each and every agency can be found in these volumes. The number of hearings and equivalent public meetings (sometimes called investigations) has increased dramatically during the past forty years, largely

Period of Government Expansion	Response of Presidency to Expansion
Nixon (1969–73): Increased Social Security benefits; expansion of diplomacy; price controls; new regulatory programs	Centralization and further specialization of White House staff; Office of Management and Budget (OMB) created; decentralization of urban and welfare programs; formation of cabinet-level coordinating councils on wages and prices and domestic policy; "indexing" of Social Security to eliminate annual legislative adjustments; enhanced use of FBI surveillance of administrators
Carter (1977–80): post-Watergate	New Departments of Energy and Education; civil service reformed; zero-base budgeting; intense effort to reduce paperwork of the bureaucracy; first to impose cost-benefit analysis on regulation; first major effort to "deregulate" government
Reagan (1980–85): Dramatic expansion of defense budget; growth of national trade deficit	Director of OMB promoted to cabinet status; expansion of OMB power of regulatory review; formation of cabinet councils; expanded cost-benefit test for regulations
Bush (1989–91): Decision to put costs of Gulf War and S&L bail-out "off-budget," outside deficit-control calculations; deficits continue to mount	More power given to OMB over total budget deficits, along with broad discretion to adjust agency budget targets to economic conditions
Clinton (1993–95): Continued deficit increases, despite reduction efforts; health care reforms and welfare reforms involve expansion, not contraction, of budgets and bureaucracies	National Performance Review to "reinvent government," with powers to the vice president; Procurement Reform Act

because there is more government to oversee.[36]

Another form of legislative oversight is con-

ducted by individual members of Congress. This is all part of Congress's "case work," and much of legislative oversight is for individual constituents seeking everything from honest information to favoritism. Some legislation and other good results may come from these acts of oversight by individual representatives and senators, but the greater influence of case work is to particularize the process, bringing the focus of administration away from good policy and responsible management to

[36]For figures on the frequency and character of oversight, see Lawrence Dodd and Richard Schott, *Congress and the Administrative State* (New York: Wiley, 1979), p. 169. See also Norman Ornstein et al., *Vital Statistics on Congress, 1987–88* (Washington, DC: Congressional Quarterly Press, 1987), pp. 161–62. For a valuable and skeptical assessment of legislative oversight of administration, see James W. Fesler and Donald F. Kettl, *The Politics of the Administrative Process* (Chatham, NJ: Chatham House, 1991), Chapter 11.

individual interests.

Obviously the best approach is for Congress to spend more of its time clarifying its legislative intent and less of its time on committee or individual oversight. If the intent of the law were clear, Congress could then count on the president to maintain a higher level of bureaucratic responsibility, because bureaucrats are more responsive to clear legislative guidance than to anything else. Nevertheless, this is not a neat and sure solution, because Congress and the president can still be at odds, and when they are at odds, bureaucrats have an opportunity to evade responsibility by playing one branch off against the other.

Bureaucracy is here to stay. The administration of a myriad of government functions and responsibilities in a large, complex society will always require "rule by desks and offices" (the literal meaning of "bureaucracy"). No "reinvention" of government, however well conceived or executed, can alter that basic fact, nor can it resolve the problem of reconciling bureaucracy in a democracy. President Clinton's National Performance Review has accomplished some impressive things: the national bureaucracy has become somewhat smaller, and in the next few years, it will become smaller still; government procedures are being streamlined and are under tremendous pressure to become even more efficient. But these efforts are no guarantee that the bureaucracy itself will become more malleable. Congress will not suddenly change its practice of loose and vague legislative draftsmanship. Presidents will not suddenly discover new reserves of power or vision to draw more tightly the reins of responsible management. No deep solution can be found in quick fixes. As with all complex social and political problems, the solution to the problem of bureaucracy in a democracy lies mainly in a sober awareness of the nature of the problem. This awareness enables people to avoid fantasies and myths about the abilities of a democratized presidency—or the potential of a reform effort, or the magical powers of the computer, or the populist rhetoric of a new Congress—to change the nature of governance by bureaucracy.

IN BRIEF BOX

HOW THE THREE BRANCHES REGULATE BUREAUCRACY

The president may	appoint and remove agency heads.
	reorganize the bureaucracy (with congressional approval).
	make changes in agencies' budget proposals.
	initiate or adjust policies that would alter the bureaucracy's activities.
Congress may	pass legislation that alters the bureaucracy's activities.
	abolish existing programs.
	investigate bureaucratic activities and force bureaucrats to testify about them.
	influence presidential appointments of agency heads and other officials.
The judiciary may	rule on whether bureaucrats have acted within the law and require policy changes to comply with the law.
	force the bureaucracy to respect the rights of individuals through hearings and other proceedings.
	rule on the constitutionality of all rules and regulations.

CHAPTER REVIEW

The foundations for presidential government were set down in the Constitution, which provided for a unitary executive and made the president head of state as well as head of government. The first section of this chapter reviewed the powers of each: the head of state with its military, judicial, and diplomatic powers; and the head of government with its executive, military, and legislative powers. But the presidency was subordinated to congressional government during the nineteenth century and part of the twentieth, as the national government took part in few domestic functions and was inactive or sporadic in foreign affairs.

The second section of the chapter showed the rise of modern presidential government following the long period of congressional government. There is no mystery in the shift to government centered on the presidency. Congress built the modern presidency essentially in the 1930s by delegating to it not only the power to implement the vast new programs of the New Deal but also by delegating its own legislative power to make policy. The cabinet, the other top presidential appointments, the White House staff, and the Executive Office of the President are some of the impressive formal resources of presidential power.

The third section focused on the president's informal resources, in particular the president's political party, the supportive group coalitions, access to the media, and, through that, access to the millions of Americans who make up the general public. These resources are not cost-free or risk-free. A good relationship with the public is the president's most potent modern resource, but the polls reveal that the public's rating of presidential performance tends to go down with time. Only international actions or events can boost presidential performance ratings, and then only briefly. This means that presidents may be tempted to use foreign policy for domestic purposes, which is not a good foundation for the task of taming the federal bureaucracy. For the president, the bureaucracy is a problem second only to foreign affairs.

The chapter concluded with an assessment of how well the two political branches (the executive and the legislative) make the bureaucracy accountable to the people it serves and controls. The president attempts to maintain accountability through management—largely through the cabinet, the White House staff, and the OMB. But each president's failure to achieve a satisfactory level of political accountability is marked by the willingness of Congress to give the next president more management help. Congress has basically two tools to meet its own responsibilities for maintaining bureaucratic accountability: clear legislation and legislative oversight. Legislative oversight breaks down into committee oversight and individual oversight. The ideal approach to bureaucratic accountability is statutes with clear legislative intent and presidents who respect that intent and see that it is imposed through management staff in the agencies themselves. "Bureaucracy in a democracy" was the theme of this section of the chapter not because we have succeeded in democratizing bureaucracies but because it is the never-ending task of politics in a democracy.

TIME LINE ON THE PRESIDENCY	
Events	**Institutional Developments**
George Washington elected first president (1789)	President establishes powers in relation to Congress (1789)

Events	Institutional Developments
Thomas Jefferson elected president (1800)	**1800** Orderly transfer of power from Federalists to Jeffersonian Republicans (1801)
"Midnight" judicial appointments by John Adams before he leaves office (1801)	*Marbury v. Madison* holds that Congress and the president are subject to judicial review (1803)
Republican caucus nominates James Madison, who is elected president (1808)	Congress dominates presidential nominations through "King Caucus" (1804–1831)
Andrew Jackson elected president (1828)	Strengthening of presidency; nominating conventions introduced (1830s)
Period of weak presidents (Martin Van Buren, William Harrison, James Polk, Zachary Taylor, Franklin Pierce, James Buchanan) (1836–1860)	
Abraham Lincoln elected president (1860)	**1860** "Constitutional dictatorship"during Civil War and after (1861–1865)
Impeachment of President Andrew Johnson (1868)	Congress takes back initiative for action (1868–1933)
Industrialization, big railroads, big corporations (1860s–1890s)	*In re Neagle*—Court holds to expansive inference from Constitution on rights, duties, and obligations of president (1890)
World War I (1914–1918)	
Congress fails to approve Wilson's League of Nations (1919–1920)	**1920**
	Budget and Accounting Act; Congress provides for an executive budget (1921)
FDR proposes New Deal programs to achieve economic recovery from the Depression (1933)	Congress adopts first New Deal programs; epoch of presidential government (1930s)
U.S. in World War II (1941–1945)	*U.S. v. Pink*—Court confirms legality of executive agreements in foreign relations (1942)
Korean War without declaration (1950–1953)	**1950** *Steel Seizure* case holds that president's power must be authorized by statute and is not inherent in the presidency (1952)
Gulf of Tonkin Resolution (1964); U.S. troop buildup begins in Vietnam (1965)	Great Society program enacted; president sends troops to Vietnam without consulting Congress (1965)
	1970
Watergate affair (1972); Watergate cover-up revealed (1973–1974)	Congressional resurgence begins—War Powers Act (1973); Budget and Impoundment Act (1974)
Nixon becomes first president to resign; Gerald Ford succeeds after Nixon's resignation (1974)	

Events	Institutional Developments
Reagan's election begins new Republican era of "supply side" economics, deregulation, and military buildup (1980–1988)	*INS v. Chadha*—Court holds legislative veto to be unconstitutional (1983) Gramm-Rudman Act seeks to contain deficit spending (1985)
Iran-Contra affair revealed (1986–1987)	
Bush elected on "no new taxes" pledge (1988)	End of cold war puts new emphasis on foreign policy (1989)
1990	
	Military actions in Iraq and Somalia may define post–cold war foreign policy (1991–1992)
Clinton's election temporarily ends "divided government"; "reinventing government" plan launched by Clinton (1993)	Clinton achieves deficit reduction (1993), but fails on health care and middle-class tax reform (1994)
Republican takeover of both houses of Congress puts Clinton on defensive (1994)	National Performance Review, led by Vice President Gore, puts reinvention plan in action, streamlines procedures, and eliminates jobs (1993–1996)
Clinton re-elected, but so is Republican majority in Congress, extending "divided government" at least until 1998 (1996)	Congress gives president line-item veto (1996); line-item veto declared unconstitutional by District Court (1997)

KEY TERMS

accountability The obligation to justify the discharge of duties in the fulfillment of responsibilities to a person or persons in higher authority; to be answerable to that authority for failing to fulfill the assigned duties and responsibilities.

bureaucracy The complex structure of offices, tasks, rules, and principles of organization that are employed by all large-scale institutions to coordinate effectively the work of their personnel.

cabinet The secretaries, or chief administrators, of the major departments of the federal government. Cabinet secretaries are appointed by the president with the consent of the Senate.

delegated powers Constitutional powers that are assigned to one governmental agency but that are exercised by another agency with the express permission of the first.

electoral college The presidential electors from each state who meet in their respective state capitals after the popular election to cast ballots for president and vice president.

executive agreement An agreement between the president and another country, which has the force of a treaty but does not require the Senate's "advice and consent."

implementation The efforts of departments and agencies to translate laws into specific bureaucratic routines.

interpretation Process wherein bureaucrats implement ambiguous statutes, requiring agencies to make educated guesses as to what Congress or higher administrative authorities intended.

Kitchen Cabinet An informal group of advisers to whom the president turns for counsel and guidance. Members of the official cabinet may or may not also be members of the Kitchen Cabinet.

legislative clearance   A process that enables the president to require all agencies of the executive branch to submit through the budget director all requests for new legislation along with estimates of their budgetary needs.

line-item veto   Power that allows a governor (or the president) to strike out specific provisions (lines) of bills that the legislature passes. Without a line-item veto, the governor (or president) must accept or reject an entire bill.

mandate (electoral)   A claim by a victorious candidate that the electorate has given him or her special authority to carry out promises made during the campaign.

National Security Council (NSC)   A presidential foreign policy advisory council composed of the president, the vice president, the secretaries of state, defense, and the treasury, the attorney general, and other officials invited by the president. The NSC has a staff of foreign-policy specialists.

oversight   The effort by Congress, through hearings, investigations, and other techniques, to exercise control over the activities of executive agencies.

paper trail   Written accounts by which the process of decision making and the participants in a decision can, if desired, be later reconstructed. Often called "red tape."

patronage   The resources available to higher officials, usually opportunities to make partisan appointments to offices and to confer grants, licenses, or special favors to supporters.

pocket veto   A presidential veto wherein the president takes no formal action on a bill. If Congress adjourns within ten days of passing a bill, and the president does not sign it, the bill is considered to be vetoed.

rallying effect   The generally favorable reaction of the public to presidential actions taken in foreign policy or, more precisely, decisions made during international crises.

veto   The president's constitutional power to turn down acts of Congress. A presidential veto may be overridden by a two-thirds vote of each house of Congress.

FOR FURTHER READING

Arnold, Peri E. *Making the Managerial Presidency: Comprehensive Organization Planning.* Princeton: Princeton University Press, 1986.

Bryner, Gary. *Bureaucratic Discretion.* New York: Pergamon Press, 1987.

Corwin, Edward S. *The President: Office and Powers,* 3rd rev. ed. New York: New York University Press, 1957.

Drew, Elizabeth. *On the Edge: The Clinton Presidency.* New York: Simon & Schuster, 1994.

Heclo, Hugh. *A Government of Strangers.* Washington, DC: Brookings Institution, 1977.

Hill, Larry B., ed. *The State of Public Bureaucracy.* Armonk, NY: M. E. Sharpe, 1992.

Lowi, Theodore J. *The Personal President: Power Invested, Promise Unfulfilled.* Ithaca: Cornell University Press, 1985.

Lynn, Naomi B., and Aaron Wildavsky. *Public Administration—The State of the Discipline.* Chatham, NJ: Chatham House, 1990.

Milkis, Sidney M. *The President and the Parties: The Transformation of the American Party System since the New Deal.* New York: Oxford University Press, 1993.

Nathan, Richard. *The Plot That Failed: Nixon's Administrative Presidency.* New York: Wiley, 1975.

Neustadt, Richard E. *Presidential Power: The Politics of Leadership from Roosevelt to Reagan,* rev. ed. New York: Free Press, 1990.

Pfiffner, James P. *The Modern Presidency.* New York: St. Martin's Press, 1994.

Polsby, Nelson, and Aaron Wildavsky. *Presidential Elections,* 8th ed. New York: Free Press, 1991.

Ripley, Randall B., and Grace A. Franklin. *Congress, the Bureaucracy and Public Policy,* 5th ed. Pacific Grove, CA: Brooks/Cole, 1991.

Rubin, Irene S. *The Politics of Public Budgeting,* 2nd ed. Chatham, NJ: Chatham House, 1993.

Skowronek, Stephen. *The Politics Presidents Make: Presidential Leadership from John Adams to George Bush.* Cambridge, MA: Harvard University Press, 1993.

Spitzer, Robert. *President and Congress: Executive Hegemony at the Crossroads of American Government.* New York: McGraw-Hill, 1993.

Wildavsky, Aaron. *The New Politics of the Budget Process,* 2nd ed. New York: HarperCollins, 1992.

Wilson, James Q. *Bureaucracy: What Government Agencies Do and Why They Do It.* New York: Basic Books, 1989.

Wood, Dan B. *Bureaucratic Dynamics: The Role of Bureaucracy in a Democracy.* Boulder, CO: Westview, 1994.

CHAPTER 7

The Federal Courts: Least Dangerous Branch or Imperial Judiciary?

ℰVERY YEAR nearly 25 million cases are tried in American courts and one American in every nine is directly involved in litigation. Cases can arise from disputes between citizens, from efforts by government agencies to punish wrongdoing, or from citizens' efforts to prove that a right provided them by law has been infringed upon as a result of government action— or inaction. Many critics of the American legal system assert that Americans have become much too ready to use the courts for all purposes, and perhaps they have. But the heavy use that Americans make of the courts is also an indication of the extent of conflict in American society. And given the existence of social conflict, it is far better that Americans seek to settle their differences through the courts rather than by fighting or feuding.

In this chapter, we will first examine the judicial process, including the types of cases that the federal courts consider. Second, we will assess the organization and structure of the federal court system as well as the flow of cases through the courts. Third, we will consider judicial review and how it makes the Supreme Court a "lawmaking body." Fourth, we will examine various influences on the Supreme Court. Finally, we will ana-

lyze the role and power of the federal courts in the American political process, looking in particular at the growth of judicial power in the United States. The framers of the American Constitution called the Court the "least dangerous branch" of American government. Today, it is not unusual to hear friends and foes of the Court alike refer to it

CORE OF THE ARGUMENT

- The power of judicial review makes the Supreme Court more than a judicial agency; it also makes the Court a major lawmaking body.
- The dominant influences shaping Supreme Court decisions are the philosophies and attitudes of the members of the Court and the solicitor general's control over cases involving the government.
- The role and power of the federal courts, particularly the Supreme Court, have been significantly strengthened and expanded over the last fifty years.

as the "imperial judiciary."[1] Before we can understand this transformation and its consequences, however, we must look in some detail at America's judicial process.

THE JUDICIAL PROCESS

Originally, a "court" was the place where a sovereign ruled—where the king and his entourage governed. Settling disputes between citizens was part of governing. According to the Bible, King Solomon had to settle the dispute between two women over which of them was the mother of the child both claimed. Judging is the settling of disputes, a function that was slowly separated from the king and the king's court and made into a separate institution of government. Courts have taken over from kings the power to settle controversies by hearing the facts on both sides and deciding which side possesses the greater merit. But since judges are not kings, they must have a basis for their authority. That basis in the United States is the Constitution and the law. Courts decide cases by hearing the facts on both sides of a dispute and applying the relevant law or principle to the facts. (See the In Brief Box for an explanation of the various types of laws and disputes.)

Cases and the Law

Court cases in the United States proceed under three broad categories of law: criminal law, civil law, and public law.

Cases of *criminal law* are those in which the government charges an individual with violating a statute that has been enacted to protect the public health, safety, morals, or welfare. In criminal cases, the government is always the *plaintiff* (the party that brings charges) and alleges that a criminal violation has been committed by a named *de-*

fendant. Most criminal cases arise in state and municipal courts and involve matters ranging from traffic offenses to robbery and murder. Another large and growing body of federal criminal law deals with such matters as tax evasion, mail fraud, and the sale of narcotics. Defendants found guilty of criminal violations may be fined or sent to prison.

Cases of *civil law* involve disputes among individuals or between individuals and the government where no criminal violation is charged. Unlike criminal cases, the losers in civil cases cannot be fined or sent to prison, although they may be required to pay monetary damages for their actions. In a civil case, the one who brings a complaint is the plaintiff and the one against whom the complaint is brought is the defendant. The two most common types of civil cases involve contracts and torts. In a typical contract case, an individual or corporation charges that is has suffered because of another's violation of a specific agreement between the two. For example, the Smith Manufacturing Corporation may charge the Jones Distributors failed to honor an agreement to deliver raw materials at a specified time, causing Smith to lose business. Smith asks the court to order Jones to compensate it for the damage allegedly suffered. In a typical tort case, one individual charges that he or she has been injured by another's negligence or malfeasance. Medical malpractice suits are one example of tort cases.

In deciding civil cases, courts apply statutes (laws) and legal *precedent* (prior decisions). State and federal statutes, for example, often govern the conditions under which contracts are and are not legally binding. Jones Distributors might argue that it was not obliged to fulfill its contract with the Smith Corporation because actions by Smith, such as the failure to make promised payments, constituted fraud under state law. Attorneys for a physician being sued for malpractice, on the other hand, may search for prior instances in which courts ruled that actions similar to those of their client did not constitute negligence. Such

[1]See Richard Neely, *How Courts Govern America* (New Haven: Yale University Press, 1981).

IN BRIEF BOX

TYPES OF LAWS AND DISPUTES

Type of law	Type of case or dispute	Form of case
Criminal law	Cases arising out of actions that violate laws protecting the health, safety, and morals of the community. The government is always the plaintiff.	*U.S. (or state) v. Jones* *Jones v. U.S. (or state)*, if Jones lost and is appealing
Civil law	"Private law," involving disputes between citizens or between government and citizen where no crime is alleged. Two general types are contract and tort. *Contract cases* are disputes that arise over voluntary actions. *Tort cases* are disputes that arise out of obligations inherent in social life. Negligence and slander are examples of torts.	*Smith v. Jones* *New York v. Jones* *U.S. v. Jones* *Jones v. New York*
Public law	All cases where the powers of government or the rights of citizens are involved. The government is the defendant. *Constitutional law* involves judicial review of the basis of a government's action in relation to specific clauses of the Constitution as interpreted in Supreme Court cases. *Administrative law* involves disputes of the statutory authority, jurisdiction, or procedures of administrative agencies.	*Jones v. U.S. (or state)* *In re Jones* *Smith v. Jones*, if a license or statute is at issue in their private dispute

precedents are applied under the doctrine of *"stare decisis,"* a Latin phrase meaning "let the decision stand."

A case becomes a matter of the third category, *public law,* when a plaintiff or defendant in a civil or criminal case seeks to show that their case involves the powers of government or rights of citizens as defined under the Constitution or by statute. One major form of public law is constitutional law, under which a court will examine the government's actions to see if they conform to the Constitution as it has been interpreted by the judiciary. Thus, what began as an ordinary criminal case may enter the realm of public law if a defen-

dant claims that his or her constitutional rights were violated by the police. Another important arena of public law is administrative law, which involves disputes over the jurisdiction, procedures, or authority of administrative agencies. Under this type of law, civil litigation between an individual and the government may become a matter of public law if the individual asserts that the government is violating a statute or abusing its power under the Constitution. For example, land owners have asserted that federal and state restrictions on land use constitute violations of the Fifth Amendment's restrictions on the government's ability to confiscate private property. Recently, the

Supreme Court has been very sympathetic to such claims, which effectively transform an ordinary civil dispute into a major issue of public law.

Most of the important Supreme Court cases we will examine in this chapter involve judgments concerning the constitutional or statutory basis of the actions of government agencies. As we shall see, it is in this arena of public law that the Supreme Court's decisions can have significant consequences for American politics and society.

Types of Courts

In the United States, systems of courts have been established both by the federal government and by the governments of the individual states. Both systems have several levels, as shown in Figure 7.1. More than 99 percent of all court cases in the United States are heard in state courts. The overwhelming majority of criminal cases, for example, involve violations of state laws prohibiting such actions as murder, robbery, fraud, theft, and assault. If such a case is brought to trial, it will be heard in a state *trial court,* in front of a judge and sometimes a jury, who will determine whether the defendant violated state law. If the defendant is convicted, he or she may appeal the conviction to a higher court, such as a state *appellate court,* and from there to a state's *supreme court.* Similarly, in civil cases, most litigation is brought in the courts established by the state in which the activity in question took place. For example, a patient bringing suit against a physician for malpractice would file the suit in the appropriate court in the state where the alleged malpractice occurred. The judge hearing the case would apply state law and

FIGURE 7.1

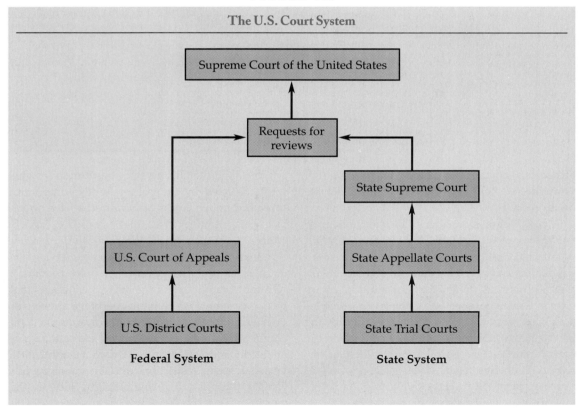

The U.S. Court System

Supreme Court of the United States

Requests for reviews

State Supreme Court

U.S. Court of Appeals

State Appellate Courts

U.S. District Courts

State Trial Courts

Federal System

State System

state precedent to the matter at hand. (It should be noted that in both criminal and civil matters, most cases are settled before trial through negotiated agreements between the parties. In criminal cases these agreements are called *plea bargains.*)

Although each state has its own set of laws, these laws have much in common from state to state. Murder and robbery, obviously, are illegal in all states, although the range of possible punishments for those crimes varies from state to state. Some states, for example, provide for capital punishment (the death penalty) for murder and other serious offenses; other states do not. As we saw in Chapter 4, however, some acts that are criminal offenses in one state may be legal in another state. Prostitution, for example, is legal in some Nevada counties, although it is outlawed in all other states. Considerable similarity among the states is also found in the realm of civil law. In the case of contract law, most states have adopted the *Uniform Commercial Code* in order to reduce interstate differences. In areas such as family law, however, which covers such matters as divorce and child custody arrangements, state laws vary greatly.

Cases are heard in the federal courts if they involve federal laws, treaties with other nations, or the U.S. Constitution; these areas are the official *jurisdiction* of the federal courts. In addition, any case in which the U.S. government is a party is heard in the federal courts. If, for example, an individual is charged with violating a federal criminal statute, such as evading the payment of income taxes, charges would be brought before a federal judge by a federal prosecutor. Civil cases involving the citizens of more than one state and in which more than fifty thousand dollars is at stake may be heard in either the federal or the state courts, usually depending upon the preference of the plaintiff.

Federal courts serve another purpose in addition to trying cases within their jurisdiction: that of hearing appeals from state-level courts. Individuals found guilty of breaking a state criminal law, for example, can appeal their convictions to a federal court by raising a constitutional issue and asking a federal court to determine whether the state's actions were consistent with the requirements of the U.S. Constitution. An appellant might assert, for example, that the state court denied him or her the right to counsel, imposed excessive bail, or otherwise denied the appellant *due process.* Under such circumstances, an appellant can ask the federal court to overturn his or her conviction. Federal courts are not obligated to accept such appeals and will do so only if they feel that the issues raised have considerable merit and if the appellant has exhausted all possible remedies within the state courts. (This procedure is discussed in more detail later in this chapter.) The decisions of state supreme courts may also be appealed to the U.S. Supreme Court if the state court's decision has conflicted with prior U.S. Supreme Court rulings or has raised some important question of federal law. Such appeals are accepted by the U.S. Supreme Court at its discretion.

Although the federal courts hear only a small fraction of all the civil and criminal cases decided each year in the United States, their decisions are extremely important. It is in the federal courts that the Constitution and federal laws that govern all Americans are interpreted and their meaning and significance established. Moreover, it is in the federal courts that the powers and limitations of the increasingly powerful national government are tested. Finally, through their power to review the decisions of the state courts, it is ultimately the federal courts that dominate the American judicial system.

FEDERAL JURISDICTION

The overwhelming majority of court cases are tried not in federal courts but in state and local courts under state common law, state statutes, and local ordinances. Of all cases heard in the United States in 1994, federal district courts (the lowest federal level) received 280,000. Although this number is up substantially from the 87,000 cases heard in 1961, it still constitutes under 1 percent of the judiciary's business. The federal courts of appeal listened to 48,815 cases in 1994, and the U.S. Supreme Court reviewed 4,621 in its 1993–1994 term. Only 99 cases were given full-dress Supreme Court review (the nine justices actually sitting *en banc*—in full court—and hearing the lawyers argue the case).[2]

The Lower Federal Courts

Most of the cases of original federal jurisdiction are handled by the federal district courts. The federal district courts are trial courts of general jurisdiction, and their cases are, in form, indistinguishable from cases in the state trial courts.

There are eighty-nine district courts in the fifty states, plus one in the District of Columbia and one in Puerto Rico, and three territorial courts. In

an effort to deal with a greatly increased court workload, in 1978, Congress increased the number of district judgeships from 400 to 517. District judges are assigned to district courts according to the workload; the busiest of these courts may have as many as twenty-eight judges.

Besides the district courts, there are also some federal courts with original jurisdiction over specific classes of cases. The U.S. Court of Claims has jurisdiction over disputes about compensation when property has been taken for a public use, cases alleging that a government agency has not properly observed its contracts, and claims by employees for back pay. The U.S. Tax Court handles cases arising out of enforcement of the Internal Revenue (income tax) Code. The Customs Court also handles tax cases, but mainly those involving tariffs. The disputes are most often over the value that ought to be put on imported merchandise for tariff purposes. Original jurisdiction over patent infringement cases is given to an administrative agency, the U.S. Patent and Trademark Office.

[2]U.S. Bureau of the Census, *Statistical Abstract of the United States 1995* (Washington, DC: Government Printing Office, 1995), p. 206.

BOX 7.1

Federal Laws and Federal Cases

SINCE ALL COMMON LAW and most statutory laws in the American federal system are of state and local origin, it is not surprising that over 99 percent of all cases are tried in state and local courts. The relatively few federal cases can be grouped into three categories:

1. *Civil cases involving "diversity of citizenship."* The Constitution provides for federal jurisdiction whenever a citizen of one state brings suit against a citizen of another state. Congressional legislation requires that the amount at issue be more than $50,000. Otherwise the case is handled by a regular state court in the state where the grievance occurs.
2. *Civil cases where an agency of the federal government is seeking to enforce federal laws that provide for civil, not criminal, penalties.* These laws can range from bankruptcy laws to admiralty and maritime laws to occupational and consumer safety laws, environmental protection laws, and energy conservation and development laws.
3. *Cases where federal criminal statutes are involved or where issues of public law have been made of state criminal cases.* State prisoner petitions alleging mistreatment, unfair trial, or abridgement of civil rights represent the largest source of criminal cases coming before the federal appellate courts.

The Appellate Courts

Roughly 10 percent of all lower court and agency cases are accepted for review by the federal appeals courts and by the Supreme Court in its capacity as an appellate court. The country is divided into twelve judicial circuits, each of which has a U.S. Court of Appeals.

Except for cases selected for review by the Supreme Court, decisions made by the appeals courts are final. Because of this finality, certain safeguards have been built into the system. The most important is the provision of more than one judge for every appeals case. Each court of appeals has from three to fifteen permanent judgeships, depending on the workload of the circuit. Although normally three judges hear appealed cases, in some instances a larger number of judges sit together *en banc.*

Another safeguard is provided by the assignment of a Supreme Court justice as the circuit justice for each of the eleven circuits. Since the creation of the appeals courts in 1891, the circuit justice's primary duty has been to review appeals arising in the circuit in order to expedite Supreme Court action. The most frequent and best-known action of circuit justices is that of reviewing requests for stays of execution when the full Court is unable to do so—mainly during the summer, when the Court is in recess.

The Supreme Court

The Supreme Court is America's highest court. Article III of the Constitution vests "the judicial power of the United States" in the Supreme Court, and this court is supreme in fact as well as form. The Supreme Court is made up of a chief justice and eight associate justices. The *chief justice* presides over the Court's public sessions and conferences. In the Court's actual deliberations and decisions, however, the chief justice has no more authority than his or her colleagues. Each justice casts one vote. To some extent, the influence of the chief justice is a function of his or her own leadership ability. Some chief justices, such as the late Earl Warren, have been able to lead the court in a new direction. In other instances, a forceful associate justice, such as the late Felix Frankfurter, are the dominant figures on the Court.

The Constitution does not specify the number of justices that should sit on the Supreme Court; Congress has the authority to change the Court's size. In the early nineteenth century, there were six Supreme Court justices; later there were seven. Congress set the number of justices at nine in 1869, and the Court has remained that size ever since. In 1937, President Franklin D. Roosevelt, infuriated by several Supreme Court decisions that struck down New Deal programs, asked Congress to enlarge the court so that he could add a few sympathetic

IN BRIEF BOX

FEDERAL JURISDICTION

Lower Federal Courts	Appellate Courts	Supreme Court
Federal district courts are trial courts of general jurisdiction. U.S. Court of Claims U.S. Tax Court Customs Court	There are twelve U.S. Courts of appeals, which review roughly 10 percent of all lower court and agency cases.	Reviews lower court decisions, state legislation, and acts of Congress where a substantial issue of public law is involved.

CONCEPT MAP 7.1

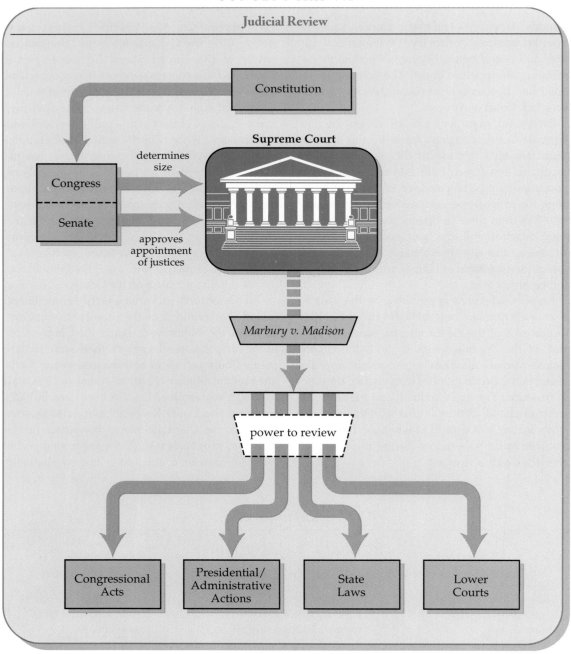

Judicial Review

Constitution

Supreme Court

Congress

determines
size

Senate

approves
appointment
of justices

Marbury v. Madison

power to review

Congressional
Acts

Presidential/
Administrative
Actions

State
Laws

Lower
Courts

justices to the bench. Although Congress balked at Roosevelt's "court packing" plan, the Court gave in to FDR's pressure and began to take a more favorable view of his policy initiatives. The president, in turn, dropped his efforts to enlarge the Court. The Court's surrender to FDR came to be known as "the switch in time that saved nine."

JUDICIAL REVIEW

The Supreme Court has the power of *judicial review*—the authority and the obligation to review any lower court decision where a substantial issue of public law is involved. The disputes can be over the constitutionality of federal or state laws, over the propriety or constitutionality of the court procedures followed, or over whether public officers are exceeding their authority. The Supreme Court's power of judicial review has come to mean review not only of lower court decisions but also of state legislation and acts of Congress (see Concept Map 7.1) For this reason, if for no other, the Supreme Court is more than a judicial agency—it is also a major lawmaking body.

The Supreme Court's power of judicial review over lower court decisions has never been at issue. Nor has there been any serious quibble over the power of the federal courts to review administrative agencies in order to determine whether their actions and decisions are within the powers delegated to them by Congress. There has, however, been a great deal of controversy occasioned by the Supreme Court's efforts to review acts of Congress and the decisions of state courts and legislatures.

Judicial Review of Acts of Congress

Since the Constitution does not give the Supreme Court the power of judicial review of

BOX 7.2

Marbury v. Madison

THE 1803 SUPREME COURT DECISION handed down in *Marbury v. Madison* established the power of the Court to review acts of Congress. The case arose over a suit filed by William Marbury and seven other people against Secretary of State James Madison to require him to approve their appointments as justices of the peace. These had been last-minute ("midnight judges") appointments of outgoing President John Adams. Chief Justice Marshall held that although Marbury and the others were entitled to their appointments, the Supreme Court had no power to order Madison to deliver them.

Marshall reasoned that constitutions are framed to serve as the "fundamental and paramount law of the nation." Thus, he argued, with respect to the legislative action of Congress, the Constitution is a "superior . . . law, unchangeable by ordinary means." He concluded that an act of Congress that contradicts the Constitution must be judged void.

As to the question of whether the Court was empowered to rule on the constitutionality of legislative action, Marshall responded emphatically that it is "the province and duty of the judicial department to say what the law is." Since the Constitution is the supreme law of the land, he reasoned, it is clearly within the realm of the Court's responsibility to rule on the constitutionality of legislative acts and treaties. This principle has held sway every since.

SOURCES: Gerald Gunther, Constitutional Law (Mineola, NY: Fountain Press, 1980), pp. 9–11; and Marbury v. Madison, 1 Cr. 137 (1803).

congressional enactments, the Court's exercise of it is something of a usurpation. Though Congress and the president have often been at odds with the Court, its legal power to review acts of Congress has not been seriously questioned since 1803 and the case of *Marbury v. Madison* (see Box 7.2). One reason is that judicial power has been accepted as natural even though not specifically intended by the framers of the Constitution. Another reason is that the Supreme Court has rarely reviewed the constitutionality of the acts of Congress, especially in the past fifty years. When such acts do come up for review, the Court makes a self-conscious effort to give them an interpretation that will make them constitutional.

Judicial Review of State Actions

The power of the Supreme Court to review state legislation or other state action and to determine its constitutionality is neither granted by the Constitution nor inherent in the federal system. But the logic of the **supremacy clause** of Article VI of the Constitution, which declares it and laws made under its authority to be the supreme law of the land, is very strong. Furthermore, in the Judiciary Act of 1789, Congress conferred on the Supreme Court the power to reverse state constitutions and laws whenever they are clearly in conflict with the U.S. Constitution, federal laws, or treaties.[3] This power gives the Supreme Court jurisdiction over all of the millions of cases handled by American courts each year.

The supremacy clause of the Constitution not only established the federal Constitution, statutes, and treaties as the "supreme law of the land," but also provided that "the Judges in every State shall be bound thereby, any Thing in the Constitution or Laws of the State to the Contrary notwithstanding." Under this authority, the Supreme Court has frequently overturned state constitutional provisions or statutes and state court decisions that it feels are counter to rights or privileges guaranteed under the Constitution or federal statutes (see Box 7.3).

How Cases Reach the Supreme Court

Given the millions of disputes that arise every year, the job of the Supreme Court would be impossible if it were not able to control the flow of cases and its own case load. Its original jurisdiction is only a minor problem. The original jurisdiction includes (1) cases between the United States and one of the fifty states, (2) cases between two or more states, (3) cases involving foreign ambassadors or other ministers, and (4) cases brought by one state against citizens of another state or against a foreign country. The most important of these cases are disputes between states over land, water, or old debts. Generally, the Supreme Court deals with these cases by appointing a "special master," usually a retired judge, to actually hear the case and present a report. The Supreme Court then allows the states involved in the dispute to present arguments for or against the master's opinion.[4]

RULES OF ACCESS   Over the years, the courts have developed specific rules that govern which cases within their jurisdiction they will and will not hear. In order to have access to the courts, cases must meet certain criteria. These rules of access can be broken down into three major categories: case or controversy, standing, and mootness.

Article III of the Constitution and Supreme Court decisions define judicial power as extending only to "cases and controversies." This means that the case before a court must be an actual controversy, not a hypothetical one, with two truly adversarial parties. The courts have interpreted this language to mean that they do not have the power to render advisory opinions to legislatures or agencies about the constitutionality of pro-

---

[3]This review power was affirmed by the Supreme Court in Martin v. Hunter's Lessee, 1 Wheaton 304 (1816).

[4]Walter F. Murphy, "The Supreme Court of the United States," in *Encyclopedia of the American Judicial System*, ed. Robert J. Janosik (New York: Scribner's, 1987).

BOX 7.3

Miranda v. Arizona

THROUGHOUT THE 1950s AND 1960s, increasingly vocal critics decried what they viewed as an alarming rise in "judicial activism" on the part of the Supreme Court. In a series of controversial rulings, the Court, led by Chief Justice Earl Warren, handed down sweeping rulings in controversial areas such as racial discrimination, school prayer, reapportionment, and rights of the accused. Few cases aroused more ire than that of the 1966 case of *Miranda v. Arizona.*

Ernesto Miranda was a poorly educated indigent of limited mental capabilities who had confessed to kidnapping and raping an eighteen-year-old woman. Miranda's confession provided key evidence of his complicity, but his conviction was challenged on the grounds that he had not been informed of his constitutional rights to remain silent and to have counsel during police questioning, as stated in the Fifth and Sixth amendments, respectively.

By a 5-to-4 vote, the Supreme Court overturned Miranda's conviction, ruling that his confession was inadmissible in the absence of prior warnings from the police. "Prior to any questioning," the Court said, "the person must be warned that he has a right to remain silent, that any statement he does make may be used against him, and that he has a right to the presence of an attorney, either retained or appointed." The decision was based on the understanding that custodial interrogation of suspects not allowed to have lawyers present made it extremely difficult for a suspect to assert the right to avoid self-incrimination.

Critics raged that these new rules amounted to judicial invasion of local police houses, that they tied the hands of law enforcement officials and balanced the scales of justice too heavily in favor of criminals. But the Supreme Court and others noted that the FBI had followed these procedures for years without a problem. Indeed, suspects often waived their rights and confessed. Studies of police behavior and criminal prosecutions after *Miranda* indicated that police were not prevented from doing their jobs.

Still, the *Miranda* decision did not sit well with many who felt that an individual who probably belonged in jail could be freed on a "technicality." President Richard Nixon won election in 1968 in part on a campaign of "law and order" that was based partially on Court rulings like *Miranda.* In the same year, Congress passed the Omnibus Crime Control and Safe Streets Act, Title II of which was aimed at curtailing suspect rights by allowing submission of confessions and other incriminating evidence if offered voluntarily but without Miranda warnings.

Despite protracted controversy and the appointment to the Supreme Court of more conservative justices, the Miranda principle has become an integral part of the law enforcement process and an essential means for protecting basic rights, including the presumption of innocence, for all suspects. What some labeled derisively as legal "technicalities" are basic procedural safeguards that provide protection from the exercise of arbitrary government power.

SOURCE: Liva Baker, *Miranda: Crime, Law, and Politics* (New York: Atheneum, 1983).

posed laws or regulations. Furthermore, even after a law is enacted, the courts will generally refuse to consider its constitutionality until it is actually applied.

Parties to a case must also have *standing,* that

is, they must show that they have a substantial stake in the outcome of the case. The traditional requirement for standing has been to show injury to oneself; that injury can be personal, economic, or even aesthetic, for example. In order for a

BOX 7.4

Access to the Courts: The Rules of Standing

OVER THE YEARS, in order to manage the many cases that come before it, the Supreme Court has developed rules governing which cases it can and cannot properly hear. The rules of access can be broken down into three major categories: (1) case or controversy, (2) standing, and (3) mootness.

(1) *Case or controversy:* The Constitution provides the judiciary with the power to decide various "cases" and "controversies," and the Supreme Court has taken this language to mean that it does not have the power to render advisory opinions. In *Muskrat v. United States* (1911), the Court extended the rule to eliminate feigned controversy. The case before the court must be a real controversy, with two truly adversarial parties; even after a law is enacted, the courts will generally refuse to consider its constitutionality until it is actually applied. The major exception to this rule is the so-called declaratory judgment, in which a statute is deemed to be unconstitutional on its face. In the case of *Ada v. Guam Society of Obstetricians and Gynecologists,* for example, a federal appeals court in San Francisco struck down a 1990 Guam statute that made performing an abortion a felony.* The statute was challenged immediately after its enactment, and before it could actually be enforced, by Guam physicians who feared prosecution if they performed abortions. The federal appeals court declared that the statute, on its face, represented a violation of the constitutional protection of the right to abortion established in *Roe v. Wade.* In November 1992, the U.S. Supreme Court, with three justices dissenting, refused to give the case further consideration.

(2) *Standing:* To have standing is to be the proper person to bring a suit, and the basic requirement for standing is to show injury to oneself. In order for a group or class of people to have standing, each member must show injury. The Court's definition of injury has changed over the years; it has expanded from the narrow reading of the term—personal and/or economic harm—to include such values as "aesthetic and environmental well-being" (*Sierra Club v. Morton* [1972]).

(3) *Mootness:* There are two time-factor requirements that must be met for the Court to hear a case. The Court must feel that the issue is ready to be heard—that the issue is still not too abstract, that all other possible remedies have been exhausted, that the matter has been absorbed into the national consciousness. Conversely, it is also necessary that the case not be moot—that the particular problem has not already been resolved by other means. The Court began to relax its rules on mootness in cases where the situation was likely to come up again. For example, under the original definition of mootness, it was usually impossible to challenge election rules since the election was almost sure to be over by the time the case reached the appellate courts. But the Court began to hear some such cases if the issue was likely to be repeated in later elections (*Moore v. Ogilvie* [1969]). And as the Court pointed out in *Roe v. Wade* (1973), the major abortion case, questions relating to pregnancy could never be appealed if the older standards of mootness were to be applied, since the case would surely take longer than the pregnancy.

*See *Congressional Quarterly Weekly Report,* 5 December 1992, p. 3751.

group or class of people to have standing (as in class action suits), each member must show specific injury. This means that a general interest in the environment, for instance, does not provide a group with sufficient basis for standing.

The Supreme Court also uses a third criterion in determining whether it will hear a case: that of **mootness.** In theory, this requirement disqualifies cases that are brought too late—after the relevant facts have changed or the problem has been re-

PROCESS BOX 7.1

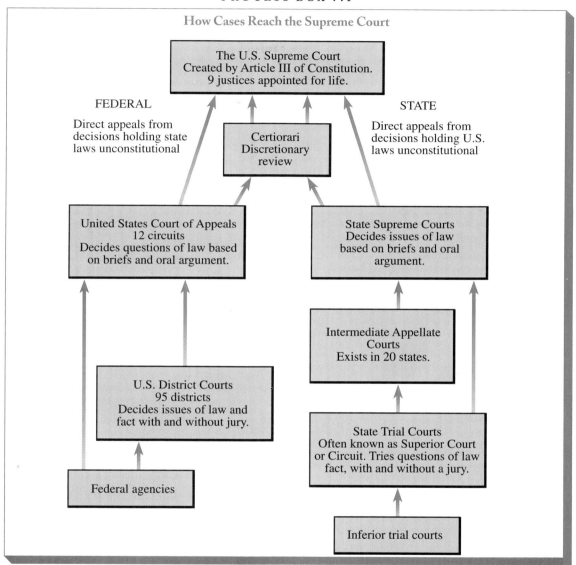

How Cases Reach the Supreme Court

The U.S. Supreme Court
Created by Article III of Constitution.
9 justices appointed for life.

FEDERAL

Direct appeals from
decisions holding state
laws unconstitutional

Certiorari
Discretionary
review

STATE

Direct appeals from
decisions holding U.S.
laws unconstitutional

United States Court of Appeals
12 circuits
Decides questions of law based
on briefs and oral argument.

State Supreme Courts
Decides issues of law
based on briefs and oral
argument.

U.S. District Courts
95 districts
Decides issues of law and
fact with and without jury.

Intermediate Appellate
Courts
Exists in 20 states.

Federal agencies

State Trial Courts
Often known as Superior Court
or Circuit. Tries questions of law
fact, with and without a jury.

Inferior trial courts

solved by other means. The criterion of mootness, however, is subject to the discretion of the courts, which have begun to relax the rules of mootness, particularly in cases where a situation that has been resolved is likely to come up again. In the abortion case *Roe v. Wade*, for example, the Supreme Court rejected the lower court's argu-

ment that because the pregnancy had already come to term, the case was moot. The Court agreed to hear the case because no pregnancy was likely to outlast the lengthy appeals process.

Putting aside the formal criteria, the Supreme Court is most likely to accept cases that involve conflicting decisions by the federal circuit courts, cases that present important questions of civil rights or civil liberties, and cases in which the federal government is the appellant. Ultimately, however, the question of which cases to accept can come down to the preferences and priorities of the justices. If a group of justices believes that the Court should intervene in a particular area of policy or politics, they are likely to look for a case or cases that will serve as vehicles for judicial intervention. For many years, for example, the Court was not interested in considering challenges to affirmative action or other programs designed to provide particular benefits to minorities. In recent years, however, several of the Court 's more conservative justices have been eager to push back the limits of affirmative action and racial preference, and have therefore accepted a number of cases that would allow them to do so. In 1995, the Court's decision in *Adarand Constructors v. Pena, Missouri v. Jenkins,* and *Miller v. Johnson* placed new restrictions on federal affirmative action programs, school desegregation efforts, and attempts to increase minority representation in Congress through the creation of "minority districts" (see Chapter 9).[5] Similarly, because some justices have felt that the Court had gone too far in the past in restricting public support for religious ideas, the Court accepted the case of *Rosenberger v. University of Virginia.* This case was brought by a Christian student group against the University of Virginia, which had refused to provide student activities fund support for the group's magazine, *Wide Awake.* Other student publications received subsidies from the activities fund, but university policy prohibited grants to religious groups. Lower courts supported the university, finding that support for the magazine would violate the Constitution's prohibition against government support for religion. The Supreme Court, however, ruled in favor of the students' assertion that the university's policies amounted to support for some ideas but not others. The Court said this violated the First Amendment.[6]

WRITS Decisions handed down by lower courts can today reach the Supreme Court in one of three ways: through a writ of *certiorari;* in the case of convicted state prisoners, through a writ of *habeas corpus;* or on a writ of appeal. A writ is a court document conveying an order of some sort. In recent years, an effort has been made to give the Court more discretion regarding the cases it chooses to hear. Before 1988, the Supreme Court was obligated to review cases on a writ of appeal. This has since been eliminated, and the Court now has virtually complete discretion over what cases it will hear.

Most cases reach the Supreme Court through the ***writ of certiorari,*** which is granted whenever four of the nine justices agree to review a case. The Supreme Court was once so inundated with appeals that in 1925 Congress enacted laws giving it some control over its caseload with the power to issue writs of *certiorari.* Rule 10 of the Supreme Court's own rules of procedure defines *certiorari* as "not a matter of right, but of sound judicial discretion . . . granted only where there are special and important reasons therefor." The reasons provided for in Rule 10 are

1. Where a state court has made a decision that conflicts with previous Court decisions.
2. Where a state court has come up with an entirely new federal question.
3. Where one court of appeals has rendered a decision in conflict with another.
4. Where there are other inconsistent rulings between two or more courts or states.
5. Where a single court of appeals has sanctioned too great a departure by a lower court from normal judicial proceedings (a reason rarely given).

[5]Adarand Constructors v. Pena, 115 S.Ct. 2097 (1995); Missouri v. Jenkins, 115 S.Ct. 2573 (1995); Miller v. Johnson, 115 S.Ct. 2475 (1995).

[6]Rosenberger v. University of Virginia, 115 S.Ct. 2510 (1995).

JUDICIAL REVIEW

Appellate courts are courts that exist solely to hear cases on appeal and, therefore, have no original jurisdiction. The exception to this rule is the Supreme Court, the highest appellate court in the country, which has original jurisdiction over cases between the states and cases involving foreign ambassadors and foreign countries. Most other cases begin at the inferior trial courts or lower level courts, and then reach the Supreme Court in one of three ways:

Writ of Appeal	Writ of Certiorari	Writ of Habeas Corpus
A right available to all litigants	Not considered a right to all litigants	A fundamental safeguard of individual rights designed to enable an accused person to challenge arbitrary detention and to force an open trial before a judge
The Supreme Court accepts cases on appeal when it believes that it must do so	Cases heard when: state court decision conflicts with previous Supreme Court decisions; a new federal question has been raised; and if there have been inconsistent rulings between two or more states or courts of appeals	Cases appealed on a writ of *habeas corpus* are left to judicial discretion
Such cases are those in which a state law directly conflicts with the Constitution or a federal law, or where the United States is party to a civil suit	Most cases reach the Supreme Court on a writ of *certiorari*	
These situations occur rarely. The Court often remands the cases to a lower court rather than fully reviewing them	Cases appealed this way are left to judicial discretion where four of the nine justices must agree to hear the case	

The writ of **habeas corpus** is a fundamental safeguard of individual rights. Its historical purpose is to enable an accused person to challenge arbitrary detention and to force an open trial before a judge. But in 1867, Congress's distrust of Southern courts led it to confer on federal courts the authority to issue writs of *habeas corpus* to prisoners already tried or being tried in state courts, where the constitutional rights of the prisoner were possibly being violated. This writ gives state prisoners a second channel toward Supreme Court review in case their direct appeal from the

TABLE 7.1

Supreme Court Justices, 1995 (in order of seniority)

Name	Year of Birth	Prior Experience	Appointed By	Year of Appointment
William H. Rehnquist Chief Justice	1924	Assistant Attorney General	Nixon*	1972
John Paul Stevens	1916	Federal Judge	Ford	1975
Sandra Day O'Connor	1930	State Judge	Reagan	1981
Antonin Scalia	1936	Law Professor, Federal Judge	Reagan	1986
Anthony Kennedy	1937	Federal Judge	Reagan	1988
David Souter	1940	Federal Judge	Bush	1990
Clarence Thomas	1948	Federal Judge	Bush	1991
Ruth Bader Ginsburg	1933	Federal Judge	Clinton	1993
Stephen Breyer	1938	Federal Judge	Clinton	1994

*Appointed chief justice by Reagan in 1986.

highest state court fails. The writ of *habeas corpus* is discretionary; that is, the Court can decide which cases it will review.

The In Brief Box on page 189 explains the major differences between the writs of *certiorari*, *habeas corpus*, and appeal.

Judicial Review and Lawmaking

When courts of original jurisdiction apply existing statutes or past cases directly to citizens, the effect is the same as legislation. Lawyers study judicial decisions in order to discover underlying principles, and they advise their clients accordingly. Often the process is nothing more than reasoning by analogy; the facts in a particular case are so close to those in one or more previous cases that the same decision should be handed down.

The appellate courts, however, are in another realm. When a court of appeals hands down its decision, it accomplishes two things. First, of course, it decides who wins—the person who won in the lower court or the person who lost in the lower court. But at the same time, it expresses its decision in a manner that provides guidance to the lower courts for handling future cases in the

same area. Appellate judges try to give their reasons and rulings in writing so the "administration of justice" can take place most of the time at the lowest judicial level. They try to make their ruling or reasoning clear, so as to avoid confusion, which can produce a surge of litigation at the lower levels. These rulings can be considered laws, but they are laws governing the behavior only of the judiciary. Decisions by appellate courts affect citizens by giving them a cause of action or by taking it away from them. That is, they open or close access to the courts.

INFLUENCES ON SUPREME COURT DECISIONS

The judiciary is conservative in its procedures, but its impact on society can be radical. That impact depends on a variety of influences, two of which stand out above the rest. The first influence is the individual members of the Supreme Court, their attitudes, and their relationships with each other. The second is the Justice Department, especially the solicitor general, who regulates the flow of cases involving public law issues.

The Supreme Court Justices

If any individual judges in the country influence the federal judiciary, they are the Supreme Court justices (see Table 7.1). Often in American history, presidents have sought to gain influence over the Court through the justices they appoint but, just as often, have been disappointed. For instance, the Court's decision in *Roe v. Wade* prohibiting states from outlawing abortion was written by Justice Harry Blackmun, a Nixon appointee who had been expected to take conservative positions.[7] By the time of his retirement in 1994, Blackmun had become the most liberal member of the Supreme Court. Ironically, Justice Byron White, who retired in 1993, had become one of the more conservative members of the Court despite having been appointed by liberal president John F. Kennedy. Such ideological migrations show how difficult it is for presidents to shape the courts through the appointment process.

Republican presidents Ronald Reagan and George Bush both assigned a high priority to the creation of a judiciary more sympathetic to conservative ideas and interests. Influenced by their five appointees, the Court has grown more conservative over the past fifteen years, modifying many high-court decisions of the previous thirty years in the areas of civil rights, criminal procedures, and abortion.

In 1993, the Library of Congress made public the papers of the late Justice Thurgood Marshall, long a champion of civil rights. The papers reveal not only his disappointment with the conservative direction of the Court, but also the key role played by Reagan's appointees in bringing about that change. For one, the papers reveal how close the Court came to overturning *Roe* in its 1989 *Webster* decision. Chief Justice William Rehnquist's early drafts would have overturned *Roe*, but he had the support of only three other justices, Antonin Scalia, Anthony Kennedy, and Byron White, and needed Sandra Day O'Connor for a majority.

She ultimately decided not to support overturning *Roe*, and Rehnquist was forced to write a narrower ruling in the *Webster* case.[8]

Bill Clinton's election in 1992 and re-election in 1996 seemed to reduce the possibility of much further rightward drift on the part of the Court. During Clinton's first year in office, Justice Byron White, the conservative bloc's lone Democrat, announced his desire to retire. After a long search, the president nominated a Federal Appeals Court judge, Ruth Bader Ginsburg, to succeed White. Ginsburg was known as a moderate liberal. She had a long record of support for abortion rights and women's rights. As a federal appeals court judge, however, she often sided with the government in criminal cases and did not hesitate to vote against affirmative action plans she deemed to be too broad.

During her first term on the Court, Ginsburg was most frequently aligned with Souter and generally strengthened the Court's moderate center, especially cases dealing with the issues of religious exercise and abortion.[9]

In 1994, President Clinton named Federal Appeals Court Judge Stephen Breyer to succeed retiring Justice Harry Blackmun. Breyer was generally viewed as another judicial moderate, unlikely to change the Court's present direction. And indeed, in 1995, 1996, and 1997, the Court continued on a conservative course in some areas, issuing rulings that placed limits on affirmative action, school desegregation, voting rights, the separation of church and state, and the power of the national government vis-à-vis the states.[10]

---

[7]Roe v. Wade, 410 U.S. 113 (1973).

[8]Webster v. Reproductive Health Services, 109 S.Ct. 3040 (1989). See also Joan Biskupic, "The Marshall Files: How an Era Ended in Civil Rights Law," *Washington Post*, 24 May 1993, p. 1; and Benjamin Weiser and Bob Woodward, "Roe's Eleventh-Hour Reprieve: 89 Drafts Show Court Poised to Strike Down Abortion Ruling," *Washington Post*, 23 May 1993, p. 1.

[9]Joan Biskupic, "Justices Follow a Mostly Conservative Course," *Washington Post*, 4 July 1994, p. 1.

[10]See Adarand Constructors v. Pena, 115 S.Ct. 2097 (1995); Miller v. Johnson, 63 USLW 4726 (1995); Missouri v. Jenkins, 115 S.Ct. 2038 (1995); U. S. v. Lopez, 115 S.Ct. 1624 (1995); Bush v. Vera 116 S.Ct. 1941 (1996); Shaw v. Hunt 64 USLW 4437 (1996); Abrams v. Johnson 95-1425 (1997); Rosenberger v.

Thurgood Marshall and Clarence Thomas
From Helping Others to Self-Help

As the first and second African Americans to serve on the Supreme Court, Thurgood Marshall and Clarence Thomas both claimed humble origins rooted in America's troubled racial past. Marshall was the great-grandson of a slave; Thomas was a sharecropper's grandson. Yet their public careers represent diametrically opposed views on how the law should treat disadvantaged citizens.

Born and raised in a Baltimore family of modest means but grand ambitions, Marshall graduated from Howard Law School and began a legal practice specializing in cases defending blacks mistreated by the legal system. In 1938, he became head of legal services for the National Association for the Advancement of Colored People (NAACP). In the 1940s and 1950s, he spearheaded legal efforts to end discrimination, arguing thirty-two cases before the Supreme Court (including *Brown v. Board of Education*). After Marshall had served on the U.S. Court of Appeals and as President Lyndon Johnson's solicitor general, he was elevated by Johnson to the Supreme Court in 1967.

Clarence Thomas's appointment to the high court by President George Bush in 1991 reinforced the Court's more conservative tendencies. His early education in a Catholic seminary had instilled in Thomas the belief that hard work and individual initiative could overcome racial discrimination and other adversities. Ironically, Thomas won admission to Yale Law School on a program aimed at recruiting blacks and others from disadvantaged backgrounds. His rapid rise included service in the Missouri attorney general's office. In his early work, Thomas carefully avoided race-related issues, but the Reagan administration named him head of the Equal Employment Opportu-

THURGOOD MARSHALL

The exceptions to the Court's conservative course have been in the areas of free speech, gay rights, and women's rights. In the Court's most important recent free speech case, *Reno v. American Civil Liberties Union*, the Communications Deency Act, a federal law restricting indecent material on the internet, was struck down as a violation of free speech.[11] In the 1996 case of *Virginia v. United States* the Court ruled that Virginia Military Institute's exclusion of women constituted a violation of the constitutional guarantee of equal protection. And, in the case of *Romer v. Evans* the Court declared that states may not prohibit local governments from writing ordinances that protect homosexuals from discrimination.[12] In these decisions, the Court appeared to be making a distinc-

---

University of Virginia, 94-329 (1995); Agostini v. Felton 96-522 (1997); Printz v. U.S. 95-1478 (1997); Mack v. U.S. 95-1503 (1997); City of Boerne v. Flores 95-2074 (1997).

[11]Reno v. A.C.L.U. 96-5611 (1997).
[12]Virginia v. U.S. 64 USLW 4638 (1996); Romer v. Evans 116 S.Ct. 1620 (1996).

nity Commission, the agency that enforces laws against discrimination. Thomas then served briefly on the court of appeals before his ascension to the Supreme Court.

In his many opinions from the bench, Marshall championed government efforts to eliminate discrimination through such means as busing to achieve racial balance in schools and the implementation of affirmative action programs designed to provide educational and employment opportunities for those who had been historically closed out of certain areas. Thomas has been a strong critic of such programs. In a 1987 law journal article, for example, Thomas criticized the landmark *Brown* case; later he sharply attacked Marshall himself, saying that it was wrong for Marshall to dwell on slavery during the commemoration of the Constitution's bicentennial.

Thomas himself ran afoul of the nation's heightened sensitivity to discrimination and fair treatment when a former employee, Oklahoma law school professor Anita Hill, leveled charges of sexual harassment against him that riveted the nation's attention.

On the Court, Thomas's conservative philosophy has stood in stark contrast to Marshall's liberal philosophy. Unlike the man he succeeded, Thomas favors the death penalty (including limiting death penalty appeals) and limiting the rights of the accused, opposes abortion rights, and in general has sided with the conservative activist wing of the Court.

Justice Marshall sought to focus the powers of government to assist those who have benefited least from the American system. Justice Thomas argues that self-help and limited government interference provide the most appropriate remedy for injustice. Both of these arguments will continue to find support in American courts.

CLARENCE THOMAS

SOURCE: Richard Kluger, *Simple Justice* (New York: Vintage Books, 1975).

tion between affirmative action—or positive governmental action on behalf of a minority group—and equal protection, meaning equality before the law. Liberals argue that equal protection is not enough to vindicate the rights of minorities that have long suffered from discriminatory treatment. The current Supreme Court majority, however, does not appear to accept this view.

Thus, while the 1992 and 1996 elections had seemed to offer new possibilities for the expansion of judicial liberalism, by 1997 the Court's more conservative justices—Rehnquist, Scalia, and Thomas—appeared to have increased their influence. The political struggles of the 1980s and 1990s amply illustrate the importance of who sits on the Supreme Court. Is abortion a fundamental right or a criminal activity? How much separation must there be between church and state? Does the use of the Voting Rights Act to increase minority representation constitute a violation of the rights of whites? The answers to these and many other questions cannot be found in the words of the Constitution. They must be located, instead, in the hearts of the judges who interpret that text.

BOX 7.5

Dissenting Opinion

DISSENTING OPINIONS DIFFER significantly in form from majority opinions. A dissenting opinion points out the fallacies in the majority's reasoning and attempts to lay the groundwork for limiting or overruling the majority opinion in the future. Because a dissenting judge need not hold together a majority of the Court, such an opinion is often quite direct in its criticism of the majority. For example, in *New York v. Quarles* (1984), Justice Marshall began his dissent with the observation that "[t]he majority's treatment of the legal issues presented in this case is no less troubling than its abuse of the facts."

In *Bowers v. Hardwick* (1986), the Supreme Court was asked to decide whether a Georgia statute prohibiting sodomy violated a constitutional right to privacy. Hardwick, a Georgia male, had been cited for violating the statute by engaging in consensual sexual activity with another male in Hardwick's home. The majority of the Court upheld the Georgia statute, ruling that the constitutional right of privacy protected the traditional family unit and did not protect conduct between homosexuals when that conduct offended "traditional Judeo-Christian values." The following passage is excerpted from the dissenting opinion of Justice Blackmun:

> This case is no more about "a fundamental right to engage in homosexual sodomy," as the Court purports to declare . . . than *Stanley v. Georgia* was about a fundamental right to watch obscene movies, or *Katz v. United States* was about a fundamental right to place interstate bets from a telephone booth. Rather, this case is about "the most comprehensive rights and the right most valued by civilized men," namely, "the right to be let alone" (*Olmstead v. United States*).

> * * *

> Like Justice Holmes, I believe that "[i]t is revolting to have no better reason for a rule of law than that it was laid down in the time of Henry IV. It is still more revolting if the grounds upon which it was laid down have vanished long since, and the rule simply persists from blind imitation of the past" (Holmes, *The Path of the Law*). I believe we must analyze respondent's claim in the light of the values that underlie the constitutional right to privacy. If that right means anything, it means that, before Georgia can prosecute its citizens for making choices about the most intimate aspects of their lives, it must do more than assert that the choice they have made is an "abominable crime not fit to be named among Christians" (*Herring v. State*).

> * * *

> I can only hope that . . . the Court soon will reconsider its analysis and conclude that depriving individuals of the right to choose for themselves how to conduct their intimate relationships poses a far greater threat to the values most deeply rooted in our Nation's history than tolerance of nonconformity could ever do. Because I think the Court today betrays those values, I dissent.

OPINION WRITING   When the Court reaches a decision on a case, it renders an *"opinion."* The Court issues both a majority opinion and a minority, or *dissenting, opinion.* The assignment to write the majority opinion in an important constitutional case is an opportunity for the chosen justice to exercise great influence on the Court. The assignment is made by the chief justice, or by the senior associate justice in the majority when the chief justice is a dissenter. But it is not a simple procedure. Serious thought has to be given to the impression the case will make on lawyers and on the public and to the probability that one justice's opinion will be more widely accepted than another's.

One of the more dramatic instances of this tactical consideration occurred in 1944, when Chief Justice Harlan F. Stone chose Justice Felix Frankfurter to write the opinion in the "white primary" case, *Smith v. Allwright*. The chief justice believed that this sensitive case, which curtailed the Southern practice of prohibiting black participation in nominating primaries, required the efforts of the most brilliant and scholarly jurist on the Court. But the day after Stone made the assignment, Justice Robert H. Jackson wrote a letter to Stone urging a change of assignment. In it Jackson argued that Frankfurter, a foreign-born Jew from New England, would not win the South with his opinion, regardless of its brilliance. Stone accepted the advice and substituted Justice Stanley Reed, an American-born Protestant from Kentucky, who was a Southern Democrat in good standing.[13]

DISSENT   Ironically, the most dependable way an individual justice can exercise a direct and clear influence on the Court is to write a dissenting opinion. Because there is no need to please a majority, dissenting opinions can be more eloquent and less guarded than majority opinions (see Box 7.4). Indeed, some of the greatest writing in the history of the Court is found in dissents, and some of the most famous justices, such as Oliver Wendell Holmes and Louis D. Brandeis earlier in this cen-

[13]*Smith v. Allwright*, 321 U.S. 649 (1944).

tury, and liberal Justice William O. Douglas in more recent years, were notable dissenters. In the single 1952–1953 Court term, Douglas wrote dissenting opinions in thirty-five cases. In the 1958–1959 term, he wrote eleven dissents. During the latter term, Justices Felix Frankfurter and John Harlan wrote thirteen and nine dissents, respectively.

Dissent plays a special role in the work and impact of the Court because it amounts to an appeal to lawyers all over the country to keep bringing cases of the sort at issue. Therefore, an effective dissent influences the flow of cases through the Court as well as the arguments that will be used by lawyers in later cases. Even more important, dissent emphasizes the fact that, although the Court speaks with a single opinion, it is the opinion only of the majority—and one day the majority might go the other way.

Individual Supreme Court justices thus have a certain amount of influence by virtue of their participation in choosing cases and in constituting a majority—or a dissenting minority—on the decisions. Since four justices must vote to grant *certiorari*, however, there are only three ways a single justice can significantly influence the judicial process: (1) by writing an eloquent dissenting opinion, (2) by issuing a stay of execution pending full Court review, and (3) by issuing a writ of habeas corpus, temporarily removing a criminal case from state jurisdiction until the Court can

IN BRIEF BOX

INFLUENCES ON SUPREME COURT DECISIONS

The Justices	Controlling the Flow of Cases
The ideologies of the justices have a great influence on the decisions of the Court. These ideologies are made known through opinion writing. Dissenting opinions can be more eloquent and less guarded than majority opinions and they indicate to lawyers that there is a sympathetic ear on the Court for such cases, thus encouraging such cases to be brought to the Court again.	The solicitor general exercises a great deal of control over what cases are heard by the Supreme Court. He or she has the power to screen cases long before they approach the Supreme Court level and can write an *amicus curiae* brief so as to enter a case even when the federal government is not a litigant.

determine its merits. The latter two powers lead to temporary stoppage pending review by the full Court.

Controlling the Flow of Cases—The Role of the Solicitor General

If any single person has greater influence than the individual justices over the work of the Supreme Court, it is the **solicitor general** of the United States. The solicitor general is third in status in the Justice Department (below the attorney general and the deputy attorney general, who serve as the government's chief prosecutors) but is the top government defense lawyer in almost all cases before the appellate courts where the government is a party. Although others can regulate the flow of cases, the solicitor general has the greatest control, with no review of his or her actions by any higher authority in the executive branch. More than half the Supreme Court's total workload consists of cases under the direct charge of the solicitor general. Even the bland description in the *U.S. Government Manual* cannot mask the extraordinary importance of this official:

> The Solicitor General is in charge of representing the Government in the Supreme Court. He decides what cases the Government should ask the Supreme Court to review and what position the Government should take in cases before the Court; he supervises the preparation of the Government's Supreme Court briefs and other legal documents and the conduct of the oral arguments in the Court and argues most of the important cases himself. The Solicitor General's duties also include deciding whether the United States should appeal in all cases it loses before the lower courts.[14]

The solicitor general exercises especially strong influence by screening cases long before they approach the Supreme Court; the justices rely on the solicitor general to "screen out undeserving litigation and furnish them with an agenda to govern-

ment cases that deserve serious consideration."[15] Agency heads may lobby the president or otherwise try to circumvent the solicitor general, and a few of the independent agencies have a statutory right to make direct appeals, but these are almost inevitably doomed to **per curiam** rejection—rejection through a brief, unsigned opinion by the whole Court—if the solicitor general refuses to participate.

The solicitor general can enter a case even when the federal government is not a direct litigant by writing an **amicus curiae** ("friend of the court") brief. A "friend of the court" is not a direct party to a case but has a vital interest in its outcome. Thus, when the government has such an interest, the solicitor general can file an *amicus curiae,* or the Court can invite such a brief because it wants an opinion in writing. The solicitor general also has the power to invite others to enter cases as *amici curiae.*

JUDICIAL POWER AND POLITICS

One of the most important institutional changes to occur in the United States during the past half-century has been the striking transformation of the role and power of the federal courts, those of the Supreme Court in particular. Understanding how this transformation came about is the key to understanding the contemporary role of the courts in America.

Traditional Limitations on the Federal Courts

For much of American history, the power of the federal courts was subject to five limitations.[16] First, courts were constrained by judicial rules of standing that limited access to the bench (see Box 7.4, page 186). Claimants who simply disagreed

---

[14]*United States Government Organization Manual* (Washington, DC: Government Printing Office, 1985).

[15]Robert Scigliano, *The Supreme Court and the Presidency* (New York: Free Press, 1971), p. 162. For an interesting critique of the solicitor general's role during the Reagan administration, see Lincoln Caplan, "Annals of the Law," *New Yorker,* 17 August 1987, pp. 30–62.

[16]For limits on judicial power, see Alexander Bickel, *The Least Dangerous Branch* (Indianapolis: Bobbs-Merrill, 1962).

with governmental action or inaction could not obtain access. Access to the courts was limited to individuals who could show that they were directly affected by the government's behavior in some area. This limitation on access to the courts diminished the judiciary's capacity to forge links with important political and social forces. Second, courts were traditionally limited in the kind of relief they could provide. In general, courts acted only to offer relief or assistance to individuals and not to broad social classes, again inhibiting the formation of alliances between the courts and important social forces.

Third, courts lacked enforcement powers of their own and were compelled to rely upon executive or state agencies to ensure compliance with their edicts. If the executive or state agencies were unwilling to assist the courts, judicial enactments could go unheeded, as was illustrated when President Andrew Jackson declined to enforce Chief Justice John Marshall's 1832 order to the state of Georgia to release two missionaries it had arrested on Cherokee lands. Marshall asserted that the state had no right to enter the lands of the Cherokees without their assent.[17] Jackson is reputed to have said, "John Marshall has made his decision, now let *him* enforce it."

Fourth, federal judges are appointed by the president (with the consent of the Senate). As a result, the president and Congress can shape the composition of the federal courts and ultimately, perhaps, the character of judicial decisions. Finally, Congress has the power to change both the size and the jurisdiction of the Supreme Court and other federal courts. In many areas, federal courts obtain their jurisdiction not from the Constitution but from the congressional statutes. On a number of occasions, Congress has threatened to take matters out of the Court's hands when it was unhappy with the Court's rulings on certain cases.[18] For example, on one memorable occasion,

presidential and congressional threats to expand the size of the Court—Franklin Roosevelt's "court packing" plan—encouraged the justices to drop their opposition to New Deal programs.

As a result of these five limitations on judicial power, through much of their history the chief function of the federal courts has been to provide judicial support for executive agencies and to legitimate acts of Congress by declaring them to be consistent with constitutional principles. Only on rare occasions did the federal courts actually dare to challenge Congress or the executive.[19]

Two Judicial Revolutions

Since the Second World War, however, the role of the federal judiciary has been strengthened and expanded. There have actually been two judicial revolutions in the United States since World War II. The first and most visible of these was the substantive revolution in judicial policy. In policy areas, including school desegregation, legislative apportionment, and criminal procedure, as well as obscenity, abortion, and voting rights, the Supreme Court was at the forefront of a series of sweeping changes in the role of the U.S. government and, ultimately, in the character of American society.[20]

But at the same time that the courts were introducing important policy innovations, they were also bringing about a second, less visible revolution. During the 1960s and 1970s, the Supreme Court and other federal courts instituted a series of changes in judicial procedure that fundamentally expanded the power of the courts in the United States. First, the federal courts liberalized the concept of standing to permit almost any group to bring its case before the federal bench. This change has given the courts a far greater role

[17]Worcester v. Georgia, 6 Peters 515 (1832).
[18]See Walter Murphy, *Congress and the Court* (Chicago: University of Chicago Press, 1962).

[19]Robert Dahl, "The Supreme Court and National Policy Making," *Journal of Public Law* 6 (1958), p. 279.
[20]Martin Shapiro, "The Supreme Court: From Warren to Burger," in *The New American Political System*, ed. Anthony King (Washington, DC: American Enterprise Institute, 1978).

DEBATING THE ISSUES

Interpreting the Constitution and Original Intent

*J*UDGES BEAR THE RESPONSIBILITY *of interpreting the meaning and applicability of the Constitution, written over two hundred years ago, to modern society. The application of constitutional principles to modern problems is inherently difficult because of disagreements over what the founders intended and over how the Constitution's words ought to apply to issues and problems unimagined in the eighteenth century.*

Former federal judge Robert H. Bork argues in favor of the "original intent" approach, urging judges to stick as closely to the Constitution's text and original meaning as possible. Constitutional scholar Leonard W. Levy counters that original intent, even if it could be divined, is an inadequate and inappropriate way to deal with constitutional interpretation.

BORK

What was once the dominant view of constitutional law—that a judge is to apply the Constitution according to the principles intended by those who ratified the document—is now very much out of favor among the theorists of the field. . . .

In truth, only the approach of original understanding meets the criteria that any theory of constitutional adjudication must meet in order to possess democratic legitimacy. Only that approach is consonant with the design of the American Republic. . . .

. . . The original understanding is . . . manifested in the words used and in secondary materials, such as debates at the conventions, public discussion, newspaper articles, dictionaries in use at the time, and the like.

The search for the intent of the lawmaker is the everyday procedure of lawyers and judges when they apply a statute, a contract, a will, or the opinion of a court. . . . Lawyers and judges should seek in the Constitution what they seek in other legal texts: the original meaning of the words. . . .

A judge, no matter on what court he sits, may never create new constitutional rights or destroy old ones. Any time he does so, he violates the limits of his own authority and, for that reason, also violates the rights of the legislature and the people. . . .

The role of a judge committed to the philosophy of original understanding is not to "choose a level of ab-

in the administrative process than ever before. Many federal judges are concerned that federal legislation in areas such as health care reform would create new rights and entitlements that would give rise to a deluge of court cases. "Any time you create a new right, you create a host of disputes and claims," warned Barbara Rothstein, chief judge of the federal district court in Seattle, Washington.[21]

Second, the federal courts broadened the scope of relief to permit action on behalf of broad categories or classes of persons in "class action" cases, rather than just on behalf of individuals.[22] A *class action suit* permits large numbers of persons with common interests to join together under a representative party to bring or defend a lawsuit.

Third, the federal courts began to employ so-

[21]Toni Locy, "Bracing for Health Care's Caseload," *Washington Post*, 22 August 1994, p. A15.

[22]See "Developments in the Law—Class Actions," *Harvard Law Review* 89 (1976), p. 1318.

straction." Rather, it is to find the meaning of a text—a process which includes finding its degree of generality, which is part of its meaning—and to apply that text to a particular situation. . . . The equal-protection clause [for example] was adopted in order to protect freed slaves, but its language, being general, applies to all persons.[1]

LEVY

James Madison, Father of the Constitution and of the Bill of Rights, rejected the doctrine that the original intent of those who framed the Constitution should be accepted as an authoritative guide to its meaning. "As a guide in expounding and applying the provisions of the Constitution . . . the debates and incidental decisions of the Convention can have no authoritative character." . . . We tend to forget the astounding fact that Madison's Notes were first published in 1840, fifty-three years after the Constitutional Convention had met. . . . What mattered to them [the founders] was the text of the Constitution, construed in the light of conventional rules of interpretation, the ratification debates, and other contemporary expositions. . . . Original intent is an unreliable concept because it assumes the existence of one intent. . . . The entity we call "the Framers" did not have a collective mind. . . . In fact, they disagreed on many crucial matters. . . .

Fifty years ago . . . Jacobus tenBroek asserted, rightly, that "the intent theory . . . inverts the judicial process." . . . Original intent . . . makes the judge "a mindless robot whose task is the utterly mechanical function" of using original intent as a measure of constitutionality. In the entire history of the Supreme Court . . . no Justice employing the intent theory has ever written a convincing and reliable study.

The Court has the responsibility of helping regenerate and fulfill the noblest aspirations for which the nation stands. It must keep constitutional law constantly rooted in the great ideals of the past yet in a state of evolution in order to realize them. . . . Chief Justice Earl Warren . . . declared, "We serve only the public interest as we see it, guided only by the Constitution and our own consciences." That, not the original intent of the Framers, is our reality.[2]

[1]Robert H. Bork, "The Case against Political Judging," *National Review,* 8 December 1989, pp. 23–28.
[2]Leonard W. Levy, *Original Intent and the Framers' Constitution* (New York: Macmillan, 1988), pp. 1–2, 294, 388, 396, 398.

called structural remedies, in effect retaining jurisdiction of cases until the court's mandate had actually been implemented to its satisfaction.[23] The best-known of these instances was Federal Judge W. Arthur Garrity's effort to operate the Boston school system from his bench in order to ensure its desegregation. Between 1974 and 1985, Judge Garrity issued fourteen decisions relating to different aspects of the Boston school desegregation plan that had been developed under his authority and put into effect under his supervision.[24] In its 5-to-4 decision in the 1990 case of *Missouri v. Jenkins*, the Supreme Court held that federal judges could actually order local governments to increase taxes to remedy such violations of the Constitution as school segregation.[25] This decision upheld an order by a federal district judge,

[23]See Donald Horowitz, *The Courts and Social Policy* (Washington, DC: Brookings Institution, 1977).

[24]Moran v. McDonough, 540 F. 2nd 527 (1 Cir., 1976; *cert denied* 429 U.S. 1042 [1977]).
[25]Missouri v. Jenkins, 110 S.Ct. 1651 (1990).

Russel G. Clark, to the Kansas City, Missouri, school board to adopt a "magnet" school plan that would lessen segregation in the schools. Potentially, this decision claims for the judiciary the power to levy taxes—a power normally seen as belonging to elected legislatures.

Through these three judicial mechanisms, the federal courts paved the way for an unprecedented expansion of national judicial power. In essence, liberalization of the rules of standing and expansion of the scope of judicial relief drew the federal courts into linkages with important social interests and classes, while the introduction of structural remedies enhanced the courts' abilities to serve these constituencies. Thus, during the 1960s and 1970s, the power of the federal courts expanded in the same way that the power of the executive expanded during the 1930s—through links with constituencies, such as civil rights, consumer, environmental, and feminist groups, that staunchly defended the Supreme Court in its battles with Congress, the executive, or other interest groups.

The Reagan and Bush administrations, of course, sought to end the relationship between the Court and liberal political forces. As we have seen, the conservative judges appointed by these Republican presidents modified the Court's position in areas such as abortion, affirmative action, and judicial procedure—though not as completely as some conservatives had hoped. Interestingly, however, the Court has not been eager to surrender the expanded powers carved out by its liberal predecessors. In a number of decisions during the 1980s and 1990s, the Court was willing to make use of its expanded powers on behalf of interests it favored.[26]

In the important 1992 case of *Lujan v. Defenders of Wildlife*, the Court seemed to retreat to a concep-

tion of standing more restrictive than that affirmed by liberal activist jurists.[27] Rather than an example of judicial restraint, however, the *Lujan* case was actually a direct judicial challenge to congressional power. The case involved an effort by an environmental group, the Defenders of Wildlife, to make use of the 1973 Endangered Species Act to block the expenditure of federal funds being used by the governments of Egypt and Sri Lanka for public works projects. Environmentalists charged that the projects threatened the habitats of several endangered species of birds and, therefore, that the expenditure of federal funds to support the projects violated the 1973 act. The Interior Department claimed that the act affected only domestic projects.[28]

The Endangered Species Act, like a number of other pieces of liberal environmental and consumer legislation enacted by Congress, encourages citizen suits—suits by activist groups not directly harmed by the action in question—to challenge government policies they deem to be inconsistent with the act. Justice Scalia, however, writing for the Court's majority, reasserted a more traditional conception of standing, requiring those bringing suit against a government policy to show that the policy is likely to cause *them* direct and imminent injury.

Had Scalia stopped at this point, the case might have been seen as an example of judicial restraint. Scalia went on, however, to question the validity of any statutory provision for citizen suits. Such legislative provisions, according to Justice Scalia, violate Article III of the Constitution, which limits the federal courts to consideration of actual "cases" and "controversies." This interpretation would strip Congress of its capacity to promote the enforcement of regulatory statutes by encouraging activist groups not di-

---

[26]Mark Silverstein and Benjamin Ginsberg, "The Supreme Court and the New Politics of Judicial Power," *Political Science Quarterly* 102 (Fall 1987), pp. 371–88.

[27]Lujan v. Defenders of Wildlife, 112 S.Ct. 2130 (1992).
[28]Linda Greenhouse, "Court Limits Legal Standing in Suits," *New York Times*, 13 June 1992, p. 12.

rectly affected or injured to be on the lookout for violations that could provide the basis for lawsuits. This enforcement mechanism—which conservatives liken to bounty hunting—was an extremely important congressional instrument and played a prominent part in the enforcement of such pieces of legislation as the 1990 Americans with Disabilities Act (see Chapter 4). Thus, the *Lujan* case offers an example of judicial activism rather than of judicial restraint; even the most conservative justices are reluctant to surrender the powers now wielded by the Court.

CHAPTER REVIEW

Millions of cases come to trial every year in the United States. The great majority—nearly 99 percent—are tried in state and local courts. The types of law are civil law, criminal law, and public law. Cases are heard at the state level before three types of courts: trial court, appellate court, and (state) supreme court.

There are three kinds of federal cases: (1) civil cases involving diversity of citizenship, (2) civil cases where a federal agency is seeking to enforce federal laws that provide for civil penalties, and (3) cases involving federal criminal statutes or where state criminal cases have been made issues of public law.

The organization of the federal judiciary provides for original jurisdiction in the federal district courts, the U.S. Court of Claims, the U.S. Tax Court, the Customs Court, and federal regulatory agencies.

Each district court is in one of the twelve appellate districts, called circuits, presided over by a court of appeals. Appellate courts admit no new evidence; their rulings are based solely on the records of the court proceedings or agency hearings that led to the original decision. Appeals court rulings are final unless the Supreme Court chooses to review them.

The Supreme Court has some original jurisdiction, but its major job is to review lower court decisions involving substantial issues of public law. Supreme Court decisions can be reversed by Congress and the state legislatures, but this seldom happens. There is no explicit constitutional authority for the Supreme Court to review acts of Congress. Nonetheless, the 1803 case of *Marbury v. Madison* established the Court's right to review congressional acts. The supremacy clause of Article VI and the Judiciary Act of 1789 give the Court the power to review state constitutions and laws.

Cases reach the Court mainly through the writ of *certiorari*. The Supreme Court controls its caseload by issuing few writs and by handing down clear leading opinions that enable lower courts to resolve future cases without further review.

Judge-made law is like a statute in that it articulates the law as it relates to future controversies. It differs from a statute in that it is intended to guide judges rather than the citizenry in general.

The judiciary as a whole is subject to two major influences: (1) the individual members of the Supreme Court, who have lifetime tenure; and (2) the Justice Department—particularly the solicitor general, who regulates the flow of cases.

The influence of an individual member of the Supreme Court is limited when the Court is polarized, and close votes in a polarized Court impair the value of the decision rendered. Writing the majority opinion for a case gives a justice an opportunity to influence the judiciary. But the need to frame an opinion in such a way as to develop majority support on the Court may limit such opportunities. Dissenting opinions can have more impact than the majority opinion; they stimulate a continued flow of cases around that issue. The solicitor general is the most important single influence outside the Court itself because he or she controls the flow of cases brought by the Justice Department and also shapes the argument in those cases.

In recent years, the importance of the federal judiciary—the Supreme Court in particular—has increased substantially as the courts have developed new tools of judicial power and forged alliances with important forces in American society.

TIME LINE ON THE JUDICIARY	
Events	**Institutional Developments**
George Washington appoints John Jay chief justice (1789–1795)	Judiciary Act creates federal court system (1789)
1800	
John Marshall appointed chief justice (1801)	*Marbury v. Madison* provides for judicial review (1803)
States attempt to tax the second Bank of the U.S. (1818)	*McCulloch v. Maryland*—Court upholds supremacy clause, broad construction of necessary and proper clause; denies right of states to tax federal agencies (1819)
Andrew Jackson appoints Roger Taney chief justice; Taney Court expands power of states (1835)	*Barron v. Baltimore*—Court rules that only the federal government and not the states are limited by the U.S. Bill of Rights (1833)
1850	
Period of westward expansion; continuing conflict and congressional compromises over slavery in the territories (1830–1850s)	*Dred Scott v. Sandford*—Court rules that federal government cannot exclude slavery from the territories (1857)
Civil War (1861–1865)	*Slaughter-House Cases*—Court limits scope of Fourteenth Amendment to newly freed slaves; states retain right to regulate state businesses (1873)
Reconstruction (1867–1877)	
Self-government restored to former Confederate states (1877)	
1890	
"Jim Crow" laws spread throughout Southern states (1890s)	*Plessy v. Ferguson*—Court upholds doctrine of "separate but equal" (1896)
World War I; wartime pacifist agitation in U.S. (1914–1918)	*Abrams v. U.S.* (1919) and *Gitlow v. N.Y.* (1925) apply First Amendment to states and limit free speech by "clear and present danger" test
Red Scare; postwar anarchist agitation (1919–1920)	

Events	Institutional Developments
1930	
FDR's New Deal (1930s)	Court invalidates many New Deal laws, e.g., *Shechter Poultry Co. v. U.S.* (1935)
Court-packing crisis—proposal to increase the number of Supreme Court justices defeated by Congress (1937)	Court reverses position, upholds most of New Deal, e.g., *NLRB v. Jones & Laughlin Steel* (1937)
U.S. enters World War II (1941–1945)	*Korematsu v. U.S.*—Court approves sending Japanese-Americans to internment camps (1944)
1950	
Korean War (1950–1953)	*Youngstown Sheet & Tube Co. v. Sawyer*—Court rules that president's steel seizure must be authorized by statute (1952)
Earl Warren appointed chief justice (1953)	
Civil Rights movement (1950s and 1960s)	*Brown v. Board of Ed.*—Court holds that school segregation is unconstitutional (1954)
	Court begins nationalization of the Bill of Rights—*Baker v. Carr* (1962); *Gideon v. Wainwright* (1963); *Escobedo v. Ill.* (1964); *Miranda v. Arizona* (1966), etc.
Consumer, environmental, feminist, and antinuclear movements (1960s–1990s)	*Flast v. Cohen*—Court permits class action suits (1968)
Warren Burger appointed chief justice (1969)	
1970	
Right-to-life movement (1970s–1990s)	*Roe v. Wade*—Court strikes down state laws making abortion illegal (1973)
Affirmative action programs (1970s–1990s)	*U.S. v. Nixon*—Court limits executive privilege (1974)
Court arbitrates conflicts between Congress and president (1970s–1980s)	*Univ. of Calif. v. Bakke*—Court holds that race may be taken into account but limits use of quotas (1978)
William Rehnquist appointed chief justice (1986)	*Bowsher v. Synar*—Court invalidates portion of Gramm-Rudman Act (1986); *Morrison v. Olson*—Court upholds constitutionality of special prosecutor (1988)
	Reagan and Bush appointees create a Republican Court (1980–1991)
1990	
Bush appoints David Souter (1990) and Clarence Thomas (1991) to the Supreme Court	Souter, O'Connor, and Kennedy form moderate bloc (1992)
Clinton appoints Ruth Bader Ginsburg (1993) and Stephen Breyer (1994) to the Supreme Court	

KEY TERMS

amicus curiae   Literally, "friend of the court"; individuals or groups who are not parties to a lawsuit but who seek to assist the court in reaching a decision by presenting additional briefs.

appellate court   A court that hears the appeals of trial court decisions.

chief justice   Justice on the Supreme Court who presides over the Court's public sessions.

civil law   A system of jurisprudence, including private law and governmental actions, to settle disputes that do not involve criminal penalties.

class action suit   A lawsuit in which large numbers of persons with common interests join together under a representative party to bring or defend a lawsuit, such as hundreds of workers together suing a company.

criminal law   The branch of law that deals with disputes or actions involving criminal penalties (as opposed to civil law). It regulates the conduct of individuals, defines crimes, and provides punishment for criminal acts.

defendant   The individual or organization against whom a complaint is brought in criminal or civil cases.

dissenting opinion   Decision written by a justice in the minority in a particular case in which the justice wishes to express his or her reasoning in the case.

due process   To proceed according to law and with adequate protection for individual rights.

en banc   As a panel; involving all the judges on a court.

habeas corpus   A court order demanding that an individual in custody be brought into court and shown the cause for detention. *Habeas corpus* is guaranteed by the Constitution and can be suspended only in cases of rebellion or invasion.

judicial review   Power of the courts to declare actions of the legislative and executive branches invalid or unconstitutional. The Supreme Court asserted this power in *Marbury v. Madison.*

jurisdiction   The authority of a court to initially consider a case. Distinguished from appellate jurisdiction, which is the authority to hear appeals from a lower court's decision.

mootness   A criterion used by courts to screen cases that no longer require resolution.

opinion   The written explanation of the Supreme Court's decision in a particular case.

per curiam   Decision by an appellate court, without a written opinion, that refuses to review the decision of a lower court; amounts to a reaffirmation of the lower court's opinion.

plaintiff   The individual or organization who brings a complaint in court.

plea bargains   Negotiated agreements in criminal cases in which a defendant agrees to plead guilty in return for the state's agreement to reduce the severity of the criminal charge the defendant is facing.

precedents   Prior cases whose principles are used by judges as the bases for their decisions in present cases.

public law   Cases in private law, civil law, or criminal law in which one party to the dispute argues that a license is unfair, a law is inequitable or unconstitutional, or an agency has acted unfairly, violated a procedure, or gone beyond its jurisdiction.

solicitor general   The top government lawyer in all cases before the appellate courts where the government is a party.

standing   The right of an individual or organization to initiate a court case.

stare decisis   Literally "let the decision stand." A previous decision by a court applies as a precedent in similar cases until that decision is overruled.

supremacy clause   Article VI of the Constitution, which states that laws passed by the national government and all treaties are the supreme laws of the land and superior to all laws adopted by any state or any subdivision.

supreme court   The highest court in a particular state or in the United States. This court primarily serves an appellate function.

trial court   The first court to hear a criminal or civil case.

Universal Commercial Code   A set of standards for contract law recognized by all states that greatly reduces interstate differences in the practice of contract law.

writ of *certiorari*   A decision of at least four of the nine Supreme Court justices to review a decision of a lower court; from the Latin "to make more certain."

FOR FURTHER READING

Abraham, Henry. *The Judicial Process,* 6th ed. New York: Oxford University Press, 1993.

Bickel, Alexander. *The Least Dangerous Branch.* Indianapolis: Bobbs-Merrill, 1962.

Blasi, Vincent. *The Burger Court: The Counter-Revolution That Wasn't.* New Haven: Yale University Press, 1983.

Bryner, Gary, and Dennis L. Thompson. *The Constitution and the Regulation of Society.* Provo, UT: Brigham Young University Press, 1988.

Carp, Robert, and Ronald Stidham. *The Federal Courts.* Washington, DC: Congressional Quarterly Press, 1985.

Davis, Sue. *Justice Rehnquist and the Constitution.* Princeton: Princeton University Press, 1989.

Faulkner, Robert K. *The Jurisprudence of John Marshall.* Princeton: Princeton University Press, 1968.

Goldman, Sheldon, and Thomas P. Jahnige. *The Federal Courts as a Political System.* New York: Harper & Row, 1985.

Graber, Mark A. *Transforming Free Speech: The Ambiguous Legacy of Civil Libertarianism.* Berkeley: University of California Press, 1991.

Hamilton, Charles V. *The Bench and the Ballot: Southern Federal Judges and Black Voters.* New York: Oxford University Press, 1973.

History of the Supreme Court of the United States. 9 vols. New York: Macmillan, 1981.

Maveety, Nancy. *Representation Rights and the Burger Years.* Ann Arbor: University of Michigan Press, 1991.

McCann, Michael W. *Rights at Work.* Chicago: University of Chicago Press, 1994.

Mezey, Susan G. *No Longer Disabled: The Federal Courts and the Politics of Social Security Disability.* New York: Greenwood Press, 1988.

Nardulli, Peter F., James Eisenstein, and Roy B. Fleming. *The Tenor of Justice: Criminal Courts and the Guilty Plea.* Urbana: University of Illinois Press, 1988.

Neely, Richard. *How Courts Govern America.* New Haven: Yale University Press, 1981.

O'Brien, David M. *Storm Center: The Supreme Court in American Politics,* 2nd ed. New York: W. W. Norton, 1990.

Rosenberg, Gerald. *The Hollow Hope: Can Courts Bring about Social Change?* Chicago: University of Chicago Press, 1991.

Rubin, Eva. *Abortion, Politics, and the Courts.* Westport, CT: Greenwood Press, 1982.

Scigliano, Robert. *The Supreme Court and the Presidency.* New York: Free Press, 1971.

Silverstein, Mark. *Judicious Choices: The New Politics of Supreme Court Confirmations.* New York: W. W. Norton, 1994.

Stimson, Shannon C. *The American Revolution in the Law: Anglo-American Jurisprudence before John Marshall.* Princeton, NJ: Princeton University Press, 1990.

Tribe, Laurence. *Constitutional Choices.* Cambridge: Harvard University Press, 1985.

Wolfe, Christopher. *The Rise of Modern Judicial Review.* New York: Basic Books, 1986.

PART 3

POLITICS AND POLICY

CHAPTER 8

Public Opinion and the Media

I*N JANUARY 1991*, after American-led coalition forces achieved a swift victory over Iraq, President George Bush's level of public approval soared to an unprecedented 91 percent. Many commentators assumed that Bush would be re-anointed, rather than merely re-elected, in 1992. Indeed, several leading Democratic presidential aspirants decided there would be no point in challenging Bush in the coming presidential race. Only a year later, however, Bush's poll standing had fallen below 50 percent. By the late summer of 1992, the Democratic presidential candidate, Bill Clinton, had opened a commanding lead over Bush in the polls, who by then could barely muster a 40 percent approval rating.

After his election to the presidency, Clinton, too, found that public opinion could be quite fickle. By May 1993, only one hundred days after his inauguration, Clinton's approval ratings had fallen sharply. According to a May 4–6 New York Times/CBS News poll, 50 percent of Americans disapproved of the way Clinton was handling the economy while only 38 percent approved. Only a month earlier, nearly half of all respondents to the same poll question had approved of Clinton's economic performance, while only 37 percent had disapproved.[1]

[1]Gwen Ifill, "As Ratings Stall, Clinton Tries Tune-Up," *New York Times*, 10 May 1993, p. A16.

Consistent with the pattern discussed in Chapter 6, Clinton's public approval rating briefly increased by eleven points, to nearly 50 percent, in June 1993 after he ordered a cruise missile attack on Iraqi intelligence headquarters. The attack was in retaliation for an alleged Iraqi plot to assassinate former president George Bush. Clinton attributed his improved poll standing not to the missile attack but to what he termed better public understanding of his economic program. Within a few days, however, Clinton's approval rating

> ### CORE OF THE ARGUMENT
>
> - Opinions are shaped by individuals' characteristics but also by institutional, political, and governmental forces.
> - Among the most important influences shaping public opinion are the media. The media have tremendous power to shape the public agenda and our images of politicians and policies.
> - The political power of the media has increased considerably through the growing prominence of investigative reporting.
> - In general, the government's actions are consistent with public preferences.

dropped back to its previous 38-percent level. Clinton's approval rating continued to linger in this range during most of 1994. Indeed, despite the nation's strong economic performance during the first half of 1994, the majority of those polled even disapproved of the president's handling of the economy.[2] By 1996, however, President Clinton's popular standing seemed to have been fully restored. In the weeks prior to the November 1996, presidential elections, Clinton's lead in the polls over his Republican challenger, Senator Robert Dole, was as high as twenty-one points. Pundits began to predict a Clinton landslide.

Commentators and social scientists carefully plotted these massive changes in public opinion and pondered their causes. Significantly, however, no analyst charting these shifts in popular sentiment was so bold as to ask whether public opinion was right or wrong—whether it made sense or nonsense. Rather, public opinion was viewed as a sort of natural force that, like the weather, affected everything but was itself impervious to human intervention and immune to criticism.

Public opinion has become the ultimate standard against which the conduct of contemporary governments is measured. In the democracies, especially in the United States, both the value of government programs and the virtue of public officials are typically judged by the magnitude of their popularity. Twentieth-century dictatorships, for their part, are careful at least to give lip service to the idea of popular sovereignty in their countries, if only to bolster public support at home and to maintain a favorable image abroad.

In this chapter, we will examine the role of public opinion in American politics. First, we will look at the institutions and processes that help to shape public opinion in the United States, most notably the "marketplace of ideas" in which opinions compete for acceptance, and the news media. Second, we will assess the government's role in shaping American public opinion. Third, we will

address the problem of measuring opinion. Finally, we will consider the issue of governmental responsiveness to citizens' opinions.

THE MARKETPLACE OF IDEAS

Opinions are products of individuals' personalities, social characteristics, and interests. But opinions are also shaped by institutional, political, and governmental forces that make it more likely that citizens will hold some beliefs and less likely that they will hold others. In the United States and the other Western democracies, opinions and beliefs compete for acceptance in what is sometimes called the *marketplace of ideas*. In America, it is mainly the hidden force of the market that determines which opinions and beliefs will flourish and which will fall by the wayside. Thus, to understand public opinion in the United States, it is important to understand the origins and operations of this "idea market."

Origins of the Idea Market

During the nineteenth century, almost every Western government initiated the creation of a national forum in which the views of all classes of people could be exchanged. Westerners often equate freedom of opinion and expression with the absence of state interference. Western freedom of opinion, however, is not the unbridled freedom of some state of nature. It is, rather, the structured freedom of a public forum constructed and maintained by the state. The creation and maintenance of this forum, this marketplace of ideas, has required nearly two centuries of extensive governmental effort in the areas of education, communication, and jurisprudence.

First, in the nineteenth century, most Western nations engaged in intense efforts to impose a single national language upon their citizens. In the United States, massive waves of immigration during the nineteenth century meant that millions

[2]Richard Morin, "Clinton Ratings Decline Despite Rising Economy," *Washington Post,* 9 August 1994, p. 1.

of residents spoke no English. In response, the American national government, as well as state and local governments, made vigorous efforts to impose the English language upon these newcomers. Schools were established to provide adults with language skills. At the same time, English was the only language of instruction permitted in the public elementary and secondary schools. Knowledge of English became a prerequisite for American citizenship.

Second, and closely related to the problem of a common language, was the matter of literacy. Prior to the nineteenth century, few people were able to read or write. These skills were, for the most part, limited to the upper strata. Communication among the majority of people depended upon word of mouth, a situation hardly conducive to the spread of ideas across regional, class, or even village or neighborhood boundaries. During the nineteenth and twentieth centuries, all Western governments actively sought to expand popular literacy. With the advent of universal, compulsory education, children were taught to read and write the national language. Together with literacy programs for adults, including extensive efforts by the various national military services to instruct uneducated recruits, this educational process led to the gradual reduction of illiteracy in the industrial West.

A third facet of the construction of the marketplace of ideas was the development of communications mechanisms. During the early nineteenth century, governments built hundreds of thousands of miles of roads, opening lines of communication among the various regions and between cities and countryside. Road building was followed later in the century by governmental promotion of the construction of rail and telegraph lines, further facilitating the exchange of goods, persons, and, not least important, ideas and information among previously disparate and often isolated areas. Such internal improvements constituted the single most important activity undertaken by the American central government both before and after the Civil War. During the twenti-

eth century, all Western regimes promoted the development of radio, telephone, television, and the complex satellite-based communications networks that today link the world.

The final key component of the construction of a free market of ideas was, and is, legal protection for free expression of ideas. This last factor is, of course, what most clearly distinguished the construction of the West's idea market from the efforts of authoritarian regimes. The cumulative result of all these governmental efforts was the gradual destruction of internal barriers to communication in every Western nation, and the construction of a forum in which the views of all groups and strata could easily be exchanged.

The Idea Market Today

The operation of the idea market in the United States today has meant that individuals are continually exposed to concepts and information that originate outside their own region, class, or ethnic community. It is this steady exposure over time that leads members of every social group to acquire at least some of the ideas and perspectives embraced by the others. Given continual exposure to the ideas of other strata, it is virtually impossible for any group to resist some modification of its own beliefs.

COMMON FUNDAMENTAL VALUES Today most Americans share a common set of political beliefs and opinions. First, Americans generally believe in *equality of opportunity.* That is, they assume that all individuals should be allowed to seek personal and material success. Moreover, Americans generally believe that such success should be linked to personal effort and ability rather than family, "connections," or other forms of special privilege. Second, Americans strongly believe in individual freedom. They typically support the notion that governmental interference with individuals' lives and property should be kept to the minimum consistent with the general welfare (although in recent years Americans have grown accustomed to greater levels of governmental intervention than would have been deemed appropriate by the founders of liberal theory). Third, most Americans believe in democracy. They presume that every person should have the opportunity to take part in the nation's governmental and policy-making processes and to have some "say" in determining how they are governed.[3]

One indication that Americans of all political stripes share these fundamental political values is the content of the acceptance speeches delivered by Bill Clinton and Bob Dole upon receiving their parties' presidential nominations in 1996. Clinton and Dole differed on many specific issues and policies. Yet, the political visions they presented reveal an underlying similarity. A major emphasis of both candidates was equality of opportunity. Clinton referred frequently to opportunity in his speech, even beginning the speech with a poignant story about the importance of equality of opportunity in his own life.

> I never met my father. He was killed in a car wreck on a rainy road three months before I was born . . . After that my mother had to support us . . . My mother taught me. She taught me about family and hard work and sacrifice . . . We must have a government that expands opportunity . . . We offer our people a new choice based on old values. We offer opportunity . . . Old fashioned Americans for a new time. Opportunity. Responsibility. Community.

Dole, for his part, proclaimed,

> And the guiding light of my administration will be that in this country we have no rank order by birth, no claim to favoritism by race, no expectation of judgement other than it be evenhanded. We cannot guarantee the outcome, but we shall guarantee the opportunity.

Thus, however much the two candidates differed in means and specifics, both seemed to share this fundamental American value.

Agreement on fundamental political values, though certainly not absolute, is probably more widespread in the United States than anywhere else in the Western world. During the course of Western political history, competing economic, social, and political groups put forward a variety of radically divergent views, opinions, and political philosophies. America was never socially or economically homogeneous. But two forces that were extremely powerful and important sources of ideas and beliefs elsewhere in the world were relatively weak or absent in the United States.

First, the United States never had the feudal aristocracy like the one that dominated so much of European history. Second, for reasons including America's prosperity and the early availability of political rights, no Socialist movements comparable to those that developed in nineteenth-century Europe were ever able to establish themselves in the United States. As a result, during the course of American history, there existed neither an aristocracy to assert the virtues of inequality, special privilege, and a rigid class structure, nor a powerful American Communist or Socialist party to challenge the desirability of limited government and individualism.[4]

AGREEMENT AND DISAGREEMENT ON ISSUES
Agreement on fundamentals, however, by no means implies that Americans do not differ with one another on a wide variety of issues. American political life is characterized by vigorous debate on economic, foreign policy, and social policy issues; race relations; environmental affairs; and a host of other matters. Differences of political opinion are to some extent linked to divergences in various groups' economic and political positions and to their histories and experiences. People's political opinions are often associated with

---

[3]For a discussion of the political beliefs of Americans, see Harry Holloway and John George, *Public Opinion* (New York: St. Martin's Press, 1986). See also Paul R. Abramson, *Political Attitudes in America* (San Francisco: W. H. Freeman, 1983).

[4]See Louis Hartz, *The Liberal Tradition in America* (New York: Harcourt, Brace, 1955).

such variables as income, education, and occupation. Similarly, factors such as race, gender, ethnicity, age, religion, and region, which not only influence individuals' interests but also shape their experiences and upbringing, have enormous influence upon their beliefs and opinions. For example, individuals whose incomes differ substantially have different views on the desirability of a number of important economic and social programs. In general, the poor—who are the chief beneficiaries of these programs—support them more strongly than the well-to-do Americans whose taxes pay for the programs. Similarly, blacks and whites have different views on questions of civil rights and civil liberties—presumably reflecting differences of interest and historical experience. In recent years, many observers have begun to take note of a number of differences between the views expressed by men and those supported by women, especially on foreign policy questions, where women appear to be much more concerned with the dangers of war, and on social welfare issues, where women show more concern than men for the problems of the poor and unfortunate. Quite conceivably these differences—known collectively as the "gender gap"—reflect the results of differences in the childhood experiences and socialization of men and women in America.

LIBERALISM AND CONSERVATISM Many Americans describe themselves as either liberal or conservative in political orientation. Historically these terms were defined somewhat differently than they are today (see Concept Map 8.1). As recently as the nineteenth century, a liberal was an individual who favored freedom from state control, while a conservative was someone who supported the use of governmental power and favored continuation of the influence of church and aristocracy in national life.

Today, the term *liberal* has come to imply support for political and social reform; support for extensive governmental intervention in the economy; the expansion of federal social services;

more vigorous efforts on behalf of the poor, minorities, and women; and greater concern for consumers and the environment. In social and cultural areas, liberals generally support abortion rights, are concerned with the rights of persons accused of crime, support decriminalization of drug use, and oppose state involvement with religious institutions and religious expression. In international affairs, liberal positions are usually seen as including support for arms control, opposition to the development and testing of nuclear weapons, support for aid to poor nations, opposition to the use of American troops to influence the domestic affairs of developing nations, and support for international organizations such as the United Nations.

By contrast, the term *conservative* today is used to describe those who generally support the social and economic status quo and are suspicious of efforts to introduce new political formulae and economic arrangements. Conservatives believe strongly that a large and powerful government poses a threat to citizens' freedom. Thus, in the domestic arena, conservatives generally oppose the expansion of governmental activity, asserting that solutions to social and economic problems can be developed in the private sector. Conservatives particularly oppose efforts to impose government regulation on business, pointing out that such regulation is frequently economically inefficient and costly and can ultimately lower the entire nation's standard of living. As to social and cultural positions, many conservatives oppose abortion, support school prayer, are more concerned for the victims than the perpetrators of crimes, oppose school busing, and support traditional family arrangements. In international affairs, conservatism has come to mean support for the maintenance of American military power.

Often political observers search for logical connections among the various positions identified with liberalism or with conservatism, and they are disappointed or puzzled when they are unable to find a set of coherent philosophical principles that define and unite the several elements of

CONCEPT MAP 8.1

Liberalism versus Conservatism	
LIBERAL	**CONSERVATIVE**

OLD

18th & 19th centuries

Old Liberalism

Tenets: Individual above all, the pursuit of happiness, free market, capitalism

Justification for government: Intervention only against conduct that is palpably harmful in its consequences

Examples (& people): Libertarians (Adam Smith)

Today would support: Privatization, deregulation, end of welfare state, abortion rights

Old Conservatism

Tenets: Morality above all, the individual is subordinate to morality, in society and politics

Justification for government: Intervention against conduct deemed good or evil in itself

Examples (& people): Religious conservatives (anti-evolutionists), Southern conservatives who favored community and state rights (John Calhoun)

Today would support: School prayer, right to life

NEW

20th century

New Liberalism

Tenets: Same as above, but more statist

Justification for government: Same as Box 1, but with a lower threshold: the theory of harm is enough

Examples (& people): Traditional Democratic party, unions (Mario Cuomo, Jay Rockefeller, Richard Gephardt)

Would support: Broad health coverage, minimum wage, gun control, abortion rights

New Conservatism

Tenets: Same as above

Justification for government: Same as above

Examples (& people): Neo-conservatives, Heritage Foundation, converts from Left and liberal groups (Irving Kristol, Thomas Sowell, Jeane Kirkpatrick)

Would support: Interventionist foreign policy, capital punishment, anti-affirmative action, deregulation

either of these sets of beliefs. On the liberal side, for example, what is the logical connection between opposition to U.S. government intervention in the affairs of foreign nations and calls for greater intervention in America's economy and society? On the conservative side, what is the logical relationship between opposition to governmental regulation of business and support for a ban on abortion? Indeed, the latter would seem to be just the sort of regulation of private conduct that conservatives claim to abhor.

Frequently, the relationships among the various elements of liberalism or the several aspects of conservatism are *political* rather than *logical*. One underlying basis of liberal views is that all or most represent criticisms of or attacks on the foreign and domestic policies and cultural values of the business and commercial strata that have been prominent in the United States for the past century. In some measure, the tenets of contemporary conservatism represent this elite's defense of its positions against its enemies, who include organized labor, minority groups, and some intellectuals and professionals. Thus, liberals attack business and commercial elites by advocating more governmental regulation, including consumer protection and en-

vironmental regulation, opposition to military weapons programs, and support for expensive social programs. Conservatives counterattack by asserting that governmental regulation of the economy is ruinous and that military weapons are needed in a changing world, and they seek to stigmatize their opponents for showing no concern for the rights of "unborn" Americans.[5]

Of course, it is important to note that many people who call themselves liberals or conservatives accept only part of the liberal or conservative ideology. During the 1980s, many political commentators asserted that Americans were becoming increasingly conservative in their political orientations. Indeed, it was partly in response to this view that the Democrats in 1992 selected a presidential candidate drawn from the party's moderate wing. Although it appears that Americans have adopted more conservative outlooks on some issues, their views in other areas have remained largely unchanged or even become more

[5]For a discussion of this conflict, see Benjamin Ginsberg and Martin Shefter, "A Critical Realignment? The New Politics, the Reconstituted Right, and the Election of 1984," in *The Elections of 1984*, ed. Michael Nelson (Washington, DC: Congressional Quarterly Press, 1985), pp. 1–26.

TABLE 8.1

Have Americans Become More Conservative?

	1972	1978	1980	1982	1984	1986	1988	1992
Percentage responding "yes" to the following questions:								
Should the government help minority groups?	30%	25%	16%	21%	27%	26%	13%	27%
Should the government see to it that everyone has a job and a guaranteed standard of living?	27	17	22	25	28	25	24	30
Should abortion never be permitted?	9	10	18	13	13	13	12	12
Should the government provide fewer services and reduce spending?	NA	NA	27	32	28	24	25	33

NA = Not asked
SOURCE: Center for Political Studies of the Institute for Social Research, University of Michigan. Data made available through the Inter-University Consortium for Political and Social Research.

liberal in recent years (see Table 8.1). Thus, many individuals are liberal on social issues but conservative on economic issues. There is nothing illogical about these mixed positions. They indicate the relatively open and fluid character of American political debate.

The idea market has created a common ground for Americans in which discussion of issues is encouraged and based on common understandings. Despite the many and often sharp divisions that exist in the twentieth century—between liberals and conservatives, different income groups, different regional groups—most Americans see the world through similar lenses.

SHAPING PUBLIC OPINION

In many areas of the world, governments determine which opinions their citizens may or may not express. People who assert views that their rulers do not approve of may be subject to imprisonment—or worse. Americans and the citizens of the other Western democracies are fortunate to live in nations where freedom of opinion and expression are generally taken for granted.

Freedom of opinion, however, does not mean that all ideas and opinions flourish. Both private groups and the government itself today attempt to influence which opinions do take hold in the public imagination.

Few ideas spread spontaneously. Usually, whether they are matters of fashion, science, or politics, ideas must be vigorously promoted to become widely known and accepted. For example, the clothing, sports, and entertainment fads that occasionally seem to appear from nowhere and sweep the country before being replaced by some new trend are almost always the product of careful marketing campaigns by some commercial interest, rather than spontaneous phenomena. Even in the sciences, generally considered *the* bastions of objectivity, new theories, procedures, and findings are not always accepted simply and immedi-

ately on their own merit. Often, the proponents of a new scientific principle or practice must campaign within the scientific community on behalf of their views. Like their counterparts in fashion and science, successful—or at least widely held—political ideas are usually the products of carefully orchestrated campaigns by government or by organized groups and interests, rather than the results of spontaneous popular enthusiasm.

Government Management of Issues

All governments attempt, to a greater or lesser extent, to influence, manipulate, or manage their citizens' beliefs. In the United States, some efforts have been made by every administration since the nation's founding to influence public sentiment. But efforts to shape opinion did not become a routine and formal official function until World War I, when the Wilson administration created a censorship board, enacted sedition and espionage legislation, and attempted to suppress groups that opposed the war, like the International Workers of the World (IWW) and the Socialist party. Eugene Debs, a prominent Socialist and a presidential candidate, was arrested and convicted of having violated the Espionage Law, and he was sentenced to ten years in prison for delivering a speech that defended the IWW.

At the same time, however, World War I was the first modern industrial war, and it required a total mobilization of popular effort on the home front for military production. The war effort required the government to persuade the civilian population to bear the costs and make the sacrifices needed to achieve industrial and agricultural, as well as military, success. The Committee on Public Information (CPI), chaired by journalist and publicist George Creel, organized a massive public relations and news management program aimed at promoting popular enthusiasm for the war effort. This program included the dissemination of favorable news, the publication of patriotic pamphlets, films, photos, cartoons, bulletins, and periodicals, and the organization of "war expositions" and speakers' tours. Special labor programs were aimed at maintaining the loyalty and productivity of the workforce. Many of the CPI's staff were drawn from the major public relations firms of the time.[6]

The extent to which public opinion is actually affected by governmental public relations efforts is probably limited. The government—despite its size and power—is only one source of information and evaluation in the United States. Very often, governmental claims are disputed by the media, by interest groups, and, at times by opposing forces within the government itself.

Often, too, governmental efforts to manipulate public opinion backfire when the public is made aware of the government's tactics. Thus, in 1971, the United States government's efforts to build popular support for the Vietnam War were hurt when CBS News aired its documentary "The Selling of the Pentagon," which revealed the extent and character of government efforts to sway popular sentiment. In this documentary, CBS demonstrated the techniques, including planted news stories and faked film footage, that the government had used to misrepresent its activities in Vietnam. These revelations, of course, had the effect of undermining popular trust in all government claims. During the 1991 Persian Gulf War, the U.S. military was much more concerned with the accuracy of its assertions.

A hallmark of the Clinton administration has been the steady use of campaign techniques like those used in election campaigns to bolster popular enthusiasm for White House initiatives. The president established a "political war room" in the Executive Office Building similar to the one that operated in his campaign headquarters. Representatives from all departments meet in the war room every day to discuss and coordinate the president's public relations efforts. Many of the same

consultants and pollsters who directed the successful Clinton campaign have been employed in the selling of the president's programs.[7]

Indeed, the Clinton White House has made more sustained and systematic use of *public opinion* polling than any previous administration. For example, during his presidency Bill Clinton has relied heavily on the polling firm of Penn & Schoen to help him decide which issues to emphasize and what strategies to adopt. During the 1995–1996 budget battle with Congress, the White House commissioned polls almost every night to chart changes in public perceptions about the struggle. Poll data suggested to Clinton that he should present himself as struggling to save Medicare from Republican cuts. Clinton responded by launching a media attack against what he claimed were GOP efforts to hurt the elderly. This proved to be a successful strategy and helped Clinton defeat the Republican budget.[8] The administration, however, has asserted that it uses polls only as a check on its communications strategy.[9]

Of course, at the same time that the Clinton administration has worked diligently to mobilize popular support, its opponents have struggled equally hard to mobilize popular opinion against the White House. A host of public and private interest groups opposed to President Clinton's programs crafted public relations campaigns designed to generate opposition to the president. For example, in 1994, while Clinton campaigned to bolster popular support for his health care reform proposals, groups representing small business and segments of the insurance industry, among others, developed their own publicity campaigns that ultimately convinced many Americans that Clinton's initiative posed a threat to their own health care. These opposition

---

[6]See George Creel, *How We Advertised America* (New York: Harper and Brothers, 1920).

[7]Gerald F. Seib and Michael K. Frisby, "Selling Sacrifice," *Wall Street Journal,* 5 February 1993, p. 1.

[8]Michael K. Frisby, "Clinton Seeks Strategic Edge with Opinion Polls," *Wall Street Journal,* 24 June 1996, p. A16.

[9]James Carney, "Playing by the Numbers," *Time,* 11 April 1994, p. 40.

JAMES CARVILLE AND MARY MATALIN
All's Fair in Love, War, and Politics

THE TUMULTUOUS 1992 PRESIDENTIAL CAMPAIGN contained many dramatic elements, including George Bush's surprising drop in the polls following the Persian Gulf War, and Bill Clinton's phoenix-like rise in the polls in the summer and fall before the election. The candidates' campaign managers labored unceasingly throughout the campaign to swing public sentiment their way. Yet, like a made-for-television movie, this pitched political battle between the Bush and Clinton camps included a melodramatic element: the real-life romance between Clinton's top strategist, James Carville, and Bush's political director, Mary Matalin.

James Carville began his political career in his home state of Louisiana. A mediocre student at Louisiana State University, Carville completed his undergraduate degree in seven years (interrupted by service in the Marines) and acquired a law degree in 1973. After working on several state political campaigns, Carville struck out on his own as a political consultant in 1982, working for state Democratic candidates around the country. Carville acquired a national reputation in 1991 when he engineered the come-from-behind Pennsylvania Senate victory of unknown Democratic Harris Wofford against former attorney general Richard Thornburgh.

JAMES CARVILLE

The Clinton campaign posed a similar challenge in that Clinton was little known and given little chance of winning. Carville brought to the campaign two key principles: the campaign should respond immediately to any charges or attacks and the campaign should stay focused on its own core message and not allow itself to be forced on the defensive. These tactics were crucial to Clinton's winning effort.

Mary Matalin is also considered a rising young star in the world of campaign management. Brought up on the South Side of Chicago, the daughter of a steel-mill worker, Matalin also took seven years to complete her undergraduate degree and then had early experience in Illinois political campaigns. In the 1980s, she did political work with the

campaigns played an important role in the eventual defeat of the president's proposal.

Often, claims and counterclaims by the government and its opponents are aimed chiefly at elites and opinion makers rather than directly at the public. For example, many of the television ads about the health care debate were aired primarily in and around Washington and New York City, where they were more likely to be seen by persons influential in politics, business, and the media. The presumption behind this strategy is

that such individuals are likely to be the key decision makers on most issues.

Private Groups and the Shaping of Public Opinion

Political issues and ideas seldom emerge spontaneously from the grass roots. We have already seen how the government tries to shape opinion. In addition, the ideas that become prominent in political life are developed and spread by impor-

Republican National Committee in Washington, D.C. Her big break came when she was credited with designing Bush's winning strategy in the important Michigan caucuses during the 1988 Republican nominating season. Matalin acknowledges having learned much from Republican campaign wizard Lee Atwater, who was credited with successfully guiding the Reagan and Bush campaigns of the 1980s.

In the race against Clinton, Matalin was considered among the toughest and most loyal campaign leaders in the Bush camp. Despite taking some flak for saying that the Clinton campaign had to control its "bimbo eruptions" (a reference to allegations of womanizing by Clinton), Matalin was one of Bush's most effective campaign operatives. Unlike the Clinton campaign, however, the Bush campaign faced organizational problems, including indecisiveness about which direction the campaign should take.

Both Carville and Matalin are considered tough, quick-witted, plain-speaking, hard-working partisans. Their romantic relationship began after meeting at a Washington dinner party in 1991. In public, both agreed to suspend their relationship during the campaign. Yet gossip columnists reported that they continued to see each other throughout the campaign. When asked if they fought about politics, Matalin responded, "In terms of intense disagreements that we've had, politics ranks pretty much in the middle." When Matalin was criticized for the "bimbo" remark, Carville expressed public sympathy for her plight.

MARY MATALIN

After the campaign, the two left for an extended European vacation, and in 1993, they married. Carville has maintained his partnership with a Washington-based political consulting firm, continues occasional campaign work, and serves as a part-time adviser to Clinton and other Democrats. Matalin became co-host of a political talk show. In 1994, the two published their joint memoir. Their book, *All's Fair,* provides a detailed insider's account of the 1992 presidential campaigns. But the book is also highly critical of media analysis and bias in presidential campaign coverage. Politics aside, Carville and Matalin vow that continued partisanship will not interfere with love.

SOURCE: James Carville and Mary Matalin, *All's Fair: Love, War, and Running for President* (New York: Random House and Simon and Schuster, 1994).

tant economic and political groups searching for issues that will advance their causes. One example is the "right-to-life" issue that has inflamed American politics over the past twenty years. Its proponents seek to outlaw abortions and overturn the Supreme Court's *Roe v. Wade* decision.

The notion of right-to-life was developed and heavily promoted by conservative politicians who saw the issue of abortion as a means of uniting Catholic and Protestant conservatives and linking both groups to the Republican coalition, at that time led by President Reagan. These politicians convinced Catholic and evangelical Protestant leaders that they shared similar views on the question of abortion, and they worked with religious leaders to focus public attention on the negative issues in the abortion debate. To advance their cause, leaders of the movement sponsored well-publicized Senate hearings, where testimony, photographs, and other exhibits were presented to illustrate the violent effects of abortion procedures.

At the same time, publicists for the movement

produced leaflets, articles, books, and films, such as *The Silent Scream*, to highlight the agony and pain ostensibly felt by the unborn during abortion procedures. Finally, Catholic and evangelical Protestant religious leaders were organized to denounce abortion from their church pulpits and, increasingly, from their electronic pulpits on the Christian Broadcasting Network (CBN) and various other television forums available for religious programming. Religious leaders also organized demonstrations, pickets, and disruptions at abortion clinics throughout the nation.[10] Abortion rights remains a potent issue; it even influenced the 1994 health care debate.

Among President Clinton's most virulent critics have been leaders of the religious Right, who were outraged by his support for abortion and gay rights. Conservative religious leaders like the Rev. Jerry Falwell and Pat Robertson, leader of the Christian Coalition, have used their television programs to attack the president's programs and to mount biting personal attacks both on Clinton and on his wife, Hillary Rodham Clinton. Other conservative groups not associated with the religious Right have also launched sharp assaults against the president. Nationally syndicated talk-show host Rush Limbaugh is a constant critic of the Clinton administration.

Typically, ideas are best marketed by groups with access to financial resources, public or private institutional support, and sufficient skill or education to select, develop, and draft ideas that will attract interest and support. Thus, the development and promotion of conservative themes and ideas in recent years has been greatly facilitated by the millions of dollars that conservative corporations and business organizations, such as the Chamber of Commerce and the Public Affairs Council, spend each year on public information and what is now called in corporate circles "issues management." In addition, conservative businesses have contributed millions of dollars to such conservative institutions as the Heritage Foundation, the Hoover Institution, and the American Enterprise Institute.[11] Many of the ideas that helped those on the right influence political debate were first developed and articulated by scholars associated with these institutions.

Although they do not usually have access to financial assets that match those available to their conservative opponents, liberal intellectuals and professionals have ample organizational skills, access to the media, and practice in creating, communicating, and using ideas. During the past three decades, the chief vehicle through which liberal intellectuals and professionals have advanced their ideas has been the "public interest group," an institution that relies heavily upon voluntary contributions of time, effort, and interest on the part of its members. Through groups like Common Cause, the National Organization for Women, the Sierra Club, Friends of the Earth, and Physicians for Social Responsibility, intellectuals and professionals have been able to use their organizational skills and educational resources to develop and promote ideas.[12]

Often, research conducted in universities and in liberal "think tanks" like the Brookings Institution provides the ideas upon which liberal politicians rely. For example, the welfare reform plan introduced by the Clinton administration in 1994 originated with the work of Harvard professor David Ellwood. Ellwood's academic research led him to the idea that the nation's welfare system would be improved if services to the poor were expanded in scope, but limited in duration. His idea was taken up by the 1992 Clinton campaign, which was

[10]See Gillian Peele, *Revival and Reaction* (Oxford, England: Clarendon Press, 1985). Also see Connie Paige, *The Right-to-Lifers* (New York: Summit, 1983).

[11]See David Vogel, "The Power of Business in America: A Reappraisal," *British Journal of Political Science* 13 (January 1983), pp. 19–44.
[12]See David Vogel, "The Public Interest Movement and the American Reform Tradition," *Political Science Quarterly* 96 (Winter 1980), pp. 607–27.

searching for a position on welfare that would appeal to both liberal and conservative Democrats.

Journalist and author Joe Queenan correctly observed that although political ideas can erupt spontaneously, they almost never do. Instead,

> issues are usually manufactured by tenured professors and obscure employees of think tanks. . . . It is inconceivable that the American people, all by themselves, could independently arrive at the conclusion that the depletion of the ozone layer poses a dire threat to our national well-being, or that an immediate, across-the-board cut in the capital-gains tax is the only thing that stands between us and the economic abyss. The American people do not have that kind of sophistication. *They have to have help.*[13]

Whatever their particular ideology or interest, those groups that can muster the most substantial financial, institutional, educational, and organizational resources—or, as we shall see later, access to government power—are also best able to promote their ideas in the marketplace. Obviously, these resources are most readily available to upper-middle-and upper-class groups. As a result, their ideas and concerns are most likely to be discussed and disseminated by books, films, newspapers, magazines, and the electronic media. As we shall see, upper-income groups dominate the marketplace of ideas, not only as producers and promoters, but also as consumers of ideas. In general, and particularly in the political realm, the print and broadcast media and the publishing industry are most responsive to the tastes and views of the more "upscale" segments of the potential audience.

The Media

Among the most important forces shaping public opinion are the national news media. The content and character of news and public affairs program-

ming—what the media choose to present and how they present it—can have the most far-reaching political consequences. Media disclosures can greatly enhance—or fatally damage—the careers of public officials. Media coverage can rally support for—or intensify opposition to—national policies. The media can shape and modify, if not fully form, public perceptions of events, issues, and institutions.

Shaping Events

In recent American political history, the media have played a central role in at least three major events. First, the media were critically important factors in the Civil Rights movement of the 1950s and 1960s. Television pictures showing peaceful civil rights marchers attacked by club-swinging police helped to generate sympathy among Northern whites for the civil rights struggle and greatly increased the pressure on Congress to bring an end to segregation.[14]

Second, the media were instrumental in compelling the Johnson and Nixon administrations to negotiate an end to the Vietnam War. Beginning in 1967, the national media portrayed the war as misguided and unwinnable and, as a result, helped to turn popular sentiment against continued American involvement.[15]

Third, the media were central actors in the Watergate affair, which ultimately forced President Richard Nixon, landslide victor in the 1972 presidential election, to resign from office in disgrace. It was the relentless series of investigations launched by the *Washington Post,* the *New York Times,* and the major television networks that led to the disclosures of the various abuses of which Nixon was guilty and ultimately forced Nixon to choose between resignation and almost certain impeachment.

---

[13]Joe Queenan, "Birth of a Notion," *Washington Post,* 20 September 1992, p. C1.

[14]David Garrow, *Protest at Selma* (New Haven: Yale University Press, 1978).

[15]See Todd Gitlin, *The Whole World Is Watching* (Berkeley: University of California Press, 1980).

How a News Story Is Prepared

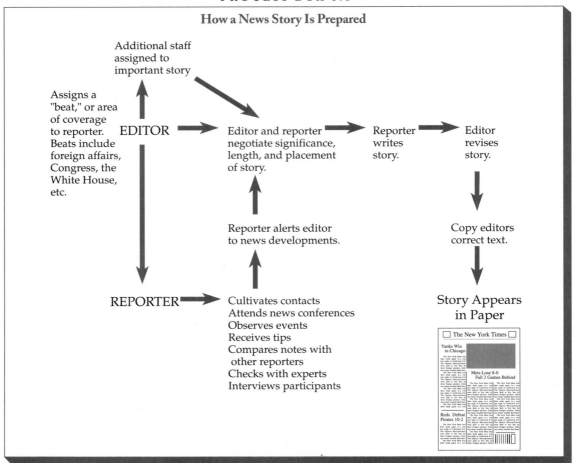

The Sources of Media Power

The power of the media stems from several sources. First, the media help to set the agenda for political discussion. Groups and forces that wish to bring their ideas before the public in order to generate support for policy proposals or political candidacies must somehow secure media coverage. If the media are persuaded that an idea is newsworthy, then they may declare it an "issue" that must be resolved or a "problem" to be solved, thus clearing the first hurdle in the policy-making process. On the other hand, if an idea lacks or loses media appeal, its chance of resulting in new programs or policies is diminished. Some ideas seem to surface, gain media support for a time, lose media appeal, and then resurface. For example, crime was an issue during the 1988 and 1992 presidential campaigns, but was ignored in 1996.

A second source of the media's power is their influence as interpreters and evaluators of events and political results. For example, media interpretations may often determine how people perceive an election outcome. In 1968, despite the growing strength of the opposition to his Viet-

SOURCES OF MEDIA POWER

Setting the agenda for political discussion: Groups wishing to generate support for policy proposals or political candidacies must secure media coverage. The media must be persuaded that an item is newsworthy.

Interpretation and evaluation: The media's interpretation of an event or political action can sometimes determine how people perceive the event or result.

Shaping perceptions of leaders: Most citizens will never meet their political leaders, but will base opinions of these leaders on their media images. The media has a great deal of control over how a person is portrayed or whether an individual even receives public attention.

nam War policies, incumbent President Lyndon Johnson won two-thirds of the votes cast in New Hampshire's Democratic presidential primary. His rival Senator Eugene McCarthy received less than one-third. The broadcast media, however, declared the outcome to have been a great victory for McCarthy, who was said to have done much better than "expected" (or at least expected by the media). His "defeat" in New Hampshire was one of the factors that persuaded Johnson to withdraw from the 1968 presidential race.

Finally, the media have a good deal of power to shape popular perceptions of political leaders. Most citizens will never meet Bill Clinton or Al Gore or Newt Gingrich. Popular perceptions and evaluations of these individuals are based upon their media images. Obviously, through public relations and other techniques, politicians seek to cultivate favorable media images. But the media have a good deal of discretion over how individuals are portrayed, or how they are allowed to portray themselves.

In the case of political candidates, the media have considerable influence over whether or not a particular individual will receive public attention and will be taken seriously as a viable contender, and whether the public will perceive a candidate's performance favorably. Thus, if the media find a candidate interesting, they may treat him or her as a serious contender even though the facts of the matter seem to suggest otherwise. For ex-

ample, in 1992, the broadcast media found Ross Perot to be an incredible novelty. Here was a self-made billionaire with oversized ears who was determined to challenge the American political establishment. Some members of the press depicted Perot as a potential Mussolini, while others portrayed him as a wealthy Harry Truman. Nevertheless, from the beginning, Perot received enormous media attention, which helped to make his quixotic candidacy a serious threat to the two major parties.[16]

In a similar vein, the media may declare that a candidate has "*momentum,*" a mythical property that the media confer upon candidates they admire. Momentum has no substantive meaning—it is simply a media prediction that a particular candidate will do even better in the future than in the past. Such media prophecies can become self-fulfilling as contributors and supporters jump on the bandwagon of the fortunate candidate.

In 1992, for example, when Bill Clinton's poll standings surged in the wake of the Democratic National Convention (see Chapter 9), the media determined that Clinton had enormous momentum. In fact, nothing that happened during the remainder of the race led the media to change its collective judgment. Even when George Bush's poll standing began to improve, many news stories pointed to Bush's inability to gain momentum.

[16]See Carl Bernstein, "The Idiot Culture," *New Republic,* 8 June 1992, pp. 22–28.

The Media: How Influential Are They?

*I*N RECENT YEARS *an important political argument has emerged over the real or imagined political power of the media. Commentators, politicians, and others routinely attribute vast influence to the American media; yet many who study the matter argue that claims about media power are exaggerated.*

Newspaper editor Michael J. O'Neill summarizes the thinking of many critics as he describes the media's reach and influence. On the basis of his study of media coverage of Congress, media analyst Stephen Hess argues that the media's actual power is less than most assume.

O'NEILL

The extraordinary powers of the media, most convincingly displayed by network television and the national press, have been mobilized to influence major public issues and national elections, to help diffuse the authority of Congress and to disassemble the political parties—even to make Presidents or to break them. Indeed, the media now weigh so heavily on the scales of power that some political scientists claim we are upsetting the historic checks and balances invented by our forefathers. . . . This is flattering, of course, because all newspapermen dream of being movers and shakers and the thought that we may actually be threatening the national government is inspirational. In several respects, it is also true. . . .

No longer are we just the messengers, observers on the sidelines, witch's mirrors faithfully telling society how it looks. Now we are deeply imbedded in the democratic process itself, as principal actors rather than bit players or mere audiences. . . . Thanks mainly to television, we are often partners in the creation of news—unwilling and unwitting partners, perhaps, but partners nonetheless. . . .

In ways that Jefferson and Hamilton never intended nor could even imagine, Americans now have the whole world delivered to them every day, in pulsating, living color—all of life swept inside their personal horizon.[1]

While there is no way to ascertain what impact this coverage had on the race, at the very least, Republican contributors and activists must have been discouraged by the constant portrayal of their candidate as lacking—and the opposition as possessing—this magical "momentum." In 1996, the national media portrayed Bob Dole's candidacy as hopeless almost from the very beginning. Coverage of the Republican convention and the October debates emphasized Clinton's "insurmountable" lead. The media's coverage of Dole's campaign became a self-fulfilling prophecy of his defeat.[17]

Of course, what the media confer they can also take away. Soon after his "momentum" carried

Bill Clinton to victory in the 1992 election, the new president became the target of fierce attacks by prominent members of the national media. After a series of miscues during his first month in office, previously friendly commentators described Clinton as "incredibly inept," as "stumbling," and as a man with the "common sense of a gnat." Clinton went, according to one prominent journalist, "from *Time's* 'Man of the Year' to punching bag of the week." Some analysts suggested that the media were trying to compensate for their earlier enthusiastic support for Clinton.[18]

Media power to shape images is not absolute. Other image-makers compete with and indeed do

[17]See Howard Kurtz, "No Debate About It: TV Analysts Say Clinton's a Winner," *Washington Post*, 18 October 1996, p. D1.

[18]Howard Kurtz, "Media Pounce on Troubles as Pendulum Swings Again," *Washington Post*, 1 February 1993, p. 1.

Hess

There is no shortage of claims for the power of the press on Capitol Hill. . . . So many knowledgeable people, including senators, tell us that this is so that surely it must be so.

The most obvious reason why influence is attributed to the media is that the members of Congress, and especially their staffs, are incorrigible news junkies. . . .

The problem is that cause and effect are so difficult to match up. . . .

During the year I spent as an observer at the Senate, I did not see any cause and effect. I saw a lot of reporters writing stories. I saw a lot of bills being voted up or down. The stories often helped explain the votes, but I do not think the stories caused the votes. . . .

Ultimately, a lot more people and groups have an interest in noting the power of the press than in showing that media power sometimes may be akin to that of the Wizard of Oz. . . . There are also certain participants in the governmental process who must find it useful to blame "media power" for their own failures or frustrations. Books about the power that is will always sell better than those about the power that is not. And finally, there are media researchers whose entitlements in the world of conference going and journal articles . . . will be in direct proportion to our colleagues' sense that we are writing about one of the real power players in public policy. This then becomes a collective bias of which readers should be aware. Beware.[2]

---

[1]Michael J. O'Neill, "The Power of the Press." A presidential address to the American Society of Newspaper Editors, 1982, reprinted in *The Mass Media: Opposing Viewpoints* (St. Paul, MN: Greenhaven Press, 1988), pp. 150–51.
[2]Stephen Hess, *The Ultimate Insiders: U.S. Senators and the National Media* (Washington, DC: Brookings Institution, 1986), pp. 100–112.

---

manipulate the media by planting stories and rumors and staging news events. Some politicians are so adept at communicating with the public and shaping their own images that the media seem to have little effect upon them. For example, for six years Ronald Reagan appeared to have the ability to project such a positive image to millions of Americans that media criticism had little or no effect upon his popularity. The media came to refer to Reagan as the "Teflon-coated" president— criticisms never seemed to "stick" (although eventually even Reagan's Teflon coating chipped and cracked).

While the power of the media to shape perceptions is not unlimited, it is substantial. Portrayals of "bumbling" Jerry Ford, "tricky" Dick Nixon,

and "cry baby" Ed Muskie helped to shape our images of these individuals and to shorten their political careers. Similarly, media investigations of Richard Nixon, 1984 Democratic vice-presidential candidate Geraldine Ferraro, Vice President Spiro Agnew, and others sealed their political fates. Equally important, media interpretation of events can actually overpower and re-create reality, as in the "victorious" North Vietnamese Tet offensive and in Lyndon Johnson's "loss" in the 1968 New Hampshire primary.

Candidates Try to Turn the Tables

During the 1992 presidential campaign, candidates developed a number of techniques designed to take control of the image-making process away from journalists and media executives. Among the most important of these techniques were the many town meetings and television talk and entertainment show appearances that all the major candidates made. Frequent exposure on such programs as *Larry King Live* and *Today* gave candidates an opportunity to shape and focus their own media images and to overwhelm any negative image that might be projected by the media.

Members of the national news media responded by aggressively investigating and refuting many of the candidates' claims. Each of the major television networks, for example, aired regular critical analysis of the candidates' speeches, television commercials, and talk show appearances. In 1996, the media subjected Bob Dole's tax cut proposal to intensive scrutiny, suggesting that it was based on faulty economic assumptions. This type of political coverage serves the public interest by subjecting candidates' claims to scrutiny and refuting errors and distortions. At the same time, such critical coverage serves the interests of the news media by enhancing their own control over political imagery and perceptions and, thus, the power of the media vis-à-vis other political actors and institutions in the United States. We shall examine this topic next, as we consider the development and significance of investigative reporting.

The Rise of Investigative Reporting

The political power of the news media has greatly increased in recent years through the growing prominence of "investigative reporting"—a form of journalism in which the media adopt an adversarial posture toward the government and public officials.

During the nineteenth century, American newspapers were completely subordinate to the political parties. Newspapers depended upon official patronage—legal notices and party subsidies—for their financial survival and were controlled by party leaders. (A vestige of that era survived into the twentieth century in such newspaper names as the *Springfield Republican* and the *St. Louis Globe-Democrat*.) At the turn of the century, with the development of commercial advertising, newspapers became financially independent. This made possible the emergence of a formally nonpartisan press.

Presidents were the first national officials to see the opportunities in this development. By communicating directly to the electorate through newspapers and magazines, Theodore Roosevelt and Woodrow Wilson established political constituencies for themselves independent of party organizations and strengthened their own power relative to Congress. President Franklin Roosevelt used the radio, most notably in his famous fireside chats, to reach out to voters throughout the nation and to make himself the center of American politics (see Box 8.1). FDR was also adept at developing close personal relationships with reporters that enabled him to obtain favorable news coverage despite the fact that in his day a majority of newspaper owners and publishers were staunch conservatives. Following Roosevelt's example, subsequent presidents have all sought to use the media to enhance their popularity and power. For example, through televised news conferences, President John F. Kennedy mobilized public support for his domestic and foreign policy initiatives.

During the 1950s and 1960s, a few members of Congress also made successful use of the media—especially television—to mobilize national support for their causes. Senator Estes Kefauver of Tennessee became a major contender for the presidency and won a place on the 1956 Democratic national ticket as a result of his dramatic televised hearings on organized crime. Senator Joseph McCarthy of Wisconsin made himself a powerful national figure through his well-publicized investigations of alleged Communist infiltration of key American institutions. These senators, however, were more exceptional than typical. Through the

BOX 8.1

The First Fireside Chat
March 12, 1933

I WANT TO TALK for a few minutes with the people of the United States about banking—with the comparatively few who understand the mechanics of banking but more particularly with the overwhelming majority who use banks for the making of deposits and the drawing of checks. I want to tell you what has been done in the last few days, why it was done, and what the next steps are going to be. I recognize that the many proclamations from State capitols and from Washington, the legislation, the treasury regulations, etc., couched for the most part in banking and legal terms, should be explained for the benefit of the average citizen. I owe this in particular because of the fortitude and good temper with which everybody has accepted the inconvenience and hardships of the banking holiday. I know that when you understand what we in Washington have been about I shall continue to have your cooperation as fully as I have had your sympathy and help during the past week. . . .

After all, there is an element in the readjustment of our financial system more important than currency, more important than gold, and that is the confidence of the people. Confidence and courage are the essentials of success in carrying out our plan. You people must have faith; you must not be stampeded by rumors or guesses. Let us unite in banishing fear. We have provided the machinery to restore our financial system; it is up to you to support and make it work.

It is your problem no less than it is mine. Together we cannot fail.

---

mid-1960s, the executive branch continued to generate the bulk of news coverage, and the media served as a cornerstone of presidential power.

The Vietnam War shattered this relationship between the press and the presidency. During the early stages of U.S. involvement, American officials in Vietnam who disapproved of the way the war was being conducted leaked information critical of administrative policy to reporters. Publication of this material infuriated the White House, which pressured publishers to block its release—on one occasion, President Kennedy went so far as to ask the *New York Times* to reassign its Saigon correspondent. The national print and broadcast media—the network news divisions, the national news weeklies, the *Washington Post,* and the *New York Times*—discovered, however, that there was an audience for critical coverage among segments of the public skeptical of administration policy.

As the Vietnam conflict dragged on, critical media coverage fanned antiwar sentiment. Moreover, growing opposition to the war among liberals encouraged some members of Congress, most notably Senator J. William Fulbright, chair of the Senate Foreign Relations Committee, to break with the president. In turn, these shifts in popular and congressional sentiment emboldened journalists and publishers to continue to present critical news reports. Through this process, journalists developed a commitment to "investigative reporting," while a constituency emerged that would rally to the defense of the media when it came under White House attack.

This pattern endured through the 1970s and into the 1990s. Political forces opposed to presidential policies, many members of Congress, and the national news media began to find that their interests often overlapped. Liberal opponents of the Nixon, Carter, Reagan, and Bush administrations welcomed news accounts critical of the conduct of executive agencies and officials in foreign affairs and in such domestic areas as race relations, the environment, and regulatory policy. In addition, many senators and representatives found it politically advantageous to champion causes favored by the antiwar, consumer, or environmental movements because, by conducting televised hearings on such issues, they were able to mobilize national constituencies, to become national figures, and in a number of instances to become serious contenders for their party's presidential nomination.

Aggressive use of the techniques of investigation, publicity, and exposure has allowed the national media to enhance their autonomy and carve out a prominent place for themselves in American government and politics. Increasingly, media coverage has come to influence politicians' careers, the mobilization of political constituencies, and the fate of issues and causes. Inasmuch as members of Congress and groups opposed to presidential policies in the 1970s and 1980s benefited from the growing influence of the press, they were prepared to rush to its defense when it came under attack. This constituency could be counted upon to denounce any move by the White House or its supporters to curb media influence as an illegitimate offer to manage the news, chill free speech, and undermine the First Amendment. It was the emergence of these overlapping interests, more than an ideological bias, that has often led to an alliance between liberal political forces and the national news media.

This confluence of interests was in evidence during the 1996 presidential campaign. Most journalists endeavored to be evenhanded in their coverage of the candidates. As we saw above, the media subjected all the major campaigns to regular scrutiny and criticism. However, as several studies have since indicated, during the course of the campaign the media tended to be more critical of Dole and more supportive of Clinton. Republican economic proposals were generally dismissed by the media as gimmickry. Republican

efforts to question President Clinton's ethics—a topic the media had enjoyed probing during the previous years—were rejected as inappropriate for a serious national campaign. Even the Republican National Convention was dismissed, not without cause, as a staged event not worthy of much news coverage. A major network news program, *Nightline*, showed its disdain for the GOP's convention by leaving before the convention ended, host Ted Koppel proclaiming, "Nothing surprising has happened."[19] One British observer wrote in reaction to these events, "Dole got his most sympathetic and in-depth coverage when he fell off the stage in Chico, California."[20] This was an almost inevitable outgrowth of the *de facto* alliance that developed over a number of years between the media and liberal forces. Like any longstanding relationship, this one tends to shape the attitudes and perceptions of the participants. Without any need for overt bias or sinister conspiracy, journalists tend naturally to provide more favorable coverage to liberal politicians and causes.

The link between substantial segments of the media and liberal interest groups is by no means absolute. Indeed, over the past several years a conservative media complex has emerged in opposition to the liberal media. This complex includes two major newspapers, the *Wall Street Journal* and the *Washington Times*, several magazines, such as the *American Spectator*, and a host of conservative radio and television talk programs. The emergence of this complex has meant that liberal policies and politicians are virtually certain to come under attack even when the "liberal media" is sympathetic to them. For example, charges that President Clinton and his wife were involved in financial improprieties as partners in the Whitewater Development Corporation, as well as allegations that, while governor, Clinton had sexually harassed an Arkansas state employee, Paula

[19]Clarence Page, "Party, Media Get Their Chances," *Memphis Commercial Appeal*, 20 August 1996, p. 8A.
[20]Mark Steyn, "The Big Turn-Off," *Sunday Telegraph*, 13 October 1996, p. 36.

Jones, were first publicized by the conservative press. Though the mainstream "liberal" media may have been slow to begin their coverage of the Whitewater and Paula Jones stories, once the allegations began to receive attention, the *Washington Post*, the *New York Times*, and the major television networks quickly devoted substantial investigative resources and time to them. In due course, the "liberal" media probably gave the Whitewater and Jones charges just as much play as the "conservative" media, often with just as little regard for hard evidence.[21]

At the same time, the increasing decay of party organizations (see Chapter 10) has made politicians even more dependent upon favorable media coverage. National political leaders and journalists have had symbiotic relationships at least since FDR's presidency, but initially politicians were the senior partners. They benefited from media publicity, but they were not totally dependent upon it as long as they could still rely on party organizations to mobilize votes. Journalists, on the other hand, depended upon their relationships with politicians for access to information, and would hesitate to report stories that might antagonize valuable sources. Reporters feared exclusion from the flow of information in retaliation. Thus, for example, they did not publicize potentially embarrassing information, widely known in Washington, about the personal lives of such figures as Franklin Roosevelt and John F. Kennedy.

With the decline of party, the balance of power between politicians and journalists has been reversed. Now that politicians have become heavily dependent upon the media to reach their constituents, journalists no longer fear that their access to information can be restricted in retaliation for negative coverage.

By the mid-1990s, many commentators were beginning to wonder whether the media had become too critical and adversarial in their coverage of public figures and events. In Chapter 15, we shall look again at the role the media play in contemporary American politics and consider some of its more—and less—positive implications.

MEASURING PUBLIC OPINION

As recently as fifty years ago, American political leaders gauged public opinion by people's applause or cheers and by the presence of crowds in meeting places. This direct exposure to the people's views did not necessarily produce accurate knowledge of public opinion. It did, however, give political leaders confidence in their public support—and therefore confidence in their ability to govern by consent.

Abraham Lincoln and Stephen Douglas debated each other seven times in the summer and autumn of 1858, two years before they became presidential nominees. Their debates took place before audiences in parched cornfields and courthouse squares. A century later, the presidential debates, although seen by millions, take place before a few reporters and technicians in television studios that might as well be on the moon. The public's response cannot be experienced directly. This distance between leaders and followers is one of the agonizing problems of modern democracy. The media send information to millions of people, but they are not yet as efficient at getting information back to leaders. Is government by consent possible where the scale of communication is so large and impersonal? In order to compensate for the decline in their ability to experience public opinion for themselves, leaders have turned to science, in particular to the science of opinion polling.

It is no secret that politicians and public officials make extensive use of *public opinion polls* to help them decide whether to run for office, what policies to support, how to vote on important legislation, and what types of appeals to make in their campaigns. President Lyndon Johnson was

[21]Howard Kurtz, "The Media and the Fiske Report," *Washington Post*, 3 July 1994, p. A4.

famous for carrying the latest Gallup and Roper poll results in his hip pocket, and it is widely believed that he began to withdraw from politics because the polls reported losses in public support. All recent presidents and other major political figures have worked closely with polls and pollsters.

Constructing Public Opinion from Surveys

The population in which pollsters are interested is usually quite large. To conduct their polls they choose a *sample* of the total population. The selection of this sample is important. Above all, it must be representative; the views of those in the sample must accurately and proportionately reflect the views of the whole. To a large extent, the validity of the poll's results depends on the sampling pro-

cedure used, several of which are described in the In Brief Box below.

The degree of reliability in polling is a function of sample size. The same sample is needed to represent a small population as to represent a large population. The typical size of a sample ranges from 450 to 1,500 respondents. This number, however, reflects a trade-off between cost and degree of precision desired. The degree of accuracy that can be achieved with even a small sample can be seen from the polls' success in predicting election outcomes.

Table 8.2 shows how accurate two of the major national polling organizations have been in predicting the outcomes of presidential elections. In only three instances between 1952 and 1996 did the final October poll of a major pollster predict

IN BRIEF BOX

METHODS OF MEASURING PUBLIC OPINION

Interpreting Mass Opinion from Mass Behavior and Mass Attributes

Consumer behavior: predicts that people tend to vote against the party in power during a downslide in the economy

Group demographics: can predict party affiliation and voting by measuring income, race, and type of community (urban or rural)

Getting Public Opinion Directly from the People

Person-to-person: form impressions based on conversations with acquaintances, aides, and associates

Selective polling: form impressions based on interviews with a few representative members of a group or groups

Bellwether districts: form impressions based on an entire community that has a reputation for being a good predictor of the entire nation's attitudes

Constructing Public Opinion from Surveys

Quota sampling: respondents are chosen because they match a general population along several significant dimensions, such as geographic region, sex, age, and race

Probability sampling: respondents are chosen without prior screening, based entirely on a lottery system

Area sampling: respondents are chosen as part of a systematic breakdown of larger homogeneous units into smaller representative areas

Haphazard sampling: respondents are chosen by pure chance with no systematic method

Systematically biased sampling: respondents are chosen with a hidden or undetected bias toward a given demographic group

Two Pollsters and Their Records (1948–1992)

	HARRIS	GALLUP	ACTUAL OUTCOME
1996			
Clinton	51%	52%	49%
Dole	39	41	41
Perot	9	7	8
1992			
Clinton	44%	44%	43%
Bush	38	37	38
Perot	17	14	19
1988			
Bush	51%	53%	54%
Dukakis	47	42	46
1984			
Reagan	56%	59%	59%
Mondale	44	41	41
1980			
Reagan	48%	47%	51%
Carter	43	44	41
Anderson		8	
1976			
Carter	48%	48%	51%
Ford	45	49	48
1972			
Nixon	59%	62%	61%
McGovern	35	38	38
1968			
Nixon	40%	43%	43%
Humphrey	43	42	43
G. Wallace	13	15	14
1964			
Johnson	62%	64%	61%
Goldwater	33	36	39
1960			
Kennedy	49%	51%	50%
Nixon	41	49	49
1956			
Eisenhower	NA	60%	58%
Stevenson		41	42
1952			
Eisenhower	47%	51%	55%
Stevenson	42	49	44
1948			
Truman	NA	44.5%	49.6%
Dewey		49.5	45.1

All figures except those for 1948 are rounded. NA = Not asked.
SOURCES: Data from the Gallup Poll, the Harris Survey (New York: Chicago Tribune—New York News Syndicate, various press releases 1964–96). Courtesy of the Gallup Organization and Louis Harris & Associates.

the wrong outcome; and in all three instances—Harris in 1968 and Gallup in 1976, as well as Roper in 1960—the actual election was extremely close and the prediction was off by no more than two percentage points.

Even with reliable sampling procedures, problems can occur. Validity can be adversely affected by poor question format, faulty ordering of questions, inappropriate vocabulary, ambiguity of questions, or questions with built-in biases. Often, seemingly minor differences in the wording of a question can convey vastly different meanings to respondents and, thus, produce quite different response patterns.

For example, for many years the University of Chicago's National Opinion Research Center has asked respondents whether they think the federal government is spending too much, too little, or about the right amount of money on "assistance for the poor." Answering the question posed this way, about two-thirds of all respondents seem to believe that the government is spending too little. However, the same survey also asks whether the government spends too much, too little, or about the right amount for "welfare." When the word "welfare" is substituted for "assistance for the poor," about half of all respondents indicate that too much is being spent by the government.[22]

In the early days of a political campaign when voters are asked which candidates they do, or do not, support, the answer they give often has little significance, because the choice is not yet salient to them. Their preference may change many times before the actual election. This is part of the explanation for the phenomenon of the post-convention "bounce" in the popularity of presidential candidates, which was observed after the 1992 and 1996 Democratic and Republican national conventions. In general, presidential candidates can expect about a five-percentage-point bounce in their poll standings immediately after a national convention, though the effects of the bounce tend to dis-

appear rapidly. In 1996, Bob Dole trailed Bill Clinton by as much as twenty-two points before the Republican convention but pulled to within seven points of Clinton after. This dramatic post-convention bounce, however, was completely erased a short month later. In the aftermath of the Democratic convention Clinton moved to a twenty-one-point lead, almost precisely where he had been before the Republican convention.[23] Analysis of focus group data suggests that Dole's temporary bounce was almost entirely the result of a positive voter reaction to his wife, Elizabeth, who made a major speech at the GOP convention. Faced with the reality of having to vote for Bob rather than Elizabeth Dole, many voters reconsidered their enthusiastic reaction.[24] Respondents' preferences reflected the amount of attention a candidate had received during the conventions rather than strongly held views.

Salient interests are interests that stand out beyond others, that are of more than ordinary concern to respondents in a survey or to voters in the electorate. Politicians, social scientists, journalists, or pollsters who assume something is important to the public, when in fact it is not, are creating an *illusion of saliency*. This illusion can be created and fostered by polls despite careful controls over sampling, interviewing, and data analysis. In fact, the illusion is strengthened by the credibility that science gives survey results.

The problem of saliency has become especially acute as a result of the proliferation of media polls. The television networks and major national newspapers all make heavy use of opinion polls. Increasingly, polls are being commissioned by local television stations and local and regional newspapers as well.[25] On the positive side, polls allow journalists to make independent assessments of political realities—assessments not influ-

[22]Michael Kagay and Janet Elder, "Numbers Are No Problem for Pollsters, Words Are," *New York Times,* 9 August 1992, p. E6.

[23]Michael X. Delli Carpini, "The Voter Bounce," *Memphis Commercial Appeal,* 15 September 1996, p. 4B.
[24]Jamie Dettmer, "Focus Group Rates Conclaves," *Washington Times,* 23 September 1996, p. 6.
[25]See Thomas E. Mann and Gary Orren, eds., *Media Polls in American Politics* (Washington, DC: Brookings Institution, 1992).

PROCESS BOX 8.2

How a Poll Is Conducted

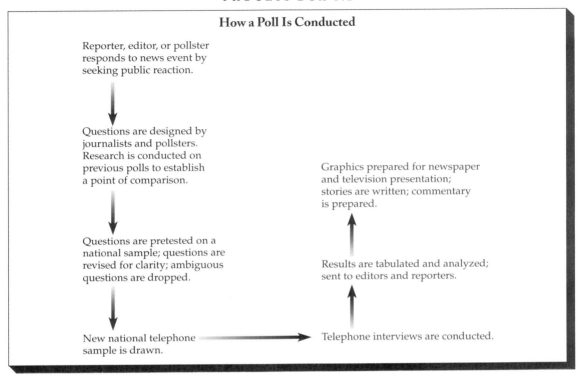

Reporter, editor, or pollster responds to news event by seeking public reaction.

Questions are designed by journalists and pollsters. Research is conducted on previous polls to establish a point of comparison.

Graphics prepared for newspaper and television presentation; stories are written; commentary is prepared.

Questions are pretested on a national sample; questions are revised for clarity; ambiguous questions are dropped.

Results are tabulated and analyzed; sent to editors and reporters.

New national telephone sample is drawn.

Telephone interviews are conducted.

enced by the partisan claims of politicians.

At the same time, however, media polls can allow journalists to make news when none really exists. Polling diminishes journalists' dependence upon news makers. A poll commissioned by a news agency can provide the basis for a good story even when candidates, politicians, and other news makers refuse to cooperate by engaging in newsworthy activities. Thus, on days when little or nothing is actually taking place in a political campaign, poll results, especially apparent changes in candidate margins, can provide voters with exciting news. In 1996, hundreds of news stories focused on the magnitude of Clinton's lead over Dole and on the post-convention "bounce" in poll standings shown by the two candidates. As we saw above, the polls were inaccurate in their electoral predictions, and the post-election bounce was, as always, a transient phenomenon. In effect,

a huge percentage of pre-election news coverage was literally a waste of paper and ink.

Interestingly, because rapid and dramatic shifts in candidate margins tend to take place when voters' preferences are least fully formed, horse race news is most likely to make the headlines when it is actually least significant.[26] In other words, media interest in poll results is inversely related to the actual salience of voters' opinions and the significance of the polls' findings. However, by influencing perceptions, especially those of major contributors, media polls can influence political realities.

The most noted, but least serious, of polling problems is the *bandwagon effect*, which occurs when polling results influence people to support

[26]For an excellent and reflective discussion by a journalist, see Richard Morin, "Clinton Slide in Survey Shows Perils of Polling," *Washington Post*, 29 August 1992, p. A6.

the candidate marked as the probable victor. Some scholars argue that this bandwagon effect can be offset by an "underdog effect" in favor of the candidate who is trailing in the polls.[27] However, a candidate who demonstrates a lead in the polls usually finds it considerably easier to raise campaign funds than a candidate whose poll standing is poor. With these additional funds, poll leaders can often afford to pay for television time and other campaign activities that will cement their advantage. For example, Bill Clinton's substantial lead in the polls during much of the summer of 1992 helped the Democrats raise far more money than in any previous campaign, primarily from interests hoping to buy access to a future President Clinton. For once, the Democrats were able to outspend the usually better-heeled Republicans. Thus, the *appearance* of a lead, according to the polls, helped make Clinton's lead a reality. Much the same effect was seen in 1996, when Clinton's lead in the polls caused many Republicans to write off the contest as hopeless weeks before the election.

Public Opinion, Political Knowledge, and the Importance of Ignorance

Many people are distressed to find public opinion polls not only unable to discover public opinion, but also unable to avoid producing unintentional distortions of their own. No matter how hard they try, no matter how mature the science of opinion polling becomes, politicians forever may remain substantially ignorant of public opinion.

Although knowledge is good for its own sake, and knowledge of public opinion may sometimes produce better government, ignorance also has its uses. It can, for example, operate as a restraint on the use of power. Leaders who think they know what the public wants are often autocratic rulers.

Leaders who realize that they are always partially in the dark about the public are likely to be more modest in their claims, less intense in their demands, and more uncertain in their uses of government power. Their uncertainty may make them more accountable to their constituencies because they will be more likely to continue searching for consent.

One of the most valuable benefits of survey research is actually "negative knowledge"—knowledge that pierces through irresponsible claims about the breadth of opinion or the solidarity of group or mass support. Because this sort of knowledge reveals the complexity and uncertainty of public opinion, it can help make citizens less gullible, group leaders less strident, and politicians less deceitful. This fact alone gives public opinion research, despite its great limitations, an important place in the future of American politics.[28]

PUBLIC OPINION AND GOVERNMENT POLICY

In democratic nations leaders should pay attention to public opinion, and most evidence suggests that they do. There are many instances in which public policy and public opinion do not coincide, but in general the government's actions are consistent with citizens' preferences. One study, for example, found that between 1935 and 1979, in about two-thirds of all cases, significant changes in public opinion were followed within one year by changes in government policy consistent with the shift in the popular mood.[29] Other studies have come to similar conclusions.

In addition, there are always areas of disagreement between opinion and policy. For example,

[27]See Michael Traugott, "The Impact of Media Polls on the Public," in Mann and Orren, eds., *Media Polls in American Politics,* pp. 125–49.

[28]For a fuller discussion of the uses of polling and the role of public opinion in American politics, see Benjamin Ginsberg, *The Captive Public* (New York: Basic Books, 1986).
[29]Benjamin I. Page and Robert Y. Shapiro, "Effects of Public Opinion on Policy," *American Political Science Review* 77 (March 1983), pp. 175–90.

the majority of Americans favored stricter governmental control of handguns for years before Congress finally adopted the modest restrictions on firearms purchases embodied in the 1994 Brady Bill and the Crime Control Act. Similarly, most Americans—blacks as well as whites—oppose school busing to achieve racial balance, yet such busing continues to be used extensively throughout the nation. Most Americans are far less concerned with the rights of the accused than the federal courts seem to be. Most Americans oppose U.S. military intervention in other nations' affairs, yet interventions continue to take place and often win public approval after the fact.

Several factors can contribute to a lack of consistency between opinion and governmental policy. First, the nominal majority on a particular issue may not be as intensely committed to its preference as the adherents of the minority viewpoint. An intensely committed minority may often be more willing to commit its time, energy, efforts, and resources to the affirmation of its opinions than an apathetic, even if large, majority. In the case of firearms, for example, although the proponents of gun control are in the majority by a wide margin, most do not regard the issue as one of critical importance to themselves and are not willing to commit much effort to advancing their cause. The opponents of gun control, by contrast, are intensely committed, well organized, and well financed, and as a result are usually able to carry the day.

A second important reason that public policy and public opinion may not coincide has to do with the character and structure of the American system of government. The framers of the American Constitution, as we saw in Chapter 2, sought to create a system of government that was based upon popular consent but that did not invariably and automatically translate shifting popular sentiments into public policies. As a result, the American governmental process includes arrangements such as an appointed judiciary that can produce policy decisions that may run contrary to prevailing popular sentiment—at least for a time.

When all is said and done, however, there can be little doubt that in general the actions of the American government do not remain out of line with popular sentiment for very long. A major reason for this is, of course, the electoral process, to which we shall next turn.

CHAPTER REVIEW

All governments claim to obey public opinion, and in the democracies politicians and political leaders actually try to do so.

The American government does not directly regulate opinions and beliefs in the sense that dictatorial regimes often do. Opinion is regulated by an institution that the government constructed and that it maintains—the marketplace of ideas. In this marketplace, opinions and ideas compete for support. In general, opinions supported by upper-class groups have a better chance of succeeding than those views that are advanced mainly by the lower classes.

Americans share a number of values and viewpoints but often classify themselves as liberal or conservative in their basic orientations. The meaning of these terms has changed greatly over the past century. Once liberalism meant opposition to big government. Today liberals favor an expanded role for the government. Once conservatism meant support for state power and aristocratic rule. Today conservatives oppose almost all government regulation.

Although the United States relies mainly on market mechanisms to regulate opinion, even our government intervenes to some extent, seeking to influence particular opinions and, more important, the general climate of political opinion, often by trying to influence media coverage of events.

Another important force shaping public opinion is the news media, which help to determine the agenda or focus of political debate and to shape popular understanding of political events. The power of the media stems from their having the freedom to present information and opinion

critical of government, political leaders, and policies. Free media are essential ingredients of popular government.

The scientific approach to learning public opinion is called polling. Through polling, elections can be accurately predicted; polls also provide information on the bases and conditions of voting decisions and make it possible to assess trends in attitudes and the influence of ideology on attitudes.

TIME LINE ON PUBLIC OPINION AND THE MEDIA

Events		Institutional Developments
Alien and Sedition Acts attempt to silence opposition press (1798)	**1800**	Newspapers and pamphlets serve leaders (early 1800s)
New printing presses introduced, allowing cheaper printing of more newspapers (1820s–1840s)		Expansion of popular press; circulation of more newspapers, magazines, and books (1840s)
First transmission of telegraph message between cities (from Baltimore to Washington) (1844)		Nation begins to be linked by telegraph communications network (1840s)
Creation of Associated Press (AP) (1848)		
	1850	
Completion of telegraph connections across country to San Francisco (1861)		Birth of advertising industry—scientific manipulation of public opinion (1880s)
Democrats denounce polling as a Republican plot (1896)		Advertising industry makes press financially free of parties; beginnings of an independent, nonpartisan press (1880s)
Publisher William R. Hearst sparks Spanish-American War (1898)		Circulation war between Hearst's *N.Y. Journal* and Pulitzer's *N.Y. World* leads to "yellow journalism"—sensationalized reporting (1890s)
Rise of large corporations and municipal corruption spark Progressive reform efforts (1880s–1890s)		Beginning of "muckraking"—exposure by journalists of social evils (1890s)
First news bulletins transmitted over radio; regular radio programs introduced (1920)	**1920**	Beginning of radio broadcasting (1920s)
NBC links radio stations into network (1926)		Regulation of broadcasting industry begins with Federal Radio Commission (1927)
Great Depression (1929–1933)		*Near v. Minnesota*—Supreme Court holds that government cannot exercise prior restraint (1931)
Literary Digest poll predicts Hoover will defeat Roosevelt (1932)		Federal Communications Act creates Federal Communications Commission (FCC) (1934)

Events	Institutional Developments
Franklin D. Roosevelt uses radio "fireside chats" to assure the nation and restore confidence (1930s)	
Gallup and Roper use sample surveys in national political polls (1936)	Growth of national polls (1930s–1950s)
	Television is introduced (late 1940s–1950s)

1950

Televised Senate hearings (1950s)	Computer analysis of polls (1959)
Televised Kennedy-Nixon debate (1960)	Fairness doctrine governing TV coverage (1960s)
John F. Kennedy uses televised news conference to mobilize public support for his policies (1961–1963)	Beginning of extended national television news coverage (1963)
	Development of exit polls (1960s)
"Daisy Girl" commercial helps defeat Goldwater and elect Lyndon Johnson president (1964)	*N.Y. Times v. Sullivan* asserts "actual malice" standard in libel cases involving public officials (1964)
Vietnam War; American officials in Vietnam leak information to the press (1960s–early 1970s)	Vietnam War first war to receive extended television coverage, which contributes to expansion of opposition to the war (1965–1973)
	TV spot ads become candidates' major weapons (1960s–1990s)
	Red Lion Broadcasting v. U.S. establishes "right of rebuttal" (1969)
	Media attack governmental opinion manipulation (1960s–1970s)
	Era of investigative reporting and critical journalistic coverage of government (1960s–1990s)

1970

Pentagon Papers on Vietnam War published by *N.Y. Times* and *Washington Post* (1971)	*N.Y. Times v. U.S.*—Supreme Court rules against prior restraint in *Pentagon Papers* case (1971)
Televised Watergate hearings (1973–1974)	
Exit polls used to predict presidential elections before polls closed on West coast (1976–1988)	

1980

Unsuccessful libel suits by Israeli General Ariel Sharon against *Time* magazine (1984) and by General William Westmoreland against CBS News (1985)	FCC stops enforcing fairness doctrine (1985)
Televised Iran-Contra hearings (1987)	

Events	Institutional Developments
1990	
Live coverage of Persian Gulf War (1990)	Media access controlled by military throughout Persian Gulf conflict (1990–1991)
Candidates use talk show appearances, "infomercials," televised town meetings during campaign (1992)	Politicians create new media formats to pitch themselves and their programs; era of permanent campaign (1992)
President Clinton uses town meetings and media appeals to bolster popular support for programs; Congress lobbies by mobilizing popular pressure (1993)	Members of presidential campaign staffs join White House staff to bolster public support for programs (1993)
Talk radio programs help Republicans defeat Democrats in congressional elections (1994)	

Key Terms

bandwagon effect A situation wherein reports of voter or delegate opinion can influence the actual outcome of an election or a nominating convention.

conservative Today this term refers to those who generally support the social and economic status quo and are suspicious of efforts to introduce new political formulae and economic arrangements. Conservatives believe that a large and powerful government poses a threat to citizens' freedom.

equality of opportunity A universally shared American ideal that all people should have the freedom to use whatever talents and wealth they have to reach their fullest potential.

illusion of saliency Impression conveyed by polls that something is important to the public when actually it is not.

liberal A liberal today generally supports political and social reform; extensive governmental intervention in the economy; the expansion of federal social services; more vigorous efforts on behalf of the poor, minorities, and women; and greater concern for consumers and the environment.

marketplace of ideas The public forum in which beliefs and ideas are exchanged and compete.

momentum A media prediction that a particular candidate will do even better in the future than in the past.

public opinion Citizens' attitudes about political issues, personalities, institutions, and events.

public opinion polls Scientific instruments for measuring public opinion.

sample A small group selected by researchers to represent the most important characteristics of an entire population.

For Further Reading

Asher, Herbert. *Polling and the Public: What Every Citizen Should Know.* Washington, DC: Congressional Quarterly Press, 1988.

Bennett, W. Lance. *Public Opinion in American Politics.* New York: Harcourt Brace Jovanovich, 1980.

Braestrup, Peter. *Big Story: How the American Press and Television Reported and Interpreted the Crisis of Tet 1968 in Vietnam and Washington,* Abridged ed. Novato, CA: Presidio, 1994.

Cook, Timothy. *Making Laws and Making News: Media Strategies in the House of Representatives.* Washington, DC: Brookings Institution, 1989.

Erikson, Robert S., Norman Luttbeg, and Kent Tedin. *American Public Opinion: Its Origins, Content and Impact.* New York: Wiley, 1980.

Gallup, George. *The Pulse of Democracy.* New York: Simon and Schuster, 1940.

Ginsberg, Benjamin. *The Captive Public: How Mass Opinions Promotes State Power.* New York: Basic Books, 1986.

Graber, Doris. *Mass Media and American Politics.* Washington, DC: Congressional Quarterly Press, 1989.

Hess, Stephen. *Live from Capitol Hill: Studies of Congress and the Media.* Washington, DC: Brookings Institution, 1991.

Holloway, Harry, and John George. *Public Opinion: Coalitions, Elites, and Masses.* New York: St. Martin's Press, 1986.

Joslyn, Richard A. *Mass Media and Elections.* Reading, MA: Addison-Wesley, 1984.

Lippmann, Walter. *Public Opinion.* New York: Harcourt, Brace, 1922.

Lipset, Seymour M., and William Schneider. *The Confidence Gap: Business, Labor, and Government in the Public Mind*, rev. ed. Baltimore: Johns Hopkins University Press, 1987.

Margolis, Michael, and Gary A. Mauser. *Manipulating Public Opinion.* Pacific Grove, CA: Brooks/Cole, 1989.

Mueller, John. *Policy and Opinion in the Gulf War.* Chicago: University of Chicago Press, 1994.

Nacos, Brigitte L. *The Press, Presidents, and Crises.* New York: Columbia University Press, 1990.

Neuman, W. Russell. *The Paradox of Mass Politics: Knowledge and Opinion in the American Electorate.* Cambridge: Harvard University Press, 1986.

Owen, Diana. *Media Messages in American Presidential Elections.* Westport, CT: Greenwood, 1991.

Smith, Craig A., and Cathy B. Smith. *The White House Speaks: Presidential Leadership as Persuasion.* Westport, CT: Greenwood, 1994.

Sullivan, John L., James Piereson, and George E. Marcus. *Political Tolerance and American Democracy.* Chicago: University of Chicago Press, 1982.

CHAPTER 9

Elections

O VER THE PAST two centuries, elections have come to play a significant role in the political processes of most nations. The forms that elections take and the purposes they serve, however, vary greatly from nation to nation. The most important difference among national electoral systems is that some provide the opportunity for opposition while others do not. Democratic electoral systems, such as those that have evolved in the United States and western Europe, allow opposing forces to compete against and even to replace current office holders. Authoritarian electoral systems, by contrast, do not allow the defeat of those in power. In the authoritarian context, elections are used primarily to mobilize popular enthusiasm for the government, to provide an outlet for popular discontent and to persuade foreigners that the regime is legitimate—i.e., that it has the support of the people. In the former Soviet Union, for example, citizens were required to vote even though no opposition to Communist Party candidates was allowed.

In democracies, elections can also serve as institutions of legitimation and as safety valves for social discontent. But beyond these functions, democratic elections facilitate popular influence, promote leadership accountability, and offer groups in society a measure of protection from the abuse of governmental power. Citizens exercise influence through elections by determining who should control the government (see Concept Map 9.1). The chance to decide who will govern serves as an opportunity for ordinary citizens to make choices about the policies, programs, and directions of government action. In the United States,

CORE OF THE ARGUMENT

- Elections are important because they promote accountability in elected officials and facilitate popular influence in the governmental process.
- The government exerts a measure of control over the electoral process by regulating the composition of the electorate, translating voters' choices into electoral decisions, and insulating day-to-day government from the impact of those decisions.
- The strongest influences on voters' decisions are partisan loyalty, issue and policy concerns, and candidate characteristics.
- Ordinary voters have little influence on the political process today.

CONCEPT MAP 9.1

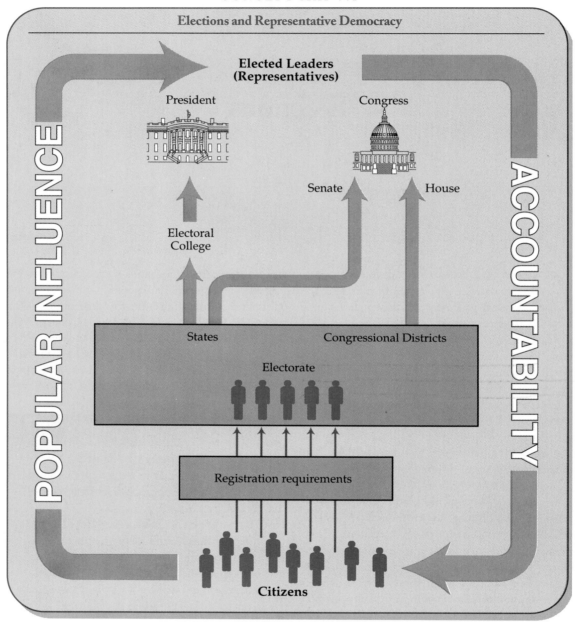

Elections and Representative Democracy

Elected Leaders
(Representatives)

President   Congress

Senate   House

POPULAR INFLUENCE   ACCOUNTABILITY

Electoral
College

States   Congressional Districts

Electorate

Registration requirements

Citizens

for example, recent Democratic and Republican candidates have differed significantly on issues of taxing, social spending, and governmental regulation. As American voters have chosen between the two parties' candidates, they have also made choices about these issues.

Elections promote leadership accountability because the threat of defeat at the polls exerts pressure on those in power to conduct themselves in a responsible manner and to take account of popular interests and wishes when they make their decisions. As James Madison observed in the *Federalist Papers*, elected leaders are "compelled to anticipate the moment when their power is to cease, when their exercise of it is to be reviewed, and when they must descend to the level from which they were raised, there forever to remain unless a faithful discharge of their trust shall have established their title to a renewal of it."[1] It is because of this need to anticipate that elected officials constantly monitor public opinion polls as they decide what positions to take on policy issues.

Finally, the right to vote, or *suffrage,* can serve as an important source of protection for groups in American society. The passage of the 1965 Voting Rights Act, for example, enfranchised millions of African Americans in the South, paving the way for the election of thousands of new black public officials at the local, state, and national levels and ensuring that white politicians could no longer ignore the views and needs of African Americans. The Voting Rights Act was one of the chief spurs for the elimination of many overt forms of racial discrimination as well as for the diminution of racist rhetoric in American public life.

Despite the potential importance of the suffrage, tens of millions of Americans routinely fail to exercise their right to vote. *Turnout* in recent presidential elections has barely reached 50 percent of those eligible, while congressional elections draw only about one-third of the potential

electorate. As we shall see, low levels of voter participation have important implications for the American political process. While voting participation in the U.S. is low, the participation of wealthy and powerful interests in electoral politics appears to be at an all-time high. Campaign spending by candidates, parties, interest groups, and wealthy individuals achieved a new record, reaching the $2 billion mark in the 1996 presidential election, just as voter turnout dropped to its lowest level since 1924. These two facts, taken together, should lead us to look carefully at the relationship between the *principles* and *practices* of American democratic politics.

In this chapter, we will look first at what distinguishes voting from other forms of political activity. Second, we will examine the formal structure and setting of American elections. Third, we will see how—and what—voters decide when they take part in elections. Fourth, we will discuss the consequences of elections, especially electoral realignment, to try to make sense of contemporary American electoral politics. Fifth, we will focus on recent national elections. Finally, we will assess the place of elections in the American political process.

POLITICAL PARTICIPATION

In the twentieth century, voting is viewed as the normal form of mass political activity. Yet, ordinary people took part in politics long before the introduction of the election or any other formal mechanism of popular involvement in political life. If there is any natural or spontaneous form of mass political participation, it is the riot rather than the election. Indeed, the urban riot and the rural uprising were a major part of life in western Europe prior to the nineteenth century, and in eastern Europe until the twentieth. In eighteenth-century London, for example, one of the most notorious forms of popular political action was the "illumination." Mobs would march up and down the street demanding that householders express

[1]Clinton Rossiter, ed., *The Federalist Papers* (New York: New American Library, 1961), No. 57, p. 352.

support for their cause by placing a candle or lantern in a front window. Those who refused to illuminate in this way risked having their homes torched by the angry crowd. This eighteenth-century form of civil disorder may well be the origin of the expression "to shed light upon" an issue.

The fundamental difference between voting and rioting is that voting is a socialized and institutionalized form of mass political action.[2] When, where, how, and which individuals participate in elections are matters of public policy rather than questions of spontaneous individual choice. With the advent of the election, control over the agenda for political action passed at least in part from the citizen to the government.

In an important study of participation in the United States, Sidney Verba and Norman Nie define political participation as consisting of "activities 'within the system'—ways of influencing politics that are generally recognized as legal and legitimate."[3] Governments try very hard to channel and limit political participation to actions "within the system." Even with that constraint, however, the right to political participation is a tremendous advancement in the status of citizens on two levels. At one level, it increases the probability that they will regularly affect the decisions that governments make. On another level, it reinforces the concept of the individual as independent from the state.

Those holding power are willing to concede the right to participate in the hope that it will encourage citizens to give their consent to being governed. This is a calculated risk for citizens. They give up their right to revolt in return for the right to participate regularly. They can participate, but only in ways prescribed by the government. Outside the established channels, their participation can be suppressed or disregarded. It is also a calculated risk for the politician, who may

be forced into certain policy decisions or forced out of office altogether by citizens exercising their right to participate. This risk is usually worth taking, since in return, governments acquire consent, and through consent citizens become supporters of government action.[4]

REGULATING THE ELECTORAL PROCESS

The compromise between rulers and ruled that is at the heart of the voting process is, perhaps, best illustrated by the rule governing electoral institutions. While elections allow citizens a chance to participate in politics, they also allow the government a chance to exert a good deal of control over when, where, how, and which of its citizens will participate. Electoral processes are governed by a variety of rules and procedures that allow government an excellent opportunity to regulate and control popular involvement. Three general forms of regulation have played especially important roles in the electoral history of the Western democracies. First, governments often attempt to regulate who can vote in order to diminish the influence of groups they deem to be undesirable. Second, governments frequently seek to manipulate the translation of voters' choices into electoral outcomes. Third, virtually all governments attempt to insulate the policy-making process from electoral intervention through regulation of the relationship between the ballot box and the organization of government.

Electoral Composition

Perhaps the oldest and most obvious device used to regulate voting and its consequences is manipulation of the electorate's composition. In the first elections in western Europe, for example, the suffrage was generally limited to property owners

---

[2]For a fuller discussion, see Benjamin Ginsberg, *The Consequences of Consent* (New York: Random House, 1982).
[3]Sidney Verba and Norman Nie, *Participation in America* (New York: Harper & Row, 1972), pp. 2–3.

[4]See Ginsberg, *Consequences of Consent.*

and others who could be trusted to vote in a manner acceptable to those in power. Property qualifications in France prior to 1848 limited the electorate to 240,000 of some 7 million men over the age of twenty-one.[5] No women were permitted to vote. During the same era, other nations manipulated the electorate's composition by assigning unequal electoral weights to different classes of voters. The 1831 Belgian constitution, for example, assigned individuals anywhere from one to three votes depending upon their property holdings, education, and position.[6] But even in the context of America's ostensibly universal and equal suffrage in the twentieth century, the composition of the electorate is still subject to manipulation. Until recent years, some states tried to manipulate the vote by the discriminatory use of *poll taxes* and literacy tests or by such practices as the placement of polls and the scheduling of voting hours to depress participation by one or another group. The most important example of the regulation of the American electorate's composition in recent history was the requirement that people register in person. That changed only in 1993 with passage of the Motor Voter bill.

Levels of voter participation in twentieth-century American elections are quite low by comparison to those of the other Western democracies.[7] Indeed, voter participation in presidential elections in the United States has barely averaged 50 percent recently. Turnout in the 1996 presidential election was 48.8 percent, the lowest turnout rate since 1924. During the nineteenth century, by contrast, voter turnout in the United States was extremely high. Records, in fact, indicate that in some counties as many as 105 percent of those eligible voted in presidential elections. Some proportion of this

total obviously was artificial—a result of the widespread corruption that characterized American voting practices during that period. Nevertheless, it seems clear that the proportion of eligible voters actually going to the polls was considerably greater in nineteenth-century America than it is today.

As Figure 9.1 indicates, the critical years during which voter turnout declined across the United States were between 1890 and 1910. These years coincide with the adoption of laws across much of the nation requiring eligible citizens to appear personally at a registrar's office to register to vote some time prior to the actual date of an election. Personal registration was one of several "Progressive" reforms initiated at the turn of the century. The ostensible purpose of registration was to discourage fraud and corruption. But to many Progressive reformers, "corruption" was a code word, referring to the type of politics practiced in the large cities where political parties had organized immigrant and ethnic populations. Reformers not only objected to this corruption, but they also opposed the growing political power of these urban populations and their leaders.

Personal registration imposed a new burden upon potential voters and altered the format of American elections. Under the registration systems adopted after 1890, it became the duty of individual voters to secure their own eligibility. This duty could prove to be a significant burden for potential voters. During a personal appearance before the registrar, individuals seeking to vote were (and are) required to furnish proof of identity, residence, and citizenship. While the inconvenience of registration varied from state to state, usually voters could register only during business hours on weekdays. Many potential voters could not afford to lose a day's pay in order to register. Second, voters were usually required to register well before the next election, in some states up to several months earlier. Third, since most personal registration laws required a periodic purge of the election rolls, ostensibly to keep them up-to-date, voters often had to re-register to maintain their

[5]Stein Rokkan, *Citizens, Elections, Parties* (New York: David McKay, 1970), p. 149.

[6]John A. Hawgood, *Modern Constitutions since 1787* (New York: D. Van Nostrand, 1939), p. 148.

[7]See Walter Dean Burnham, "The Changing Shape of the American Political Universe," *American Political Science Review* 59 (1965), pp. 7–28.

FIGURE 9.1

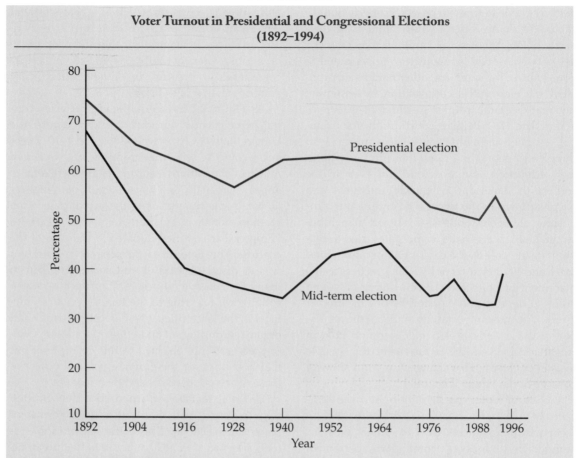

Voter Turnout in Presidential and Congressional Elections (1892–1994)

SOURCES: For 1892 to 1958, Erik Austin and Jerome Clubb, *Political Facts of the United States since 1789* (New York: Columbia University Press, 1986), pp. 378–79; for 1960–1992, Bureau of the Census, *Statistical Abstract of the United States* (Washington, DC: Government Printing Office, 1992); for 1994, U.S. Newswire, 11 November 1994.

eligibility. Thus, although personal registration requirements helped to diminish the widespread electoral corruption that accompanied a completely open voting process, they also made it much more difficult for citizens to participate in the electoral process.

Registration requirements particularly depress participation on the part of those with little education and low incomes, for two reasons. First, the simple obstacle of registering on weekdays during business hours is most difficult for working-class persons to overcome. Second, and more im-

portant, registration requires a greater degree of political involvement and interest than does the act of voting itself. To vote, a person need only be concerned with the particular election campaign at hand. Requiring individuals to register before the next election forces them to make a decision to participate on the basis of an abstract interest in the electoral process rather than a simple concern with a specific campaign. Such an abstract interest in electoral politics is largely a product of education. Those with relatively little education may become interested in political events because of a

IN BRIEF BOX

ELECTORAL COMPOSITION

Manipulation of the electorate's composition is a device used to regulate voting and its consequences.

Past methods by which voter participation was limited	Current limits on participation
property ownership and literacy requirements poll taxes race and gender restrictions placement of polls and scheduling of polling hours voter registration rules	There are no official limits (other than the age requirement), except that a voter must be an American citizen. However, any voter registration rules tend to depress voting on the part of the poor and uneducated.

particular campaign, but by that time it may be too late to register. As a result, personal registration requirements not only diminish the size of the electorate but also tend to create an electorate that is, in the aggregate, better educated, higher in income and social status, and composed of fewer African Americans and other minorities than the citizenry as a whole. Presumably this is why the elimination of personal registration requirements has not always been viewed favorably by some conservatives.[8]

Over the years, voter registration restrictions have been modified somewhat to make registration easier. In 1993, for example, Congress approved and President Clinton signed the "Motor Voter" bill to ease voter registration by allowing individuals to register when they applied for driver's licenses as well as in public assistance and military recruitment offices.[9] A similar bill had been vetoed by President George Bush in 1992. Republicans objected to the bill because they feared it would increase registration by the poor and minority voters who generally tend to support the Democrats. Experience suggests, how-

ever, that *any* registration rules, however liberal, tend to depress voting on the part of the poor and uneducated.

Translating Voters' Choices into Electoral Outcomes

With the exception of America's personal registration requirements, contemporary governments generally do not try to limit the composition of their electorates. Instead, they prefer to allow everyone to vote and then to manipulate the outcome of the election. This is possible because there is more than one way to decide the relationship between individual votes and electoral outcomes. There are any number of possible rules that can be used to determine how individual votes will be translated into collective electoral decisions. Two types of regulations are especially important: the rules that set the criteria for victory and the rules that define electoral districts.

THE CRITERIA FOR WINNING In some nations, to win a seat in the parliament or other representative body, a candidate must receive a simple majority (50% + 1) of all the votes cast in the relevant district. This type of electoral system is called a *majority system* and was used in the primary elections of most Southern states until

[8]See Kevin Phillips and Paul H. Blackman, *Electoral Reform and Voter Participation* (Washington, DC: American Enterprise Institute, 1975).
[9]Helen Dewar, "'Motor Voter' Agreement Is Reached," *Washington Post*, 28 April 1993, p. A6.

IN BRIEF BOX

WHO WINS?
TRANSLATING VOTERS' CHOICES INTO ELECTORAL OUTCOMES

Majority System
Winner must receive a simple majority (50 percent plus one)
Example: formerly used in primary elections in the South

Plurality System
Winner is the candidate who receives the most votes, regardless of the percentage
Example: currently used in almost all general elections throughout the country

Proportional Representation
Winners are selected to a representative body in the proportion to the votes their party received
Example: used in New York City in the 1930s, resulting in several Communist seats on the City Council

recent years. Generally, majority systems have a provision for a second or "runoff" election among the two top candidates if the initial contest drew so many contestants that none received an absolute majority of the votes cast.

In other nations, candidates for office need not receive an absolute majority of the votes cast to win an election. Instead, victory is awarded to the candidate who receives the most votes in a given election regardless of the actual percentage of votes this represents. Thus, a candidate who receives 40 percent or 30 percent or 20 percent of the votes cast may win the contest so long as no rival receives more votes. This type of electoral process is called a *plurality system,* and it is the system used in almost all general elections in the United States.

Most European states employ a third form of electoral system, called *proportional representation.* Under proportional rules, competing political parties are awarded legislative seats roughly in proportion to the percentage of the popular vote that they receive. For example, a party that won 30 percent of the votes would receive roughly 30 percent of the seats in the parliament or other representative body. In the United States, proportional representation is used by many states in presidential primary elections. In these primaries, candidates for the Democratic and Re-

publican nominations are awarded convention delegates in rough proportion to the percentage of the popular vote they receive in the primary.

ELECTORAL DISTRICTS   Despite the use of proportional representation and the occasional use of majority voting systems, most electoral contests in the United States are decided on the basis of plurality rules.

Congressional district boundaries in the United States are redrawn by governors and state legislatures every ten years, after the decennial census determines the number of House seats to which each state is entitled. Rather than seeking to manipulate the criteria for victory, American politicians have usually sought to influence electoral outcomes by manipulating the organization of electoral districts. This is called *gerrymandering* in honor of nineteenth-century Massachusetts Governor Elbridge Gerry, who was alleged to have designed a district in the shape of a salamander to promote his party's interests. The principle is a simple one. Different distributions of voters among districts produce different electoral outcomes; those in a position to control the arrangements of districts are also in a position to manipulate the results. For example, until recent years, gerrymandering to dilute the voting strength of

PROCESS BOX 9.1

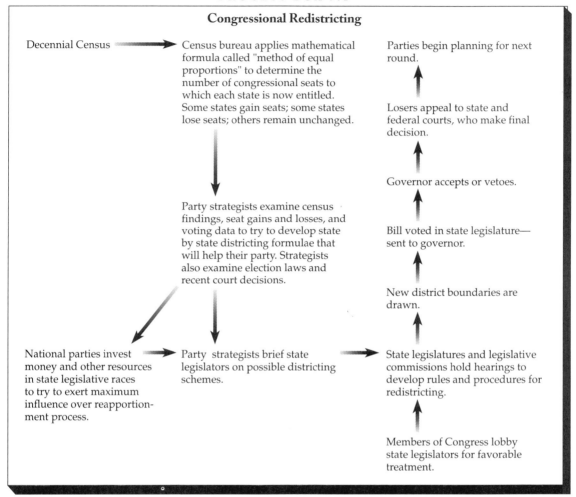

Congressional Redistricting

Decennial Census → Census bureau applies mathematical formula called "method of equal proportions" to determine the number of congressional seats to which each state is now entitled. Some states gain seats; some states lose seats; others remain unchanged.

Party strategists examine census findings, seat gains and losses, and voting data to try to develop state by state districting formulae that will help their party. Strategists also examine election laws and recent court decisions.

National parties invest money and other resources in state legislative races to try to exert maximum influence over reapportionment process.

Party strategists brief state legislators on possible districting schemes.

State legislatures and legislative commissions hold hearings to develop rules and procedures for redistricting.

Members of Congress lobby state legislators for favorable treatment.

New district boundaries are drawn.

Bill voted in state legislature—sent to governor.

Governor accepts or vetoes.

Losers appeal to state and federal courts, who make final decision.

Parties begin planning for next round.

racial minorities was a tactic employed by many state legislatures. One of the more common strategies involved redrawing congressional boundary lines in such a way as to divide and disperse a black population that otherwise would have constituted a majority within the original district.

This form of *racial gerrymandering,* sometimes called "cracking," was used in Mississippi during the 1960s and 1970s to prevent the election of an African American to Congress. Historically, the black population in Mississippi was clustered in the western half of the state, along the Mississippi Delta. From 1882 until 1966, the delta was one congressional district. Although blacks constituted a clear majority within the district (66 percent in 1960), the continuing election of white representatives was assured simply because blacks were denied the right to register and vote. With Congress's passage of the Voting Rights Act of 1965, however, the Mississippi state legislature moved swiftly to minimize the potential voting power of African Americans by redrawing congressional district lines in such a way as to fragment the African American population in the delta into four of the state's five congressional districts. Mississippi's gerrymandering scheme was preserved in the state's redistricting plans in 1972 and 1981 and helped to prevent the election of any African American representative until 1986, when Mike Espy became the first African American since Reconstruction to represent Mississippi in Congress.

In recent years, the federal government has encouraged what is sometimes called *"benign gerrymandering,"* designed to increase minority representation in Congress. The 1982 amendments to the Voting Rights Act of 1965 foster the creation of legislative districts with predominantly African American or Hispanic American populations by requiring states, when possible, to draw district lines that take account of concentrations of African American and Hispanic American voters. These amendments were initially supported by Democrats who assumed that minority-controlled districts would guarantee the election of Democratic members of Congress. Republicans championed them, too, hoping that if minority voters were concentrated in particular districts, Republican prospects in other districts would be enhanced.[10] This practice is sometimes called "stacking."

The 1993 Supreme Court decision in *Shaw v. Reno,* however, opened the way for challenges by white voters to the drawing of these districts. In the 5-to-4 majority opinion, Justice O'Connor wrote that if district boundaries were so "bizarre" as to be inexplicable on any grounds other than an effort to ensure the election of minority group members to office, white voters would have reason to assert that they had been the victims of unconstitutional racial gerrymandering.[11] In the 1995 case of *Miller v. Johnson,* the Supreme Court put further limits on "benign" gerrymandering by asserting that the use of race as a "predominant factor" in creating election districts was presumptively unconstitutional. However, the Court held open the possibility that race could be *one* of the factors influencing legislative redistricting.[12]

Although governments do have the capacity to manipulate electoral outcomes, this capacity is not absolute. Electoral arrangements conceived to be illegitimate may prompt some segments of the electorate to seek other ways of participating in political life. Moreover, no electoral system that provides universal and equal suffrage can, by itself, long prevent an outcome favored by large popular majorities. Yet, faced with opposition short of an overwhelming majority, governments' ability to manipulate the translation of individual choices into collective decisions can be an important factor in preserving the established distribution of power.

Insulating Decision-Making Processes

Virtually all governments attempt at least partially to insulate decision-making processes from electoral intervention. The most obvious ways of doing this are confining popular elections to only some governmental positions, using various modes of indirect election, and setting lengthy terms of office. In the United States, the framers of the Constitution intended that only members of the House of Representatives would be subject to direct popular election. The president and senators were to be indirectly elected for longer terms to allow them, as the *Federalist* put it, to avoid "an unqualified complaisance to every sudden breeze of passion, or to every transient impulse which the people may receive."[13]

THE ELECTORAL COLLEGE   In the early history of popular voting, nations often made use of indirect elections. In these elections, voters would choose

[10]Roberto Suro, "In Redistricting, New Rules and New Prizes," *New York Times,* 6 May 1990, sec. 4, p. 5.

[11]Shaw v. Reno, 113 S.Ct. 2816 (1993); Linda Greenhouse, "Court Questions Districts Drawn to Aid Minorities," *New York Times,* 29 June 1993, p. 1.

[12]Miller v. Johnson, 63 USLW 4726 (1995).

[13]Clinton Rossiter, ed., *The Federalist Papers* (New York: New American Library, 1961), No. 71, p. 432.

the members of an intermediate body. These members would, in turn, select public officials. The assumption underlying such processes was that ordinary citizens were not really qualified to choose their leaders and could not be trusted to do so directly. The last vestige of this procedure in America is the *electoral college,* the group of electors who formally select the president of the United States.

When Americans go to the polls on election day, they are technically not voting directly for presidential candidates. Instead, voters within each state are choosing among slates of electors who have been elected or appointed to their positions some months earlier. The electors are pledged to support their own party's presidential candidate chosen in the presidential race. In each state (except for Maine and Nebraska), the slate that wins casts all the state's electoral votes for its party's candidate.[14] Each state is entitled to a number of electoral votes equal to the number of the state's senators and representatives combined, for a total of 538 electoral votes for the fifty states and the District of Columbia. Occasionally, an elector breaks his or her pledge and votes for the other party's candidate. For example, in 1976, when the Republicans carried the state of Washington, one Republican elector from that state refused to vote for Gerald Ford, the Republican presidential nominee. Many states have now enacted statutes formally binding electors to their pledges, but some constitutional authorities doubt whether such statutes are enforceable.

In each state, the electors whose slate has won proceed to the state's capital on the Monday following the second Wednesday in December and formally cast their ballots. These are sent to Washington, tallied by the Congress in January, and the name of the winner is formally announced. If no

candidate receives a majority of all electoral votes, the names of the top three candidates would be submitted to the House, where each state would be able to cast one vote. Whether a state's vote would be decided by a majority, plurality, or some other fraction of the state's delegates would be determined under rules established by the House.

In 1800 and 1824, the electoral college failed to produce a majority for any candidate. In the election of 1800, Thomas Jefferson, the Jeffersonian Republican Party's presidential candidate, and Aaron Burr, that party's vice presidential candidate, received an equal number of votes in the electoral college, throwing the election into the House of Representatives. (The Constitution at that time made no distinction between presidential and vice presidential candidates, specifying only that the individual receiving a majority of electoral votes would be named president.) Some members of the Federalist Party in Congress suggested that they should seize the opportunity to damage the Republican cause by supporting Burr and denying Jefferson the presidency. Federalist leader Alexander Hamilton put a stop to this mischievous notion, however, and made certain that his party supported Jefferson. Hamilton's actions enraged Burr and helped lead to the infamous duel between the two men, in which Hamilton was killed. The Twelfth Amendment, ratified in 1804, was designed to prevent a repetition of such a situation by providing for separate electoral college votes for president and vice president.

In the 1824 election, four candidates–John Quincy Adams, Andrew Jackson, Henry Clay, and William H. Crawford—divided the electoral vote; no one of them received a majority. The House of Representatives eventually chose Adams over the others, even though Jackson had won more electoral and popular votes. This choice resulted from the famous "corrupt bargain" between Adams and Henry Clay. After 1824, the two major political parties had begun to dominate presidential politics to such an extent that by December of each election year, only two candidates remained for the electors to choose

---

[14]State legislatures determine the system by which electors are selected and almost all states use this "winner-take-all" system. Maine and Nebraska, however, provide that one electoral vote goes to the winner in each congressional district and two electoral votes go to the winner statewide.

between, thus ensuring that one would receive a majority. This freed the parties and the candidates from having to plan their campaigns to culminate in Congress, and Congress very quickly ceased to dominate the presidential selection process.

On all but two occasions since 1824, the electoral vote has simply ratified the nationwide popular vote. Since electoral votes are won on a state-by-state basis, it is mathematically possible for a candidate who receives a nationwide popular plurality to fail to carry states whose electoral votes would add up to a majority. Thus, in 1876, Rutherford B. Hayes received fewer popular votes than his rival, Samuel Tilden but was declared the winner by a specially-appointed commission. In 1888, Grover Cleveland received more popular votes than Benjamin Harrison, but received fewer electoral votes.

The possibility that in some future election the electoral college will, once again, produce an outcome that is inconsistent with the popular vote has led to many calls for the abolition of this institution and the introduction of some form of direct popular election of the president. In 1992 Ross Perot's candidacy, for example, at one point opened the possibility of a discrepancy between the popular and electoral totals, and even raised the specter of an election decided in the House of Representatives. Efforts to introduce such a reform, however, are usually blocked by political forces that believe they benefit from the present system. For example, minority groups that are influential in large urban states with many electoral votes feel that their voting strength would be diminished in a direct, nationwide, popular election. At the same time, some Republicans believe that their party's usual presidential strength in the South and the West gives them a distinct advantage in the electoral college. There is little doubt, however, that an election resulting in a discrepancy between the electoral and popular outcomes would create irresistible political pressure to eliminate the electoral college and introduce direct popular election of the president.

FREQUENCY OF ELECTIONS   Somewhat less obvious are the insulating effects of electoral arrangements that permit direct, and even frequent, popular election of public officials, but tend to fragment the impact of elections upon the government's composition. In the United States, for example, the constitutional provision of staggered terms of service in the Senate was designed to diminish the impact of shifts in electoral sentiment upon the Senate as an institution. Since only one-third of its members were to be selected at any time, the composition of the institution would be partially protected from changes in electoral preferences.

SIZE OF ELECTORAL DISTRICTS   The division of the nation into relatively small, geographically based constituencies for the purpose of selecting members of the House of Representatives was, in part, designed to have a similar effect. Representatives were to be chosen frequently. And although not prescribed by the Constitution, the fact that each was to be selected by a discrete constituency was thought by Madison and others to diminish the government's vulnerability to mass popular movements.

In a sense, the House of Representatives was compartmentalized in the same way that a submarine is divided into watertight sections to confine the impact of any damage to the vessel. First, by dividing the national electorate into small districts, the importance of local issues would increase. Second, the salience of local issues would mean that a representative's electoral fortunes would be more closely tied to factors peculiar to his or her own district than to national responses to issues. Third, given a geographical principle of representation, national groups would be somewhat fragmented while the formation of local forces that might or might not share common underlying attitudes would be encouraged. No matter how well represented individual constituencies might be, the influence of voters on national policy questions would be fragmented.

THE BALLOT   Prior to the 1890s, voters cast ballots according to political parties. Each party printed its own ballots, listed only its own candidates for each office, and employed party workers to distribute its ballots at the polls. This ballot format virtually prevented split-ticket voting. Because only one party's candidates appeared on any ballot, it was very difficult for a voter to cast anything other than a *straight party vote.*

The advent of a new, neutral ballot represented a significant change in electoral procedure. The new ballot was prepared and administered by the state rather than the parties. Each ballot was identical and included the names of all candidates for office. This ballot reform made it possible for voters to make their choices on the basis of the individual rather than the collective merits of a party's candidates. Because all candidates for the same office now appeared on the same ballot, voters were no longer forced to choose a straight party ticket. This give rise to the phenomenon of *split-ticket voting* in American elections.

Prior to the reform of the ballot, it was not uncommon for an entire incumbent administration to be swept from office and replaced by an entirely new set of officials. In the absence of a real possibility of split-ticket voting, any desire on the part of the electorate for change could be expressed only as a vote against all candidates of the party in power. Because of this, there always existed the possibility, particularly at the state and local levels, that an insurgent slate committed to policy change could be swept into power. The party ballot thus increased the potential impact of elections upon the governments' composition. Although this potential may not always have been realized, the party ballot at least increased the chance that electoral decisions could lead to policy changes. By contrast, because it permitted choice on the basis of candidates' individual appeals, ticket splitting led to increasingly divided partisan control of government.

Taken together, regulation of the electorate's composition, the translation of voters' choices into electoral decisions, and the impact of those decisions upon the government's composition allow those in power a measure of control over mass participation in political life. These techniques do not necessarily have the effect of diminishing citizens' capacity to influence their rulers' conduct. Rather, these techniques are generally used to *influence electoral influence.*

HOW VOTERS DECIDE

Thus far, we have focused on the election as an institution. But, of course, the election is also a process in which millions of individuals make decisions and choices that are beyond the government's control. Whatever the capacity of those in power to organize and structure the electoral process, it is these millions of individual decisions that ultimately determine electoral outcomes. Sooner or later the choices of voters weigh more heavily than the schemes of electoral engineers.

The Bases of Electoral Choice

Three types of factors influence voters' decisions at the polls: partisan loyalty, issue and policy concerns, and candidate characteristics.

PARTISAN LOYALTY   Many studies have shown that most Americans identify more or less strongly with one or the other of the two major political parties. Partisan loyalty was considerably stronger during the 1940s and 1950s than it is today. But even now most voters feel a certain sense of identification or kinship with the Democratic or Republican party. This sense of identification is often handed down from parents to children and is reinforced by social and cultural ties. Partisan identification predisposes voters in favor of their party's candidates and against those of the opposing party. At the level of the presidential contest, issues and candidate personalities may become very important, although even here many Americans supported Bob Dole or Bill Clinton because of partisan loyalty. But partisanship is more likely to assert itself in the less visible races, where issues and the candidates are not as well known. State legislative races, for example, are often decided by voters' party ties. Once formed, voters' partisan loyalties seldom change. Voters tend to keep their party affiliations unless some crisis causes them to reexamine the bases of their loyalties and to conclude that they have not given their support to the appropriate party. During these relatively infrequent periods of electoral change, millions of voters can change their party ties. For example, at the beginning of the New Deal era between 1932 and 1936, millions of former Republicans transferred their allegiance to Franklin Roosevelt and the Democrats.

ISSUES   Issues and policy preferences are a second factor influencing voters' choices at the polls. Voters may cast their ballots for the candidate whose position on economic issues they believe to be closest to their own. Similarly, they may select the candidate who has what they believe to be the best record on foreign policy. Issues are more important in some races than others. If candidates actually "take issue" with one another, that is, articulate and publicize very different positions on important public questions, then voters are more likely to be able to identify and act upon whatever policy preferences they may have. The 1964 presidential election, pitting conservative Republican Barry Goldwater against liberal Democrat Lyndon Johnson, was one in which each candidate vigorously promoted a perspective on the role of government and shape of national policy very different from the one asserted by his opponent. Voters elected Johnson, basing their choices on the issues.

The 1980 and 1984 contests won by Ronald Reagan, the most conservative American president of the postwar period, were also very heavily issue oriented, with Reagan emphasizing tax policy, social policy, and foreign policy positions different from prior American governmental commitments. In response, many voters based their choices on issue and policy preferences. In 1996, Democratic candidate Bill Clinton emphasized the health of the nation's economy and what he termed Republican efforts to cut Medicare and other entitlement programs as he sought re-election. Republican Robert Dole emphasized his plan for a 15-percent tax cut. Some Republicans urged Dole to focus on the issue of Clinton's alleged ethical lapses. Dole, however, declined to make personal character an issue until the closing days of the campaign. Most voters turned out not to be interested in the character issue and supported Clinton because of the apparent health of the economy during the president's first term.

The ability of voters to make choices on the bases of issue or policy preferences is diminished if competing candidates do not differ substantially or do not focus their campaigns on policy matters. Very often, candidates deliberately take the safe course and emphasize topics that will not be offensive to any voters. Thus, candidates often trumpet their opposition to corruption, crime, and inflation. Presumably, few voters favor these things. While it may be perfectly reasonable for candidates to take the safe course and remain as inoffensive as possible, this candidate strategy makes it extremely difficult for voters to make their issue of policy preferences the bases for their choices at the polls.

CANDIDATE CHARACTERISTICS   Candidates' personal attributes always influence voters' decisions. Some analysts claim that voters prefer tall candidates to short candidates, candidates with shorter names to candidates with longer names, and candidates with lighter hair to candidates with darker hair. Perhaps these rather frivolous criteria do play some role. But the more important candidate characteristics that affect voters' choices are race, ethnicity, religion, gender, geography, and social background. Voters presume

HOW VOTERS DECIDE: THREE FACTORS INFLUENCE VOTERS' DECISIONS AT THE POLLS

Partisan loyalty—Most Americans identify with either the Democratic or Republican party and will vote for candidates accordingly. Party loyalty rarely changes and is most influential in less visible electoral contests, such as on the state or local level where issues and candidates are less well known.

Issues—Voters may choose a candidate whose views they agree with on a particular issue that is very important to them, even if they disagree with the candidate in other areas. It is easier for voters to make choices based on issues if candidates articulate very different positions and policy preferences.

Candidate characteristics—Voters are more likely to identify with and support a candidate who shares their background, views, and perspectives; therefore, race, ethnicity, religion, gender, geography, and social background are characteristics that influence how people vote. Personality characteristics such as honesty and integrity have become more important in recent years.

that candidates with similar backgrounds to their own are likely to share their views and perspectives. Moreover, they may be proud to see someone of their ethnic, religious, or geographic background in a position of leadership. This is why, for many years, politicians sought to "balance the ticket," making certain that their party's ticket included members of as many important groups as possible. In 1988, for example, Dukakis named Texas Senator Lloyd Bentsen as his running mate to balance the ticket with a conservative Southerner. George Bush, in turn, selected Dan Quayle to appeal to younger and more conservativevoters.

Just as a candidate's personal characteristics may attract some voters, they may repel others. Many voters are prejudiced against candidates of certain ethnic, racial, or religious groups. And many voters—both men and women—continue to be reluctant to support the political candidacies of women, although this appears to be changing.

Voters also pay attention to candidates' personality characteristics, such as their "decisiveness," "honesty," and "vigor." In recent years, integrity has become a key election issue. During the 1992 campaign, George Bush accused Bill Clinton of

seeking to mislead voters about his anti–Vietnam War activities and his efforts to avoid the draft during the 1960s. This, according to Bush, revealed that Clinton lacked the integrity required of a president. Clinton, in turn, accused Bush of resorting to mudslinging because of his poor standing in the polls—an indication of Bush's own character deficiencies.

All candidates seek, through polling and other mechanisms, to determine the best image to project to the electorate. At the same time, the communications media—television in particular—exercise a good deal of control over how voters perceive candidates. During the 1992 campaign, the candidates developed a number of techniques designed to take control of the image-making process away from the media. Among the chief instruments of this "spin control" was the candidate talk-show appearance used very effectively by both Ross Perot and Bill Clinton. And in 1996, the Republican and Democratic parties both sought to stage-manage their national conventions to control media coverage. As we shall see, however, no candidate was fully able to circumvent media scrutiny.

Elections in Recent American History: From FDR to Bill Clinton

America's modern political history begins with President Franklin D. Roosevelt. Between 1896 and 1932, the Republicans had been the nation's majority party. After his election in 1932, however, Roosevelt worked to build a coalition of political forces that would make the Democratic party the dominant force in American politics.

The New Deal Coalition and Its Disruption

Franklin Roosevelt's New Deal coalition was composed of unionized labor, members of urban ethnic groups, Southerners, Northern blacks, middle-class liberals, and, ultimately, important sectors of the American business community. Roosevelt and his successors won and maintained the support of these groups by building governmental institutions and enacting policies that served their needs and interests. For example, New Deal labor legislation confirmed the support of organized labor for the Democratic party; Roosevelt's welfare and social service programs won the loyalty of Northern blacks and members of urban ethnic groups; Southerners benefited from New Deal farm programs; middle-class liberals benefited from the expansion of white-collar employment in the public sector as well as from New Deal programs in areas such as education and the arts; segments of the business community benefited from New Deal support for free trade and, later, from the expansion of industrial production in the World War II and postwar periods.[15]

This New Deal coalition dominated the government and politics of the United States until the 1960s, when it was shattered by conflicts over race relations, the Vietnam War, and the government's fiscal and regulatory policies. These conflicts drove apart the various groups that had made up the New Deal coalition and set the stage for new forces to attempt to reconstruct a governing coalition in the United States. Thus, today, middle-class liberals, organized labor, and blacks have vied for influence within the Democratic party, and have sought to use that party as a vehicle through which to secure power on the national level. However, segments of the business community, social and religious conservatives, upper-middle-class suburbanites, Southern whites, and many Northern blue-collar workers have united in a reconstituted coalition of the political Right within the Republican party.

Over the past thirty years, segments of the Democratic coalition have pursued a variety of electoral strategies. In 1968, liberal Democrats supported Eugene McCarthy's attempt to win the Democratic presidential nomination. In 1972, Democratic liberals forged an alliance with blacks that succeeded in securing the Democratic presidential nomination for George McGovern but was routed again in the general election by the Republicans. In 1976, liberals, in alliance with organized labor, played a key role in bringing about Jimmy Carter's presidential victory. This alliance between labor and liberals collapsed in 1980, when liberals spurned both Carter and Reagan and essentially boycotted the presidential contest—throwing away their votes in support of John Anderson's hopeless independent candidacy.

In 1984, Walter Mondale sought to build a strong and lasting alliance between liberals, blacks, and organized labor. Republicans, however, charged Mondale with pandering to "special interests" and routed him in the election. In 1988, Massachusetts Governor Michael Dukakis, seeking to win support from all elements of the party while not offending independents and Republicans, stressed the themes of competence and lead-

---

[15]See Thomas Ferguson, "From Normalcy to New Deal: Industrial Structure, Party Competition, and American Public Policy in the Great Depression," *International Organization* 38 (Winter 1984), pp. 42–94.

ership and sought to eschew commitments on substantive programs. However, he also could not escape being depicted as a politician with commitments to constituencies and causes that could be served only at the expense of the taxpayer and middle America. And, once again, the Democrats lost the presidential contest.

The Reconstituted Right

Under the leadership of Ronald Reagan, the reconstituted Right became the dominant force in American electoral politics in the 1980s. During the 1980 election campaign, Reagan fashioned a set of programs and policies designed to link the disparate forces of the political Right to one another and to his presidential campaign. First, Reagan promised middle-class suburbanites that he would trim social programs, cut taxes, and bring inflation under control—whatever the cost in terms of blue-collar employment. Second, Reagan promised social and religious conservatives that he would support "pro-family," anti-abortion, and school prayer legislation. Third, Reagan promised white Southerners and other opponents of the civil rights revolution an end to federal support for affirmative action, minority quotas, and other programs designed to aid blacks. Fourth, Reagan promised American business a relaxation of the environmental rules and other forms of "new regulation" that liberals had succeeded in enacting during the 1970s. Finally, Reagan promised the defense industry greatly increased rates of military spending.

Under Reagan's leadership, the Republican party scored a decisive victory in the 1980 presidential election, won control of the Senate, and substantially increased its representation in the House. Once in office, Reagan was able to begin fulfilling many of his campaign promises during his first term. The upper and upper-middle classes realized substantial savings from Reagan's tax reduction programs. Inflation was brought under control, although the cost of doing so was

the deepest recession since the 1930s. Defense spending increased dramatically. The federal regulatory climate became somewhat more favorable to business. The rate of increase in domestic social spending diminished. The federal government's efforts on behalf of minorities and the poor were reduced.[16]

Finally, under Reagan's auspices, some legislation was enacted to promote school prayer, various federal agencies began to reduce their backing for abortion, and Reagan himself continued to offer moral support and encouragement to the various groups of social and religious conservatives who had championed his candidacy. As a result of what must be seen as a generally successful record of service to the coalition that elected him, Reagan increased his support among the forces that had initially placed him in office. In the 1984 election, Reagan's share of the vote rose within all of the major segments of the electorate that had backed him in 1980. This enabled Reagan to win 59 percent of the popular vote in 1984, and to carry forty-nine states.

The electoral dominance of Reagan's coalition seemed to be reaffirmed in 1988 with the victory of Reagan's vice president, George Bush. Although Bush and his running mate, Dan Quayle, were generally perceived to be weak campaigners, they were able to maintain the unity of the Reagan coalition by castigating the Democrats for their liberalism. Thus, Bush won 54 percent of the popular vote and carried forty states. In the electoral college, Bush's margin was 426 to 112.

By the end of George Bush's term in office, however, the Reagan coalition had begun to unravel. The two key elements in the electoral appeal of Reaganism had been prosperity at home and strength abroad. But these two key elements did not last. The nation became mired in one of the longest economic downturns in recent

[16]See Lester Salamon and Michael Lund, eds., *The Reagan Presidency and the Governing of America* (Washington, DC: Urban Institute Press, 1985).

CAROL MOSELEY-BRAUN AND NEWT GINGRICH
Two Insurgencies

NATIONAL POLITICS IN THE 1990s offered little comfort to defenders of the status quo. The congressional races of 1992 and 1994 produced startling changes in Congress. One of the most distinctive milestones of the 1992 congressional races was the election of an unprecedented six women to the U.S. Senate (a seventh joined the Senate in a special election in 1993) and 47 to the House. Among the new women senators was the first African American woman ever to serve, Carol Moseley-Braun. In 1994 the status quo was further rocked by a Republican takeover in both houses of Congress, a move led in the House of Representatives by Newt Gingrich. Two years later, the Republicans retained control of Congress for the first time in 68 years.

Moseley-Braun grew up on Chicago's South Side, attended public schools, graduated from the University of Illinois, and received her law degree from the University of Chicago. She began her career as an assistant attorney general and then won election to the Illinois state legislature, where she served for ten years. She was serving as recorder of deeds for Cook County in 1991 when, along with millions of other TV viewers, she became outraged at what she saw as the unfair treatment of Anita Hill by the all-white, all-male Senate Judiciary Committee during Supreme Court Justice Clarence Thomas's nomination hearings (Hill testified that she had been sexually harassed by Thomas). That outrage focused on Illinois's senior senator, Democrat Alan Dixon, when he voted in favor of Thomas's confirmation. The night after the Senate confirmation vote, Moseley-Braun was deluged with calls from friends urging her to mount a Senate campaign.

Despite Dixon's wide popularity in Illinois, Moseley-Braun upset the two-term incumbent in a Democratic primary by capitalizing on the country's anti-incumbent mood. The primary victory catapulted her into the national spotlight, where she went on to defeat the Republican candidate.

Upon entering the Senate, Moseley-Braun immediately staked out a prominent liberal agenda that included support for ending the ban on gays in the military, passage of family leave and voter-registration reforms, and economic assistance for inner cities. She has also championed efforts to crack down on "deadbeat dads"—fathers who fail to pay child support—and gained Senate approval of a measure to prohibit the Small Business Administration from giving grants to those who fail to pay child support.

Never one to shrink from a fight, Moseley-Braun took on the Senate's most conservative member, Jesse Helms, in a successful effort to withhold federal recognition of a Southern group that identified with the Confederacy. She also landed a seat on the Judiciary Committee, ending its days as a white male bastion. In 1995, Moseley-Braun switched to the Finance Committee, where she could have a more direct impact on health and family issues.

CAROL MOSELEY-BRAUN

Newt Gingrich has been in the vanguard of a revolution of a different sort. Born in Pennsylvania, but raised in Georgia, Gingrich was educated at Emory and Tulane Universities, earning a Ph.D. in history from the latter in 1971. After teaching history for several years, he joined the House of Representatives as a Republican in 1978, where he quickly became known for his brash, abrasive, contentious style. In an environment in which collegiality, respect, and deference were considered necessary to win advancement, Gingrich waged what was labeled "guerrilla warfare against the Democrats." For example, he and fellow conservative Republicans used C-SPAN (the televised proceedings of Congress) to harshly criticize the Democrats in a highly public and therefore embarrassing manner.

Gingrich was among the first to criticize Democratic House Speaker Jim Wright in 1989 for alleged ethics problems, including questions surrounding a suspicious book deal. In the face of mounting criticism, Wright resigned his House seat.

Also in 1989, Gingrich pursued and won the number-two position in his party, House minority whip. Using his position, Gingrich raised campaign money under an umbrella organization called GOPAC to cultivate and fund a new generation of conservative Republican House candidates around the country who could effectively challenge entrenched Democrats. That effort culminated in the 1994 election, when a rising Republican tide swept 73 Republicans into the House (33 of whom were recruited by Gingrich's organization), giving the Republicans a majority for the first time since 1954. With the retirement of Republican Minority Leader Robert Michel, Gingrich was elevated to the position of Speaker in 1995.

Almost immediately, Gingrich pushed for a new conservative agenda, and won early legislative successes with House passage of many of the key elements of the Republican Contract with America. Yet many of these proposals died in the Republican-held, but more cautious Senate, or by the pen of presidential vetoes. Political conflict between congressional Republicans and Democratic President Clinton reached a climax when the two branches failed to agree on the 1996 federal budget. For a record-setting nine months, the government endured two shutdowns and no budget. In the wake of mounting public criticisms aimed mostly at congressional Republicans, a compromise was finally reached. The following year, Congress and the prresident reached agreement on the 1997 budget before the October 1 deadline.

In 1996 and 1997, Gingrich adopted a decidedly more restrained and conciliatory approach, both because the Republican margin in the House diminished in the 1996 elections, and because Gingrich's negative ratings in national polls were higher than those of any other national political figure. Gingrich's task during Clinton's second term would be to balance more carefully the zeal of his loyalists in the House with the need to seek compromise with a Democratic president.

NEWT GINGRICH

SOURCE: Burdett A. Loomis, *The Contemporary Congress* (New York: S Martin's Press, 1996).

decades, and the Soviet Union collapsed, bringing an end to the cold war and diminishing the threat of a nuclear holocaust.

The poor performance of the American economy during his term in office eroded Bush's popularity and divided the Republican coalition.

Democratic Triumph

These cracks in the Republican coalition provided the Democrats with their best opportunity in two decades to capture the White House. First, however, they had to put their own party's house in order. Since the early 1970s, Democratic candidates had been handicapped by problems of a liberal ideology and racial issues. During this period, moderate Democrats had argued that the party needed to present a more centrist image if it hoped to be competitive in national elections. The major organizational vehicle for the centrists was the Democratic Leadership Council (DLC), an organization based in Washington and funded by business firms with ties to the Democratic party. Throughout the Reagan and Bush years, the DLC organized networks of state and local party officials and sought to develop political themes that could bring about a measure of party unity *and* appeal to the national electorate.[17]

In 1992, the DLC and its moderate allies were able to dominate the Democratic party's presidential nominating processes as well as its national convention. The party chose as its presidential and vice presidential candidates Governor Bill Clinton and Senator Al Gore, both founding members of the DLC. The platform adopted at the party's national convention was widely perceived to be the most conservative in decades, stressing individual responsibility and private enterprise while implicitly criticizing welfare recipients. Though the platform mentioned the importance of protecting the rights of women, gays, and mi-

norities, gone were the calls for expanded rights for criminals and welfare recipients that had provided Republicans with such convenient political targets in previous years.

Democrats sought to deal with their party's racial divisions by keeping black politicians and racial issues at arm's length and relying upon economic appeals to woo both working-class white and black voters. Democratic strategists calculated that black voters and politicians would have no choice but to support the Democratic ticket. Given the nation's economic woes, which afflicted blacks even more than whites, Democratic leaders reasoned that they did not need to appeal explicitly for black support. This freed the party to seek the votes of conservative whites. One step in this direction was, of course, the creating of a ticket headed by two Southerners. Democrats hoped that the Clinton-Gore ticket would appeal directly to the Southern white voters who once had been Democratic stalwarts but had made the Deep South a Republican bastion during the Reagan years.

Clinton went out of his way to assure conservative whites in both the North and the South that, unlike previous Democratic candidates, he would not cater to blacks. He thus became the first Democratic presidential candidate in two decades who was neither burdened by an excessively liberal image nor plagued by the party's racial division. With Democratic strategists believing they had stabilized the party's traditional Southern, African American, and blue-collar base, Clinton and his allies moved to expand the Democratic coalition into Republican electoral territory— business and the middle class. For this purpose, the Democrats fashioned an economic message designed to appeal to business and the middle class without alienating the party's working-class constituency.

Against the backdrop of the continuing economic recession and Republican disarray, the Democrats' economic program and new posture of moderation on racial issues and ideology helped

[17]For a discussion, see Thomas Edsall, "The Democrats Pick a New Centerpiece," *Washington Post National Weekly Edition*, 24 August 1992, p. 14.

PROCESS BOX 9.2

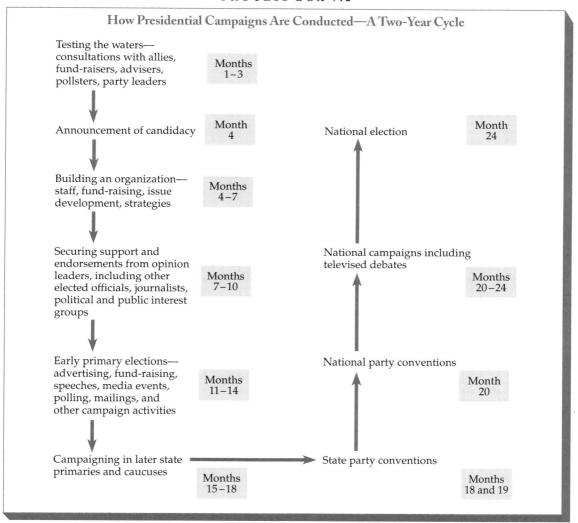

How Presidential Campaigns Are Conducted—A Two-Year Cycle

Testing the waters—consultations with allies, fund-raisers, advisers, pollsters, party leaders — Months 1–3

Announcement of candidacy — Month 4

National election — Month 24

Building an organization—staff, fund-raising, issue development, strategies — Months 4–7

Securing support and endorsements from opinion leaders, including other elected officials, journalists, political and public interest groups — Months 7–10

National campaigns including televised debates — Months 20–24

Early primary elections—advertising, fund-raising, speeches, media events, polling, mailings, and other campaign activities — Months 11–14

National party conventions — Month 20

Campaigning in later state primaries and caucuses — Months 15–18

State party conventions — Months 18 and 19

the Clinton-Gore ticket take a commanding lead in the polls in August 1992, after the Democratic National Convention. The Republican ticket's difficulties became fully evident during the nationally televised presidential and vice presidential debates in October. While the Democratic candidates focused on the nation's economic distress, constantly reminding voters of the need for programs and policies designed to improve the na-

tion's economy, Bush and Quayle had considerable difficulty articulating an affirmative message and were left to talk about character. Not surprisingly, the debates attracted few new voters to the Republican camp.

The Clinton-Gore ticket achieved a comfortable victory, winning 43 percent of the popular vote and 370 electoral votes. Bush and Quayle received 38 percent of the popular vote and only

FIGURE 9.2

Distribution of Electoral Votes in the 1996 Election

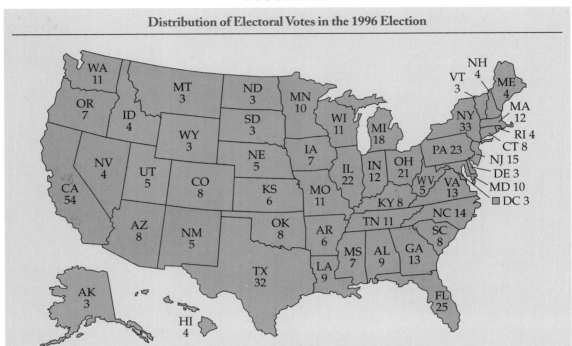

For Clinton/Gore (D) (379 Total)
For Dole/Kemp (R) (159 Total)

SOURCE: Congressional Quarterly American Voter '96 Web site: http:/voter96.cqalert.com/elect/results.htm

168 electoral votes. Economic recession, the end of the cold war, and the Democrats' newfound moderation on matters of race and ideology combined to oust the Republicans from the White House for the first time in twelve years.

The 1996 Election

In 1996, President Bill Clinton won a solid victory in the national presidential election to become the first Democratic president re-elected for a second term since Lyndon Johnson defeated Barry Goldwater in 1964, and the first to be re-elected for a second full term since Franklin Roosevelt's 1936 landslide. Clinton won 49 percent of the popular vote and carried 31 states, for a total of 379 elec-

toral votes. Republican challenger Bob Dole won only 41 percent of the popular vote and carried 19 states, with 159 electoral votes. Reform Party candidate Ross Perot, who had won 19 percent of the popular vote in 1992, dropped to 8 percent in 1996.

Clinton ran well in traditionally Democratic constituencies. Voters with incomes below $30,000 supported Clinton by a margin of 56 to 33 percent. By contrast, those earning more than $75,000 gave Dole their support by a 50-to-42 percent margin. Eighty-three percent of African Americans voted for Clinton. Those voters who call themselves liberals gave Clinton 78 percent of their votes. Americans who said Medicare and Social Security were their major concerns gave Clinton 67 percent of their votes. Finally, as has been the case in most recent elections, the 1996 results showed a significant "gender gap": 54 percent of women voted for Clinton, but only 44 percent of men did so.[18]

Despite Clinton's solid victory, Democratic Senate and House candidates did not fare especially well in 1996. Republicans actually gained two Senate seats to give the GOP a 55-to-45 majority in the upper chamber. In House races, Democrats gained 8 seats, falling far short of the 19 that would have been needed to recapture control of the House of Representatives. Republicans had a 227-to-205 House majority in the 105th Congress.

Poll data suggests that some voters deliberately split their tickets in order to prevent either political party from fully controlling the government. Ironically, many voters chose Clinton in part as a reaction to Newt Gingrich and the Republican-led 104th Congress. Having decided to vote for Clinton, however, some of these individuals voted for Republican congressional candidates because they feared that a Democratic president plus a Democratic Congress would mean the enactment of expensive new federal programs.[19] Nearly one in seven, or more than 6 million voters who supported Clinton simultaneously gave their vote to a Republican congressional candidate.

Against the backdrop of a nation at peace and a robust economy, ideal conditions for re-election, Clinton demonstrated once again that he is a polished, articulate, and vigorous campaigner, particularly in front of the television cameras. Republican nominee Bob Dole, on the other hand, although he was an able and effective senator, seemed to lack the media savvy and public relations skills needed by a modern presidential candidate.

As recently as the summer of 1995, Clinton's chances for re-election had seemed poor. He had been widely blamed for the Democrats' loss of both houses of Congress in 1994 and had been forced to the sidelines for a while as the GOP legislative juggernaut pushed forward in 1995.[20] After the 1994 elections, however, Clinton and his advisers developed a strategy to bolster the president's political image. This strategy called for Clinton to move sharply to the political right to occupy a middle ground between liberal congressional Democrats and conservative congressional Republicans. Thus Clinton advocated a series of tax-cut initiatives (the "middle class bill of rights"), called for tough anti-crime measures, embraced the idea of voluntary school prayer, spoke out against sex and violence on television, dropped much of his opposition to Republican welfare reform proposals, and advocated "family values" in a series of public addresses.

Clinton's shift to the right outraged many of his liberal advisers. However, his strategy successfully robbed the Republicans of their most potent issues in the 1996 elections.[21] The 1995–96 budget battle in which congressional Republicans forced two partial shutdowns of federal agencies allowed Clinton to portray himself as a moderate, willing to compromise, while congressional Republicans were pilloried as militant radicals by the national media. "The most important event of 1995," said Democratic pollster Geoff Garin, "was that the Republicans vacated the center in a radical way, and President Clinton was very smart and very effective in filling the vacuum and occupying the center in American politics."[22]

---

[18]Data are drawn from exit poll results reported in the *Washington Post*, 6 November 1996, p. B7.

[19]See David Broder, "Parceling Out Power to Both Parties," *Washington Post*, 6 November 1996, p. B1.

[20]Jon Healey, "Declining Fortunes: President's Leadership Role Eclipsed by Vigor and Unity of GOP Majority," *Congressional Quarterly Weekly Report*, Vol. 54, No. 4 (27 January 1996), pp. 193–98.

[21]Elizabeth Drew, *Showdown: The Struggle Between the Gingrich Congress and the Clinton White House* (New York: Simon & Schuster, 1996).

[22]John F. Harris, "Clinton Had Ingredients for Victory a Year Ago," *Washington Post*, 4 November 1996, p.1.

Do Elections Matter?

Reviewing the recent history of American elections only tells us who won and, perhaps, why they won. It cannot tell us much about the larger place of elections in the American political process. Unfortunately, recent political trends raise real questions about the continuing ability of ordinary Americans to influence their government through electoral politics.

The Decline of Voting

Despite the sound and fury of contemporary American politics, one very important fact stands out: Participation in the American political process is abysmally low. Politicians in recent years have been locked in intense struggles. As we saw in Chapter 5, partisan division in Congress has reached its highest level of intensity since the nineteenth century. Nevertheless, millions of citizens have remained uninvolved. For every American who voted in the bitterly fought 1994 congressional races, for example, two stayed home.

This lack of popular involvement is sometimes attributed to the shortcomings of American citizens—many millions do not go to the trouble of registering and voting. In actuality, however, low levels of popular participation in American politics are as much (or more) the fault of politicians as of voters. Even with America's personal registration rules, higher levels of political participation could be achieved if competing political forces made a serious effort to mobilize voters. Unfortunately, however, contending political forces in the United States have found ways of attacking their opponents that do not require them to engage in voter mobilization, and many prefer to use these methods than to endeavor to bring more voters to the polls. The low levels of popular mobilization that are typical of contemporary American politics are very much a function of the way that politics is conducted in the United States today.

For most of U.S. history, elections were the main arenas of political combat. In recent years, however, elections have become less effective as ways of resolving political conflicts in the United States. Today's political struggles are frequently waged elsewhere, and crucial policy choices tend to be made outside the electoral realm. Rather than engage voters directly, contending political forces rely on such weapons of institutional combat as congressional investigations, media revelations, and judicial proceedings. In contemporary America, electoral success often fails to confer the capacity to govern, and political forces, even if they lose at the polls or do not even compete in the electoral arena, have been able to exercise considerable power. However, neither side has made much effort to mobilize *new* voters, to create strong local party organizations, or in general, to make full use of the electoral arena to defeat its enemies.

The 1993 **Motor Voter bill** was, at best, a very hesitant step in the direction of expanded voter participation. This act requires all states to allow voters to register by mail when they renew their driver's licenses (twenty-eight states already had similar mail-in procedures) and provides for the placement of voter registration forms in motor vehicle, public assistance, and military recruitment offices. Motor Voter did result in some increases in voter registration. Thus far, however, few of these newly registered individuals have actually gone to the polls to cast their ballots. In 1996, the percentage of newly registered voters who appeared at the polls actually dropped.[23] Mobilization requires more than the distribution of forms.

It is certainly not true that politicians don't know how to mobilize new voters and expand electoral competition. Voter mobilization is hardly a mysterious process. It entails an investment of funds and organizational effort to register voters actively and bring them to the polls on election day. Occasionally, politicians demonstrate that

---

[23]Peter Baker, "Motor Voter Apparently Didn't Drive Up Turnout," Washington Post, 6 November 1996, p. B7.

they *do* know how to mobilize voters if they have a strong enough incentive. For example, a massive get-out-the-vote effort by Democrats to defeat neo-Nazi David Duke in the 1991 Louisiana gubernatorial election led to a voter turnout of over 80 percent of those eligible—twice the normal turnout level for a Louisiana election. And in the 1990s it was the GOP, through its alliance with conservative religious leaders, that made the more concerted effort to bring new voters into the electorate. This effort was limited in scope, but it played an important part in the Republican Party's capture of both houses of Congress in 1994. The GOP's gains from this limited strategy of mobilization demonstrate what could be achieved from a fuller mobilization of the national electorate. Significantly, in 1996, while voter turnout dropped, campaign expenditures by parties, candidates, and interest groups rose sharply.

The 1996 national elections were widely thought to have been the most expensive in American history, with many estimates placing total campaign spending on the part of candidates, parties, and interest groups at more than $2 billion. During the course of the presidential campaign, media accounts suggested that both parties had accepted improper campaign contributions from foreign donors. Democratic National Committee official John Huang was compelled to resign in the wake of revelations connecting him with millions of dollars in contributions from Indonesian business interests. Obviously, neither party devoted much energy to mobilizing new voters, preferring, instead, to work within the boundaries of the established electorate.

The important role played by private funds in American politics affects the balance of power among contending social groups. Politicians need large amounts of money to campaign successfully for major offices. This fact inevitably ties their interests to the interests of the groups and forces that can provide this money. In a nation as large and diverse as the United States, to be sure, campaign contributors represent many different groups and often represent clashing interests. Business groups, labor groups, environmental groups, and pro-choice and right-to-life forces all contribute millions of dollars to political campaigns. Through such PACs as EMILY's List, women's groups contribute millions of dollars to women running for political office. One set of trade associations may contribute millions to win politicians' support for telecommunications reform, while another set may contribute just as much to block the same reform efforts. Insurance companies may contribute millions of dollars to Democrats to win their support for changes in the health care system, while physicians may contribute equal amounts to prevent the same changes from becoming law.

Despite this diversity of contributors, however, not all interests play a role in financing political campaigns. Only those interests that have a good deal of money to spend can make their interests known in this way. These interests are not monolithic, but neither do they completely reflect the diversity of American society. The poor, the destitute, and the downtrodden also live in America and have an interest in the outcome of political campaigns. Who is to speak for them?

Both sides give lip service to the idea of fuller popular participation in political life. Politicians and their upper-middle-class constituents in both camps, however, have access to a variety of different political resources—the news media, the courts, universities, and interest groups, to say nothing of substantial financial resources. As a result, neither side has much need for or interest in political tactics that might, in effect, stir up trouble from below. Both sides prefer to compete for power without engaging in full-scale popular mobilization. Without mobilization drives that might encourage low-income citizens or minorities to register and to actually vote, the population that does vote tends to be wealthier, whiter, and better-educated than the population as a whole. There are marked differences in voter turnout linked to ethnic group, education level, and employment status. This trend has created a political

Do Elections and Voting Matter?

*M*OST *A*MERICANS *take pride in the country's annual election rituals, pointing out that few nations of the world have mechanisms for transferring power in such a smooth and peaceful fashion. Critics of American elections argue, however, that the differences between the candidates and political parties are marginal, if not nonexistent; that elections and campaigns are more spectacle and show than about real power; and that elections pacify the electorate more than they encourage true citizenship.*

Political scientists Gerald M. Pomper and Susan S. Lederman argue that elections in fact do meet the criteria for meaningful political exercises. Political scientist Howard L. Reiter, on the other hand, argues that voting is at best a poor method for translating preferences into policies and, worse, that voting tends to channel citizens toward a relatively harmless political act and away from other more effective methods of political expression.

POMPER AND LEDERMAN

The first necessity for meaningful elections is an organized party system. . . . Without a choice between at least two competing parties, the electorate is powerless to exert its influence.

A related vital requirement is for free competition between the parties. The voters must be able to hear diverse opinions and be able to make an uncoerced choice. . . . Nomination and campaigning must be available to the full range of candidates, and the means provided for transmitting their appeals to the electorate. . . .

Elections in the United States do largely meet the standards of meaningful popular decisions; true voter influence exists. The two parties compete freely with one another, and the extent of their competition is spreading to virtually all states. Access to the voters is open to diverse candidates, and no party or administration can control the means of communication. Suffrage is virtually universal, and voters have fairly simple choices to make for regular offices. In the overwhelming number of cases, voting is conducted honestly. . . .

Whatever the future may hold, present conditions in the United States do enable the voters to influence,

process whose class bias is so obvious and egregious that, if it continues, may force Americans to begin adding a qualifier when they describe their politics as democratic. Perhaps the terms "semi-democratic," "quasi-democratic," or "neo-democratic" are in order to describe a political process in which ordinary voters have as little influence as they do in contemporary America.

THE CONSEQUENCES OF CONSENT

Voting choices and electoral outcomes can be extremely important in the United States. Yet, to observe that there can be relationships between vot-

ers' choices, leadership composition, and policy outputs is only to begin to understand the significance of democratic elections, rather than to exhaust the possibilities. Important as they are, voters' choices and electoral results may still be less consequential for government and politics than the simple fact of voting itself. The impact of electoral decisions upon the governmental process is, in some respects, analogous to the impact made upon organized religion by individuals' being able to worship at the church of their choice. The fact of worship can be more important than the particular choice. Similarly, the fact of mass electoral participation can be more significant than what or how the citizens decide once they participate. Thus, electoral participation has important

but not control, the government. The evidence . . . does not confirm the most extravagant expectations of popular sovereignty. Neither are elections demonstrably dangerous or meaningless. Most basically, we have found the ballot to be an effective means for the protection of citizen interests. Elections in America ultimately provide only one, but the most vital, mandate.[1]

REITER

Most of the major issues in American history have been resolved not by elections but by other historical forces. . . . Elections are not very good ways of expressing the policy views of the people who actually vote. Elections are even less effective as a means of carrying out the policy views of all citizens. . . .

Politics, we are encouraged to believe, occurs once a year in November, and for most adults it occurs only once every four years. We are able to discharge our highest civic function by taking a few minutes to go into a booth and flip a few levers once every four years. Although we are all free to engage in other political activities, such as collective action, writing to officials or working on campaigns, most adults are quite content to limit their political activity to that once-in-a-quadrennium lever flip. And if we think of voting as the crown jewel of our liberties, we will not think that citizenship requires anything else.

All in all, the message that elections send us is to be passive about politics. Don't take action that involves any effort, don't unite with other citizens to achieve political goals, just respond to the choice that the ballot box gives us. In a strange way, then, elections condition us *away* from politics. A nation which defines its precious heritage in terms of political rights discourages its citizens from all but the *least* social, *least* public, and *least* political form of activity. This should raise the most profound questions for us. Why should we as a society discourage political activism? What is the real role that voting plays in our politics?[2]

[1]Gerald M. Pomper and Susan S. Lederman, *Elections in America: Control and Influence in Democratic Politics*, 2nd ed. (New York: Longman, 1980), pp. 223–25.
[2]Howard L. Reiter, *Parties and Elections in Corporate America* (New York: St. Martin's Press, 1987), pp. 1–3, 9.

consequences in that it socializes and institutionalizes political action.

First, democratic elections socialize political activity. Voting is not a natural or spontaneous phenomenon. It is an institutionalized form of mass political involvement. That individuals vote rather than engage in some other form of political behavior is a result of national policies that create the opportunity to vote and discourage other political activities relative to voting. Elections transform what might otherwise consist of sporadic, citizen-initiated acts into a routine public function. This transformation expands and democratizes mass political involvement. At the same time, however, elections help to preserve the government's stability by containing and channeling away potentially more disruptive or dangerous forms of mass political activity. By establishing formal avenues for mass participation and accustoming citizens to their use, government reduces the threat that volatile, unorganized involvement can pose to the established order.

Second, elections bolster the government's power and authority. Elections help to increase popular support for political leaders and for the regime itself. The formal opportunity to participate in elections serves to convince citizens that the government is responsive to their needs and wishes. Moreover, elections help to persuade citizens to obey. Electoral participation increases popular acceptance of taxes and military service upon which the government depends. Even if popular voting can influence the behavior of those in power, voting serves simultaneously as a form of co-optation. Elections—particularly democratic elections—substitute consent for coercion as the foundation of governmental power.

Finally, elections institutionalize mass influence in politics. Democratic elections permit citizens to routinely select and depose public officials, and elections can serve to promote popular influence over officials' conduct. But however effective this electoral sanction may be, it is hardly the only means through which citizens can reward or punish public officials for their actions. Spontaneous or privately organized forms of political activity, or even the threat of their occurrence, can also induce those in power to heed the public's wishes. The alternative to democratic elections is not clearly and simply the absence of popular influence; it can be unregulated and unconstrained

popular intervention into government. It is often precisely because spontaneous forms of mass political activity can have too great an impact upon the actions of government that elections are introduced. Walter Lippmann, a journalist who helped to pioneer the idea of public opinion voicing itself through the press via the "opinion-editorial," or op-ed, page, once observed that "new numbers were enfranchised because they had power, and giving them the vote was the least disturbing way of letting them exercise their power."[24] The vote can provide the "least disturbing way" of allowing ordinary people to exercise power. If the people had been powerless to begin with, elections would never have been introduced.

Thus, although citizens can secure enormous benefits from their right to vote, government secures equally significant benefits from allowing them to do so.

Chapter Review

Allowing citizens to vote represents a calculated risk on the part of power holders. On the one hand, popular participation can generate consent and support for the government. On the other hand, the right to vote may give ordinary citizens more influence in the governmental process than political elites would like.

Voting is only one of the many possible types of political participation. The significance of voting is that it is an institutional and formal mode of political activity. Voting is organized and subsidized by the government. This makes voting both more limited and more democratic than other forms of participation.

All governments regulate voting to influence its effects. The most important forms of regulation include regulation of the electorate's composition, regulation of the translation of voters' choices into electoral outcomes, and insulation of policymaking processes from electoral intervention.

Voters' choices are based on partisanship, issues, and candidates' personalities. Which of

these criteria will be most important varies over time and depends upon the factors and issues that opposing candidates choose to emphasize in their campaigns.

Voters' choices have had particularly significant consequences during periods of critical electoral realignment. During these periods, which have occurred roughly every thirty years, new electoral coalitions have formed, new groups have come to power, and important institutional and policy changes have occurred. The last such critical period was associated with Franklin Roosevelt's New Deal.

Whatever voters decide, elections are important because they socialize political activity, increase governmental authority, and institutionalize popular influence in political life.

[24]Walter Lippmann, *The Essential Lippmann,* eds. Clinton Rossiter and James Lare (New York: Random House, 1965), p. 12.

TIME LINE ON ELECTIONS

Events		Institutional Developments
George Washington elected president (1789)		Federalists in control of national government (1789–1800)
Thomas Jefferson elected president (1800)	1800	First electoral realignment—Jeffersonian Republicans defeat Federalists (1800)
Andrew Jackson elected president; beginning of party government (1828)		Second realignment—Jacksonian Democrats take control of White House and Congress (1828)
		Presidential nominating conventions introduced (1830s)
Whigs win; William Henry Harrison elected president (1840)		Whig party forms (1830s)
Lincoln elected (1860); South secedes (1860–1861)		Civil War realignment—Republican party founded (1856); Whig party destroyed (1860)
Civil War (1861–1865)		
Reconstruction (1867–1877)		Under Reconstruction Acts, blacks enfranchised in South (1867)
	1870	Fifteenth Amendment forbids states to deny voting rights based on race (1870)
Contested presidential election—Hayes versus Tilden (1876); Republican Rutherford Hayes elected by electoral vote of 185–184 (1876)		Hayes's election leads to an end of Reconstruction; voting rights of South restored (1877)
		Southern blacks lose voting rights through poll taxes, literacy tests, grandfather clause (1870s–1890s)
		Progressive reforms—direct primaries, civil service reform, Australian ballot, registration requirements; voter participation drops sharply (1890s–1910s)
Republican William McKinley elected president (1896)		Realignment of 1896; Republican hegemony (1896–1932)
	1900	
		Seventeenth Amendment authorizes direct election of senators (1913)
		Nineteenth Amendment gives women right to vote (1920)
Democrat Franklin D. Roosevelt elected president (1932)		Democratic realignment (1930s)

Events		Institutional Developments
Democrat John F. Kennedy first Roman Catholic elected president (1960)	**1960**	*Baker v. Carr*—Supreme Court declares doctrine of "one man, one vote" (1962); period of reapportionment (1960s)
		Voting Rights Act (1965)
Republican Richard Nixon elected president (1968)		Breakdown of Democratic New Deal coalition (1968)
Rise of black voting in the South (1970s)		Twenty-sixth Amendment lowers voting age to eighteen (1971)
Era of new campaign technology and PACs (1970s–1980s)		Federal Election Campaign Act (1971)
Republican Ronald Reagan elected president (1980)	**1980**	New Republican era begins with election of Reagan (1980)
Geraldine Ferraro first woman on major party national ticket (1984)		Electoral stalemate; Democrats dominate Congress; Republicans control presidency (1986–1990)
Jesse Jackson first black candidate to become important presidential contender (1988)		
George Bush elected president (1988)		
Democrats regain control of Congress (1990)	**1990**	
Democrat Bill Clinton elected president; Democrats retain control of House and Senate (1992)		New rules governing voter registration adopted (1993)
Republicans take control of Congress (1994)		
Clinton re-elected president; Republicans maintain control of Congress (1996)		

KEY TERMS

benign gerrymandering Attempts to draw districts so as to create districts made up primarily of disadvantaged or underrepresented minorities.

electoral college The presidential electors from each state who meet in their respective state capitals after the popular election to cast ballots for president and vice president.

gerrymandering Apportionment of voters in districts in such a way as to give unfair advantage to one political party.

majority system Type of electoral system in which, to win a seat in the parliament or other representative body, a candidate must receive a majority of all the votes cast in the relevant district.

Motor Voter bill A legislative act passed in 1993 that requires all states to allow voters to register by mail when they renew their drivers' licenses and provides for the placement of voter registration forms in motor vehicle, public assistance, and military recruitment offices.

plurality system Type of electoral system in which, to win a seat in the parliament or other representative body, a candidate need only receive the most votes in the election, not necessarily a majority of votes cast.

poll tax   A state-imposed tax upon voters as a prerequisite for registration. Poll taxes were rendered unconstitutional in national elections by the Twenty-fourth Amendment, and in state elections by the Supreme Court in 1966.

proportional representation   A multiple-member district system that awards seats based on the percentage of the vote won by each candidate. By contrast, the "winner-take-all" system of elections awards the seat to the one candidate who wins the most votes.

racial gerrymandering   Redrawing congressional boundary lines in such a way as to divide and disperse a racial minority population that otherwise would constitute a majority within the original district.

split-ticket voting   The practice of casting ballots for the candidates of at least two different political parties in the same election. Voters who support only one party's candidates are said to vote a straight party ticket.

straight party vote   The practice of casting ballots for candidates of only one party.

suffrage   The right to vote; also called franchise.

turnout   The percentage of eligible individuals who actually vote.

For Further Reading

Andersen, Kristi. *The Creation of a Democratic Majority: 1928–1936.* Chicago: University of Chicago Press, 1979.

Black, Earl, and Merle Black. *The Vital South: How Presidents Are Elected.* Cambridge, MA: Harvard University Press, 1992.

Brady, David. *Critical Elections and Congressional Policymaking.* Stanford, CA: Stanford University Press, 1988.

Carmines, Edward G., and James Stimson. *Issue Evolution: The Racial Transformation of American Politics.* Princeton: Princeton University Press, 1988.

Conway, M. Margaret. *Political Participation in the United States.* Washington, DC: Congressional Quarterly Press, 1985.

Dinkin, Robert J. *Campaigning in America: A History of Election Practices.* Westport, CT: Greenwood Press, 1989.

Fowler, Linda. *Candidates, Congress, and the American Democracy.* Ann Arbor: University of Michigan Press, 1994.

Fowler, Linda, and Robert D. McClure. *Political Ambition: Who Decides to Run for Congress.* New Haven: Yale University Press, 1989.

Ginsberg, Benjamin, and Martin Shefter. *Politics by Other Means: Institutional Conflict and the Declining Significance of Elections in America.* New York: Basic Books, 1990.

Jackson, Brooks. *Honest Graft: Big Money and the American Political Process.* New York: Alfred A. Knopf, 1988.

Jamieson, Kathleen H. *Eloquence in an Electronic Age: The Transformation of Political Speechmaking.* New York: Oxford University Press, 1988.

Niemi, Richard, and Herbert Weisberg. *Controversies in American Voting Behavior.* Washington, DC: Congressional Quarterly Press, 1984.

Norrander, Barbara. *Super Tuesday: Regional Politics and Presidential Primaries.* Lexington: University of Kentucky Press, 1992.

Piven, Frances Fox, and Richard A. Cloward. *Why Americans Don't Vote.* New York: Pantheon, 1988.

Pohlmann, Marcus. *Black Politics in Conservative America.* New York: Longman, 1990.

Reed, Adolph. *The Jesse Jackson Phenomenon.* New Haven: Yale University Press, 1987.

Reichley, A. James, ed. *Elections American Style.* Washington, DC: Brookings Institution, 1987.

Sorauf, Frank. *Inside Campaign Finance: Myths and Realities.* New Haven, CT: Yale University Press, 1992.

Stanley, Harold. *Voter Mobilization and the Politics of Race: The South and Universal Suffrage, 1952–1984.* New York: Praeger, 1987.

Tate, Katherine. *From Protest to Politics: The New Black Voters in American Elections.* Cambridge, MA: Harvard University Press, 1994.

Wilcox, Clyde. *God's Warriors: The Christian Right in Twentieth-Century America.* Baltimore, MD: Johns Hopkins University Press, 1991.

Witt, Linda, Karen Paget, and Glenna Matthews. *Running as a Woman: Gender and Power in American Politics.* New York: Free Press, 1994.

CHAPTER 10

Political Parties

WE OFTEN REFER to the United States as a nation with a "two-party system." By this we mean that in the United States the Democratic and Republican parties compete for office and power. Most Americans believe that party competition contributes to the health of the democratic process. Certainly, we are more than just a bit suspicious of those nations that claim to be ruled by their people but do not tolerate the existence of opposing parties.

The idea of party competition was not always accepted in the United States. In the early years of the Republic, parties were seen as threats to the social order. In his 1796 "Farewell Address," President George Washington warned his fellow citizens to shun partisan politics:

> Let me warn you in the most solemn manner against the baneful effects of the spirit of party generally. This spirit exists under different shapes in all government, more or less stifled, controlled, or repressed, but in those of the popular form it is seen in its greatest rankness and is truly their worst enemy.

Often, those in power viewed the formation of political parties by their opponents as acts of

treason that merited severe punishment. Thus, in 1798, the Federalist party, which controlled the national government, in effect sought to outlaw its Jeffersonian Republican opponents through the infamous Alien and Sedition Acts, which, among other things, made it a crime to publish or say anything that might tend to defame or bring into disrepute either the president or the Congress (see Box 10.1). Under this law, fifteen peo-

CORE OF THE ARGUMENT

- Today the Democratic and Republican parties dominate the American two-party political system.
- The most important functions of American political parties are facilitating nominations and elections and organizing the institutions of national government.
- The role of parties in electoral politics has declined in the United States over the last thirty years.
- New political technology has strengthened the advantage of wealthier political groups.

BOX 10.1

Alien and Sedition Acts:
A Party's Attempt to Suppress the Opposition

In 1798, war seemed likely to break out between the United States and France. The overt purpose of the Alien and Sedition Acts was to protect the government against subversive activities by foreigners in the country—particularly the French. Their covert purpose, however, was to suppress Jefferson's and Madison's Republican party, which was rapidly gaining strength in its opposition to the Federalists.

The four pieces of legislation collectively referred to as the Alien and Sedition Acts are (1) the Naturalization Act, passed June 18, 1798; (2) the Act Concerning Aliens, passed June 25, 1798; (3) the Act Respecting Alien Enemies, passed July 6, 1798; and (4) the Act for the Punishment of Certain Crimes (the Sedition Act), passed July 14, 1798.

The Alien Enemies Act never went into effect, because it was contingent on the declaration of war. The Alien Act, which gave the president power to order out of the country all aliens he considered a threat to national security, was never enforced. Nonetheless, it is believed to have been responsible for the departure of many of the French. Since most naturalized citizens became Republicans, this act may have functioned to diminish the number of potential Republicans. In extending the period of residence required for naturalization from five to fourteen years, the Naturalization Act was an obvious move to weaken the Republican party.

The Sedition Act had the most serious legal implications. It was designed to suppress critics of the administration by limiting their freedom of speech and of the press. It was used to indict approximately fifteen persons. Although fewer than half of those indicted were ever brought to trial, several prominent Republican journalists were convicted. By 1802, all but the Alien Enemies Act had either expired or been repealed.

ple—including several Republican newspaper editors—were arrested and convicted.[1]

These efforts to outlaw political parties obviously failed. By the nineteenth century American politics was dominated by powerful *party "machines"* that inspired enormous voter loyalty, controlled electoral politics, and, through elections, exercised enormous influence over government and policy in the United States. In recent years, as we shall see, these party machines have all but disappeared. Electoral politics has become a candidate-centered" affair in which individual "candidates for office build their own campaign organiza-

tions, while voters make choices based more upon their reactions to the candidates than upon loyalty to the parties. Party organization, as we saw in Chapter 5, continues to be an important factor within the Congress. Even in the Congress, however, the influence of party leaders is based more upon ideological affinity than any real power over party members. The weakness of the party system is an important factor in understanding contemporary American political patterns.[2]

In this chapter, we will examine the realities underlying these changing conceptions. First, we

[1]See Richard Hofstadter, *The Idea of a Party System* (Berkeley: University of California Press, 1969).

[2]For an excellent discussion of the role of political parties in the United States see John J. Coleman, *Party Decline in America: Policy, Politics, and the Fiscal State* (Princeton, NJ: Princeton University Press, 1996).

will evaluate America's two-party system, and assess the similarities and differences between the parties. Second, we will discuss the functions of the parties. Finally, we will address the significance and changing role of parties in American politics today.

THE TWO-PARTY SYSTEM IN AMERICA

Political parties, like interest groups, are organizations seeking influence over government. Ordinarily, they can be distinguished from interest groups on the basis of their orientation. A party seeks to control the entire government by electing its members to office and thereby controlling the government's personnel. Interest groups usually accept government and its personnel as a given and try to influence government policies through them.

Political parties as they are known today developed along with the expansion of suffrage and can be understood only in the context of elections. The two are so intertwined that American parties actually take their shape from the electoral process. They were formed because there were elections to run. The shape of party organization in the United States has followed a simple rule: For every district where an election is held, there should be some kind of party unit (see Figure 10.1).

Compared to political parties in Europe, parties in the United States have always seemed weak. They have no criteria for party membership—no cards for their members to carry, no obligatory participation in any activity, no notion of exclusiveness. And today, they seem weaker than ever: they inspire less loyalty and are less able to control nominations. Some people are even talking about a "crisis of political parties," as though party politics was being abandoned. But there continues to be at least some substance to party organizations in the United States.

Although George Washington deplored partisan politics, the two-party system emerged early in the history of the new Republic. Beginning with the Federalists and the Jeffersonian Republicans in the early 1800s, two major parties would dominate national politics, although which particular two parties they were would change with the times and issues. This two-party system has culminated in today's Democrats and Republicans. The evolution of American political parties is shown in Process Box 10.1.

The Democrats

When the Jeffersonian party splintered in 1824, Andrew Jackson emerged as the leader of one of its four factions. In 1830, Jackson's group became the Democratic party. This new party had the strongest national organization of its time and presented itself as the party of the common man. Jacksonians supported reductions in the price of public lands and a policy of cheaper money and credit. Laborers, immigrants, and settlers west of the Alleghenies were quickly attracted to it.

From 1828, when Jackson was elected president, to 1860, the Democratic party was the dominant force in American politics. For all but eight of those years, the Democrats held the White House. In addition, a Democratic majority controlled the Senate for twenty-six years and the House for twenty-four years during the same time period. Nineteenth-century Democrats emphasized the importance of interpreting the Constitution literally, upholding states' rights, and limiting federal spending.

In 1860, the issue of slavery split the Democrats along geographic lines. In the South, many Democrats served in the Confederate government. In the North, one faction of the party (the Copperheads) opposed the war and advocated negotiating a peace with the South. Thus, for years after the war, Republicans denounced the Democrats as the "party of treason."

FIGURE 10.1

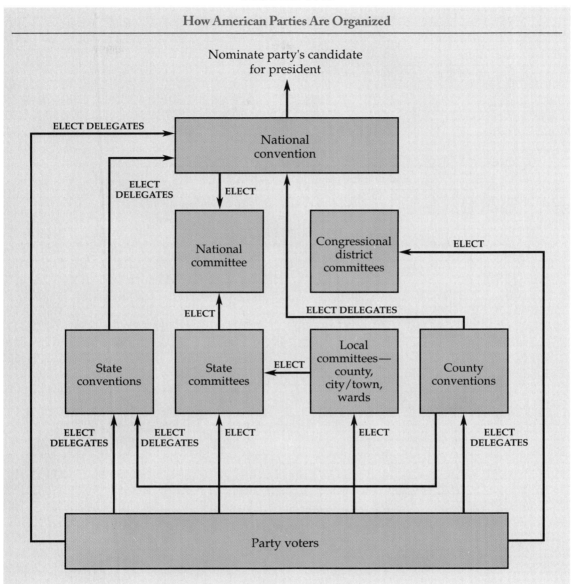

How American Parties Are Organized

The Democratic party was not fully able to regain its political strength until the Great Depression. In 1932, Democrat Franklin D. Roosevelt entered the White House. Subsequently, the Democrats won control of Congress as well. Roosevelt's New Deal coalition, composed of Catholics, Jews, African Americans, farmers, intellectuals, and members of organized labor,

How the U.S. Party System Evolved

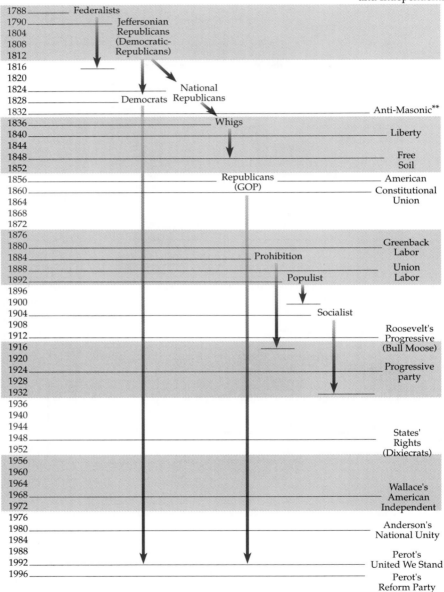

Third Parties*
and Independents

1788 — Federalists
1790 — Jeffersonian Republicans (Democratic-Republicans)
1804
1808
1812
1816
1820
1824
1828 — Democrats
National Republicans
1832 — Anti-Masonic**
1836 — Whigs
1840 — Liberty
1844
1848 — Free
1852 — Soil
1856 — Republicans (GOP) — American
1860 — Constitutional Union
1864
1868
1872
1876
1880 — Greenback Labor
1884 — Prohibition
1888 — Union Labor
1892 — Populist
1896
1900
1904 — Socialist
1908
1912 — Roosevelt's Progressive (Bull Moose)
1916
1920
1924 — Progressive party
1928
1932
1936
1940
1944
1948 — States' Rights (Dixiecrats)
1952
1956
1960
1964
1968 — Wallace's American Independent
1972
1976
1980 — Anderson's National Unity
1984
1988
1992 — Perot's United We Stand
1996 — Perot's Reform Party

*Or in some cases, fourth party; most of these are one-term parties.

**The Anti-Masonics not only had the distinction of being the first third party, but it was also the first party to hold a national nominating convention and the first to announce a party platform.

dominated American politics until the 1970s and served as the basis for the party's expansion of federal power and efforts to remedy social problems.

The Democrats were never fully united. In Congress, Southern Democrats often aligned with Republicans in the so-called conservative coalition rather than with members of their own party. But the Democratic party remained America's majority party, usually controlling Congress and the White House, for nearly four decades after 1932. By the 1980s, the Democratic coalition faced serious problems. The once-Solid South often voted for the Republicans, along with many blue-collar Northern voters. On the other hand, the Democrats increased their strength among African American voters and women. The Democrats maintained a strong base in the bureaucracies of the federal government and the states, in labor unions, and in the not-for-profit sector of the economy. During the 1980s and 1990s, moderate Democrats were able to take control of the party nominating process and sought to broaden middle-class support for the party. This helped the Democrats elect a president in 1992. In 1994, however, the unpopularity of Democratic President Bill Clinton led to the loss of the Democrats' control of both houses of Congress for the first time since 1946. In 1996, Clinton was able to win re-election to a second term over the weak opposition of Republican candidate Robert Dole. Democrats were, however, unable to dislodge their GOP rivals from the leadership of either house of Congress.

The Republicans

The 1854 Kansas-Nebraska Act overturned the Missouri Compromise of 1820 and the Compromise of 1850, which had barred the expansion of slavery in the American territories. The Kansas-Nebraska Act gave each territory the right to decide whether or not to permit slavery. Opposition to this policy galvanized antislavery groups and led them to create a new party, the Republicans.

It drew its membership from existing political groups—former Whigs, Know-Nothings, Free Soilers, and antislavery Democrats. In 1856, the party's first presidential candidate, John C. Fremont, won one-third of the popular vote and carried eleven states.

The early Republican platforms appealed to commercial as well as antislavery interests. The Republicans favored homesteading, internal improvements, the construction of a transcontinental railroad, and protective tariffs, as well as the containment of slavery. In 1858, the Republican party won control of the House; in 1860, the Republican presidential candidate, Abraham Lincoln, was victorious.

For almost seventy-five years after the North's victory in the Civil War, the Republicans were America's dominant political party. Between 1860 and 1932, Republicans occupied the White House for fifty-six years, controlled the Senate for sixty years, and the House for fifty. During these years, the Republicans came to be closely associated with big business. The party of Lincoln became the party of Wall Street.

The Great Depression, however, ended Republican supremacy. The voters held Republican President Herbert Hoover responsible for the economic catastrophe, and by 1936, the party's popularity was so low that Republicans won only eighty-nine seats in the House and seventeen in the Senate. The Republican presidential candidate, Governor Alfred M. Landon of Kansas, carried only two states. The Republicans won only four presidential elections between 1932 and 1980, and they controlled Congress for only four of those years (1947–1949 and 1953–1955).

The Republican party has widened its appeal over the last four decades. Groups previously associated with the Democratic party—particularly blue-collar workers and Southern Democrats—have been increasingly attracted to Republican presidential candidates (for example, Dwight D. Eisenhower, Richard Nixon, Ronald Reagan, and

COMPARING THE 1996 REPUBLICAN AND DEMOCRATIC PLATFORMS

A Choice for Voters

ONE OF THE MOST common complaints heard from voters is that "there's not a dime's worth of difference" between the major political parties. If this charge is true, it lends fuel to the fires of critics who say that the political parties have failed in their most important job—to provide voters with a real choice. Yet an examination of the party platforms from the 1996 presidential elections reveals major differences on almost every issue. Even though the platforms are not binding on the candidates, they do provide a good view of the opinions of the two parties' core leaders.

After four years with Democratic President Bill Clinton, the Democratic platform gave the economy high praise: "Today, America is moving forward. The economy is stronger, the deficit is lower and the Government is smaller." The Republican verdict was very different: "We cannot go on like this. For millions of families, the American dream is fading." In their platform Democrats called for an end to "something-for-nothing tax cuts." Republicans called for "a 15 percent reduction in tax rates." The parties were a little closer on balancing the federal budget, with the Democrats supporting a balanced budget by 2002, and Republicans calling for a balanced-budget constitutional amendment.

On social issues, party differences were even greater. The Democrats advocated continued support for existing abortion rights for

George Bush). Yet, Republicans generally did not do as well at the state and local levels and had little chance of capturing a majority in either the House or Senate. The Watergate scandal of the Nixon administration was a setback to the party's efforts to increase its political power. In 1980, under the leadership of Ronald Reagan, the Republicans began to mount a new bid to become the nation's majority party, but the Iran-Contra scandal damaged Reagan's popularity. Reagan's successor, George Bush, was voted out after one term in office, mainly in response to voters' concerns about the economy. In 1994, the Republican party finally won a majority in both houses of Congress.

During the 1990s, conservative religious groups, who had been attracted to the Republican camp by its opposition to abortion and support for school prayer, made a concerted effort to expand their influence within the party. This effort led to conflict between these members of the "religious Right" and more traditional "country-club" Republicans, whose major concerns were matters such as taxes and federal regulation of business. This coalition swept the polls in 1994 and maintained its control of both houses of Congress in 1996. The GOP's 1996 presidential standard bearer, Senator Robert Dole, however, went down to defeat partly because Democrats were able to

women, whereas the Republican platform supported a constitutional amendment banning all abortions. The Democratic platform called for an end to discrimination "against gay men and lesbians"; Republicans rejected efforts to extend civil rights to "cover sexual preference." On affirmative action, the Democrats argued that "We should mend it, not end it." The Republicans argued for achieving "equal rights without quotas or other forms of preferential treatment."

On education, the Democrats emphasized support for the nation's public schools. The Republicans supported use of federal money to assist parents who wish to send their children to private schools. On the environment, the Democrats called for a continued reliance on government regulations to protect the environment, while the Republicans urged more consideration of private property rights. On gun control, the

Democrats maintained support for a waiting period for purchase of handguns and a ban on assault weapons. The Republicans expressed support for "a right to bear arms" and mandatory penalties for those found guilty of committing crimes with guns. In the area of government support for the arts, the Democrats pledged continued support and continued funding for the Corporation for Public Broadcasting. The Republicans called for an end to all government financing of these activities.

Even in foreign policy, the parties disagreed. The Democrats stated their opposition to revival of the missile defense system known as "Star Wars," whereas the Republicans supported development of such a system.

If this comparison reveals anything, it is that the Democratic and Republican parties stand far apart on key issues of the day.

portray Republican social conservatives as dangerous "extremists."[3]

Electoral Alignments and Realignments

In the United States, party politics has followed a fascinating pattern (see Figure 10.2). Typically, during the course of American political history, the national electoral arena has been dominated by one party for a period of roughly thirty years. At the conclusion of this period, the dominant party has been supplanted by a new party in what political scientists call a *critical electoral realignment.* The realignment is typically followed by a long period in which the new party is the dominant political force in the United States—not necessarily winning every election but generally maintaining control of the Congress and usually of the White House as well.[4]

Although there are some disputes among scholars about the precise timing of these critical

[3]James Bennet, "Liberal Use of 'Extremist' is the Winning Strategy," *New York Times,* 7 November 1996, p. B1.

[4]See Walter Dean Burnham, *Critical Elections and the Mainsprings of American Electoral Politics* (New York: W. W. Norton, 1970). See also James L. Sundquist, *Dynamics of the Party System* (Washington, DC: Brookings Institution, 1983).

FIGURE 10.2

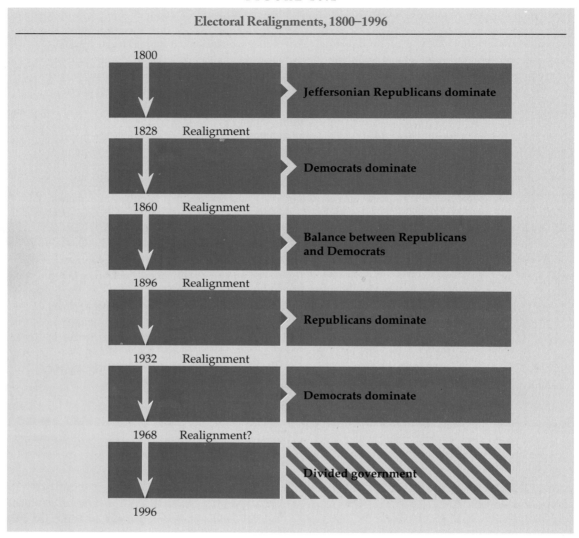

Electoral Realignments, 1800–1996

1800

Jeffersonian Republicans dominate

1828   Realignment

Democrats dominate

1860   Realignment

Balance between Republicans and Democrats

1896   Realignment

Republicans dominate

1932   Realignment

Democrats dominate

1968   Realignment?

Divided government

1996

realignments, there is general agreement that at least five have occurred since the founding of the American Republic. The first took place around 1800 when the Jeffersonian Republicans defeated the Federalists and became the dominant force in American politics. The second realignment occurred in about 1828, when the Jacksonian Democrats took control of the White House and the Congress. The third period of realignment cen-

tered on 1860. During this period, the newly founded Republican party led by Abraham Lincoln won power, in the process destroying the Whig party, which had been one of the nation's two major parties since the 1830s. During the fourth critical period, centered on the election of 1896, the Republicans reasserted their dominance of the national government, which had been weakening since the 1880s. The fifth realignment took place during the period 1932–1936 when the Democrats, led by Franklin Delano Roosevelt, took control of the White House and Congress and, despite sporadic interruptions, maintained control of both through the 1960s.

Historically, realignments occur when new issues combined with economic or political crises persuade large numbers of voters to re-examine their traditional partisan loyalties and permanently shift their support from one party to another (see Concept Map 10.1). For example, during the 1850s, diverse regional, income, and business groups supported one of the two major parties, the Democrats or the Whigs, on the basis of their positions on various economic issues, such as internal improvements, the tariff, monetary policy, and banking. This economic alignment was shattered during the 1850s. The newly formed Republican party campaigned on the basis of opposition to slavery and, in particular, opposition to the expansion of slavery into the territories. The issues of slavery and sectionalism produced divisions within both the Democratic and the Whig parties, ultimately leading to the dissolution of the latter, and these issues compelled voters to re-examine their partisan allegiances. Many Northern voters who had supported the Whigs or the Democrats on the basis of their economic stands shifted their support to the Republicans as slavery replaced tariffs and economic concerns as the central item on the nation's political agenda. Many Southern Whigs shifted their support to the Democrats. The new sectional alignment of forces that emerged was solidified by the trauma of the Civil War and persisted almost to the turn of the century.

In 1896, this sectional alignment was at least partially supplanted by an alignment of political forces based on economic and cultural factors. During the economic crises of the 1880s and 1890s, the Democrats forged a coalition consisting of economically hard-pressed Midwestern and Southern farmers, as well as small-town and rural economic interests. These groups tended to be descendants of British Isles, Dutch, and Hessian fundamentalist Protestants. The Republicans, on the other hand, put together a coalition comprising most of the business community, industrial workers, and city dwellers. In the election of 1896, Republican candidate William McKinley, emphasizing business, industry, and urban interests, decisively defeated Democrat William Jennings Bryan, who spoke for sectional interests, farmers, and fundamentalism. Republican dominance lasted until 1932.

Such periods of critical realignment in American politics have had extremely important institutional and policy results. Realignments occur when new issue concerns coupled with economic or political crises weaken the established political elite and permit new groups of politicians to create coalitions of forces capable of capturing and holding the reins of governmental power. The construction of new governing coalitions during these realigning periods has effected major changes in American governmental institutions and policies. Each period of realignment represents a turning point in American politics. The choices made by the national electorate during these periods have helped shape the course of American political history for generations.[5]

Similarities and Differences Today

One of the most familiar observations about American politics is that the two major parties try to be all things to all people and are therefore indistinguishable from each other. Data and experience give some support to this observation. The wide range of interests within the Democratic party today can be represented by liberals such as Richard Gephardt and by conservatives such as Charles Stenholm. The 1992 and 1996 Democratic presidential ticket consisted of two moderates, Bill Clinton and Al Gore, who appealed successfully

[5]Benjamin Ginsberg, *The Consequences of Consent* (New York: Random House, 1982), Chapter 4.

CONCEPT MAP 10.1

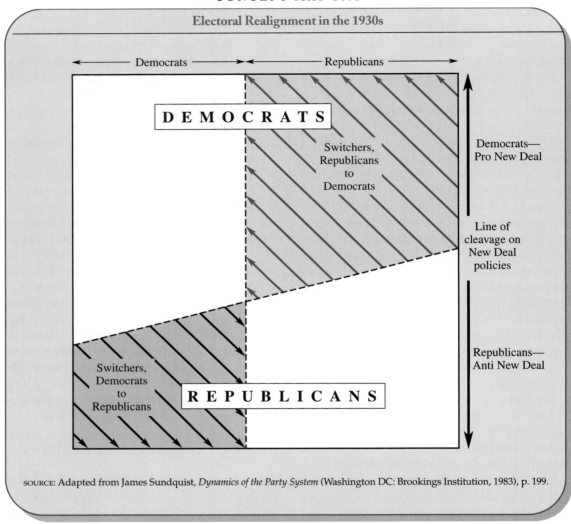

Electoral Realignment in the 1930s

Democrats → ← Republicans

DEMOCRATS

Switchers,
Republicans
to
Democrats

Democrats—
Pro New Deal

Line of
cleavage on
New Deal
policies

Switchers,
Democrats
to
Republicans

REPUBLICANS

Republicans—
Anti New Deal

SOURCE: Adapted from James Sundquist, *Dynamics of the Party System* (Washington DC: Brookings Institution, 1983), p. 199.

for the votes of many conservative Democrats and moderate Republicans. A similar spectrum exists within the Republican party, as represented by liberals such as Constance Morella and conservatives like Newt Gingrich, although in the 1980s and 1990s, liberal Republicans became something of an endangered species.

Parties in the United States are not programmatic or ideological, as they have sometimes been in England or in other parts of Europe. But this does not mean there are no differences between them. During the Reagan era, important differences emerged between the positions of Democratic and Republican party leaders on a number of key issues, and these differences are still apparent today. The national leadership of the Republican party supports high levels of military spending, cuts in social programs, tax relief for middle- and upper-income voters, tax incentives to businesses, and the "social agenda" backed by members of conservative religious denominations.

The national Democratic leadership, on the other hand, supports expanded social welfare spending, cuts in military spending, increased regulation of business, and a variety of consumer and environmental programs. In 1990, for example, most Republicans supported President Bush's policies in the Persian Gulf, while most Democrats initially opposed the president's use of American military force against Iraq—at least until the president's policies succeeded. These differences reflect differences in philosophy as well as differences in the core constituencies to which the parties seek to appeal. The Democratic party at the national level seeks to unite organized labor, the poor, members of racial minorities, and liberal upper-middle-class professionals. The Republicans, by contrast, appeal to business, upper-middle- and upper-class groups in the private sector, and social conservatives.

Minor Parties

The United States is always said to have a two-party system, and Americans usually assume that only the candidates nominated by one of the two major parties have any chance of winning. Voters who would prefer a third-party candidate may feel compelled, nonetheless, to vote for the major-party candidate whom they regard as the "lesser of the two evils," to avoid wasting their vote in a futile gesture. Third-party candidates must struggle—usually without success—to overcome the perception that they cannot win. Thus, in 1996, some voters who favored Ross Perot gave their votes to Bob Dole or Bill Clinton on the presumption that Perot was not really electable.

As many scholars have pointed out, third-party prospects are also hampered by America's *single-member-district* plurality election system. In many other nations, several individuals can be elected to represent each legislative district. This is called a system of *multiple-member districts.* With this type of system, the candidates of weaker parties have a better chance of winning at least some seats. For their part, voters are less concerned about wasting ballots and usually more willing to support minor-party candidates.

Reinforcing the effects of the single-member district, plurality voting rules (as was noted in Chapter 9) generally have the effect of setting what could be called a high threshold for victory. To win a plurality race, candidates usually must secure many more votes than they would need under most European systems of proportional representation. For example, to win an American plurality election in a single-member district where there are only two candidates, a politician must win more than 50 percent of the votes cast. To win a seat from a European multiple-member district under proportional rules, a candidate may need to win only 15 or 20 percent of the votes cast. This high American threshold discourages minor parties and encourages the various political factions that might otherwise form minor parties to minimize their differences and remain within the major-party coalitions.

It would nevertheless be incorrect to assert (as some scholars have maintained) that America's single-member plurality election system is the major cause of our historical two-party pattern. All that can be said is that American election law depresses the number of parties likely to survive over long periods of time in the United States. There is nothing magical about two. Indeed, the single-member plurality system of election can also discourage second parties. After all, if one party consistently receives a large plurality of the vote, people may eventually come to see their vote *even for the second party* as a wasted effort. This happened to the Republican party in the Deep South before World War II.

TABLE 10.1

Parties and Candidates in 1996

CANDIDATE	PARTY	VOTE TOTAL*	% OF VOTE*
Bill Clinton	Democrat	45,628,667	49.16%
Bob Dole	Republican	37,869,435	40.80
Ross Perot	Reform	7,874,283	8.48
Ralph Nader	Green	580,627	.63
Harry Browne	Libertarian	470,818	.51
Howard Phillips	U.S. Taxpayers	178,779	.19
John Hagelin	Natural Law	110,194	.12
Monica Moorehead	Workers World	29,118	.03
Marsha Feinland	Peace and Freedom	22,593	.02
James Harris	Socialist Workers	11,513	.01
Charles Collins	Independent	7,234	.00
Dennis Peron	Grassroots	5,503	.00
Mary Hollis	Socialist	3,376	.00
Jerry White	Socialist Equality	2,752	.00
Diane Templin	Independent American	1,875	.00
Earl Dodge	Independent	1,198	.00
Peter Crane	Independent	1,105	.00
Ralph Forbes	Independent	861	.00
John Birrenbach	Independent Grassroots	760	.00
Isabell Masters	Independent	737	.00
Steve Michael	Independent	407	.00
Other candidates	—	5,575	.00
TOTAL		92,807,410	100.00%

*With 99 percent of votes tallied.
SOURCE: *USA Today*, 8–10 November 1996, p. 8A.

Despite these obstacles, every presidential election brings out a host of minor-party hopefuls (see Table 10.1). Few survive until the next contest.

FUNCTIONS OF THE PARTIES

Parties perform a wide variety of functions. They are mainly involved in nominations and elections—providing the candidates for office, getting out the vote, and facilitating mass electoral choice. They also influence the institutions of government—providing the leadership and organization of the various congressional committees.

Nominations and Elections

Nomination is the process of selecting one party candidate to run for each elective office. The nominating process can precede the election by many months, as it does when the many candidates for the presidency are eliminated from consideration through a grueling series of debates and state primaries until there is only one survivor in each party—the party's nominee. Nomination is the parties' most serious and difficult business. In the course of American political history, the parties have used three modes of nomination—the caucus,

THE NOMINATING PROCESS

Nomination by Caucus
 Party leaders and active members gather informally to agree upon a candidate (common in the eighteenth and early nineteenth centuries)

Nomination by Convention
 Party leaders and delegates chosen by party members meet formally to vote for the nomination (a more formalized caucus that took shape in the 1830s)

Nomination by Primary Election
 Every party member has a vote in an election that determines the nomination

Independent Candidates
 Candidates must file a petition with a minimum number of signatures

the convention, and the primary election (see the In Brief Box above).

THE CAUCUS In the eighteenth and early nineteenth centuries, nominations were informal, without rules or regulations. Local party leaders would simply gather all the party activists, and they would agree on the person, usually from among themselves, who would be the candidate. The meetings where candidates were nominated were generally called *caucuses*. Informal nominations by caucus sufficed for the parties until widespread complaints were made about cliques of local leaders or state legislators dominating all the nominations and leaving no place for the other party members who wanted to participate. Beginning in the 1830s, nominating conventions were proposed as a reform that would enable the mass membership of a party to express its will.

NOMINATION BY CONVENTION A nominating convention is a formal caucus bound by a number of rules that govern participation and nominating procedures. Conventions are meetings of delegates elected by party members from the relevant county (county convention) or state (state convention). Delegates to each party's national convention (which nominates the party's presidential candidate) are chosen by party members on a

state-by-state basis; there is no single national delegate selection process.

Historically, the great significance of the convention mode of nomination was its effect on the presidential selection process and on the presidency itself. For more than fifty years after America's founding, the nomination of presidential candidates was dominated by meetings of each party's congressional delegations, meetings that critics called "King Caucus." In the early 1830s, when the major parties adopted the national nominating convention, they broke the power of King Caucus. This helped to give the presidency a mass popular base. Nevertheless, reformers in the early twentieth century regarded nominating conventions as instruments of "boss rule." They proposed replacing conventions with primaries, which provide for direct choice by the voters at an election some weeks or months before the general election.

NOMINATION BY PRIMARY ELECTION In primary elections, party members select the party's nominees directly rather than selecting convention delegates who then select the nominees. Primaries are far from perfect replacements for conventions, since it is rare that more than 25 percent of the enrolled voters participate in them. Nevertheless, they are replacing conventions as the dominant method of nomination.[6] At the present time, only a small number of states, including Connecticut, Delaware, and Utah, provide for state conventions to nominate candidates for statewide offices, and even these states combine them with primaries whenever a substantial minority of delegates vote for one of the defeated aspirants.

Primary elections are of two types—closed and open. In a *closed primary,* participation is limited to individuals who have declared their affiliation by registering with the party. In an *open primary,* individuals declare their party affiliation on the actual day of the primary election—they simply go to the polling place and ask for the ballot of a particular party. The open primary allows each voter an opportunity to consider candidates and issues before deciding whether to participate and in which party's con-

test to participate. Open primaries, therefore, are less conducive than closed contests to strong political parties. But in either case, primaries are more open than conventions or caucuses to new issues and new candidates.

INDEPENDENT CANDIDATES   The types of nominating processes are summarized in the In Brief Box, which indicates that the convention and primary methods are not the only ways that candidates can get on the ballot. State laws extend the right of *independent candidacy* to individuals who do not wish to be nominated by political parties or who are unable to secure a party nomination.

Although nomination by a political party is complicated, the independent route to the ballot is even more difficult. For almost all offices in all states, the law requires more signatures for independent nomination than for party designation. Table 10.2 shows some of the special difficulties of getting on the ballot as an independent candidate in New York State. The candidate for a party's nomination to Congress in New York must get

---

[6]For a discussion of some of the effects of primary elections, see Peter F. Galderisi and Benjamin Ginsberg, "Primary Elections and the Evanescence of Third Party Activity in the United States," in *Do Elections Matter?* ed. Benjamin Ginsberg and Alan Stone (Armonk, NY: M. E. Sharpe, 1986), pp. 115–30.

TABLE 10.2

Getting on the Ballot in New York State		
	NUMBER OF SIGNATURES REQUIRED FOR NOMINATING PETITIONS	
OFFICE SOUGHT	**PARTY DESIGNATION**	**INDEPENDENT NOMINATION**
Governorship or other statewide office	20,000 or 5% of enrolled voters of party, whichever is less	20,000 or 5% of registered voters, whichever is less
Mayoralty of large city*	2,000	5% of last election vote for governor in city
County office*	1,500	1,500
City council	500	1,500
Congress	1,250	3,500
State senate	1,000	3,000
State assembly	500	1,500

*Outside the city of New York. For New York City, 5,000 signatures are required.
SOURCE: *New York State Political Calendar, 1988–1989* (Albany, NY: Fort Orange Press). Adapted by permission.

1,250 valid signatures within the congressional district, while the independent candidate must get 3,500 signatures.

The Role of the Parties in Getting Out the Vote

The actual election period begins immediately after the nominations. Historically, this has been a time of glory for the political parties, whose popular base of support is fully displayed. All the paraphernalia of party committees and all the committee members are activated into local party work forces.

The first step in the electoral process involves voter registration. This aspect of the process takes place all year round. There was a time when party workers were responsible for virtually all of this kind of electoral activity, but they have been supplemented (and in many states virtually displaced) by civic groups such as the League of Women Voters, unions, and chambers of commerce.

Those who have registered have to decide on election day whether to go to the polling place, stand in line, and actually vote for the various candidates and referenda on the ballot. Political parties, candidates, and campaigning can make a big difference in convincing the voters to vote.

On any general election ballot, there are likely to be only two or three candidacies where the nature of the office and the characteristics and positions of the candidates are well known to voters. But what about the choices for judges, the state comptroller, the state attorney general, and many other elective positions? And what about referenda? This method of making policy choices is being used more and more as a means of direct democracy. A *referendum* may ask: Should there be a new bond issue for financing the local schools? Should there be a constitutional amendment to increase the number of county judges? The famous "Proposition 13" on the 1978 California ballot was a referendum to reduce local property taxes. It started a taxpayer revolt that

spread to many other states. By the time it had spread, most voters knew where they stood on the issue. But the typical referendum question is one on which few voters have clear and knowledgeable positions. Parties and campaigns help most by giving information when voters must choose among obscure candidates and vote on unclear referenda.

Facilitation of Mass Electoral Choice

Parties facilitate mass electoral choice. As the late Harvard political scientist V. O. Key pointed out long ago, the persistence over time of competition between groups possessing a measure of identity and continuity is a necessary condition for electoral control.[7] Party identity increases the electorate's capacity to recognize its options. Consistent party division organizes voters in a way necessary to sustain any popular influence in the governmental process. In the absence of party division, the voter is, in Key's words, confronted constantly by "new faces, new choices," and little basis exists for "effectuation of the popular will."[8]

Even more significant, however, is the fact that party organization is generally an essential ingredient for effective electoral competition by groups lacking substantial economic or institutional resources. Party building has typically been the strategy pursued by groups that must organize the collective energies of large numbers of individuals to counter their opponents' superior material means or institutional standing. Historically, disciplined and coherent party organizations were generally developed first by groups representing the political aspirations of the working class. Parties, French political scientist Maurice Duverger notes, "are always more developed on the Left than on the Right because they are always more necessary on the Left than on the Right."[9]

[7]V. O. Key, *Southern Politics* (New York: Random House, 1949), Chapter 14.
[8]Ibid.
[9]Maurice Duverger, *Political Parties* (New York: Wiley, 1954), p. 426.

In the United States, the first mass party was built by the Jeffersonians as a counterweight to the superior social, institutional, and economic resources of the incumbent Federalists. In a subsequent period of American history, the efforts of the Jacksonians to construct a coherent mass party organization were impelled by a similar set of circumstances. Only by organizing the power of numbers could the Jacksonian coalition hope to compete successfully against the superior resources mobilized by its adversaries.

The political success of party organizations forced their opponents to copy them in order to meet the challenge. It was, as Duverger points out, "contagion from the Left" that led politicians of the Center and Right to attempt to build strong party organizations.[10] These efforts were sometimes successful. In the United States during the 1830s, the Whig party, which was led by northeastern business interests, carefully copied the organizational techniques devised by the Jacksonians. The Whigs won control of the national government in 1840. But even when groups nearer the top of the social scale responded in kind to organizational efforts by their opponents, the effect nonetheless was to give lower-class groups an opportunity to compete on a more equal footing.

If no one is organized, middle- and upper-class factions almost inevitably have a substantial competitive edge over their lower-class rivals. But if both sides are organized, the net effect is still to erode the relative advantage of the well-off. Parties of the Right, moreover, were seldom actually able to equal the organizational coherence of their working-class opposition. As Duverger and others have observed, middle- and upper-class parties generally failed to construct organizations as effective as those built by their working-class foes, who typically commanded larger and more easily disciplined forces.

While political parties continue to be significant in the United States, the role of party organi-

zations in electoral politics has clearly declined over the past three decades. This decline, and the partial replacement of the party by new forms of electoral technology, is one of the most important developments in twentieth-century American politics.

The Parties' Influence on National Government

The ultimate test of the party system is its relationship to and influence on the institutions of national government. Thus, it is important to examine the party system in relation to Congress and the president.

THE PARTIES AND CONGRESS   Congress, in particular, depends more on the party system than is generally recognized. First, the speakership of the House is a party office. All the members of the House take part in the election of the Speaker. But the actual selection is made by the majority party. When the majority party caucus presents a nominee to the entire House, its choice is then invariably ratified in a straight party-line vote.

The committee system of both houses of Congress is also a product of the two-party system. Although the rules organizing committees and the rules defining the jurisdiction of each are adopted like ordinary legislation by the whole membership, all other features of the committees are shaped by parties. For example, each party is assigned a quota of members for each committee, depending upon the percentage of total seats held by the party. On the rare occasions when an independent or third-party candidate is elected, the leaders of the two parties must agree against whose quota this member's committee assignments will count.

The assignment of individual members to committees is a party decision. Each party has a "committee on committees" to make such decisions. Permission to transfer from one committee to another is also a party decision. Moreover, advancement up the committee ladder toward the

[10]Ibid., Chapter 1.

chair is a party decision. Since the late nineteenth century, most advancements have been automatic—based upon the length of continual service on the committee. This seniority system has existed only because of the support of the two parties, and each party can depart from it by a simple vote. During the 1970s, both parties reinstituted the practice of reviewing each chair—voting anew every two years on whether each chair would be continued. Few chairpersons have actually been removed, but notice has been served that the seniority system is no longer automatic and has thereby reminded everyone that all committee assignments are party decisions. Thus, although party leaders no longer can control the votes of many members, the party system itself remains an important factor.

The continuing importance of parties in Congress became especially evident after the Republicans won control of Congress in 1994. During the first few months of the 104th Congress, the Republican leadership was able to maintain nearly unanimous support among party members on vote after vote as it sought to implement the GOP's legislative agenda. By the end of 1995, however, splits within the party began to surface over issues such as welfare reform and balancing the budget.

During the great 1995–1996 budget struggle between President Clinton and Speaker Gingrich, cracks began to develop within the Republican coalition, and the GOP ended the 104th Congress far less united than it had been at the outset. After the 1996 national elections, Republicans retained control of both houses of Congress. However, the GOP seemed to lack the ideological fervor that had helped to bring about an unprecedented level of party unity in 1994. Moreover, Speaker Gingrich, who had been the driving force behind the Republican "Contract with America," was compelled to devote some of his attention to dealing with Democratic efforts to prove he had violated Congressional ethics rules. As a result, Republican party unity in the 105th Congress never approached its earlier levels. No longer forced to confront a united GOP, the Democrats, too, split into their various wings and factions. Partisanship was important in the 105th Congress, but it was no longer all-important.

WEAKENING OF PARTY ORGANIZATION

Opposition to party politics was the basis for a number of the institutional reforms of the American political process at the turn of the twentieth century during the so-called Progressive Era. Many Progressive reformers were motivated by a sincere desire to rid politics of corruption and to improve the quality and efficiency of government in the United States. But simultaneously, from the perspective of middle- and upper-class Progressives and the financial, commercial, and industrial elites with which they were often associated, the weakening or elimination of party organization would also mean that power could more readily be acquired and retained by those with wealth, position, and education.

The list of anti-party reforms of the Progressive Era is a familiar one. Ballot reform took away the parties' privilege of printing and distributing ballots and thus introduced the possibility of split-ticket voting. The introduction of nonpartisan local elections eroded grassroots party organization. The extension of "merit systems" for administrative appointments stripped party organizations of their vitally important access to patronage and thus reduced their ability to recruit workers. The development of the direct primary reduced party leaders' capacity to control candidate nominations. These reforms obviously did not destroy political parties as entities, but taken together they did substantially weaken party organizations in the United States.

After the turn of the century, the organizational strength of American political parties gradually diminished. Between the two world wars, organization remained the major tool available to contending electoral forces, but in most areas of the country the "reformed" state and local parties that survived the Progressive Era gradually lost their organizational vitality and coherence, and they became less effective campaign tools. While most areas of the nation continued to boast Democratic and Republican party groupings, reform meant the elimination of the permanent mass organizations that had been the parties' principal campaign weapons.

High-Tech Politics

As a result of Progressive reform, American party organizations entered the twentieth century with rickety substructures. As the use of civil service, primary elections, and other Progressive innovations spread, the strength of party organizations eroded. By the end of World War II, political scientists were already bemoaning the absence of party discipline and "party responsibility" in the United States. This erosion of the parties' organizational strength set the stage for the introduction of new political techniques that represented radical departures from the campaign practices perfected during the nineteenth century. In place of workers and organization, contending forces began to employ intricate electronic communications techniques to attract supporters. This new political technology includes five basic elements.

1. *Polling.* Surveys of voter opinion provide the information that candidates and their staffs use to craft campaign strategies. Candidates use polls to select issues, to assess their own strengths and weaknesses (as well as those of the opposition), to check voter response to the campaign, and to determine the degree to which various constituent groups are susceptible to campaign appeals. In recent years, pollsters have become central figures in most national campaigns. Indeed, Stanley Greenberg, who polled for the 1992 Clinton campaign, became part of Clinton's inner circle of advisers and ultimately played a role in major policy decisions. Virtually all contemporary campaigns for national and statewide office,

as well as many local campaigns, make extensive use of opinion surveys. As we saw in Chapter 8, President Clinton used polling extensively both during and after the 1996 presidential election, using the results to shape his rhetoric and guide his policy initiatives.

2. *The broadcast media.* Extensive use of the electronic media, television in particular, has become the hallmark of the modern political campaign. One commonly used broadcast technique is the thirty- or sixty-second television spot advertisement that permits the candidate's message to be delivered to a target audience before uninterested or hostile viewers can psychologically, or physically, tune it out. Famous recent examples are George Bush's "Willie Horton" ad in the 1988 presidential campaign, which portrayed Michael Dukakis as soft on crime by showing a frightening close-up picture of Mr. Horton, a convicted felon who raped a woman while on a weekend furlough from a Massachusetts prison, and Lyndon Johnson's famous "daisy girl" ad in 1964, discussed in detail in Box 10.2.

Television spot ads and other media techniques are designed to establish candidate name recognition, to create a favorable image of the candidate and a negative image of the opponent, to link the candidate with desirable groups in the community, and to communicate the candidate's stands on selected issues. These spot ads can have an important electoral impact. Generally, media campaigns attempt to follow the guidelines indicated by a candidate's polls, emphasizing issues and personal characteristics that appear important in the poll data.

The broadcast media are now so central to modern campaigns that most candidates' activities are tied to their media strategies.[11] Candidate activities are designed expressly to stimulate television news coverage. For instance, members of Congress running for re-election or for president

[11]Larry J. Sabato, *The Rise of Political Consultants* (New York: Basic Books, 1981).

BOX 10.2

The Daisy Girl

On September 7, 1964, NBC's *Monday Night at the Movies* was interrupted by what came to be one of the most famous and controversial political commercials ever shown on American television. In this ad, a little girl with long, light brown hair stood in a field picking daisy petals. As she pulled the petals, she counted, "1-2-3. . . ." As she counted, the voice of an announcer in the background counted backward, "10-9-8. . . ." As the count continued, the announcer's voice became louder and the girl's voice more muted, until the girl reached 10 and the announcer counted down to 0. At that point, a blinding nuclear explosion destroyed everything, with President Johnson saying, "These are the stakes: To make a world in which all of God's children can live or go into the dark. We must either love each other or we must die." The announcer then urged viewers to vote for President Johnson on November 3. The ad was cut after one use, but the use of short spots has continued.

SOURCE: Photo courtesy of the Lyndon Baines Johnson Presidential Library.

almost always sponsor committee or subcommittee hearings to generate publicity. In recent years, Senate hearings on hunger, crime, health, and defense have been used mainly to attract television cameras.

The 1992 presidential election introduced three new media techniques: the talk show interview, the "electronic town hall" meeting, and the "infomercial." Candidates used television and radio interview programs such as *Larry King Live* and Rush Limbaugh's radio program to reach mass audiences. From the perspective of the candidates, these television and radio appearances offered excellent opportunities to appeal for the support of millions of potential voters. Because

these are entertainment programs, viewers are perceived to be more relaxed and, hence, potentially more susceptible to candidates' appeals. Some programs allow listeners or viewers to call in, and this gives candidates a chance to demonstrate that they are responsive to ordinary people and sympathetic to their problems.

Similarly, the "town meeting" format gave a candidate the chance to appear in a hall with a group of ordinary citizens, answer their questions, and listen to their ideas. Bill Clinton felt that he was very effective in this format and insisted that one of the presidential debates be organized as a town meeting. After the election, Clinton hosted a series of televised meetings on the economy and promised to continue to make himself available to the public during his presidency. He and his political aides viewed the town meeting as an excellent mechanism for bolstering public support.

Talk show appearances and town meetings, moreover, allow candidates to avoid the twin problems usually associated with political use of the media—cost and filtering. Normally, candidates must spend hundreds of thousands—even millions—of dollars for the use of commercial television time, while press conferences and news program *"sound bite"* appearances leave candidates at the mercy of media interpretations and possible unfriendly editing. The talk show format gives candidates a free opportunity to present themselves and their ideas—often in the company of a congenial host—to millions of Americans without the media filtering or editorial revision that might undermine their presentations.

In addition to making talk show appearances, independent candidate Ross Perot purchased several thirty-minute network television slots to present detailed expositions of his ideas and programs. In the early days of television, candidates often scheduled fifteen- or even thirty-minute presentations. This format, however, was abandoned because of its cost and because only a candidate's strongest supporters would take the time to watch such a long presentation. In essence, candidates were paying a great deal of money to preach to the already converted.

In recent years, however, changes in television cost structures have made thirty-minute slots available at relatively reasonable prices. To the surprise of many analysts, Perot was able to attract large audiences for his detailed discussions of the nation's budget deficit and other economic topics. Perhaps the well-educated electorate of the 1990s is more willing than was the electorate of the 1950s to devote its time and attention to discourse and explanation. If so, in the years to come we may see the thirty-second spot ad give way more and more to the thirty- or even sixty-minute infomercial.

The most dramatic use of the electronic media in contemporary electoral politics is the televised debate. Televised presidential debates began with the 1960 Kennedy-Nixon clash. Today, candidates for many public offices hold debates during the weeks prior to the election. These presidential debates are typically held so late in the campaign season that they usually do not change many votes. Most viewers have already decided which candidate they will support and tend to use the debate to confirm their choice. Generally, viewers will perceive the candidate they already favor as the winner of the debate. This is especially true for viewers with strong partisan leanings. Thus Republicans, as a rule, thought that Bob Dole was the stronger performer in the 1996 presidential debates, whereas Democrats were convinced that Bill Clinton was.

Nevertheless, the debates do allow candidates to reach the few viewers who have not fully made up their minds about the election. Moreover, the debates can enhance the credibility of lesser-known candidates. Thus, in 1960, a little-known senator, Jack Kennedy, was able to use a solid debate performance to become a credible (and eventually victorious) candidate in a race against his much better known and more experienced rival, Richard Nixon. In 1996, Bob Dole hoped to use the presidential debates to reduce Bill Clinton's lead in the race. Dole's performance, however, was not sufficiently strong to affect the outcome.

3. *Phone banks.* Through the broadcast media, candidates communicate with voters *en masse* and impersonally. Phone banks, on the other hand, allow campaign workers to make personal contact with hundreds of thousands of voters. Personal contacts of this sort are thought to be extremely effective. Again, poll data serve to identify the groups that will be targeted for phone calls. Computers select phone numbers from areas in which members of these groups are concentrated. Staffs of paid or volunteer callers, using computer-assisted dialing systems and prepared scripts, place calls to deliver the candidate's message. The targeted groups are generally those

PROCESS BOX 10.2

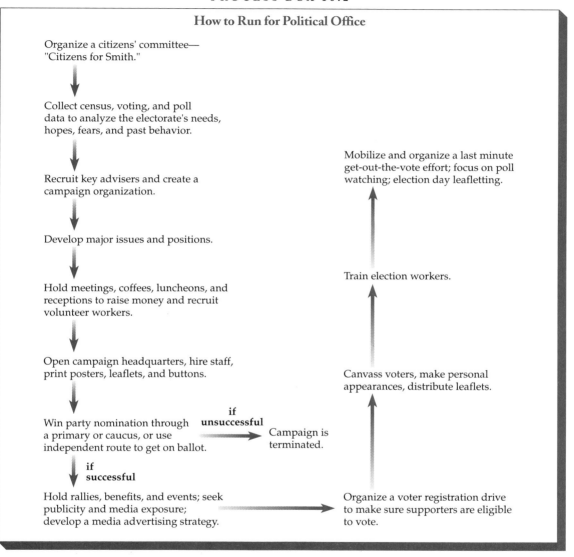

How to Run for Political Office

Organize a citizens' committee—
"Citizens for Smith."

Collect census, voting, and poll
data to analyze the electorate's needs,
hopes, fears, and past behavior.

Recruit key advisers and create a
campaign organization.

Develop major issues and positions.

Hold meetings, coffees, luncheons, and
receptions to raise money and recruit
volunteer workers.

Open campaign headquarters, hire staff,
print posters, leaflets, and buttons.

Win party nomination through
a primary or caucus, or use
independent route to get on ballot.

if unsuccessful → Campaign is terminated.

if successful

Hold rallies, benefits, and events; seek
publicity and media exposure;
develop a media advertising strategy.

Organize a voter registration drive
to make sure supporters are eligible
to vote.

Canvass voters, make personal
appearances, distribute leaflets.

Train election workers.

Mobilize and organize a last minute
get-out-the-vote effort; focus on poll
watching; election day leafletting.

identified by polls as either uncommitted or weakly committed, as well as strong supporters of the candidate who are contacted simply to encourage them to vote.

Phone banks are used extensively in pivotal contests. Before the 1980 Iowa caucuses, for example, Democratic and Republican presidential hopefuls placed a total of more than 3 million phone calls to Iowa's 1.7 million registered voters.

During the same year, former President Carter was reported to have personally placed between twenty and forty calls every night to homes in key primary and caucus states. On some New Hampshire blocks, a dozen or more residents eventually received telephone calls from the president.[12]

[12]Sabato, *Rise of Political Consultants*, p. 218.

4. *Direct mail*. Direct mail serves both as a vehicle for communicating with voters and as a mechanism for raising funds. The first step in a direct mail campaign is the purchase or rental of a computerized mailing list of voters deemed to have some particular perspective or social characteristic. Often sets of magazine subscription lists or lists of donors to various causes are employed. For example, a candidate interested in reaching conservative voters might rent subscription lists from the *National Review*, *Human Events*, or *Conservative Digest*; a candidate interested in appealing to liberals might rent subscription lists from the *New York Review of Books* or the *New Republic*. Considerable fine-tuning is possible. After obtaining the appropriate mailing lists, candidates usually send pamphlets, letters, and brochures describing themselves and their views to voters believed to be sympathetic. Different types of mail appeals are made to different electoral subgroups.

In addition to its use as a political advertising medium, direct mail has also become an important source of campaign funds. Computerized mailing lists permit campaign strategists to pinpoint individuals whose interests, background, and activities suggest that they may be potential donors to the campaign. Letters of solicitation are sent to these potential donors. Some of the money raised is then used to purchase additional mailing lists. Direct mail solicitation can be enormously effective.[13]

5. *Professional public relations*. Modern campaigns and the complex technology upon which they rely are typically directed by professional public relations consultants. Virtually all serious contenders for national and statewide office retain the services of professional campaign consultants. Increasingly, candidates for local office, too, have come to rely upon professional campaign managers. Consultants offer candidates the expertise necessary to conduct accurate opinion polls, produce television commercials, organize

direct mail campaigns, and make use of sophisticated computer analyses.

Several of the components of this "new" political technology were developed long before World War II. Professional public relations firms first became involved in electoral politics in 1934, when the firm of Whittaker and Baxter helped to defeat novelist Upton Sinclair's Socialist candidacy in the California gubernatorial race by charging that Sinclair was a Communist. The firm was hired by California business interests. Primitive opinion polls were used in American elections as early as 1824, and relatively sophisticated surveys were employed extensively during the 1880s and 1890s.

After the Second World War, however, the introduction of television and the computer provided the mechanisms that became the electronic heart of the modern campaign. These innovations coincided with a growing realization on the part of politicians and activists that the capacity of traditional party organizations to mobilize voters had greatly diminished. As this realization spread, a small number of candidates began to experiment with new campaign methods. Even the initial trickle of political techniques was generally more effective than the more traditional campaign efforts that could be mounted by the now-debilitated party organizations.

In a number of well-publicized congressional, senatorial, and gubernatorial campaigns during the postwar years, candidates using the new campaign methods decisively defeated rivals who continued to rely on the older organizational techniques. The successful campaigns mounted by Richard Nixon, who relied on professional public relations firms in the 1948 California Senate race, and Jacob Javits, who made brilliant use of poll data in his 1948 New York congressional race, were vivid examples of the power of technology.

The number of technologically oriented campaigns increased greatly after 1971. The Federal Elections Campaign Act of 1972 prompted the creation of large numbers of political action com-

---

[13]Ibid., p. 250.

mittees (PACs) by a host of corporate and ideological groups. This development increased the availability of funds to political candidates—conservative candidates in particular—which meant in turn that the new technology could be used more extensively.

Initially, the new techniques were employed mainly by individual candidates who often made little or no effort to coordinate their campaigns with those of other political aspirants sharing the same party label. For this reason, campaigns employing the new technology sometimes came to be called "candidate-centered" efforts, as distinguished from the traditional party-coordinated campaign. Nothing about the new technology, however, precluded its use by political party leaders seeking to coordinate a number of campaigns. In recent years, party leaders—Republicans in particular—have learned to make good use of modern campaign technology. The difference between the old and new political methods is not that the latter is inherently candidate-centered while the former is strictly a party tool. Rather, the difference is a matter of the types of political resources upon which each method depends.

From Labor-Intensive to Capital-Intensive Politics

With the new political techniques the party organization became less important, resulting in a shift from labor-intensive to capital-intensive campaigns. Campaign tasks once performed by masses of party workers with some cash now require fewer personnel but a great deal more money. The new political style depends on polls, computers, and other electronic paraphernalia. Of course, even when workers and organization were the key electoral tools, money had considerable political significance. Nevertheless, during the nineteenth century, national political campaigns in the United States employed millions of people. Indeed, as many as 2.5 million individuals were employed in political work during the

1880s.[14] The direct cost of campaigns, therefore, was relatively low. For example, in 1860, Abraham Lincoln spent only $100,000—which was approximately twice the amount spent by his chief opponent, Stephen Douglas.

Modern campaigns depend heavily on money. Each element of the new political technology is enormously expensive. A sixty-second spot announcement on prime-time network television costs hundreds of thousands of dollars each time it is aired. Opinion surveys can be quite expensive; polling costs in a statewide race can easily reach or exceed the six-figure mark. Campaign consultants can charge substantial fees.

A direct mail campaign can eventually become an important source of funds but is very expensive to initiate. The inauguration of a serious national direct mail effort requires at least $1 million in "front end cash" to pay for mailing lists, brochures, letters, envelopes, and postage.[15] While the cost of televised debates is covered by the sponsoring organizations and the television stations and is therefore free to the candidates, even debate preparation requires substantial staff work and research, and, of course, money.

It is the expense of the new technology that accounts for the enormous cost of recent American national elections. In 1996, political candidates spent a total of more than $1.6 billion on election campaigns. The average winning candidate in a campaign for a seat in the House of Representatives spent more than $500,000; the average winner in a senatorial campaign spent $4 million.[16] The 1996 Democratic and Republican presidential candidates, along with independent candidate Ross Perot, each received $60 million in public funds to run their campaigns. Clinton and Dole were also helped by tens of millions of dollars in

[14]M. Ostrogorski, *Democracy and the Organization of Political Parties* (New York: Macmillan, 1902).

[15]Timothy Clark, "The RNC Prospers, the DNC Struggles as They Face the 1980 Election," *National Journal*, 27 October 1980, p. 1619.

[16]Federal Election Commission (FEC) reports.

IN BRIEF BOX

HIGH TECH POLITICS

Polling—Candidates use polls to select issues, to assess their own strengths and weaknesses, and to check voter response.

Broadcast media—Television spot ads are the most common use of television by candidates. Ads establish name recognition, communicate the candidate's stand on issues, and link the candidate to desirable groups in the community. The televised debate is another long-standing use of the media. New media techniques include the talk show interview, the "electronic town hall" meeting, and the "infomercial."

Phone banks—Through phone banks, campaign workers make personal contact with hundreds of thousands of voters.

Direct mail—Direct mail serves as a fund-raising tool and as a means of communicating a candidate's ideas. The choice of mailing lists is very important.

Professional public relations—Professional campaign consultants offer expertise in how best to utilize the above-mentioned methods. Virtually all national and statewide candidates and more and more local political candidates rely on consultants.

so-called independent expenditures on the part of corporate and ideological *political action committees (PACs).* As long as such political expenditures are not formally coordinated with a candidate's campaign, they are considered to be constitutionally protected free speech and are not subject to legal limitation or even reporting requirements. Likewise, independent spending by political parties is also considered to be an expression of free speech.[17]

Federal Election Commission data suggest that approximately one-fourth of the private funds spent on political campaigns in the United States is raised through small, direct-mail contributions; about one-fourth is provided by large, individual gifts; and another fourth comes from contributions from PACs. The remaining fourth is drawn from the political parties and from candidates' personal or family resources.[18]

In recent years, Congress has sought to regulate campaign finance. The Supreme Court, how-

ever, has limited the effect of this legislation by declaring unconstitutional any absolute limits on the freedom of individuals to spend their own money on campaigns.[19] The Federal Elections Campaign Act of 1971 imposed contribution limits and provided for full disclosure of all campaign receipts and expenditures (see Box 10.3).

Throughout the 1990s, a number of pieces of legislation have proposed additional restrictions on the private funding of campaigns. Political reform has been blocked, however, because the two major parties disagree over the form it should take. The Republicans have developed a very efficient direct-mail apparatus and would be willing to place limits on the role of PACs. The Democrats, by contrast, depend more heavily on PACs and fear that limiting their role would hurt the party's electoral chances.

In recent years, expenditures by political parties and by interest groups have undermined the significance of the Federal Elections Campaign Act. Since these forms of spending are not subject

[17]Buckley v. Valeo, 424 U.S. 1 (1976); Colorado Republican Party v. Federal Election Commission, 64 U.S.L.W. 4663 (1996).
[18]FEC reports.

[19]Buckley v. Valeo, 421 U.S. 1 (1976).

BOX 10.3

Federal Campaign Finance Regulation

Campaign Contributions

No individual may contribute more than $1,000 to any one candidate in any single election. Individuals may contribute as much as $20,000 to a national party committee and up to $5,000 to a political action committee. Full disclosure is required by candidates of all contributions over $100. Candidates may not accept cash contributions over $100.

Political Action Committees

Any corporation, labor union, trade association, or other organization may establish a political action committee (PAC). PACs must contribute to the campaigns of at least five different candidates and may contribute as much as $5,000 per candidate in any given election.

Presidential Elections

Candidates in presidential primaries may receive federal matching funds if they raise at least $5,000 in each of twenty states. The money raised must come in contributions of $250 or less. The amount raised by candidates in this way is matched by the federal government, dollar for dollar, up to a limit of $5 million. In the general election, major-party candidates' campaigns are carefully funded by the federal government. Candidates may spend no money beyond their federal funding. But independent groups may spend money on behalf of a candidate so long as their efforts are not directly tied to the official campaign. Minor-party candidates may be entitled to partial federal funding.

Federal Election Commission (FEC)

The six-member FEC supervises federal elections, collects and publicizes campaign finance records, and investigates violations of federal campaign finance law.

to regulation so long as they are not directly coordinated with individual candidates, donors have come to give much more of their money to the parties, or to spend it directly on behalf of candidacies they favor. Campaign spending by the two parties in 1996 reached a total of $650 million.[20] Nearly half was in the form of unregulated *"soft money"* nominally spent without coordination with the candidates. If this pattern continues, political parties may grow in power relative to the individual candidates for office, leading the U.S. in the direction of a stronger party system.

Certainly "people power" is not irrelevant to modern political campaigns. Candidates continue to utilize the political services of tens of thousands of volunteer workers. Nevertheless, in the contemporary era, even the recruitment of volunteer campaign workers has become a matter of electronic technology. Employing a technique called "instant organization," paid telephone callers use phone banks to contact individuals in areas targeted by a computer (which they do when contacting potential voters, as we discussed before). Volunteer workers are recruited from among these individuals. A number of campaigns—Richard Nixon's 1968 presidential campaign was the first—have successfully used this technique.

[20]Michael Duffy and Nancy Gibbs, "The Money Mess," *Time*, 11 October 1996, p. 33.

DEBATING THE ISSUES

The State of the Parties: Decaying or Revitalized?

*M*ANY POLITICAL OBSERVERS *have complained in recent years that America's political parties are dying. Both politicians and voters seem less concerned and less interested in party labels and party loyalty, a fact that, if true, means weaker and fewer links between citizens and the government. Yet not everyone agrees. Some argue that parties play a greater role in government than ever, as seen for example in recent sharp party clashes between the Republican-controlled Congress and the Democratic president. In the essays below, the political scientists William E. Hudson and Gerald M. Pomper summarize the arguments for and against decaying political parties.*

HUDSON

Political parties have grown weaker organizationally in the past few decades, as have voter attachments to them. More voters, particularly among the higher educated and more affluent . . . are ticket splitters, voting for different political parties in a single election. With an electorate indifferent to party, those holding elective office are more apt to ignore party discipline and vote independently, behavior that only reinforces the electorate's perception that party labels do not matter. . . .

In the United States today, political parties have become increasingly marginalized as election vehicles. Because state election laws continue to make ballot access easier for party nominees and because enough voters retain party identification to give such nominees an automatic pool of support, candidates still seek the party label, but attaching the label tends to be all that parties contribute to the process. Modern campaigns have become candidate centered rather than party centered. Individual candidates build their personal campaign organizations, using professional campaign managers and funds they have raised themselves. . . . Party attachments tend to be deemphasized, and party officials, as opposed to personal campaign advisers, are not involved in the process. Unfortunately for democracy, this new candidate-centered style of campaigning has undermined equal representation.[1]

POMPER

I want to dispute [the] common assertion, that American parties have become weakened, irrelevant, and impotent. To the contrary, . . . parties are increasingly rooted in distinct voter coalitions, [are] stronger organiza-

The displacement of organizational methods by the new political technology has the most far-reaching implications for the balance of power among contending political groups. Labor-intensive organizational tactics allowed parties whose chief support came from groups nearer the bottom of the social scale to use the numerical superiority of their forces as a partial counterweight to the institutional and economic resources more readily available to the opposition. The capital-intensive technological format, by contrast, has

given a major boost to the political fortunes of those whose supporters are better able to furnish the large sums needed to compete effectively.[21]

[21]For discussions of the consequences, see Thomas Edsall, *The New Politics of Inequality* (New York: W. W. Norton, 1985). See also Thomas Edsall, "Both Parties Get the Company's Money—But the Boss Backs the GOP," *Washington Post National Weekly Edition*, 16 September 1986, p. 14; and Benjamin Ginsberg, "Money and Power: The New Political Economy of American Elections," in *The Political Economy*, ed. Thomas Ferguson and Joel Rogers (Armonk, NY: M. E. Sharpe, 1984).

tionally, and clearly relevant to the policy issues facing the nation. . . . the thesis of party decline fails because it rests on a flawed theoretical foundation. The thesis depends on a view of parties as collectivities of voters. In this view, parties are weaker because fewer voters are strongly identified with the parties, and fewer are consistent supporters at the ballot box.

The problem with this argument is that parties are not properly considered as collections of voters. . . . Voters are not members of the party organization, but rather its clientele. . . . We do better to think of the parties as seekers of voters. . . . We can point to a few indicators that the major parties. . . . will be able to maintain themselves in the electoral marketplace. There are at least the following signs of party strengthening in the electorate:

Party identification, the proportion of strong identifiers, and affect toward the parties have all risen, after the decline of the 1970s.

There is strong continuity in the electoral coalitions of the parties during the period of 1976–1992. . . .

In the election of 1992, strong party loyalty is evident in individual-level data. Clinton won not only all states carried by Dukakis in 1988, but the overwhelming proportion of Dukakis's supporters (83 percent), and of self-identified Democrats (77 percent).

In 1992, only 23.9 percent of the congressional districts voted for different parties for president and the U.S. House, the lowest proportion in four decades. . . .

We can see the emergence of stable voter coalitions and strengthened party organizations. Maybe, just maybe, and just in time, we can now observe an emerging "semi-responsible party government."[2]

---

[1] William E. Hudson, *American Democracy in Peril* (Chatham, NJ: Chatham House, 1995), pp. 41, 152.
[2] Gerald M. Pomper, "Alive! The Political Parties after the 1980–1992 Presidential Elections," *American Presidential Elections*, ed. Harvey L. Schantz (Albany, NY: SUNY Press, 1996), pp. 135, 140–41, 151–52.

Indeed, the new technology permits financial resources to be more effectively harnessed and exploited than was ever before possible.

In a political process lacking strong party organizations, the likelihood that groups that do not possess substantial economic or institutional resources can acquire some measure of power is severely diminished. Dominated by the new technology, electoral politics becomes a contest in which the wealthy and powerful have a decided advantage.

Is the Party Over?

Of course, the Democratic and Republican parties still exist. The contemporary parties, however, differ from their predecessors. In recent decades, the Democrats and Republicans have become entrenched in distinct segments of the national governmental apparatus. The Democrats have a hold on federal social service, labor and regulatory agencies, and government bureaucracies and nonprofit organizations on the state and local levels that help administer national social programs. This entrenchment has its roots in Franklin D. Roosevelt's New Deal and Lyndon Johnson's Great Society programs, which expanded the size and institutional capacities of the national government's domestic agencies. These developments have transformed the Democratic party from a political force based upon state and local party machines into one grounded in the domestic bureaucracy.

In 1993, the Democrats sought to entrench themselves still further in the domestic state apparatus. The three chief vehicles for this effort were President Clinton's economic policy proposals, health care reform proposals, and political reform initiatives. Clinton's economic package entailed substantial tax increases and cuts in military spending. In this way, the administration hoped to make additional revenues available for Democratic social programs and agencies that had been starved for funding through twelve years of Republican rule.

Clinton's unsuccessful health care reform proposals promised to create an enormous new set of agencies and institutions that would permit Democrats to expand substantially their influence over an area representing nearly 15 percent of the domestic economy, while simultaneously attaching major constituency groups to the Democratic party. This is why Republicans opposed his effort so furiously.

Finally, Clinton proposed changes in campaign spending rules that would generally work to the advantage of liberal public-interest groups and Democratic incumbents. He signed the "Motor Voter" bill, which potentially could bring larger numbers of mainly Democratic poor and minority voters to the polls. And he proposed reforms of the Hatch Act that would permit employees of the heavily Democratic federal civil service to play a larger role in the political process.[22]

Taken together, these proposals represented a bold effort to ensure continuing Democratic control of the government. Adoption of these proposals would have solidified the Democratic party's institutional base in the bureaucracies of the executive branch while making it all the more difficult for Republicans to dislodge the Democrats through electoral methods. For these reasons, Republicans blocked Clinton's legislative proposals.

The Republicans, in turn, control the national security apparatus, sectors of the economy that benefit from military spending, and those segments of American society threatened by the welfare and regulatory state built by the Democrats. This was one of the major factors behind the efforts of the Reagan administration to increase levels of defense spending while reducing domestic social spending. In essence, Reagan sought to direct the flow of federal funds into agencies and institutions associated with the Republicans while reducing the flow of funds into those sectors of the government in which the Democrats were entrenched.

During the budget debates of the late 1980s and early 1990s, congressional Democrats sought to reverse this state of affairs by diminishing funding for the national security sector and increasing funding levels for the domestic social and regulatory sectors. But proponents of defense spending were able to block demands for sharp cuts in the military. When the Democrats regained the White House in 1992, they renewed attacks on the military and national security sectors. Not only did President Clinton propose substantial cuts in military spending, but he and some congressional Democrats were also sharply critical of the military for closing its eyes to the sexual abuse of women and prohibiting the recruitment and retention of gay and lesbian personnel. These criticisms can, in part, be interpreted as an effort by

---

[22]Chuck Alston, "Democrats Flex New Muscle with Trio of Election Bills: Some Republicans Say That 'Motor Voter,' Campaign Finance, and Hatch Act Bills Add Up to Permanent Power Grab," *Congressional Quarterly Weekly Report*, 20 March 1993, pp. 643–45.

Democrats to undermine an institution that had become a Republican fiefdom.

To a considerable extent, this competitive entrenchment of Republicans and Democrats is a substitute for mass electoral mobilization as a means of securing power in the United States today. This is one reason why high levels of partisan conflict coexist with low rates of voter participation in contemporary American politics. To today's parties, traditional electoral politics is only one arena of political combat. In between elections, the Democrats and Republicans engage in institutional struggles with outcomes every bit as important as the verdict at the ballot box. We will discuss the impact of this situation in depth in Chapter 14.

CHAPTER REVIEW

Political parties seek to control government by controlling its personnel. Elections are their means to this end. Thus, parties take shape from the electoral process. The formal principle of party organization is this: For every district in which an election is held—from the entire nation to the local district, county, or precinct—there should be some kind of party unit.

The two-party system dominates U.S. politics. Today, on individual issues, the two parties differ little from each other. In general, however, Democrats lean more to the left on issues and Republicans more to the right. Even though party affiliation means less to Americans than it once did, partisanship remains important. What ticket-splitting there is occurs mainly at the presidential level.

Third parties are short-lived for several reasons. They have limited electoral support, the tradition of the two-party system is strong, and a major party often adopts their platforms. Single-member districts with two competing parties also discourage third parties.

Nominating and electing are the basic functions of parties. Originally nominations were made in party caucuses, and individuals who ran as independents had a difficult time getting on the ballot. In the 1830s, dissatisfaction with the cliquish caucuses led to nominating conventions. Although these ended the "King Caucus" that controlled the nomination of the presidential candidates, and thereby gave the presidency a popular base, they too proved unsatisfactory. Primaries have now more or less replaced the conventions. There are both closed and open primaries. Closed primaries are more supportive of strong political parties than open primaries. Contested primaries sap party strength and financial resources, but they nonetheless serve to resolve important social conflicts and recognize new interest groups. Winning at the top of a party ticket usually depends on the party regulars at the bottom getting out the vote. At all levels, the mass communications media are important. Mass mailings, too, are vital in campaigning. Thus, campaign funds are crucial to success.

Congress is organized around the two-party system. The House speakership is a party office. Parties determine the makeup of congressional committees, including their chairs, which are no longer based entirely on seniority.

In recent years, the role of parties in political campaigns has been partially supplanted by the use of new political technologies. These include the broadcast media, polling, professional public relations, phone banks, and direct mail fund-raising and advertising. These techniques are enormously expensive and have led to a shift from labor-intensive to capital-intensive politics. This shift works to the advantage of political forces representing the well-to-do. The parties currently have also entrenched themselves in government agencies and sectors of the national economy.

TIME LINE ON POLITICAL PARTIES

Events	Institutional Developments
Parties form in Congress (1790s)	Washington peacefully assumes the presidency (1789)
Washington's farewell address warns against parties (1796)	First party system—Federalists versus Jeffersonian Republicans (1790s)
Republican Thomas Jefferson elected president (1800)	**1800** Federalists try to retain power by Alien and Sedition Acts (1798) and by appointing "midnight judges" (1801)
Jefferson renominated by congressional caucus; re-elected by a landslide (1804)	Congressional caucuses nominate presidential candidates from each party (1804–1831)
Republican James Monroe re-elected president; no Federalist candidate; no caucuses called (1820)	Destruction of Federalists; period of one-partyism; "era of good feelings" (1810s–1830s)
	Republican party splinters into National Republicans (Adams) and Democratic Republicans (Jackson) (1824)
Democrat Andrew Jackson elected president, ushering in "era of common man" (1828)	Democrats use party rotation to replace National Republicans in government positions (1829)
National nominating conventions held by Democrats and National Republicans (1831)	**1830** National nominating conventions replace caucuses as methods of selecting presidential candidates from each party (1830s)
Whig presidential candidates lose to Democratic candidate Martin Van Buren (1836)	Second party system—Whig party forms in opposition to Jackson—Democrats versus Whigs (1830s–1850s)
Whig William Henry Harrison elected president (1840)	Whigs gain presidency and majority in Congress; both parties organized down to the precinct level (1840)
Republican Abraham Lincoln elected president (1860)	**1850** Third party system; destruction of Whigs; creation of Republicans—Democrats versus Republicans (1850s–1890s)
Civil War (1861–1865)	
Reconstruction (1867–1877)	
Era of groups and movements; millions of southern and eastern European immigrants arrive in U.S. (1870s–1890s)	**1890** Fourth party system; both the Democratic and the Republican parties are rebuilt along new lines (1890s–1930s)
Republican William McKinley elected president; Democrats decimated (1896)	Shrinking electorate; enactment of Progressive reforms (registration laws, primary elections, Australian ballot, civil service reform); decline of party machines; emergence of one-party states (1890s)

Events		Institutional Developments
Democrat Franklin D. Roosevelt elected president (1932)	**1930**	Fifth party system; period of New Deal Democratic dominance (1930s–1960s)
	1960	
Democratic convention—party badly damaged; Republican Richard Nixon elected president (1968)		Disruption of New Deal coalition; decay of party organizations (1968)
		Federal Election Campaign Act regulates campaign finance (1972)
Watergate scandal (1972–1974)		Introduction of new political techniques (1970s and 1980s)
Nixon resigns (1974)		
Republican Ronald Reagan elected president; Republican presidential ascendancy begins (1980) Republican George Bush elected president (1988)	**1980**	Efforts by Republicans to build a national party structure (1980s)
		Continuation of divided government, with Democrats controlling Congress and Republicans the White House (1980s–1992)
Partisan struggle over budget and Persian Gulf War (1990–1991)	**1990**	
Democrat Bill Clinton elected president (1992)		High levels of congressional party unity as Republicans seek to enact ambitious legislative program (1995)
Republicans win control of House and Senate (1994)		
Bill Clinton re-elected president (1996)		Divided government continues, with Republicans controlling Congress and Democrats the White House (1994–1998)

KEY TERMS

caucus (political)   A normally closed meeting of a political or legislative group to select candidates, plan strategy, or make decisions regarding legislative matters.

closed primary   A primary election in which voters can participate in the nomination of candidates, but only of the party in which they are enrolled for a period of time prior to primary day.

critical electoral realignment   The point in history when a new party supplants the ruling party, becoming in turn the dominant political force. In the United States, this has tended to occur roughly every thirty years.

multiple-member district   An electorate that selects all candidates at large from the whole district; each voter is given the number of votes equivalent to the number of seats to be filled.

nomination   The process through which political parties select their candidate for election to public office.

open primary   A primary election in which the voter can wait until the day of the primary to choose which party to enroll in to select candidates for the general election.

party machines   Local party organizations that control urban politics by mobilizing voters to elect the machines' candidates.

political action committee (PAC)   A private group that raises and distributes funds for use in election campaigns.

political parties   Organized groups that attempt to influence the government by electing their members to important government offices.

referendum   The practice of referring a measure proposed or passed by a legislature to the vote of the electorate for approval or rejection.

single-member district   An electorate that is allowed to elect only one representative from each district; the normal method of representation in the United States.

soft money   Money contributed directly to political parties for voter registration and organization.

sound bite   A word or phrase that is meant to convey a larger meaning or image; used by political candidates to briefly describe their stand on issues.

For Further Reading

Aldrich, John H. *Why Parties?: The Origin and Transformation of Party Politics in America.* Chicago: University of Chicago Press, 1995.

Chambers, William N., and Walter Dean Burnham. *The American Party Systems: Stages of Political Development.* New York: Oxford University Press, 1975.

Coleman, John J. *Party Decline in America: Policy, Politics, and the Fiscal State.* Princeton, NJ: Princeton University Press, 1996.

Grimshaw, William J. *Bitter Fruit: Black Politics and the Chicago Machine, 1931–1991.* Chicago: University of Chicago Press, 1992.

Hofstadter, Richard. *The Idea of a Party System: The Rise of Legitimate Opposition in the United States, 1780–1840.* Berkeley: University of California Press, 1969.

Kayden, Xandra, and Eddie Mahe, Jr. *The Party Goes On: The Persistence of the Two-Party System in the United States.* New York: Basic Books, 1985.

Lawson, Kay, and Peter Merkl. *When Parties Fail: Emerging Alternative Organizations.* Princeton: Princeton University Press, 1988.

Milkis, Sidney. *The President and the Parties: The Transformation of the American Party System since the New Deal.* New York: Oxford University Press, 1993.

Polsby, Nelson W. *Consequences of Party Reform.* New York: Oxford University Press, 1983.

Sabato, Larry. *PAC Power.* New York: W. W. Norton, 1984.

Sabato, Larry. *The Rise of Political Consultants.* New York: Basic Books, 1981.

Shafer, Byron, ed. *Beyond Realignment: Interpreting American Electoral Eras.* Madison: University of Wisconsin Press, 1991.

Smith, Eric R. *The Unchanging American Voter.* Berkeley: University of California Press, 1989.

Sorauf, Frank J. *Party Politics in America.* Boston: Little, Brown, 1984.

Sundquist, James. *Dynamics of the Party System.* Washington, DC: Brookings Institution, 1983.

Wattenberg, Martin. *The Decline of American Political Parties, 1952–1988.* Cambridge: Harvard University Press, 1989.

CHAPTER 11

Groups and Interests

AMERICANS often worry about the power of special interests. Many believe that organized groups, pursuing special agendas, dominate the governmental and policy-making process. Senator Edward Kennedy once said that Americans sometimes feel they have the "best Congress that money can buy." Certainly, a good deal of what Americans see and read about their nation's politics seems to confirm this pessimistic view.

In 1996, thousands of special interest groups donated over $1.5 billion to political parties and candidates at the national, state, and local levels. Business groups raised $242 million, mainly for Republicans, while organized labor donated $35 million to Democratic candidates and spent another $35 million directly to campaign for Democrats.[1] In response to charges that both he and President Bill Clinton were allowing major campaign contributors—including foreign firms—too much influence in the political process, Republican presidential candidate Bob Dole called for new campaign spending rules that would abolish large private contributions and prohibit noncitizens from contributing money to American political candidates.[2] Democrats immediately questioned Dole's sincerity, noting that the former Senate majority leader had personally raised some $100 million in campaign funds during the course of his long political career. While the two

[2]Thomas B. Edsall, "Dole Outlines Changes for Political Financing," *New York Times*, 21 October 1996, p. 1.

CORE OF THE ARGUMENT

- Interest groups are organized to influence government decisions.
- Interest groups have proliferated over the last thirty years as a result of the expansion of the federal government and the "new politics" movement.
- Interest groups use various strategies to promote their goals, including going public, lobbying, gaining access to key decision makers, using the courts, and influencing electoral politics.
- Though interest groups sometimes promote public concerns, they more often represent narrow interests.

---

[1]Leslie Wayne, "Business Is Biggest Campaign Spender, Study Says," *New York Times*, 18 October 1996, p. 1.

parties traded charges, Democratic fund-raiser John Huang was being forced to resign from the Democratic National Committee campaign staff amid allegations that he funneled millions of dollars in contributions from a wealthy Indonesian family into Democratic campaign coffers.[3]

Fund-raising activities hardly pause after an election. Members of both parties must immediately begin frantic rounds of fund-raising to prepare for the next race. On just one day in 1995 studied by the *Wall Street Journal*, twelve Republican and Democratic members of Congress raised a total of $650,000 in preparation for the 1996 elections, through a series of Washington fund-raising events attended chiefly by corporate lobbyists. Within six months of the 1994 elections, House members had already raised more than $45 million to prepare for the 1996 races.[4]

Does this sea of special-interest money affect the behavior of our elected leaders? The answer often seems to be that it does. In June 1994, President Clinton, who previously had called for "relying less on black-tie dinners and more on brown-bag lunches" for fund raising, was criticized for hosting a $1,500-per-person black-tie dinner designed to raise $2 million for Democratic candidates.[5] The dinner, which organizers called "An American Celebration," included among its honorary co-chairs Dwayne O. Andreas, board chair of the Archer Daniels Midland Company (ADM), a huge agricultural firm that is very dependent upon federal policy and very generous to both political parties. Andreas paid $100,000 for the privilege of being listed as a dinner co-chair, although he never actually attended the affair. A week later, ADM won a major political victory when the Environmental Protection Agency (EPA), with the urging of the White House, ruled

that a substantial share of the gasoline sold in the United States by 1996 must contain corn-based ethanol. ADM controls 60 percent of America's ethanol production and stood to gain millions of dollars from the EPA's decision (which was overturned by a federal court in 1995).[6] The White House denied any connection between ADM's contributions and the favorable EPA ruling.

The framers of the American Constitution feared the power that could be wielded by organized interests. Yet they believed that interest groups thrived because of freedom—the freedom that all Americans enjoyed to organize and express their views. To the framers, this problem presented a dilemma—indeed, the dilemma of freedom versus power that is central to our text. If the government were given the power to regulate or in any way to forbid efforts by organized interests to interfere in the political process, the government would in effect have been given the power to suppress freedom. The solution to this dilemma was presented by James Madison:

> . . . Take in a greater variety of parties and interest [and] you make it less probable that a majority of the whole will have a common motive to invade the rights of other citizens. . . . [Hence the advantage] enjoyed by a large over a small republic.[7]

According to Madisonian theory, a good constitution encourages multitudes of interests so that no single interest can ever tyrannize the others. The basic assumption is that competition among interests will produce balance, with all the interests regulating each other.[8] Today, this Madisonian principle is called *pluralism.*

There are tens of thousands of organized groups in the United States, ranging from civic associations to huge nationwide groups like the Na-

[3]David Sanger and James Sterngold, "Fund Raiser for Democrats Now Faces Harsh Spotlight," *New York Times,* 21 October 1996, p. 1.
[4]Phil Kuntz, "A Day in Washington Is Just Another Day to Raise More Dollars," *Wall Street Journal,* 23 October 1995, p. 1.
[5]Michael Wines, "Clinton under Attack on Big Contributions," *New York Times,* 22 June 1994, p. 1.

[6]Timothy Noah, "EPA Came Through for Archer-Daniels-Midland Soon after Andreas's Role at Presidential Dinner," *Wall Street Journal,* 6 July 1994, p. A20.
[7]Clinton Rossiter, ed., *The Federalist Papers* (New York: New American Library, 1961), No. 10, p. 83.
[8]Ibid.

tional Rifle Association, whose chief cause is opposition to restrictions on gun ownership, or Common Cause, a public interest group that advocates a variety of liberal political reforms. The huge number of *interest groups* competing for influence in the U.S., however, does not mean that all *interests* are fully and equally represented in the American political process. As we shall see, the political deck is heavily stacked in favor of those interests able to organize and to wield substantial economic, social, and institutional resources on behalf of their cause. This means that within the universe of interest-group politics it is political power—not some abstract conception of the public good—that is likely to prevail. Moreover, this means that interest-group politics, taken as a whole, is a political format that works more to the advantage of some types of interests than others. In general, a politics in which interest groups predominate is a politics with a distinctly upper-class bias (see Concept Map 11.1).

In this chapter, we will examine some of the antecedents and consequences of interest-group politics in the United States. First, we will seek to understand the character of the interests promoted by interest groups. Second, we will assess the growth of interest-group activity in recent American political history, including the emergence of "public interest" groups. Finally, we will review and evaluate the strategies that competing groups use in their struggle for influence.

CHARACTER OF INTEREST GROUPS

Individuals form groups in order to increase the chance that their views will be heard and their interests treated favorably by the government. *Interest groups* are organized to influence governmental decisions. There are an enormous number of interest groups in the United States, and millions of Americans are members of one or more groups, at least to the extent of paying dues or attending an occasional meeting.

What Interests Are Represented

Interest groups come in as many shapes and sizes as the interests they represent. When most people think about interest groups, they immediately think of groups with a direct economic interest in governmental actions. These groups are generally supported by groups of producers or manufacturers in a particular economic sector. Examples of this type of group include the National Petroleum Refiners Association, the American Farm Bureau Federation, and the National Federation of Independent Business, which represents small business owners. At the same time that broadly representative groups like these are active in Washington, specific companies, like Shell Oil, International Business Machines, and General Motors, may be active on certain issues that are of particular concern to them.

Labor organizations are equally active lobbyists. The AFL-CIO, the United Mine Workers, and the Teamsters are all groups that lobby on behalf of organized labor. In recent years, lobbies have arisen to further the interests of public employees, the most significant among these being the American Federation of State, County, and Municipal Employees.

Professional lobbies like the American Bar Association and the American Medical Association have been particularly successful in furthering their own interests in state and federal legislatures. Financial institutions, represented by organizations like the American Bankers Association and the National Savings & Loan League, although frequently less visible than other lobbies, also play an important role in shaping legislative policy.

Recent years have witnessed the growth of a powerful *"public interest"* lobby purporting to represent interests whose concerns are not likely to be addressed by traditional lobbies. These groups have been most visible in the consumer protection and environmental policy areas, although public interest groups cover a broad range of issues. The

CONCEPT MAP 11.1

Interest Group Pluralism

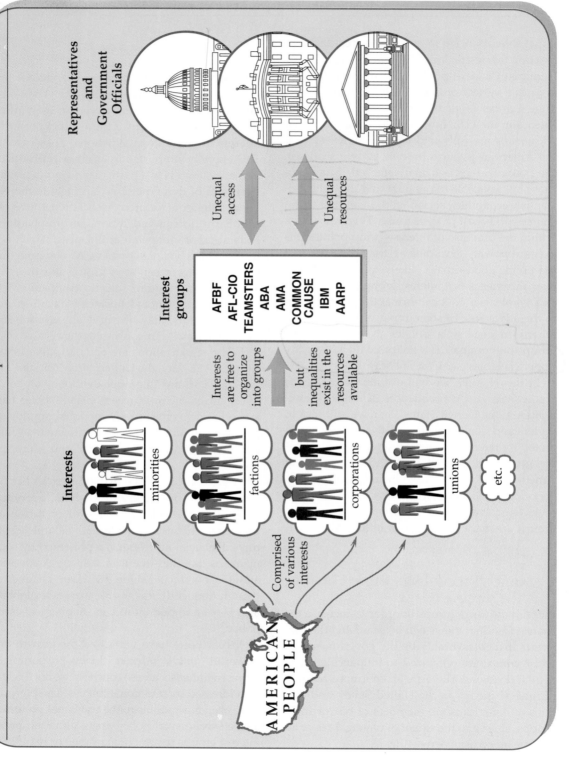

IN BRIEF BOX

CHARACTER OF INTEREST GROUPS

What Interests Are Represented
  Economic interests—American Farm Bureau Federation
  Labor organizations—AFL-CIO, United Mine Workers, Teamsters
  Professional lobbies—American Bar Association, American Medical Association
  Financial institutions—American Bankers Association, National Savings & Loan League
  Public interest groups—Common Cause, Union of Concerned Scientists
  Public sector lobby—National League of Cities

Organizational Components
  attracting and keeping members
  fundraising to support their infrastructure and their lobbying efforts
  leadership and decision-making structure
  agency that carries out the group's tasks

Characteristics of Members
  Interest groups tend to attract members from the middle and upper-middle classes because
    these people are more likely to have the time, the money, and the inclination to take part in
    such associations. People from less advantaged socioeconomic groups need to be organized
    on the massive scale of political parties.

National Resources Defense Council, the Union of Concerned Scientists, and Common Cause are all examples of public interest groups.

The perceived need for representation on Capitol Hill has generated a public sector lobby in the past several years, including the National League of Cities and the "research" lobby. The latter group comprises think tanks and universities that have an interest in obtaining government funds for research and support, and it includes such prestigious institutions as Harvard University, the Brookings Institution, and the American Enterprise Institute. Indeed, many universities have expanded their lobbying efforts even as they have reduced faculty positions and course offerings.[9]

Organizational Components

Although there are many interest groups, most share certain key organizational components.

[9]Betsy Wagner and David Bowermaster, "B.S. Economics," *Washington Monthly* (November 1992), pp. 19–22.

First, all groups must attract and keep members. Usually, groups appeal to members not only by promoting political goals or policies they favor but also by providing them with direct economic or social benefits. Thus, for example, the American Association of Retired Persons (AARP), which promotes the interests of senior citizens, at the same time offers members a variety of insurance benefits and commercial discounts. Similarly, many groups whose goals are chiefly economic or political also seek to attract members through social interaction and good fellowship. Thus, the local chapters of many national groups provide their members with a congenial social environment while collecting dues that finance the national offices' political efforts.

Second, every group must build a financial structure capable of sustaining an organization and funding the group's activities. Most interest groups rely on annual membership dues and voluntary contributions from sympathizers. Many also sell some ancillary services, such as insurance and vacation tours, to members. Third, every group must have a leadership and decision-making structure. For some groups, this structure is very simple. For others, it can be quite elaborate and involve hundreds of local chapters that are melded into a national apparatus. Finally, most groups include an agency that actually carries out the group's tasks. This may be a research organization, a public relations office, or a lobbying office in Washington or a state capital.

One example of a successful interest group is the National Rifle Association (NRA). Founded in 1871, the NRA claims a membership of over three million. It employs a staff of 350 and manages an operating budget of $5.5 million. Organized ostensibly to "promote rifle, pistol and shotgun shooting, hunting, gun collecting, home firearm safety and wildlife conservation," the organization has been highly effective in mobilizing its members to block attempts to enact gun control measures, even though such measures are supported by 80 percent of the Americans who are asked about them in opinion polls. The NRA provides numerous benefits to its members, like sporting magazines and discounts on various types of equipment, and it is therefore adept in keeping its members enrolled and active. Though the general public may support gun control, this support is neither organized nor very intense. This allows the highly organized NRA to prevail, even though its views are those of a minority. Although the enactment of the Brady bill, which requires a waiting period for firearms purchases, and the 1994 crime bill, which banned the sale of several types of assault weapons, were defeats of the NRA's agenda, the organization remains one of the most effective lobbies in the nation.

The Characteristics of Members

Membership in interest groups is not randomly distributed in the population. People with higher incomes, higher levels of education, and management or professional occupations are much more likely to become members of groups than those who occupy lower rungs on the socioeconomic ladder.[10] Well-educated, upper-income business and professional people are more likely to have the time and the money, and to have acquired through the educational process the concerns and skills needed to play a role in a group or association. Moreover, for business and professional people, group membership may provide personal contacts and access to information that can help advance their careers. At the same time, of course, corporate entities—businesses and the like—usually have ample resources to form or participate in groups that seek to advance their causes.

The result is that interest-group politics in the United States tends to have a very pronounced upper-class bias. Certainly, there are many interest groups and political associations that have a working-class or lower-class membership—labor organizations or welfare-rights organizations, for example—but the great majority of interest groups and their members are drawn from the middle and upper-middle classes. In general, the "interests" served by interest groups are the interests of society's "haves." Even when interest groups take opposing positions on issues and policies, the conflicting positions they espouse usually reflect divisions among upper-income strata rather than conflicts between the upper and lower classes.

In general, to obtain adequate political representation, forces from the bottom rungs of the socioeconomic ladder must be organized on the massive scale associated with political parties. Parties can organize and mobilize the collective energies of large numbers of people who, as individuals, may have very limited resources. Interest groups, on the other hand, generally organize smaller numbers of the better-to-do. Thus, the relative importance of political parties and interest

---

[10]Kay Lehman Schlozman and John T. Tierney, *Organized Interests and American Democracy* (New York: Harper & Row, 1986), p. 60.

groups in American politics has far-ranging implications for the distribution of political power in the United States. As we saw in Chapter 10, political parties have declined in influence in recent years. Interest groups, on the other hand, as we shall see shortly, have become much more numerous, active, and influential.

THE PROLIFERATION OF GROUPS

Over the past thirty years, there has been an enormous increase both in the number of interest groups seeking to play a role in the American political process and in the extent of their opportunity to influence that process. The explosion of interest-group activity during the past quarter century has three basic origins: first, the expansion of the role of government during this period; second, the coming of age of a new and dynamic set of political forces in the United States—a set of forces that has relied heavily on "public interest" groups to advance their causes; and third, a revival of grassroots conservatism in American politics.

The Expansion of Government

Modern governments' extensive economic and social programs have powerful politicizing effects, often sparking the organization of new groups and interests. The activities of organized groups are usually viewed in terms of their effects upon governmental action. But interest-group activity is often as much a consequence as an antecedent of governmental programs. Even when national policies are initially responses to the appeals of pressure groups, government involvement in any area can be a powerful stimulus for political organization and action by those whose interests are affected. A *New York Times* report, for example, noted that during the 1970s, expanded federal regulation of the automobile, oil, gas, education, and health care industries impelled each of these interests to increase substantially its efforts

to influence the government's behavior. These efforts, in turn, had the effect of spurring the organization of other groups to augment or counter the activities of the first.[11]

Similarly, federal social programs have occasionally sparked political organization and action on the part of clientele groups seeking to influence the distribution of benefits and, in turn, the organization of groups opposed to the programs or their cost. In the same vein, federal programs and court decisions in such areas as abortion and school prayer were the stimuli for political action and organization by fundamentalist religious groups. Thus, the expansion of government in recent decades has also stimulated increased group activity and organization.

One contemporary example of a proposed government program that sparked intensive organization and political action by affected interests is the case of health care reform. Soon after his election, President Clinton announced the formation of a health care task force charged with developing plans for a complete overhaul of the nation's medical care system. Claiming that the escalating cost of health care represented a national social and economic crisis, Clinton and other Democratic strategists also believed that the creation of a vast federal health care program would provide them with the opportunity to link major constituency groups to the Clinton administration and the Democratic party for years to come.

While the health care plan was being formulated, major efforts were launched by various groups of physicians, hospitals, pharmaceutical and insurance companies, nurses, mental health professionals, and even chiropractors. Every group claimed to speak for the public interest, although, curiously, each group's understanding of the public interest differed from the others in some significant detail.

[11]John Herbers, "Special Interests Gaining Power as Voter Disillusionment Grows," *New York Times*, 14 November 1978.

The administration denounced all these special interest activities. At one point, Clinton rejected a plea from the American Medical Association to be included in the health care reform planning process.[12] At the same time, however, the administration organized its own public relations campaign to sell health care reform to the public and to Congress.

Clinton presumed (correctly) that congressional Republicans would bitterly oppose this major effort to expand the Democratic party's political base and institutional power. Clearly, Republicans would not accept the president's version of the public interest any more readily than he would accept the health care industry's corporate interests as *the* public interest.

The New Politics Movement and Public Interest Groups

The second factor accounting for the explosion of interest group activity in recent years was the emergence of a new set of forces in American politics that can collectively be called the "New Politics movement."

The **New Politics movement** is a coalition of upper-middle-class professionals and intellectuals that formed during the 1960s in opposition to the Vietnam War and racial inequality. In more recent years, the forces of New Politics have focused their attention on such issues as environmental protection, women's rights, and nuclear disarmament. This movement was spearheaded by young members of the upper middle class for whom the Civil Rights and antiwar movements were formative experiences, just as the Great Depression and World War II had been for their parents. The crusade against racial discrimination and the Vietnam War led these young men and women to become conscious of themselves, and to define themselves, as a political force in opposition to the

public policies and politicians associated with the nation's postwar regime.

Members of the New Politics movement constructed or strengthened "public interest" groups such as Common Cause, the Sierra Club, the Environmental Defense Fund, Physicians for Social Responsibility, the National Organization for Women, and the various organizations formed by consumer activist Ralph Nader. Through these groups, New Politics forces were able to influence the media, the Congress, and even the judiciary, and to enjoy a remarkable degree of success during the late 1960s and early 1970s in securing the enactment of policies they favored while undermining the powers and prerogatives of many members of the postwar governing coalition.

New Politics activists also played a major role in securing the enactment of environmental, consumer, and occupational health and safety legislation. This represented a dramatic change in the thrust of federal regulatory policy, whose primary function previously had been to restrict price competition in regulated industries, enabling firms in these industries to reap handsome profits and to pay above-market wages to their employees. In addition, environmental and community activists defeated numerous public works projects and, along with anti-nuclear activists, they have played an important role in restricting the growth of the multi-billion-dollar nuclear power industry.

Environmental and consumer legislation in particular opened up avenues for participation by public interest groups in the political process. Turning to the courts to enforce their assertions, public interest groups were frequently able to put a halt to federally funded projects that they found objectionable.

New Politics groups sought to distinguish themselves from other interest groups—business groups, in particular—by styling themselves as "public interest" organizations to suggest that they served the general good rather than their own selfish interest. These groups' claims to rep-

---

[12]Robert Pear, "White House Shuns Bigger A.M.A. Voice in Health Changes," *New York Times*, 5 March 1993, p. 1.

resent *only* the public interest should be viewed with caution, however. Quite often, goals that are said to be in the general or public interest are also or indeed primarily in the particular interest of those who espouse them. For example, environmental controls and consumer regulations not only serve a general interest in air and water quality and public safety, they also represent a way of attacking and weakening the New Politics movement's political rivals, especially big business and organized labor, by imposing restrictions on the manner in which goods can be produced, on capital investment, and on the flow of federal resources to these interests.

The term "public interest" has become so ubiquitous that it is not uncommon to find decidedly private interests seeking to hide under its cloak. For example, in 1996, the *Washington Post* looked into the finances of one public interest group, "Contributions Watch." The group, presenting itself as an independent and nonpartisan organization working for campaign finance reform, released a study purporting to detail millions of dollars in political contributions to Democratic candidates by trial lawyers. The implication was that the lawyers' groups had made the contributions as part of their effort to defeat Republican tort law reform proposals. The *Post*'s investigation revealed that Contributions Watch was created by a professional lobbying firm, State Affairs Co. The lobbying firm had been retained by a major Washington law firm, Covington and Burling, on behalf of its client, Philip Morris Tobacco. The giant tobacco company had sought the cover of public interest to mask an attack on its enemies, the trial lawyers, who are presently bringing billions of dollars in damage suits against the tobacco companies.[13] Contribution Watch insisted that its report was accurate.

This example underscores the often ambiguous character of claims that a policy serves the public interest. The public interest is a concept that should be used cautiously. Claims that a group and its programs only serve some abstract public interest must always be viewed with a healthy measure of skepticism.[14]

Conservative Interest Groups

The third factor associated with the expansion of interest-group politics in contemporary America has been an explosion of grassroots conservative activity. For example, the Christian Coalition, whose major focus is opposition to abortion, has nearly 2 million active members organized in local chapters in every state. Twenty of the state chapters have full-time staff and fifteen have annual budgets over $200,000.[15] The National Taxpayers Union has several hundred local chapters. The National Federation of Independent Business (NFIB) has hundreds of active local chapters throughout the nation, particularly in the Midwest and Southeast. Associations dedicated to defending "property rights" are organized at the local level throughout the West. Right-to-life groups are organized in virtually every U.S. congressional district. Even proponents of the rather exotic principle of "home schooling" are organized through the Home School Legal Defense Association (HSLDA), which has 75 regional chapters that, in turn, are linked to more than 3,000 local support groups. Much of this organizational complexity emerged after President Ronald Reagan left office in 1988. Thousands of conservative activists who had gone to Washington to work in the Reagan administration returned to their homes still eager to be involved in conservative politics.

[13]Ruth Marcus, "Tobacco Lobby Created Campaign 'Watchdog,'" *Washington Post*, 30 September 1996, p. 1.

[14]See Benjamin Ginsberg, *The Captive Public* (New York: Basic Books, 1986), Chapter 4. See also David Vogel, "The Public Interest Movement and the American Reform Tradition," *Political Science Quarterly* 95 (Winter 1980), pp. 607–27.

[15]Rich Lowry, "How the Right Rose," *National Review* 66, 11 December 1995, pp. 64–76.

These former officials, who formed what came to be called the "Reagan Diaspora," played a leading role in organizing conservative groups at the local level. For example, lawyers who formerly worked for the Reagan administration are responsible for establishing most of the several dozen conservative public-interest law centers currently active in the U.S. Similarly, members of the Reagan Diaspora have been active in establishing conservative policy organizations, forums, centers, and associations, as well as local chapters of national conservative organizations. This has helped produce an explosion in conservative groups at the state and local levels.[16]

These local conservative organizations were energized by the political struggles that took place during the Bush and Clinton years. Fights over environmental regulation stimulated organization and activity on the part of property rights groups throughout the West, including the organization of armed "citizens' militias," which have been implicated in several acts of violence in recent years. Disputes regarding the Family Medical Leave Act during the Bush presidency and fights over the employer mandates of the Clinton administration's health care reform proposals drew hundreds of thousands of small business owners into the political arena under the auspices of the NFIB. Employer mandates would have required employers to pay much of the cost of their employees' health care coverage, and this outraged most owners of small businesses. In its struggle against employer mandates, the NFIB organized meetings and community forums around the country, and its members began a relentless campaign of letters, telephone calls, and faxes to members of Congress arguing that small business would be ruined by the requirement.[17] During the debates over the Clinton administration's health care proposal, the NFIB's membership rolls grew at the expense of business organizations, like the U.S. Chamber of Commerce, that sought to reach accommodations with the administration.

In a similar vein, battles over the restrictions on gun ownership in the Clinton administration's 1993 crime bill helped the National Rifle Association (NRA) energize local gun owners groups throughout the country. The struggle over a proposed amendment to the 1993 education bill, which would have placed additional restrictions on home schooling, helped the HSLDA enroll thousands of active new members in its regional and local chapters. After an intense campaign, HSLDA succeeded in both defeating the amendment and in enhancing the political awareness and activism of its formerly quiescent members. And, of course, the ongoing struggles over abortion and school prayer have helped the Christian Coalition, the Family Research Council, and other organizations comprising the Christian Right to expand the membership rolls of their state and local organizations. Anti-abortion forces, in particular, are organized at the local level throughout the U.S. and are prepared to participate in political campaigns and legislative battles.

The development of local conservative organizations has been greatly facilitated by the emergence of conservative communications media throughout the U.S. (see also Chapter 8). The most important element of this media is conservative talk radio—discussion programs run by conservative commentators, often featuring conservative politicians and activists as guests, and inviting listener commentary via telephone. Some talk-radio programs are nationally syndicated. The most important of the nationally-syndicated radio hosts of course is Rush Limbaugh, whose program is heard on more than 600 local radio stations. In addition, Limbaugh's syndicated television program is seen on more than 200 local T.V. stations. Other national commentators include former Reaganite operatives Oliver North and G. Gordon Liddy, and also James Dobson, whose

---

[16]Ibid.
[17]Theda Skocpol, *Boomerang: Clinton's Health Security Effort and the Turn against Government in U.S. Politics* (New York: W.W. Norton, 1996).

IN BRIEF BOX

PROLIFERATION OF INTEREST GROUPS

Expansion of government—As the government expands and establishes more programs and agencies to treat different problems, interest groups crop up in response. Once established, groups try to influence government as it develops policy, not only after a policy has been implemented.

Public interest groups—Developed largely by members of the New Politics movement who wished to show that their concern was for the public good, not for their own selfish interests. They have focused their attention on environmental protection, women's rights, nuclear disarmament, and consumer rights.

Conservative interest groups—These groups have grown enormously during the political struggles of the Bush and Clinton years and have been fed by the growth of conservative talk radio. Such groups include the National Taxpayers Union, the Christian Coalition, and the Home School Legal Defense Association.

program—"Focus on the Family"—reaches nearly five million listeners every week and discusses social issues from a conservative Christian perspective. These programs, along with Pat Robertson's Christian Broadcasting Network, focus on national issues and endeavor to present a conservative perspective on national events.

These nationally-syndicated radio and television programs have helped conservatives to promote their ideas on the national level. The emergence of local conservative talk-radio programs in virtually every media market in the nation has been even more important in stimulating grassroots activism. Such programs broadcast in large markets (e.g., programs run by Bob Grant in New York and Michael Reagan in Los Angeles), as well as in smaller cities (e.g., the programs of Blanquita Cullum in Richmond, Virginia, Kirby McClure in Seattle, Washington, Ron Smith in Baltimore, Maryland, and Ray Appleton in Fresno, California.). And rural areas in the Midwest are reached by such programs as Jerry Hughes' "Washington on Trial" on the People's Radio Network.

Local and regional talk-radio programs focus on the activities of grassroots groups and often invite local conservative activists to appear as guests. These programs can be extremely effective in mobilizing support for local electoral and lobbying efforts as well as encouraging local groups to participate in national campaigns. To foster such political mobilization, the House Republican Conference faxes daily news updates to hundreds of local radio hosts who, in turn, urge their listeners to call or write local and national legislators about such issues as lobby reform, welfare reform, and balancing the federal budget.

In addition, local anti-abortion and property rights protests are publicized on talk radio, as are the meeting times and places for grassroots conservative organizations. Talk radio has been such an effective communications network for the conservative movement in recent years that the Democrats have singled it out for attack. For example, in the aftermath of the bombing of the Oklahoma City federal building in 1995, President Clinton asserted that conservative talk-radio hosts were responsible for inspiring violence against government facilities and officials.

This extensive organization has meant that conservatives not only have been able to bring pressure to bear upon the national government, but also have become a real presence in the corridors of state capitols, county seats, and city halls. For example, spurred by conservative groups and conservative radio programs, legislators in all fifty states have introduced property rights legislation. Eighteen states have already enacted laws requiring a "takings impact analysis," before any new government regulation affecting property can go into effect.[18] Such legislation is designed to diminish the ability of state and local governments to enact land use restrictions for environmental or planning purposes. In a similar vein, 17 states, pressed by local conservative groups, have recently enacted legislation protecting or expanding the rights of gun owners.[19]

STRATEGIES: THE QUEST FOR POLITICAL POWER

As we saw, people form interest groups in order to improve the probability that they and their interests will be heard and treated favorably by the government. The quest for political influence or power takes many forms, but among the most frequently used strategies are: going public, lobbying, establishing access to key decision makers, using the courts, and going partisan. These strategies do not exhaust all the possibilities, but they paint a broad picture of groups competing for power through the maximum utilization of their resources (see Process Box 11.1).

Going Public

Going public is a strategy that attempts to mobilize the widest and most favorable climate of opinion. Many groups consider it imperative to maintain this climate at all times, even when they have no issue to fight about. An increased use of this kind of strategy is usually associated with modern advertising. As early as the 1930s, political analysts were distinguishing between the "old

lobby" of direct group representation before Congress and the "new lobby" of public relations professionals addressing the public at large to reach Congress.[20]

One of the best-known ways of going public is the use of institutional advertising. A casual scanning of important mass circulation magazines and newspapers will provide numerous examples of expensive and well-designed ads by the major oil companies, automobile and steel companies, other large corporations, and trade associations. The ads show how much these organizations are doing for the country, for the protection of the environment, or for the defense of the American way of life. Their purpose is to create and maintain a strongly positive association between the organization and the community at large in the hope that these favorable feelings can be drawn on as needed for specific political campaigns later on.

Another form of going public is the **grassroots lobbying** campaign. In such a campaign, a lobby group mobilizes its members and their families throughout the country to write to their representatives in support of the group's position. For example, in 1993, lobbyists for the Nissan Motor Company sought to organize a "grassroots" effort to prevent President Clinton from raising tariffs on imported minivans, including Nissan's Pathfinder model. Nissan's twelve hundred dealers across the nation, as well as the dealers' employees and family members, were urged to dial a toll-free number that would automatically generate a prepared mailgram opposing the tariff to be sent to the president and each of the dealers' senators. The mailgram warned that the proposed tariff increase would hurt middle-class auto purchasers and small businesses like the dealership itself.[21]

Among the most effective users of the grassroots lobby effort in contemporary American poli-

[18]Neil Peirce, "Second Thoughts About Takings Measure," *Baltimore Sun*, 18 December 1995, p. 13A.

[19]Chris Warden, "A GOP Revolution That Wasn't," *Investor's Daily*, 2 January 1996, p. A1.

[20]E. Pendleton Herring, *Group Representation before Congress* (New York: McGraw-Hill, 1936).

[21]Michael Weisskopf and Steven Mufson, "Lobbyists in Full Swing on Tax Plan," *Washington Post*, 17 February 1993, p. 1.

PROCESS BOX 11.1

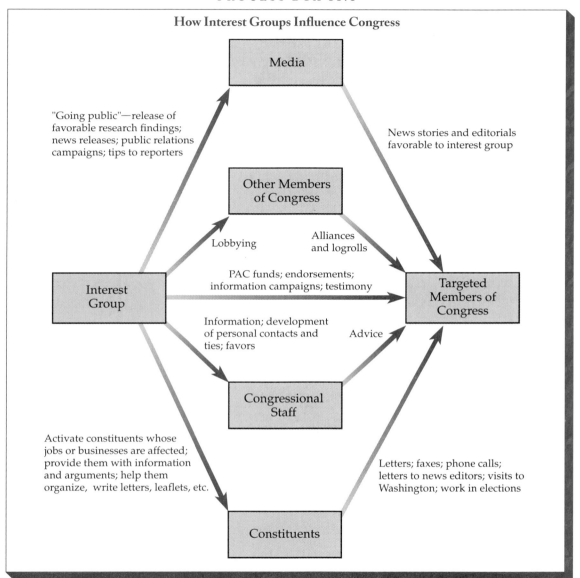

How Interest Groups Influence Congress

tics is the religious Right. Networks of evangelical churches have the capacity to generate hundreds of thousands of letters and phone calls to Congress and the White House. For example, the religious Right was outraged when President Clinton announced soon after taking office that he planned to end the military's ban on gay and lesbian soldiers. The Reverend Jerry Falwell, an evangelist leader, called upon viewers of his television program to dial a telephone number that would add their names to a petition urging Clinton to retain the ban on gays in the military.

CESAR CHAVEZ AND PAT ROBERTSON
Grassroots Populism

GRASSROOTS POLITICS takes many forms in America. One could scarcely find two more different grassroots activists than Cesar Chavez and Pat Robertson.

Cesar Chavez was the son of migrant farmers who harvested crops in Arizona and California. Chavez had long dreamed of organizing migrant workers, who typically labored under the most oppressive and exploitative circumstances. In 1962, he began to organize California grape pickers. In 1966, his group merged with another to form the United Farm Workers Organizing Committee. Shortly after the merger, they won their first big victory: wine grape growers recognized the UFWOC as the official bargaining agent for the workers. Renamed the United Farm Workers (UFW) in 1973, the organization attracted national attention, calling for boycotts on lettuce, grapes, and other produce as a means of forcing growers to make concessions concerning migrant worker safety, wages, and working conditions.

Chavez abhorred violence, finding success in nonviolent grassroots tactics such as picketing, marches, boycotts, fasting, and other legal direct-action methods borrowed from other movement leaders like Mohandas Gandhi and Martin Luther King, Jr. Chavez and his group won some important victories by turning national attention to the plight of migrant workers whose labors brought fresh produce to the rest of the country. In the 1980s, the UFW lost some organizing struggles to the Teamsters Union. Yet Chavez continued to exert key influence, engaging, for example, in a protracted fast in 1988 to draw attention to the use of pesticides considered harmful to both farm workers and consumers. The years of fasting took their toll, however; Chavez died from heart failure in 1993.

Television evangelist turned presidential candidate Gordon M. "Pat" Robertson applied his own grassroots approach to Republican party politics in the 1980s and 1990s. The son of a United States senator, Pat Robertson at first turned his back on politics to start his own

CESAR CHAVEZ

Within a few hours, 24,000 persons had called to support the petition.[22]

Has grassroots campaigning been overutilized? One story in the *New York Times* forces us to ask that question. Ten giant companies in the financial services, manufacturing, and high-tech industries began a grassroots campaign in 1992 and

[22]Michael Weisskopf, "Energized by Pulpit or Passion, the Public Is Calling," *Washington Post*, 1 February 1993, p. 1.

spent millions of dollars over the next three years to influence a decision in Congress to limit the ability of investors to sue for fraud. Retaining an expensive consulting firm, these corporations paid for the use of specialized computer software to persuade Congress that there was "an outpouring of popular support for the proposal." Thousands of letters from individuals flooded Capitol Hill. Many of those letters were written and sent by people who sincerely believed that investor

ministry. In the early 1970s, Robertson took over a run-down television station in Virginia in order to "claim it for the Lord." Within a decade, he had built a television ministry that reached about 30 million homes on the Christian Broadcast Network (CBN) and grossed $200 million per year. Robertson's face became well known because of his television program "The 700 Club." Robertson's electronic grassroots support provided the basis for his move into national politics.

In 1987, Robertson announced that he would seek the Republican nomination for the presidency. Few considered his candidacy serious at first, but once again Robertson demonstrated what the *New York Times* called "awesome organizing ability." Emphasizing family values in his speeches, Robertson activated thousands of fundamentalist Christians, many of whom had never before been involved in politics. In the early party primaries and caucuses, where personal involvement counts the most, Robertson's supporters raised money from small donors and turned out for caucuses and primary elections. To the surprise of most pundits, Robertson finished second in the 1988 Iowa caucuses, and scored well in several primaries.

Yet much of what Robertson said aroused suspicion, including his assertions that only Christians and Jews were fit to govern and that both God and Satan had spoken directly to him, and that the world would end soon. He was labeled as quick-tempered and intolerant by critics, and in the long run his campaign faded. Despite his controversial views, Robertson has remained an important force in the Republican party, serving as a keynote speaker at its 1992 national convention. Robertson's fundamentalist Christian organizing tactics have subsequently spread to other Christian political organizations seeking to win local elections around the country.

As the accomplishments of both Chavez and Robertson illustrate, an individual or movement that can demonstrate its ability to rally significant numbers of motivated citizens to attract national attention or raise money can win important political concessions. Even in the modern media age, grassroots politics matters.

PAT ROBERTSON

SOURCE: Mark P. Petracca, ed., *The Politics of Interests* (Boulder: Westview Press, 1992).

lawsuits are often frivolous and should be curtailed. But much of the mail was phony, generated by the Washington-based campaign consultants; the letters came from people who had no strong feelings or even no opinion at all about the issue. More and more people, including leading members of Congress, are becoming quite skeptical of such methods, charging that these are not genuine grassroots campaigns but instead represent *"Astroturf lobbying"* (a play on the name of an ar-

tificial grass used on many sports fields). Such "Astroturf" campaigns have increased in frequency in recent years as members of Congress grow more and more skeptical of Washington lobbyists and far more concerned about demonstrations of support for a particular issue by their constituents. But after the firms mentioned above spent millions of dollars and generated thousands of letters to members of Congress, they came to the somber conclusion that "it's more effective to have 100 letters from your district where constituents took the time to write and understand the issue," because "Congress is sophisticated enough to know the difference."[23]

Lobbying

Lobbying is an attempt by an individual or a group to influence the passage of legislation by exerting direct pressure on members of the legislature. The First Amendment to the Constitution provides for the right to "petition the Government for a redress of grievances." But as early as the 1870s, "lobbying" became the common term for petitioning—and it is an accurate one. Petitioning cannot take place on the floor of the House or Senate. Therefore, petitioners must confront members of Congress in the lobbies, giving rise to the term "lobbying."

The Federal Regulation of Lobbying Act defines a lobbyist as "any person who shall engage himself for pay or any consideration for the purpose of attempting to influence the passage or defeat of any legislation to the Congress of the United States." Each lobbyist must register with the clerk of the House and the secretary of the Senate. Further legislation enacted in December 1995, requires all individuals lobbying the national government to register and disclose whom they represent, whom they lobby, what they are lobbying for, and how much they are paid. It is estimated currently that fewer than one-third of Washington's professional lobbyists are registered. The new law also prohibits certain types of nonprofit organizations that receive federal grants or contracts from using public funds for the purpose of lobbying the government. This portion of the law was intended by Republicans to dampen the lobbying activities of liberal public-interest groups.

Lobbyists badger and buttonhole legislators, administrators, and committee staff members with facts about pertinent issues and facts or claims about public support of them.[24] Lobbyists can serve a useful purpose in the legislative and administrative process by providing this kind of information. In 1978, during debate on a bill to expand the requirement for lobbying disclosures, Democratic Senators Edward Kennedy of Massachusetts and Dick Clark of Iowa joined with Republican Senator Robert Stafford of Vermont to issue the following statement: "Government without lobbying could not function. The flow of information to Congress and to every federal agency is a vital part of our democratic system."[25] But they also added that there is a dark side to lobbying—one that requires regulation.

The business of lobbying is uneven and unstable. Some groups send their own loyal members to Washington to lobby for them. These representatives usually possess a lot of knowledge about a particular issue and the group's position on it, but they have little knowledge about or experience in Washington or national politics. They tend not to remain in Washington beyond the campaign for their issue.

Other groups, including foreign governments, hire lobbyists with a considerable amount of Washington wisdom. These professional lobbyists, who live in the Washington area, are often lawyers, or former members of Congress, or former employees of government agencies. For example, three former members of Congress, Tom Downey, Marty Russo, and Ed Jenkins, effectively lobbied the House Ways and Means Committee—a committee on which all three had served—on behalf of the prescription drug industry. Lobbyists like them seek to maintain close relationships with government agencies, members of Congress, and congressional staffers.

[23]Jane Fritsch, "The Grass Roots, Just a Free Phone Call Away," *New York Times,* 23 June 1995, pp. A1, A22.

[24]For discussions of lobbying, see Allan J. Cigler and Burdett A. Loomis, eds., *Interest Group Politics* (Washington, DC: Congressional Quarterly Press, 1983). See also Jeffrey M. Berry, *Lobbying for the People* (Princeton: Princeton University Press, 1977).

[25]"The Swarming Lobbyists," *Time,* 7 August 1978, p. 15.

The lobby industry in Washington is growing. At least eighteen hundred associations employing more than forty thousand persons are located in Washington. New groups are moving in all the time, relocating from Los Angeles, Chicago, and other important cities. More than two thousand individuals are registered with Congress as lobbyists, and many local observers estimate that the actual number of people engaged in important lobbying (part-time or full-time) is closer to fifteen thousand. In addition to the various unions, commodity groups, and trade associations, the important business corporations keep their own representatives in Washington.

Gaining Access

Lobbying is an effort by outsiders to exert influence on Congress or government agencies by providing them with information about issues, support, and even threats of retaliation. **Access** is actual involvement in the decision-making process. It may be the outcome of long years of lobbying, but it should not be confused with lobbying. If lobbying has to do with "influence on" a government, access has to do with "influence within" it. Many interest groups resort to lobbying because they have insufficient access or insufficient time to develop access.

One interesting example of a group that had access but lost it, turned to lobbying, and later used a strategy of "going public" is the dairy farmers. Through the 1960s, the dairy industry was part of the powerful coalition of agricultural interests that had full access to the Congress and to the Department of Agriculture. During the 1960s, a series of disputes broke out between the dairy farmers and the producers of corn, grain, and other agricultural commodities over commodities prices. Dairy farmers, whose cows consume grain, prefer low commodities prices while grain producers obviously prefer to receive high prices. The commodities producers won the battle, and Congress raised commodities prices, in part at the expense of the dairy farmers. In the 1970s, the dairy farmers left the agriculture coalition, set up their own lobby and political action groups, and became heavily involved in public relations campaigns and both congressional and presidential elections. The dairy farmers encountered a number of difficulties in pursuing their new "outsider" strategies. Indeed, the political fortunes of the dairy operations were badly hurt when they were accused of making illegal contributions to President Nixon's re-election campaign in 1972.

Access is usually a result of time and effort spent cultivating a position within the inner councils of government. This method of gaining access often requires the sacrifice of short-run influence. For example, many of the most important organized commodity interests in agriculture devote far more time and resources cultivating the staff and trustees of state agriculture schools and county agents back home than buttonholing members of Congress or federal bureaucrats in Washington.

Figure 11.1 is a sketch of one of the most important access patterns in recent American political history: that of the defense industry. Each of these patterns is almost literally a triangular shape, with one point in an executive branch program, another point in a Senate or House legislative committee or subcommittee, and a third point in some highly stable and well-organized interest group. The points in the *"iron triangle"* are mutually supporting; they count as access only if they last over a long period of time. For example, access to a legislative committee or subcommittee requires that at least one member of it support the interest group in question. This member also must have built up considerable seniority in Congress. An interest group cannot feel comfortable about its access to Congress until it has one or more of its "own" people with ten or more years of continuous service on the relevant committee or subcommittee.

A very important example of access politics in action is the military-industrial complex—a

FIGURE 11.1

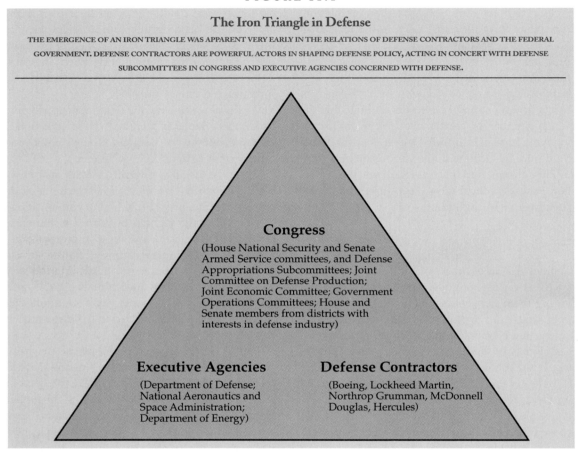

The Iron Triangle in Defense

THE EMERGENCE OF AN IRON TRIANGLE WAS APPARENT VERY EARLY IN THE RELATIONS OF DEFENSE CONTRACTORS AND THE FEDERAL GOVERNMENT. DEFENSE CONTRACTORS ARE POWERFUL ACTORS IN SHAPING DEFENSE POLICY, ACTING IN CONCERT WITH DEFENSE SUBCOMMITTEES IN CONGRESS AND EXECUTIVE AGENCIES CONCERNED WITH DEFENSE.

Congress

(House National Security and Senate Armed Service committees, and Defense Appropriations Subcommittees; Joint Committee on Defense Production; Joint Economic Committee; Government Operations Committees; House and Senate members from districts with interests in defense industry)

Executive Agencies

(Department of Defense; National Aeronautics and Space Administration; Department of Energy)

Defense Contractors

(Boeing, Lockheed Martin, Northrop Grumman, McDonnell Douglas, Hercules)

notion put forth by President Eisenhower in his farewell address in January 1961. The military-industrial complex is a pattern of relationships among manufacturers, the Defense Department, and Congress that has emerged out of America's vast peacetime involvement in international military and economic affairs. More than four years before Eisenhower's farewell address, the House Armed Services Committee conducted a survey of the postmilitary careers of retired officers above the rank of major. The survey disclosed that more than 1,400 officers, including 261 at the rank of general or its equivalent in the navy, had left the armed forces directly for employment by one

of the hundred leading defense contractors.[26] This same pattern was at the heart of the military procurement scandal that rocked the Reagan administration in 1988, when the news media and congressional investigators revealed that some defense contractors had systematically overcharged the Pentagon for military hardware and supplies.

During the Reagan and Bush administrations, the military-industrial complex became more

[26]U.S. Congress, House of Representatives, *Report of the Subcommittee for Special Investigations of the Committee on Armed Services*, 96th Congress, 1st session (Washington, DC: Government Printing Office, 1960), p. 7.

closely linked to the Republican White House than to the Democratic Congress. Indeed, Republicans in the executive branch saw the military-industrial complex as an institutional base that could serve the Republican party in much the same way that the welfare and regulatory agencies of the domestic state served the Democrats. Thus, military and defense agencies, linked to industries and regions of the country that benefited economically from high levels of defense spending, could enhance Republican political strength in the same way that domestic agencies, their clients in the public and not-for-profit sectors, and the beneficiaries of domestic spending programs strengthened the Democrats.

Access to centers of power in Washington can also be secured through the services of certain important Washington lawyers and lobbyists. These individuals can, for a fee, provide access to key members of Congress and to the White House. "Influence peddling" is the negative term for this sale or rental of access that goes on openly in Washington. Former commerce secretary Ron Brown, for example, was an important Washington lawyer-lobbyist, earning nearly one million dollars annually for his services to corporate clients and foreign governments, before joining the administration. Brown's ties to a variety of corporate interests raised many questions about President Clinton's wisdom in appointing him—questions that Brown and his supporters angrily rebutted.[27]

Using the Courts (Litigation)

Interest groups sometimes turn to litigation when they lack access or when they are dissatisfied with government in general or with a specific government program and feel they have insufficient influence to change the situation. They can use the courts to affect public policy in at least three ways: (1) by bringing suit directly on behalf of the group

itself, (2) by financing suits brought by individuals, or (3) by filing a companion brief as *amicus curiae* (literally "friend of the court") to an existing court case.

Among the most significant modern illustrations of the use of the courts as a strategy for political influence are those that accompanied the "sexual revolution" of the 1960s and the emergence of the movement for women's rights. Beginning in the mid-sixties, a series of cases was brought into the federal courts in an effort to force definition of a right to privacy in sexual matters. The case began with a challenge to state restrictions on obtaining contraceptives for nonmedical purposes, a challenge that was effectively made in *Griswold v. Connecticut*, where the Supreme Court held that states could neither prohibit the dissemination of information about nor prohibit the actual use of contraceptives by married couples. That case was soon followed by *Eisenstadt v. Baird*, in which the Court held that the states could not prohibit the use of contraceptives by single persons any more than they could prohibit their use by married couples. One year later, the Court held, in the 1973 case of *Roe v. Wade*, that states could not impose an absolute ban on voluntary abortions. Each of these cases, as well as others, was part of the Court's enunciation of a constitutional doctrine of privacy.[28]

The 1973 abortion case sparked a controversy that brought conservatives to the fore on a national level. These conservative groups made extensive use of the courts to whittle away the scope of the privacy doctrine. They obtained rulings, for example, that prohibit the use of federal funds to pay for voluntary abortions. And in 1989, right-to-life groups used a strategy of litigation that significantly undermined the *Roe v. Wade* decision in the case of *Webster v. Reproductive Health Services* (see Chapter 4), which restored the right of states to place restrictions on abortion.[29]

[27]William Raspberry, "Why Did Ron Brown Become a Target?" *Washington Post*, 20 January 1993, p. A21.

[28]Griswold v. Connecticut, 381 U.S. 479 (1965); Eisenstadt v. Baird, 405 U.S. 438 (1972); Roe v. Wade, 410 U.S. 113 (1973).
[29]Webster v. Reproductive Health Services, 109 S.Ct. 3040 (1989).

INTEREST GROUP STRATEGIES

Going Public
 Especially via advertising; also through boycotts, strikes, rallies, marches, and sit-ins,
  generating positive news coverage

Lobbying
 Influencing the passage or defeat of legislation
 Three types of lobbyists:
 Amateur—loyal members of a group seeking passage of legislation that is currently under
  scrutiny
 Paid—often lawyers or professionals without a personal interest in the legislation who are not
  lobbyists full time
 Staff—employed by a specific interest group full time for the express purpose of influencing or
  drafting legislation

Access
 Development of close ties to decision makers on Capitol Hill

Litigation
 Taking action through the courts, usually in one of three ways:
 Filing suit against a specific government agency or program
 Financing suits brought against the government by individuals
 Filing companion briefs as *amicus curiae* (friend of the court) to existing court cases

Partisan Politics
 Giving financial support to a particular party or candidate
 Congress passed the Federal Election Campaign Act of 1971 to try to regulate this practice by
  limiting the amount of funding interest groups can contribute to campaigns

---

Another extremely significant set of contemporary illustrations of the use of the courts as a strategy for political influence is found in the history of the NAACP. The most important of these court cases was, of course, *Brown v. Board of Education of Topeka*, in which the U.S. Supreme Court held that legal segregation of the schools was unconstitutional.[30]

Business groups are also frequent users of the courts because of the number of government programs applied to them. Litigation involving large businesses is most mountainous in such areas as taxation, antitrust, interstate transportation, patents, and product quality and standardization.

Groups will also sometimes seek legislation designed to help them secure their aims through litigation. During the 1970s, for example, Congress fashioned legislation meant to make it easier for environmental and consumer groups to use the courts. Several regulatory statutes, such as the 1973 Endangered Species Act, contained "citizen suit" provisions, in effect, giving environmental groups the right to bring suits challenging the decisions of executive agencies and the actions of business firms in environmental cases even if the groups bringing suit were not being directly harmed by the governmental or private action in question. Such suits, moreover, could be financed by the expedient of "fee shifting"—that is, environmental or consumer groups could pay for

---

[30]Brown v. Board of Education of Topeka, 347 U.S. 483 (1954).

successful suits by collecting legal fees and expenses from their opponents.

In its decision in the 1992 case of *Lujan v. Defenders of Wildlife* (see Chapter 7), the Supreme Court seemed to question the constitutionality of citizen suit provisions. Justice Scalia indicated that such provisions violated Article III of the U.S. Constitution, which limits the jurisdiction of the federal courts to actual cases and controversies.[31] This means that only persons directly affected by a case can bring it before the court. If the Court were to continue to take this position, the capacity of public interest groups to employ a strategy of litigation would be diminished. Congress, however, has continued to write legislation designed to assist groups in achieving their aims through litigation.

Using Electoral Politics

Many interest groups decide that it is far more effective to elect the right legislators than to try to influence the incumbents through lobbying or through a changed or mobilized mass opinion. Interest groups can influence elections by two means: financial support funded through political action committees, and campaign activism.

POLITICAL ACTION COMMITTEES   By far the most common electoral strategy employed by interest groups is that of giving financial support to the parties or to particular candidates. But such support can easily cross the threshold into outright bribery. Therefore, Congress has occasionally made an effort to regulate this strategy. A recent effort was the Federal Election Campaign Act of 1971 (amended in 1974). This act limits campaign contributions and requires that each candidate or campaign committee itemize the full name and address, occupation, and principal business of each person who contributes more than $100.

These provisions have been effective up to a point, considering the rather large number of embarrassments, indictments, resignations, and criminal convictions in the aftermath of the Watergate scandal.

The Watergate scandal, itself, was triggered by the illegal entry of Republican workers into the office of the Democratic National Committee in the Watergate apartment building. But an investigation quickly revealed numerous violations of campaign finance laws, involving millions of dollars in unregistered cash from corporate executives to President Nixon's re-election committee. Many of these revelations were made by the famous Ervin committee, whose official name was the Senate Select Committee to Investigate the 1972 Presidential Campaign Activities.

Reaction to Watergate produced further legislation on campaign finance in 1974 and 1976, but the effect has been to restrict individual rather than interest group campaign activity. Individuals may now contribute no more than $1,000 to any candidate for federal office in any primary or general election. A political action committee (PAC), however, can contribute $5,000, provided it contributes to at least five different federal candidates each year. Beyond this, the laws permit corporations, unions, and other interest groups to form PACs and to pay the costs of soliciting funds from private citizens for the PACs.

Electoral spending by interest groups has been increasing steadily despite the flurry of reform following Watergate. Table 11.1 presents a dramatic picture of the growth of PACs as the source of campaign contributions. The dollar amounts for each year indicate the growth in electoral spending. The number of PACs has also increased significantly—from 480 in 1972 to almost 4,000 in 1995 (see Table 11.2). Although the reform legislation of the early and mid-1970s attempted to reduce the influence of special interests over elections, the effect has been almost the exact opposite. Opportunities for legally influencing campaigns are now widespread.

---

[31]Lujan v. Defenders of Wildlife , 112 S.Ct. 2130 (1992); see also Linda Greenhouse, "Court Limits Legal Standing in Suits," *New York Times,* 13 June 1992, p. 12.

TABLE 11.1

PAC Spending

YEARS	CONTRIBUTIONS
1977–1978 (est.)	$ 77,800,000
1979–1980	131,153,384
1981–1982	190,173,539
1983–1984	266,822,476
1985–1986	339,954,416
1987–1988	364,201,275
1989–1990	372,100,000
1991–1992	402,300,000
1993–1994	387,426,957

SOURCE: Federal Election Commission.

Indeed, PACs and campaign contributions provide organized interests with such a useful tool for gaining access to the political process that interests of all political stripes are now willing to suspend their conflicts and rally to the defense of political action committees when they come under attack. This support has helped to make the present campaign funding system highly resistant to reform. For example, in May 1996, the Senate considered a bipartisan campaign finance bill sponsored by Senators John McCain (R-Ariz.), Russell Feingold (D-Wisc.), and Fred Thompson (R-Tenn.), which would have abolished political action committees. The bill was staunchly opposed by a coalition of business groups, labor unions, liberal groups like EMILY's List, and conservative groups like Americans for Tax Reform. Though these groups disagree on many substantive matters, they agreed on the principle that abolition of PACs would "diminish the ability of average citizens to join together to have their voices heard." A less positive interpretation was offered by Common Cause president Ann McBride, a proponent of abolishing PACs, who characterized the pro-PAC alliance as an example of "labor and business coming together and agreeing on the one thing that they can agree on, which is maintaining the status quo and their ability to use money to buy outcomes on Capitol Hill."[32]

Given the enormous costs of television commercials, polls, computers, and other elements of the new political technology (see Chapter 10), most politicians are eager to receive PAC contributions and are at least willing to give a friendly hearing to the needs and interests of contributors. It is probably not the case that most politicians

[32]Ruth Marcus, "Campaign Finance Proposal Drawing Opposition from Diverse Group," *Washington Post,* 1 May 1996, p. A12.

TABLE 11.2

Political Action Committee Growth, 1974–1995

AS OF:	CORPO-RATE	LABOR	TRADE	NON-CONNECTED	COOP-ERATIVE	CORP. W/O STOCK	TOTAL
12/31/74	89	201	318				608
12/31/78	785	217	453	162	12	24	1,653
12/31/80	1,206	297	576	376	42	56	2,551
12/31/84	1,682	394	698	1,053	52	130	4,009
12/31/86	1,744	384	745	1,077	56	151	4,157
12/31/92	1,735	347	770	1,145	56	142	4,195
12/31/93	1,715	338	767	1,011	55	139	4,025
12/31/94	1,660	333	792	980	53	136	3,954
7/01/95	1,670	334	804	1,002	43	129	3,982

SOURCE: Federal Election Commission.

simply sell their services to the interests that fund their campaigns. But there is considerable evidence to support the contention that interest groups' campaign contributions do influence the overall pattern of political behavior in Congress and the state legislatures.[33]

A recent lawsuit, for example, brought to light documents recording the activities of the General Electric Company's political action committee over a ten-year period. The PAC made hundreds of thousands of dollars in donations to congressional and senatorial campaigns for individuals who were or could be "helpful" to the company. One House member was given money because company officials felt that his help in protecting a $20 million GE project "alone justifies supporting him."[34]

PACs provide more than just the financial support that individual candidates receive. Under present federal law, there is no restriction on the amount that individuals and interests can contribute directly to the parties for voter registration, grassroots organizing, and other party activities not directly linked to a particular candidate's campaign. Such contributions, called soft money, allow individuals and interest groups to circumvent restrictions on campaign contributions. Critics argue that soft money contributions allow wealthy donors to have unfair influence in the political process. Perhaps this potential does not exist. However, soft money also provides the national and state parties with the means to engage in voter registration and turnout drives. In 1996, the U.S. Supreme Court ruled in the case of *Colorado Republican Party v. Federal Election Commission* that the government could not restrict political parties' use of soft money.[35]

Often, the campaign spending of activist groups is carefully kept separate from party and candidate organizations in order to avoid the restrictions of federal campaign finance laws. So long as a group's campaign expenditures are not coordinated with those of a candidate's own campaign, the group is free to spend as much money as it wishes. Such expenditures are viewed as "issues advocacy" and are protected by the First Amendment and thus not subject to statutory limitation.[36]

In 1996, as mentioned previously, organized labor budgeted $35 million for independent efforts to elect pro-union congressional candidates. At the same time, business groups sought to coordinate their activities through an alliance informally known as "the Coalition." Prominent members of the Coalition included the Chamber of Commerce, the National Federation of Independent Business, the National Association of Manufacturers, the National Association of Wholesale Distributors, and the National Restaurant Association. Coalition members spent tens of millions of dollars on radio and television advertising in support of conservative congressional candidates.

CAMPAIGN ACTIVISM   Financial support is not the only way that organized groups seek influence through electoral politics. Sometimes, activism can be even more important than campaign contributions. Campaign activism on the part of conservative groups played a very important role in bringing about the Republican capture of both houses of Congress in the 1994 congressional elections. For example, Christian Coalition activists played a role in many races, including ones in which Republican candidates were not overly identified with the religious Right. One post-election study suggested that more than 60 percent of the over 600 candidates supported by the Christian Right were successful in state, local, and congressional

[33]See Benjamin Ginsberg and John Green, "The Best Congress Money Can Buy," in *Do Elections Matter?* ed. Benjamin Ginsberg and Alan Stone (Armonk, NY: M.E. Sharpe, 1986).

[34]Charles Babcock, "GE Files Offer Rare View of What PACs Seek to Buy on Capitol Hill," *Washington Post*, 1 June 1993, p. A10.

[35]Filed as Colorado Republican Federal Campaign Committee v. Jones, 95-489 (1996).

[36]Ruth Marcus, "Outside Groups Pushing Election Laws into Irrelevance," *Washington Post*, 8 August, 1996, p. A9.

DEBATING THE ISSUES

PACs and Politics

*T*HE ATTEMPT *to reform campaign finance laws in the early 1970s had an unintended effect: It prompted an explosion in the number and influence of political action committees (PACs), organizations formed by corporations, unions, trade associations, and other entities to raise and distribute campaign contributions. Now numbering in the thousands, PACs are perfectly legal, yet are often condemned for corrupting the political process and providing incumbents with even more political advantages. (PACs rarely contribute to challengers since they have little chance of defeating incumbents.)*

Campaign finance expert Herbert Alexander defends PACs, arguing that the case against them is exaggerated. Public interest activist Fred Wertheimer summarizes the objections to PACS.

ALEXANDER

Seen in historical perspective, political action committees represent a functional system for political fundraising that developed, albeit unintentionally, from efforts to reform the political process. PACs represent an expression of an issue politics that resulted from attempts to remedy a sometimes unresponsive political system. And they represent an institutionalization of the campaign fund solicitation process that developed from the enactment of reform legislation intended to increase the number of small contributors. . . . PAC supporters . . . should question the unarticulated assumptions at the basis of much anti-PAC criticism. Money is not simply a necessary evil in the political process. By itself money is neutral. . . . There is nothing inherently immoral or corrupting about corporate or labor contributions of money. . . . All campaign contributions are not attempts to gain special favors. . . . Money is not the sole, and often not even the most important, political resource. . . . Curbing interest group contributions will not free legislators of the dilemma of choosing between electoral necessity and legislative duty. . . . A direct dialogue between candidates and individual voters without interest group influence is not possible in a representative democracy. . . . The freedom to join in

races in 1994.[37] The efforts of conservative Republican activists to bring voters to the polls is one major reason that turnout among Republicans exceeded Democratic turnout in a midterm election for the first time since 1970. This increased turnout was especially marked in the South, where the Christian Coalition was most active. In many congressional districts, Christian Coalition efforts on behalf of the Republicans were augmented by grassroots campaigns launched by the National Rifle Association (NRA) and the National Federation of Independent Business (NFIB). The NRA

had been outraged by Democratic support for gun control legislation, while the NFIB had been energized by its campaign against employer mandates in the failed Clinton health care reform initiative. Both groups are well organized at the local level and were able to mobilize their members across the country to participate in congressional races.

In 1996, by contrast, it was the Democrats who benefitted from campaign activism. Organized labor made a major effort to mobilize its members for the campaign. Conservative activists, on the other hand, were not enthusiastic about GOP presidential candidate Bob Dole or his running mate Jack Kemp and failed to mobilize their forces for a maximum campaign effort. Dole be-

[37]Richard L. Burke, "Religious-Right Candidates Gain as GOP Turnout Rises," *New York Times*, 12 November 1994, p. 10.

common cause with other citizens remains indispensable to our democratic system. The pursuit of self-interest is . . . a condition, not a problem.[1]

WERTHEIMER

The growth of PACs and the increased importance of PAC money have had a negative effect on two different parts of the political process—congressional elections and congressional decision making. First, PAC money tends to make congressional campaigns less competitive because of the overwhelming advantage enjoyed by incumbents in PAC fund-raising. The ratio of PAC contributions to incumbents over challengers in 1984 House races was 4.6 to 1.0; in the Senate, incumbents in 1984 enjoyed a 3.0 to 1.0 advantage in PAC receipts [comparable ratios hold for subsequent elections]. . . . The advantage enjoyed by incumbents is true for all kinds of PAC giving—for contributions by labor groups, corporate PACs, and trade and membership PACs. . . .

Second, there is a growing awareness that PAC money makes a difference in the legislative process, a difference that is inimical to our democracy. PAC dollars are given by special interest groups to gain special access and special influence in Washington. Most often PAC contributions are made with a legislative purpose in mind. . . .

Common Cause and others have produced a number of studies that show a relationship between PAC contributions and legislative behavior. The examples run the gamut of legislative decisions. . . .

PAC gifts do not guarantee votes or support. PACs do not always win. But PAC contributions do provide donors with critical access and influence; they do affect legislative decisions and are increasingly dominating and paralyzing the legislative process.[2]

[1]Herbert Alexander, "The Case for PACs," Public Affairs Council monograph (Washington, DC, 1983).
[2]Fred Wertheimer, "Campaign Finance Reform: The Unfinished Agenda," *The Annals of the American Academy of Political and Social Science* 486 (July 1986), pp. 92–93.

latedly recognized his need for the support of these activists, but was never able to energize them in sufficient numbers to affect the outcome of the election.[38]

GROUPS AND INTERESTS— THE DILEMMA

James Madison wrote that "liberty is to faction what air is to fire."[39] By this he meant that the or-ganization and proliferation of interests were inevitable in a free society. To seek to place limits on the organization of interests, in Madison's view, would be to limit liberty itself. Madison believed that interests should be permitted to regulate themselves by competing with one another. So long as competition among interests was free, open, and vigorous, there would be some balance of power among them and none would be able to dominate the political or governmental process.

There is considerable competition among organized groups in the United States. For example, pro-choice and anti-abortion forces continue to be locked in a bitter struggle. Nevertheless, interest-group politics is not as free of bias as Madisonian

[38]John Harwood, "Dole Presses Hot-Button Issues to Try to Rouse GOP Activists Missing from Campaign So Far," *Wall Street Journal*, 16 October 1996, p. A22.
[39]Rossiter, ed., *The Federalist Papers*, No. 10, p. 78.

theory might suggest. Though the weak and poor do occasionally become organized to assert their rights, interest-group politics is generally a form of political competition in which the wealthy and powerful are best able to engage.

Moreover, though groups sometimes organize to promote broad public concerns, interest groups more often represent relatively narrow, selfish interests. Small, self-interested groups can be organized much more easily than large and more diffuse collectives. For one thing, the members of a relatively small group—say, bankers or hunting enthusiasts—are usually able to recognize their shared interests and the need to pursue them in the political arena. Members of large and more diffuse groups—say, consumers or potential victims of firearms—often find it difficult to recognize their shared interests or the need to engage in collective action to achieve them.[40] This is why causes presented as public interests by their proponents often turn out, upon examination, to be private interests wrapped in a public mantle.

Thus, we have a dilemma to which there is no ideal answer. To regulate interest-group politics is, as Madison warned, to limit freedom and to expand governmental power. Not to regulate interest-group politics, on the other hand, may be to ignore justice. Those who believe that there are simple solutions to the problems of political life would do well to ponder this problem.

[40]Mancur Olson, Jr., *The Logic of Collective Action* (Cambridge: Harvard University Press, 1971).

Chapter Review

Efforts by organized groups to influence government and policy are becoming an increasingly important part of American politics. The expansion of government over the past several decades has fueled an expansion of interest-group activity. In recent years upper-middle-class Americans have organized public interest groups to vie with more specialized interests. All groups use a number of strategies to gain power.

Going public is an effort to mobilize the widest and most favorable climate of opinion. Advertising is a common technique in this strategy.

Lobbying is the act of petitioning legislators. Lobbyists—individuals who receive some form of compensation for lobbying—are required to register in the House and Senate. In spite of an undeserved reputation for corruption, they serve a useful function, providing members of Congress with a vital flow of information.

Access is participation in government. Groups with access have less need for lobbying. Most groups build up access through great effort. They work years to get their members into positions of influence on congressional committees.

Litigation sometimes serves interest groups when other strategies fail. Groups may bring suit on their own behalf, finance suits brought by individuals, or file *amicus curiae* briefs.

Groups engage in electoral politics either by embracing one of the major parties, usually through financial support or through a nonpartisan strategy. Interest groups' campaign contributions now seem to be flowing into the coffers of candidates at a faster rate than ever before.

TIME LINE ON INTEREST GROUPS

Events	Institutional Developments
Early trade associations and unions formed (1820s and 1830s)	Term "lobbyist" is first used (1830)
Citizen groups and movements form—temperance (1820s), antislavery (1810–1830), women's (1848), abolition (1850s)	Local regulations restricting or forbidding manufacture and sale of alcohol (1830–1860); several states pass laws granting women control over their property (1839–1860s)

1850

Civil War (1861–1865)	
	Lobbying is recognized in law and practice (1870s)
Development of agricultural groups, including the Grange (1860s–1870s)	Grangers successfully lobby for passage of "Granger laws" to regulate rates charged by railroads and warehouses (1870s)

1880

Farmers' Alliances and Populists (1880s–1890s)	Beginnings of labor and unemployment laws (1880s)
American Federation of Labor (AFL) formed (1886)	Election of candidates pledged to farmers (1890s)
Middle-class Progressive movement and trade associations (1890s)	Women's suffrage granted by Wyoming, Colorado, Utah, Idaho (1890s)
Growth of movement for women's suffrage (1890s)	Laws for direct primary, voter registration, regulation of business (1890s–1910s)

1900

Strengthening of women's movements—temperance (1890s) and suffrage (1914)	
World War I (1914–1918)	Prohibition (Eighteenth) Amendment ratified (1919)
American Farm Bureau Federation (1919); farm bloc (1920s)	Nineteenth Amendment gives women the vote (1920)
Growth of trade associations (1920s)	Corrupt practices legislation passed; lobbying registration legislation (1920s)
Teapot Dome scandal (1924)	Farm bloc lobbies for farmers (1921–1923)
CIO is formed (1938)	Wagner National Labor Relations Act (1935)

1940

U.S. in World War II (1941–1945)	Federal Regulation of Lobbying Act (1946)
Postwar wave of strikes in key industries (1945–1946)	Taft-Hartley Act places limits on unions (1947)

Events		Institutional Developments
	1950	
AFL and CIO merge (1955)		
Senate hearings into labor racketeering (1950s)		Landrum-Griffin Act to control union corruption (1959)
Civil Rights movement—boycotts, sit-ins, vote drives (1957), March on Washington (1963)		Passage of Civil Rights acts (1957, 1960, 1964), Voting Rights Act (1965)
National Organization for Women (NOW) formed (1966)		
Vietnam War: antiwar movement (1965–1973)	**1970**	End of draft (1973)
Watergate scandal (1972–1974)		Campaign spending legislation leads to PACs (1970s)
Pro-life and pro-choice groups emerge (post-1973)		*Roe v. Wade* (1973)
Public interest groups formed (1970s–1980s)		Consumer, environmental, health, and safety legislation (1970s)
Moral Majority formed (late 1970s)		Ethics in Government Act (1978)
Pentagon procurement scandal (1988)		PACs help to elect conservative candidates (1980s)
		Further regulation of lobbying (1980s)
Keating Five investigation (1990–1991)	**1990**	
Intense efforts by interest groups to influence Clinton health care and economic proposals (1993)		Clinton proposals to restrict corporate lobbying activities (1993)
		Expanded use of new technologies for grassroots lobby efforts (1993)

KEY TERMS

access The actual involvement of interest groups in the decision-making process.

Astroturf lobbying A negative term used to describe group-directed and exaggerated grassroots lobbying.

going public A strategy that attempts to mobilize the widest and most favorable climate of opinion.

grassroots lobbying A lobbying campaign in which a group mobilizes its membership to contact government officials in support of the group's position.

interest group A group of people organized around a shared belief or mutual concern who try to influence the government to make policies promoting their belief or respectful of their concerns.

iron triangle The stable and cooperative relationships that often develop between a congressional committee, an administrative agency, and one or more supportive interest groups. Not all of these relationships are triangular, but the iron triangle is the most typical.

lobbying Strategy by which organized interests seek to influence the passage of legislation by exerting direct pressure on members of the legislature; this term is derived from having to wait in the lobbies just outside the floor of the legislature, where outsiders are not permitted.

New Politics movement Political movement that began in the 1960s and 1970s, made up of professionals and intellectuals for whom the Civil Rights and antiwar movements were formative experiences. The New Politics movement strengthened public-interest groups.

pluralism The theory that all interests are and should be free to compete for influence in the government.

The outcome of this competition is compromise and moderation.

public interest groups Lobbies that claim they serve the general good rather than their own particular interest, such as consumer protection or environmental lobbies.

FOR FURTHER READING

Cigler, Allan J., and Burdett A. Loomis, eds. *Interest Group Politics.* Washington, DC: Congressional Quarterly Press, 1983.

Clawson, Dan, Alan Neustadtl, and Denise Scott. *Money Talks: Corporate PACs and Political Influence.* New York: Basic Books, 1992.

Costain, Anne. *Inviting Women's Rebellion: A Political Process Interpretation of the Women's Movement.* Baltimore, MD: Johns Hopkins University Press, 1992.

Day, Christine. *What Older Americans Think: Interest Groups and Aging Policy.* Princeton: Princeton University Press, 1990.

Goldfield, Michael. *The Decline of Organized Labor in the United States.* Chicago: University of Chicago Press, 1987.

Hansen, John Mark. *Gaining Access: Congress and the Farm Lobby, 1919–1981.* Chicago: University of Chicago Press, 1991.

Heinz, John P., et al. *The Hollow Core: Private Interests in National Policy Making.* Cambridge, MA: Harvard University Press, 1993.

Lowi, Theodore J. *The End of Liberalism.* New York: W. W. Norton, 1979.

Moe, Terry M. *The Organization of Interests.* Chicago: University of Chicago Press, 1980.

Olsen, Mancur, Jr. *The Logic of Collective Action: Public Goods and the Theory of Groups.* Cambridge: Harvard University Press, 1971.

Olzak, Susan. *The Dynamics of Ethnic Competition and Conflict.* Stanford, CA: Stanford University Press, 1992.

Paige, Connie. *The Right-to-Lifers.* New York: Summit, 1983.

Petracca, Mark, ed. *The Politics of Interests: Interest Groups Transformed.* Boulder, CO: Westview, 1992.

Pope, Jacqueline. *Biting the Hand That Feeds Them: Women on Welfare at the Grass Roots Level.* New York: Praeger, 1989.

Schlozman, Kay Lehman, and John T. Tierney. *Organized Interests and American Democracy.* New York: Harper & Row, 1986.

Staggenborg, Suzanne. *The Pro-Choice Movement: Organization and Activism in the Abortion Conflict.* New York: Oxford University Press, 1991.

Truman, David. *The Governmental Process: Political Interests and Public Opinion.* New York: Alfred A. Knopf, 1951.

Vogel, David. *Fluctuating Fortunes.* New York: Basic Books, 1989.

CHAPTER 12

Introduction to Public Policy

*T*RY AS WE MAY to have a system of limited government, where freedom and control are balanced, control must be the first priority. Without public order—that is, a predictable and relatively safe society—our freedom would not count for much.

The most deliberate form of government control we call "public policy." *Public policy* is an officially expressed intention backed by a sanction, and that sanction can be a reward or a punishment. A public policy may also be called a law, a rule, a statute, an edict, a regulation, an order. Today, "public policy" is the preferred term, probably because it conveys more of an impression of flexibility and compassion than other terms. But citizens, especially students of political science, should never forget that "policy" and "police" have common origins. Both derive from *polis* and *polity*, which refer to the political community, and "political community" is another, more positive term for public order. A public policy is thus composed of two parts—(1) one or more goals; and (2) some kind of a sanction. The first has to do with the purposes of government. The second is concerned with the means of achieving those purposes. Governments adopt many policies to pursue many goals, which is why Congress is so busy

all the time. In contrast, there are very few types of sanctions to provide government with the means of fulfilling those purposes. We call these sanctions "techniques of control" to indicate the coercive aspect of policy. We deal with these in the first section of this chapter precisely because there are so few of them. The second section of this chapter will discuss some examples of actual policy goals that are served by these techniques of control.

TECHNIQUES OF CONTROL

Techniques of control are to policy makers roughly what tools are to a carpenter. There are a limited number of techniques; there is a logic or an orderliness to each of them; and there is an accumulation of experience that helps us know if a certain technique is likely to work. There is no unanimous agreement on technique, just as carpenters will disagree about the best tool for a task. But we offer here a workable elementary handbook of techniques that will be useful for analyzing all policies.

The In Brief Box opposite lists important techniques of control available to policy makers. They

IN BRIEF BOX

TECHNIQUES OF PUBLIC CONTROL

Types of Techniques	Techniques	Definitions and Examples
Promotional techniques	Subsidies and grants of cash, land, etc.	"Patronage" is the promotion of private activity through what recipients consider "benefits" (example: in the nineteenth century the government encouraged westward settlement by granting land to those who went west)
	Contracting	Agreements with individuals or firms in the "private sector" to purchase goods or services
	Licensing	Unconditional permission to do something that is otherwise illegal (franchise, permit)
Regulatory techniques	Criminal penalties	Heavy fines or imprisonment; loss of citizenship
	Civil penalties	Less onerous fines, probation, exposure, restitution
	Administrative regulation	Setting interest rates, maintaining standards of health, investigating and publicizing wrongdoing
	Subsidies, contracting, and licensing	Regulatory techniques when certain conditions are attached (example: the government refuses to award a contract to firms that show no evidence of affirmative action in hiring)
	Regulatory taxation	Taxes that keep consumption or production down (liquor, gas, cigarette taxes)
	Expropriation	"Eminent domain"—the power to take private property for public use
Redistributive techniques	Fiscal use of taxes	Altering the distribution of money by changing taxes or tax rules
	Fiscal use of budgeting	Deficit spending to pump money into the economy when it needs a boost; creating a budget surplus through taxes to discourage consumption in inflationary times
	Fiscal use of credit and interest (monetary techniques)	Changing interest rates to affect both demand for money and consumption. When rates are low it is easy to borrow and thus invest and consume

are grouped into three categories—promotional, regulatory, and redistributive techniques. In this section, the specifics of each will be discussed and explained. Each category of policy is associated with a different kind of politics. In other words, since these techniques are different ways of using government, each type is likely to develop a distinctive pattern of power.

Promotional Techniques

Promotional techniques are the carrots of public policy. Their purpose is to encourage people to do something they might not otherwise do, or to get people to do more of what they are already doing. Sometimes the purpose is merely to compensate people for something done in the past. As the

CORE OF THE ARGUMENT

- Governments establish public order with three techniques of control: promotional, regulatory, and redistributive policies.
- Promotional techniques bestow benefits, regulatory techniques directly control individual conduct, and redistributive techniques manipulate the entire economy.
- Social policies fall into two main categories: welfare policies, intended to address materially problems of poverty and dependency; and civil rights policies, intended to address problems of inequality.
- The Social Security Act of 1935 distinguished between two kinds of welfare policies: contributory programs, generally called "social security," to which people must pay in order to receive benefits; and noncontributory programs, also called "welfare" or "public assistance," for which eligibility is determined by means testing.
- Affirmative action, the legislative effort to redress inequality of results as well as inequality of opportunity, has become a significant but controversial element of federal social policy.

In Brief Box demonstrates, promotional techniques can be classified into at least three separate types—subsidies, contracts, and licenses.

SUBSIDIES *Subsidies* are simply government grants of cash, goods, services, or land. Although subsidies are often denounced as "giveaways," they have played a fundamental role in the history of government in the United States. As we discussed in Chapter 3, subsidies were the dominant form of public policy of the national government throughout the nineteenth century. They continue to be an important category of public policy at all levels of government. The first planning document ever written for the national gov-

ernment, Alexander Hamilton's *Report on Manufactures*, was based almost entirely on Hamilton's assumption that American industry could be encouraged by federal subsidies and that these were not only desirable but constitutional.

The thrust of Hamilton's plan was not lost on later policy makers. Subsidies in the form of land grants were given to farmers and to railroad companies to encourage western settlement. Substantial cash subsidies have traditionally been given to commercial shipbuilders to help build the commercial fleet and to guarantee the use of the ships as military personnel carriers in time of war.

Subsidies have always been a technique favored by politicians because subsidies can be treated as "benefits" that can be doled out in response to many demands that might otherwise produce profound conflict. Subsidies can, in other words, be used to buy off the opposition.

So widespread is the use of the subsidy technique in government that it takes encyclopedias to keep track of them all. Indeed, for a number of years, one company published an annual *Encyclopedia of U.S. Government Benefits*, a thousand-page guide to benefits

> for every American—from all walks of life. . . . [R]ight now, there are thousands of other American Taxpayers who are missing out on valuable Government Services, simply because they do not know about them. . . . Start your own business. . . . Take an extra vacation. . . . Here are all the opportunities your tax dollars have made possible.[1]

Another secret of the popularity of subsidies is that those who receive the benefits do not perceive the controls inherent in them. In the first place, most of the resources available for subsi-

[1] Roy A. Grisham and Paul McConaughty, eds., *Encyclopedia of U.S. Government Benefits* (Union City, NJ: William H. Wise, 1972). The quote is taken from the dust jacket. A comparable guide published by the *New York Times* is called *Federal Aid for Cities and Towns* (New York: Quadrangle Books, 1972). It contains 1,312 pages of federal government benefits that cities and towns, rather than individuals, can apply for.

dies come from taxation. (In the nineteenth century, there was a lot of public land to distribute, but that is no longer the case.) Second, the effect of any subsidy has to be measured in terms of what people *would be doing* if the subsidy had not been available. For example, many thousands of people settled in lands west of the Mississippi only because land subsidies were available. Hundreds of research laboratories exist in universities and corporations only because certain types of research subsidies from the government are available. And finally, once subsidies exist, the threat of their removal becomes a very significant technique of control.

CONTRACTING   Like any corporation, a government agency must purchase goods and services by contract. The law requires open bidding for a substantial proportion of these contracts because government contracts are extremely valuable to businesses in the private sector and because the opportunities for abuse are great. But contracting is more than a method of buying goods and services. Contracting is also an important technique of policy because government agencies are often authorized to use their **contracting power** as a means of encouraging corporations to improve themselves, as a means of helping to build up whole sectors of the economy, and as a means of encouraging certain desirable goals or behavior, such as equal employment opportunity.

For example, the infant airline industry of the 1930s was nurtured by the national government's lucrative contracts to carry airmail. A more recent example is the use of contracting to encourage industries, universities, and others to engage in research and development.

The power of contracting was of great significance for administrations like those of Reagan and Bush because of their commitment to "privatization." When a presidential administration wants to turn over as much government as possible to the private sector, it may seek to terminate a government program and leave the activity to private companies to pick up. That would be true privatization. But in most instances, true privatization is neither sought nor achieved. Instead, the government program is transferred to a private company to provide the service *under a contract with the government,* paid for by the government, and supervised by a government agency. In this case, privatization is only a euphemism. Government by contract has been around for a long time and has always been seen by business as a major source of economic opportunity.

LICENSING   A *license* is a privilege granted by a government to do something that it otherwise considers to be illegal. For example, state laws make practicing medicine or driving a taxi illegal without a license. The states then create a board of doctors and a "hack bureau" to grant licenses for the practice of medicine or for the operation of a cab to all persons who have met the particular qualifications specified in the statute or by the agency.

Like subsidies and contracting, licensing has two sides. One is the giveaway side, making the license a desirable object of patronage. The other side of licensing is the control or regulatory side.

Regulatory Techniques

If promotional techniques are the carrots of public policy, **regulatory techniques** can be considered the sticks. Regulation comes in several forms, but every regulatory technique shares a common trait—direct government control of conduct. The conduct may be regulated because people feel it is harmful to others, or threatens to be, such as drunk driving or false advertising. Or the conduct may be regulated because people think it's just plain immoral, whether it is harming anybody or not, such as prostitution, gambling, or drinking. Because there are many forms of regulation, we have subdivided them here: (1) police regulation, through civil and criminal penalties, (2) administration regulation, and (3) regulatory taxation.

POLICE REGULATION   "Police regulation" is not a technical term, but we use it for this category because these techniques come closest to the tradition exercise of *police power*. After a person's arrest and conviction, these techniques are administered by courts and, where necessary, penal institutions. They are regulatory techniques.

Civil penalties usually refer to fines or some other form of material restitution (such as public service) as a sanction for violating civil laws or such common law principles as negligence. Civil penalties can range from a $5 fine for a parking violation to a heavier penalty for late payment of income taxes to the much more onerous penalties for violating antitrust laws against unfair competition or environmental protection laws against pollution. *Criminal penalties* usually refer to imprisonment but can also involve heavy fines and the loss of certain civil rights and liberties, such as the right to vote or the freedom of speech.

ADMINISTRATIVE REGULATION   Police regulation addresses conduct considered immoral. In order to eliminate such conduct, strict laws have been passed and severe sanctions enacted. But what about conduct that is not considered morally wrong but has harmful consequences? There is, for example, nothing morally wrong with radio or television broadcasting. But broadcasting on a particular frequency or channel is regulated by government because there would be virtual chaos if everybody could broadcast on any frequency at any time.

This kind of conduct is thought of less as *policed* conduct and more as *regulated* conduct. When conduct is said to be regulated, the purpose is rarely to eliminate the conduct but rather to influence it toward more appropriate channels, toward more appropriate locations, or toward certain qualified types of persons, all for the purpose of minimizing injuries or inconveniences. This type of regulated conduct is sometimes called *administrative regulation* because the controls are given over to administrative agencies rather than

to the police. Each regulatory agency in the executive branch has extensive powers to keep a sector of the economy under surveillance and also has powers to make rules dealing with the behavior of individual companies and people. But these administrative agencies have fewer powers of punishment than the police and the courts have, and the administrative agencies generally rely on the courts to issue orders enforcing the rules and decisions made by the agencies.

Sometimes a government will adopt administrative regulation if an economic activity is considered so important that it is not to be entrusted to competition among several companies in the private sector. This is the rationale for the regulation of local or regional power companies. A single company, traditionally called a "utility," is given an exclusive license (or franchise) to offer these services, but since the one company is made a legal monopoly and is protected from competition by other companies, the government gives an administrative agency the power to regulate the quality of the services rendered, the rates charged for those services, and the margin of profit that the company is permitted to make.

At other times, administrative regulation is the chosen technique because the legislature decides that the economy needs protection from itself— that is, it may set up a regulatory agency to protect companies from destructive or predatory competition, on the assumption that economic competition is not always its own solution. This is the rationale behind the Federal Trade Commission, which has the responsibility of watching over such practices as price discrimination or pooling agreements between companies when their purpose is to eliminate competitors.

Subsidies, licensing, and contracting are listed a second time in the In Brief Box on page 335 because although these techniques can be used strictly as promotional policies, they can also be used as techniques of administrative regulation. It all depends on whether the law sets serious conditions on eligibility for the subsidy, license, or contract. To put it another way, the threat of losing a valuable subsidy, license, or contract can be used by the government as a sanction to improve compliance with the goals of regulation. For example, the threat of removal of the subsidies called "federal aid to education" has had a very significant influence on the willingness of schools to cooperate in the desegregation of their student bodies and faculties. For another example, social welfare subsidies (benefits) can be lowered to encourage or force people to take low-paying jobs, or they can be increased to placate people when they are engaging in political protest.[2]

Like subsidies and licensing, government contracting can be an entirely different kind of technique of control when the contract or its denial is used as a reward or punishment to gain obedience in a regulatory program. For example, Presidents Kennedy and Johnson initiated the widespread use of executive orders, administered by the Office of Federal Contract Compliance in the Department of Labor, to prohibit racial discrimination by firms receiving government contracts.[3] The value of these contracts to many private corporations was so great that they were quite willing to alter if not eliminate racial discrimination in employment practices if that was the only way to qualify to bid for government contracts. Today it is common to see on employment advertisements the statement, "We are an equal opportunity employer."

REGULATORY TAXATION   Taxation is generally understood to be a fiscal technique, and it will be

discussed as such below. But in many instances, the primary purpose of the tax is not to raise revenue but to discourage or eliminate an activity altogether by making it too expensive for most people. For example, since the end of Prohibition, although there has been no penalty for the production or sale of alcoholic beverages, the alcohol industry has not been free from regulation. First, all alcoholic beverages have to be licensed, allowing only those companies that are "bonded" to put their product on the market. Federal and state taxes on alcohol are also made disproportionately high, on the theory that, in addition to the revenue gained, less alcohol will be consumed.

We may be seeing a great deal more regulation by taxation in the future for at least the following reasons. First, it is a kind of hidden regulation, acceptable to people who in principle are against regulation. Second, it permits a certain amount of choice. For example, a heavy tax on gasoline or on smokestack and chemical industries (called an "effluent tax") will encourage drivers and these companies to regulate their own activities by permitting them to decide how much pollution they can afford. Third, advocates of regulatory taxation believe it to be more efficient than other forms of regulation, requiring less bureaucracy and less supervision.

EXPROPRIATION   *Expropriation*—seizing private property for a public use—is a widely used technique of control in the United States, especially in land-use regulation. Almost all public works, from highways to parks to government office buildings, involve the forceful taking of some private property in order to assemble sufficient land and the correct distribution of land for the necessary construction. The vast Interstate Highway Program required expropriation of thousands of narrow strips of private land. "Urban redevelopment" projects often require city governments to use the powers of seizure in the service of private developers, who actually build the urban projects on land that would be far too

---

[2]For an evaluation of the policy of withholding subsidies to carry out desegregation laws, see Gary Orfield, *Must We Bus?* (Washington, DC: Brookings Institution, 1978). For an evaluation of the use of subsidies to encourage work or to calm political unrest, see Frances Fox Piven and Richard Cloward, *Regulating the Poor: The Functions of Public Welfare* (New York: Random House, 1971).

[3]For an evaluation of Kennedy's use of this kind of executive power, see Carl M. Brauer, *John F. Kennedy and the Second Reconstruction* (New York: Columbia University Press, 1977), especially Chapter 3.

PROCESS BOX 12.1

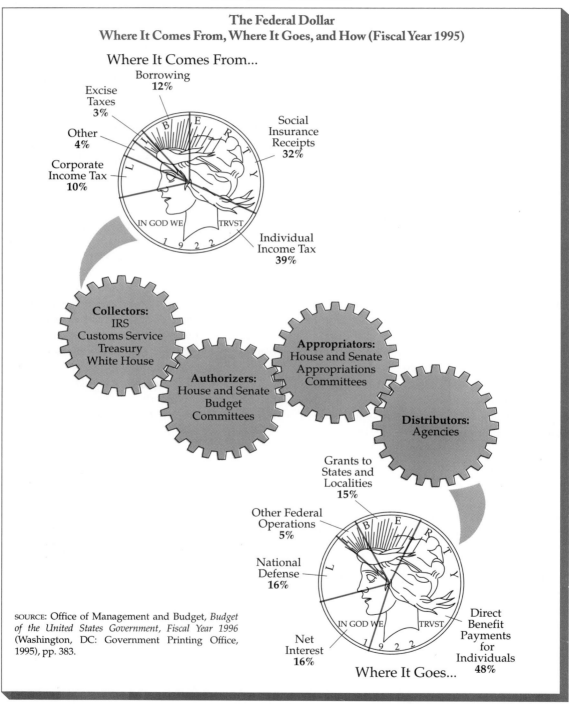

The Federal Dollar
Where It Comes From, Where It Goes, and How (Fiscal Year 1995)

Where It Comes From...

Borrowing
12%

Excise
Taxes
3%

Other
4%

Corporate
Income Tax
10%

Social
Insurance
Receipts
32%

Individual
Income Tax
39%

Collectors:
IRS
Customs Service
Treasury
White House

Authorizers:
House and Senate
Budget
Committees

Appropriators:
House and Senate
Appropriations
Committees

Distributors:
Agencies

Grants to
States and
Localities
15%

Other Federal
Operations
5%

National
Defense
16%

Net
Interest
16%

Direct
Benefit
Payments
for
Individuals
48%

Where It Goes...

SOURCE: Office of Management and Budget, *Budget of the United States Government, Fiscal Year 1996* (Washington, DC: Government Printing Office, 1995), pp. 383.

expensive if purchased on the open market. Private utilities that supply electricity and gas to individual subscribers are given powers to take private property whenever a new facility or a right-of-way is needed.

We generally call the power to expropriate *eminent domain*.[4] The Fifth Amendment of the U.S. Constitution surrounds this expropriation power with important safeguards against abuse, so that government agencies in the United States are not permitted to use that power except through a strict due process, and they must offer "fair market value" for the land sought. Another form of expropriation is forcing individuals to work for a public purpose—for example, drafting people for service in the armed forces.

Redistributive Techniques

Redistributive techniques are usually of two types—fiscal and monetary—but they have a common purpose: to control people by manipulating the entire economy rather than by regulating people directly. As observed earlier, regulatory techniques focus upon individual conduct. The regulatory rule may be written to apply to the whole economy: "Walking on the grass is not permitted," or "Membership in a union may not be used to deny employment, nor may a worker be fired for promoting union membership." Nevertheless, the regulation focuses on individual strollers or individual employers who might walk on the grass or discriminate against a trade union member. In contrast, techniques are redistributive if they seek to control conduct more indirectly by altering the conditions of conduct or manipulating the environment of conduct.

FISCAL TECHNIQUES *Fiscal techniques* of control are the government's taxing and spending powers. Personal and corporate income taxes, which raise most government revenues, are the most prominent examples. While the direct purpose of taxes is to raise revenue, each type of tax has a different impact on the economy, and government can plan for that impact. For example, although the main reason given for increasing the Social Security tax (which is an income tax) under President Carter was to keep Social Security solvent, a big reason for it in the minds of many legislators was that it would reduce inflation by shrinking the amount of money people could spend on goods and services.

Likewise, President Clinton's commitment in his 1992 campaign to a "middle-class tax cut" was motivated by the goal of encouraging economic growth through increased consumption. Soon after the election, upon learning that the deficit was far larger than had earlier been reported, he had to break his promise of such a tax cut. Nevertheless, the idea of a middle-class tax cut is still an example of a fiscal policy aimed at increased consumption, because of the theory that people in middle-income brackets will tend to spend a high proportion of unexpected earnings or windfalls, rather than saving or investing them.[5]

MONETARY TECHNIQUES *Monetary techniques* also seek to influence conduct by manipulating the entire economy through the supply or availability of money. The *Federal Reserve Board* (the Fed) can adopt what is called a "hard money policy" by increasing the interest rate it charges member banks (called the *discount rate*). Another monetary policy is one of increasing or decreasing the *reserve requirement*, which sets the actual proportion of deposited money that a bank must keep "on demand" as it makes all the rest of the deposits available as new loans. A third important technique used by the Fed is *open market*

[4]For an evaluation of the politics of eminent domain, see Theodore Lowi and Benjamin Ginsberg, *Policide* (New York: Macmillan, 1976), especially Chapters 11 and 12, written by Julia and Thomas Vitullo-Martin.

[5]For a fascinating behind-the-scenes look at how and why President Clinton abandoned his campaign commitment to tax cuts and economic stimulus, and instead accepted the fiscal conservatism advocated by the Federal Reserve and its chair, Alan Greenspan, see Bob Woodward, *The Agenda: Inside the Clinton White House* (New York: Simon & Schuster, 1994).

operations—the buying and selling of Treasury securities to absorb excess dollars or to release more dollars into the economy.

SPENDING POWER AS FISCAL POLICY Perhaps the most important redistributive technique of all is the most familiar one—the *"spending power"*—which is a combination of subsidies and contracts. These techniques can be used for policy goals far beyond the goods and services bought and the individual conduct regulated.

One of the most important examples of the national government's use of purchasing power as a fiscal or redistributive technique is found in another of the everyday activities of the Federal Reserve Board. As mentioned above, the Fed goes into the "open market" to buy and sell government bonds in order to increase or decrease the amount of money in circulation. By doing so, the Fed can raise or lower the prices paid for goods and the interest rate paid on loans.

SUBSTANTIVE USES OF PUBLIC POLICIES

The Welfare State as Fiscal and Social Policy

Government involvement in the relief of poverty and dependency was insignificant until the twen-tieth century because of Americans' antipathy to government and because of their confidence that all of the deserving poor could be cared for by private efforts alone. This traditional approach crumbled in 1929 in the wake of the Depression, when some misfortune befell nearly everyone. Americans finally confronted the fact that poverty and dependency could be the result of imperfections of the economic system itself, rather than a result of individual irresponsibility. Americans held to their distinction between the deserving and undeserving poor but significantly altered these standards regarding who was deserving and who was not. And once the idea of an imperfect system was established, a large-scale public approach became practical not only to alleviate poverty but also to redistribute wealth and to manipulate economic activity through fiscal policy.

The architects of the original Social Security system in the 1930s were probably well aware that a large welfare system can be good *fiscal* policy. When the economy is declining and more people are losing their jobs or are retiring early, welfare payments go up automatically, thus maintaining consumer demand and making the "downside" of the business cycle shorter and shallower. Conversely, during periods of full employment or high levels of government spending, when inflationary pressures can mount, welfare taxes take an extra bite out of consumer dollars,

IN BRIEF BOX

THE WELFARE STATE AS FISCAL AND SOCIAL POLICY

Fiscal policy—When the economy is declining and more and more people have less money to spend, welfare payments increase, which helps maintain consumer spending, thus shortening the "downside" of the business cycle. On the other hand, if inflation is threatening, then welfare taxes absorb some consumer dollars, having a (desired) dampening effect on an economy that is growing too quickly.

Social policy—Contributory programs were established in recognition of the fact that not all people have the means to establish financial security, i.e., save for the future. These programs are financed by taxation and can be considered "forced savings." Noncontributory programs provide assistance to those who cannot provide for themselves.

tending to dampen inflation, flattening the "upside" of the economy.

However, the authors of Social Security were more aware of the *social* policy significance of the welfare state. They recognized that a large proportion of the unemployment, dependency, and misery of the 1930s was due to the imperfections of a large, industrial society and occurred through no fault of the victims of these imperfections. They also recognized that opportunities to achieve security, let alone prosperity, were unevenly distributed in our society. This helps ex-

plain how the original Social Security laws came to be called—both by supporters and by critics— "the welfare state." The 1935 Social Security Act provided for two separate categories of welfare— *contributory* and *noncontributory*. Table 12.1 outlines the key programs in each of these categories.

CONTRIBUTORY PROGRAMS *Contributory programs* are financed by taxation in a way that can be called "forced savings." These programs are what most people have in mind when they refer to Social Security or social insurance. Under the

TABLE 12.1

Public Welfare Programs

TYPE OF PROGRAM	STATUTORY BASIS	YEAR ENACTED	NUMBER OF RECIPIENTS IN 1995 (IN MILLIONS)	FEDERAL OUTLAYS IN 1995 (IN BILLIONS)
Contributory (Insurance) System				
Old Age, Survivors, and Disability Insurance	Social Security Act (SSA), Title II	1935	43.3	$334.2
Medicare	SSA Title XVIII	1965	37.1	173.3
Unemployment compensation	SSA Title III	1935	8.9	23.9
Noncontributory (Public Assistance) System				
Medicaid	SSA Title XIX	1965	36.4	96.4
Food stamps	Food Stamp Act	1964	27.2	25.7
Aid to Families with Dependent Children	SSA Title IV	1935	5.1	16.9
Supplemental Security Income (cash assistance for aged, blind, disabled)	SSA Title XVI	1974	6.3	28.2
Housing assistance to low-income families	National Housing Act	1937	NA	23.3
School Lunch Program	National School Lunch Act	1946	37.3	7.6
Training and employment program	Job Training Partnership Act	1982	NA	3.7

NA=Not available.
SOURCE: Office of Management and Budget, *The Budget of the United States Government, Fiscal Year 1995* (Washington, DC: Government Printing Office, 1995), Historical Tables, pp. 176, 217–19; Mid-session Review of the 1995 Budget, pp. 27–28.

original old-age insurance program, the employer and the employee were each required to pay equal amounts, which in 1937 were set at 1 percent of the first $3,000 of wages, to be deducted from the paycheck of each employee and matched by the same amount from the employer. This percentage has increased over the years; the total contribution is now 7.65 percent subdivided as follows: 6.20 percent on the first $65,400 of income for the Social Security benefits and an additional 1.45 percent on all earnings for Medicare.[6]

Social Security is a rather conservative approach to welfare. In effect, the Social Security (FICA) tax is a message that people cannot be trusted to save voluntarily in order to take care of their own needs. But in another sense, it is quite radical. Social Security is not real insurance; workers' contributions do not accumulate in a personal account like an annuity. Consequently, contributors do not receive benefits in proportion to their own contributions, and this means that there is a redistribution of wealth occurring. In brief, contributory Social Security mildly redistributes wealth from higher- to lower-income people, and it quite significantly redistributes wealth from young to old people and from younger workers to older retirees.

NONCONTRIBUTORY PROGRAMS *Noncontributory programs* are also known as public assistance programs. Historically, the two most important ones were aid to the aged, blind, and disabled—now grouped together as *Supplemental Security Income* (SSI)—and *Aid to Families with Dependent Children* (AFDC). Both programs were "means tested," requiring the applicant to show some definite need for assistance and an inability to provide for it.

Over the years, coverage expanded and benefits increased in both contributory and noncontrib-

utory programs and through cash and in-kind benefits. Congress increased Social Security benefits every two or three years during the 1950s and 1960s. The biggest single expansion in contributory programs since 1935 was the establishment in 1965 of *Medicare*, which provides substantial medical services to elderly persons who are already eligible to receive old-age, survivors, and disability insurance under the original Social Security system. In 1972, Congress decided to end the grind of biennial legislation by establishing *indexing*, whereby benefits paid out under contributory programs would be modified annually by *cost of living adjustments* (COLAs) based on changes in the Consumer Price Index, so that benefits would increase automatically as the cost of living rose. But, of course, Social Security taxes (contributions) also increased after almost every benefit increase. This made Social Security, in the words of one observer, "a politically ideal program. It bridged partisan conflict by providing liberal benefits under conservative financial auspices."[7]

The noncontributory public assistance categories also made their most significant advances during the 1960s. The largest single category of expansion was the establishment in 1965 of *Medicaid*, which extended medical services to all low-income persons who had already established eligibility through *"means testing"* under AFDC.

The expansion of all types of benefits and the expansion of the number of persons eligible to receive them added tremendously to the costs of noncontributory welfare programs. Meanwhile, important demographic changes were adding costs to the contributory programs and at the same time were reducing the amount of revenue raised by Social Security taxes. The most important demographic change was an increase in the number of elderly Americans relative to the number of individuals in the workforce. Between the 1950s and the 1980s, the ratio between the two

---

[6]The figures cited are for 1997. Although on paper the employer is taxed, this is all part of "forced savings," because in reality the employer's contribution is nothing more than a mandatory wage supplement that the employee never sees or touches before it goes into the trust fund held exclusively for the contributory programs.

[7]Edward J. Harpham, "Fiscal Crisis and the Politics of Social Security Reform," in *The Attack on the Welfare State*, ed. Anthony Champagne and Edward Harpham (Prospect Heights, IL: Waveland Press, 1984), p. 13.

dropped from a high of eighteen workers for every one retired eligible beneficiary to four workers for every retired eligible beneficiary.[8] This obviously added greatly to the gap between

welfare contributions and welfare obligations which in 1973 was defined as a "fiscal crisis."

Consensus gradually formed for a long-term solution, and in 1977 Congress adopted a series of tax increases extending over thirteen years, the

[8]From *Social Security Bulletins,* quoted in Gary Freeman and Paul Adams, "The Politics of Social Security," in *The Political Economy of Public Policy,* ed. Alan Stone and Edward Harpham

(Beverly Hills, CA: Sage Publications, 1982), p. 245.

PROCESS BOX 12.2

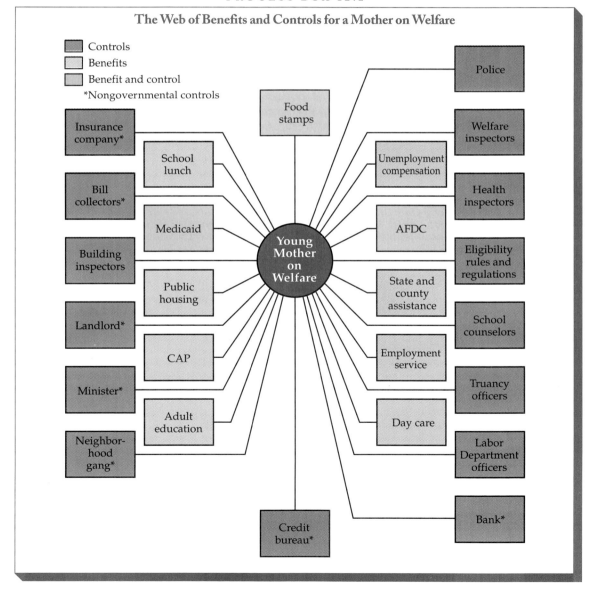

The Web of Benefits and Controls for a Mother on Welfare

DEBATING THE ISSUES

Welfare Reform

*I*N *1996, Congress passed and the president signed a sweeping welfare reform bill. Among other things, the new law cut $55 billion from federal welfare programs over six years, imposed strict work requirements on able-bodied adults, and ended federal guarantees of cash assistance to poor children. Yet debate continues to rage over such provisions as work requirements and other restrictions; even in 1996, one American child in five under the age of 18 lived in poverty. Political scientist Lawrence M. Mead defends work requirements as a way of breaking welfare dependency, while social analysts Richard A. Cloward and Frances Fox Piven argue that such "reform" is simply another name for punishing the poor.*

MEAD

Liberal reformers presume that welfare recipients fail to work because they face special "barriers," notably a lack of jobs, child-care, and training opportunities. If government provided more of these things, liberals assert, welfare work levels would rise. That is a misconception. Research has shown that the presumed impediments rarely keep people from working, at least in low-skilled, low-paid jobs. The main reason for nonwork, rather, is the reluctance of many recipients to take such jobs. The main task of welfare work policy is to overcome that reluctance. While this probably requires some new services, it above all requires more clear-cut *requirements* that recipients work in return for benefits. Those who favor increased benefits are seeking not so much to promote work as to advance the traditional liberal interest in social equality. . . .

The work issue has come to the fore for a good reason: Nonwork is the immediate cause of much poverty and dependency today. There is still a tendency to see the poor simply as victims entitled to government redress. That view is most plausible for the elderly and disabled poor, whom society does not expect to work. But, it is implausible for families headed by able bodied people of working age, whom society does expect to work. . . .

It is true that most poor families have some earnings, yet remain needy. But few of these families have members working full-time. Many more people are poor for lack of work than despite work. Moreover, for the vast majority of workers, poverty is uncommon or transient. Fewer than 3 percent of able-bodied, working-age adults lived in poor households with any earnings in 1970, and only 15 percent of these—or 0.3 percent of all working-age adults—were also poor in 1980. . . .

The great question is how to get more of the employable poor to participate in the economy, in any kind of job, not how to improve those jobs. . . . For it is the *working* people that government would help by raising job quality, and who also have the greatest power to help themselves. Liberals and conservatives can dispute whether working people really need help from government. They ought to agree that dependent adults should at least become workers.[1]

final one taking effect January 1, 1990. Thus, during the 1980s, instead of a deficit, the Social Security Trust Fund began producing surpluses. In 1989, the Social Security surplus—contributions received in excess of benefits paid out—reached over $50 billion. The annual surplus was projected to go up to $200 billion by the year 2002. Around the year 2020 the ratio of retirees to workers will require a drawing down of the surpluses. But by then, there will only be IOUs and not cash in the trust fund. Why? To avoid raising income and sales taxes, the Bush and Reagan administrations

CLOWARD AND PIVEN

[Workfare] proposals reflect a rising tide of antiwelfare rhetoric, whose basic argument is that people receiving public assistance become trapped in a "cycle of dependency.". . . The national press announces that dependency has reached epidemic proportions. According to these accounts, rising unemployment, declining wage levels and disappearing fringe benefits need not concern anyone. "The old issues were economic and structural," [Lawrence] Mead says, and "the new ones are social and personal." . . .

But there is no economically and politically practical way to replace welfare with work at a time when the labor market is saturated with people looking for jobs. Unemployment averaged 4.5 percent in the 1950s, 4.7 percent in the 1960s, 6.1 percent in the 1970s and 7.2 percent in the 1980s, and job prospects look no better in the 1990s. The labor market is flooded with immigrants from Asia and Latin American, and growing numbers of women have taken up jobs to shore up family income as wages decline. Confronted with an increasingly globalized economy, corporations are shedding workers or closing domestic plants and opening new ones in Third World countries with cheap labor. Meanwhile, defense industries are making huge workforce cuts. . . .

Because most mothers who receive Aid to Families with Dependent Children are unskilled, they can command only the lowest wages and thus cannot adequately support their families, a problem that will grow worse as wages continue to decline. According to the Census Bureau, 14.4 million year-round, full-time workers 16 years of age or older (18 percent of the total) had annual earnings below the poverty level in 1990, up from 10.3 million (14.6 percent) in 1984 and 6.6 million (12.3 percent) in 1974. There is no reason to think that A.F.D.C. mothers can become "self-sufficient" when growing millions of currently employed workers cannot. In a study of the finances of welfare families, sociologists Christopher Jencks and Kathryn Edin found that "single mothers do not turn to welfare because they are pathologically dependent on handouts or unusually reluctant to work—they do so because they cannot get jobs that pay better than welfare.". . .

Despite workfare's record of failure, an aura of optimism still permeates the literature on welfare reform. . . . As sociologist Sanford Schram points out, these [workfare] initiatives serve "symbolic purposes at the expense of substantive benefits."

Politicians understand the value of this symbolism, however, and rush to divert voter discontent over rising unemployment and falling wage levels by focusing on "welfare reform," knowing that welfare mothers, a majority of whom are black and Hispanic, make convenient scapegoats.[2]

[1]Lawrence M. Mead, "Jobs for the Welfare Poor: Work Requirements Can Overcome the Barriers," *Policy Review,* Winter 1990.
[2]Richard A. Cloward and Frances Fox Piven, "Punishing the Poor, Again: The Fraud of Workfare," *The Nation,* 24 May 1993.

borrowed from the Social Security Trust Fund by selling it U.S. bonds—essentially IOUs. This could compromise the Social Security system in the future by producing high inflation, which, because of their fixed incomes, hurts the elderly most of all.

President Clinton was elected on a platform of "putting people first," but deficit realities significantly revised the meaning of that promise. His most positive achievement was the increase in 1994 in the Earned Income Tax Credit, by which working households with children can file through their income tax returns for an income supplement if their annual earned incomes are below $20,000. Yet aside from this one benefit increase, Clinton's campaign promise to "end welfare as we know it" had led to no concrete policies by 1995. In 1994, Clinton had proposed a new welfare plan whose key provisions would require 400,000 welfare recipients to find jobs by the year 2000, and would cut off benefits after two years to those who refused to work or to join job-training programs. These were bold proposals, and Clinton's plan did represent a radical departure from traditional federal welfare policies. But his plan was overtaken by the Republican landslide in the 1994 elections, and by 1995 the Republican Congress had proposed even more radical changes in welfare policies: forcing 1.5 million welfare recipients to work by the year 2000, denying public aid to legal immigrants who are not citizens and granting states wide discretion to run welfare programs according to their own wishes.

Nevertheless, the stalemate over welfare was still not to be broken until the waning days of the 104th Congress and the approach of the 1996 presidential campaign. The Personal Responsibility and Work Opportunity Act was signed into law on August 22, 1996, and it went far beyond anything the pundits could have imagined. It was made possible by unusual Republican cohesion in Congress and by the president's decision to endorse the Republican bill, based largely on his fear of public repudiation at the polls in November.

The new law replaces the sixty-one-year-old program of AFDC and its education/work training program, known as JOBS, with block grants to the states over a five-year period for *Temporary Assistance to Needy Families (TANF)*. The Act imposes not only the five-year time limit on the TANF benefits but also requires work after two years of benefits. It also requires community service after two months of benefits, unless the state administrators agree to an exemption of the rule. Many additional requirements for eligibility are spelled out in the law. And the states are under severe obligation to impose all these requirements on the threat of losing their TANF federal grants. The two other important public assistance programs, food stamps and Medicaid, were implicated but not eliminated in the Act. The food stamp program became a "simplified food stamp program," which applies many of the same TANF restrictions as outlined before. Moreover, differences in food stamp benefits from state to state will be permitted to vary even more greatly than variations in cash benefits.

Medicaid was the least affected by the new law.[9] Republicans had hoped to overhaul Medicaid as part of the 1996 welfare reform bill, but a veto threat from President Clinton convinced them that they should let that portion of the bill die in order to save the rest. With continued Republican control of Congress, it is virtually certain we have not heard the last of Medicaid reform. But we have also not heard the last of welfare reform. Even before he signed the bill, Clinton vowed to make it more palatable after the election, saying in one public comment "I think it can be easily fixed." Clinton has no inclination at all to restore welfare as the *entitlement* it was under AFDC. Rather, he has committed himself to changing a few of the controversial but less important aspects of the law. For example, he wants to ease up on the severity of the restrictions in the law against legal immigrants. And he has expressed a commitment to change the provisions that made it difficult for able-bodied adults without dependents to receive food stamps if they are not working. But even this may be difficult, because, as one observer put it, most of the $54.6 billion the welfare law hopes to save over the upcoming six years comes not from AFDC savings

---

[9]The best outline of the provisions of this very long and complex welfare reform law will be found in Vee Burke, "New Welfare Law: Comparison of the New Block Grant Program with Aid to Families with Dependent Children," Library of Congress, Congressional Research Service, 26 August 1996.

SUBSTANTIVE USES OF PUBLIC POLICIES

but from cuts in food stamps and aid to legal immigrants—"the very provisions the administration is trying to revise."[10]

Imperfections in Society: Changing the Rules of Inequality

A capitalist employer will always prefer the most efficient worker at the lowest price and will want to fire or refuse to hire the least efficient. How, then, do we account for the fact that a disproportionate number of African Americans, Hispanic Americans, women, and other minorities are found in poverty in America?[11] This has to be explained by the *social rules* that are shaped by the personal prejudices of individuals and the traditions of communities. Employers may share in these prejudices, but that would be a departure from rational economic behavior. As long as prejudice exists, there will be biases in the composition of the poverty class, unless public policies—that is, regulatory policies—intervene.

As observed in Chapter 4, equal protection of the laws might have been established and implemented by the courts alone. But after a decade of

frustration, the courts and Congress ultimately came to the conclusion that the task of changing the social rules would require legislative and administrative, as well as judicial, action. Table 12.2 provides an overview of the efforts by Congress to make equal protection of the laws a reality. Three civil rights acts were passed during the first decade after the 1954 Supreme Court decision in *Brown v. Board of Education.* But these acts were of only marginal importance. The first two, in 1957 and 1960, established that the Fourteenth Amendment of the Constitution, adopted almost a century earlier, could no longer be ignored, particularly in regard to voting. The third, the Equal Pay Act of 1963, was more important, but it was concerned with women in the public sector and consequently did not touch the question of racial discrimination or discrimination in the private sector.

By far the most important piece of legislation passed by Congress was the Civil Rights Act of 1964. It not only put some teeth in the voting rights provisions of the 1957 and 1960 acts, but also went far beyond voting to attack discrimination in public accommodations, segregation in the schools, and, at long last, the discriminatory conduct of employers in hiring, promoting, and laying off their employees. Discrimination against women was also included, extending the important 1963 provisions. The 1964 act seemed bold at the time, revolutionary to some, but it was enacted ten years after the Supreme Court had declared racial discrimination "inherently unequal" under the Fifth and Fourteenth amendments. And it was enacted after blacks had demonstrated time after time that discrimination was no longer acceptable. The choice in 1964 was not between congressional action or inaction but between legal action or expanded violence.

The 1964 legislation declared discrimination by private employers and state governments (school boards, etc.) illegal, then went even further to provide for administrative agencies to help the courts implement these laws. Title IV of the

---

[10]Jeffrey L. Katz, "Small Change," *The New Republic,* 9 December 1996, p. 15. Katz estimates that cuts in the food stamp distribution could save about $23 billion through 2002; and the savings on the immigrants' provisions would be about the same, including the savings on food stamp distribution to them as well as restrictions on the access of low-income aged, blind, and disabled to SSI.

[11]For example, although many African Americans have improved their economic situations in the past decades, as a group African Americans remain economically deprived. In 1992, the per capita income for white Americans was $15,981; for blacks, it was just $9,296. In 1992, one-seventh of the U.S. population—37 million people—lived in what the government defines as poverty (for a family of four, an income of less than about $14,000). But while 11.6 percent of all whites lived below the poverty level, 33.3 percent of all African Americans lived in poverty. Furthermore, while one in six white children lives in poverty, almost half of all black children, or 46.3 percent, live in poverty. These inequalities of distribution apply not only to blacks but also to Hispanic Americans; in 1992, for example, 29.3 percent of all Hispanics, and 38.8 percent of Hispanic children, lived in poverty. See Bureau of the Census, *Statistical Abstract of the United States 1994,* (Washington, DC: Government Printing Office, 1994), p. 475.

TABLE 12.2

Key Provisions of Federal Civil Rights Laws (1957–1991)

Civil Rights Act of 1957	Established the Commission on Civil Rights to monitor civil rights progress.
	Elevated the importance of the Civil Rights Division of the Department of Justice, headed by an assistant attorney general. Made it a federal crime to attempt to intimidate a voter or to prevent a person from voting.
Civil Rights Act of 1960	Increased the sanction against obstruction of voting or of court orders enforcing the vote.
	Established federal power to appoint referees to register voters wherever a "pattern or practice" of discrimination was found by a federal court.
Equal Pay Act of 1963	Banned wage discrimination on the basis of sex in jobs requiring equal skill, effort, and responsibility. Exceptions involved employee pay differentials based on factors other than sex, such as merit or seniority.
Civil Rights Act of 1964	*Voting:* Title I made attainment of a sixth-grade education (in English) a presumption to literacy.
	Public accommodations: Title II barred discrimination in any commercial lodging of more than five rooms for transient guests and in any service station, restaurant, theater, or commercial conveyance. The complainant could bring suit against the establishment or the attorney general could take the initiative if he or she saw a "pattern or practice" of discrimination.
	Public schools: Title IV empowered the attorney general to sue for desegregation whenever a segregation complaint was found meritorious. Title VI authorized the withholding of federal aid from segregated schools.
	Private employment: Title VII outlawed discrimination in a variety of employment practices on the basis of race, religion, and sex (sex added for the first time in an area other than wage discrimination). Established the Equal Employment Opportunity Commission (EEOC) to enforce the law but required it to defer enforcement to state or local agencies for sixty days following each complaint.
Civil Rights Act of 1965	*Voting rights only:* Empowered the attorney general, with the Civil Service Commission, to appoint voting examiners to replace local registrars wherever fewer than 50 percent of the persons of voting age had voted in the 1964 presidential election and to suspend all literacy tests where they were used as a tool for discrimination.

1964 act, for example, authorized the executive branch, through the Justice Department, to implement federal court orders to desegregate schools, and to do so without having to wait for individual parents to bring complaints. Title VI vastly strengthened the role of the executive branch and the credibility of court orders by providing that federal grants-in-aid to state and local governments for education be withheld from any school system practicing racial segregation.

In the decade following the 1964 Civil Rights Act, the Justice Department brought legal action against more than five hundred school districts. During the same period, administrative agencies filed actions against six hundred school districts, threatening to suspend federal aid to education unless real desegregation steps were taken. At the same time, the federal government filed more than four hundred antidiscrimination suits in federal courts against hotels, restaurants, taverns, gas stations, and other "public accommodations" under Title II.[12]

Title VII, the fair employment title of the 1964 act, declared job discrimination illegal. This title

---

[12]For a review of these suits, see Richard Kluger, *Simple Justice* (New York: Random House, 1975), p. 759 and Chapters 25 and 26.

TABLE 12.2 (CONTINUED)

Key Provisions of Federal Civil Rights Laws (1957–1991) (continued)

Civil Rights Act of 1968	*Open housing:* Made it a crime to refuse to sell or rent a dwelling on the basis of race or religion, if a bona fide offer had been made, or to discriminate in advertising or in the terms and conditions of sale or rental. Administered by the Department of Housing and Urban Development, but the burden of proof is on the complainant, who must seek local remedies first, where they exist.
Amendments of 1970 to Voting Rights Act	Extended 1965 act and included some districts in Northern states.
Equal Employment Opportunity Act of 1972	Increased coverage of the Civil Rights Act of 1964 to include public-sector employees. Gave EEOC authority to bring suit against persons engaging in "pattern or practice" of employment discrimination.
Amendments of 1975 to Voting Rights Act	Extended 1965 act and broadened antidiscrimination measures to include protection for language minorities (e.g., Hispanics, Native Americans).
Amendments of 1978 to Civil Rights Act of 1964	Prohibited discrimination in employment on the basis of pregnancy or related disabilities. Required that pregnancy or related medical conditions be treated as disabilities eligible for medical and liability insurance.
Amendments of 1982 to Voting Rights Act	Extended 1965 act and strengthened antidiscrimination measures by requiring only proof of *effect* of discrimination, not *intent* to discriminate.
Americans with Disabilities Act of 1990	Extended to people with disabilities protection from discrimination in employment and public accommodations similar to the protection given to women and racial, religious, and ethnic minorities by the 1964 Civil Rights Act. Required that public transportation systems, other public services, and telecommunications systems be accessible to those with disabilities. As of 1997, employers are required to make "reasonable accommodations" for workers suffering from psychiatric illnesses like depression, schizophrenia, and manic depression.
Civil Rights Act of 1991	Reversed several Court decisions that had made it harder for women and minorities to seek compensation for job discrimination. It put back on the employer the burden of proof to show that a discriminatory policy was a business necessity.

covered all employers of more than fifteen employees, all governmental agencies, and also trade unions. Some of the powers to enforce fair employment practices were delegated to the Justice Department's Civil Rights Division and others to a new agency created in the 1964 act, the Equal Employment Opportunity Commission (EEOC). It is also important to note the use here of another "technique of control" identified earlier in this chapter: By executive order, these agencies had the power to revoke public con-

tracts for goods and services and to refuse to award contracts for goods and services to any private company that could not guarantee that its rules for hiring, promoting, and firing were nondiscriminatory.[13]

[13]Although 1964 was the most important year for civil rights law, it was not the only important year. In 1965, Congress significantly strengthened legislation protecting voting rights. For a comprehensive analysis and evaluation of the Voting Rights Act, see Bernard Grofman and Chandler Davidson, eds., *Controversies in Minority Voting: The Voting Rights Act in Perspective* (Washington, DC: Brookings Institution, 1992).

W. E. B. DuBois and Booker T. Washington:
Competing Paths to Equality

Two of the most important founders of the modern civil rights movement shared the same goal—equality for African Americans—but differed markedly on how best to achieve that goal.

William Edward Burghardt (better known as W. E. B.) DuBois, born in Massachusetts in 1868, entered the academic world via Fisk University and Harvard University, where his doctoral dissertation on the slave trade was the first volume published in the Harvard Historical Studies series. DuBois taught at many universities, wrote numerous books, and founded the National Association for the Advancement of Colored People (NAACP).

Booker T. Washington was born a Virginia slave in 1856. After the Civil War, Washington worked in coal mines and salt furnaces. In 1872, he was admitted to the Hampton Institute, an industrial school for blacks. Five years later he became a teacher there. In 1881, Washington established and headed the Tuskegee Institute in Alabama, a school, modeled on Hampton, that emphasized vocational trades for blacks, including farming, carpentry, mechanical skills, and teaching. Eventually, Washington became a prominent political figure, and an adviser to Presidents Theodore Roosevelt and William H. Taft.

DuBois's philosophy of race relations emphasized the importance of black self-sufficiency and excellence, urging cultivation of a "talented tenth" that could excel and lead other blacks. And as early as 1903, he predicted that "the problem of the twentieth century is the problem of the color line." Washington, on the other hand, espoused the view that blacks should seek "through compromise, an emergence

W. E. B. DuBois

Affirmative Action

Unfortunately, the civil rights laws work best for middle-class victims, because they have the education, the self-confidence, and the resources to pursue their grievances through law and politics. But as they succeed, they move away not only from lower-paying jobs but also from segregated neighborhoods, and they deprive their former neighbors of their example and their leadership, underscoring the plight of those who remain.[14] *Affirmative action* was supposed to be the answer.

Most affirmative action comes not from new legislation but from more vigorous and positive interpretations of existing legislation arising out of feelings on the part of many that positive actions are necessary to overcome long years of discrimination. President Johnson put the case powerfully in 1965: "You do not take a person who, for years, has been hobbled by chains . . . and then say you are free to compete with all the others, and still just believe that you have been completely fair."[15] Consequently, one of the first affir-

[14]William Julius Wilson, *The Truly Disadvantaged* (Chicago: University of Chicago Press, 1987).

[15]From Lyndon B. Johnson, *The Vantage Point* (New York: Holt, Rinehart, and Winston, 1971), p. 166.

into an economic, social, and cultural stability never quite equal to the white man's." This philosophy led Washington to state that blacks were better off by getting practical vocational education than by seeking college training. DuBois did not reject the need for vocational education, but he took sharp issue with Washington's willingness to accept an inferior and segregated status for blacks.

Not surprisingly, Washington's views found wider acceptance among white Americans, which won him influence among the nation's political leaders. Washington also promoted his views through his financial control of various black newspapers. Washington avoided endorsing controversial political causes, although he did funnel money secretly to support lawsuits to fight discrimination in the courts. Toward the end of his life, his influence declined as the views of organizations such as the NAACP acquired greater respect.

BOOKER T. WASHINGTON

DuBois never backed down from his advocacy of political and social equality. For many years, he worked for the NAACP and edited its publication called *The Crisis*. In 1950, he unsuccessfully ran for U.S. senator from New York on the American Labor party ticket. Disillusioned with American party politics, DuBois joined the Communist party and traveled extensively in China and the Soviet Union. In 1961, the aged man moved to Ghana, to direct the writing of the *Encyclopedia Africana*.

Both DuBois and Washington believed that their philosophies would ultimately help eradicate inequality. The course chosen by DuBois, however, more closely foreshadowed the civil rights struggles of years to come.

SOURCES: Booker T. Washington, *Up from Slavery* (New York: Corner House, 1971; orig. published in 1901); W. E. B. DuBois, *The Souls of Black Folk* (New York: Signet Classics, 1969; orig. published in 1903).

mative action programs was President Johnson's War on Poverty, begun in 1964. Its aim was to help people in underprivileged and ghetto neighborhoods form organizations with a leadership that could speak for the people in those neighborhoods. The ultimate goal of these "Community Action Programs" was to provide more assistance and at the same time teach the poor how to organize to compete more effectively in political as well as economic life.

The War on Poverty has been subjected to a good deal of valid criticism. But there is no denying that some of the various redistributive programs that Congress included as part of the War

on Poverty did reach poor neighborhoods. The Job Corps and food stamps did have a positive effect on the overall level of poverty. Head Start did redistribute educational opportunities for individuals in those neighborhoods. And the Community Action Programs did in fact bring political experience and leadership skills to unprecedented numbers of black and other minority residents of poor and hitherto isolated neighborhoods.[16]

[16] For a criticism of the administrative methods used, see Theodore J. Lowi, *The End of Liberalism* (New York: W. W. Norton, 1979), Chapter 8. For a very positive account of the amount of money spent and the impact made, see John Schwarz, *America's Hidden Success* (New York: W. W. Norton, 1988), pp. 34–50.

Affirmative action also took the form of efforts by the agencies in the Department of Health, Education, and Welfare to shift their focus from "desegregation" to "integration." Federal agencies—sometimes with court orders and sometimes without them—required school districts to present plans for busing children across district lines, for pairing schools, for closing certain schools, and for redistributing faculties as well as students, under pain of loss of grants-in-aid from the federal government. The guidelines issued for such plans literally constituted preferential treatment to compensate for past discrimination.

Affirmative action was also initiated in the area of employment opportunity. The Equal Employment Opportunity Commission often has required plans whereby employers must attempt to increase the number of their minority employees, and the Office of Federal Contract Compliance in the Department of Labor has used the threat of contract revocation for the same purpose.

The constitutionality of these legislative efforts at affirmative action were to a great extent upheld. The *Bakke* (1978) case, already dealt with in Chapter 4, permitted universities to continue to use racial categorizations and to take minority status into consideration as long as it was used as a *guideline* for social diversity and not as a mathematically defined ratio.[17] This was followed two years later in a Supreme Court decision upholding the "minority business enterprise" provisions of federal law, requiring that 10 percent of federal funds granted for local public works projects must be used to procure services or supplies from businesses owned by minority group members.[18] This principle was reaffirmed in 1990, giving Congress a broader latitude than states and localities when authorizing affirmative-action programs.[19] In that spirit, affirmative action had been em-

braced quite positively by the federal government, many of the states, and many private companies all during the 1970s. But in the 1980s, the situation changed. Ronald Reagan became "the first president in the post–World War II period to reverse this trend of an increasingly active government role in . . . redressing the consequences of past discrimination." Budgets and staff of key civil rights agencies were cut to the bone. Busing was opposed. Government cases against school segregation, housing discrimination, and job discrimination dropped to a fraction of the cases brought under previous administrations. And, although federal court decisions upheld the use of statistics on the "effect" of discrimination as a basis for Justice Department initiatives in filing "pattern or practice" suits to open opportunities for minorities, the Justice Department under President Reagan virtually terminated such suits, focusing instead on individual cases where actual intent to discriminate could be proven.

President Bush continued in the Reagan direction. He vetoed the Civil Rights Act of 1990 as a "quota bill" (although he accepted essentially the same bill in 1991). Most important, though, he "relentlessly" appointed known social conservatives to the federal courts "with the same energy that Ronald Reagan did."[20] And his single appointment to the Supreme Court, Clarence Thomas, who replaced civil rights advocate Thurgood Marshall, is an opponent of anything that has to do with affirmative action.

As noted at the end of Chapter 4, President Clinton reversed the trend by somewhat stronger support for civil rights in the belief that meaningful equality of opportunity must include redress of historical inequalities. But a storm was gathering. It had begun in 1989, with the Supreme Court declaring unconstitutional an ordinance of the

---

[17]*Regents of the University of California v. Bakke,* 438 U.S. 265 (1978).

[18]*Fullilove v. Klutznick,* 448 U.S. 448 (1980).

[19]*Metro Broadcasting Inc. v. Federal Communications Commission,* 497 U.S. 547 (1990).

[20]An observation by Nan Aron of the liberal Alliance for Justice, quoted in Ruth Marcus, "Using the Bench to Bolster a Conservative Team," *Washington Post National Weekly Edition,* 25 February–3 March 1991, p. 31.

city of Richmond, which provided that 30 percent of its contracting work should go to minority-owned businesses. The Court not only invalidated this ordinance on the grounds that it was a strict numerical quota that had been forbidden a decade earlier but went further to declare that *all* racial classifications ought to be considered suspect and therefore subject to "strict scrutiny." Moreover, the Court said that it was "obvious that [the] program is not narrowly tailored to remedy the effects of prior discrimination." This was an entirely new rule.[21] *Richmond v. Croson* was significantly strengthened and extended in a conservative direction in 1995, when the Supreme Court held that the "strict scrutiny" applied to state and local affirmative action decisions through the Fourteenth Amendment was to be incorporated (in reverse) into the Fifth Amendment and applied to equivalent decisions by the national government. This strengthened the *Richmond* case and also, for all practical purposes, reversed the policy of federal set-asides by holding that "benign" federal racial classifications "like those of the State, must serve a compelling governmental interest, and must be narrowly tailored to further that interest."[22] The mood in Congress against any program that could be called "social engineering" was already forcing Clinton to back off from plans aimed at the inner city and what had come to be called the underclass. The 1994 Republican takeover of Congress, coupled with the adverse Supreme Court decisions prompted Clinton to order the Justice Department to do a full-scale review of affirmative action, and their conclusion was not a happy one for the administration. In strict, policy-oriented terms, no program could

any longer be "justified solely by reference to general societal discrimination, general assertions of discrimination in a particular sector or industry, or a statistical underrepresentation of minorities in a sector or industry. . . . Without more, these are impermissible bases for affirmative action."[23] Meanwhile, the gathering storm of political controversy was coming into focus in California, with Proposition 209, a referendum proposal for the 1996 election. Prop 209 provides that "The state shall not discriminate against, or grant preferential treatment to, any individual or group on the basis of race, sex, color, ethnicity, or national origin in the operation of public employment, public education, or public contracting. . . ." This was going to cause a serious problem for President Clinton, who, up until that moment, was holding by his 1995 statement of support of affirmative-action policy: "mend it, don't end it." Presidential candidate Robert Dole, a longstanding supporter of civil rights, including affirmative action, had already switched his position to support Prop 209, and California public opinion was also moving in that direction. For Clinton to take a pro-affirmative action position and make this a major campaign issue in California would endanger his support in the state, an absolutely essential state for his re-election. Clinton simply backed off from the issue, and had the very good luck of a Dole decision to stay away from it also.

This leaves affirmative action largely in limbo as a public policy. Proposition 209 is being copied by other states, but the impact will be delayed, possibly for several years, as the legal/constitutional status of such measures is tested in the courts. But though in limbo, affirmative action is not dead. Others are trying to find more accommodating, "nonexclusionary" approaches to affirmative action based on highly specialized definitions of individual need rather than classifications. And some federal judges have actually settled

---

[21] *City of Richmond v. J. A. Croson Co.*, 488 U.S. 469 (1989). For an excellent study of the case and an evaluation of its consequences for the nation at large and the city of Richmond, see W. Avon Drake and Robert D. Holsworth, *Affirmative Action and the Stalled Quest for Black Progress* (Urbana: University of Illinois Press, 1996). This idea of "narrow tailoring" was going to add additional burdens to those trying to justify an affirmative action decision.

[22] *Adarand Constructors Inc. v. Pena*, 115 S.Ct. 2097 (1995).

[23] Quoted in unauthored editorial, "The Race Gap," *The New Republic*, 14 August 1995, p. 7.

local legal disputes by obliging state bodies to go further in reflecting the ethnic composition of local populations. Meanwhile, many large companies are moving even more vigorously than public-sector agencies. Levi Strauss has been hiring people according to their ability to fill "demographic gaps" in their work force; Hughes Aircraft and Lockheed Martin give managers a bonus if they hit various "diversity targets." Pacific Gas and Electric publicly endorsed affirmative action during the California campaign, and Pacific Bell, Southern California Edison, and Kaiser Permanente all encouraged their employees to favor the same. As the British journal *The Economist* put it, "The public sector's assorted affirmative action officers may find that the best way to save their pet schemes lies in privatization."[24]

Finally, since the Supreme Court has put affirmative action under "strict scrutiny" without declaring it unconstitutional, many opportunities remain. Although some outspoken African American intellectuals have come out against affirmative action programs, most civil rights leaders and their organizations continue to be of the opinion that such programs are absolutely essential. And, despite the vote in California and the support in other states for similar actions, a sizable portion of private sector employers find affirmative action good policy for themselves. Many who favor affirmative *actions* but oppose affirmative *action* are of the faith that no government intervention is necessary. Others continue to believe that spontaneous private action is a necessary but insufficient condition, which needs legislative and administrative support. But virtually every American would agree that the issue must be understood in order to change the rules determining who shall be poor, because poverty is almost surely the status to which people are doomed if they get no assistance to break out of the historically shaped circle of poverty.

[24]The quote and source for the several other affirmative action efforts in this paragraph: Editorial, "Affirmative Action in California: Not Over Till It's Over," *The Economist*, 16 November 1996, p. 27.

Chapter Review

Madison set the tone for this chapter in *The Federalist*, No. 51, in three sentences of prose that have more the character of poetry:

> Justice is the end of government.
> It is the end of civil society.
> It ever has been and ever will be
>   pursued
>   Until it be obtained,
> Or until liberty be lost in the pursuit.

Our economic system is the most productive ever developed, but it is not perfect—and many policies have been adopted over the years to deal with its imperfections. The first section of this chapter provided an introduction to the "techniques of control" that all policies embody. Policy is the purposive and deliberate aspect of government in action. But if policy is to come anywhere near obtaining its stated goal (clean air, stable prices, equal employment opportunity), it must be backed up by some kind of sanction—the ability to reward or punish—coupled with some ability to administer or implement those sanctions. The "techniques of control" were presented in three categories—promotional techniques, regulatory techniques, and redistributive techniques. These techniques are found in the multitude of actual policies adopted by legislatures and implemented by administrative agencies. Good policy analysis consists largely of identifying the techniques of control and choosing the policies that seek to manipulate "the economy as a system." Redistributive techniques usually come in the form of (1) monetary policies, which are concerned with control of banks, currency, and credit; (2) fiscal policies, which have to do with taxing and spending; and (3) welfare policies, which have the dual purpose of stabilizing the economy while providing a safety net for dependent and poor people.

The final section looked at imperfections in our society and how public policies have succeeded or failed in dealing with these imperfections, particularly in the distribution of opportunities. Although the welfare state itself has a great deal to do with the distribution of opportunities, this section was concerned with civil rights. An important distinction was made between policies concerning the elimination of discrimination versus policies concerning "affirmative action" aimed at overcoming and compensating for the results of discrimination in the past. Considerable progress has been made in the former but little in the latter. Civil rights laws have been helpful to women and members of minority groups who were already in the middle class of Americans. But their success in taking advantage of the civil rights laws served to increase the distance between themselves and the lower-income members of the same groups. Affirmative action policies are aimed precisely at the groups left behind, but these policies have produced a great deal of controversy. The struggle over the effort to bring solutions to these groups of people and the controversy over the permissibility of quotas will influence the agenda of public policy well into the next century.

TIME LINE ON PUBLIC POLICY

Events	Institutional Developments
Alexander Hamilton's *Report on Manufactures* presents the first comprehensive statement of the policies necessary for American economic development (1791)	Regulatory policies reserved to the states: policies controlling property, land use, education, morality, marriage, criminal conduct (1790s–1990s)
1800	
Territorial expansion, western settlement (1800s)	Promotional policies used by national government to encourage national commerce: tariffs (1792); land grants, internal improvements, shipping subsidies, etc. (1800s)
Civil War (1861–1865)	Reconstruction; military occupation of South; return to normal promotional policies (1870s)
Growth and mechanization of industry; formation of corporations; commercialization of agriculture (1860s–1890s)	National government adopts first regulatory policies—Interstate Commerce Act (1887), Sherman Antitrust Act (1890)
Abuses of workers and farmers; unionization; progressive reform movement (1880s–1890s)	
1900	
Airplane, automobile, electrification, and mass production create another "industrial revolution" (1900s–1920s)	Supreme Court declares income tax unconstitutional (1895); Sixteenth Amendment provides for income tax (1913)

Events		Institutional Developments
	1900	
		Congress establishes Federal Reserve System (1913); Federal Trade Commission (1914)
World War I (1914–1918)		Mobilization of entire economy for war
Stock market crash (1929); Great Depression (1929–1930s)		Demobilization and return to status quo (1920s)
	1930	
Franklin Roosevelt elected; initiates the New Deal (1932)		New Deal policies: bank rescue, relief for unemployed, many new regulatory agencies, agriculture relief policies, Social Security Act, National Labor Relations Act (1933–1936)
	1940	
U.S. in Worl<None>d War II; total mobilization of society and economy (1941–1945)		GI Bill of Rights for educational and vocational training (1944); National School Lunch Program (1946); housing policies; Council of Economic Advisers and commitment to "full employment planning" (1946–1947)
Postwar demobilization; strikes; fear of inflation and depression (1945–1946)		
	1950	
Civil Rights Movement (1950s and 1960s)		*Brown v. Board of Education*—Court rules against school segregation (1954)
Soviets launch *Sputnik* (1957)		First federal aid to education—National Defense Education Act (1958)
	1960	
Growth of government (1960s); Kennedy assassinated; Johnson assumes presidency (1963)		Equal pay for women (1963); Civil Rights Act establishes EEOC (1964); Food Stamp Act (1964); Elementary and Secondary School Act (1965); Voting Rights Act, Medicare and Medicaid (1965); War on Poverty (1964–1968)
Vietnam War and "confidence gap" (1965–1973)	**1970**	Indexing of welfare benefits (1972); Supplemental Security Income (SSI) (1974)
Richard Nixon elected (1968); administrative reorganization (1968–1974)		
Energy crisis; rise of "stagflations" (1973)		EEOC strengthened, especially for women (1972)
Reaction begins against regulation (1978–1980)	**1980**	Deregulation through executive management (1980s)
Ronald Reagan elected (1980)		Deregulation of securities (1975), railroads (1976 and 1980), airlines (1978–1981), banking (1980), motor carriers (1980)

Events		Institutional Developments
	1980	
		Executive Order 12291 mandates presidential oversight of all regulatory proposals (1981)
Public reaction against social policies as well as regulation (1980s)		Health and housing programs cut (1981–1984); increased (1986–1988)
		Historic tax cuts (1981)
George Bush elected (1988)		
Public sentiment for some reregulation begins to mount (1990)	**1990**	Bush vetoes most new regulation but accepts Clean Air Act (1990) and Americans with Disabilities Act (1991), and favors abortion regulation (1989–1992)
		Clinton health care plan fails in Congress (1994)
Bill Clinton elected, promising reforms of welfare and health care (1992)		Congress and Clinton develop welfare reform proposals (1995)
Republicans win control of Congress (1994)		

KEY TERMS

administrative regulation   Rules made by regulatory agencies and commissions.

affirmative action   A policy or program designed to redress historic injustices committed against racial minorities and other specified groups by making special efforts to provide members of these groups with access to educational and employment opportunities.

Aid to Families with Dependent Children (AFDC)   Federal funds, administered by the states, for children living with parents or relatives who fall below state standards of need.

contracting power   The power of government to set conditions on companies seeking to sell goods or services to government agencies.

contributory programs   Social programs financed in whole or in part by taxation or other mandatory contributions by their present or future recipients. The most important example is Social Security, which is financed by a payroll tax.

cost of living adjustments (COLAs)   Changes made to the level of benefits based on the rate of inflation.

discount rate   The interest rate charged by the Federal Reserve when commercial banks borrow in order to expand their lending operations; an effective tool of monetary policy.

eminent domain   The right of government to take private property for public use, with reasonable compensation awarded for the property.

entitlement   Eligibility for benefits by virtue of a category of benefits defined by legislation.

expropriation   Confiscation of property with or without compensation.

Federal Reserve Board   The governing board of the Federal Reserve System is comprised of a chair and six other members, appointed by the president with the consent of the Senate.

fiscal techniques   The government's use of taxing, monetary, and spending powers to manipulate the economy.

indexing   Periodic adjustments of welfare payments, wages, or taxes, tied to the cost of living.

license   Permission to engage in some activity that is otherwise illegal, such as hunting or practicing medicine.

means testing   Procedure by which potential beneficiaries of a public assistance program establish their eligibility by demonstrating a genuine need for the assistance.

Medicaid   A federally financed, state-operated program providing medical services to low-income people.

Medicare　National health insurance for the elderly and for the disabled.

monetary techniques　Efforts to regulate the economy through manipulation of the supply of money and credit. America's most powerful institution in the area of monetary policy is the Federal Reserve Board.

noncontributory programs　Social programs that provide assistance to people based on demonstrated need rather than any contribution they have made.

open market operations　The buying and selling of government securities to help finance government operations and to loosen or tighten the total amount of credit circulating in the economy.

police power　Power reserved to the state to regulate the health, safety, and morals of its citizens.

promotional technique　A technique of control that encourages people to do something they might not otherwise do, or to continue an action or behavior. Three types of promotional techniques are subsidies, contracts, and licenses.

public policy　A law, rule, statute, or edict that expresses the government's goals and provides for rewards and punishments to promote their attainment.

redistributive techniques　Techniques—fiscal or monetary—designed to control people by manipulating the entire economy rather than by regulating people directly.

regulatory techniques　Techniques that government uses to control the conduct of the people.

reserve requirement　The amount of liquid assets and ready cash that the Federal Reserve requires banks to hold to meet depositors' demands for their money.

Social Security　A contributory welfare program into which working Americans contribute a percentage of their wages, and from which they receive cash benefits after retirement.

spending power　A combination of subsidies and contracts that the government can use to redistribute income.

subsidies　Government grants of cash or other valuable commodities, such as land, to individuals or organizations; used to promote activities desired by the government, to reward political support, or to buy off political opposition.

Supplemental Security Income (SSI)　A program providing a minimum monthly income to people who pass a "means test" and who are sixty-five or older, blind, or disabled. Financed form general revenues rather than from Social Security contributions.

Temporary Assistance to Needy Families (TANF)　A policy by which states are given block grants by the federal government in order to create their own programs for public assistance.

For Further Reading

Bullock, Charles, III, and Charles M. Lamb. *Implementation of Civil Rights Policy.* Monterey, CA: Brooks/Cole, 1984.

Chubb, John, and Paul Peterson, eds. *Can the Government Govern?* Washington, DC: Brookings Institution, 1988.

Derthick, Martha. *Agency under Stress: The Social Security Administration in American Government.* Washington, DC: Brookings Institution, 1990.

Foreman, Christopher. *Signals from the Hill: Congressional Oversight and the Challenge of Social Regulation.* New Haven: Yale University Press, 1988.

Grofman, Bernard, and Chandler Davidson, eds. *Controversies in Minority Voting: The Voting Rights Act in Perspective.* Washington, DC: Brookings Institution, 1992.

Gutmann, Amy. *Democracy and the Welfare State.* Princeton: Princeton University Press, 1988.

Heilbroner, Robert. *The Nature and Logic of Capitalism.* New York: W. W. Norton, 1985.

Lemann, Nicholas. *The Promised Land: The Great Black Migration and How It Shaped America.* New York: Alfred A. Knopf, 1991.

Lenno, Rhonda F. *Class Struggle and the New Deal: Industrial Labor, Industrial Capital, and the State.* Lawrence: University of Kansas Press, 1988.

Levi, Margaret. *Of Rule and Revenue.* Berkeley: University of California Press, 1988.

Marmor, Theodore R., Jerry L. Mashaw, and Phillip L. Harvey. *America's Misunderstood Welfare State.* New York: Basic Books, 1990.

Orfield, Gary, and Carole Ashkinaze. *The Closing Door: Conservative Policy and Black Opportunity.* Chicago: University of Chicago Press, 1991.

Paul, Ellen. *Equity and Gender: The Comparable Worth Debate.* New Brunswick, NJ: Transaction, 1989.

Piven, Frances Fox, and Richard A. Cloward. *Regulating the Poor*. New York: Pantheon, 1971.

Rubin, Irene S. *The Politics of Public Budgeting—Getting and Spending, Borrowing and Balancing*. Chatham, NJ: Chatham House, 1990.

Sawhill, Isabel. *Challenge to Leadership—Economic and Social Issues for the Next Decade*. Washington, DC: Urban Institute Press, 1988.

Self, Peter. *Government by the Market? The Politics of Public Choice*. Boulder, CO: Westview, 1994.

Stone, Alan. *Wrong Number: The Break Up of AT&T*. New York: Basic Books, 1989.

Tatalovich, Raymond, and Byron Daynes, eds. *Social Regulatory Policy: Moral Controversies in American Politics*. Boulder, CO: Westview Press, 1988.

Vogel, David. *Fluctuating Fortunes: The Political Power of Business in America*. New York: Basic Books, 1989.

Weir, Margaret, Ann Orloff, and Theda Skocpol. *The Politics of Social Policy in the United States*. Princeton: Princeton University Press, 1988.

CHAPTER 13

Foreign Policy and World Politics

*E*VER SINCE Franklin Roosevelt's dramatic "First Hundred Days" in 1933, there has by tradition been a "honeymoon period" during which presidents address America's needs and Congress is expected to cooperate in a bipartisan spirit. Yet for most presidents, the honeymoon is short, if there is one at all. The interruption in the happy marriage is usually foreign policy.

President Clinton was by background and temperament a domestic president, and he marched into Washington with a bulging domestic portfolio. Yet within hours of his election in November, he discovered how sensitive foreign affairs can be. Because Clinton had supported political asylum for Haiti's immigrants during his campaign, his election produced a fever of boatbuilding on the island. As president, Clinton was forced to reverse his stand before Florida became flooded with immigrants. It was a harsh reminder of how easily foreign policy can trump domestic policy.

Most American presidents have been domestic politicians who set out to make their place in the history books through domestic policy achievements. Despite their limited experience with for-

eign affairs, all presidents since 1945 have been confronted with major foreign policy issues soon after taking office. They have had to spend inordinate amounts of time on foreign policy throughout their tenure, and most of their legacy, for better and for worse, is in foreign policy.

This chapter will explore American foreign policy, the changing attitudes of presidents and other Americans toward world politics, and the place of America in world affairs. Although modern presidents cannot escape the demands of foreign policy and world politics, this has not always been the case in our nation's history, as we shall see in this chapter.

We will begin with the players, those who make and shape foreign policy. Next, we lay out the world of nation-states and why they present such a serious challenge to each other. From there, we will trace out the history of America's place in the world of nation-states and how that history has influenced our contemporary foreign policies. Then we will identify and evaluate the six basic instruments of American foreign policy. Finally, we will look at actual roles the United States has attempted to play in world affairs.

CORE OF THE ARGUMENT

- The United States is a nation-state in a world of nation-states, each of which claims sovereignty over its own affairs but lacks perfect security.
- Certain values—fear of centralized power and of foreign entanglements—have traditionally shaped American foreign policy; today these values find expression in the intermingling of domestic and foreign policy institutions and the tendency toward unilateralism.
- American foreign policy is carried out through certain instruments, including diplomacy, the United Nations, the international monetary structure, economic aid, collective security, and military deterrence.
- In the conduct of foreign policy, nations can play one of several roles: the Napoleonic role, the Holy Alliance role, the balance-of-power role, and the economic expansionist role.
- The United States plays different roles in foreign affairs, depending on what it seeks to achieve in a particular situation; the Holy Alliance role seems to be the most typical American role in the post–Cold War era.

THE PLAYERS: THE MAKERS AND SHAPERS OF FOREIGN POLICY

Although the power of the American people over foreign policy is impossible to overestimate, "the people" should not be given all the credit or all the blame for actual policies and their outcomes. As in domestic policy, foreign policy making is a highly pluralistic arena. First there are the official players, those who comprise the "foreign policy establishment"; these players and the agencies they head can be called the actual "makers" of foreign policy.

But there are other major players, less official but still influential. We call these the "shapers."

Who Makes Foreign Policy?

THE PRESIDENT Although many foreign policy decisions can be made without so much as the president's fingerprint on them, these decisions must be made and implemented in the name of the president. In the cases of Iran-Contra and Iran-Bosnia, much of the action took place far from the White House and was hidden from the president. But those decisions and actions were taken to further a goal that the president wanted. That all foreign policies come from the president is a necessity in making any foreign policy. All heads of state must have some confidence that each head of state has enough power and stability to negotiate, to make agreements, and to keep those agreements.

THE BUREAUCRACY The major foreign policy players in the bureaucracy are the secretaries of the departments of State, Defense, and the Treasury; the Joint Chiefs of Staff (JCOS), especially the chair of the JCOS; and the director of the Central Intelligence Agency (CIA). A separate unit in the bureaucracy comprised of these people and a few others is the National Security Council (NSC), whose main purpose is to iron out the differences among the key players and to integrate their positions in order to confirm or reinforce a decision the president wants to make in foreign policy or military policy. In the Clinton administration, the secretary of commerce has also become an increasingly important foreign policy maker, with the rise and spread of economic globalization. Clinton's first secretary of commerce, Ron Brown, was not the first to be active in promoting world trade, but he may well have been the most vigorous and successful up to now.

In addition to these top cabinet-level officials, key lower-level staff members have policy-making influence as strong as that of the cabinet secretaries—some may occasionally exceed cabinet influence. These include the two or three specialized national security advisers in the White House, the staff of the NSC (headed by the national security adviser), and a few other career bureaucrats in the departments of State and Defense whose influence varies according to their specialty and to the foreign policy issue at hand.

CONGRESS   In foreign policy makings, Congress has to be subdivided into three parts. The first part is the Senate. For most of American history, the Senate was the only important congressional foreign policy player because of its constitutional role in reviewing and approving treaties. The treaty power is still the primary entrée of the Senate into foreign policy making. But since World War II and the continual involvement of the United States in international security and foreign aid, Congress as a whole has become a major foreign policy maker because most modern foreign policies require financing, which requires both the House of Representatives and the Senate. Congress has also become increasingly involved in foreign policy making because of the increasing use by the president of *executive agreements* to conduct foreign policy. Executive agreements have the force of treaties but do not require prior approval by the Senate. They can, however, be revoked by action of both chambers of Congress.

The third congressional player is the foreign policy and military policy committees: in the Senate these are the Foreign Relations Committee and the Armed Services Committee; in the House, these are the International Affairs Committee and the Armed Services Committee. Usually, a few members of these committees who have spent years specializing in foreign affairs become trusted members of the foreign policy establishment and are actually makers rather than mere shapers of foreign policy. In fact, several members of Congress have left to become key foreign affairs cabinet members.[1]

Who Shapes Foreign Policy?

The shapers of foreign policy are the nonofficial, informal players, but they are typically people or groups that have great influence in the making of foreign policy. Of course, the influence of any given group varies according to the party and the ideology that is dominant at a given moment.

INTEREST GROUPS   Far and away the most important category of nonofficial player is the interest group—that is, the interest groups to whom one or more foreign policy issues are of long-standing and vital relevance. The type of interest group with the reputation for the most influence is the economic interest group. Yet the myths about their influence far outnumber and outweigh the realities. The actual influence of organized economic interest groups in foreign policy varies enormously from issue to issue and year to year. Most of these groups are "single-issue" groups and are therefore most active when their particular issue is on the agenda. On many of the broader and more sustained policy issues, such as the *North American Free Trade Agreement (NAFTA)* or the general question of American involvement in international trade, the larger interest groups, sometimes called "peak associations," find it difficult to maintain tight enough control of their many members to speak with a single voice. The most systematic study of international trade policies and their interest groups concluded that the leaders of these large, economic interest groups spend more time maintaining consensus among their members than they do actually lobbying

---

[1]Under President Bush, for example, Dick Cheney left the House to become secretary of defense; under President Clinton, Senator Lloyd Bentsen and Representative Les Aspin left Congress to become the secretaries of the treasury and defense, respectively.

Congress or pressuring major players in the executive branch.[2] The more successful economic interest groups, in terms of influencing foreign policy, are the narrower, single-issue groups such as the tobacco industry, which over the years has successfully kept American foreign policy from putting heavy restrictions on international trade in and advertising of tobacco products, and the computer hardware and software industries, which have successfully hardened the American attitude toward Chinese piracy of intellectual property rights.

Another type of interest group with a well-founded reputation for influence in foreign policy is made up of people with strong attachments and identifications to their country of national origin. The interest group with the reputation for greatest influence is American Jews, whose family and emotional ties to Israel make them one of the most alert and potentially one of the most active interest groups in the whole field of foreign policy. But note once again how narrowly specialized that interest is—it focuses almost entirely and exclusively on policies toward Israel. Similarly, Americans of Irish heritage, despite having resided in the United States for two, three, or four generations, still maintain a vigilance about American policies toward Ireland and Northern Ireland; many even contribute to the activities of the Irish Republican Army. Many other ethnic and national interest groups wield similar influence over American foreign policy.

A third type of interest group, one with a reputation that has been growing in the past two decades, is the human rights interest group. Such groups are made up of people who, instead of having self-serving economic or ethnic interests in foreign policy, are genuinely concerned for the welfare and treatment of people throughout the world—particularly those who suffer under harsh political regimes. A relatively small but often quite influential example is Amnesty International, whose exposés of human rights abuses have altered the practices of many regimes around the world.

A related type of group with a fast-growing influence is the ecological or environmental group, sometimes called the "greens." Groups of this nature often depend more on demonstrations than on the usual forms and strategies of influence in Washington—lobbying and using electoral politics, for example. Demonstrations in strategically located areas can have significant influence on American foreign policy. One good example of this is the opposition that relatively small environmental protection groups in the United States raised against American contracts to buy electrical power from the Canadian province of Quebec: The group opposed the ecological effect of the enlarged hydroelectric power dams that were going to have to be built in order to accommodate American demands.[3]

THE MEDIA   Here again, myth may outweigh truth about media influence in foreign policy. The most important element of the policy influence of the media is the speed and scale with which the media can spread political communications. In that factor alone, the media's influence is growing—more news reaches more people faster, and people's reaction times are therefore shorter. When we combine this ability to communicate faster with the "feedback" medium of public opinion polling, it becomes clear how the media have become so influential—they enable the American people to reach

[2]Raymond A. Bauer, Ithiel de Sola Pool, and Lewis Anthony Dexter, *American Business and Public Policy: The Politics of Foreign Trade*, 2nd ed. (Chicago: Aldine-Atherton, 1972).

[3]Brenda Holzinger, "Power Politics: Public Policy, Federalism, and Hydroelectric Power," unpublished Ph.D. dissertation, Cornell University, 1997.

IN BRIEF BOX

MAKERS AND SHAPERS OF FOREIGN POLICY

Makers
   the president
   the bureaucracy (secretaries of State, Defense, and the Treasury; the Joint Chiefs of Staff, and the
      director of the Central Intelligence Agency)
   Congress (Senate approves treaties, both chambers vote on financing, foreign policy, and
      military policy committees in each chamber)
Shapers
   interest groups (economic, cultural/ethnic groups, human rights groups, environmental
      groups)
   the media

the president and the other official makers of foreign policy.[4]

There is one other aspect of media influence to consider. Many unhappy politicians complain bitterly of "media bias." The complaint most often heard is that journalists have a liberal (anti-Republican) bias. Although this general complaint has never been adequately documented, one aspect of media bias has been shown. Using survey evidence, Michael Robinson demonstrated that reliance on television as a source of news gave people negative attitudes toward public policies and especially toward government and public officials.[5] Robinson called this attitude "videomalaise." A later study found, in addition, that "television news in particular has an inherent bias toward reporting negative and critical informa-

tion. In other words, 'videomalaise' [is] as much a product of the medium as of the message."[6] One probable influence of the media on foreign as well as domestic policy has been to make the American people far more cynical and skeptical than they would otherwise have been. Beyond that, however, the influence of any medium of communication or any one influential journalist or news program varies from case to case.

Putting It Together

What can we say about who really makes American foreign policy? First, except for the president, the influence of players and shapers varies from case to case—this is a good reason to look with some care at each example of foreign policy in this chapter. Second, since the one constant influence is the centrality of the president in foreign policy making, it is best to evaluate other actors and factors as they interact with the president.[7] Third, the reason influence varies from case to case is that each case arises under different conditions and

[4]For further discussion of the vulnerability of modern presidents to the people through the media, see Theodore Lowi, *The Personal President: Power Invested, Promise Unfulfilled* (Ithaca, NY: Cornell University Press, 1985); Jeffrey K. Tulis, *The Rhetorical Presidency* (Princeton, NJ: Princeton University Press, 1987); Samuel Kernell, *Going Public: New Strategies of Presidential Leadership* (Washington, DC: CQ Press, 1986); Richard Rose, *The Postmodern President: The White House Meets the World* (Chatham, NJ: Chatham House, 1988); and George C. Edwards, *The Public Presidency: The Pursuit of Popular Support* (New York: St. Martin's, 1983).

[5]Michael J. Robinson, "Public Affairs Television and the Growth of Political Malaise: The Case of 'TV Selling of the Pentagon,'" *American Political Science Review* 70, no. 2 (June 1976), p. 425.

[6]Seymour Martin Lipset and William Schneider, *The Confidence Gap: Business, Labor, and Government in the Public Mind* (New York: Free Press, 1983), p. 405.

[7]A very good brief outline of the centrality of the president in foreign policy will be found in Paul E. Peterson, "The President's Dominance in Foreign Policy Making," *Political Science Quarterly* 109, no. 2 (Summer 1994), pp. 215, 234.

CONCEPT MAP 13.1

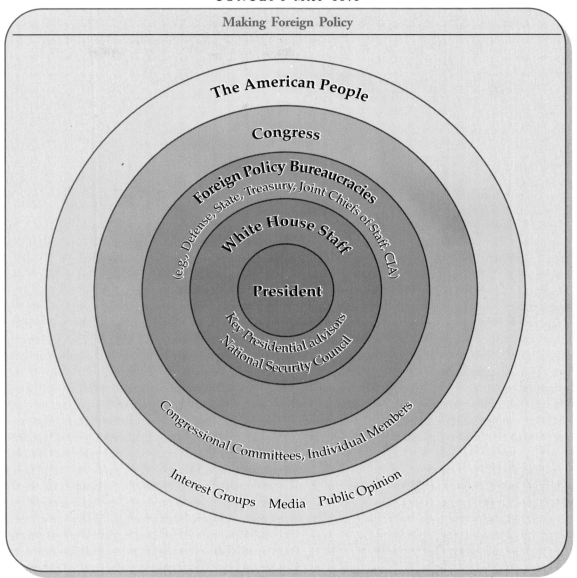

Making Foreign Policy

The American People

Congress

Foreign Policy Bureaucracies

(e.g., Defense, State, Treasury, Joint Chiefs of Staff, CIA)

White House Staff

President

Key Presidential advisors
National Security Council

Congressional Committees, Individual Members

Interest Groups   Media   Public Opinion

with vastly different time constraints: for issues that arise and are resolved quickly, the opportunity for influence is limited. Fourth, foreign policy experts will usually disagree about the level of influence any player or type of player has on policy making.

But just to get started, let's make a few tentative generalizations and then put them to the test with the substance and experience reported in the remainder of this chapter. First, when an important foreign policy decision has to be made under conditions of crisis—where "time is of the essence"—the influence of the presidency is at its strongest. Second, under those time constraints, access to the decision is limited almost exclusively to the narrowest definition of the "foreign policy establishment." The arena for participation is tiny; any discussion at all is limited to the officially and constitutionally designated players. To put this another way, in a crisis, the foreign policy establishment works as it is supposed to.[8] As time becomes less restricted, even when the decision to be made is of great importance, the arena of participation expands to include more government players and more nonofficial, informal players—the most concerned interest groups and the most important journalists. In other words, the arena becomes more pluralistic, and therefore less distinguishable from the politics of domestic policy making. Third, because there are so many other countries with power and interests on any given issue, there are severe limits on the choices the United States can make. As one author concludes, in foreign affairs, "policy takes precedence over politics."[9] Thus, even though foreign policy making in noncrisis situations may more closely resemble the pluralistic politics of domestic policy making, foreign policy making is still a narrower arena with fewer participants.

THE SETTING: A WORLD OF NATION-STATES

A nation is a population of individuals bound to each other by a common past, a common language, or other cultural ties that draw these individuals together and distinguish them from other peoples. When such a nation has sufficient self-consciousness to organize itself also into a political entity, it is generally referred to as a *nation-state.* But why form a nation-state? As Hans Morgenthau, one of the most eminent students of the nation-state, noted, "The most elementary function of the nation-state is the defense of the life of its citizens and of their civilization. A political organization that is no longer able to defend these values . . . must yield, either through peaceful transformation or violent destruction, to one capable of that defense."[10]

For at least two centuries, nation-states have effectively defended their populations, and the attraction to forming nation-states does not seem to have waned as a third century approaches. There were fifty-four nation-states at the beginning of the twentieth century. In 1945, when the United Nations (U.N.) was founded, there were sixty-seven, of which fifty-one were U.N. charter members. By the end of 1994, the total number U.N. member states stood at 184.

Yet the profusion of nation-states presents a paradox: They arise out of a concern for self-defense, but they tend to draw each other into war. Why? As people form themselves into nation-states as a means of defense, they become unified only by isolating themselves from other nations. By doing so, each nation deprives itself of information about the motives and interests of other nations. Modern means of transportation and communication have made the world smaller but not better acquainted. Mutual ignorance has tended to breed hostility because each nation-state conducts its foreign policy on the assumption that every country will pursue its interests at the expense of others.

The national purpose or national interest of the nation-state is said to be the maintenance of its

---

[8]One confirmation of this will be found in Theodore Lowi, *The End of Liberalism,* 2nd ed. (New York: W. W. Norton, 1979), pp. 127–30; another will be found in Stephen Krasner, "Are Bureaucracies Important?" *Foreign Policy* 7 (Summer 1972), pp. 159–79. However, it should be added that Krasner was writing his article in disagreement with Graham T. Allison, "Conceptual Models and the Cuban Missile Crisis," *American Political Science Review* 63, no. 3 (September 1969), pp. 689–718.

[9]Peterson, "The President's Dominance in Foreign Policy," p. 232.

[10]Hans J. Morgenthau, *The Purpose of American Politics* (New York: Knopf, 1960), pp. 169–70.

sovereignty. Sovereignty can be defined as respect by other nations for the claim by a government that it has conquered its territory and is the sole authority over its population.

Obviously, no nation-state is completely sovereign. In 1973, even the most powerful nation-states were brutally reminded of the fragility of their sovereignty when the Organization of Petroleum Exporting Countries (OPEC) adopted a common foreign policy to control the price of oil on the world market, and the price of oil quadrupled. The fragility of sovereignty was also shown when Iraq occupied Kuwait in 1990 and then had its own sovereignty violated by a large U.N. military force.

The power of a nation-state can be measured roughly according to the number and size of its *client states*, states that have the capacity to carry out their own foreign policy most of the time, but that still depend upon the interests of one or more of the major powers.[11] By that standard, the United States is the greatest nation-state, but it is not the only one. For most of this century, the Soviet Union was virtually America's equal; the Russian Republic will probably regain much of its status by early in the twenty-first century. The People's Republic of China, Japan, and the oil-rich Arab states are also powerful nation-states.

THE VALUES IN AMERICAN FOREIGN POLICY

When President Washington was preparing to leave office in 1796, he crafted with great care, and with the help of Alexander Hamilton and James Madison, a farewell address that is one of the most memorable documents in American history. We have already had occasion to look at a portion of Washington's farewell address, because in it he gave some stern warnings against political parties (see Chapter 10). But Washington's greater concern was to warn the nation against foreign influence:

> History and experience prove that foreign influence is one of the most baneful foes of republican government. . . . The great rule of conduct for us in regard to foreign nations is, in extending our commercial relations to have with them as little *political* connection as possible. So far as we have already formed engagements let them be fulfilled with perfect good faith. Here let us stop. . . . There can be no greater error than to expect or calculate upon real favors from nation to nation. . . . Trust to temporary alliances for extraordinary emergencies, [but in all other instances] steer clear of permanent alliances with any portion of the foreign world. . . . Such an attachment of a small or weak toward a great and powerful nation dooms the former to be the satellite of the latter. [emphasis in original.][12]

With the exception of a few leaders such as Thomas Jefferson and Thomas Paine, who were eager to take sides with the French against all others, Washington was probably expressing sentiments shared by most Americans. In fact, during most of the nineteenth century, American foreign policy was to a large extent no foreign policy. But Americans were never isolationist, if isolationism means the refusal to have any associations with the outside world. Americans were eager for trade and for treaties and contracts facilitating trade. Americans were also expansionists, but their vision of expansionism was limited to filling up the North American continent only.

Three familiar historical factors help explain why Washington's sentiments became the

---

[11]At least one nation-state in the middle of the continuum, Switzerland, is not a client state. Switzerland's sovereignty is well guarded by most other states in order to maintain at least one country where diplomacy and business can take place no matter how chaotic international relations may be. But most of the nation-states in this middle category are best understood as client states.

[12]A full version of the text of the farewell address, along with a discussion of the contribution to it made by Hamilton and Madison, will be found in Daniel J. Boorstin, ed., *An American Primer* (Chicago: University of Chicago Press, 1966), vol. 1, pp. 192–210. This editing is by Richard B. Morris.

tradition and the source of American foreign policy values. The first was the deep anti-statist ideology shared by most Americans in the nineteenth century and into the twentieth century. Although we witness widespread anti-statism today, in the form of calls for tax cuts, deregulation, privatization, and other efforts to "get the government off our backs," such sentiments were far more intense in the past, when many Americans opposed foreign entanglements, a professional military, and secret diplomacy. The second factor was federalism. The third was the position of the United States in the world as a client state. Most nineteenth-century Americans recognized that if the United States became entangled in foreign affairs, national power would naturally grow at the expense of the states, and so would the presidency at the expense of Congress. Why? Because foreign policy meant having a professional diplomatic corps, professional armed forces with a general staff—and secrets. This meant professionalism, elitism, and remoteness from citizens. Being a client state gave us the luxury of being able to keep our foreign policy to a minimum. Moreover, maintaining American sovereignty was in the interest of the European powers, because it prevented any one of them from gaining an advantage over the others in the Western Hemisphere.

Legacies of the Traditional System

Two identifiable legacies flowed from the long tradition based on anti-statism, federalism, and client status. One is the intermingling of domestic and foreign policy institutions. The second is unilateralism—America's willingness to go it alone. Each of these reveals a great deal about the values behind today's conduct of foreign policy.

INTERMINGLING OF DOMESTIC AND FOREIGN POLICY Because the major European powers once policed the world, American political leaders could treat foreign policy as a mere extension of domestic policy. The *tariff* is the best example. A tax on one

category of imported goods as a favor to interests in one section of the country would directly cause friction elsewhere in the country. But the demands of those adversely affected could be met without directly compromising the original tariff, by adding a tariff to still other goods that would placate those who were complaining about the original tariff. In this manner, Congress was continually adding and adjusting tariffs on more and more classes of commodities.

An important aspect of the treatment of foreign affairs as an extension of domestic policy was amateurism. Unlike many other countries, Americans refused to develop a tradition of a separate foreign service composed of professional people who spent much of their adult lives in foreign countries, learning foreign languages, absorbing foreign cultures, and developing a sympathy for foreign points of view. Instead, Americans have tended to be highly suspicious of any American diplomat or entrepreneur who spoke sympathetically of any such foreign viewpoints.[13] No systematic progress was made to create a professional diplomatic corps until after the passage of the Foreign Service Act of 1946.

UNILATERALISM Unilateralism, not isolationism, was the American posture toward the world until the middle of the twentieth century. Isolationism means to try to cut off contacts with the outside, to be a self-sufficient fortress. American was never isolationist; it preferred *unilateralism,* or "going it alone." Americans have always been more likely to rally around the president in support of direct action rather than for a sustained, diplomatic involvement.

The Great Leap—Thirty Years Late

The traditional era of U.S. foreign policy came to an end with World War I for several important

---

[13]E. E. Schattschneider, *Politics, Pressures, and the Tariff* (Englewood Cliffs, NJ: Prentice-Hall, 1935).

reasons. First, the "balance of power" system[14] that had kept the major European powers from world war for a hundred years had collapsed.[15] In fact, the great powers themselves had collapsed internally. The most devastating of all wars up to that time had ruined their economies, their empires, and, in most cases, their political systems. Second, the United States was no longer a client state but in fact one of the great powers. Third, as we saw in earlier chapters, the United States was soon to shed its traditional domestic system of federalism with its national government of almost pure promotional policy. Thus, virtually all the conditions that contributed to the traditional system of American foreign policy had disappeared. Yet there was no discernible change in America's approach to foreign policy in the period between World War I and World War II. After World War I, as one foreign policy analyst put it, "the United States withdrew once more into its insularity. Since America was unwilling to use its power, that power, for purposes of foreign policy, did not really exist."[16]

The Great Leap in foreign policy was finally made thirty years after conditions demanded it and only then after another world war, to which America's post–World War I behavior had undoubtedly contributed. This is not said with the intent merely to criticize—for who knows how different the world would have been if America had been more engaged in world affairs during the interwar years. The observation is made to emphasize the strength of the traditional pattern,

so strong as to resist change in the face of compelling conditions.

Pressure for a new tradition came into direct conflict with the old. The new tradition required foreign entanglements; the old tradition feared them deeply. The new tradition required diplomacy; the old distrusted it. The new tradition required acceptance of antagonistic political systems; the old embraced democracy and was aloof from all else.

The values of the new tradition were all apparent during the *cold war.* Instead of unilateralism, the United States pursued *multilateralism,* entering into treaties with other nations to achieve its foreign policy goals. The most notable of these treaties is that which formed the *North Atlantic Treaty Organization (NATO)* in 1948, which allied the United States, Canada, and most of Western Europe. With its NATO allies, the United States practiced a two-pronged policy in dealing with its rival, the Soviet Union: *containment* and *deterrence.* Fearing that the Soviet Union was bent on world domination, the United States fought wars in Korea and Vietnam to "contain" Soviet power. And in order to deter a direct attack against itself or its NATO allies, the United States developed a multi-billion-dollar nuclear arsenal capable of destroying the Soviet Union many times over.

The primary instruments of foreign policy in the new, post–World War II tradition can also be seen as six case studies in the balancing of the old tradition against the demands for a new tradition. Each is a dramatic illustration of how traditional values shaped the instruments America would use to fashion its new place in the world as the leading imperial power.

THE INSTRUMENTS OF MODERN AMERICAN FOREIGN POLICY

Any nation-state has at hand certain instruments, or tools, to use in implementing its foreign policy.

[14]"Balance of power" was the primary foreign policy role played by the major European powers during the nineteenth century, and it is a role available to the United States in contemporary foreign affairs, a role occasionally adopted but not on a world scale. This is the third of the four roles identified and discussed later in this chapter.

[15]The best analysis of what he calls the "100 years' peace" will be found in Karl Polanyi, *The Great Transformation* (New York: Rinehart, 1944; Beacon paperback edition, 1957), pp. 5ff.

[16]John G. Stoessinger, *Crusaders and Pragmatists: Movers of Modern American Foreign Policy* (New York: W. W. Norton, 1985), pp. 21, 34.

GEORGE KENNAN AND HENRY KISSINGER
Architects of American Foreign Policy

TWO OF THE MOST IMPORTANT and influential figures in American foreign policy never held elective office. Known more for their intellect than for their use of political power, both George Kennan and Henry Kissinger developed powerful paradigms for the conduct of American foreign policy.

George Kennan, a career foreign service officer and expert on the Soviet Union, spent many years studying Soviet languages and politics. While serving as second-in-command at the American embassy in Moscow at the end of World War II, Kennan was asked for advice about postwar Soviet intentions from policy makers in Washington. His response was an 8,000-word telegram in which he attacked America's spirit of cooperation with the Soviets. Kennan believed that the U.S.S.R. viewed the world as divided into two camps, socialist and capitalist, and that in such a "bipolar" world there could be no peaceful coexistence. Therefore, the United States had two choices: (1) resist Soviet efforts to undermine the Western coalition, or (2) buy time until the Soviet Union changed from within.

This telegram became the blueprint for America's postwar policy in what has been labeled the cold war. Fearing he had succeeded too well, however, Kennan published an article a year later in the journal *Foreign Affairs* under the pseudonym Mr. X, in which he argued that the U.S.S.R. was not out to dominate the world. Rather, he asserted, the Soviets wanted a ring of sympathetic nations around their country as a buffer against future attacks (remembering that over the centuries the Soviets had been attacked and devastated numerous times by invading armies). Kennan's conclusion to his article literally became American policy for the next two decades: "The main element of any United States policy toward the Soviet Union must be that of a long-term patient but firm and vigilant *containment* of Russian expansive tendencies" (emphasis added).

GEORGE KENNAN

Any instrument is neutral, capable of serving many goals. There have been many instruments of American foreign policy, and we can deal here only with those instruments we deem to be most important in the modern epoch: diplomacy, the United Nations, the international monetary structure, economic aid, collective security, and military deterrence. Each of these instruments will be evaluated in this section for its utility in the conduct of American foreign policy, and each will be assessed in light of the history and development of American values.

Diplomacy

We begin this treatment of instruments with diplomacy because it is the instrument to which all other instruments should be subordinated, although they seldom are. **Diplomacy** is the representation of a government to other foreign gov-

Like Kennan's, Henry Kissinger's path to foreign policy grew from intellect and experience. As a Harvard Ph.D. and professor, Kissinger wrote extensively in the 1950s and 1960s on American-Soviet policy and the role of nuclear weapons. Impressed with his ideas, foreign policy experts in the Eisenhower, Kennedy, and Johnson administrations sought Kissinger's advice as a so-called defense intellectual. In 1969, Kissinger was selected by newly elected President Richard Nixon to serve as his national security adviser. Together, Nixon and Kissinger changed the shape of U.S. foreign policy. While taking a hard line on the Vietnam War, Kissinger orchestrated Nixon's historic trips to China and the Soviet Union in 1972, ushering in an era of "détente" between the superpowers. He was also instrumental in reaching an important agreement with the Soviets to limit nuclear arms, known as SALT I (the first Strategic Arms Limitation Treaty). Kissinger sought to implement his longstanding belief in "power politics"—namely, that the only international relations that really matter are those between the world's big and powerful nations, and that the problems of smaller nations are best viewed in terms of how they affect the superpowers. Although this philosophy was helpful in guiding improved U.S.-Soviet relations, it contributed to mistakes in Vietnam.

HENRY KISSINGER

Through a combination of intellect and an unexcelled talent for bureaucratic politics, Kissinger dominated foreign-policy making during the Nixon and Ford administrations. (He was named secretary of state in 1973.) After Ford's defeat in 1976, Kissinger began a consulting firm that helped provide access to top governmental and corporate leaders for his clients, which have included China and other nations. In contrast, George Kennan withdrew from public life, in part because of his disenchantment with the course of foreign policy in the 1950s and 1960s. As a scholar and researcher affiliated with the Institute for Advanced Study in Princeton, Kennan continued to garner respect for his intellect and perspectives on the policy he had helped create.

SOURCE: Fred Kaplan, *The Wizards of Armageddon* (New York: Simon and Schuster, 1983).

ernments. Its purpose is to promote national values or interests by peaceful means. According to Hans Morgenthau, "a diplomacy that ends in war has failed in its primary objective."[17]

The first effort to create a modern diplomatic service in the United States was made through the Rogers Act of 1924, which established the initial framework for a professional foreign service staff. But it took World War II and the Foreign Service Act of 1946 to forge the foreign service into a fully professional diplomatic corps.

Diplomacy, by its very nature, is overshadowed by spectacular international events, dramatic initiatives, and meetings among heads of state or their direct personal representatives. The traditional American distrust of diplomacy continues today, albeit in weaker form. Impatience

[17]Hans Morgenthau, *Politics among Nations,* 2nd ed. (New York: Knopf, 1956), p. 505.

with or downright distrust of diplomacy has been built not only into all the other instruments of foreign policy but also into the modern presidential system itself.[18] So much personal responsibility has been heaped upon the presidency that it is difficult for presidents to entrust any of their authority or responsibility in foreign policy to professional diplomats in the State Department and other bureaucracies. And the American practice of appointing political friends and campaign donors to major ambassadorial positions does not inspire trust. During his first year in office, President Bush named eighty-seven ambassadorial appointees, forty-eight of whom were important political contributors. President Clinton appointed even fewer professional diplomats to ambassadorships than either President Reagan or President Bush.[19]

Electoral politics is not the only kind of politics affecting the nature and timing of ambassadorial appointments. The Republican chair of the Senate Foreign Relations Committee, Jesse Helms, blocked eighteen of President Clinton's ambassadorial nominations for most of the 1995 congressional session, demanding that Clinton agree to merge three independent foreign policy agencies with the State Department. Although Helms did not win everything he demanded from President Clinton, he did gain some important concessions in return for his approval of the ambassadors during the last days before Congress recessed in December 1995.[20]

Distrust of diplomacy has also produced a tendency among all recent presidents to turn frequently to military and civilian personnel outside the State Department to take on a special diplomatic role as direct personal representatives of the president. As discouraging as it is to those who have dedicated their careers to foreign service to

have political hacks appointed over their heads, it is probably even more discouraging when they are displaced from a foreign policy issue as soon as relations with the country they are posted in begin to heat up. When a special personal representative is sent abroad to represent the president, that envoy holds a status higher than that of the local ambassador, and the embassy becomes the envoy's temporary residence and base of operation. Despite the impressive professionalization of the American foreign service—with advanced training, competitive exams, language requirements, and career commitment—this practice of displacing career ambassadors with political appointees and with special personal presidential representatives continues. For instance, when President Clinton sought in 1994 to make a final diplomatic attempt to persuade Haiti's military dictator to relinquish power to the country's freely elected president before dispatching U.S. military forces to the island, he sent a team of three personal representatives—former president Jimmy Carter, Senator Sam Nunn, and former chairman of the Joint Chiefs of Staff Colin Powell.

The significance of diplomacy and its vulnerability to domestic politics may be better appreciated as we proceed to the other instruments. Diplomacy was an instrument more or less imposed on Americans as the prevailing method of dealing among nation-states in the nineteenth century. The other instruments to be identified and assessed below are instruments that Americans self-consciously crafted for themselves to take care of their own chosen place in the world affairs of the second half of the twentieth century. They are, therefore, more reflective of American culture and values than is diplomacy.

The United Nations

The utility of the **United Nations (U.N.)** to the United States as an instrument of foreign policy can too easily be underestimated. During the first decade or more after its founding in 1945, the

---

[18]See Lowi, *The Personal President*, pp. 167–69.

[19]Dick Kirschten, "Life Jacket, Anyone?" *National Journal* 26 (25 June 1994), p. 1501.

[20]"Senate Slashes Agency Budgets, Confirms Eighteen Ambassadors," *Congressional Quarterly*, 16 December 1995, p. 3821.

United Nations was a direct servant of American interests. The most spectacular example of the use of the United Nations as an instrument of American foreign policy was the official U.N. authorization and sponsorship of intervention in Korea with an international "peacekeeping force" in 1950. Thanks to the Soviet boycott of the United Nations at that time, which deprived the U.S.S.R. of its ability to use its veto in the Security Council of the U.N., the United States was able to conduct the Korean War under the auspices of the United Nations.

The United States provided 40 percent of the U.N. budget in 1946 (its first full year of operation) and 28.1 percent of the $1.1 billion U.N. budget in 1994–1995.[21] Many Americans feel that the United Nations does not give good value for the investment. But any evaluation of the United Nations must take into account the purpose for which the United States sought to create it: to achieve power without diplomacy. After World War II, when the United States could no longer remain aloof from foreign policy, the nation's leaders sought to use its power to create an international structure that could be run with a minimum of regular diplomatic involvement—so that Americans could return to their normal domestic pursuits. As one constitutional scholar characterized the founding in 1787, so we could say of America's effort to found the United Nations—it sought to create "a machine that would go of itself."[22]

The U.N. may have gained a new lease on life in the post–cold war era, first with its performance in the Gulf War and then with its role in Somalia. Although President Bush's immediate reaction to Iraq's invasion of Kuwait was unilateral, he quickly turned to the U.N. for sponsorship. The U.N. General Assembly initially adopted resolutions condemning the invasion and approving the full blockade of Iraq. Once the blockade was seen as having failed to achieve the unconditional withdrawal demanded by the U.N., the General Assembly adopted further resolutions authorizing the twenty-nine-nation coalition to use force if, by January 15, 1991, the resolutions were not observed. The Gulf War victory was a genuine U.N. victory. The cost of the operation was estimated at $61.1 billion. First authorized by the U.S. Congress, actual U.S. outlays were offset by pledges from the other participants—the largest shares coming from Saudi Arabia ($15.6 billion), Kuwait ($16 billion), Japan ($10 billion), and Germany ($6.5 billion). The final U.S. costs were estimated at a maximum of $8 billion.[23]

Whether or not the U.N. is able to maintain its central position in future border and trade disputes, demands for self-determination, and other provocations to war depends entirely upon the character of each dispute. The Gulf War was a special case because it was a clear instance of invasion of one country by another that also threatened the control of oil, which is of vital interest to the industrial countries of the world. But in the case of Somalia, although the conflict violated the world's conscience, it did not threaten vital national interests outside the country's region. The United States had propped up Somalia's government for years for purely cold war purposes, but abandoned its dictatorial regime in 1990 and left it to a chaotic civil war involving many warlords, tribal leaders, and gangs of marauding youths. Late in 1992, thousands of American soldiers

[21]In 1994, the next four biggest contributors were Japan (11.9 percent), Germany (8.6 percent), Russia (6.4 percent), and France (5.7 percent). These figures do not include many specific U.N. operations and organizations, nor the U.S. contributions to these programs. See the *Statesman's Yearbook, 1994–95* (London: Macmillan, 1994), p. 6; and the *1995 Information Please Almanac* (Boston: Houghton Mifflin, 1994), pp. 73, 299.

[22]Michael Kammen, *A Machine That Would Go of Itself: The Constitution in American Culture* (New York: Alfred A. Knopf, 1986).

[23]There was, in fact, an angry dispute over a "surplus" of at least $2.2 billion, on the basis of which Japan and others demanded a rebate. *Report of the Secretary of Defense to the President and Congress* (Washington, DC: Government Printing Office, 1992), p. 26.

under U.N. sponsorship were dispatched with almost no advance preparation of the public for a limited military intervention to make the country safe enough for humanitarian aid. One expert on diplomatic affairs characterized the operation as the affirmation of an important principle (and possibly a new U.N. precedent): "Once a country utterly loses its ability to govern itself, it also loses its claim to sovereignty and should become a ward of the United Nations."[24]

But Somalia also suggests how fragile the American commitment to such "wars of conscience" can be. After a bloody firefight in October 1993, in which more than a dozen American soldiers were killed and some of their bodies dragged through the streets of Mogadishu—scenes that shocked American television viewers—President Clinton announced his intention to withdraw all American forces from Somalia. That withdrawal was completed on March 31, 1994.

Somalia was the first conflict for which U.N. troops were brought in for strictly humanitarian purposes. The next was in the former Yugoslavia. When Yugoslavia's communist regime collapsed in the early 1990s, the country broke apart into historically ethnically distinct regions. In one of these, Bosnia, a fierce war broke out between Muslims, Croatians, and Serbians. From the outset, all outside parties urged peace, and United Nations troops were deployed to create "safe havens" in several Bosnian cities and towns. Yet despite his campaign criticism of President Bush for not doing more to stop the bloodshed in Bosnia, President Clinton was also unable to muster support for a more active policy. Faced with resistance from NATO allies and from Russia, and with the unwillingness of the American people to risk the lives of U.S. soldiers over an issue not vital to U.S. interests, Clinton gave up his stern warnings and accepted the outcome: the in-

ternational community's failure to prevent Serbs from waging a war of aggression and genocide.

Not until November 1995, after still another year of frustration and with U.N. peacekeeping troops in increasingly serious danger from both sides in the Yugoslav civil war, was President Clinton able to achieve a ceasefire and a peace agreement in Dayton, Ohio, among the heads of the warring factions.

Despite the difficulty of restoring peace, the U.N. and its peacekeeping troops did an extraordinary job in the former Yugoslavia, dealing both with the intransigence of the warring parties and with the disagreement among the European powers about how to deal with a vicious and destructive civil war in their own neighborhood. This and other recent U.N. interventions show the promise and the limits of the U.N. as an instrument of foreign policy in the post–cold war era. Although the United States can no longer control U.N. decisions, as it could in the U.N.'s early days, the U.N. continues to function as a useful instrument of American foreign policy.[25]

The International Monetary Structure

Fear of a repeat of the economic devastation that followed World War I brought the United States together with its allies (except the U.S.S.R.) to Bretton Woods, New Hampshire, in 1944 to create a new international economic structure for the postwar world. The result was two institutions: the International Bank for Reconstruction and Development (commonly called the World Bank) and the International Monetary Fund.

The World Bank was set up to finance long-term capital. Leading nations took on the obliga-

---

[24]Strobe Talbott, "America Abroad," *Time*, 14 December 1992, p. 35.

[25]Not all American policy makers agree that the U.N. is a worthy instrument of American policy. The U.N. is on the verge of bankruptcy, no thanks to the United States, which owes the U.N. nearly $1.5 billion in dues. For a review, see Barbara Crossette, "U.N., Facing Bankruptcy, Plans to Cut Payroll by Ten Percent," *New York Times*, 6 February 1996, p. A3.

tion of contributing funds to enable the World Bank to make loans to capital-hungry countries. (The U.S. quota has been about one-third of the total.)

The *International Monetary Fund (IMF)* was set up to provide for the short-term flow of money. After the war, the dollar, instead of gold, was the chief means by which the currencies of one country would be "changed into" currencies of another country for purposes of making international transactions. To permit debtor countries with no international balances to make purchases and investments, the IMF was set up to lend dollars or other appropriate currencies to needy member countries to help them overcome temporary trade deficits. For many years after World War II, the IMF, along with U.S. foreign aid, in effect constituted the only international medium of exchange.

Economic Aid

Commitment to rebuilding war-torn countries came as early as commitment to the basic postwar international monetary structure. This is the way President Franklin Roosevelt put the case in a press conference in November 1942, less than one year after the United States entered World War II:

> Sure, we are going to rehabilitate [other nations after the war]. Why? . . . Not only from the humanitarian point of view . . . but from the viewpoint of our own pocketbooks, and our safety from future war.[26]

The particular form and timing for enacting American foreign aid was heavily influenced by Great Britain's sudden decision in 1947 that it would no longer be able to maintain its commitments to Greece and Turkey (full proof that America would now have to *have* clients rather than *be* one). Within three weeks of that announcement, President Truman recommended a $400-million direct aid program for Greece and Turkey, and by mid-May of 1947, Congress approved it. Since President Truman had placed the Greece-Turkey action within the larger context of a commitment to help rebuild and defend all countries the world over, wherever the leadership wished to develop democratic systems or to ward off communism, the Greek-Turkish aid was followed quickly by the historically unprecedented program that came to be known as the Marshall Plan, named in honor of Secretary of State (and former five-star general) George C. Marshall.[27]

The *Marshall Plan*—officially known as the European Recovery Plan (ERP)—was essential for the rebuilding of war-torn Europe. By 1952, the United States had spent over $34 billion for the relief, reconstruction, and economic recovery of Western Europe. The emphasis was shifted in 1951, with passage of the Mutual Security Act, to building up European military capacity. Of the $48 billion appropriated between 1952 and 1961, over half went for military assistance, the rest for continuing economic aid. Over those years, the geographic emphasis of U.S. aid also shifted toward South Korea, Taiwan, the Philippines, Vietnam, Iran, Greece, and Turkey—that is, toward the rim of communism. In the 1960s, the emphasis shifted once again, toward what became known as the Third World. From 1962 to 1975, over $100 billion was sent, mainly to Latin America for economic assistance. Other countries of Africa and Asia were also brought in.[28]

Many critics have argued that foreign aid is really aid for political and economic elites, not for

---

[26]Quoted in John Lewis Gaddis, *The United States and the Origins of the Cold War* (New York: Columbia University Press, 1972), p. 21.

[27]The best account of the decision and its purposes will be found in Joseph Jones, *The Fifteen Weeks* (New York: Viking, 1955).

[28]Robert A. Pastor, *Congress and the Politics of U.S. Foreign Economic Policy* (Berkeley: University of California Press, 1980), pp. 256–80.

the people. Although this is to a large extent true, it needs to be understood in a broader context. If a country's leaders oppose distributing food or any other form of assistance to its people, there is little the United States, or any aid organization, can do, short of terminating the assistance. Goods have to be exchanged across national borders before they can reach the people who need them. Needy people would probably be worse off if the United States cut off aid altogether. The lines of international communication must be kept open. That is why diplomacy exists, and foreign aid can facilitate diplomacy, just as diplomacy is needed to help get foreign aid where it is most needed.

Another important criticism of U.S. foreign aid policy is that it has not been tied closely enough to U.S. diplomacy. The original Marshall Plan was set up as an independent program outside the State Department and had its own separate missions in each participating country. Essentially, "ERP became a Second State Department."[29] This did not change until the program was reorganized as the Agency for International Development (AID) in the early 1960s. Meanwhile, the Defense Department has always had principal jurisdiction over that substantial proportion of economic aid that goes to military assistance. The Department of Agriculture administers the commodity aid programs, such as Food for Peace. Each department has in effect been able to conduct its own foreign policy, leaving many foreign diplomats to ask, "Who's in charge here?"

That brings us back to the history of U.S. efforts to balance traditional values with the modern needs of world leadership. Economic assistance is an instrument of American foreign policy, but it has been less effective than it might have been because of the inability of American politics to overcome its traditional opposition to foreign entanglements and build a unified foreign policy— something that the older nation-states would call a foreign ministry. The U.S. has undoubtedly

made progress, but those outside its borders still often wonder who is in charge.

Collective Security

In 1947, most Americans hoped that the United States could meet its world obligations through the United Nations and economic structures alone. But most foreign-policy makers recognized that it was a vain hope even as they were permitting and encouraging Americans to believe it. They had anticipated the need for military entanglements at the time of drafting the original U.N. charter by insisting upon language that recognized the right of all nations to provide for their mutual defense independently of the United Nations. And almost immediately after enactment of the Marshall Plan, the White House and a parade of State and Defense Department officials followed up with an urgent request to the Senate to ratify and to Congress to finance mutual defense alliances.

At first quite reluctant to approve treaties providing for national security alliances, the Senate ultimately agreed with the executive branch. The first collective security agreement was the Rio Treaty (ratified by the Senate in September 1947), which created the Organization of American States (OAS). This was the model treaty, anticipating all succeeding collective security treaties by providing that an armed attack against any of its members "shall be considered as an attack against all the American States," including the United States. A more significant break with U.S. tradition against peacetime entanglements came with the North Atlantic Treaty (signed in April 1949), which created the North Atlantic Treaty Organization (NATO). ANZUS, a treaty tying Australia and New Zealand to the United States, was signed in September 1951. Three years later, the Southeast Asia Treaty created the Southeast Asia Treaty Organization (SEATO).

In addition to these multilateral treaties, the United States entered into a number of bilateral

---

[29]Quoted in Lowi, *The End of Liberalism*, 2nd ed., p. 162.

treaties—treaties between two countries. As one author has observed, the United States has been a *producer* of security while most of it allies have been *consumers* of security.[30] Figure 13.1 demonstrates that the United States has consistently devoted a greater percentage of its gross domestic product (GDP) to defense than have its NATO allies and Japan.

This pattern has continued in the post–cold war era, and its best illustration is in the Persian Gulf War, where the United States provided the initiative, the leadership, and most of the armed

forces, even though its allies were obliged to reimburse over 90 percent of the cost.

It is difficult to evaluate collective security and its treaties, because the purpose of collective security as an instrument of foreign policy is prevention, and success of this kind has to be measured according to what did *not* happen. The critics have argued that U.S. collective security treaties posed a threat of encirclement to the Soviet Union, forcing it to produce its own collective security, particularly the Warsaw Pact.[31] Nevertheless, no

[31]The Warsaw Pact was signed in 1955 by the Soviet Union, the German Democratic Republic (East Germany), Poland, Hungary, Czechoslovakia, Romania, Bulgaria, and Albania. Albania later dropped out. The Warsaw Pact was terminated in 1991.

[30]George Quester, *The Continuing Problem of International Politics* (Hinsdale, IL: Dryden Press, 1974), p. 229.

FIGURE 13.1

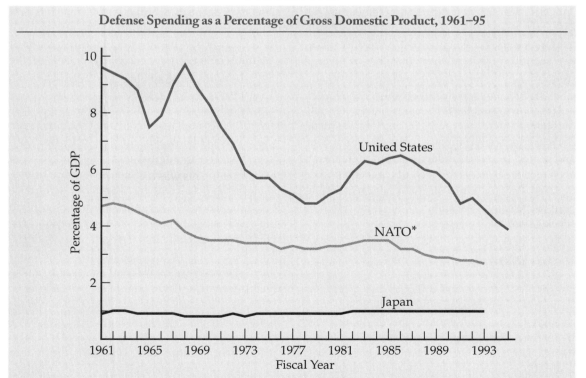

Defense Spending as a Percentage of Gross Domestic Product, 1961–95

SOURCES: Office of Management and Budget, *Budget of the United States Government, Fiscal Year 1995, Historical Tables* (Washington, DC: Government Printing Office, 1994), pp. 39–42; *SIPPRI Yearbook* (Stockholm, Sweden: Stockholm International Peace Research Institute, various years), 1979: pp. 36–37, 46–47; 1986: pp. 243–44; 1994: pp. 396, 560.

one can deny the counterargument that the world has enjoyed more than forty-five years without world war.

Although the Soviet Union has collapsed, Russia has emerged from a period of confusion and consolidation signaling its determination to play once again an active role in regional and world politics. The challenge for the United States and NATO in coming years will be how to broaden membership in the alliance to include the nations of Eastern Europe and some of the former Soviet republics without antagonizing Russia, which might see such an expansion of NATO as a new era of encirclement. The Partnership for Peace has served as a loosely defined first step toward full membership for these nations, which want NATO's protection against possible Russian expansionism.

NATO's ability to assist in implementing the uncertain peace in the Bosnian civil war will be a genuine test of the viability of NATO, and collective security in general, now that the cold war is over. NATO and the other mutual security organizations throughout the world are likely to survive. But these organizations are going to be less like military alliances and more like economic associations to advance technology, reduce trade barriers, and protect the world environment. Another form of collective security may well have emerged from the 1991 Persian Gulf War, with nations forming temporary coalitions under U.N. sponsorship to check a particularly aggressive nation.

Military Deterrence

For the first century and a half of its existence as an independent republic, the United States held strongly to a "Minuteman" theory of defense: Maintain a small corps of professional officers, a few flagships, and a small contingent of marines; leave the rest of defense to the state militias. In case of war, mobilize as quickly as possible, taking advantage of the country's immense size and its separation from Europe to gain time to mobilize.

The United States applied this policy as recently as the post–World War I years and was beginning to apply it after World II, until the new policy of preparedness won out. The cycle of demobilization-remobilization was broken, and in its place the United States adopted a new policy of constant mobilization and preparedness: *deterrence*, or the development and maintenance of military strength as a means of discouraging attack. After World War II, military deterrence against the Soviet Union became the fundamental American foreign policy objective, requiring a vast commitment of national resources. With preparedness as the goal, peacetime defense expenditures grew steadily.

However, the size of the defense budget has not been central to the consideration of deterrence as an instrument of foreign policy. Whether arms expenditures are motivated by a bilateral struggle between the United States and the Soviet Union or by a confrontation with a variety of potential aggressors, as has happened in the 1990s, the goal is not military dominance as such but *deterrence from any attack at all*. The Iraqi invasion of Kuwait proved that whatever had deterred the Soviet Union from aggression was not necessarily translatable into post–cold war conflicts. The victory against Iraq may lead to technologies and policies of deterrence more appropriate to the post–cold war world. But deterrence is still the name of the game, and the resumption and escalation of arms sales throughout the world, and especially in the Middle East since the Gulf War, suggest that the United States and other powers will have a real struggle to make deterrence work. There continues to be a kind of "arms race," but that race now tends to be not for quantitative but for technologically qualitative superiority.

For over a century after Napoleon brought to the world the first mass citizen armies, military capacity in the Western world was measured quantitatively. Technology was, of course, always important. Technological superiority helped to make possible the domination of the Western powers over their non-Western colonies and the domination of small U.S. armed contingents over Native Americans. But it was probably not until World War II that technology became the key to the military's value as an instrument of foreign policy. From then on, the technological tail began to wag the military dog. And it is not merely a question of adding technology by giving each soldier an automatic weapon and an

IN BRIEF BOX

INSTRUMENTS OF FOREIGN POLICY

Diplomacy
The representation of a government to other foreign governments
Designed to promote national values or interests by peaceful means, mainly discussion

United Nations
International peacekeeping structure created by the United States in the 1940s as response to World War II (originally a goal set by President Woodrow Wilson after World War I)
Often used as a tool to further the aims of American foreign policy (e.g., Korean War, Persian Gulf War)

International Monetary Structure
Formation of the World Bank (International Bank for Reconstruction and Development) and the International Monetary Fund (IMF) in response to economic devastation following World War II
World Bank set up to make long-term loans to countries for capital investment
IMF created to provide for short-term flows of money to facilitate trade (fund made up of gold and currencies of each member country)

Economic Aid
The first economic assistance plan of any importance was the Marshall Plan (European Recovery Plan) set up to rebuild Europe after World War II
Economic assistance has no doubt been a cornerstone in American foreign policy toward Third World countries, especially during the 1960s and early 1970s when the United States sent over $100 billion to Latin America to thwart the advance of communism

Collective Security
Mutual defense alliances set up after World War II
Agreement that an attack against a member country would be considered as an attack against all member countries
The first treaty calling for a mutual security alliance was the Rio Treaty (OAS) between United States and various Central and South American countries, Mexico, and Haiti. Other examples are NATO, ANZUS, SEATO

Military Deterrence
Mobilization of troops during peacetime combined with a willingness to expand defense budget
The "balance of terror" or Mutually Assured Destruction (MAD) between superpowers during the cold war
Post–cold war continuation of race in technical innovation and arms sales

electronic communications device. Technology means a policy of planned technological innovation. Probably the most important outcome of the Persian Gulf War, especially from the military point of view, is that most of this expensive technology—laser-guided bombs, cruise missiles, satellite reconnaissance, computerized coordination of battles—worked as well as its supporters had claimed. This will likely enhance the credibility of using military technology as the primary deterrent in the world.

The policy of planned technological innovation is called research and development (R&D). R&D is certainly not limited to national defense. American industries spend billions of dollars on R&D annually, and many nonmilitary agencies of the federal government engage in some R&D. But nowhere is R&D such a high priority as in the modern American military establishment. The U.S. government and private industry together spend about $150 billion a year on R&D "covering everything from mapping the human genome to exploring the frontiers of physics. That is about 3 percent of America's gross domestic product, and about the same percentage that Japan and Germany spend."[32] But there the similarity ends. Germany and Japan devote almost all of their R&D to civilian projects; the United States spends about 40 percent of its R&D on military projects. This amounted to $47.8 billion in 1992, up from $18.4 billion in 1980.[33] There is an additional "hidden" R&D military budget in the private manufacture of military hardware. It is difficult to determine just where R&D ends and manufacturing begins; nevertheless, it is certain that R&D takes a significant bite of each private defense production contract.

The end of the cold war raised public expectations for a "peace dividend" at last, after nearly a decade of the largest peacetime defense budget increases in U.S. history. Many defense experts, liberal and conservative, feared what they called a budget "free-fall," not only because deterrence was still needed but also because severe and abrupt cuts could endanger private industry in many friendly foreign countries as well as in the United States.

The Persian Gulf War brought both points dramatically into focus. First, the Iraqi invasion of Kuwait revealed the size, strength, and advanced modern technological base not only of the Iraqi armed forces but of other countries, Arab and non-Arab, including the capability, then or soon, to make atomic weapons and other weapons of massive destructive power. Moreover, the demand for advanced weaponry was intensifying. The decisive victory of the United States and its allies in the Gulf War, far from discouraging the international arms trade, gave it fresh impetus. Following the Gulf War victory, *Newsweek* reported that "industry reps quickly realized that foreign customers would now be beating a path to their doors, seeking to buy the winning weaponry." The Soviet Union at one time led the list of major world arms sellers, and Russia and several other republics of the former Soviet Union have continued to make international arms sales, particularly since now there are "no ideological limitations" in the competition for customers.[34] The United States now leads the list of military weapons exporters, followed by Russia, France, Great Britain, and China. Thus, some shrinkage of defense expenditure has been desirable, but Democrats and Republicans alike agree that this reduction must be guided by the continuing need to maintain U.S. and allied credibility as a deterrent to post–cold war arms races.

As to the second point, domestic pressures join international demands to fuel post–cold war de-

---

[32]Michael Lubell, "Getting the Right Mix on R&D," *New York Times*, 27 December 1992, sec. 3, p. 11.

[33]The R&D budget totals include the Department of Defense, Department of Energy (military related), and the National Aeronautics and Space Administration. See *Statistical Abstract of the United States: 1990*, pp. 331, 584.

[34]"Arms for Sale," *Newsweek*, 8 April 1991, pp. 22–27.

fense spending. Each cut in military production and each closing of a military base or plant translates into a significant loss of jobs. Moreover, the conversion of defense industries to domestic uses is not a problem faced by the United States alone. Figure 13.2 conveys a dramatic picture of the "international relations" of the production of one single weapons system, the F-16 fighter airplane.

All of this suggests that the threat of the arms race and international conflicts persists even in the post–cold war era. It also suggests that the United States is an important part of the problem as well as the most essential part of the solution. The only real hope for a significant reduction in the international demand for arms will come from changes in the general political and economic environment. But such changes do not happen spontaneously. On the international level, genuine reduction in the demand for arms will require diplomacy; try as we might, power without diplomacy can never be a permanent solution. And this must in turn be accompanied by economic growth, not only in the United States but everywhere.

FIGURE 13.2

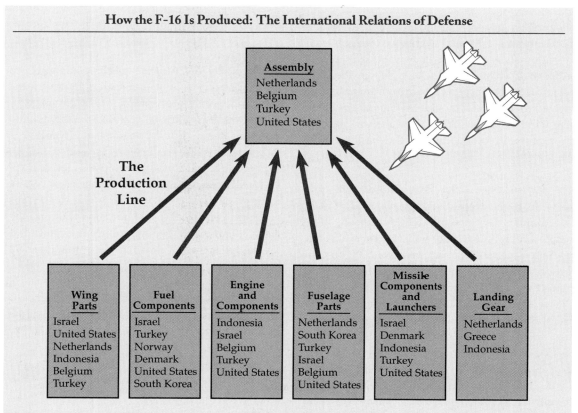

How the F-16 Is Produced: The International Relations of Defense

The Production Line

Assembly
Netherlands
Belgium
Turkey
United States

Wing Parts	**Fuel Components**	**Engine and Components**	**Fuselage Parts**	**Missile Components and Launchers**	**Landing Gear**
Israel	Israel	Indonesia	Netherlands	Israel	Netherlands
United States	Turkey	Israel	South Korea	Denmark	Greece
Netherlands	Norway	Belgium	Turkey	Indonesia	Indonesia
Indonesia	Denmark	Turkey	Israel	Turkey	
Belgium	United States	United States	Belgium	United States	
Turkey	South Korea		United States		

SOURCES: U.S. Congress, Office of Technology Assessment, *Arming Our allies: Cooperation and Competition in Defense Technology,* Series OTA-ICS-449 (Washington, DC: Government Printing Office, May 1990), pp. 42–43. Information provided by the primary manufacturer, General Dynamics Corporation.

ROLES NATIONS PLAY

Although each president has hundreds of small foreign fires to fight and can choose whichever instruments of policy best fit each particular situation, the primary foreign policy problem any president faces is choosing an overall role for the country in foreign affairs. Roles help us to define a situation in order to control the element of surprise in international relations. Surprise is in fact the most dangerous aspect of international relations, especially in a world made smaller and more fragile by advances in and the proliferation of military technology.

Choosing a Role

The problem of choosing a role can be understood by identifying a limited number of roles played by nation-states in the past. Four such roles will be drawn from history—the Napoleonic, the Holy Alliance, the balance-of-power, and the economic expansionist roles. Although the definitions given here will be exaggerations of the real world, they do capture in broad outline the basic choices available.

THE NAPOLEONIC ROLE The *Napoleonic role* takes its name from the role played by postrevolutionary France under Napoleon. The French at that time felt not only that their new democratic system of government was the best on earth but also that France would not be safe until democracy was adopted universally. If this meant intervention into the internal affairs of France's neighbors, and if that meant warlike reactions, then so be it. President Woodrow Wilson expressed a similar viewpoint when he supported the U.S. declaration of war in 1917 with his argument that "the world must be made safe for democracy." Obviously such a position can be adopted by any powerful nation as a rationalization for intervening at its convenience in the internal affairs of another country. But it can also be

sincerely espoused, and in the United States it has from time to time enjoyed broad popular consensus. The U.S. played the Napoleonic role most recently in ousting Philippine dictator Ferdinand Marcos (February 1986), Panamanian leader Manuel Noriega (December 1989), the Sandinista government of Nicaragua (February 1990), and the military rulers of Haiti (September 1994).

THE HOLY ALLIANCE ROLE The concept of the *Holy Alliance role* emerged out of the defeat of Napoleon and the agreement by the leaders of Great Britain, Russia, Austria, and Prussia to preserve the social order against *all* revolution, including democratic revolution, at whatever cost. (Post-Napoleonic France also joined it.) The Holy Alliance made use of every kind of political instrument available—including political suppression, espionage, sabotage, and outright military intervention—to keep existing governments in power. The Holy Alliance role is comparable to the Napoleonic role in that each operates on the assumption that intervention into the internal affairs of other countries is justified for the maintenance of peace. But Napoleonic intervention is motivated by fear of dictatorship, and it can accept and even encourage revolution. In contrast, Holy Alliance intervention is antagonistic to any form of political change, even when this means supporting an existing dictatorship.[35] Because the Holy Alliance role became more important after the cold war ended, illustrations of this role will be given later in the chapter.

THE BALANCE-OF-POWER ROLE The *balance-of-power role* is basically an effort by the major powers to play off against each other so that no

---

[35]For a thorough and instructive exposition of the original Holy Alliance pattern, see Paul M. Kennedy, *The Rise and Fall of the Great Powers: Economic Change and Military Conflict from 1500 to 2000* (New York: Random House, 1987), pp. 159–60. And for a comparison of the Holy Alliance role with the balance-of-power role, to be discussed next, see Polanyi, *The Great Transformation*, pp. 5–11 and 259–62.

great power or combination of great and lesser powers can impose conditions on others. The most relevant example of the use of this strategy is found in the nineteenth century, especially the latter half. The feature of the balance-of-power role that is most distinct from the two previously identified roles is that this role accepts the political system of each country, asking no questions except whether the country will join an alliance and will use its resources to ensure that each country will respect the borders and interests of all the others.[36]

THE ECONOMIC EXPANSIONIST ROLE   The *economic expansionist role,* also called the capitalist role, shares with the balance-of-power role the attitude that the political system or ideology of a country is irrelevant; the only question is whether a country has anything to buy or sell and whether its entrepreneurs, corporations, and government agencies will honor their contracts. Governments and their armies are occasionally drawn into economic expansionist relationships in order to establish, reopen, or expand trade relationships, and to keep the lines of commerce open. But the role is political, too. The point can

be made that the economic expansionist role was the role consistently played by the United States in Latin and Central America, until the cold war (perhaps in the 1960s and beyond) pushed us toward the Holy Alliance role with most of those countries.

Like arms control, however, economic expansion does not happen spontaneously. In the past, economic expansion owed a great deal to military backing, because contracts do not enforce themselves, trade deficits are not paid automatically, and new regimes do not always honor the commitments made by regimes they replace. The only way to expand economic relationships is through diplomacy.

Roles for America Today

Although "making the world safe for democracy" was used to justify the U.S. entry into World War I, it was taken more seriously after World War II, when at last the United States was willing to play a more sustained part in world affairs. The Napoleonic role was most suited to America's view of the postwar world. To create the world's ruling regimes in the American image would indeed give Americans the opportunity to return to their private pursuits, for if all or even most of the world's countries were governed by democratic

[36]Felix Gilbert et al., The Norton History of Modern Europe (New York: W. W. Norton, 1971), pp. 1222–24.

IN BRIEF BOX

THE ROLES NATIONS PLAY

Napoleonic role—a country feels that in order to safeguard its form of government (i.e., democracy), it must ensure (by force if necessary) that other countries adopt the same form of government

Holy Alliance role—using every political instrument available to keep existing governments in power, whatever form those governments may take; keeping peace is more important than promoting one particular form of government

balance-of-power role—major powers play off against each other so that no one power or combination of powers can impose conditions on others

economic expansionist role—being primarily concerned with what other countries have to buy or to sell and with their dependability in honoring contracts, regardless of their form of government

constitutions, there would be no more war, since no democracy would ever attack another democracy—or so it has been assumed.[37]

MAKING THE WORLD SAFE FOR DEMOCRACY The emergence of the Soviet Union as a superpower was the overwhelming influence on American foreign policy thinking in the post–World War II era. The distribution of power in the world was "bipolar," and Americans saw the world separated in two, with an "iron curtain" dividing the communist world from the free world. Immediately after the war, American's foreign policy goal had been "pro-democracy," a Napoleonic role dominated by the Marshall Plan and the genuine hope for a democratic world. This quickly shifted toward a Holy Alliance role, with "containment" as the primary foreign policy criterion.[38] Containment was fundamentally a Holy Alliance concept. According to foreign-policy expert Richard Barnet, during the 1950s and 1960s, "the United States used its military or paramilitary power on an average of once every eighteen months either to prevent a government deemed undesirable from coming to power or to overthrow a revolutionary or reformist government considered inimical to America's interests."[39] Although Barnet did not refer to Holy Alliance, his description fits the model perfectly.

During the 1970s, the United States played the Holy Alliance role less frequently, not so much because of the outcome of the Vietnam War as because of the emergence of a multipolar world. In 1972, the United States accepted (and later recognized) the communist government of the People's Republic of China and broke forever its pure bipolar, cold war view of world power distribution. Other powers became politically important as well, including Japan, the European Economic Community (now the European Union), India, and, depending on their own resolve, the countries making up the Organization of Petroleum Exporting Countries (OPEC). The United States experimented with all four of the previously identified roles, depending on which was appropriate to a specific region of the world. In the Middle East, America tended to play an almost classic balance-of-power role, by appearing sometimes cool in its relations with Israel and by playing off one Arab country against another. The United States has been able to do this despite the fact that every country in the Middle East recognizes that for cultural, domestic, and geostrategic reasons, the United States has always considered Israel as its most durable and important ally in the region and has unwaveringly committed itself to Israel's survival in a very hostile environment. President Nixon introduced balance-of-power considerations in the Far East by "playing the China card." In other parts of the world, particularly in Latin America, America tended to hold to the Holy Alliance and Napoleonic roles.

This multipolar phase ended after 1989, with the collapse of the Soviet Union and the end of the cold war. Soon thereafter the Warsaw Pact collapsed too, ending armed confrontation in Europe. With almost equal suddenness, the popular demand for "self-determination" produced several new nation-states and the demand for still more. On the one hand, it is indeed good to witness the re-emergence of some twenty-five major nationalities after anywhere from forty-five to seventy-five years of suppression On the other hand, policy makers with a sense of history are aware that this new world order bears a strong resemblance to the world of 1914. Then, the trend was known as "Balkanization." Balkanization meant nationhood and self-determination, but it also meant war. The Soviet Union after World

[37]For a summary of the entire literature about the "democratic peace," see Henry S. Farber and Joanne Gowa, "Politics and Peace," *International Security* 20, no. 2 (Fall 1995), pp. 123–46. See also Jack Levi, "Domestic Politics and War," *Journal of Interdisciplinary History* 18, no. 4 (Spring 1988), pp. 653–73.

[38]The original theory of containment was articulated by former ambassador and scholar George Kennan in a famous article published under the Pseudonym Mr. X, "The Sources of Soviet Conduct," *Foreign Affairs* 25 (1947), p. 556.

[39]Richard Barnet, "Reflections," *New Yorker,* 9 March 1987, p. 82.

War I and Yugoslavia after World War II kept more than twenty nationalities from making war against each other for several decades. In 1989 and the years that followed, the world was caught unprepared for the dangers of a new disorder that the re-emergence of these nationalities produced.

It should also be emphasized that the demand for nationhood emerged with new vigor in many other parts of the world—the Middle East, South and Southeast Asia, and South Africa. Perhaps we are seeing worldwide Balkanization; we should not overlook the re-emergence of the spirit of nationhood among ethnic minorities in Canada and the United States.

MAKING THE WORLD SAFE FOR DEMOCRACY AND MARKETS   The abrupt end of the cold war unleashed another dynamic factor, the globalization of markets; one could call it the globalization of capitalism. This is good news, but it has its problematic side because the free market can disrupt nationhood. Although the globalization of markets is enormously productive, countries like to enjoy its benefits while attempting at the same time to prevent international economic influences from affecting local jobs, local families, and established class and tribal relationships.

This struggle between capitalism and nationhood produces a new kind of bipolarity in the world. The old world order was shaped by *external bipolarity*—of West versus East. This seems to have been replaced by *internal bipolarity*, wherein each country is struggling to make its own hard policy choices to preserve its cultural uniqueness while competing effectively in the global marketplace.

Approval of the North American Free Trade Agreement (NAFTA) serves as the best example of this struggle within the United States. NAFTA was supported by a majority of Democrats and Republicans on the grounds that a freer, global market was in America's national interest. But even as NAFTA was being embraced by large bipartisan majorities in Congress, three important

factions were rising to fight it. Former presidential candidate Pat Buchanan led a large segment of conservative Americans to fight NAFTA because, he argued, communities and families would be threatened by job losses and by competition from legal and illegal immigrant workers. Another large faction, led by Ross Perot, opposed NAFTA largely on the theory that American companies would move their operations to Mexico, where labor costs are lower. Organized labor also joined the fight against NAFTA.

The global market is here to stay and American values have changed enough to incorporate it, despite the toll it may take on community and family tradition. Meanwhile, many of the elements of foreign policy created during the cold war still exist because they turned out to be good adjustments to the modern era. The Marshall Plan and the various forms of international economic aid that succeeded it continue to this day. Although appropriations for foreign aid have been shrinking, only a small minority of members of the Senate and the House favor the outright abolition of foreign aid programs. NATO and other collective security arrangements continue, as do some aspects of containment, even though there is no longer a Soviet Union, because collective security arrangements have, as we shall see, proven useful in dealing with new democracies and other nations seeking to join the global market. Even though the former Soviet Union is now more often an ally than an adversary, the United States still quite frequently uses unilateral and multilateral means of keeping civil wars contained within their own borders, so that conflict does not spread into neighboring states. America is practicing a new form of containment, but one that is based on the values and institutions of cold war containment.

Another traditional value that has been updated and given fresh application is the American commitment to "making the world safe for democracy." By this, Woodrow Wilson and eventually all Americans intended that we would fight foreign wars only to keep violent conflicts and

■ DEBATING THE ISSUES ■

American Foreign Policy: Self-Interest or Idealism?

With the end of the cold war and the breakup of the Soviet Union, many foreign policy experts are reassessing America's role in the world community. Some argue that it is time to focus our attention and resources more directly on our own problems and needs. Others argue that this is no time for the United States to abandon its world leadership role.

Economist Alan Tonelson defends what he labels an "interest-based" foreign policy for America. Such a position emphasizes placing American needs first and advocates foreign interventions only when they serve our interests. Foreign-policy specialist Joshua Muravchik, on the other hand, rejects the realist view of Tonelson and others; he maintains that America has both a right and an obligation to extend democratic values around the world.

TONELSON

The United States cannot hope to achieve the desired level of security and prosperity by underwriting the security and prosperity of countries all over the world, and by enforcing whatever global norms of economic and political behavior this ambition requires. . . . It must therefore distinguish between what it must do that is absolutely essential for achieving this more modest set of objectives and those things it might do that are not essential. It must, in other words, begin to think in terms not of the whole world's well-being but rather of purely national interests. . . .

. . . An interest-based U.S. foreign policy would firmly subordinate international activism and the drive for world leadership to domestic concerns. Indeed, it would spring from new and more realistic ideas about what can be expected of a country's official foreign policy in the first place. . . An interest-based approach would also reject the idea that meeting a set of global responsibilities can be the lodestar of U.S. foreign policy. . . . An interest-based foreign policy would acknowledge that the citizens of a democracy have every right to choose whatever foreign policy they please. . . .

The new foreign policy certainly would not preclude acting on principle. But it would greatly de-emphasize conforming to abstract standards of behavior. In fact, the new foreign policy would shy away from any over-

corrupting foreign influences away from our shores. That particular value has been refashioned to mean "making the world safe for democracy and markets," which requires that American policy look more closely at and act more directly upon the domestic institutions of other countries, so that there will be more trade outlets as well as more stable and less warlike regimes. This, too, is a modern application of an older faith—the belief that democracies may compete economically with each other but will never go to war against each other. The question remains, however, what are the implications of internal bipolarity for the role

the United States is going to play in the post–cold war world?

THE INTERNATIONAL ARMS TRADE   Another indication of America's post–Cold War role is the new arms race—that is, the international market in military products—and the growing importance of the Holy Alliance role in America's effort to produce a "new world order." The primary incentive in the international sale of military products is to keep the American defense industry alive and prosperous in the face of cuts in the defense budget. The United States today is the world's biggest

arching strategy of or conceptual approach to international relations. . . . Its only rule of thumb would be "whatever works" to preserve or enhance America's security and prosperity. . . .[1]

MURAVCHIK

Although many state actions aim to defend interests, many do not. Some are motivated by altruism. The United States rushes aid to the victims of flood, famine, or other catastrophe wherever these occur for no motive other than human sympathy. Several other countries do the same. Various states offer asylum to the persecuted, provide good offices for the mediation of distant disputes, and even contribute troops to international peacekeeping forces, all for reasons that are essentially humanitarian. . . . The realists are left with the argument that it is wrong to foist our ways—that is, democracy—on others. In saying this the realists suddenly are arguing in moral terms. Their point, however, entails a logical fallacy. The reason it is wrong to impose something on others, presumably, is because it violates their will. But absent democracy, how can their will be known? Moreover, why care about violating people's will unless one begins with the democratic premise that popular will ought to be sovereign?

This argument implies that people prefer to be ruled by an indigenous dictator than to be liberated through foreign influence. The realists will have a hard time explaining this to the people of Panama who danced in the streets when U.S. invaders ousted dictator Manuel Noriega. . . .

The examples of Panama, Japan, Germany, the Dominican Republic, and Grenada notwithstanding, to foist democracy on others does not ordinarily mean to impose it by force. Nor does it mean to seek carbon copies of American institutions. . . . If individuals are obliged to abide by certain moral rules, can they be exempted from those rules when they act collectively with others in the name of the nation?[2]

---

[1]Alan Tonelson, "What Is the National Interest?" *The Atlantic*, July 1991, pp. 37, 39.
[2]Joshua Muravchik, *Exporting Democracy: Fulfilling America's Destiny* (Washington, DC: AEI Press, 1991), pp. 25, 34–36.

producer and exporter of advanced weaponry. In 1993, for instance, 73 percent of new arms deals in the Third World came from America, and the value of American arms sales to Third World nations totalled $14.8 billion.[40] Many other countries also manufacture military materials, and a tremendous proportion of their military goods are for export. These countries are Brazil (over 80 percent for export), Italy (62 percent), Israel (47 percent), Spain (41 percent), the United Kingdom (40 percent), and Sweden (24 percent).[41] This means that each of these economies has a heavy stake in the international arms market. It also means that the United States and Russia in particular have a double stake in the maintenance of that market, because they profit not only from their own exports but from royalties they earn on the exports of the

---

[40]Two sales to wealthy but vulnerable Middle East nations accounted for 80 percent of this total: Saudi Arabia paid $9.5 billion for 72 F-15 jet fighters from McDonnell Douglas, and Kuwait paid $2.2 billion for 256 M1-A2 tanks from General Dynamics. See "Look Who's Dominating the Arms Trade," *New York Times*, 20 August 1994, p. A22.

[41]See U.S. Congress, Office of Technology Assessment, *Global Arms Trade* (Washington, DC: Government Printing Office, June 1991).

other countries, since most of the weapons and weapons components that these smaller countries manufacture are under license from the United States or Russia.[42]

Until 1991, Iraq was the biggest importer of military goods. Between 1983 and 1988, the U.S. Arms Control and Disarmament Agency could identify $40 billion worth of arms bought by Iraq on the international market. And Iraq will almost certainly return in the near future to major status as a purchaser. Meanwhile, the largest importers today are Saudi Arabia ($26 billion imported during the same five years), India ($15 billion during the same period), Syria ($13 billion), and Iran ($12 billion).[43]

Why are these countries buying so much advanced military material? In some instances there are actual arms races. Just as the United States and the Soviet Union used weaponry as a deterrent against each other, so smaller, neighboring countries use their weaponry as a deterrent against one another. The value of weapons importation for these countries can be seen in the regular use the United States and the United Nations make of restrictions and embargoes on weapons as sanctions against "misbehaving" countries.

Another reason is that many of the most despotic regimes view a big military presence as an essential means of maintaining control of their own populations. And all too often, the United States has cooperated in this aspect of the arms trade, even encouraging it as part of its Holy Alliance role. Supporting existing regimes was a key aspect of the original Holy Alliance of the nineteenth century, and it remains a key aspect of it in the post–cold war world today. The United States will never wholly approve of despotic regimes and is rarely even comfortable with benevolent but undemocratic ones. But America finds itself supporting distasteful regimes because it likes world stability more than it dislikes undemocratic regimes. And this attitude makes the Holy Alliance role a lot easier to play, because it is an attitude with which its European allies are historically comfortable.

A Holy Alliance role will never relieve the United States of the need for diplomacy, however. In fact, diplomacy becomes all the more important because despotic regimes eventually fail and in the process attempt to thrust their problems on their neighbors. The dissolution of Yugoslavia and the struggles of a concert of nations to stop the genocidal ethnic struggle there testify to the limits of the Holy Alliance role. The painstaking efforts of the Clinton administration to reach a diplomatic settlement with North Korea over its efforts to develop nuclear weapons also testify to the continuing importance of diplomacy. This is not to argue that war is never justifiable or that peace can always be achieved through discussions among professional diplomats or purchased by compromise or appeasement. It is only to argue that there are severe limits on how often a country like the United States can engage in Holy Alliances. When leaders in a democracy engage in unilateral or multilateral direct action, with or without military force, they must have overwhelming justification. In all instances, the political should dominate the military. That is what diplomacy is all about. In 1952, the distinguished military career of General Douglas MacArthur was abruptly terminated when President Truman dismissed him for insubordination. At issue was MacArthur's unwillingness to allow the military in Korea to be subordinated to politicians and diplomats. MacArthur's argument was "In war, there is no substitute for victory."[44] But he was overlooking the prior question and therefore missed the very point that should guide any foreign policy: Is there a substitute for war?

---

[42]The license is a sale to a foreign company by, for example, a U.S. company, of the right to manufacture one of its products. This is subject to approval by the departments of Defense and State.

[43]See U.S. Congress, Office of Technology Assessment, *Global Arms Trade*, pp. 4–7.

[44]Address, joint meeting of Congress, 10 April 1951.

CHAPTER REVIEW

This chapter began by raising some dilemmas about forming foreign policy in a democracy like the United States. Skepticism about foreign entanglements and the secrecy surrounding many foreign policy issues form the basis of these dilemmas. Although we cannot provide solutions to the foreign policy issues that the United States faces, we can provide a well-balanced analysis of the problems of foreign policy. This analysis is based on the five basic dimensions of foreign policy: the players, the setting, the values, the instruments, and the roles.

The first section of this chapter looked at the players in foreign policy: the makers and the shapers. The influence of institutions and groups varies from case to case, with the important exception of the president. Since the president is central to all foreign policy, it is best to assess how other actors interact with the president. In most instances, this interaction involves only the narrowest element of the foreign policy establishment. The American people have an opportunity to influence foreign policy, but primarily through Congress or interest groups.

Foreign policy is also guided by developments within the international system. The United States operates as a nation-state in a world of nation-states whose ignorance of each other breeds distrust and hostility. The purpose of foreign policy is to defend national sovereignty against other nation-states that are conducting their foreign policy for the same purpose.

The next section, on values, traced the history of American values that had a particular relevance to American perspectives on the outside world. We found that the American fear of a big government applied to foreign as well as domestic governmental powers. The founders and the active public of the founding period all recognized that foreign policy was special, that the national government had special powers in its dealings with foreigners, and that presidential

supremacy was justified in the conduct of foreign affairs. The only way to avoid the big national government and presidential supremacy was to avoid the foreign entanglements that made foreign policy, diplomacy, secrecy, and presidential discretion necessary. Americans held on to their "anti-statist" tradition until World War II, long after world conditions cried out for American involvement. And even as it became involved in world affairs, the U.S. held on tightly to the legacies of 150 years of tradition: the intermingling of domestic and foreign policy institutions, and unilateralism, the tendency to "go it alone" when confronted with foreign conflicts.

We then looked at the instruments—that is, the tools—of American foreign policy. These are the basic statutes and the institutions by which foreign policy has been conducted since World War II: diplomacy, the United Nations, the international monetary structure, economic aid, collective security, and military deterrence. Although Republicans and Democrats look at the world somewhat differently, and although each president has tried to impose a distinctive flavor on foreign policy, they have all made use of these basic instruments, and that has given foreign policies a certain continuity. When Congress created these instruments after World War II, the old tradition was still so strong that it moved Congress to try to create instruments that would do their international work with a minimum of diplomacy—a minimum of human involvement. This is what we called power without diplomacy.

The next section concentrated on the role or roles the president and Congress have sought to play in the world. To help simplify the tremendous variety of tactics and strategies that foreign policy leaders can select, we narrowed the field down to four categories of roles nations play, suggesting that there is a certain amount of consistency and stability in the conduct of a nation-state in its dealings with other nation-states. These were labeled according to actual roles that diplomatic historians have identified in the history of major Western nation-states: The Napoleonic, Holy Alliance, balance-of-power, and economic expansionist roles. We also attempted to identify and assess the role of the United States in the post–cold war era, essentially the Holy Alliance role. But whatever its advantages may be, the Holy Alliance approach will never allow the United States to conduct foreign policy without diplomacy. America is tied inextricably to the perils and ambiguities of international relationships, and diplomacy is still the monarch of all available instruments of foreign policy.

We conclude by returning to the dilemma we raised in the chapter's introduction: In a democracy like the United States, who should make foreign policy? The chapter provided numerous case studies to seek an answer to this question. We believe that between the extremes of isolationism and total power resting with the president resides a middle ground where the American people can express their will through the members of Congress. The national interest can be defined only through debate and deliberation, which we hope will serve as the foundations for the formation of foreign policy in the American democracy.

TIME LINE ON FOREIGN POLICY

Events		Institutional Developments
Treaties with Britain and Spain establish recognition of U.S. sovereignty (1795)		U.S. attempts to steer clear of foreign alliances; pursues neutrality policy (1790s)
Louisiana Purchase from France (1803)	**1800**	
War of 1812, despite American attempts to maintain neutrality (1812)		Monroe Doctrine to prevent further European colonization in Western Hemisphere (1823)
U.S. reaches diplomatic settlement with Great Britain over Northwest Territory; Oregon Treaty sets northern U.S. border at the 49th parallel (1846)		Manifest Destiny doctrine leads to war with Mexico (1840s); Mexican War first successful offensive war (1846–1848)
War with Mexico, ending in Mexico's giving up claim to Texas and ceding California and New Mexico to U.S. (1846–1848)		
Civil War (1861–1865)	**1860**	
U.S. purchases Alaska from Russia; Midway Islands annexed (1867)		
First Inter-American Conference between U.S. and Latin American nations (1889–1890)		Unilateralism prevails (1870s–1890s)
Spanish-American War; treaty leads to U.S. annexation of Puerto Rico, Guam, Philippines; Hawaii annexed (1898)		Reciprocal agreements between U.S. and Latin American nations (1890)
		U.S. concern with world markets after closing of American frontier (1890s)

Events		Institutional Developments
	1900	
World War I (1914–1918)		U.S. does not join the League of Nations (1919)
		Rogers Act recognizes foreign service officers as part of government career system (1924)
U.S. in World War II (1941–1945)		U.N. established (1945)
Bretton Woods conference (1944)		Foreign Service Act creates a professional diplomatic corps (1946)
Soviets develop A-bomb (1949)		Cold war and containment—Truman Doctrine (1947); Marshall Plan (1947); OAS (1947); NATO (1949); Mutual Security (1951); SEATO (1954)
Korean War (1950–1953)	**1950**	
U.S. intervenes in Iran (1953); in Guatemala (1954)		
Soviets launch *Sputnik* (1957); first U.S. satellite (1958)		U.S. and Soviets race to the moon (1957–1969)
	1960	
Bay of Pigs Invasion (1961); Cuban Missile Crisis (1962)		U.S. and Soviets face off in Cuba (1962)
		Nuclear Test-Ban Treaty (1963)
U.S. builds up troops in Vietnam (1965–1973)		Détente between U.S. and Soviet Union (1970s)
Nixon visits China (1972)		U.S.-Soviet Trade Agreement (1972)
Arab oil embargo (1973–1974)		End of U.S. military draft (1973)
		Termination of Bretton Woods system (1973)
U.S. intervenes in Chile (1974)		
Camp David summit (1978)		Panama Canal Treaty (1978)
U.S. formally recognizes China (1979)		
Iranian hostage crisis (1979–1981)		SALT II Agreement (1979–1981)
	1980	SALT II repudiated (1981)
Grenada invasion (1983)		SDI ("Star Wars") commitment (1980s)
First Reagan–Gorbachev summit (1985)		Policy of covert action in Latin America (1980s)
Iran-Contra affair (1986–1987)		INF Treaty (1988)
Panama invaded (1989)		
Collapse of Soviet system; Berlin Wall dismantled (1989)		NATO/Warsaw Pact withdrawals begin (1989)
Germany reunified (1990)	**1990**	Eastern Europe adopts capitalism (1990)

Events	Institutional Developments
War in Persian Gulf (1991)	Efforts to cut defense spending; 29-nation U.N. coalition conducts blockade and invasion of Iraq (1990–1991)
Communist rule in U.S.S.R. and Yugoslavia ends (1991)	
U.N.-sponsored humanitarian intervention in Somalia (1992)	
Crisis in Bosnia (1993–1995)	Clinton-Yeltsin summit cements U.S.-Russian ties (1993)
	Clinton favors collective approach rather than leadership role in Bosnia; acts unilaterally against Iraq; takes lead in G7 talks (1993)
	Clinton unilaterally sends troops to Haiti and offers loan guarantees to Mexico (1994)

Key Terms

balance-of-power role The strategy whereby many countries form alliances with one or more other countries in order to counterbalance the behavior of other, usually more powerful, nation-states.

client state A nation-state dependent upon a more powerful nation-state but still with enough power and resources to be able to conduct its own foreign policy up to a point.

cold war The period of struggle between the United States and the former Soviet Union between the late 1940s and 1990.

containment The policy used by the United States during the cold war to restrict the expansion of communism and limit the influence of the Soviet Union.

deterrence The development and maintenance of military strength as a means of discouraging attack.

diplomacy The representation of a government to other foreign governments.

economic expansionist role The strategy often pursued by capitalist countries to adopt foreign policies that will maximize the success of domestic corporations in their dealings with other countries.

executive agreement An agreement between the president and another country, which has the force of a treaty but does not require the Senate's "advice and consent."

Holy Alliance role A strategy pursued by a super-power to prevent any change in the existing distribution of power among nation-states, even if this requires intervention into the internal affairs of another country in order to keep a ruler from being overthrown.

International Monetary Fund (IMF) An institution established in 1944 at Bretton Woods, New Hampshire, to provide loans to needy member countries and to facilitate international monetary exchange.

Marshall Plan The U.S. European Recovery Plan, in which over $34 billion was spent for relief, reconstruction, and economic recovery of Western Europe after World War II.

multilateralism A foreign policy that seeks to encourage the involvement of several nation-states in coordinated action, usually in relation to a common adversary, with terms and conditions usually specified in a multi-country treaty, such as NATO.

Napoleonic role Strategy pursued by a powerful nation to prevent aggressive actions against itself by improving the internal state of affairs of a particular country, even if this means encouraging revolution in that country.

nation-state A political entity consisting of a people with some common cultural experience (nation), who also share a common political authority (state), recognized by other sovereignties (nation-states).

North American Free Trade Agreement (NAFTA) An agreement among Canada, the United States, and Mexico that promotes economic cooperation and abolishes many trade restrictions between the three countries.

North Atlantic Treaty Organization (NATO) A treaty organization, comprising the United States, Canada, and most of Western Europe, formed in 1948 to counter the perceived threat from the Soviet Union.

sovereignty Supreme and independent political authority.

tariff A tax placed on imported goods.

unilateralism A foreign policy that seeks to avoid international alliances, entanglements, and permanent commitments in favor of independence, neutrality, and freedom of action.

United Nations The organization of nations founded in 1945, mainly to serve as a channel for negotiation and a means of settling international disputes peaceably. It has had frequent successes in providing a forum for negotiation and on some occasions a means of preventing international conflicts from spreading. On a number of occasions, the U.N. has been a convenient cover for U.S. foreign policy goals.

FOR FURTHER READING

Crabb, Cecil V., and Kevin V. Mulcahy. *Presidents and Foreign Policymaking: From FDR to Reagan.* Baton Rouge: Louisiana State University Press, 1986.

Gilpin, Robert. *The Political Economy of International Relations.* Princeton, NJ: Princeton University Press, 1987.

Graubard, Stephen, ed. "The Exit from Communism." *Daedalus* 121, no. 2 (Spring 1992).

Graubard, Stephen, ed. "The Quest for World Order." *Daedalus* 124, no. 3 (Summer 1995).

Greenfield, Liah. *Nationalism: Five Roads to Modernity.* Cambridge, MA: Harvard University Press, 1993.

Keller, William W. *Arm in Arm: The Political Economy of the Global Arms Race.* New York: Basic Books, 1995.

Kennan, George F. *Around the Cragged Hill—A Personal and Political Philosophy.* New York: W. W. Norton, 1993.

Kennedy, Paul M. *The Rise and Fall of the Great Powers: Economic Change and Military Conflict from 1500 to 2000.* New York: Random House, 1987.

LaFeber, Walter. *The American Age: United States Foreign Policy at Home and Abroad since 1750.* New York: W. W. Norton, 1989.

Smist, Frank J., Jr. *Congress Oversees the U.S. Intelligence Community, 1947–1994*, 2nd ed. Knoxville: University of Tennessee Press, 1994.

U.S. Congress. *Report of the Congressional Committees Investigating the Iran-Contra Affair.* New York: Random House, 1988.

Wirls, Daniel. *Buildup: The Politics of Defense in the Reagan Era.* Ithaca, NY: Cornell University Press, 1992.

CHAPTER 14

Can the Government Govern?

*A*s we approach the twenty-first century, America faces many problems. It no longer seems able to provide enough jobs or an adequate standard of living for many of its citizens as the gap between rich and poor grows larger. Now that America is the world's largest debtor, its economy and economic policy are increasingly vulnerable to the wishes of foreign bondholders.[1] America's educational system is widely viewed as deserving failing marks. Millions of Americans lack adequate housing, health care, or child care. American cities are plagued by crime and drugs.

In many instances, programs that are intended to deal with these problems turn out to be more symbol than substance. For example, in 1994, Congress enacted an anti-crime bill in response to the public's growing concern with violence. The bill outlawed the sale of nineteen types of assault weapons and called for more than $30 billion in federal spending. It was touted by its sponsors as providing funds that would allow municipalities throughout the country to hire 100,000 more police officers. These might seem to be important

steps in enhancing public safety. Unfortunately, however, there is some doubt that this legislation had much impact upon the nation's crime problem. First, the number of additional police officers that might conceivably be hired because of the

---

CORE OF THE ARGUMENT

- America's contemporary political process is the source of many of the government's present problems.
- The role of interest groups in the political process has increased in the last couple of decades.
- The power structure's governing philosophy reflects a "turn against government."
- Divided government has become nearly permanent, resulting in a two-party duopoly and increasingly incremental and symbolic politics.
- Existing political forces depend on "politics by other means"—forms of conflict that neither require nor encourage citizen involvement.
- A stronger party system is the most effective cure for America's political woes.

---

[1]Douglas R. Sease and Constance Mitchell, "World's Bond Buyers Gain Huge Influence over U.S. Fiscal Plans," *Wall Street Journal*, 6 November 1992, p. 1.

crime control act is closer to 20,000 than to the 100,000 initially promised.[2] As for the ban on nineteen types of assault weapons, 650 types of semi-automatic rifles were exempted from the prohibition, as were any type of assault weapon already owned at the time the bill was passed.

Second, as Republican critics pointed out, nearly one-third of the funds promised by the bill were allocated for social programs called "crime prevention," but whose precise relationship to crime control is not clear. For example, funds are allocated for "midnight sports leagues" and arts, crafts, and dance programs for inner city neighborhoods. Supporters of these programs argue that they provide young people with constructive activities. But however meritorious these activities may be, there is no evidence indicating that such programs help to reduce crime. Other portions of the bill were pure congressional pork with no relationship to crime; one provision called for the creation of a task force to study the introduction of non-indigenous plant and animal species into Hawaii.[3]

In essence, the 1994 crime bill was mainly an exercise in symbolic politics. For the Democrats, support for the bill was an opportunity to show that they could be tough on crime. For the Republicans, opposition to the bill was an opportunity to show that they could be tough on Democrats. As Representative Cynthia McKinney (D-Ga.) said, the bill contained "an ounce of prevention, a pound of punishment and a ton of politics."[4]

In such areas as health care, housing, and education, the U.S. government has found it difficult to formulate or implement effective programs and policies. In 1993 and 1994, Republicans defeated President Clinton's initiatives in the areas of social policy and health care. In 1995 and 1996, with the GOP in control of Congress, a major welfare reform bill was enacted (see Chapters 3 and 12). President Clinton, however, was able to block Republican initiatives in the realms of deficit reduction, regulatory reform, and tort reform.

Despite a general realization that the Medicare program is in danger of collapse, politicians thus far have been unwilling to do more than charge one another with frightening senior citizens. Moreover, despite a general realization that America's debt problem still needs to be brought under greater control through some combination of tax increases and spending cuts, America's political leadership has been, thus far, incapable of fully swallowing the bitter medicine of fiscal discipline. To be sure, annual deficit spending has declined somewhat in the past several years, but mostly as a result of a thriving economy that has produced more tax revenues. In 1995, congressional Republicans introduced a budget resolution they claimed would actually balance the federal budget by 2002. The Republican proposal, however, was defeated in the 1995–1996 budget showdown between Congress and President Clinton (see Chapter 5).

Today, Congress and the White House seem unable to agree whether to raise taxes, slash taxes, cut spending, or increase spending. At times, different aspects of federal policy seem to be aimed at each of these objectives simultaneously. An excellent volume of essays published in 1989 by Washington's prestigious Brookings Institution was aptly entitled, *Can the Government Govern?* The short answer to this complex question was a very clear "No!"[5] Now, nearly ten years later, we would still answer "No!"

One major reason for our present problems is that over the past several decades an un-

---

[2]William Claiborne, "On the Street, Bill's Effectiveness on Crime Reduction is Debatable," *Washington Post*, 20 August 1994, p. A5.

[3]"This is Governing?" *Wall Street Journal*, 23 August 1994, p. A12.

[4]Ann Devroy, "House Passes $30 Billion Crime Bill," *Washington Post*, 22 August 1994, p. 1.

[5]John Chubb and Paul Peterson, eds., *Can the Government Govern?* (Washington, DC: Brookings Institution, 1989).

healthy and fundamentally undemocratic political process has developed in the United States. The framers of the Constitution believed that a strong government rested most securely upon a broad and active popular base. "I would raise the federal pyramid to a considerable altitude," said Pennsylvania delegate James Wilson. "Therefore, I would give it as broad as a base as possible." As we saw in Chapter 1, concern for the new government's power and stability was a main reason that the framers established representative institutions and permitted political participation on the part of ordinary citizens. For much of U.S. history, the "federal pyramid," indeed, rested upon a relatively broad base of vigorous—often tumultuous—popular participation, with most major issues debated, fought, and ultimately resolved in the electoral arena. America's democratic politics, in turn, provided political leaders with a base of support from which to develop and implement programs, contend with powerful entrenched interests, and during times of crisis, such as the Civil War and World War II, ask their fellow citizens for the exertions and sacrifices needed in order for the nation to survive. As the framers had intended, democratic politics protected citizens' liberties *and* helped promote governance.

In recent decades, however, as noted in Chapter 9, popular participation in American political life has declined sharply. Despite a much-ballyhooed increase in voter registration, only 49 percent of eligible Americans bothered to vote in the 1996 presidential election, and barely 39 percent turned out for the 1994 congressional races. At the same time, the political parties that once mobilized voters and imparted a measure of unity to the scattered pieces of the American governmental structure have decayed (see Chapter 10), making it very difficult, if not impossible, to create a coherent government through the American electoral process.

Both reflecting and reinforcing these changes in the character of elections, the contending politi-

cal forces in the United States have come to rely heavily on forms of political conflict that neither require nor encourage much in the way of citizen involvement. In recent years, many of the most important national political struggles have been fought largely outside the electoral arena rather than through competitive electoral contests. In fact, in contemporary America, electoral results themselves have at times been negated or reversed by political forces that were not satisfied with the outcomes.

This process has been compounded by the existence of a new power structure in the United States today. The predominant political philosophy guiding the political process is one based on former President Ronald Reagan's dictum that "government is the problem, not the solution." Many of our elected leaders profess a hostility to "big government" (at least at the national level). The irony is that the anti-government coalition has been unsuccessful in realizing its goals. Divided government, a political phenomenon that has been nearly permanent over the last couple of decades, has resulted in a political process that prevents real governmental innovation. Changes in public policy have been quite marginal. Politics has become largely symbolic rather than substantive.

America's contemporary political process—characterized by low voter turnout, weak parties, increasing power of interest groups, and the rise of a "politics by other means"—has narrowed the base upon which the "federal pyramid" rests and is the source of many of our government's present problems. As we shall see in this chapter, this political process is increasingly undemocratic, is increasingly hostile to change, fragments political power, and fails to provide elected officials with the strong and stable political base they need to govern effectively. The result is public policy that is hollow and symbolic. Most important, America's contemporary political patterns undermine the ability of elected officials to bring about or even to take account of the public good.

Let us now look critically at the pieces of America's political process and then consider their implications for our government's capacity to govern. We will first look at the rise of interest groups and interest-group liberalism, examining how groups funded with extraordinary amounts of money are subverting the political process. Second, we will examine the new power structure and how it embodies a turn against government. Third, we will assess the impact of divided government on the political process and how its permanent form has contributed to the rise of incremental and symbolic politics. Next, we will look at the declining importance of popular voting and the rise of new forms of conflict in the United States. Finally, we will attempt to ascertain why there are no easy solutions for America's current political problems. But a sober awareness of the problems is a healthy start. In seeking to answer the question "Can the government govern?" we hope to lead readers toward a sense of how the government's capacity to govern can be restored.

A GOVERNMENT OF INTERESTS

The Democratic party of the New Deal era was the party of innovation; it created new national government programs in response to the needs and demands of the American people. With so much government growth promoted by the party, each component of the New Deal coalition had a reasonable expectation of political rewards. This meant that the New Deal coalition held itself together to a large extent through patronage, or through the expectation of patronage—promotional policies that benefited a particular group within the coalition.

A patronage policy simply authorizes a government agency to take whatever funds are budgeted to it and dispense them to individuals, companies, or groups to encourage new building, to fund the provision of a particular service, or to encourage a private individual to take an initiative that he or

she might not otherwise take. Sometimes these funds are distributed via a contract for work to be done or goods to be bought, as in a contract with a private construction company to build a bridge. At other times, these funds are dispensed in the form of a grant to an individual, for research or a particular artistic project, for example.

Abuse of such policies gave them a bad reputation. Patronage came to imply abuse and outright corruption; and patronage or promotion policies were given an ugly label: pork-barrel policies, a name probably inspired by the pre–Civil War practice of distributing chunks of salt pork to slaves out of huge barrels.[6] But the labels should not be allowed to overshadow the prominence and the utility of promotional or patronage policies.

As we saw in Chapter 12, such policies predominated in Congress throughout the nineteenth century. They were an important part of national government policy under dual federalism (see Chapter 3). Such "pork-barrel" policies can be broken up into smaller pieces and distributed to a maximum number of persons or groups. And just as the image of a pork barrel best describes these policies, so "logrolling" best describes the politics behind these policies. In Chapter 5, we defined logrolling as a political relationship between two or more persons who have absolutely nothing in common. In logrolling, the understanding is that "if you will support me on issue A, I will support you on any other issue you want; just tell me when and how you want me to vote."[7] These logrolling relationships worked well in Congress in the nineteenth century, and congressional committees and political parties flourished through their ability to gain and maintain political support through logrolling relationships.

[6]William Safire, *Safire's Political Dictionary* (New York: Random House, 1978), p. 553.
[7]These policy categories and their associated political patterns were first laid out in Theodore J. Lowi, "American Business, Public Policy, Case-Studies, and Political Theory," *World Politics* 16, no. 4 (July 1964), pp. 677–715.

The Democratic party of the New Deal was in essence a nineteenth-century patronage party, albeit modernized by the addition of important programs like Social Security that distributed benefits on a national level. And since the New Deal Democrats were committed to the expansion of the national government, the availability of patronage was considerable for the groups involved. The distribution of rewards as determined by congressional committees and implemented by bureaucratic agencies allowed the Democrats to maintain their power in Congress for decades. In fact, the iron-triangle relationships between congressional committees and subcommittees, bureaucratic agencies, and interest groups became more and more stable over time (see Chapter 11).

As a governing philosophy, patronage worked well for the New Deal Democrats for a long time. Problems began, however, when the principle became less of "to each according to his need" and more of "to each according to his claim." The influence of interest groups became so strong that their demands became rights. In essence, the government turned over its authority to make policy to the interest groups. Furthermore, in order to maintain their political power as well as to distribute benefits as widely as possible, New Deal liberals began to appease virtually every interest. The liberalism of the New Deal became what we call *interest-group liberalism*—a decadent politics based upon the accommodation of claims.[8] The influence of interest-group liberalism can be found in the policies and politics of every Congress and every administration since the presidency of John F. Kennedy.

The problem with interest-group liberalism is that, although its practitioners may have been successful in achieving their legislative aims, as a principle of government, it is self-defeating. It promotes the interest of the individual (or the individual group) at the expense of the greater society. It transforms every claim into a right. It precludes the development of priorities, even among members of the same party. And in the end, it weakens popular control over government, thus altering the balance between freedom and power.

Several examples of the failures of interest-group liberalism can be drawn from the first term of Bill Clinton's presidency. The absence of priorities in Clinton's policy agenda is echoed in his approach to the policy-making process. The distinguished journalist William Greider observed that

> [Clinton] . . . made common cause with selected power blocs—congressional barons of the Democratic party and major corporate-financial interests normally aligned with the Republicans as well as those right-of-center Southern Democrats. . . . The strategy assumed that once Clinton had satisfied their particular needs, these forces would help him to prevail on crucial reform issues. Instead, they ate his lunch.[9]

Greider went on to say that even Clinton's commitment to campaign and lobbying reform was marginal, because "instead of flogging Congress and the entrenched interests on the scandal of political money, Clinton ceded the issue to congressional Democrats, who, not surprisingly, do not wish to alter the status quo since it works for them."[10]

The Violent Crime Control and Law Enforcement Act of 1994 is a clear example of Clinton's surrender to interest-group liberalism. Although one of the genuine liberal aims of the original bill was to make it unlawful to "manufacture, transfer, or possess a semiautomatic weapon," the 650 exemptions alluded to earlier were in fact concessions to the interests of the manufacturers and dealers of such weapons, who clearly had a large stake in the matter.

---

[8]The concept of *interest-group liberalism* was introduced in Lowi, "The Public Philosophy: Interest-Group Liberalism," *American Political Science Review* (March 1967), vol. 61, pp. 5–24.

[9]William Greider, "Clinton at Midterm: What Went Wrong?" *Rolling Stone*, 3 November 1994, p. 48.
[10]The various quotes are from ibid., p. 108.

Health Care Reform and Interest-Group Politics

Clinton's health care reform proposals are another example of interest-group interference. Health care, it was hoped, could do for the Clintonians what Social Security had done for Franklin Roosevelt and his Democratic party in the 1930s—it would provide millions of voters with an ongoing incentive to support the Democrats while providing the party with a major new institutional base through which to manage the domestic economy.

Clinton's task force, led by First Lady Hillary Rodham Clinton, deliberated in secret. Indeed, for a time, even the composition of the group was secret. This secrecy, however, did not prevent hundreds of groups with interests in the health care field from conducting massive lobbying campaigns for and against. Major efforts were launched by various groups of physicians, hospitals, pharmaceutical and insurance companies, nurses, mental health professionals, and even chiropractors. Every group claimed to speak for the public interest, although, curiously, each group's understanding of the public interest differed in some significant detail.

Major insurance companies, including Prudential, Aetna, and Cigna, organized as the Alliance for Managed Competition, enthusiastically supported what was generally seen as the president's preferred health care option. Large insurers liked the idea of managed competition because, as envisioned by the president, this system promised to give them virtually full control of the nation's health care system at the expense of physicians and smaller insurance concerns.[11] Indeed, the major insurers had worked for years to shape the health care debate by their involvement in the so-called Jackson Hole Group, which pioneered the notion of managed competition.

Smaller insurance companies, not surprisingly, sought to resist this effort by the giants to put them out of business. Their lobby, the Health Insurance Association of America (HIAA), led by a former member of Congress, Willie Gradison, mounted a grassroots campaign against managed competition. The most memorable element of this effort was a $12-million series of thirty-second television spots featuring "Harry and Louise," actors depicting a middle-aged American couple who raise questions about President Clinton's health care plan. Harry and Louise proved so effective in creating public doubt about the plan that, at one point, the chair of the House Ways and Means Committee felt compelled to make a number of concessions to the HIAA in exchange for its agreement to keep Harry and Louise off the air while that committee considered health care legislation.[12]

In a similar vein, pharmaceutical manufacturers sponsored an advertising campaign designed to convince Americans that their own health could not be maintained without a healthy prescription-drug industry.[13] Pharmaceutical industry representatives also lobbied congressional committees that were considering health care legislation. The industry's goal was to eliminate from the administration's proposal the requirement that drug companies rebate to the government a portion of their earnings from the federal Medicare program to help finance health care reform. Though the rebate plan could not be defeated entirely, lobbyists representing brand-name drug companies convinced the House Ways and Means Committee to shift part of the rebate requirement to the rival generic-drug industry. The brand-name manufacturers were able to secure this victory by assembling a powerful team of lobbyists with direct access to the Ways and Means Committee. These lobbyists included former Ways and Means Committee members Thomas Downey, Ed Jenkins, and Marty Russo,

---

[11]Robin Toner, "Lobbyists Scurry for a Place on the Health-Reform Train," *New York Times*, 20 March 1993, p. 1.

[12]Michael Weisskopf, "Harry, Louise to Vacation During Hearings," *Washington Post*, 24 May 1994, p. 1.

[13]Howard Kurtz, "For Health Care Lobbies, a Major Ad Operation," *Washington Post*, 13 April 1993, p. D1.

former Ways and Means counsel Thomas Schlicht, and former Ways and Means staff director Ken Bowler.[14]

The most effective lobbying effort directed against the president's health care proposal was mounted by owners of small businesses. They objected to the chief mechanism through which Clinton proposed to finance the new health care system—the employer mandate—which would require employers to pay much of the cost of their employees' health care coverage. The National Federation of Independent Business (NFIB) mobilized its members to pressure their representatives in Congress. Members of three congressional committees considering health care legislation, the Senate Finance Committee and the House Energy and Commerce and Ways and Means committees, received particular attention. Two other congressional committees that were writing health care bills, the House and Senate labor committees, were seen by the NFIB as too liberal to be influenced. NFIB members and lobbyists organized meetings and community forums in their districts, and began a relentless campaign of letters, telephone calls, and faxes to committee members, arguing that small business would be ruined and the local economy destroyed by employer mandates. Largely as a result of these efforts, the House Energy and Commerce Committee was unable to approve any health care bill. The Senate Finance Committee approved a bill without employer mandates. Only the House Ways and Means Committee overcame NFIB resistance. Peter Stark, chair of the Ways and Means subcommittee on health, described the NFIB members as "greedy, inconsiderate folks . . . simply without any social conscience."[15] Lobbying efforts by the NFIB were among the most important factors leading to the defeat of comprehensive health care reform proposals in 1994.

Money and Politics

One study called the health care reform plan "the most heavily lobbied legislative initiative in recent U.S. history." Altogether, over $100 million was spent to influence the outcome of the debate, most of it by groups opposed to the initiative. Then again, $100 million might seem a drop in the bucket compared to the amount spent in the 1996 election. As we saw in Chapter 9, more than $2 billion was spent by candidates, parties, and interest groups.

The important role played by private funds in American politics affects the balance of power among contending social groups. Politicians need large amounts of money to campaign successfully for major offices. This fact inevitably ties their interests to the interests of the groups and forces that can provide this money. In a nation as large and diverse as the United States, to be sure, campaign contributors represent many different groups and often represent clashing interests. Business groups, labor groups, environmental groups, and pro-choice and right-to-life forces all contribute millions of dollars to political campaigns. Through such PACs as EMILY's List, women's groups contribute millions of dollars to women running for political office. One set of trade associations may contribute millions to win politicians' support for telecommunications reform, while another set may contribute just as much to block the same reform efforts. Insurance companies may contribute millions of dollars to Democrats to win their support for changes in the health care system, while physicians may contribute equal amounts to prevent the same changes from becoming law.

Despite this diversity of contributors, however, not all interests play a role in financing political campaigns. Only those interests that have a good deal of money to spend can make their interests known in this way. These interests are not monolithic, but nor do they completely reflect the diversity of American society. The poor, the destitute, and the downtrodden also live in America and have an interest in the outcome of political campaigns. Who is to speak for them?

[14]Michael Weisskopf, "Generics Lose in Health Bill Drug War," *Washington Post*, 2 July 1994, p. 1.

[15]Neil A. Lewis, "Lobbying for Small Business Owners Puts Big Dent in Health Care," *New York Times*, 6 July 1994, p. 1.

The Turn against Government

One important reason that health care reform failed is the campaign waged against it by the various interest groups opposed to its measures. But another important reason for its failure was the ideological opposition coming from the right wing of the Republican party. To Clinton Democrats, health care reform represented an opportunity to build a broad coalition of future electoral support. To conservative Republicans, health care reform represented the growth of big government and inefficient bureaucracy. Republicans are, in principle, opposed to the growth of government and the use of government for political purposes. Clinton's health care plan gave conservative Republicans the means to unite around a cohesive agenda. With patronage and growth ruled out, what was left to hold Republicans together? The key cementing factor seemed (and continues to seem) to be the principle of negation of government.

Negating the National Government

The principle of negation has two important dimensions. The first focuses on cutting the *national* government. Since before the New Deal, Republicans have supported reducing the size and scope of government. Yet while Republicans have professed this antipathy to "big government," they have done very little actually to reduce its size. Recall from Chapter 1 Ronald Reagan's inaugural pledge to curb the growth of the federal government, accompanying that pledge with the most memorable expression of his philosophy: "Government is the problem, not the solution." At the same time, he covered his retreat by making it clear that his intention was not "to do away with government." And that was much closer to the truth.

DEVOLUTION   The single most dramatic policy choice made in these recent years of Republican national hegemony left the *net amount of govern-* *ment* the same or possibly larger: the 1996 "welfare reform bill" (officially the Personal Responsibility Act [PRA]), put in quotes here because it was much more devolution than reform (see also Chapter 3). PRA virtually terminated the entire means-tested welfare program, more properly called Aid to Families with Dependent Children (AFDC), as a national program of entitlements. But instead of truly terminating it, Congress turned it over to the states, giving them proportionately the same federal welfare grants as before but with more discretion as to how to administer them. PRA did in fact cut the size of the *national* government by devolving welfare to the states, and that national downsizing will continue as the federal block grants get smaller. However, the law also provided for new national mandates and new state responsibilities. These include the well-known work requirements, which render people ineligible for benefits unless they find work or show evidence of searching for work within two years. Less well-known and less appreciated are the requirements that all mothers on welfare cooperate in identifying the biological father of their child in order to force him to contribute to child support; and that they must continue this cooperation to help continue enforcement of child support. The act also requires that, as a condition of receiving welfare, unmarried teenage mothers must live under adult supervision. There are also provisions for punishment for states whose nonmarital birthrates and abortion rates do not show some evidence of decline. Thus, the new so-called welfare reform law replaced the means test with a morality test. Many millions of Americans probably approve, and enactment of PRA by the Republican-Conservative majority (including many Democrats) probably directly reflects public opinion. But whether a person approves or disapproves of the new welfare provisions, the fact of the matter is that *all of the new requirements and criteria for eligibility for welfare benefits must be implemented by government agencies.* The new law simply converted the detested welfare bureaucrats into welfare police. Once again, even those who sentimentally support such a transformation must recognize that this is government, and in order to implement these new provisions, there might be even more government intrusion than before, whether that is measured in increased personnel and budget or not.

TERMINATING GOVERNMENT PROGRAMS Negation as a public philosophy has been validated and reinforced by the times in which we live. With the collapse of the New Deal coalition, the epoch of government growth was over. No major new programs were established after the Great Society binge of the late 1960s and early 1970s (including, as we've seen, national health care). But during the same time period, few programs were eliminated either. The only programs that have actually been terminated were the Civil Aeronautics Board (CAB) under President Carter, the Comprehensive Employment Training Administration under President Reagan, and the Interstate Commerce Commission (ICC) in 1996 under President Clinton. It should be recalled also that President Reagan admitted publicly in 1984 that he was giving up on his 1980 campaign promise to abolish the departments of Education and Energy; and in the 1990s, the Republicans gave up once again on their concerted effort to abolish the Department of Commerce. A few major programs were substantially gutted by the 104th Congress—agriculture price supports, telephone and cable regulation, and welfare entitlements within AFDC. But even here, the agencies were left in place, and the phasing out of these programs was going to take several years.

A Policy of No Policies

It appears that thus far the Republicans have been unsuccessful in scaling back government as a whole, even while trying to diminish the national government. Another tactic that conservatives have utilized in recent years is trying to keep the national government from getting any larger by not adopting new programs. Here, then, is the second dimension of negation: a policy of no policies.

In recent years, the Republicans' policy of no policies has been elevated to the level of political philosophy. With the 104th Congress, this philosophy reached new heights. Early in the congressional session, Republicans raised expectations that their "Contract with America" would bring great change to Washington. Ironically, historians will actually remember the 104th Congress as one of the least productive in modern history. The first session passed fewer bills than any Congress since 1933. Altogether, the 104th Congress enacted only 67 bills into law, compared to 210 in the 103rd Congress. The slow trickle of legislation surviving the 104th Congress is just one more symptom of Republican leaders embracing a "policy of no policies." This philosophy was taken to an extreme at the end of 1995 during the budget impasse with President Clinton that led to a temporary shutdown of the national government. Republicans thought the country would be better off without government, but the American people, it turned out, did not agree and the shutdown decision backfired on the Republicans. In 1997, when congressional Republicans began negotiating with President Clinton on the budget, there was much more evidence of bipartisanship and conciliation. But budget compromises reveal another condition of our government's incapacity to govern. When our elected leaders find something to agree on besides negation, it's often symbolic and inconsequential. Much was reported about the bipartisan spirit that allowed President Clinton and congressional Republicans to agree about deficit reduction. But the talk of accomplishment becomes lost in what amounts to marginal reductions. Changes in public policy, when they do occur, are often incremental and the results are often more symbolic than substantive.

We shall see more of the details immediately below, because these patterns go beyond the current ideology of negation of national government. They are virtually built into the new and extreme form of separation of powers that we have come to call divided government.

The Politics of Divided Government

The public's response to the government shutdown at the end of 1995 sent a message to the Republicans in Congress: Some government programs are necessary and desired. Following the failure of President Clinton's health care initiative, some congressional Democrats continued to press for federal health programs and some Republicans, fearing the public's scorn and their chances for re-election, found room for bipartisan agreement. On August 21, 1996, the Health Insurance Portability and Accountability Act was signed into law by President Clinton. The bill, sponsored by liberal Democrat Ted Kennedy of Massachusetts and moderate Republican Nancy Kassebaum of Kansas, required insurance companies to carry over coverage to employees who lost or changed their jobs. The Kennedy-Kassebaum bill was hailed as a triumph of bipartisanship. In spite of divided government, compromise could be reached and "progress" could be made toward the good of the American people. But, as one scholar of the health care reform debate said, the Kennedy-Kassebaum bill was "incremental" progress at best and "exhibited a high ratio of hype to accomplishment."

> Republicans and Democrats both touted Kennedy-Kassebaum during the 1996 campaign; the Democrats, especially, boasted that this legislation was a breakthrough toward enhanced health security for tens of millions of Americans. But the sober truth is otherwise. Once we get down to the nitty-gritty, it turns out that Kennedy-Kassebaum merely guarantees employees who are lucky enough already to be covered through a previous job the right to buy some kind of continuing coverage should they switch jobs or lose employment. That's nice, but insurance companies can still charge higher prices for lesser-quality coverage than the person had under the old employer plan. Thus many people who think they are going to be helped will be in for a rude surprise. At the very moment that their family's finances are under greatest stress, they will have to ante up huge sums for continuing coverage of marginal quality.

> Kennedy-Kassebaum does nothing to help laid-off employees pay for continuing health coverage. And of course it also does nothing to extend coverage to those who currently lack employer-provided insurance and nothing to prevent employers from charging more for existing coverage or deciding to discontinue health benefits. Such trends continue apace, and a recent study sponsored by the American Hospital Association estimates that the ranks of the approximately 40 million Americans without health insurance in 1995 will grow to 45.5 million "by the time the next president takes office in 2001."[16]

The Kennedy-Kassebaum bill is indicative of the problems with our political process. Divided government has become institutionalized and as a result we have a permanent two-party government, with each party satisfied with the status quo and not open to innovation. When facing re-election, our elected leaders react by working toward bipartisan compromise and innovative policies so that they can claim to the American people that government is helping them in their lives, but in most cases, the rhetoric is better than the reality. For reasons discussed earlier, innovation in government is nearly impossible. Permanently divided government has brought us incremental change and symbolic politics. We now turn to these three phenomena in order to better understand our government's incapacity to govern.

Divided Government

Between 1946 and 1998 (the end of the 105th Congress), thirty-two of the fifty-two years (almost 62 percent) were years of divided government, in which one branch was controlled by the Republican party and the other branch was controlled by the Democratic party. (This includes the first six Reagan years when Republicans controlled the presidency and the Senate but not the House of Representatives.) Of the

---

[16]Theda Skocpol, *Boomerang: Health Care Reform and the Turn against Government* (New York: W. W. Norton, 1997), pp. 194–195.

thirty years between 1968 and 1998, twenty-four years—80 percent—were years of divided government. And in the eighteen years since the election of Ronald Reagan, sixteen years—89 percent—were years of *divided government.*

At first, divided government didn't seem to matter very much. Presidents continued to turn out proposals, and Congress continued to pass legislation.[17] But a closer look, in particular at the past eighteen years, reveals another pattern entirely, and it matters a great deal because it appears to be the culmination of virtually a new American political system with a new kind of party system. We still have essentially a two-party system, but we do not have party government in the traditional sense based on electoral competition. Party government once meant one-party government, with control of the entire government apparatus alternating between the two major parties, depending upon national and congressional electoral majorities. What we have now—and have had for long enough to consider it institutionalized—is *dual*-party government, *with each party nested in one of the branches.* This is better understood not as party government or as two-party government but as *duopoly government.*

With fully confirmed expectations (based upon a probability of over 80 percent) that each party will control one of the branches, each party operates as a *majority party.* After a while, each party begins to act like a majority party and the leaders of both parties develop a special kind of majority mentality. In fact, this is a highly anti-innovation type of mentality, comparable to the situation as it is understood in a duopolistic or oligopolistic economy.[18] With a guaranteed position, or market share, there is a strong tendency to be risk averse.

As one important economics text puts it, "the key feature of oligopoly is that sellers take one another's actions into account in making price and output decisions."[19] In other words, "If it ain't broke, don't fix it!" "Don't quit while you're ahead." The same tendency can be observed in the political sphere, because political duopolists can easily know each other's basic interests without collusion and can cooperate without conspiracy. They can pick specialized and limited areas of competition and thereby avoid all-out competition that might harm the competitor but risks harming oneself as well. And we saw in Chapter 11 that competition from third parties is not a threat.

The following is a very telling observation by Ross Perot, a champion of competition and third parties, in his capacity as an expert on business and competition. While he served as a member of the board of directors of General Motors, he had publicly expressed his dismay at the automobile industry's oligopolistic behavior since World War II:

> . . . The entire American automobile industry had a big respite from competition. . . . [I]t got so bad that [the Big Three companies] tried to get divisions [within their own company] to compete with one another— Chevrolet compete with Pontiac, Oldsmobile with Buick, and so on. . . . I don't like that, and I say "Fellows, that's intramural sports . . . You don't even tackle there, you just touch the guy. . . . You don't even play with pads." . . . You don't understand competition.[20]

There is no reason to expect otherwise in the behavior of parties and their competition for political power. Each competitor has a vested interest in the other, and each has a vested interest in keeping additional competitors out of the political market altogether. From this perspective, we can also see that when each party has a high

---

[17]For an exhaustive coverage of most of this epoch, see David R. Mayhew, *Divided We Govern: Party Control, Lawmaking, and Investigations, 1946–1990* (New Haven: Yale University Press, 1991).

[18]An oligopoly is defined as a market situation in which there are only a few important sellers who produce all, or most, of the entire industry's output. Duopoly is a special case of oligopoly, a two-firm oligopoly.

[19]Robert H. Frank, *Microeconomics and Behavior* (New York: McGraw-Hill, 1991), p. 444.

[20]Quoted in Walter Adams and James Brock, eds., *The Structure of American Industry* (New York: Prentice Hall, 1995), pp. 80–81.

DEBATING THE ISSUES

Is Divided Government a Blessing in Disguise

*T*HE SITUATION *where one political party controls the presidency and the other party controls Congress is called "divided government." The name itself suggests that control divided between the parties invites governmental gridlock and paralysis, yet it has been the norm in recent decades—from 1968 to 1996, the United States has had a divided government for all but six years.*

Political analyst James L. Sundquist argues that divided control erodes the ability to govern. Political scientist David R. Mayhew asserts that, at least in the post–World War II era, divided control is not an impediment to governing.

SUNDQUIST

Those who believe that a basic weakness of the United States government is the recurrent conflict and deadlock between the executive and legislative branches must turn, at the outset, to the problem of divided government.

When one party controls the executive branch and the opposing party has the majority in one or both houses of Congress, all of the normal difficulties of attaining harmonious and effective working relationships between the branches are multiplied manifold. For, by the nature of party competition in a democracy, the business of political parties is to oppose each other. Competition between the two major parties in the United States is a constant of political life—and it must be, as a safeguard against abuse of power and as the means of assuring the citizenry a genuine choice of leaders and of programs. In an overriding emergency, partisan competition may be set aside, but only temporarily. As soon as the crisis is surmounted, the competition must resume.

When government is divided, then, the normal and healthy partisan confrontation that occurs during debates in every democratic legislature spills over into confrontation between the branches of the government, which may render it immobile. . . . When the president sends a recommendation to the opposition-controlled Congress, the legislators are virtually compelled to reject or profoundly alter it; otherwise, they are endorsing the president's leadership as wise and sound—and, in so doing, strengthening him or his party for the next election. Conversely, if the congressional majorities initiate a measure, the president must either condemn it and use his veto or else acknowledge to the nation the prudence and creativity of his political opponents.[1]

probability of being nested in a branch, it doesn't matter very much which branch it is, as long as the probability remains high that each party will have such a sanctuary, that each will win some power in the government.

There are two ways to assess this lack of party competition and the institutionalized nature of divided government. One is to look at it as the absolute fulfillment of the separation of powers intended by the framers of the Constitution, who were clear about their intents and purposes. The system of the separation of powers was designed

to (1) prevent the legislative branch from dominating government and (2) make it difficult for the national government to make policy decisions at all. Now that the original intent has been fulfilled, the question is "Can we live with it?" This brings us to the second interpretation of this phenomenon, that it has rendered the national government virtually incapable of governing. This is, of course, a fulfillment of conservative Republicans' philosophy based on the negation of national government. One might expect the Democrats, who since the New Deal derived

MAYHEM

. . . [U]nified as opposed to divided control has not made an important difference in recent times in the incidence of two particular kinds of activity. These are, first, high-publicity investigations in which congressional committees expose alleged misbehavior in the executive branch: Such extravaganzas seem to go on regardless of conditions of party control. And second, the enactment of a standard kind of important legislation: From the Taft-Hartley Act and Marshall Plan of 1947–48 through the Clean Air Act and $490 billion deficit-reduction package of 1990, important laws have materialized at a rate largely unrelated to conditions of party control. To see this pattern, one has to . . . look at actual enactments. There, the pattern is as stated.

. . . [I]t does not seem to make all that much difference whether party control of the American government happens to be unified or divided. One reason we assume it does is that "party government" plays a role in political science somewhere between a Platonic form and a grail. When we reach for it as a standard, we draw on abstract models, presumed European practice, and well-airbrushed American experience, but we seldom take a cold look at real American experience. We forget about Franklin Roosevelt's troubles with HUAC [the House Un-American Activities Committee] and the Rules Committee, Truman's and Kennedy's domestic policy defeats, McCarthy's square-off against Eisenhower, Johnson versus Fulbright on Vietnam, and Carter's energy program and "malaise."

Political parties can be powerful instruments, but in the United States they seem to play more of a role as "policy factions" than as, in the British case, governing instruments. A party as policy faction can often get its way even in circumstances of divided control. . . . There is the obvious structural component—separation of powers—that brings on deadlock and chronic conflict, but also nudges officials toward deliberation, compromise, and super-majority outcomes.[2]

---

[1]James L. Sundquist, *Constitutional Reform and Effective Government* (Washington, DC: Brookings Institution, 1986), pp. 75–76.

[2]David R. Mayhew, *Divided We Govern: Party Control, Lawmaking, and Investigations, 1946–1990* (New Haven: Yale University Press, 1991), pp. 4, 198–99.

their power from innovation and patronage, to answer no to the question of living with the absolute separation of powers, but the reality of the two-party duopoly has led them to the contrary position. In many ways, President Clinton has become a model Republican, contributing to the consensus we now have in our political system. We know that government innovation is now out of the question. We've already seen that, in recent years, negation of the national government has been a guiding principle of governance. What else is there?

Incrementalism

Incrementalism is the means by which our elected leaders put into practice their strategy of negation. We have already reviewed the difficulty of terminating entire programs and agencies. Negation can only be accomplished in small bits and pieces, or increments. Incremental change involves decisions to cut small percentages without assessing the purpose and nature of the government program or agency in question. Cutting at the margins involves no genuine sharing of power between the president and Congress. We now have a government of bookkeepers.

The politics of incrementalism was reinforced by two laws that required, in effect, that policy decisions would not be policy decisions at all but bookkeeping decisions made at the margins of each governmental activity. The 1974 Budget and Impoundment Control Act was adopted by a Democratic Congress against a Republican president, to provide Congress with its own source of budget information and power to compete with OMB—to answer OMB item by item with mind-numbing budgetary figures on each and every governmental activity. Through a process called "reconciliation" new congressional budget committees were given the power to establish budget resolutions that set advance spending targets for agencies and large categories of agencies and that would require Congress and the executive branch to limit spending within those broad categories. Reconciliation pushed almost every policy decision into a budgetary process—to the advantage of the bookkeeping mentality.

This was reinforced by the 1985 Gramm-Rudman-Hollings legislation establishing mandatory deficit reduction figures that would produce a balanced budget by 1991. Any year the established deficit targets were not met, OMB would have to make automatic cuts *across the board* with a formula set by law to reduce the budgets of all governmental activities at a given percentage: at the margins, even if the margins were to be felt as large ones. As one authority put it, these two reforms "moved budgetary gimmickry from the sidelines to the center stage." Some say the 1974 and 1985 decisions contribute to an enhancement of presidential power, and others say that it restored to Congress more powers to retaliate, thereby maintaining the balance between the two branches. Either way, the debate between the two branches was forced and formalized toward the budgetary margins, and the alterations of relative power between the two branches would have to be considered incremental at every step of the

way. Although Gramm-Rudman is defunct today, the process lingers on.

Symbolic Politics

THE PRESIDENT   Another related way to stay within the politics of incrementalism while giving off an impression of substance is to engage in symbolic politics. From the presidential perspective, this is usually called the bully pulpit. All presidents have employed the bully pulpit strategy some of the time (even though the term was not coined until Theodore Roosevelt). But recent presidents seem to be employing it virtually all the time.[21] In its most concrete and relevant form, playing the bully pulpit means the announcement at the highest possible rhetorical level of hopelessly unrealistic proposals that convey the impression of virtually immediate effectiveness.

Significant recent examples provided by President Clinton are: commitment to putting school children in uniform; a national goal of grading local school and teaching effectiveness; computerizing all classrooms; organizing a "citizen army of a million volunteer tutors" to meet the goal of bringing all children to a genuine reading ability by the end of third grade; ordering federal agencies to recruit and hire welfare recipients even as the civil service is being "downsized." In these matters, President Clinton is merely following his predecessors, but still he is carrying to greater heights of eloquence President Bush's "thousand points of light."

Cutting the federal work force by one percent may be a laudable goal but it has to be dressed up as "reinventing government." A tax cut worth $500 a family has to constitute fulfillment of a "Middle Class Bill of Rights." If there is a "confidence gap" in the United States, there is also a

---

[21]See, for example: Jeffrey K. Tulis, *The Rhetorical Presidency* (Princeton: Princeton University Press, 1987); Samuel Kernell, *Going Public—New Strategies of Presidential Leadership* (Washington, DC: Congressional Quarterly Inc., 1986); and Theodore Lowi, *The Personal President—Power Invested, Promise Unfulfilled* (Ithaca, NY: Cornell University Press, 1985).

very deep chasm of boredom for which symbols dressed in exalted rhetoric may not be an adequate cover.[22]

THE CONTRACT WITH AMERICA Despite the president's advantage, Congress has not lost out completely in the politics of symbolism. Senators have a larger pulpit than members of the House, which is certainly why so many senators and so few members of the House are talked about as presidential contenders. But the House has made great strides in recent years, and Newt Gingrich may be an early example of a new breed of player. The Contract with America was a marvelously successful bundle of symbols that played a fundamental part in the first outright and total Republican control of both chambers of Congress since 1952. On first glance it appears enormously innovative. In reality, the Contract played incredibly well in the politics of incrementalism, with tax cuts and deficit reductions spread out so far across the whole budget and so thinned out over five to seven years that it amounted to little more than a hill of beans. The Contract was also marvelously effective as symbolism, giving Americans at least a few months of widespread political excitement as well as maintenance of Republican control of Congress for two additional years, the first succession of Republican control of Congress since 1928.

---

[22]Joe Klein offers a dramatic illustration of President Clinton's contribution to incrementalism and to the government of bookkeepers. The article also demonstrates the effect of those very same forces on Clinton himself. Klein draws a Clinton quote from *USA Today*: "One of the things I learned with Hillary is that in the absence of a genuine immediate crisis you can make more progress if you have a discernible, step-by-step plan than you can by asking Congress to do more than the system will bear." Klein also draws a meaningful quote out of Robert Reich, a close Clinton friend and former secretary of labor: "[Clinton's] got one last big election—the one for his place in history—and he seems to be making the mistake of treating it like every other election he's run. But you can't court history, or poll it, or pander to it. . . . The way to win is to be bold." Joe Klein, "The End of a Conversation— Why Has the White House Suddenly Gone so Quiet?", *New Yorker*, 12 May 1997, pp. 40–43.

THE 1997 BALANCED BUDGET AGREEMENT The much-ballyhooed balanced budget agreement of 1997 was another child of the Contract's success. It made a Republican out of President Clinton, and that provided the opportunity for an unprecedented show of bipartisanship. Leaders of both parties were able to stand before the Capitol building and later on the White House lawn to sing each other's praises, to celebrate having reached "an historic agreement" (said President Clinton), having ushered in "the beginning of a new era of freedom" (said Senate Republican Leader Trent Lott), and having produced" a dream come true" (cried budget-balance radical Republican John Kasich). But, as observed earlier, despite being able to demonstrate numerically a balanced budget by the year 2002, most of the tough decisions to cut enough spending by 2002 to compensate for the tax cuts of 1997 will not be carried out until 2000 or beyond by a new Congress and a new president. Here are some examples of deals in the great 1997 agreement: The tax cuts (which are the opposite of getting a budget to balance by making revenue equal expenditure) amount to $95 billion lost revenue over five years and $275 billion over ten years. Yet the most-costly tax credit is one for $400 per child under seventeen (up to $500 in 1999) for all taxpayers with annual earnings of less than $75,000. Another is a tax credit of $1,500 for each of the first two years of college tuition—a second minor boon for middle-income families that actually is an incentive to colleges to raise their tuition! Two other credits are unabashedly for the wealthy: a cut in the capital gains tax and a cut in estate taxes. The biggest proposed cut in expenditures ($263 billion over five years) was laid on Medicare through reduction in payments to health care providers; but the burden of this was to be in large part compensated for by adding coverage for more preventive measures and by eliminating the one important (nonincremental) provision to increase Medicare eligibility age from sixty-five to sixty-seven and a $5 co-payment for home health care visits.

RONALD REAGAN AND BILL CLINTON
Redefining the Role of Government

Debate over the size, scope, and power of the federal government dominated the American political agenda in the 1980s and 1990s. Ronald Reagan swept into office in 1980 in large part because of his promise to reduce government. Yet twelve years after Reagan's election, Bill Clinton won the presidency based on his pledge to mobilize the resources of government to attack pressing domestic problems.

Ronald Reagan's career in politics extended back to his days as an actor, when he was elected president of the Screen Actors Guild in 1947. He began his political life as a Democrat but formally switched to the Republican party in 1962. He became an ardent supporter of conservative Republican Barry Goldwater's unsuccessful bid for the presidency in 1964. Two years later Reagan was elected governor of California, a position he held for eight years. In 1976, Reagan narrowly lost the Republican nomination to incumbent Gerald Ford. Four years later, he captured the nomination and the presidency on a crest of conservative enthusiasm for less government and stronger national defense spending, defeating beleaguered incumbent Jimmy Carter.

In his inaugural address, Reagan stated unequivocally that "government is not the solution to our problem; government is the problem." During his first term in office, Reagan won major revisions in fiscal policy and secured enormous increases in military spending. During his second term, however, most of Reagan's legislative efforts were blocked by Congress, and his administration ended under the cloud of the Iran-Contra scandal. Whether viewed as successful or not, the Reagan administration redefined the American political agenda as one in which more would have to be done with less.

Although considered by many to be a supporter of big-government spending, Bill Clinton sought to adapt to the post–Reagan era of limited government by redefining the Democratic party while still

RONALD REAGAN

Meanwhile, there were far more items contributing to higher rather than lower deficits during the first four years of the 1997 agreement, and these were aimed directly at favorite Democratic and Republican constituencies. Clinton got $8 billion of expenditures more than he requested (from $16 to $24 billion) for expanding health care for poor children. Republicans, for whom adding to the expenditure side is taboo, got equally juicy benefits for their support groups through "tax expenditures" (i.e., the value in lost revenue of a tax break designed for a narrow constituency or interest group)—such as a very large but hidden tax break for Amtrak (worth an estimated $2.3 billion), a tax break for two Asian affiliates of the Amway Company (also camouflaged, and worth $200 to $300 million), and, best of all, a provision attached to the newly augmented tobacco tax that would permit tobacco companies to treat those taxes paid as a credit against the $368 billion in damages they were ordered to pay to meet future suits against damages attributable to smoking. In fact, one inde-

drawing on the party's tradition of activism. Clinton's humble Arkansas roots belied his grand ambitions. A Rhodes scholar and graduate of Yale Law School, Clinton set his sights early on a political career. He became the nation's youngest governor when first elected in 1978. After an unexpected defeat in 1980, Clinton came back two years later to recapture the office, which he held until assuming the presidency.

Despite early political setbacks, Clinton proved to be a tenacious and durable campaigner for the 1992 presidential nomination. By the time he won the Democratic nomination, he stood even with his two rivals, George Bush and Ross Perot. From the end of the Democratic convention to election day, Clinton never trailed in the polls. Sensing that the mood of the country called for governmental leadership to address such pressing domestic problems as economic decline, revamping the nation's creaking health care system, and improving America's competitiveness, Clinton promised in his inaugural address to "resolve to make our Government a place for what Franklin Roosevelt called bold, persistent experimentation."

Once in office, Clinton introduced an ambitious package of proposals, including tax and spending increases, changes in America's health care system, and reform of campaign finance and lobbying practices. His proposls were initially greeted with enthusiasm by the media, the public, and members of his own party in Congress. Within several months, however, Clinton faced intense opposition from the Republicans, large segments of the media, and even from key congressional Democrats. Analysts asked whether Clinton's difficulties resulted from the president's own errors or whether they reflected some of the more systemic problems faced by America's government today. Is government the problem, as Reagan would suggest? Or the solution, as Clinton would contend? The debate continues. . . .

BILL CLINTON

SOURCE: John Chubb and Paul Peterson, eds., *Can Government Govern?* (Washington, DC: Brookings Institution, 1989).

pendent and respected think tank, the Committee for a Responsible Federal Budget, reported that if the economy stayed near its current pace and the 1997 agreement disappeared, the budget would balance itself between 1998 and 2002—*two years before the date set in the 1997 agreement!* On the other hand, if the entire 1997 agreement becomes law and the economy does not keep up to its current steady pace, deficits will quickly begin to balloon again. Moreover, as the equally respected Concord Coalition puts it, deficits will resume their expan-

sion soon after 2002 *regardless of the state of the economy or the 1997 commitments* because the hard decisions about expenditures Congress did not make in 1997 are going to be harder and harder to make. One example will have to suffice here: Medicare. In 1997, Congress backed away from the proposal to move the eligibility age up from sixty-five in tiny increments to sixty-seven over a period as long as twenty years. As the years go by, the increments of increase will have to get larger and *non*incremental.

Epitaph for a still-born triumph: The conservative *Wall Street Journal* was only one of many important media charging that the budget deal was hardly worth the paper it was printed on:

> Our fax machines have been filling up with Republican self-praise about the new budget deal with President Clinton. But the more we learn about the fine print of this bargain, the more we wish Republicans would stop spending and start fighting.[23]

It should also be kept in mind that the great agreement of 1997 is only the Budget Reconciliation for fiscal 1998. Provisions in this bill will still have to be implemented in thirteen, or possibly even more, actual appropriation acts, and there can be many a slip. Moreover, many of the provisions are probably of the special nature that makes them subject to the president's new line-item veto power. (See Chapter 6. This power will go back before the Supreme Court for constitutional review once the president uses it, but if it is sustained, the president's use can certainly alter the budget-balancing effect.) And, probably most important, the next Congress as well as the next president can negate the whole balancing act; that is just as likely as their honoring it.

OTHER SYMBOLIC TACTICS Members of Congress employ other symbolic tactics that make action virtually impossible. One of the best of these is a rule that has existed for a long time but has come into significantly increased usage in the past decade—the so-called filibuster rule. There has been a considerable increase in the use and in the threat of filibuster, to such an extent that Senate leadership would be loathe to bring up a bill for a vote unless they were fairly certain they had sixty votes, in order to overcome the threat of filibuster.

And the threat of filibuster is virtually enough without having to go through the delays of a real one. Another, of course, is the setting of spending caps on broad categories of governmental activities, forcing a kind of zero-sum game among related agencies, such that an increase in one has to be compensated for by a decrease in one or more others, or worse, a provision for revenue enhancements to cover the increase. This not only forces the discourse toward the margins and away from the substance of government activities, as observed earlier, but it also amounts to a decision at the beginning of a congressional session to tie the hands of substantive legislative committees and congressional entrepreneurs and to inhibit any tendency toward substantial innovation.

Still other examples of decision prevention are being sought vigorously by factions in Congress that are majority size but not yet majorities large enough to pass a constitutional amendment or to overcome a Senate filibuster. The most important of these are the various forms of effort to impose a three-fifths vote requirement on all tax increases and on all substantive actions that would contribute to an increase in the deficit. The most sought-after means of this is the balanced-budget amendment, which would not only constitutionalize discourse at the margins but would put virtually all taxation and all substantive policy innovation beyond the reach of majoritarian republicanism.

Finally, there is one congressional action that warrants close scrutiny not only because of its intrinsic importance but because of the likelihood that it will be imitated. This is the Defense Base Closure and Realignment Commission established by Congress in the late 1980s. Special provision was made for the independence of this Commission by giving it the authority to make an annual listing of recommendations for military bases to be closed, with the stipulation that the House and Senate could only vote the entire list of recommendations up or down, with no additions or dele-

---

[23]*Wall Street Journal,* 9 May 1997, p. 18. Other such opinions, plus valuable data on the agreement will be found in Nancy Gibbs, "A Conspiracy of Celebration," *Time,* 11 August 1997, pp. 27–30; John Cassidy, "The Budget Boondoggle," *New Yorker,* 11 August 1997, pp. 4–5; and Ronald D. Elving and Andrew Taylor, "A Balanced-Budget Deal Won, A Defining Issue Lost," *Congressional Quarterly,* 2 August 1997, pp. 1831–1836.

tions. Congress gave itself no "line-item veto." Other such commissions in the pipeline are (1) a commission to fix the Consumer Price Index (CPI), which allegedly is overstating the rate of inflation; and (2) a commission to give America the campaign finance reform that neither party can commit to.

Symbolic politics has in fact been both a cause and an effect of important changes in the constituency of Congress. Historically, Congress was tied to a geographical base. Geography or territoriality had always been the very essence of representation in the United States. States have been the geography and therefore the constituency of senators, and the single-member district has even more closely tied House members to a system of geographic representation. That formality still exists, but the substance of geography is being subordinated to the more diffuse regional and national public opinion and campaign-finance constituencies that make the popular base of the House and the Senate very much like that of the president. To engage in symbolic politics means reaching a larger and larger public, and the cost of reaching that public require a broader and broader financial base. Thus, not only have the costs of campaigns gone up meteorically; an even more interesting and underappreciated fact is that a decreasing percentage of campaign money comes from within the state of a senator or within the home district of a member of the House. Each and every year, and with increasing frequency, incumbents and serious contestants have to make their march on the eight or ten leading financial and commercial centers of the United States. They are even being drawn toward foreign resources, even though at present that is in most circumstances treated as illegal. It costs a lot to play the game of symbolic politics, and to that extent symbolic politics is changing all the other forms of politics. And perhaps the most significant change of all is in the electoral domain, to which we turn now.

The Decline of Voting and the Rise of "Politics by Other Means"

For most of U.S. history, elections were the main arenas of political combat. In recent years, however, elections have become less effective as ways of resolving political conflicts in the United States. Today's political struggles are frequently waged elsewhere, and crucial policy choices tend to be made outside the electoral realm. Rather than engage voters directly, contending political forces rely on such weapons of institutional combat as congressional investigations, media revelations, and judicial proceedings. In contemporary America, even electoral success fails to confer the capacity to govern, and political forces, even if they lose at the polls or do not even compete in the electoral arena, have been able to exercise considerable power.

Several trends in contemporary American political life bring sharply into focus the declining significance of the electoral arena. American elections in recent decades have been characterized by strikingly low levels of voter turnout and by a decline of political competition. Since 1900, turnout in national elections has declined by 25 percentage points. As noted above, in the 1992 presidential election, only 55.9 percent of the eligible electorate went to the polls, and in the 1994 midterm congressional elections, voter turnout was a mere 39 percent. Turnout in the 1996 presidential election was 48.8 percent, the lowest turnout rate since 1924. In other Western democracies, turnout normally exceeds 80 percent.

Politics outside the Electoral Arena

As competition in the electoral arena has declined, the significance of other forms of political combat has risen. Contemporary political struggles have come increasingly to involve the criminal justice system and the courts, the national security apparatus, and the mass media. Let us look

FIGURE 14.1

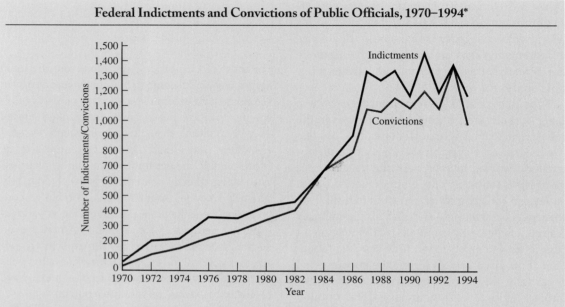

Federal Indictments and Convictions of Public Officials, 1970–1994*

*Reporting procedures for these statistics were modified in 1983, so pre- and post-1983 data are not strictly comparable.
SOURCE: Annual reports of the U.S. Department of Justice, Public Integrity Section, 1971–1988; *Statistical Abstract of the United States* (Washington, DC: Government Printing Office, 1994, 1996).

at the political role played by each of these non-electoral institutions.

THE JUDICIARY One important substitute for competition in the electoral arena is the growing political use of a powerful non-electoral weapon—the criminal justice system. Between the early 1970s and the present, there was more than a tenfold increase in the number of indictments brought by federal prosecutors against national, state, and local officials. The data given in Figure 14.1 actually understate the extent to which public officials have been subjected to criminal proceedings in recent years, because they do not include those political figures (such as Ronald Reagan's attorney general, Edwin Meese, and former Democratic House Speaker Jim Wright) who were targets of investigations that did not result in indictments.

Many of the individuals indicted have been lower-level civil servants, but large numbers have

been prominent political figures—among them more than a dozen members of Congress, several federal judges, and numerous state and local officials. Some of these indictments were initiated by Republican administrations, and their targets were primarily Democrats. At the same time, a substantial number of high-ranking Republicans in the executive branch—including former Defense Secretary Caspar Weinberger, former Assistant Secretary of State Elliott Abrams, presidential aides Michael Deaver and Lyn Nofziger, and, of course, national security official Oliver North—were the targets of criminal prosecutions stemming from allegations or investigations initiated by Democrats. Weinberger and Abrams, along with several other figures in the Iran-Contra case, were pardoned by President George Bush in December 1992, just before he left office. In justifying the pardons, Bush charged that Democrats were attempting to criminalize policy differences.

During the first two years of the Clinton administration, the powerful chair of the House Ways and Means Committee, Dan Rostenkowski (D-Ill.), was forced to give up his post after being indicted on corruption charges. In 1994 and 1995, charges of improper conduct were leveled at Agriculture Secretary Mike Espy, Transportation Secretary Henry Cisneros, and Commerce Secretary Ron Brown, among others. Espy was forced to resign in October 1994. On Capitol Hill, House Speaker Newt Gingrich and Senate Minority Leader Tom Daschle found themselves the subjects of ethics investigations.

In 1994, a special counsel was appointed by the Justice Department to investigate charges that President Clinton and his wife had engaged in illegal activities growing out of their partnership in the Whitewater Development Corporation while Clinton was governor of Arkansas. The same special counsel, Robert Fiske, also investigated the activities of a number of Clinton aides accused of making illegal contacts with the Treasury Department on behalf of the White House. In August 1994, Fiske was replaced by former federal prosecutor Kenneth Starr. Fiske had been appointed by Attorney General Janet Reno before Congress had restored the lapsed independent counsel provision of the Ethics in Government Act. Under the terms of the act, an independent counsel is appointed by a panel of federal judges. Once this portion of the act was restored by Congress, a three-judge federal panel ruled that because Fiske had been appointed to investigate Clinton by a member of Clinton's own cabinet, there was a potential for conflict of interest. Democrats, however, asserted that the Starr appointment represented an even greater conflict of interest. Starr is a Republican who has often been sharply critical of the Clinton administration.[24]

There is no particular reason to believe that the level of political corruption or abuse of power in America actually increased tenfold over the past two decades, as Figure 14.1 would seem to indi-

cate. It could be argued, however, that this sharp rise reflects a heightened level of public concern about governmental misconduct. However, as we shall see, both the issue of government ethics and the growing use of criminal sanctions against public officials have been closely linked to struggles for political power in the United States. In the aftermath of Watergate, institutions such as the office of the independent counsel were established and processes were created to investigate allegations of unethical conduct on the part of public figures. Since then, political forces have increasingly sought to make use of these mechanisms to discredit their opponents. When scores of investigators, accountants, and lawyers are deployed to scrutinize the conduct of a Bill Clinton or a Newt Gingrich, it is all but certain that something questionable will be found. The creation of these investigative processes, more than changes in the public's tolerance for government misconduct, explains why public officials are increasingly being charged with ethical and criminal violations.

The growing use of criminal indictments as a partisan weapon has helped enhance the political importance of the judiciary. The prominence of the courts has been heightened by the sharp increase in the number of major policy issues that have been fought and decided in the judicial realm rather than in the arena of electoral politics.[25] The federal judiciary has become the main institution for resolving struggles over such issues as race relations and abortion, and it has also come to play a more significant role in deciding questions of social welfare and economic policy.[26] The number of suits brought by civil rights, environmental, feminist, and other liberal groups seeking to advance their policy goals increased dramatically during the 1970s and

---

[24]David Johnston, "Appointment in Whitewater Turns into a Partisan Battle," *New York Times,* 13 August 1994, p. 1.

[25]Jeremy Rabkin, *Judicial Compulsions* (New York: Basic Books, 1989).

[26]Martin Shapiro, "The Supreme Court's 'Return' to Economic Regulation," *Studies in American Political Development* 1 (1986), pp. 91–142.

FIGURE 14.2

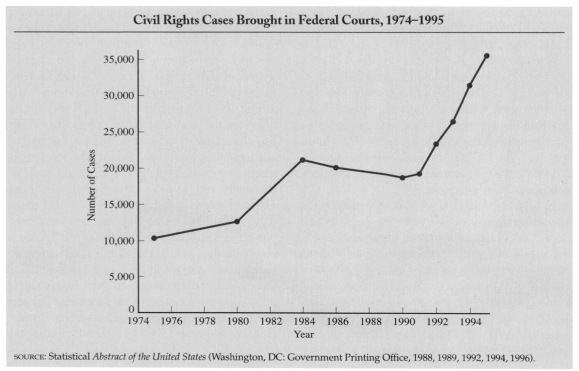

Civil Rights Cases Brought in Federal Courts, 1974–1995

SOURCE: Statistical *Abstract of the United States* (Washington, DC: Government Printing Office, 1988, 1989, 1992, 1994, 1996).

1980s—reflecting the willingness and ability of these groups to fight their battles in the judicial arena. For example, as Figure 14.2 indicates, the number of civil rights cases brought in federal courts doubled during this period. After the emergence of a conservative majority on the Supreme Court in 1989, forces from the political Right began to use litigation to implement their own policy agenda. The growing political importance of the federal judiciary explains why Supreme Court confirmation battles, such as the struggle over the Clarence Thomas nomination, came to be so bitterly fought during the Reagan and Bush administrations.[27]

THE MEDIA   Another institution whose political significance has increased dramatically is the mass media. With the decline of political parties, politicians have become almost totally dependent on the media to reach their constituents, but this dependence has made politicians extremely vulnerable to attack by and through the media. At the same time, the development of techniques of investigative reporting and critical journalism provided the modern news media with powerful weapons to use in political struggles.

The national media enhanced their autonomy and political power by aggressively investigating, publicizing, and exposing instances of official misconduct.[28] Conservative forces during the

[27]Martin Shefter, "Institutional Conflict over Presidential Appointments: The Case of Clarence Thomas," *PS: Political Science & Politics* 25, no. 4 (December 1992), pp. 676–78.

[28]Samuel P. Huntington, *American Politics: The Promise of Disharmony* (Cambridge, MA: Harvard University Press, 1981), pp. 203–10.

Nixon and Reagan years responded to media criticism by denouncing the press as biased and seeking to curb it. However, members of Congress and groups opposed to conservative presidential policies benefited from the growing influence of the press and, as noted in the preceding chapter, have been prepared to defend it when it comes under attack.

Revelation, Investigation, Prosecution

Taken together, the expanded political roles of the national news media and the federal judiciary have given rise to a major new weapon of political combat—revelation, investigation, and prosecution. The acronym for this, RIP, forms a fitting political epitaph for the public officials who have become its targets. The RIP weaponry was initially forged by opponents of the Nixon administration in their struggles with the White House, and through the Reagan years it was used primarily by congressional Democrats to attack their foes in the executive branch. In the 1980s, however, Republicans began to wield the RIP weapon against Democrats.

In 1972, after his re-election, President Nixon undertook to expand executive power at the expense of Congress by impounding funds appropriated for domestic programs and reorganizing executive agencies without legislative authorization. In addition, the White House established the so-called "plumbers" squad of former intelligence agents and mercenaries to plug leaks of information to Congress and the press, and (its opponents claimed) it sought to undermine the legitimacy of the federal judiciary by appointing unqualified justices to the Supreme Court. The administration's adversaries also charged that it tried to limit Congress's influence over foreign policy by keeping vital information from it, most notably the "secret bombing" of Cambodia from 1969 to 1973.

At the same time, Nixon sought to curtail the influence of the national news media. His administration brought suit against the New York Times in an effort to block publication of the Pentagon

Papers and threatened, using the pretext of promoting ideological diversity, to compel the national television networks to sell the local stations they owned. The president's opponents denounced the administration's actions as abuses of power—which they surely were—and launched a full-scale assault upon Richard Nixon in the Watergate controversy.

The Watergate attack began with a series of revelations in the Washington Post linking the White House to a break-in at the Watergate Hotel headquarters of the Democratic National Committee. The Post's reporters were quickly joined by scores of investigative journalists from the New York Times, Newsweek, Time, and the television networks.

As revelations of misdeeds by the Nixon White House proliferated, the administration's opponents in Congress demanded a full legislative investigation. In response, the Senate created a special committee, chaired by Senator Sam Ervin, to investigate White House misconduct in the 1972 presidential election. Investigators for the Ervin committee uncovered numerous questionable activities on the part of Nixon's aides, and these were revealed to the public during a series of dramatic, nationally televised hearings.

Evidence of criminal activity unearthed by the Ervin committee led to congressional pressure for the appointment of a special prosecutor. Ultimately, a large number of high-ranking administration officials were indicted, convicted, and imprisoned. Impeachment proceedings were initiated against President Nixon, and when evidence linking him directly to the cover-up of the Watergate burglary was found, he was forced to resign from office. Thus, with the help of the RIP weaponry, the Nixon administration's antagonists achieved a total victory in their conflict with the president. Although no subsequent president has been driven from office, opponents of presidential administrations have since used the RIP process to attack and weaken their foes in the executive branch.

CONCEPT MAP 14.1

The RIP Process

New appointment is proposed by the White House.

OPPONENTS	**SUPPORTERS**

Opponents of the appointment do an extensive background check, trying to find any negative information that may exist.

Supporters marshal evidence: the nominee's experience, judgment, knowledge, etc.

Negative information discovered about the appointee is made public through leaks, rumors, and disclosures to reporters, TV news programs, and other media outlets.

Positive information is disseminated through the media: public statements in support of nominee, etc., picked up by newspapers, TV news programs, and news magazines.

In order to follow up on the leaks, the media do further investigations and the process picks up momentum, often resulting in additional negative information.

Supporters seek to refute damaging information by providing additional positive evidence and challenging media investigations and negative allegations.

Congressional hearings

Hostile questioning due to negative information in the media.

More negative information is uncovered and publicized by the media as momentum peaks.

Supporters are gradually silenced by momentum of negative information.

Supporters drop away, when accusations aimed at nominee prove to be accurate, particularly if the nominee has broken the law.

Nominee withdraws or is defeated.

The RIP process became institutionalized when Congress adopted the 1978 Ethics in Government Act, which established procedures for the appointment of independent counsels (ini-tially called "special prosecutors") to investigate allegations of wrongdoing in the executive branch. The act also defined as criminal several forms of influence peddling in which executive officials had traditionally engaged, such as lobbying former associates after leaving office. (Such activities are also traditional on Capitol Hill, but Congress chose not to impose the restrictions embodied in the act upon its own members and staff.) Basically, Congress created new crimes that executive branch officials could be charged with. The independent counsel provision of the act lapsed during the Bush administration, but was restored by Congress in 1994.

The extent to which the RIP process had come to be a routine feature of American politics became evident during the Iran-Contra conflict when Democrats charged that the Reagan administration had covertly sold arms to Iran and used the proceeds to provide illegal funding for Nicaraguan Contra forces, in violation of the Boland Amendment, which prohibited such help. After the diversion of funds to the Contras was revealed, it was universally assumed that Congress should conduct televised hearings and the judiciary should appoint an independent counsel to investigate the officials involved in the episode. Yet this procedure is really quite remarkable: Officials who in other democracies would merely be compelled to resign from office are now threatened with criminal prosecution in the United States.

The greatest challenges to Clinton first came from the Whitewater probe, in which the president's critics charged that he and his wife had been guilty of a variety of conflicts of interest and financial improprieties while involved in a partnership with a shady Arkansas banker and real estate developer. An independent counsel was appointed to look into the charges, and Republicans demanded that congressional hearings on the issue be scheduled. Democrats opposed hearings, arguing that the Republicans merely sought to embarrass the administration prior to major congressional votes and the 1994 congressional elections. Finally, hearings were scheduled, but under very limited conditions that Democrats hoped would protect the president from potentially embarrassing disclosures.

The president's critics also questioned the circumstances under which Hillary Clinton had been able to earn a profit of more than $100,000 in a short period of time, through a series of highly risky and speculative commodities trades. Critics noted that the First Lady, who had no experience in the commodities market, had been guided by an attorney for Tyson Foods, Inc., a huge Arkansas-based poultry producer that stood to gain from the friendship of then-Governor Clinton. Although the White House denied any wrongdoing on her part, the charges produced at least the appearance of impropriety.

After the GOP took control of both houses of Congress in 1994, new investigations were launched by the House and Senate banking committees and the House oversight committee. In 1995, as he investigated the Clintons' involvement in the Whitewater matter, special counsel Kenneth Starr indicted Arkansas Governor Jim Guy Tucker and former Clinton Whitewater partners James and Susan McDougal for bank fraud and conspiracy. All three were convicted, but Starr was not immediately able to wrest incriminating testimony about the president from them. Another Clinton associate had already been sent to prison as a result of evidence turned up during the various investigations of the Clintons' business dealings in Arkansas. Former Hillary Clinton law partner and Associate U.S. Attorney General Webster Hubbell began serving a prison term in 1994 for scheming to defraud his Rose law firm partners of $482,000.

In March 1996, the scope of Starr's investigation was broadened to include the so-called "Travelgate" affair, in which the administration is alleged to have sought to cover up the details surrounding the firing of members of the White House travel office. In June 1996, the scope of Starr's investigation was expanded again to include "Filegate," allegations that the White House had improperly obtained FBI files on some 900 individuals.

The 1996 elections left the GOP in control of both houses of Congress and, thus, in a position to continue aggressively investigating the Clinton White House. During the course of the 1996 campaign the Democratic party was accused of accepting millions of dollars in improper contributions from Indonesian business interests. Republicans promised to add this matter to the long list of questions under investigation. Republicans promised to use their investigative powers to harass Clinton for the remainder of his presidency. "Clinton will be debilitated," predicted Bush White House Counsel C. Boyden Gray.[29]

While Republicans were hounding Clinton, Democrats were pressing their own investigation of Republican House Speaker Newt Gingrich. Acting on a formal complaint from Democratic House members, the House ethics committee began in 1994 to investigate whether a college course organized by Gingrich with tax-deductible contributions was actually a partisan political endeavor. This would violate federal laws prohibiting tax-exempt charities from engaging in partisan efforts.

In 1996, the committee and special counsel James M. Cole broadened the scope of their investigation to examine the relationship between the course and GOPAC, a political action committee once headed by Gingrich. GOPAC raised an enormous amount of money for Republican congressional candidates. The committee is also looking at the Progress and Freedom Foundation, a conservative think tank associated with Gingrich. At issue are whether the tax-exempt foundation was actually a shelter for partisan efforts, and whether Gingrich's college courses were actually tied to GOPAC.[30] And so, RIP continues.

POLITICS AND GOVERNANCE

Alas, there is no specific set of reforms we can propose to change a situation where the parties have become virtual obstructions to democracy. What we can do is to end on a note of warning, warning about what harm American political leaders are doing, coupled with a note of optimism that those leaders have the power of genuine democratic reform in their own hands, which they are more likely to use if they are made aware of the harm inherent in their present course. We do indeed feel that the only solution to complex political problems is awareness of the nature of the problems.

Contemporary American politics undermines governance in four ways. First, elections today fail to accomplish what must be the primary task of any leadership selection process: they fail to determine *who will govern*. An election should award the winners with the power to govern. Only in this way can popular consent be linked to effective governance. Under the fragmented system bequeathed to us by the Constitution's framers, seldom at any point in American history have all the levers of power been grasped by a unified and disciplined party or group.

Today, however, with the decay of America's political party organizations, this fragmentation has increased sharply. There are many victorious cliques and factions with little unity among them. During the Bush presidency, fragmentation and division led to a pattern of "gridlock" in which little or nothing could be accomplished in Washington. Deep factional divisions within the Democratic party, as we have seen, posed severe problems for the Clinton administration in its first two years, and a Republican majority in Congress since 1995 has continued the paralysis begun during the Bush years.

In addition to factional opposition, Clinton's efforts were hampered by the fact that many congressional Democrats have become "soloists," willing to give the administration their support only in exchange for some set of tangible benefits for themselves and the interests they represent. In the absence of party organizations and mechanisms for enforcing party discipline, there is little

[29]Owen Ulmann, "What Clinton Has to Fear from a Landslide," *Business Week*, 11 November 1996, p. 51.
[30]R. H. Melton, "Ethics Probe Reaching Critical Stage for Frustrated Gingrich," *Washington Post*, 4 November 1996, p. A17.

to prevent legislators from demanding what amounts to immediate political payoffs in exchange for their support on important pieces of legislation. The result is that all legislation effectively becomes special-interest legislation filled with loopholes and special benefits. For example, the 1993 budget contained provisions requiring that cigarettes manufactured in the United States contain 75 percent domestically grown tobacco. This provision was inserted at the behest of Senator Wendell Ford of Kentucky for the benefit of his state's tobacco farmers. Similarly, Democratic Representative James Bilbray of Nevada agreed to support the budget only after securing a tax credit designed to offset the Social Security taxes paid on employees' tips by restaurant owners—an important constituency group in his district. Texas Democrat Solomon Ortiz traded his support of the president's budget for an enlarged share of defense conversion funds for his district. The list goes on and on.[31] No wonder columnist David Broder called the resulting budget a "pastiche of conflicting goals."[32] One Clinton administration official conceded that because the budget was "driven by politics not policy," it was "not the greatest package ever."[33]

The second problem with contemporary politics is that modern governments are weak and unstable. Elected officials subjected to RIP attacks often find that their poll standing (today's substitute for an organized popular base) can evaporate overnight and their capacity to govern disappear with it. Thus, the Nixon administration was paralyzed for three years by the Watergate affair, the Reagan White House for two years by the Iran-Contra affair, the Clinton White House was distracted by Whitewater, and Newt Gingrich's pop-

ularity and leadership were compromised by attacks on his character. This is hardly a recipe for a strong government to solve America's problems.

Third, because they lack a firm popular base, politicians seldom have the capacity to confront entrenched economic or political interest groups even when the public interest seems clear. For example, early in the Bush administration, the Treasury Department's plan for resolving the crisis in the savings and loan industry involved the imposition of a fee on S&L deposits. This idea was adamantly rejected by the industry and met overwhelming resistance on Capitol Hill, where thrift institutions enjoyed a good deal of influence. The administration was compelled to disown the Treasury plan and proposed, instead, a plan in which general tax revenues would finance the bulk of the cost of the $166 billion bailout. In this way, a powerful interest, the savings and loan industry, was able to shift the burden of a major federal initiative designed for the industry's own benefit from itself to the general public.

In a similar vein, after his election in 1992, President Clinton felt compelled to reassure the nation's business community and powerful banking and financial interests that his administration would be receptive to their needs. This was a major reason that Clinton—who had campaigned as a staunch opponent of business-as-usual in Washington—named Democratic National Committee chair Ron Brown to be his secretary of Commerce and Texas Democratic Senator Lloyd Bentsen to the post of secretary of the Treasury. Brown was a veteran Washington corporate lobbyist well known to the business community. Bentsen, as chair of the Senate Finance Committee, was noted for his close and cordial relationship with banking, finance, insurance, and real estate interests.[34] President Clinton was no more eager

[31]David Rogers and John Harwood, "No Reasonable Offer Refused as Administration Bargained to Nail Down Deficit Package in House," *Wall Street Journal*, 6 August 1993, p. A12.

[32]David Broder, "Some Victory," *Washington Post*, 10 August 1993, p. A15.

[33]Hobart Rowan, "It's Not Much of a Budget," *Washington Post*, 12 August 1993, p. A27.

[34]Jill Abramson and John Harwood, "Some Say Likely Choice of Bentsen, the Insider, for Treasury Post Could Send the Wrong Signals," *Wall Street Journal*, 9 December 1992, p. A26.

than his predecessor to confront these interests. Later, to secure the enactment of his tax proposals, Clinton felt compelled to give major tax concessions to a variety of interests including aluminum producers, real estate developers, multinational corporations, and the energy industry.[35] Such moves did not always guarantee him support, however; even after Clinton made significant concessions to a variety of lobby groups, a coalition of powerful interests was able to scuttle his plan for reform of America's health care system.

Finally, the enhanced political power of non-electoral institutions means that the question of who will *not* govern is unlikely to be resolved in the electoral arena. The most important function of an election is to determine who will govern. At the same time, elections must also deprive the losing party of the power to prevent the winning party from governing effectively. Today, elections not only fail to determine who will govern but also do not definitively determine *who will not exercise power*. Given the political potency of non-electoral modes of political struggle, electoral defeat does not deprive the losing party of the power to undermine the programs and policies of the winner. Indeed, as we have seen, electoral verdicts can now be reversed outside the electoral arena.

As a result, even as the "winners" in the American electoral process do not acquire firm control of the government, so the "losers" are not deprived of power. Instead, "winners" and "losers" typically engage in a continuing struggle, which often distracts them from real national problems. For example, in 1996, House Speaker Newt Gingrich was diverted from his efforts to lead a Republican "revolution" by a barrage of ethics complaints levied against him by the Democrats.

More important, however, this struggle compels politicians to pay greater heed to the implications of policies for their domestic political battles than for collective national purposes. The Reagan and Bush administrations' tolerance of enormous budget deficits and their program of deregulation provide examples of this phenomenon. One important reason why Republican administrations were prepared to accept the economic risks of unprecedented deficits is the constraint these deficits imposed on congressional power. Similarly, the Republicans pressed for deregulation in part because the constellations of interests surrounding many regulatory policies are important Democratic bastions. This sort of political gamesmanship caused these administrations to overlook potential costs and risks of their policies. The relaxation of regulatory restraints on financial institutions permitted many S&Ls to shift from their traditional role as home mortgage lenders into potentially more lucrative but dangerously speculative areas. We all now know the results.

Concern for their institutional and political advantage can also affect the way officials respond to the initiatives of their opponents. For example, congressional Democrats regularly voted for lower levels of military spending than the two Republican administrations proposed, not because they were less committed to the nation's defense, but because the defense establishment has been an important institutional bastion of the Republicans. This reason also played a part in Democratic opposition to the 1991 Persian Gulf War.

Similarly, despite the continuing problem of America's huge budget deficit, the Clinton administration has been committed to increases in federal domestic spending. Just as Reagan and Bush had political reasons for increasing defense spending, domestic social spending is politically necessary for the Clinton administration, whatever the long-term economic risks it may entail. Indeed, despite his reputation as a "policy wonk," Clinton quickly found that it was virtually impossible to focus on questions of policy effectiveness. Purely political considerations frequently had to come first.[36] In contemporary America, political

[35]David Hilzenrath, "Bentsen Signals White House's Willingness to Deal," Washington Post, 17 May 1993, p. A4.

[36]See Jeffrey H. Birnbaum and Michael K. Frisby, "Clinton's Zigzags between Politics and Policy Explain Some Problems of His First 100 Days," *Wall Street Journal*, 29 April 1993, p. A16.

struggle is constant, leaving little room for consideration of long-term public interests.[37]

Restoring the Government's Capacity to Govern

This brings us back to where we started: the government's incapacity to govern. American government today provides minimal solutions in a democratic republic subjected constantly to maximum demands and maximum expectations. The legitimacy of an enormous democratic politics in a large republican government cannot long survive a national governmental process whose operational code is action-prevention and the adoration of bookkeepers and the bottom line. This is no appeal for another forty fat years of governmental growth that held the New Deal coalition together. It is an appeal for common sense over and against an ideologically supported denial of the capacity to govern. Something is wrong with our politics, and we have to look to our politics to find a way out.

Ronald Reagan was right, for all the wrong reasons, when he said that government is the problem, not the solution. Today, our government is in fact the problem, and it is incapable of contributing substantially to the solution. The frustrating thing is that we can almost get our hands on the problem and might even be able to cope with it if not solve it. We are in the unprecedentedly tight grip of ever more and richer interest groups confronting a party system comprised of two parties in a duopolistic, noncompetitive political market.

And the situation is self-perpetuating because of the increasing dependence of individual candidates on interest groups. We need no more evidence than the 1996 national election campaign. According to the Federal Election Commission, total political campaign expenditures for federal campaigns in the 1995–1996 election cycle (all aimed at the 1996 election) came to slightly more

than $2.7 billion—"exceeding the gross domestic product of a number of African nations."[38] Of this amount, it is estimated that the two major parties spent 27.5 percent of that total, which includes expenditures of "soft money"; and that means that almost all of the rest was raised and spent by individual candidates for president, House, and Senate, including the 19 percent of the total expenditure ($429.8 million) raised and spent by the PACs. Little of that money came from family, close friends, and dedicated believers. The rest came from the PACs, which are no more than interest groups committed to influencing elections, and from all the other organized interest groups that concern themselves more with influencing policy decisions after elections are over.

Already we can see that the crisis in campaign finance is not actually a crisis in campaign expenditure; democracy, especially in the electronic age, is expensive. The problem is not the cost of democracy but the influence of interest groups and the consequent vulnerability of all candidates and all elected representatives. The most egregious campaign finance sin of the 1996 campaign was probably President Clinton's renting out the Lincoln Bedroom. But here, as in all interest group relationships, the night's hospitality in return for cash is a small part of the problem; the rest of the problem begins the next morning when the seducer begins to test out how tight the ties are bound and how vulnerable he'll be to "when will I see you again?" once the seduction is over and the guest has left the premises.

No campaign finance laws (none at least that can pass judicial review) can solve the problem of interest group influence on vulnerable individual candidates. As James Madison would say, every cure for "faction" would be worse than the disease. Unfortunately, now that we have followed Madison's advice to "extend the sphere [in order

---

[37]For examples, see Robin Toner, "Edginess on Capitol Hill," *New York Times*, 22 August 1994, p. 1.

[38]Quote and figures from Federal Election Commission, as published in Carroll Doherty, "Inquiry on Campaign Finance—Burning with a Short Fuse," *Congressional Quarterly*, 5 April 1997, p. 768.

to] take in a greater variety of parties and interests [to] make it less probable that a majority of the whole will have a common motive to invade the rights of other citizens . . . ," and now that we have found that advice wanting, where do we go from here? Stronger parties are the only sure antidote to the mischiefs of organized interests, and we cannot ordain strong parties. Until we have them, politicians will cope with interests either by continuing to yield to them and being captured by them, or they will allow more and more of their own legislative powers to drain to other branches of government and elsewhere.

The following is a parsimonious inventory of some of the receptacles of that drainage. Some of the drainage has already taken place and may be irreversible, others are signs of drainage still in progress:

1. delegation of legislative power away from Congress to the executive, 1933–1973;
2. delegation of fiscal/monetary power from Congress and the president to an independent and self-financing Federal Reserve;
3. delegation of large chunks of national power to the states, which have actually done little in the past several decades to deserve the reputation for virtue they now enjoy, and which vary immensely in terms of their capacity and wealth to meet the added responsibilities delegated to them;
4. delegation of power to special commissions, such as the Defense Base Closure and Realignment Commission set up nearly ten years ago with the authority to make an annual listing of recommendations for military bases to be closed, with the stipulation that the House and Senate can only vote the entire list of recommendations up or down, with no deletions; others to follow: a Social Security commission, a commission on the Consumer Price Index, a campaign finance reform commission;
5. delegation of investigatory power to independent counsels, to do what Congress itself has the power and the duty to do;
6. rejection of policy making in favor of marginal analysis;
7. replacement of law with economics as the language of government;
8. displacement of policy making with bookkeeping;
9. denial of the separateness from and the integrity of the political in relation to the moral and the economic realms.

People are fond of saying that "God looks after fools, drunkards, and the United States of America." America has indeed been lucky. It came out of World War II as the only viable economy and the leading world power. It spent a lot of money rebuilding its allies and can take a great deal of credit for the number of democracies there are in the world. But the United States was also able to have its way, unilaterally, multilaterally, and through the U.N. and other international agencies. Even the Cold War, which proved so costly, had the hidden advantage of imposing certain restraints on American politics and a sense of national purpose that helped impose a certain amount of capacity to make substantive and timely public policy decisions even in times of peace. Perhaps an artificial national unity, it nevertheless contributed to the country's capacity to make policy decisions. It also contributed to the necessary correlative capacity to withstand and survive spectacular policy failures, such as the Vietnam War, without irreparable loss of legitimacy.

The United States has thus enjoyed a fair-weather system of government for nearly fifty years. But can it continue this string of fat years now that the Cold War is over and the world is a more chaotic even if less dangerous place? What will the United States do when the weather turns foul and the fat years turn to lean? Can it survive the unintended consequences of the current *mega*policy decision not to make policy decisions? Can it survive a government of bookkeepers? An ideological antipathy to government and politics?

The capacity to govern is not something a nation-state is born with—however free it is born. The capacity to govern is not something that can be provided by even the most enlightened constitutional architecture—although that is an indispensable starting point. The capacity to govern is political, and politics is very much like a physical capacity that requires a lot of practice to do well. And the capacity to govern in a democratic republic requires something else that great team athletes require beyond practice, and that is collective character, because the political system must not only continually prove itself by its successes but also sustain itself by coping with failure. Good government, in sum, requires experience with success and experience with failure, and above all, experience with trying. Use it or lose it.

TIME LINE ON POLITICS AND GOVERNANCE		
Events		**Institutional Developments**
		Long-term decline in voter turnout begins (1890)
	1960	Decay of political party organizations (1960s)
		Rise of interest-group liberalism (1960s)
		Rise of activist and adversarial media (1968)
	1970	
Watergate hearings (1973–1974)		Legislative limits on presidential power: War Powers Resolution (1973); Budget and Impoundment Control Act (1974); Ethics in Government Act (1978)
	1980	Reagan pledges to terminate departments of Education and Energy but fails (1980s)
Iran-Contra Affair (1986)		Reagan's deficits impose budgetary limits on Congress; period of intense conflict between legislative and executive branches (1980–1992)
		Gramm-Rudman mandates across-the-board budget cuts (1985)
Clarence Thomas hearings (1900)	**1990**	
Health care reform fails (1993–1994)		Democratic control of both branches ends divided government but doesn't end gridlock (1993)
Nannygate; Travelgate (1993); Whitewater investigation (1994–1997)		Republicans take control of Congress (1994); divided government returns; 104th Congress passes fewer bills than any Congress since 1933 (1995–1996)
Temporary government shutdown (1995–1996)		
Welfare "devolution" passes (1996)		Divided government continues (1996–1998)
Clinton and congressional Republicans agree to deficit-reduction plan (1997)		
Campaign fundraising by Democrats and Republicans investigated (1997)		

KEY TERMS

divided government   The condition in American government wherein the presidency is controlled by one party while the opposing party controls one or both houses of Congress.

interest-group liberalism   The theory of governance that, in principle, all claims on government resources and action are equally valid, and that all interests are equally entitled to participation in and benefits from government.

FOR FURTHER READING

Dionne, E. J., Jr. *Why Americans Hate Politics.* New York: Simon and Schuster, 1991.

Drew, Elizabeth. *On the Edge: The Clinton Presidency.* New York: Simon and Schuster, 1994.

Greider, William. *Who Will Tell the People: The Betrayal of American Democracy.* New York: Simon and Schuster, 1992.

Lowi, Theodore. *The End of Liberalism,* 2nd ed. New York: W. W. Norton, 1979.

Lowi, Theodore. *The End of the Republican Era.* Norman: University of Oklahoma Press, 1995.

Phillips, Kevin. *Boiling Point: Democrats, Republicans, and the Decline of Middle-Class Prosperity.* New York: Random House, 1993.

Rosenstone, Steven, and John Mark Hansen. *Mobilization, Participation and Democracy in America.* New York: Macmillan, 1993.

Skocpol, Theda. *Boomerang: Health Care Reform and the Turn against Government.* New York: W. W. Norton, 1997.

Sundquist, James L. *Constitutional Reform and Effective Government.* Washington, DC: Brookings Institution, 1992 rev. ed.

Woodward, Bob. *The Agenda: Inside the Clinton White House.* New York: Simon and Schuster, 1994.

APPENDIX

The Declaration of Independence

In Congress, July 4, 1776

When in the course of human events, it becomes necessary for one people to dissolve the political bands which have connected them with another, and to assume among the Powers of the earth, the separate and equal station to which the Laws of Nature and of Nature's God entitle them, a decent respect to the opinions of mankind requires that they should declare the causes which impel them to the separation.

We hold these truths to be self-evident, that all men are created equal, that they are endowed by their Creator with certain unalienable rights, that among these are Life, Liberty, and the pursuit of Happiness. That to secure these rights, Governments are instituted among Men, deriving their just powers from the consent of the governed. That whenever any Form of Government becomes destructive of these ends, it is the Right of the People to alter or to abolish it, and to institute new Government, laying its foundation on such principles and organizing its powers in such form, as to them shall seem most likely to effect their Safety and Happiness. Prudence, indeed, will dictate that Governments long established should not be changed for light and transient causes; and accordingly all experience hath shown, that mankind are more disposed to suffer, while evils are sufferable, than to right themselves by abolishing the forms to which they are accustomed. But when a long train of abuses and usurpations, pursuing invariably the same Object evinces a design to reduce them under absolute Despotism, it is their right, it is their duty, to throw off such Government, and to provide new Guards for their future security.— Such has been the patient sufferance of these Colonies; and such is now the necessity which constrains them to alter their former Systems of Government. The history of the present King of Great Britain is a history of repeated injuries and usurpations, all having in direct object the establishment of an absolute Tyranny over these States. To prove this, let Facts be submitted to a candid world.

He has refused his Assent to Laws, the most wholesome and necessary for the public good.

He has forbidden his Governors to pass Laws of immediate and pressing importance, unless suspended in their operation till his Assent should be obtained; and when so suspended, he has utterly neglected to attend to them.

He has refused to pass other Laws for the accommodation of large districts of people, unless those people would relinquish the right of Representation in the Legislature, a right inestimable to them and formidable to tyrants only.

He has called together legislative bodies at places unusual, uncomfortable, and distant from the depository of their public Records, for the sole purpose of fatiguing them into compliance with his measures.

He has dissolved Representative Houses repeatedly, for opposing with manly firmness his invasions on the rights of the people.

He has refused for a long time, after such dissolutions, to cause others to be elected; whereby the Legislative powers, incapable of Annihilation, have returned to the People at large for their exercise; the State remaining in the mean time exposed to all dangers of invasion from without, and convulsions within.

He has endeavored to prevent the population of these States; for that purpose obstructing the Laws of Naturalization of Foreigners; refusing to pass others to encourage their migrations hither, and raising the conditions of new Appropriations of Lands.

He has obstructed the Administration of Justice, by refusing his Assent to Laws for establishing Judiciary powers.

He has made Judges dependent on his Will alone, for the tenure of their offices, and the amount and payment of their salaries.

He has erected a multitude of New Offices, and sent hither swarms of Officers to harass our People, and eat out their substance.

He has kept among us, in times of peace, Standing Armies without the Consent of our legislature.

He has affected to render the Military independent of and superior to the Civil Power.

He has combined with others to subject us to a jurisdiction foreign to our constitution, and unacknowledged by our laws; giving his Assent to their Acts of pretended Legislation:

For quartering large bodies of armed troops among us:

For protecting them, by a mock Trial, from Punishment for any Murders which they should commit on the Inhabitants of these States:

For cutting off our Trade with all parts of the world:

For imposing taxes on us without our Consent:

For depriving us in many cases, of the benefits of Trial by jury:

For transporting us beyond Seas to be tried for pretended offences:

For abolishing the free System of English Laws in a neighboring Province, establishing therein an Arbitrary government, and enlarging its Boundaries so as to render it at once an example and fit instrument for introducing the same absolute rule into these Colonies:

For taking away our Charters, abolishing our most valuable Laws, and altering fundamentally the Forms of our Governments:

For suspending our own Legislatures, and declaring themselves invested with Power to legislate for us in all cases whatsoever.

He has abdicated Government here, by declaring us out of his Protection and waging War against us.

He has plundered our seas, ravaged our Coasts, burnt our towns, and destroyed the lives of our people.

He is at this time transporting large armies of foreign mercenaries to compleat the works of death, desolation, and tyranny, already begun with circumstances of Cruelty & perfidy scarcely paralleled in the most barbarous ages, and totally unworthy the Head of a civilized nation.

He has constrained our fellow Citizens taken Captive on the high Seas to bear Arms against their Country, to become the executioners of their friends and Brethren, or to fall themselves by their Hands.

He has excited domestic insurrections amongst us, and has endeavored to bring on the inhabitants of our frontiers, the merciless Indian Savages, whose known rule of warfare, is an undistinguished destruction of all ages, sexes, and conditions.

In every stage of these Oppressions We have Petitioned for Redress in the most humble terms: Our repeated Petitions have been answered only by repeated injury. A Prince, whose character is thus marked by every act which may define a Tyrant, is unfit to be the ruler of a free people.

Nor have We been wanting in attention to our British brethren. We have warned them from time to time of attempts by their legislature to extend an unwarrantable jurisdiction over us. We have reminded them of the circumstances of our emigration and settlement here. We have appealed to their native justice and magnanimity, and we have conjured them by the ties of our common kindred to disavow these usurpations, which, would inevitably interrupt our connections and correspondence. They too must have been deaf to the voice of justice and of consanguinity. We must, therefore, acquiesce in the necessity, which denounces our Separation, and hold them, as we hold the rest of mankind, Enemies in War, in Peace Friends.

WE, THEREFORE, the Representatives of the UNITED STATES OF AMERICA, in General Congress, Assembled, appealing to the Supreme Judge of the world for the rectitude of our intentions, do, in the Name, and by Authority of the good People of these Colonies, solemnly publish and declare, That these United Colonies are, and of Right ought to be FREE AND INDEPENDENT STATES; that they are Absolved from all Allegiance to the British Crown, and that all political connection between them and the State of Great Britain, is and ought to be totally dissolved; and that as Free and Independent States, they have full Power to levy War, conclude Peace, contract Alliances, establish Commerce, and to do all other Acts and Things which Independent States may of right do. And for the support of this Declaration, with a firm reliance on the Protection of Divine Providence, we mutually pledge to each other our Lives, our Fortunes, and our sacred Honor.

The foregoing Declaration was, by order of Congress, engrossed, and signed by the following members:

John Hancock

NEW HAMPSHIRE
Josiah Bartlett
William Whipple
Matthew Thornton

MASSACHUSETTS BAY
Samuel Adams
John Adams
Robert Treat Paine
Elbridge Gerry

RHODE ISLAND
Stephen Hopkins
William Ellery

CONNECTICUT
Roger Sherman
Samuel Huntington
William Williams
Oliver Wolcott

NEW YORK
William Floyd
Philip Livingston
Francis Lewis
Lewis Morris

NEW JERSEY
Richard Stockton
John Witherspoon
Francis Hopkinson
John Hart
Abraham Clark

PENNSYLVANIA
Robert Morris
Benjamin Rush
Benjamin Franklin
John Morton
George Clymer
James Smith
George Taylor
James Wilson
George Ross

DELAWARE
Caesar Rodney
George Read
Thomas M'Kean

MARYLAND
Samuel Chase
William Paca
Thomas Stone
Charles Carroll,
 of Carrollton

VIRGINIA
George Wythe
Richard Henry Lee
Thomas Jefferson
Benjamin Harrison
Thomas Nelson, Jr.
Francis Lightfoot Lee
Carter Braxton

NORTH CAROLINA
William Hooper
Joseph Hewes
John Penn

SOUTH CAROLINA
Edward Rutledge
Thomas Heyward, Jr
Thomas Lynch, Jr.
Arthur Middleton

GEORGIA
Button Gwinnett
Lyman Hall
George Walton

Resolved, That copies of the Declaration be sent to the several assemblies, conventions, and committees, or councils of safety, and to the several commanding officers of the continental troops; that it be proclaimed in each of the United States, at the head of the army.

The Constitution of the United States of America

Annotated with references to the Federalist Papers

Federalist Paper Number and Author

[PREAMBLE]

84
(Hamilton)

We the People of the United States, in Order to form a more perfect Union, establish Justice, insure domestic Tranquility, provide for the common defence, promote the general Welfare, and secure the Blessings of Liberty to ourselves and our Posterity, do ordain and establish this Constitution for the United States of America.

ARTICLE I

Section 1

[LEGISLATIVE POWERS]

10, 45
(Madison)

All legislative Powers herein granted shall be vested in a Congress of the United States, which shall consist of a Senate and House of Representatives.

Section 2

[HOUSE OF REPRESENTATIVES, HOW CONSTITUTED, POWER OF IMPEACHMENT]

39
(Madison)
45
(Madison)
52–53, 57
(Madison)

The House of Representatives shall be composed of Members chosen every second Year by the People of the several States, and the Electors in each State shall have the Quali-

52
(Madison)
60
(Hamilton)

fications requisite for Electors of the most numerous Branch of the State Legislature.

No Person shall be a Representative who shall not have attained to the Age of twenty-five Years, and been seven Years a Citizen of the United States, and who shall not, when elected, be an inhabitant of that State in which he shall be chosen.

54
(Madison)

Representatives and *direct Taxes*[1] shall be apportioned among the several States which may be included within this Union, according to their respective Numbers, *which shall be determined by adding to the whole Number of free Persons, including those bound to Service for a Term of Years,* and excluding Indians not

54
(Madison)

taxed, *three-fifths of all other Persons.*[2] The actual Enumeration shall be made within three

58
(Madison)

Years after the first Meeting of the Congress of the United States, and within every subsequent Term of ten Years, in such Manner as they shall by Law direct. The Number of Representatives shall not exceed one for every thirty Thousand, but each State shall have at

[1]Modified by Sixteenth Amendment.
[2]Modified by Fourteenth Amendment

55–56
(Madison)

Least one Representative; *and until such enumeration shall be made, the State of New Hampshire shall be entitled to chuse three, Massachusetts eight, Rhode-Island and Providence Plantations one, Connecticut five, New-York six, New Jersey four, Pennsylvania eight, Delaware one, Maryland six, Virginia ten, North Carolina five, South Carolina five, and Georgia three.*[3]

When vacancies happen in the Representation from any State, the Executive Authority thereof shall issue Writs of Election to fill such Vacancies.

79
(Hamilton)

The House of Representatives shall chuse their Speaker and other Officers; and shall have the sole Power of Impeachment.

Section 3

[THE SENATE, HOW CONSTITUTED, IMPEACHMENT TRIALS]

39, 45
(Madison),
60
(Hamilton),
62–63
(Madison)
59
(Hamilton)

The Senate of the United States shall be composed of two Senators from each State, *chosen by the Legislature thereof,*[4] for six Years; and each Senator shall have one Vote.

Immediately after they shall be assembled in Consequence of the first Election, they shall be divided as equally as may be into three Classes. The Seats of the Senators of the first Class shall be vacated at the Expiration of the second Year, of the second Class at the Expiration of the fourth Year, and of the third Class at the Expiration of the sixth Year, so that one third may be chosen every second Year: *and if*

68
(Hamilton)

vacancies happen by Resignation, or otherwise, during the Recess of the Legislature of any State, the Executive thereof may make temporary Appointments until the next Meeting of the Legislature, which shall then fill such Vacancies.[5]

62
(Hamilton),

No person shall be a Senator who shall not have attained to the Age of thirty Years, and been nine Years a Citizen of the United States, and who shall not, when elected, be an Inhabitant of that State for which he shall be chosen.

The Vice-President of the United States shall be President of the Senate, but shall have no Vote, unless they be equally divided.

[3]Temporary provision.
[4]Modified by Seventeenth Amendment.
[5]Modified by Seventeenth Amendment.

The Senate shall chuse their other Officers, and also a President pro tempore, in the Absence of the Vice-President, or when he shall exercise the Office of President of the United States.

39
(Madison),
65–67, 79
(Hamilton)
65
(Hamilton)

The Senate shall have the sole Power to try all Impeachments. When sitting for that Purpose, they shall be on Oath or Affirmation. When the President of the United States is tried, the Chief Justice shall preside: And no Person shall be convicted without the Concurrence of two-thirds of the Members present.

84
(Hamilton)

Judgment in Cases of Impeachment shall not extend further than to removal from Office, and disqualification to hold and enjoy any Office of honor, Trust or Profit under the United States: but the Party convicted shall nevertheless be liable and subject to Indictment, Trial, Judgment and Punishment, according to Law.

Section 4

[ELECTION OF SENATORS AND REPRESENTATIVES]

59–61
(Hamilton)

The Times, Places and Manner of holding Elections for Senators and Representatives, shall be prescribed in each State by the Legislature thereof; but the Congress may at any time by Law make or alter such Regulations, except as to the Places of chusing Senators.

The Congress shall assemble at least once in every Year, and such Meeting shall be on the first Monday in December, unless they shall by Law appoint a different Day.[6]

Section 5

[QUORUM, JOURNALS, MEETINGS, ADJOURNMENTS]

Each House shall be the Judge of the Elections, Returns and Qualifications of its own Members, and a Majority of each shall constitute a Quorum to do Business; but a smaller Number may adjourn from day to day, and may be authorized to compel the Attendance of absent Members, in such Manner, and under the Penalties as each House may provide.

[6]Modified by Twentieth Amendment.

Each House may determine the Rules of its Proceedings, punish its Members for disorderly Behavior, and, with the Concurrence of two-thirds, expel a Member.

Each House shall keep a Journal of its Proceedings, and from time to time publish the same, excepting such Parts as may in their Judgment require Secrecy; and the Yeas and Nays of the Members of either House on any questions shall, at the Desire of one-fifth of the present, be entered on the Journal.

Neither House, during the Session of Congress, shall, without the Consent of the other, adjourn for more than three days, nor to any other Place than that in which the two Houses shall be sitting.

Section 6

[COMPENSATION, PRIVILEGES, DISABILITIES]

The Senators and Representatives shall receive a Compensation for their Services, to be ascertained by Law, and paid out of the Treasury of the United States. They shall in all Cases, except Treason, Felony and Breach of the Peace, be privileged from Arrest during their Attendance at the Session of their respective Houses, and in going to and returning from the same; and for any Speech or Debate in either House, they shall not be questioned in any other Place.

55 (Madison), 76 (Hamilton)

No Senator or Representative shall, during the time for which he was elected, be appointed to any civil Office under the authority of the United States, which shall have been created, or the Emoluments whereof shall have been encreased during such time; and no Person holding any Office under the United States, shall be a Member of either House during his Continuance in Office.

Section 7

[PROCEDURE IN PASSING BILLS AND RESOLUTIONS]

66 (Hamilton)

All Bills for raising Revenue shall originate in the House of Representatives; but the Senate may propose or concur with Amendments as on other Bills.

69, 73 (Hamilton)

Every Bill which shall have passed the House of Representatives and the Senate, shall, before it become a Law, be presented to the President of the United States; if he approve he shall sign it, but if not he shall return it, with his Objections to that House in which it shall have originated, who shall enter the Objections at large on their Journal, and proceed to reconsider it. If after such Reconsideration two-thirds of that House shall agree to pass the Bill, it shall be sent, together with the Objections, to the other House, by which it shall likewise be reconsidered, and if approved by two-thirds of that House it shall become a Law. But in all such Cases the Votes of both Houses shall be determined by Yeas and Nays, and the Names of the Persons voting for and against the Bill shall be entered on the Journal of each House respectively. If any Bill shall not be returned by the President within ten Days (Sundays excepted) after it shall have been presented to him, the Same shall be a Law, in like Manner as if he had signed it, unless the Congress by their Adjournment prevent its Return, in which Case it shall not be a Law.

69, 73 (Hamilton)

Every Order, Resolution, or Vote to which the Concurrence of the Senate and House of Representatives may be necessary (except on a question of Adjournment) shall be presented to the President of the United States; and before the Same shall take Effect, shall be approved by him, or being disapproved by him, shall be repassed by two-thirds of the Senate and House of Representatives, according to the Rules and Limitations prescribed in the Case of a Bill.

Section 8

[POWERS OF CONGRESS]

The Congress shall have Power

30–36 (Hamilton), 41 (Madison) 56 (Madison) 42, 45, 56 (Madison)

To lay and collect Taxes, Duties, Imposts and Excises, to pay the Debts and provide for the common Defence and general Welfare of the United States; but all Duties, Imposts and excises shall be uniform throughout the United States;

To borrow Money on the Credit of the United States;

To regulate Commerce with foreign Nations, and among the several States, and with the Indian Tribes;

A 9

32
(Hamilton),
    To establish an uniform Rule of Naturalization, and uniform Laws on the subject of Bankruptcies throughout the United States;

42
(Madison)
42
(Madison)
    To coin Money, regulate the Value thereof, and of foreign Coin, and fix the Standard of Weights and Measures;

42
(Madison)
    To provide for the Punishment of counterfeiting the Securities and current Coin of the United States;

42
(Madison)
    To establish Post Offices and post Roads;

42
(Madison)
43
(Madison)
    To promote the Progress of Science and useful Arts, by securing for limited Times to Authors and Inventors the exclusive Right to their respective Writings and Discoveries;

81
(Hamilton)
42
(Madison)
    To constitute Tribunals inferior to the supreme Court;

    To define and Punish Piracies and Felonies committed on the high Seas, and Offences against the Law of Nations;

41
(Madison)
    To declare War, grant Letters of Marque and Reprisal, and make Rules concerning Captures on Land and Water;

23, 24, 26
(Hamilton),
    To raise and support Armies, but no Appropriation of Money to that Use shall be for a longer Term than two Years;

41
(Madison)
    To provide and maintain a Navy;

    To make Rules for the Government and Regulation of the land and naval forces;

29
(Hamilton)
    To provide for calling for the Militia to execute the Laws of the Union, suppress Insurrections and repel Invasions;

29
(Hamilton)
56
(Madison)
    To provide for organizing, arming, and disciplining, the Militia, and for governing such Part of them as may be employed in the Service of the United States, reserving to the States respectively, the Appointment of the Officers, and the Authority of training the Militia according to the discipline prescribed by Congress;

32
(Hamilton),
43
(Madison)
43
(Madison)
    To exercise exclusive Legislation in all Cases whatsoever, over such District (not exceeding ten Miles square) as may, by Cession of particular States, and the Acceptance of Congress, become the Seat of the Government of the United States, and to exercise like Authority over all Places purchased by the Consent of the Legislature of the State in which the Same shall be, for the Erection of Forts,

Magazines, Arsenals, dock-Yards, and other needful Buildings;—And

29, 33
(Hamilton)
44
(Madison)
    To make all Laws which shall be necessary and proper for carrying into Execution the foregoing Powers, and all other Powers vested by this Constitution in the Government of the United States, or in any Department or Officer thereof.

Section 9

[SOME RESTRICTIONS ON FEDERAL POWER]

42
(Madison)
    The Migration or Importation of such Persons as any of the States now existing shall think proper to admit, shall not be prohibited by the Congress prior to the Year one thousand eight hundred and eight, but a Tax or Duty may be imposed on such Importation, not exceeding ten dollars for each Person.[7]

83, 84
(Hamilton)
    The privilege of the Writ of *Habeas Corpus* shall not be suspended, unless when in Cases of Rebellion or Invasion the public Safety may require it.

84
(Hamilton)
    No Bill of Attainder or ex post facto Law shall be passed.

    No Capitation, or other direct, Tax shall be laid, unless in Proportion to the Census or Enumeration herein before directed to be taken.[8]

    No Tax or Duty shall be laid on Articles exported from any State.

32
(Hamilton)
    No Preference shall be given by any Regulation of Commerce or Revenue to the Ports of one State over those of another; nor shall vessels bound to, or from, one State, be obliged to enter, clear, or pay Duties in another.

    No Money shall be drawn from the Treasury, but in Consequence of Appropriations made by Law; and a regular Statement and Account of the Receipts and Expenditures of all public Money shall be published from time to time.

39
(Madison),
84
(Hamilton)
    No Title of Nobility shall be granted by the United States: And no Person holding any Office of Profit or Trust under them, shall, without the Consent of the Congress, accept of any present, Emolument, Office or Title, of any kind whatever, from any King, Prince, or foreign State.

[7]Temporary provision.
[8]Modified by Sixteenth Amendment.

Section 10

[RESTRICTIONS UPON POWERS OF STATES]

33
(Hamilton),
44
(Madison)

No State shall enter into any Treaty, Alliance, or Confederation; grant Letters of Marque and Reprisal; coin Money; emit Bills of Credit; make any Thing but gold and silver Coin a Tender in Payment of Debts; pass any Bill of Attainder, ex post facto Law, or Law impairing the Obligation of Contracts, or grant any Title of Nobility.

32
(Hamilton),
44
(Madison)

No State shall, without the Consent of the Congress, lay any Imposts or Duties on Imports or Exports, except what may be absolutely necessary for executing its inspection Laws: and the net Produce of all Duties and Imposts, laid by any State on Imports or Exports, shall be for the Use of the Treasury of the United States; and all such Laws shall be subject to the Revision and Control of the Congress.

No State shall, without the Consent of Congress, lay any Duty of Tonnage, keep Troops, or Ships of War in time of Peace, enter into any Agreement or Compact with another State, or with a foreign Power, or engage in War, unless actually invaded, or in such imminent Danger as will not admit of Delay.

ARTICLE II

Section 1

[EXECUTIVE POWER, ELECTION, QUALIFICATIONS OF THE PRESIDENT]

39
(Madison),
70, 71, 84
(Hamilton)
69, 71
(Hamilton)
39, 45
(Madison),
68, 77
(Hamilton)

The executive Power shall be vested in a President of the United States of America. *He shall hold his Office during the Term of four years and, together with the Vice-President, chosen for the same Term, be elected, as follows:*[9]

Each State shall appoint, in such Manner as the Legislature thereof may direct, a Number of Electors, equal to the whole Number of Senators and Representatives to which the State may be entitled in the Congress: but no Senator or Representative, or Person holding an Office of Trust or Profit under the United States, shall be appointed an Elector.

66
(Hamilton)

The electors shall meet in their respective States, and vote by ballot for two Persons, of whom one at least shall not be an Inhabitant of the same State with themselves. And they shall make a List of all the Persons voted for, and of the Number of Votes for each; which List they shall sign and certify, and transmit sealed to the Seat of the Government of the United States, directed to the President of the Senate. The President of the Senate shall, in the Presence of the Senate and House of Representatives, open all the Certificates, and the Votes shall then be counted. The Person having the greatest Number of Votes shall be the President, if such Number be a Majority of the whole Number of Electors appointed; and if there be more than one who have such Majority and have an equal Number of Votes, then the House of Representatives shall immediately chuse by Ballot one of them for President; and if no person have a Majority, then from the five highest on the List the said House shall in like Manner chuse the President. But in chusing the President, the Votes shall be taken by States, the Representation from each State having one Vote; A quorum for this Purpose shall consist of a Member or Members from two-thirds of the States, and a Majority of all the States shall be necessary to a Choice. In every Case, after the Choice of the President, the person having the greatest Number of Votes of the Electors shall be the Vice-President. But if there should remain two or more who have equal vote, the Senate shall chuse from them by Ballot the Vice-President.[10]

64 (Jay)

The Congress may determine the Time of chusing the Electors, and the Day on which they shall give their Votes; which Day shall be the same throughout the United States.

No Person except a natural born Citizen, or a Citizen of the United States, at the time of the Adoption of this Constitution, shall be eligible to the Office of President; neither shall any Person be eligible to that Office who shall not have attained to the Age of thirty-five

---

[9]Number of terms limited to two by Twenty-second Amendment.

[10]Modified by Twelfth and Twentieth Amendments.

Years, and been fourteen Years a Resident within the United States.

In Case of the Removal of the President from Office, or his Death, Resignation, or Inability to discharge the Powers and Duties of the said Office, the same shall devolve on the Vice-President, and the Congress may by Law provide for the Case of Removal, Death, Resignation, or Inability, both of the President and Vice-President, declaring what Officer shall then act as President, and such Officer shall act accordingly, until the Disability be removed, or a President shall be elected.

73, 79
(Hamilton)

The President shall, at stated Times, receive for his Services, a Compensation, which shall neither be encreased nor diminished during the Period for which he shall have been elected, and he shall not receive within that Period any other Emolument from the United States, or any of them.

Before he enter on the Execution of his Office, he shall take the following Oath or Affirmation:—"I do solemnly swear (or affirm) that I will faithfully execute the Office of President of the United States, and will to the best of my Ability, preserve, protect and defend the Constitution of the United States."

Section 2

[POWERS OF THE PRESIDENT]

69, 74
(Hamilton)

74
(Hamilton)

The President shall be Commander in Chief of the Army and Navy of the United States, and of the Militia of the several States, when called into the actual Service of the United States; he may require the Opinion, in writing, of the principal Officer in each of the executive Departments, upon any Subject relating to the Duties of their respective Offices, and he shall have Power to grant Reprieves and Pardons for Offences against the United States, except in Cases of Impeachment.

69
(Hamilton)
74
(Hamilton)
42
(Madison),
64 *
(Jay),
66
(Hamilton)
42
(Madison),
66, 69,
76, 77
(Hamilton)

He shall have Power, by and with the Advice and Consent of the Senate, to make Treaties, provided two-thirds of the Senators present concur; and he shall nominate, and by and with the Advice and Consent of the Senate, shall appoint Ambassadors, other public Ministers and Consuls, Judges of the

Supreme Court, and all other Officers of the United States, whose Appointments are not herein otherwise provided for, and which shall be established by Law: but the Congress may by Law vest the Appointment of such inferior Officers, as they think proper, in the President alone, in the Courts of Law, or in the Heads of Departments.

67, 76
(Hamilton)

The President shall have Power to fill up all Vacancies that may happen during the Recess of the Senate, by granting Commissions which shall expire at the End of their next Session.

Section 3

[POWERS AND DUTIES OF THE PRESIDENT]

77
(Hamilton)
69, 77
(Hamilton)
77
(Hamilton)
69, 77
(Hamilton)
42
(Madison),
69, 77
(Hamilton)
78
(Hamilton)

He shall from time to time give to the Congress Information of the State of the Union, and recommend to their Consideration such Measures as he shall judge necessary and expedient; he may, on extraordinary Occasions, convene both Houses, or either of them, and in Case of Disagreement between them, with Respect to the Time of Adjournment, he may adjourn them to such Time as he shall think proper; he shall receive Ambassadors and other public Ministers; he shall take Care that the Laws be faithfully executed, and shall Commission all the Officers of the United States.

Section 4

[IMPEACHMENT]

39
(Madison),
69
(Hamilton)

The President, Vice-President and all civil Officers of the United States shall be removed from Office on Impeachment for, and Conviction of, Treason, Bribery, or other high Crimes and Misdemeanors.

ARTICLE III

Section 1

[JUDICIAL POWER, TENURE OF OFFICE]

81, 82
(Hamilton)
65
(Hamilton)
78, 79
(Hamilton)

The judicial Power of the United States, shall be vested in one supreme Court, and in such inferior Courts as the Congress may from time to time ordain and establish. The

Judges, both of the supreme and inferior Courts, shall hold their Offices during good Behavior, and shall, at stated Times, receive for their Services, a Compensation, which shall not be diminished during their Continuance in Office.

Section 2

[JURISDICTION]

80
(Hamilton)

The judicial Power shall extend to all Cases, in Law and Equity, arising under this Constitution, the Laws of the United States, and Treaties made, or which shall be made, under their Authority;—to all Cases affecting Ambassadors, other public Ministers and Consuls;—to all Cases of admiralty and maritime Jurisdiction;—to Controversies to which the United States shall be a party;—to Controversies between two or more States;—*between a State and Citizens of another State;*—between Citizens of different States,—between Citizens of the same State claiming Lands under Grants of different States, and between a State, or the Citizens thereof, *and foreign States, Citizens or Subjects.*[11]

81
(Hamilton)

In all Cases affecting Ambassadors, other public Ministers and Consuls, and those in which a State shall be Party, the supreme Court shall have original Jurisdiction. In all the other Cases before mentioned, the supreme Court shall have appellate Jurisdiction, both as to Law and Fact, with such Exceptions, and under such Regulations as Congress shall make.

83, 84
(Hamilton)

The Trial of all Crimes, except in Cases of Impeachment, shall be by Jury; and such Trial shall be held in the State where the said Crimes shall have been committed; but when not committed within any State, the Trial shall be at such Place or Places as the Congress may by Law have directed.

Section 3

[TREASON, PROOF, AND PUNISHMENT]

43
(Madison),
84
(Hamilton)

Treason against the United States, shall consist only in levying War against them, or in adhering to their Enemies, giving them Aid and Comfort. No Person shall be convicted of Treason unless on the Testimony of two Witnesses to the same overt Act, or on Confession in open Court.

43
(Madison),
84
(Hamilton)

The Congress shall have Power to declare the Punishment of Treason, but no Attainder of Treason shall work Corruption of Blood, or Forfeiture except during the Life of the Person attained.

ARTICLE IV

Section 1

[FAITH AND CREDIT AMONG STATES]

42
(Madison)

Full Faith and Credit shall be given in each State to the public Acts, Records, and judicial Proceedings of every other State. And the Congress may by general Laws prescribe the Manner in which such Acts, Records and Proceedings shall be proved, and the Effect thereof.

Section 2

[PRIVILEGES AND IMMUNITIES, FUGITIVES]

80
(Hamilton)

The Citizens of each State shall be entitled to all Privileges and Immunities of Citizens in the several States.

A person charged in any State with Treason, Felony or other Crime, who shall flee from Justice, and be found in another State, shall on Demand of the executive Authority of the State from which he fled, be delivered up to be removed to the State having Jurisdiction of the Crime.

No person held to Service or Labour in one State, under the Laws thereof, escaping into another, shall, in Consequence of any Law or Regulation therein, be discharged from such Service or Labour, but shall be delivered up on Claim of the Party to whom such Service or Labour may be due.[12]

---

[11]Modified by Eleventh Amendment.

[12]Repeated by the Thirteenth Amendment.

Section 3

[ADMISSION OF NEW STATES]

43
(Madison)

New States may be admitted by the Congress into this Union; but no new State shall be formed or erected within the Jurisdiction of any other State; nor any State be formed by the Junction of two or more States, or Parts of States, without the Consent of the Legislatures of the States concerned as well as of the Congress.

43
(Madison)

The Congress shall have Power to dispose of and make all needful Rules and Regulations respecting the Territory or other Property belonging to the United States; and nothing in this Constitution shall be so construed as to Prejudice any Claims of the United States, or of any particular State.

Section 4

[GUARANTEE OF REPUBLICAN GOVERNMENT]

39, 43
(Madison)

The United States shall guarantee to every State in this Union a Republican Form of Government, and shall protect each of them against Invasion; and on Application of the Legislature, or of the Executive (when the Legislature cannot be convened) against domestic Violence.

ARTICLE V

[AMENDMENT OF THE CONSTITUTION]

39, 43
(Madison)
85
(Hamilton)

The Congress, whenever two-thirds of both Houses shall deem it necessary, shall propose Amendments to this Constitution, or, on the Application of the Legislatures of two-thirds of the several States, shall call a Convention for proposing Amendments, which, in either Case, shall be valid to all Intents and Purposes, as Part of this Constitution, when ratified by the Legislatures of three-fourths of the several States, or by Conventions in three-fourths thereof, as the one or the other Mode of Ratification may be proposed by the Congress; *Provided that no Amendment which may be made prior to the Year One thousand eight hundred and eight shall in any Manner affect the first*

43
(Madison)

and fourth Clauses in the Ninth Section of the first

Article;[13] and that no State, without its Consent, shall be deprived of its equal Suffrage in the Senate.

ARTICLE VI

[DEBTS, SUPREMACY, OATH]

43
(Madison)

All Debts contracted and Engagements entered into, before the Adoption of this Constitution, shall be as valid against the United States under this Constitution, as under the Confederation.

27, 33
(Hamilton),

39, 44

This Constitution, and the Laws of the United States which shall be made in Pursuance thereof; and all Treaties made, or which shall be made, under the Authority of the United States, shall be the supreme Law of the Land; and the Judges in every State shall be bound thereby, any Thing in the Constitution or Laws of any State to the Contrary notwithstanding.

27
(Hamilton),

44

The Senators and Representatives before mentioned, and the Members of the several State Legislatures, and all executive and judicial Officers, both of the United States and of the several States, shall be bound by Oath or Affirmation, to support this Constitution; but no religious Test shall be required as a Qualification to any Office or public Trust under the United States.

ARTICLE VII

[RATIFICATION AND ESTABLISHMENT]

39, 40, 43
(Madison)

The Ratification of the Conventions of nine States, shall be sufficient for the Establishment of this Constitution between the States so ratifying the Same.[14]

Done in Convention by the Unanimous Consent of the States present the Seventeenth Day of September in the Year of our Lord one

[13]Temporary provision.

[14]The Constitution was submitted on September 17, 1787, by the Constitutional Convention, was ratified by the conventions of several states at various dates up to May 29, 1790, and became effective on March 4, 1789.

thousand seven hundred and Eighty seven and of the Independence of the United States of America the Twelfth. *In Witness* whereof We have hereunto subscribed our Names,

G:⁰ WASHINGTON—
Presidt, and Deputy from Virginia

New Hampshire	JOHN LANGDON		THOS. FITZSIMONS
	NICHOLAS GILMAN		JARED INGERSOLL
			JAMES WILSON
Massachusetts	NATHANIEL GORHAM		GOUV MORRIS
	RUFUS KING	Delaware	GEO READ
			GUNNING BEDFOR JUN
Connecticut	WM SAML JOHNSON		JOHN DICKINSON
	ROGER SHERMAN		RICHARD BASSETT
			JACO: BROOM
New York	ALEXANDER HAMILTON		
		Maryland	JAMES MCHENRY
New Jersey	WIL: LIVINGSTON		DAN OF ST. THOS. JENIFER
	DAVID BREARLY		DANL CARROLL
	WM PATERSON		
	JONA: DAYTON	Virginia	JOHN BLAIR—
			JAMES MADISON JR.
Pennsylvania	B FRANKLIN		
	THOMAS MIFFLIN	North Carolina	WM BLOUNT
	ROBT MORRIS		RICHD DOBBS SPAIGHT
	GEO. CLYMER		HU WILLIAMSON
		South Carolina	J. RUTLEDGE
			CHARLES COTESWORTH PINCKNEY
			PIERCE BUTLER
		Georgia	WILLIAM FEW
			ABR BALDWIN

Amendments to the Constitution

*Proposed by Congress and Ratified
by the Legislatures of the Several States,
Pursuant to Article V of the Original Constitution.*

*Amendments I-X, known as the Bill of Rights, were proposed by Congress on September 25, 1789, and
ratified on December 15, 1791.* Federalist Papers *comments, mainly in opposition to a Bill of Rights, can
be found in #84 (Hamilton).*

AMENDMENT I

[FREEDOM OF RELIGION, OF SPEECH, AND OF THE PRESS]

Congress shall make no law respecting an establishment of religion, or prohibiting the free exercise thereof; or abridging the freedom of speech, or of the press; or the right of the people peaceably to assemble, and to petition the Government for a redress of grievances.

AMENDMENT II

[RIGHT TO KEEP AND BEAR ARMS]

A well regulated Militia, being necessary to the security of a free State, the right of the people to keep and bear Arms, shall not be infringed.

AMENDMENT III

[QUARTERING OF SOLDIERS]

No Soldier shall, in time of peace be quartered in any house, without the consent of the Owner, nor in time of war, but in a manner to be prescribed by law.

AMENDMENT IV

[SECURITY FROM UNWARRANTABLE SEARCH AND SEIZURE]

The right of the people to be secure in their persons, houses, papers, and effects, against unreasonable searches and seizures, shall not be violated, and no Warrants shall issue, but upon probable cause, supported by Oath or affirmation, and particularly describing the place to be searched, and the persons or things to be seized.

AMENDMENT V

[RIGHTS OF ACCUSED PERSONS IN CRIMINAL PROCEEDINGS]

No person shall be held to answer for a capital, or otherwise infamous crime, unless on a presentment or indictment of a Grand Jury, except in cases arising in the land or naval forces, or in the Militia, when in actual service in time of War or in public danger; nor shall any person be subject for the same offence to be twice put in jeopardy of life or limb; nor shall be compelled in any Criminal Case to be a witness against himself, nor be deprived of life, liberty, or property, without due process of law; nor shall private property be taken for public use, without just compensation.

AMENDMENT VI

[RIGHT TO SPEEDY TRIAL, WITNESSES, ETC.]

In all criminal prosecutions, the accused shall enjoy the right to a speedy and public trial, by an impartial jury of the State and district wherein the crime shall have been committed, which district shall have been previously ascertained by law, and to be informed of the nature and cause of the accusation; to be confronted with the witnesses against him; to have compulsory process for obtaining Witnesses in his favor, and to have the Assistance of Counsel for his defence.

AMENDMENT VII

[TRIAL BY JURY IN CIVIL CASES]

In suits at common law, where the value in controversy shall exceed twenty dollars, the right of trial by jury shall be preserved, and no fact tried by a jury shall be otherwise reexamined in any Court of the United States, than according to the rules of the common law.

AMENDMENT VIII

[BAILS, FINES, PUNISHMENTS]

Excessive bail shall not be required, nor excessive fines imposed, nor cruel and unusual punishments inflicted.

AMENDMENT IX

[RESERVATION OF RIGHTS OF PEOPLE]

The enumeration in the Constitution, of certain rights, shall not be construed to deny or disparage others retained by the people.

AMENDMENT X

[POWERS RESERVED TO STATES OR PEOPLE]

The powers not delegated to the United States by the Constitution, nor prohibited by it to the States, are reserved to the States respectively, or to the people.

AMENDMENT XI

[*Proposed by Congress on March 4, 1794; declared ratified on January 8, 1798.*]

[RESTRICTION OF JUDICIAL POWER]

The Judicial power of the United States shall not be construed to extend to any suit in law or equity, commenced or prosecuted against one of the United States by Citizens of another State, or by Citizens or Subjects of any Foreign State.

AMENDMENT XII

[*Proposed by Congress on December 9, 1803; declared ratified on September 25, 1804.*]

[ELECTION OF PRESIDENT AND VICE-PRESIDENT]

The Electors shall meet in their respective states, and vote by ballot for President and Vice-President, one of whom, at least, shall not be an inhabitant of the same state with themselves; they shall name in their ballots the person voted for as President, and in distinct ballots the person voted for as Vice-President, and they shall make distinct lists of all persons voted for as President, and of all persons voted for as Vice-President, and of the number of votes for each, which lists they shall sign and certify, and transmit sealed to the seat of the government of the United States, directed to the President of the Senate;—The President of the Senate shall, in presence of the Senate and House of Representatives, open all the certificates and the votes shall then be counted;—The person having the greatest number of votes for President, shall be the President, if such number be a majority of the whole number of Electors appointed; and if no person have such majority, then from the persons having the highest numbers not exceeding three on the list of those voted for as President, the House of Representatives shall choose immediately, by ballot, the President. But in choosing the President, the votes shall be taken by states, the representation from each state having one vote; a quorum for this purpose shall consist of a member or members from two-thirds of the states, and a majority of all states shall be necessary to a choice. And if the House of Representatives shall not choose a President whenever the right of choice shall devolve upon them, before the fourth day of March next following, then the Vice-President, shall act as President, as in the case of the death or other constitutional disability of the President. The person having the greatest number of votes as Vice-President, shall be the Vice-President, if such a number be a majority of the whole number of Electors appointed, and if no person have a majority, then from the two highest numbers on the list, the Senate shall choose the Vice-President; a quorum for the purpose shall consist of two-thirds of the whole number of Senators, and a majority of the whole number shall be necessary to a choice. But no person constitutionally ineligible to the office of President shall be eligible to that of Vice-President of the United States.

AMENDMENT XIII

[Proposed by Congress on January 31, 1865; declared ratified on December 18, 1865.]

Section 1

[ABOLITION OF SLAVERY]

Neither slavery nor involuntary servitude, except as a punishment for crime whereof the party shall have been duly convicted, shall exist within the United States, or any place subject to their jurisdiction.

Section 2

[POWER TO ENFORCE THIS ARTICLE]

Congress shall have power to enforce this article by appropriate legislation.

AMENDMENT XIV

[Proposed by Congress on June 13, 1866, declared ratified on July 28, 1868.]

Section 1

[CITIZENSHIP RIGHTS NOT TO BE ABRIDGED BY STATES]

All persons born or naturalized in the United States, and subject to the jurisdiction thereof, are citizens of the United States and of the State wherein they reside. No state shall make or enforce any law which shall abridge the privileges or immunities of citizens of the United States; nor shall any State deprive any person of life, liberty, or property, without due process of law; nor deny to any person within its jurisdiction the equal protection of the laws.

Section 2

[APPORTIONMENT OF REPRESENTATIVES IN CONGRESS]

Representatives shall be apportioned among the several States according to their respective numbers, counting the whole number of persons in each State, excluding Indians not taxed. But when the right to vote at any election for the choice of electors for President and Vice-President of the United States, Representatives in Congress, the Executive and Judicial officers of a State, or the members of the Legislature thereof, is denied to any of the male inhabitants of such State, being twenty-one years of age, and citizens of the United States, or in any way abridged, except for participation in rebellion, or other crime, the basis of representation therein shall be reduced in the proportion which the number of such male citizens shall bear to the whole number of male citizens twenty-one years of age in such State.

Section 3

[PERSONS DISQUALIFIED FROM HOLDING OFFICE]

No person shall be a Senator or Representative in Congress, or elector of President and Vice-President, or hold any office, civil or military, under the United States, or under any State, who, having previously taken an oath, as a member of Congress, or as an officer of the United States, or as a member of any State legislature, or as an executive or judicial officer of any State, to support the Constitution of the United States, shall have engaged in insurrection or rebellion against the same, or given aid or comfort to the enemies thereof. But Congress may by a vote of two-thirds of each House, remove such disability.

Section 4

[WHAT PUBLIC DEBTS ARE VALID]

The validity of the public debt of the United States, authorized by law, including debts incurred for payment of pensions and bounties for services in suppressing insurrection or rebellion, shall not be questioned. But neither the United States nor any State shall assume or pay any debt or obligation incurred in aid of insurrection or rebellion against the United States, or any claim for the loss or emancipation of any slave; but all such debts, obligations and claims shall be held illegal and void.

Section 5

[POWER TO ENFORCE THIS ARTICLE]

The Congress shall have power to enforce, by appropriate legislation, the provisions of this article.

AMENDMENT XV

[Proposed by Congress on February 26, 1869; declared ratified on March 30, 1870.]

Section 1

[NEGRO SUFFRAGE]

The right of citizens of the United States to vote shall not be denied or abridged by the United States or by any State on account of race, color, or previous condition of servitude.

Section 2

[POWER TO ENFORCE THIS ARTICLE]

The Congress shall have power to enforce this article by appropriate legislation.

AMENDMENT XVI

[Proposed by Congress on July 12, 1909; declared ratified on February 25, 1913.]

[AUTHORIZING INCOME TAXES]

The Congress shall have power to lay and collect taxes on incomes, from whatever source derived, without apportionment among the several States, and without regard to any census or enumeration.

AMENDMENT XVII

[Proposed by Congress on May 13, 1912; declared ratified on May 31, 1913.]

[POPULAR ELECTION OF SENATORS]

The Senate of the United States shall be composed of two Senators from each State, elected by the people thereof, for six years; and each Senator shall have one vote. The electors in each State shall have the qualifications requisite for electors of the most numerous branch of the State Legislature.

When vacancies happen in the representation of any State in the Senate, the executive authority of such State shall issue writs of election to fill such vacancies: Provided, That the Legislature of any State may empower the executive thereof to make temporary appointment until the people fill the vacancies by election as the Legislature may direct.

This amendment shall not be so construed as to affect the election or term of any Senator chosen before it becomes valid as part of the Constitution.

AMENDMENT XVIII

[Proposed by Congress December 18, 1917; declared ratified on January 29, 1919.]

Section 1

[NATIONAL LIQUOR PROHIBITION]

After one year from the ratification of this article the manufacture, sale, or transportation of intoxicating liquors within, the importation thereof into, or the exportation thereof from the United States and all territory subject to the jurisdiction thereof for beverage purposes is hereby prohibited.

Section 2

[POWER TO ENFORCE THIS ARTICLE]

The Congress and the several states shall have concurrent power to enforce this article by appropriate legislation.

Section 3

[RATIFICATION WITHIN SEVEN YEARS]

This article shall be inoperative unless it shall have been ratified as an amendment to the Constitution by the legislatures of the several states, as provided in the Constitution, within seven years from the date of the submission hereof to the states by the Congress.[15]

AMENDMENT XIX

[Proposed by Congress on June 4, 1919; declared ratified on August 26, 1920.]

[WOMAN SUFFRAGE]

The right of the citizens of the United States to vote shall not be denied or abridged by the United States or by any state on account of sex.

Congress shall have power, by appropriate legislation, to enforce this article by appropriate legislation.

AMENDMENT XX

[Proposed by Congress on March 2, 1932; declared ratified on February 6, 1933.]

Section 1

[TERMS OF OFFICE]

The terms of the President and Vice-President shall end at noon on the 20th day of January, and the terms of the Senators and Representatives at noon on the 3rd day of January, of the years in which such terms would have ended if this article had not been ratified; and the terms of their successors shall then begin.

---

[15]Repealed by the Twenty-first Amendment.

Section 2

[TIME OF CONVENING CONGRESS]

The Congress shall assemble at least once in every year, and such meeting shall begin at noon on the 3rd day of January, unless they shall by law appoint a different day.

Section 3

[DEATH OF PRESIDENT-ELECT]

If, at the time fixed for the beginning of the term of the President, the President-elect shall have died, the Vice-President-elect shall become President. If a President shall not have been chosen before the time fixed for the beginning of his term, or if the President-elect shall have failed to qualify, then the Vice-President-elect shall act as President until a President shall have qualified; and the Congress may by law provide for the case wherein neither a President-elect nor a Vice-President-elect shall have qualified, declaring who shall then act as President, or the manner in which one who is to act shall be selected, and such person shall act accordingly until a President or Vice President shall have qualified.

Section 4

[ELECTION OF THE PRESIDENT]

The Congress may by law provide for the case of the death of any of the persons from whom the House of Representatives may choose a President whenever the right of choice shall have devolved upon them, and for the case of the death of any of the persons from whom the Senate may choose a Vice-President whenever the right of choice shall have devolved upon them.

Section 5

[AMENDMENT TAKES EFFECT]

Sections 1 and 2 shall take effect on the 15th day of October following ratification of this article.

Section 6

[RATIFICATION WITHIN SEVEN YEARS]

This article shall be inoperative unless it shall have been ratified as an amendment to the Constitution by the legislatures of three-fourths of the several States within seven years from the date of its submission.

AMENDMENT XXI

[*Proposed by Congress on February 20, 1933; declared ratified on December 5, 1933.*]

Section 1

[NATIONAL LIQUOR PROHIBITION REPEALED]

The eighteenth article of amendment to the Constitution of the United States is hereby repealed.

Section 2

[TRANSPORTATION OF LIQUOR INTO "DRY" STATES]

The transportation or importation into any State, Territory, or Possession of the United States for delivery or use therein of intoxicating liquors, in violation of the laws thereof, is hereby prohibited.

Section 3

[RATIFICATION WITHIN SEVEN YEARS]

This article shall be inoperative unless it shall have been ratified as an amendment to the Constitution by conventions in the several States, as provided in the Constitution, within seven years from the date of the submission hereof to the States by the Congress.

AMENDMENT XXII

[*Proposed by Congress on March 21, 1947; declared ratified on February 26, 1951.*]

Section 1

[TENURE OF PRESIDENT LIMITED]

No person shall be elected to the office of President more than twice, and no person who has held the office of President or acted as President for more than two years of a term to which some other person was elected President shall be elected to the Office of the President more than once. But this Article shall not apply to any person holding the office of President when this Article was proposed by the Congress, and shall not prevent any person who may be holding the office of President, or acting as President, during the term within which this Article becomes operative from holding the office of President or acting as President during the remainder of such term.

Section 2

[RATIFICATION WITHIN SEVEN YEARS]

This Article shall be inoperative unless it shall have been ratified as an amendment to the Constitution by the legislatures of three-fourths of the several states within seven years from the date of its submission to the States by the Congress.

AMENDMENT XXIII

[*Proposed by Congress on June 21, 1960; declared ratified on March 29, 1961.*]

Section 1

[ELECTORAL COLLEGE VOTES FOR THE DISTRICT OF COLUMBIA]

The District constituting the seat of Government of the United States shall appoint in such manner as the Congress may direct:

A number of electors of President and Vice-President equal to the whole number of Senators and Representatives in Congress to which the District would be entitled if it were a State, but in no event more than the least populous State; they shall be in addition to those appointed by the States, but they shall be considered, for the purposes of the election of President and Vice-President, to be electors appointed by a State; and they shall meet in the District and perform such duties as provided by the twelfth article of amendment.

Section 2

[POWER TO ENFORCE THIS ARTICLE]

The Congress shall have power to enforce this article by appropriate legislation.

AMENDMENT XXIV

[*Proposed by Congress on August 27, 1963; declared ratified on January 23, 1964.*]

Section 1

[ANTI-POLL TAX]

The right of citizens of the United States to vote in any primary or other election for President or Vice-President, for electors for President or Vice-President, or for Senator or Representative of Congress, shall not be denied or abridged by the United States or any State by reasons of failure to pay any poll tax or other tax.

Section 2

[POWER TO ENFORCE THIS ARTICLE]

The Congress shall have power to enforce this article by appropriate legislation.

AMENDMENT XXV

[*Proposed by Congress on July 7, 1965; declared ratified on February 10, 1967.*]

Section 1

[VICE-PRESIDENT TO BECOME PRESIDENT]

In case of the removal of the President from office or his death or resignation, the Vice-President shall become President.

Section 2

[CHOICE OF A NEW VICE-PRESIDENT]

Whenever there is a vacancy in the office of the Vice-President, the President shall nominate a Vice-President who shall take the office upon confirmation by a majority vote of both houses of Congress.

Section 3

[PRESIDENT MAY DECLARE OWN DISABILITY]

Whenever the President transmits to the President pro tempore of the Senate and the Speaker of the House of Representatives his written declaration that he is unable to discharge the powers and duties of his office, and until he transmits to them a written declaration to the contrary, such powers and duties shall be discharged by the Vice-President as Acting President.

Section 4

[ALTERNATE PROCEDURES TO DECLARE AND TO END PRESIDENTIAL DISABILITY]

Whenever the Vice-President and a majority of either the principal officers of the executive departments, or of such other body as Congress may by law provide, transmit to the President pro tempore of the Senate and the Speaker of the House of Representatives their written declaration that the President is unable to discharge the powers and duties of his office, the Vice-President shall immediately assume the powers and duties of the office as Acting President.

Thereafter, when the President transmits to the President pro tempore of the Senate and the Speaker of the House of Representatives his written declaration that no inability exists, he shall resume the powers and duties of his office unless the Vice-President and a majority of either the principal officers of the executive departments, or of such other body as Congress may by law provide, transmit within four days to the President pro tempore of the Senate and the Speaker of the House of Representatives their written declaration that the President is unable to discharge the powers and duties of his office. Thereupon Congress shall decide the issue, assembling within 48 hours for that purpose if not in session. If the

Congress, within 21 days after receipt of the latter written declaration, or, if Congress is not in session, within 21 days after Congress is required to assemble, determines by two-thirds vote of both houses that the President is unable to discharge the powers and duties of his office, the Vice-President shall continue to discharge the same as Acting President; otherwise, the President shall resume the powers and duties of his office.

AMENDMENT XXVI

[*Proposed by Congress on March 23, 1971; declared ratified on June 30, 1971.*]

Section 1

[EIGHTEEN-YEAR-OLD VOTE]

The right of citizens of the United States, who are eighteen years of age or older, to vote shall not be denied or abridged by the United States or by any State on account of age.

Section 2

[POWER TO ENFORCE THIS ARTICLE]

The Congress shall have power to enforce this article by appropriate legislation.

AMENDMENT XXVII

[*Proposed by Congress on September 25, 1789; ratified on May 7, 1992.*]

[CONGRESSIONAL PAY RAISES]

No law varying the compensation for the services of the Senators and Representatives shall take effect until an election of Representatives shall have intervened.

The Federalist Papers

No 10: Madison

Among the numerous advantages promised by a well-constructed Union, none deserves to be more accurately developed than its tendency to break and control the violence of faction. The friend of popular governments never finds himself so much alarmed for their character and fate as when he contemplates their propensity to this dangerous vice. He will not fail, therefore, to set a due value on any plan which, without violating the principles to which he is attached, provides a proper cure for it. The instability, injustice, and confusion introduced into the public councils have, in truth, been the mortal diseases under which popular governments have everywhere perished, as they continue to be the favorite and fruitful topics from which the adversaries to liberty derive their most specious declamations. The valuable improvements made by the American constitutions on the popular models, both ancient and modern, cannot certainly be too much admired; but it would be an unwarrantable partiality to contend that they have as effectually obviated the danger on this side, as was wished and expected. Complaints are everywhere heard from our most considerate and virtuous citizens, equally the friends of public and private faith and of public and personal liberty, that our governments are too unstable, that the public good is disregarded in the conflicts of rival parties, and that measures are too often decided, not according to the rules of justice and the rights of the minor party, but by the superior force of an interested and overbearing majority. However anxiously we may wish that these complaints had no foundation, the evidence of known facts will not permit us to deny that they are in some degree true. It will be found, indeed, on a candid review of our situation, that some of the distresses under which we labor have been erroneously charged on the operation of our governments; but it will be found, at the same time, that other causes will not alone account for many of our heaviest misfortunes; and, particularly, for that prevailing and increasing distrust of public engagements and alarm for private rights which are echoed from one end of the continent to the other. These must be chiefly, if not wholly, effects of the unsteadiness and injustice with which a factious spirit has tainted our public administration.

By a faction I understand a number of citizens, whether amounting to a majority or minority of the whole, who are united and actuated by some common impulse of passion, or of interest, adverse to the rights of other citizens, or to the permanent and aggregate interests of the community.

There are two methods of curing the mischiefs of faction: the one, by removing its causes; the other, by controlling its effects.

There are again two methods of removing the causes of faction: the one, by destroying the liberty which is essential to its existence; the other, by giving to every citizen the same opinions, the same passions, and the same interests.

It could never be more truly said than of the first remedy that it was worse than the disease. Liberty is to faction what air is to fire, an aliment without which it instantly expires. But it could not be a less folly to abolish liberty, which is essential to political life, because it nourishes faction than it would be to wish the annihilation of air, which is essential to animal life, because it imparts to fire its destructive agency.

The second expedient is as impracticable as the first would be unwise. As long as the reason of man continues fallible, and he is at liberty to exercise it, different opinions will be formed. As long as the connection subsists between his reason and his self-love, his opinions and his passions will have a reciprocal influence on each other; and the former will be objects to which the latter will attach themselves. The diversity in the faculties of men, from which the rights of property originate, is not less an insuperable obstacle to a uniformity of interests. The protection of these faculties is the first object of government. From the protection of different and unequal faculties of acquiring property, the possession of different degrees and kinds of property immediately results; and from the influence of these on the sentiments and views of the respective proprietors ensues a division of the society into different interests and parties.

The latent causes of faction are thus sown in the nature of man; and we see them everywhere brought into different degrees of activity, according to the different circumstances of civil society. A zeal for different opinions concerning religion, concerning government, and many other points, as well of speculation as of practice; an attachment to different leaders ambitiously contending for pre-eminence and power; or to persons of other descriptions whose fortunes have been interesting to the human passions, have, in turn, divided mankind into parties, inflamed them with mutual animosity, and rendered them much more disposed to vex and oppress each other than to co-operate for their common good. So strong is this propensity of mankind to fall into mutual animosities that where no substantial occasion presents itself the most frivolous and fanciful distinctions have been sufficient to kindle their unfriendly passions and excite their most violent conflicts. But the most common and durable source of factions has been the various and unequal distribution of property. Those who hold and those who are without property have ever formed distinct interests in society. Those who are creditors, and those who are debtors, fall under a like discrimination. A landed interest, a manufacturing interest, a mercantile interest, a moneyed interest, with many lesser interests, grow up of necessity in civilized nations, and divide them into different classes, actuated by different sentiments and views. The regulation of these various and interfering interests forms the principal task of modern legislation and involves the spirit of party and faction in the necessary and ordinary operations of government.

No man is allowed to be judge in his own cause, because his interest would certainly bias his judgment and, not improbably, corrupt his integrity. With equal, nay with greater reason, a body of men are unfit to be both judges and parties at the same time; yet what are many of the most important acts of legislation but so many judicial determinations, not indeed concerning the rights of single persons, but concerning the rights of large bodies of citizens? And what are the different classes of legislators but advocates and parties to the causes which they determine? Is a law proposed concerning private debts? It is a question to which the creditors are parties on one side and the debtors on the other. Justice ought to hold the balance between them. Yet the parties are, and must be, themselves the judges; and the most numerous party, or in other words, the most powerful faction must be expected to prevail. Shall domestic manufacturers be encouraged, and in what degree, by restrictions on foreign manufacturers? are questions which would be differently decided by the landed and the manufacturing classes, and probably by neither with a sole regard to justice and the public good. The apportionment of taxes on the various descriptions of property is an act which seems to require the most exact impartiality; yet there is, perhaps, no legislative act in which greater opportunity and temptation are given to a predominant party to trample on the rules of justice. Every shilling with which they overburden the inferior number is a shilling saved to their own pockets.

It is in vain to say that enlightened statesmen will be able to adjust these clashing interests and render them all subservient to the public good. Enlightened statesmen will not always be at the helm. Nor, in many cases, can such an adjustment be made at all without taking into view indirect and remote considerations, which will rarely prevail over the immediate interest which one party may find in disregarding the rights of another or the good of the whole.

The inference to which we are brought is that the causes of faction cannot be removed and that relief is only to be sought in the means of controlling its *effects*.

If a faction consists of less than a majority, relief is supplied by the republican principle, which enables the majority to defeat its sinister views by regular vote. It may clog the administration, it may convulse the society; but it will be unable to execute and mask its violence under the forms of the Constitution. When a majority is included in a faction, the form of popular government, on the other hand, enables it to sacrifice to its ruling passion or interest both the public good and the rights of other citizens. To secure the public good and private rights against the danger of such a faction, and at the same time to preserve the spirit and the form of popular government, is then the great object to which our inquiries are directed. Let me add that it is the great desideratum by which alone this form of government can be rescued from the opprobrium under which it has so long labored and be recommended to the esteem and adoption of mankind.

By what means is this object attainable? Evidently by one of two only. Either the existence of the same passion or interest in a majority at the same time must be prevented, or the majority, having such coexistent passion or interest, must be rendered, by their number and local situation, unable to concert and carry into effect schemes of oppression. If the impulse and the opportunity be suffered to coincide, we well know that neither moral nor religious motives can be relied on as an adequate control. They are not found to be such on the injustice and violence of individuals, and lose their efficacy in proportion to the number combined together, that is, in proportion as their efficacy becomes needful.

From this view of the subject it may be concluded that a pure democracy, by which I mean a society consisting of a small number of citizens, who assemble and administer the government in person, can admit of no cure for the mischiefs of faction. A common passion or interest will, in almost every case, be felt by a majority of the whole; a communication and concert results from the form of government itself; and there is nothing to check the inducements to sacrifice the weaker party or an obnoxious individual. Hence it is that such democracies have ever been spectacles of turbulence and contention; have ever been found incompatible with personal security or the rights of property; and have in general been as short in their lives as they have been violent in their deaths. Theoretic politicians, who have patronized this species of government, have erroneously supposed that by reducing mankind to a perfect equality in their political rights, they would at the same time be perfectly equalized and assimilated in their possessions, their opinions, and their passions.

A republic, by which I mean a government in which the scheme of representation takes place, opens a different prospect and promises the cure for which we are seeking. Let us examine the points in which it varies from pure democracy, and we shall comprehend both the nature of the cure and the efficacy which it must derive from the Union.

The two great points of difference between a democracy and a republic are: first, the delegation of the government, in the latter, to a small number of citizens elected by the rest; secondly, the greater number of citizens and greater sphere of country over which the latter may be extended.

The effect of the first difference is, on the one hand, to refine and enlarge the public views by passing them through the medium of a chosen body of citizens, whose wisdom may best discern the true interest of their country and whose patriotism and love of justice will be least likely to sacrifice it to temporary or partial considerations. Under such a regulation it may well happen that the public voice, pronounced by the representatives of the people, will be more consonant to the public good than if pronounced by the people themselves, convened for the purpose. On the other hand, the effect may be inverted. Men of factious tempers, of local prejudices, or of sinister designs, may, by intrigue, by corruption, or by other means, first obtain the suffrages, and then betray the interests of the people. The question resulting is, whether small or extensive republics are most favorable to the election of proper guardians of the public weal; and it is clearly decided in favor of the latter by two obvious considerations.

In the first place it is to be remarked that however small the republic may be the representatives must be raised to a certain number in order to guard against the cabals of a few; and that however large it may be they must be limited to a certain number in order to guard against the confusion of a multitude. Hence, the number of representatives in the two cases not being in proportion to that of the constituents, and being proportionally greatest in the small republic, it follows that if the proportion of fit characters be not less in the large than in the small republic, the former will present a greater option, and consequently a greater probability of a fit choice.

In the next place, as each representative will be chosen by a greater number of citizens in the large than in the small republic, it will be more difficult for unworthy candidates to practise with success the vicious arts by which elections are too often carried; and the suffrages of the people being more free, will be more likely to center on men who possess the most attractive merit and the most diffusive and established characters.

It must be confessed that in this, as in most other cases, there is a mean, on both sides of which inconveniencies will be found to lie. By enlarging too much the number of electors, you render the representative too little acquainted with all their local circumstances and lesser interests; as by reducing it too much, you render him unduly attached to these, and too little fit to comprehend and pursue great and national objects. The federal Constitution forms a happy combination in this respect; the great and aggregate interests being referred to the national, the local and particular to the State legislatures.

The other point of difference is the greater number of citizens and extent of territory which may be brought within the compass of republican than of democratic government; and it is this circumstance principally which renders factious combinations less to be dreaded in the former than in the latter. The smaller the society, the fewer probably will be the distinct parties and interests composing it; the fewer the distinct parties and interests, the more frequently will a majority be found of the same party; and the smaller the number of individuals composing a majority, and the smaller the compass within which they are placed, the more easily will they concert and execute their plans of oppression. Extend the sphere and you take in a greater variety of parties and interests; you make it less probable that a majority of the whole will have a common motive to invade the rights of other citizens; or if such a common motive exists, it will be more difficult for all who feel it to discover their own strength and to act in unison with each other. Besides other impediments, it may be remarked that, where there is a consciousness of unjust or dishonorable purposes, communication is always checked by distrust in proportion to the number whose concurrence is necessary.

Hence, it clearly appears that the same advantage which a republic has over a democracy in controlling the effects of faction is enjoyed by a large over a small republic—is enjoyed by the Union over the States composing it. Does this advantage consist in the substitution of representatives whose enlightened views and virtuous sentiments render them superior to local prejudices and to schemes of injustice? It will not be denied that the representation of the Union will be most likely to possess these requisite endowments. Does it consist in the greater security afforded by a greater variety of parties, against the event of any one party being able to outnumber and oppress the rest? In an equal degree does the increased variety of parties comprised within the Union increase this security? Does it, in fine, consist in the greater obstacles opposed to the concert and accomplishment of the secret wishes of an unjust and interested majority? Here again the extent of the Union gives it the most palpable advantage.

The influence of factious leaders may kindle a flame within their particular States but will be unable to spread a general conflagration through the other States. A religious sect may degenerate into a political faction in a part of the Confederacy; but the variety of sects dispersed over the entire face of it must secure the national councils against any danger from that source. A rage for paper money, for an abolition of debts, for an equal division of property, or for any other improper or wicked project, will be less apt to pervade the whole body of the Union than a particular member of it, in the same proportion as such a malady is more likely to taint a particular county or district than an entire State.

In the extent and proper structure of the Union, therefore, we behold a republican remedy for the diseases most incident to republican government. And according to the degree of pleasure and pride we feel in being republicans ought to be our zeal in cherishing the spirit and supporting the character of federalist.

PUBLIUS

No. 51: Madison

To what expedient, then, shall we finally resort, for maintaining in practice the necessary partition of power among the several departments as laid down in the Constitution? The only answer that can be given is that as all these exterior provisions are found to be inadequate the defect must be supplied, by so contriving the interior structure of the government as that its several constituent parts may, by their mutual relations, be the means of keeping each other in their proper places. Without presuming to undertake a full development of this important idea I will hazard a few general observations which may perhaps place it in a clearer light, and enable us to form a more correct judgment of the principles and structure of the government planned by the convention.

In order to lay a due foundation for that separate and distinct exercise of the different powers of government, which to a certain extent is admitted on all hands to be essential to the preservation of liberty, it is evident that each department should have a will of its own; and consequently should be so constituted that the members of each should have as little agency as possible in the appointment of the members of the others. Were this principle rigorously adhered to, it would require that all the appointments for the supreme executive, legislative, and judiciary magistracies should be drawn from the same fountain of authority, the people, through channels having no communication whatever with one another. Perhaps such a plan of constructing the several departments would be less difficult in practice than it may in contemplation appear. Some difficulties, however, and some additional expense would attend the execution of it. Some deviations, therefore, from the principle must be admitted. In the constitution of the judiciary department in particular, it might be inexpedient to insist rigorously on the principle: first, because peculiar qualifications being essential in the members, the primary consideration ought to be to select that mode of choice which best secures these qualifications; second, because the permanent tenure by which the appointments are held in that department must soon destroy all sense of dependence on the authority conferring them.

It is equally evident that the members of each department should be as little dependent as possible on those of the others for the emoluments annexed to their offices. Were the executive magistrate, or the judges, not independent of the legislature in this particular, their independence in every other would be merely nominal.

But the great security against a gradual concentration of the several powers in the same department consists in giving to those who administer each department

the necessary constitutional means and personal motives to resist encroachments of the others. The provision for defense must in this, as in all other cases, be made commensurate to the danger of attack. Ambition must be made to counteract ambition. The interest of the man must be connected with the constitutional rights of the place. It may be a reflection on human nature that such devices should be necessary to control the abuses of government. But what is government itself but the greatest of all reflections on human nature? If men were angels, no government would be necessary. If angels were to govern men, neither external nor internal controls on government would be necessary. In framing a government which is to be administered by men over men, the great difficulty lies in this: you must first enable the government to control the governed; and in the next place oblige it to control itself. A dependence on the people is, no doubt, the primary control on the government; but experience has taught mankind the necessity of auxiliary precautions.

This policy of supplying, by opposite and rival interests, the defect of better motives, might be traced through the whole system of human affairs, private as well as public. We see it particularly displayed in all the subordinate distributions of power, where the constant aim is to divide and arrange the several offices in such a manner as that each may be a check on the other—that the private interest of every individual may be a sentinel over the public rights. These inventions of prudence cannot be less requisite in the distribution of the supreme powers of the State.

But it is not possible to give to each department an equal power of self-defense. In republican government, the legislative authority necessarily predominates. The remedy for this inconveniency is to divide the legislature into different branches; and to render them, by different modes of election and different principles of action, as little connected with each other as the nature of their common functions and their common dependence on the society will admit. It may even be necessary to guard against dangerous encroachments by still further precautions. As the weight of the legislative authority requires that it should be thus divided, the weakness of the executive may require, on the other hand, that it should be fortified. An absolute negative on the legislature appears, at first view, to be the natural defense with which the executive magistrate should be armed. But perhaps it would be neither altogether safe nor alone sufficient. On ordinary occasions it might not be exerted with the requisite firmness, and on extraordinary occasions it might be perfidiously abused. May not this defect of an absolute negative be supplied by some qualified connection between this weaker branch of the stronger department, by which the latter may be led to support the constitutional rights of the former, without being too much detached from the rights of its own department?

If the principles on which these observations are founded be just, as I persuade myself they are, and they be applied as a criterion to the several State constitutions, and to the federal Constitution, it will be found that if the latter does not perfectly correspond with them, the former are infinitely less able to bear such a test.

There are, moreover, two considerations particularly applicable to the federal system of America, which place that system in a very interesting point of view.

First. In a single republic, all the power surrendered by the people is submitted to the administration of a single government; and the usurpations are guarded against by a division of the government into distinct and separate departments. In the compound republic of America, the power surrendered by the people is first divided between two distinct governments, and then the portion allotted to each subdivided among distinct and separate departments. Hence a double security arises to the rights of the people. The different governments will control each other, at the same time that each will be controlled by itself.

Second. It is of great importance in a republic not only to guard the society against the oppression of its rulers, but to guard one part of the society against the injustice of the other part. Different interests necessarily exist in different classes of citizens. If a majority be united by a common interest, the rights of the minority will be insecure. There are but two methods of providing against this evil: the one by creating a will in the community independent of the majority—that is, of the society itself; the other, by comprehending in the society so many separate descriptions of citizens as will render an unjust combination of a majority of the whole very improbable, if not impracticable. The first method prevails in all governments possessing an hereditary or self-appointed authority. This, at best, is but a precarious security; because a power independent of the society may as well espouse the unjust views of the major as the rightful interests of the minor party, and may

possibly be turned against both parties. The second method will be exemplified in the federal republic of the United States. Whilst all authority in it will be derived from and dependent on the society, the society itself will be broken into so many parts, interests and classes of citizens, that the rights of individuals, or of the minority, will be in little danger from interested combinations of the majority. In a free government the security for civil rights must be the same as that for religious rights. It consists in the one case in the multiplicity of interests, and in the other in the multiplicity of sects. The degree of security in both cases will depend on the number of interests and sects; and this may be presumed to depend on the extent of country and number of people comprehended under the same government. This view of the subject must particularly recommend a proper federal system to all the sincere and considerate friends of republican government, since it shows that in exact proportion as the territory of the Union may be formed into more circumscribed Confederacies, or States, oppressive combinations of a majority will be facilitated; the best security, under the republican forms, for the rights of every class of citizen, will be diminished; and consequently the stability and independence of some member of the government, the only other security, must be proportionally increased. Justice is the end of government. It is the end of civil society. It ever has been and ever will be pursued until it be obtained, or until liberty be lost in the pursuit. In a society under the forms of which the stronger faction can readily unite and oppress the weaker, anarchy may as truly be said to reign as in a state of nature, where the weaker individual is not secured against the violence of the stronger; and as, in the latter state, even the stronger individuals are prompted, by the uncertainty of their condition, to submit to a government which may protect the weak as well as themselves; so, in the former state, will the more powerful factions or parties be gradually induced, by a like motive, to wish for a government which will protect all parties, the weaker as well as the more powerful. It can be little doubted that if the State of Rhode Island was separated from the Confederacy and left to itself, the insecurity of rights under the popular form of government within such narrow limits would be displayed by such reiterated oppressions of factious majorities that some power altogether independent of the people would soon be called for by the voice of the very factions whose misrule had proved the necessity of it. In the extended republic of the United States, and among the great variety of interests, parties, and sects which it embraces, a coalition of a majority of the whole society could seldom take place on any other principles than those of justice and the general good; whilst there being thus less danger to a minor from the will of a major party, there must be less pretext, also, to provide for the security of the former, by introducing into the government a will not dependent on the latter, or, in other words, a will independent of the society itself. It is no less certain than it is important, notwithstanding the contrary opinions which have been entertained, that the larger the society, provided it lie within a practicable sphere, the more duly capable it will be of self-government. And happily for the *republican cause,* the practicable sphere may be carried to a very great extent by a judicious modification and mixture of the *federal principle.*

PUBLIUS

Glossary of Terms

absolute majority Fifty percent plus one of all those eligible to vote. Absolute rather than *simple majorities* are required for some types of congressional votes.

absolutism A system of government in which the sovereign has unlimited powers; despotism.

access The actual involvement of interest groups in the decision-making process.

accountability The obligation to justify the discharge of duties in the fulfillment of responsibilities to a person or persons in higher authority; to be answerable to that authority for failing to fulfill the assigned duties and responsibilities.

administrative regulation Rules made by *regulatory agencies* and commissions.

affirmative action A policy or program designed to redress historic injustices committed against specified groups by actively promoting equal access to educational and employment opportunities.

Aid to Families with Dependent Children (AFDC) Federal funds, administered by the states, for children living with parents or relatives who fall below state standards of need.

amicus curiae Literally, "friend of the court"; individuals or groups who are not parties to a lawsuit but who seek to assist the court in reaching a decision by presenting additional briefs.

Antifederalists Those who favored strong state governments and a weak national government and who were opponents of the constitution proposed at the American Constitutional Convention of 1787.

appellate court A court that hears the appeals of trial court decisions.

appropriations The amounts approved by Congress in statutes (bills) that each unit or agency of government can spend.

area sampling A polling technique used for large cities, states, or the whole nation when a high level of accuracy is desired. The population is broken down into small, homogeneous units, such as counties; then several units are randomly selected to serve as the sample.

Articles of Confederation America's first written constitution. Adopted by the Continental Congress in 1777, the Articles of Confederation and Perpetual Union were the formal basis for America's national government until 1789, when they were supplanted by the Constitution.

Astroturf lobbying A negative term used to describe group-directed and exaggerated grassroots lobbying.

authoritarian government A system of rule in which the government recognizes no formal limits but may, nevertheless, be restrained by the power of other social institutions.

authorization The process by which Congress enacts or rejects proposed statutes (bills) embodying the positive laws of government.

autocracy   A form of government in which a single individual—a king, queen, or dictator—rules.

automatic stabilizers   A category of public policy, largely fiscal and monetary, that automatically works against inflationary and deflationary tendencies in the economy.

balance of payments   The difference between a country's total payments to foreign countries in goods, services, investments, tourist spending, etc., and its total receipts from foreign countries. An excess of imports over exports is called "the international debt," which in the United States has been growing at a rate of over $100 billion per year.

balance of power   A system of political alignments by which stability can be achieved.

balance-of-power role   The strategy whereby many countries form alliances with one or more other countries in order to counterbalance the behavior of other, usually more powerful, nation-states.

bandwagon effect   A situation wherein reports of voter or delegate opinion can influence the actual outcome of an election or a nominating convention.

bellwether district   A town or district that is a microcosm of the whole population or that has been found to be a good predictor of electoral outcomes.

benign gerrymandering   Attempts to draw election districts so as to create districts made up primarily of disadvantaged or underrepresented minorities.

bicameralism   Division of a legislative body into two chambers, houses, or branches.

bilateral treaty   Treaty made between two nations; contrast with *multilateral treaty*.

bill of attainder   A legislative act that inflicts guilt and punishment without a judicial hearing or trial; it is proscribed by Article I, Section 10, of the Constitution.

Bill of Rights   The first ten amendments to the U.S. Constitution, ratified in 1791. They ensure certain rights and liberties to the people.

binding primary   Primary election in which the candidates for election as delegates to a presidential nominating convention pledge themselves to a certain candidate and are bound to vote for that person until released from the obligation. Contrast with *preferential primary*.

bipartisan foreign policy   Based on the assumption that "politics stops at the water's edge," this is a strategy pursued by most presidents since World War II to coopt the opposition party leaders in order to minimize the amount of public criticism and the leakage of confidential information for political purposes.

bipartisanship   Close cooperation between two parties; usually an effort by the two major parties in Congress to cooperate with the president in making foreign policy.

block grants   Federal *grants-in-aid* that allow states considerable discretion in how the funds should be spent.

bureaucracy   The complex structure of offices, tasks, rules, and principles of organization that are employed by all large-scale institutions to coordinate the work of their personnel.

cabinet   The secretaries, or chief administrators, of the major departments of the federal government. Cabinet secretaries are appointed by the president with the consent of the Senate.

capitalism   An economic system in which most of the means of production and distribution are privately owned and operated for profit.

categorical grants-in-aid   Grants by Congress to states and localities, given with the condition that expenditures be limited to a problem or group specified by the national government.

caucus (congressional)   An association of members of Congress based on party, interest, or social group such as gender or race.

caucus (political)   A normally closed meeting of a political or legislative group to select candidates, plan strategy, or make decisions regarding legislative matters.

checks and balances   Mechanisms through which each branch of government is able to participate in and influence the activities of the other branches. Major examples include the presidential veto power over congressional legislation, the power of the Senate to approve presidential appointments, and judicial review of congressional enactments.

chief justice   Justice on the Supreme Court who presides over the Court's public sessions.

citizenship   The duties, rights, and privileges of being a citizen of a political unit.

civil disobedience   A form of *direct action politics* that involves the refusal to obey civil laws considered unjust. This is usually a nonviolent or passive resistance.

civil law A system of jurisprudence, including private law and governmental actions, to settle disputes that do not involve criminal penalties.

civil liberties Areas of personal freedom with which governments are constrained from interfering.

civil penalties Regulatory techniques in which fines or another form of material restitution is imposed for violating civil laws or common law principles, such as negligence.

civil rights Legal or moral claims that citizens are entitled to make upon the government to protect them from the illegal actions of other citizens and government agencies.

class action suit A lawsuit in which large numbers of persons with common interests join together under a representative party to bring or defend a lawsuit, such as hundreds of workers together suing a company.

client state A *nation-state* dependent upon a more powerful nation-state but still with enough power and resources to be able to conduct its own foreign policy up to a point.

closed primary A primary election in which voters can participate in the nomination of candidates, but only of the party in which they are enrolled for a period of time prior to primary day. Contrast with *open primary*.

closed rule Provision by the House Rules Committee limiting or prohibiting the introduction of amendments during debate.

closed shop A contract between an employer and a union in which the employer agrees to hire no worker who is not a bona fide member of that union. This was outlawed by the Taft-Hartley Act of 1947.

cloture Rule allowing a majority of two-thirds or three-fifths of the members in a legislative body to set a time limit on debate over a given bill.

coattail effect Result of voters casting their ballot for president or governor and "automatically" voting for the remainder of the party's ticket.

coercion Forcing a person to do something by threats or pressure.

cold war The period of struggle between the U.S. and the former Soviet Union between the late 1940s and 1990.

commerce power Power of Congress to regulate trade among the states and with foreign countries.

common law Law common to the realm in Anglo-Saxon history; judge-made law based on the precedents of previous lower court decisions.

concurrent power Authority possessed by both state and national governments, such as the power to levy taxes.

confederation League of independent states.

conference committee A joint committee created to work out a compromise on House and Senate versions of a piece of legislation.

congressional veto See *legislative veto*.

conscription An aspect of *coercion* whereby the government requires certain involuntary services of citizens, such as compulsory military service, known as "the draft."

conservative Today this term refers to those who generally support the social and economic status quo and are suspicious of efforts to introduce new political formulae and economic arrangements. Many conservatives also believe that a large and powerful government poses a threat to citizens' freedoms.

constituents Members of the district from which an official is elected.

constitutional government A system of rule in which formal and effective limits are placed on the powers of the government.

constitutionalism An approach to legitimacy in which the rulers give up a certain amount of power in return for their right to utilize the remaining powers.

containment The policy used by the United States during the Cold War to restrict the spread of communism and limit the influence of the Soviet Union.

contracting power The power of government to set conditions on companies seeking to sell goods or services to government agencies.

contract model A theory asserting that governments originate from general agreements among members of the public about the necessity of dealing with common problems.

contributory programs Social programs financed in whole or in part by taxation or other mandatory contributions by their present or future recipients. The most important example is *Social Security*, which is financed by a payroll tax.

control agencies Agencies that have the power to intervene in the private sphere to regulate the conduct of individuals, groups, or corporations.

cooperative federalism A type of federalism existing since the New Deal era in which *grants-in-aid* have been used strategically to encourage states and localities (without commanding them) to pursue nationally defined goals. Also known as intergovernmental cooperation.

cooptation Strategy of bringing an individual into a group by joint action of the members of that group, usually in order to reduce or eliminate the individual's opposition.

cost of living adjustments (COLAs) See *indexing*.

coup d'état Sudden, forcible overthrow of a government.

criminal law The branch of law that deals with disputes or actions involving criminal penalties (as opposed to civil law). It regulates the conduct of individuals, defines crimes, and provides punishment for criminal acts.

criminal penalties Regulatory techniques in which imprisonment or heavy fines and the loss of certain civil rights and liberties are imposed.

critical electoral realignment The point in history when a new party supplants the ruling party, becoming in turn the dominant political force. In the United States, this has tended to occur roughly every 30 years.

debt The cumulative total amount of money owed due to yearly operating *deficits*.

debt limit Ceiling established by Congress upon the total amount of debt the government can accumulate. Can be changed by Congress as need requires.

debt service Interest paid on the public debt; an "uncontrollable" budget item because the amount is determined by general interest rates.

de facto segregation Racial segregation that is not a direct result of law or government policy but is, instead, a reflection of residential patterns, income distributions, or other social factors.

defendant The individual or organization against whom a complaint is brought in criminal or civil cases.

deficit An annual debt incurred when the government spends more than it collects. Each yearly deficit adds to the nation's total *debt*.

deficit financing Usually refers to deficits that are deliberately incurred as part of an effort to fight off a deflationary phase of the business cycle. Deficits are financed by borrowing.

de jure segregation Racial segregation that is a direct result of law or official policy.

delegated powers Constitutional powers that are assigned to one governmental agency but that are exercised by another agency with the express permission of the first.

democracy A system of rule that permits citizens to play a significant part in the governmental process, usually through the election of key public officials.

deregulation A policy of reducing or eliminating regulatory restraints on the conduct of individuals or private institutions.

deterrence The development and maintenance of military strength as a means of discouraging attack.

devolution A strategy in which the national government would grant the states more authority over a range of policies currently under national government authority.

diplomacy The representation of a government to other foreign governments.

direct action politics A form of politics, such as violent politics or civil disobedience, that uses informal channels to attempt to force rulers into a new course of action.

discharge petition Procedure of the House whereby an *absolute majority* of the members can force a bill out of committee when the committee itself has refused to report it out for consideration.

discount rate The interest rate charged by the *Federal Reserve* when commercial banks borrow in order to expand their lending operations. An effective tool of monetary policy.

dissenting opinion Decision written by a justice in the minority in a particular case in which the justice wishes to express his or her reasoning in the case.

divided government The condition in American government wherein the presidency is controlled by one party while the opposing party controls one or both houses of Congress.

double jeopardy Trial more than once for the same crime. The Constitution guarantees that no one shall be subjected to double jeopardy.

dual federalism The system of government that prevailed in the United States from 1789 to 1937 in which most fundamental governmental powers were shared between the federal and state governments. Compare with *cooperative federalism*.

due process To proceed according to law and with adequate protection for individual rights.

economic expansionist role The strategy often pursued by capitalist countries to adopt foreign policies that will maximize the success of domestic corporations in their dealings with other countries.

elastic clause See *necessary and proper clause.*

electoral college The presidential electors from each state who meet in their respective state capitals after the popular election to cast ballots for president and vice president.

electorate All of the eligible voters in a legally designated area.

elite Those people at the top who exercise a major influence on decision making.

eminent domain The right of government to take private property for public use, with reasonable compensation awarded for the property.

en banc When a larger number of judges than the required minimum of three on a circuit court of appeals hear a case.

entitlement Eligibility for benefits by virtue of a category of benefits defined by legislation.

environmental impact statement Since 1969, all federal agencies must file this statement demonstrating that a new program or project will not have a net negative impact on the human or physical environment.

equality of opportunity A universally shared American ideal that all people should have the freedom to use whatever talents and wealth they have to reach their fullest potential.

equal protection clause A clause in the Fourteenth Amendment that requires that states provide citizens "equal protection of the laws."

equal time rule A Federal Communications Commission requirement that broadcasters provide candidates for the same political office an equal opportunity to communicate their messages to the public.

equity Judicial process providing a remedy to a dispute where common law does not apply.

exclusionary rule The ability of the court to exclude evidence obtained in violation of the Fourth Amendment.

exclusive powers All the powers that the states are in effect forbidden to exercise by the Constitution rest exclusively with the national government.

executive agreement An agreement between the president and another country, which has the force of a treaty but does not require the Senate's "advice and consent."

executive privilege The claim that confidential communications between a president and close advisers should not be revealed without the consent of the president.

ex post facto law "After the fact" law; law that is retroactive and that has an adverse effect on someone accused of a crime. Under Article I, Sections 9 and 10, of the Constitution, neither the state nor the national government can enact such laws; this provision does not apply, however, to civil laws.

expressed power The notion that the Constitution grants to the federal government only those powers specifically named in its text.

expropriation Confiscation of property with or without compensation.

faction Group of people with common interests, usually in opposition to the aims or principles of a larger group or the public.

fairness doctrine A Federal Communications Commission requirement for broadcasters who air programs on controversial issues to provide time for opposing views.

federalism System of government in which power is divided by a constitution between a central government and regional governments.

Federalists Those who favored a strong national government and supported the constitution proposed at the American Constitutional Convention of 1787.

Federal Reserve Board The governing board of the *Federal Reserve System* is comprised of a chair and six other members, appointed by the president with the consent of the Senate.

Federal Reserve System (Fed) Consisting of twelve Federal Reserve Banks, the Fed facilitates exchanges of cash, checks, and credit; it regulates member banks; and it uses monetary policies to fight inflation and deflation.

filibuster A tactic used by members of the Senate to prevent action on legislation they oppose by continuously holding the floor and speaking until the majority backs down. Once given the floor, senators have unlimited time to speak, and it requires a *cloture* vote of three-fifths of the Senate to end the filibuster.

fiscal techniques The government's use of taxing, monetary, and spending powers to manipulate the economy.

fiscal year The yearly accounting period, which for

the national government is October 1–September 30. The actual fiscal year is designated by the year in which it ends.

food stamps   The largest *in-kind benefits* program, administered by the Department of Agriculture, providing coupons to individuals and families who satisfy a "needs test"; the food stamps can be exchanged for food at most grocery stores.

franchise   The right to vote; see *license, suffrage*.

full faith and credit clause   Article IV, Section 1, of the Constitution provides that each state must accord the same respect to the laws and judicial decisions of other states that it accords to its own.

gerrymandering   Apportionment of voters in districts in such a way as to give unfair advantage to one political party.

going public   A strategy that attempts to mobilize the widest and most favorable climate of opinion.

government   Institutions and procedures through which a territory and its people are ruled.

grants-in-aid   A general term for funds given by Congress to state and local governments.

grassroots lobbying   A lobbying campaign in which a group mobilizes its membership to contact government officials in support of the group's position.

Great Compromise   Agreement reached at the Constitutional Convention of 1787 that gave each state an equal number of senators regardless of its population, but linked representation in the House of Representatives to population.

gridlock   Term used to describe the state of affairs when the executive and legislative branches cannot agree on major legislation and neither side will compromise.

Gross Domestic Product (GDP)   An index of the total output of goods and services. A very imperfect measure of prosperity, productivity, inflation, or deflation, but its regular publication both reflects and influences business conditions.

habeas corpus   A court order demanding that an individual in custody be brought into court and shown the cause for detention. *Habeas corpus* is guaranteed by the Constitution and can be suspended only in cases of rebellion or invasion.

haphazard sampling   A type of sampling of public opinion that is an unsystematic choice of respondents.

Holy Alliance role   A strategy pursued by a superpower to prevent any change in the existing distribution of power among *nation-states*, even if this requires intervention into the internal affairs of another country in order to keep a ruler from being overthrown.

homesteading   A national policy that permits people to gain ownership of property by occupying public or unclaimed lands, living on the land for a specified period of time, and making certain minimal improvements on that land. Also known as squatting.

home rule   Power delegated by the state to a local unit of government to manage its own affairs.

ideology   The combined doctrines, assertions, and intentions of a social or political group that justify its behavior.

illusion of central tendency   The assumption that opinions are "normally distributed"—that responses to opinion questions are heavily distributed toward the center, as in a bell-shaped curve.

illusion of saliency   Impression conveyed by polls that something is important to the public when actually it is not.

implementation   The efforts of departments and agencies to translate laws into specific bureaucratic routines.

impoundment   Efforts by presidents to thwart congressional programs that they cannot otherwise defeat by refusing to spend the funds that Congress has appropriated for them. Congress placed limits on impoundment in the Budget and Impoundment Control Act of 1974.

independent agencies   Agencies set up by Congress to be independent of direct presidential authority. Congress usually accomplishes this by providing the head or heads of the agency with a set term of office rather than allowing their removal at the pleasure of the president.

independent counsel   A prosecutor appointed under the terms of the Ethics in Government Act to investigate criminal misconduct by members of the executive branch.

indexing   Periodic adjustments of welfare payments, wages, or taxes, tied to the cost of living.

indirect election   Provision for election of an official where the voters first select the delegates or "electors," who are in turn charged with making the final choice. The presidential election is an indirect election.

inflation A consistent increase in the general level of prices.

injunction A court order requiring an individual or organization either to cease or to undertake some form of action to prevent a future injury or to achieve some desirable state of affairs.

in-kind benefits Goods and services provided to needy individuals and families by the federal government, as contrasted with cash benefits. The largest in-kind federal welfare program is *food stamps*.

interest group A group of people organized around a shared belief or mutual concern who try to influence the government to make policies promoting their belief or respectful of their concerns.

interest-group liberalism The theory of governance that, in principle, all claims on government resources and action are equally valid, and that all interests are equally entitled to participation in and benefits from government.

International Monetary Fund (IMF) An institution established in 1944 at Bretton Woods, New Hampshire, to provide loans to needy member countries and to facilitate international monetary exchange.

interpretation Process wherein bureaucrats implement ambiguous statutes, requiring agencies to make educated guesses as to what Congress or higher administrative authorities intended.

iron triangle The stable and cooperative relationships that often develop between a congressional committee or subcommittee, an administrative agency, and one or more supportive interest groups. Not all of these relationships are triangular, but the iron triangle formulation is perhaps the most typical.

judicial review Power of the courts to declare actions of the legislative and executive branches invalid or unconstitutional. The Supreme Court asserted this power in *Marbury v. Madison*.

jurisdiction The authority of a court to initially consider a case. Distinguished from appellate jurisdiction, which is the authority to hear appeals from a lower court's decision.

Kitchen Cabinet An informal group of advisers to whom the president turns for counsel and guidance. Members of the official *cabinet* may or may not also be members of the Kitchen Cabinet.

laissez-faire An economic theory first advanced by Adam Smith, it calls for a "hands off" policy by government toward the economy, in an effort to leave business enterprises free to act in their own self-interest.

legislative clearance A process that enables the president to require all agencies of the executive branch to submit through the budget director all requests for new legislation along with estimates of their budgetary needs.

legislative intent The supposed real meaning of a statute as it can be interpreted from the legislative history of the bill.

legislative supremacy The preeminence of Congress among the three branches of government, as established by the Constitution.

legislative veto A provision in a statute permitting Congress (or a congressional committee) to review and approve actions undertaken by the executive under authority of the statute. Although the U.S. Supreme Court held the legislative veto unconstitutional in the 1983 case of *Immigration and Naturalization Service v. Chadha,* Congress continues to enact legislation incorporating such a veto.

legitimacy Popular acceptance of a government and its decisions.

liberal A liberal today generally supports political and social reform; extensive governmental intervention in the economy; the expansion of federal social services; more vigorous efforts on behalf of the poor, minorities, and women; and greater concern for consumers and the environment.

license Permission to engage in some activity that is otherwise illegal, such as hunting or practicing medicine. Synonymous with franchise, permit, certificate of convenience and necessity.

line agency Department, bureau, or other unit of administration whose primary mission requires it to deal directly with the public; contrast with *staff agency*.

line-item veto Power that allows a governor (or the president) to strike out specific provisions (lines) of bills that the legislature passes. Without a line-item veto, a governor (or the president) must accept or reject an entire bill.

lobbying Strategy by which organized interests seek to influence the passage of legislation by exerting direct pressure on members of the legislature.

logrolling A legislative practice wherein reciprocal agreements are made between legislators, usually in voting for or against a bill. In contrast to bargaining, logrolling unites parties that have nothing in common but their desire to exchange support.

majority leader The elected leader of the party holding a majority of the seats in the House of Representatives or in the Senate. In the House, the majority leader is subordinate in the party hierarchy to the *Speaker*.

majority rule Rule by at least one vote more than half of those voting.

majority system A type of electoral system in which, to win a seat in the parliament or other representative body, a candidate must receive a majority of all the votes cast in the relevant district.

mandate (electoral) A claim made by a victorious candidate that the electorate has given him or her special authority to carry out campaign promises.

marketplace of ideas The public forum in which beliefs and ideas are exchanged and compete.

Marshall Plan The U.S. European Recovery Plan, in which over $34 billion was spent for relief, reconstruction, and economic recovery of Western Europe after World War II.

Marxism The system of thought developed by Karl Marx and predicated upon a history of class struggle between those who control production and distribution (the owners) and the workers, culminating in the overthrow of the owners, the redistribution of wealth and power, and the "withering away of the state."

means testing Procedure by which potential beneficiaries of a public assistance program establish their eligibility by demonstrating a genuine need for the assistance.

Medicaid A federally financed, state-operated program for medical services to low-income people.

Medicare National health insurance for the elderly and for the disabled.

military-industrial complex A concept coined by President Eisenhower in his farewell address, in which he was referring to the threats to American democracy that may arise from too close a friendship between major corporations in the defense industry and the Pentagon. This is one example of the larger political phenomenon of the *iron triangle*.

minority leader The elected leader of the party holding less than a majority of the seats in the House or Senate.

Miranda rule Principles developed by the Supreme Court in the 1966 case of *Miranda v. Arizona* requiring that persons under arrest be informed of their legal rights, including their right to counsel, prior to police interrogation.

momentum A media prediction that a particular candidate will do even better in the future than in the past.

monetary techniques Efforts to regulate the economy through manipulation of the supply of money and credit. America's most powerful institution in the area of monetary policy is the *Federal Reserve Board*.

monopoly The existence of a single firm in a market that divides all the goods and services of that market. Absence of competition.

mootness A criterion used by courts to screen cases that no longer require resolution.

Motor Voter bill A legislative act passed in 1993 that requires all states to allow voters to register by mail when they renew their drivers' licenses and provides for the placement of voter registration forms in motor vehicle, public assistance, and military recruitment offices.

multilateral treaty A treaty among more than two nations.

multilateralism A foreign policy that seeks to encourage the involvement of several nation-states in coordinated action, usually in relation to a common adversary, with terms and conditions usually specified in a multi-country treaty, such as NATO.

multiple-member constituency Electorate that selects all candidates at large from the whole district; each voter is given the number of votes equivalent to the number of seats to be filled.

multiple-member district See *multiple-member constituency*.

Napoleonic role Strategy pursued by a powerful nation to prevent aggressive actions against itself by improving the internal state of affairs of a particular country, even if this means encouraging revolution in that country. Based on the assumption that countries with comparable political systems will never go to war against each other.

National Security Council (NSC) A presidential foreign policy advisory council composed of the president, the vice president, the secretaries of state, defense, and the treasury, the attorney general, and other officials invited by the president. The NSC has a staff of foreign-policy specialists.

nationalism The widely held belief that the people who occupy the same territory have something in common, that the nation is a single community.

national supremacy A principle that asserts that national law is superior to all other law.

nation-state A political entity consisting of a people with some common cultural experience (nation), who also share a common political authority (state), recognized by other sovereignties (nation-states).

necessary and proper clause Article I, Section 8, of the Constitution, which enumerates the powers of Congress and provides Congress with the authority to make all laws "necessary and proper" to carry them out; also referred to as the "elastic clause."

new federalism Attempts by Presidents Nixon and Reagan to return power to the states through block grants.

New Jersey Plan A framework for the Constitution, introduced by William Paterson, which called for equal representation in the national legislature regardless of a state's population.

New Politics movement Political movement that began in the 1960s and 1970s, made up of professionals and intellectuals for whom the Civil Rights and antiwar movements were formative experiences. The New Politics movement strengthened public-interest groups.

nomination The process through which political parties select their candidates for election to public office.

noncontributory programs Social programs that provide assistance to people based on demonstrated need rather than any contribution they have made.

North American Free Trade Agreement (NAFTA) An agreement among Canada, the United States, and Mexico that promotes economic cooperation and abolishes many trade restrictions between the three countries.

North Atlantic Treaty Organization (NATO) A treaty organization, comprising the United States, Canada, and most of Western Europe, formed in 1948 to counter the perceived threat from the Soviet Union.

oligarchy A form of government in which a small group—landowners, military officers, or wealthy merchants—controls most of the governing decisions.

oligopoly The existence of two or more competing firms in a given market, where price competition is usually avoided because they know that they would all lose from such competition. Rather, competition is usually through other forms, such as advertising, innovation, and obsolescence.

open market operations The buying and selling of government securities, etc., to help finance government operations and to loosen or tighten the total amount of credit circulating in the economy.

open primary A primary election in which the voter can wait until the day of the primary to choose which party to enroll in to select candidates for the general election. Contrast with *closed primary*.

opinion The written explanation of the Supreme Court's decision in a particular case.

ordinance The legislative act of a local legislature or municipal commission. Puts the force of law under city charter but is a lower order of law than a statute of the national or state legislature.

overhead agency A department, bureau, or other unit of administration whose primary mission is to regulate the activities of other agencies; it generally has no direct authority over the public. Contrast with *line agency*.

oversight The effort by Congress, through hearings, investigations, and other techniques, to exercise control over the activities of executive agencies.

paper trail Written accounts by which the process of decision making and the participants in a decision can, if desired, be later reconstructed. Often called "red tape."

parochialism The conservative tendency to focus on the parish or local community. Parochialism is the opposite of cosmopolitanism.

partisanship Loyalty to a particular political party.

party machines Local party organizations that control urban politics by mobilizing voters to elect the machines' candidates.

party vote A *roll-call vote* in the House or Senate in which at least 50 percent of the members of one party take a particular position and are opposed by at least 50 percent of the members of the other party. Party votes are rare today, although they were fairly common in the nineteenth century.

patriotism Love of one's country; loyalty to one's country.

patronage The resources available to higher officials, usually opportunities to make partisan appointments to offices and to confer grants, licenses, or special favors to supporters.

per curiam Decision by an appellate court, without a written opinion, that refuses to review the decision of a lower court; amounts to a reaffirmation of the lower court's opinion.

petition Right granted by the First Amendment to citizens to inform representatives of their opinions and to make pleas before government agencies.

plaintiff The individual or organization who brings a complaint in court.

plea bargains Negotiated agreements in criminal cases in which a defendant agrees to plead guilty in return for the state's agreement to reduce the severity of the criminal charge the defendant is facing.

plebiscite A direct vote by the electorate on an issue presented to it by a government.

pluralism The theory that all interests are and should be free to compete for influence in the government. The outcome of this competition is compromise and moderation.

pluralist politics Politics in which political elites actively compete for leadership, voters choose from among these elites, and new elites can emerge in quest of leadership.

plurality system Type of electoral system in which, to win a seat in the parliament or other representative body, a candidate need only receive the most votes in the election, not necessarily a majority of votes cast.

pocket veto A presidential veto of legislation wherein the president takes no formal action on a bill. If Congress adjourns within ten days of passing a bill, and the president does not sign it, the bill is considered to be vetoed.

police power Power reserved to the state to regulate the health, safety, and morals of its citizens.

policy of redistribution An objective of the graduated income tax—to raise revenue in such a way as to reduce the disparities of wealth between the lowest and the highest income brackets.

political action committee (PAC) A private group that raises and distributes funds for use in election campaigns.

political parties Organized groups that attempt to influence the government by electing their members to important government offices.

political socialization Induction of individuals into the political culture; learning how to accept authority; learning what is legitimate and what is not.

politics Conflicts over the character, membership, and policies of any organizations to which people belong.

polity A society with an organized government; the "political system."

poll tax A state-imposed tax upon the voters as a prerequisite to registration. It was rendered unconstitutional in national elections by the Twenty-fourth Amendment and in state elections by the Supreme Court in 1966.

populism A late 1870s political and social movement of Western and Southern farmers that protested Eastern business interests.

pork barrel legislation Appropriations made by legislative bodies for local projects that are often not needed but that are created so that local representatives can win re-election in their home district.

power elite The group that is said to make the most important decisions in a particular community.

power without diplomacy Post–World War II foreign policy in which the goal was to use American power to create an international structure that could be run with a minimum of regular diplomatic involvement.

precedents Prior cases whose principles are used by judges as the bases for their decisions in present cases.

preferential primary Primary election in which the elected delegates to a convention are instructed, but not bound, to vote specifically for the presidential candidate preferred by the voters on a separate part of the ballot. Contrast with *binding primary*.

prior restraint An effort by a governmental agency to block the publication of material it deems libelous or harmful in some other way; censorship. In the United States, the courts forbid prior restraint except under the most extraordinary circumstances.

private bill A proposal in Congress to provide a specific person with some kind of relief, such as a special exemption from immigration quotas.

privileges and immunities clause Article IV of the Constitution, which provides that the citizens of any one state are guaranteed the "privileges and immunities" of every other state, as though they were citizens of that state.

probability sampling   A method used by pollsters to select a sample in which every individual in the population has a known (usually equal) probability of being selected as a respondent so that the correct weight can be given to all segments of the population.

procedural due process   The Supreme Court's efforts to forbid any procedure that shocks the conscience or that makes impossible a fair judicial system. See also *due process*.

progressive/regressive taxes   A judgment made by students of taxation about whether a particular tax hits the upper brackets more heavily (progressive) or the lower brackets more heavily (regressive).

promotional agencies   See *clientele agencies*.

promotional technique   A technique of control that encourages people to do something they might not otherwise do, or continue an action or behavior. There are three types: subsidies, contracts, and licenses.

proportional representation   A multiple-member district system that allows each political party representation in proportion to its percentage of the vote.

protective tariff   A tariff intended to give an advantage to a domestic manufacturer's product by increasing the cost of a competing imported product.

public assistance program   A noncontributory social program providing assistance for the aged, poor, or disabled. Major examples include *Aid to Families with Dependent Children* (AFDC) and *Supplemental Security Income* (SSI).

public corporation   An agency set up by a government but permitted to finance its own operations by charging for its services or by selling bonds.

public interest groups   Lobbies that claim they serve the general good rather than their own particular interest, such as consumer protection or environmental lobbies.

public law   Cases in private law, civil law, or criminal law in which one party to the dispute argues that a license is unfair, a law is inequitable or unconstitutional, or an agency has acted unfairly, violated a procedure, or gone beyond its jurisdiction.

public opinion   Citizens' attitudes about political issues, personalities, institutions, and events.

public opinion polls   Scientific instruments for measuring public opinion.

public policy   A law, rule, statute, or edict that expresses the government's goals and provides for rewards and punishments to promote their attainment.

quorum   The minimum number of members of a deliberative body who must be present in order to conduct business.

quota sampling   A type of sampling of public opinion that is used by most commercial polls. Respondents are selected whose characteristics closely match those of the general population along several significant dimensions, such as geographic region, sex, age, and race.

racial gerrymandering   Redrawing congressional boundary lines in such a way as to divide and disperse a minority population that otherwise would constitute a majority within the original district.

rallying effect   The generally favorable reaction of the public to presidential actions taken in foreign policy or, more precisely, decisions made during international crises.

random sampling   Polls in which respondents are chosen mathematically, at random, with every effort made to avoid bias in the construction of the sample.

rate regulation   Power delegated by the legislature to any regulatory agencies to set ceilings on how much railroads and other "common carriers" can charge for their services, based upon the best available estimates of a "fair return" on investments.

realigning eras   Periods during which major groups in the electorate shift their political party affiliations. Realigning eras have often been associated with long-term shifts in partisan control of the government and with major changes in public policy. One of the most important realigning eras was the period of the New Deal in the 1930s when President Franklin Roosevelt led the Democrats to a position of power that they held for more than thirty years.

reapportionment   The redrawing of election districts and the redistribution of legislative representatives due to shifts in population.

redistributive techniques   Techniques—fiscal or monetary—designed to control people by manipulating the entire economy rather than by regulating people directly.

referendum   The practice of referring a measure proposed or passed by a legislature to the vote of the electorate for approval or rejection.

regulated federalism   A form of federalism in which Congress imposes legislation on the states and localities requiring them to meet national standards.

regulation A particular use of government power, a "technique of control" in which the government adopts rules imposing restrictions on the conduct of private citizens.

regulation of entry The purpose of licensing; permission to enter a trade or market. For example, medical licensing boards determine whether a person holding a medical degree can engage in the practice of medicine, or the FCC decides to permit a radio station to commence operation.

regulatory agencies Departments, bureaus, or independent agencies whose primary mission is to eliminate or restrict certain behaviors defined as being evil in themselves or evil in their consequences.

regulatory tax A tax whose primary purpose is not to raise revenue but to influence conduct—e.g., a heavy tax on gasoline to discourage recreational driving.

regulatory techniques Techniques that government uses to control the conduct of the people.

representative democracy A system of government that provides the populace with the opportunity to make the government responsive to its views through the selection of representatives, who, in turn, play a significant role in governmental decision making.

reserve requirement The amount of liquid assets and ready cash that the *Federal Reserve* requires banks to hold to meet depositors' demands for their money.

revenue acts Acts of Congress providing the means of raising the revenues needed by the government. The Constitution requires that all such bills originate in the House.

revenue sharing A scheme to allocate national resources to the states according to a population and income formula.

revolution A complete or drastic change of government and the rules by which government is conducted.

revolutionary politics A form of politics that rejects the existing system of government entirely and attempts to replace it with a different organizational structure and a different ruling group.

right of rebuttal A Federal Communications Commission regulation giving individuals the right to have the opportunity to respond to personal attacks made on a radio or TV broadcast.

roll-call vote Vote in which each legislator's yes or no vote is recorded as the clerk calls the names of the members alphabetically.

sample A small group selected by researchers to represent the most important characteristics of an entire population.

satellites *Nation-states* that are militarily, economically, and politically subordinate to other nations.

select committee A legislative committee established for a limited period of time and for a special purpose; not a standing committee.

selective polling A sample drawn deliberately to reconstruct meaningful distributions of an entire constituency; not a random sample.

seniority Priority or status ranking given to an individual on the basis of length of continuous service in a committee in Congress.

separation of powers The division of governmental power among several institutions that must cooperate in decision making.

service agencies Departments or other bureaus whose primary mission is to promote the interests of dependent persons or to deal with their problems.

simple majority Fifty percent plus one of all those actually voting. Compare with *absolute majority*.

single-member constituency An electorate that is allowed to elect only one representative from each district; the normal method of representation in the United States.

single-member district See *single-member constituency*.

Social Security A contributory welfare program into which working Americans contribute a percentage of their wages, and from which they receive cash benefits after retirement.

soft money Money contributed directly to political parties for voter registration and organization.

solicitor general The top government lawyer in all cases before the appellate courts where the government is a party.

sound bite A word or phrase that is meant to convey a larger meaning or image; used by political candidates to briefly describe their stand on issues.

sovereignty Supreme and independent political authority.

Speaker of the House The chief presiding officer of the House of Representatives. The Speaker is elected at the beginning of every Congress on a straight *party vote*. The Speaker is the most important party and

House leader, and can influence the legislative agenda, the fate of individual pieces of legislation, and members' positions within the House.

spending power A combination of subsidies and contracts that the government can use to redistribute income.

split-ticket voting The practice of casting ballots for the candidates of at least two different political parties in the same election. Voters who support only one party's candidates are said to vote a straight party ticket.

staff agency An agency responsible for maintaining the bureaucracy, with responsibilities such as purchasing, budgeting, personnel management, or planning.

standing The right of an individual or organization to initiate a court case.

standing committee A permanent committee with the power to propose and write legislation that covers a particular subject such as finance or appropriations.

stare decisis Literally "let the decision stand." A previous decision by a court applies as a precedent in similar cases until that decision is overruled.

state A community that claims the monopoly of legitimate use of physical force within a given territory; the ultimate political authority; sovereign.

statute A law enacted by a state legislature or by Congress.

straight party vote The practice of casting ballots for candidates of only one party.

strict scrutiny Higher standard of judicial protection for speech cases and other civil liberties and civil rights cases, in which the burden of proof shifts from the complainant to the government.

subsidies Governmental grants of cash or other valuable commodities, such as land, to individuals or organizations. Subsidies can be used to promote activities desired by the government, to reward political support, or to buy off political opposition.

substantive due process A judicial doctrine used by the appellate courts, primarily before 1937, to strike down economic legislation the courts felt was arbitrary or unreasonable.

suffrage The right to vote; see also *franchise*.

Supplemental Security Income (SSI) A program providing a minimum monthly income to people who pass a "needs test" and who are sixty-five years or older, blind, or disabled. Financed from general revenues rather than from Social Security contributions.

supremacy clause Article VI of the Constitution, which states that laws passed by the national government and all treaties are the supreme laws of the land and superior to all laws adopted by any state or any subdivision.

supreme court The highest court in a particular state or in the United States. This court primarily serves an appellate function.

systematic sampling A method used in probability sampling to ensure that every individual in the population has a known probability of being chosen as a respondent—by choosing every ninth name from a list, for example.

tariff A tax placed on imported goods.

Temporary Assistance to Needy Families (TANF) A policy by which states are given block grants by the federal government in order to create their own programs for public assistance.

Three-fifths Compromise Agreement reached at the Constitutional Convention of 1787 that stipulated that for purposes of the apportionment of congressional seats, every slave would be counted as three-fifths of a person.

ticket balancing Strategy of party leaders to nominate candidates from each of the major ethnic, racial, and religious affiliations.

ticket splitting The practice of voting for candidates of different parties on the same ballot.

totalitarian government A system of rule in which the government recognizes no formal limits on its power and seeks to absorb or eliminate other social institutions that might challenge it.

treaty A formal agreement between sovereign nations to create or restrict rights and responsibilities. In the U.S. all treaties must be approved by a two-thirds vote in the Senate. See also *executive agreement*.

trial court The first court to hear a criminal or civil case.

turnout The percentage of eligible individuals who actually vote.

tyranny Oppressive and unjust government that employs cruel and unjust use of power and authority.

uncontrollables A term applied to budgetary items that are beyond the control of budgetary committees and can only be controlled by substantive legislative action by Congress itself. Some uncontrollables are actually beyond the power of the Congress, because the terms of payment are set in contracts, such as interest on the public *debt*.

unfunded mandates   Regulations or conditions for receiving grants that impose costs on state and local governments for which they are not reimbursed by the federal government.

unilateralism   A foreign policy that seeks to avoid international alliances, entanglements, and permanent commitments in favor of independence, neutrality, and freedom of action.

United Nations   The organization of nations founded in 1945, mainly to serve as a channel for negotiation and a means of settling international disputes peaceably. It has had frequent successes in providing a forum for negotiation and on some occasions a means of preventing international conflicts from spreading. On a number of occasions, the U.N. has been a convenient cover for U.S. foreign policy goals.

Universal Commercial Code   A set of standards for contract law recognized by all states that greatly reduces interstate differences in the practice of contract law.

universalization of rights   The recognition that any group—whether defined by sex, religion, race, ethnicity, or gender—has the right not to be discriminated against.

urban renewal   An important urban policy of the national government during the 1950s in which large categories of grants-in-aid were made available to cities on condition that they develop plans for removing slums and for restoring property to more valuable uses, including new housing as well as new structures for business and civic affairs.

vested interests   Fixed or established interests; interests not varying with changing conditions; privileges respected or accepted by others.

veto   The president's constitutional power to turn down acts of Congress. A presidential veto may be overridden by a two-thirds vote of each house of Congress.

Virginia Plan   A framework for the Constitution, introduced by Edmund Randolph, which called for representation in the national legislature based upon the population of each state.

whip system   Primarily a communications network in each house of Congress, whips take polls of the membership in order to learn their intentions on specific legislative issues and to assist the majority and minority leaders in various tasks.

withholding tax   Deduction by employers of a specified percentage of all wages, paid to the government in advance to guarantee payment of taxes.

writ of *certiorari*   A decision of at least four of the nine Supreme Court justices to review a decision of a lower court; from the Latin "to make more certain."

Glossary of Court Cases

Abrams v. Johnson **(1997)** The Court narrowly upheld a Georgia federal district court's redistricting plan that created only one majority black district in the state. The Court found that the plan violated neither the Voting Rights Act nor the Constitution.

Abrams v. United States **(1919)** The Supreme Court upheld the convictions of five Bolshevik sympathizers under the Espionage Act, which made it an offense to intend interference in the war with Germany. Although the defendants actually opposed American intervention in the Russian Revolution, the Court imputed to them the knowledge that their actions would necessarily impede the war effort against Germany.

Adarand Constructors v. Pena **(1995)** With this 5-to-4 decision, the Supreme Court made federal affirmative action policies subject to stricter judicial scrutiny, but avoided the fundamental question of the constitutionality of affirmative action.

Agostini v. Felton **(1997)** By a 5-to-4 decision, the Court ordered a federal district court in New York to lift an injunction established in 1985 that forbade public school teachers from entering on parochial school grounds to provide remedial education.

Arizona v. Fulminante **(1991)** A bare majority of the Rehnquist Court held that coerced confessions may be used at trial if it could be shown that other evidence was also used to support a guilty verdict. But the Court also held that in this case, the admission of a coerced confession was not "harmless error" and remanded the case for a new trial.

Baker v. Carr **(1962)** The Court held that the issue of malapportionment of election districts raised a justiciable claim under the equal protection clause of the Fourteenth Amendment. The effect of the case was to force the reapportionment of nearly all federal, state, and local election districts nationwide.

Barron v. Baltimore **(1833)** This was one of the most significant cases ever handed down by the Court. Chief Justice John Marshall confirmed the concept of "dual citizenship," wherein each American is separately a citizen of the national government and of the state government. This meant that the Bill of Rights applied only nationally, and not at the state or local level. The consequences of this ruling were felt well into the twentieth century.

Benton v. Maryland **(1969)** The Court ruled that double jeopardy was a right incorporated in the Fourteenth Amendment as a restriction on the states.

Board of Education of Oklahoma City v. Dowell **(1991)** This case, which restricted the use of court-ordered busing to achieve school integration, gave an early indication of the attitude of the new Bush Court.

Bolling v. Sharpe **(1954)** This case, which did not directly involve the Fourteenth Amendment because the District of Columbia is not a state, confronted the Court on the grounds that segregation is inherently unequal. Its victory in effect was "incorporation in reverse," with equal protection moving from the Fourteenth Amendment to become part of the Bill of Rights.

Bowers v. Hardwick **(1986)** In this case, the Supreme Court upheld a Georgia statute prohibiting sodomy, by ruling that the constitutional right of privacy protected the traditional family unit but not conduct between homosexuals when that conduct offended "traditional Judeo-Christian values."

Bowsher v. Synar **(1986)** This was the second of two cases since 1937 in which the Court invalidated an act of Congress on constitutional grounds. In this case, the Court struck down the Gramm-Rudman Act mandating a balanced federal budget, ruling that it was unconstitutional to grant the comptroller general "executive" powers.

Brandenburg v. Ohio **(1969)** The Court overturned an Ohio statute forbidding any person from urging criminal acts as a means of inducing political reform or from joining any association that advocated such activities, on the grounds that the statute punished "mere advocacy" and therefore violated the free speech provisions of the federal Constitution.

Brown v. Allen **(1953)** This case demonstrates how extremely difficult it is for state legislatures or Congress to summon up the majorities necessary to react against a Supreme Court decision. Justice Robert Jackson commented that "The Court is not final because it is infallible; the Court is infallible because it is final."

Brown v. Board of Education of Topeka, Kansas **(1954)** The Supreme Court struck down the "separate but equal" doctrine as fundamentally unequal. This case eliminated state power to use race as a criterion of discrimination in law and provided the national government with the power to intervene by exercising strict regulatory policies against discriminatory actions.

Brown v. Board of Education of Topeka, Kansas (Brown II) **(1955)** One year after *Brown*, the Court issued a mandate for state and local school boards to proceed "with all deliberate speed" to desegregate schools.

Buckley v. Valeo **(1976)** The Supreme Court limited congressional attempts to regulate campaign financing by declaring unconstitutional any absolute limits on the freedom of individuals to spend their own money on campaigns.

Bush v. Vera **(1996)** This decision upheld a district court's ruling that three new congressional districts established in Texas in 1994, two with an African-American majority and one with a Hispanic majority, were unconstitutional because race was the predominant factor used to create them.

Cable News Network v. Noriega **(1990)** The doctrine of "no prior restraint" was weakened when the Supreme Court held that Cable News Network (CNN) could be restrained from broadcasting supposedly illegally obtained tapes of conversations between former Panamanian leader Manuel Noriega and his lawyer until the trial court had listened to the tapes and had determined whether such a broadcast would violate Noriega's right to a fair trial.

Chicago, Burlington, and Quincy Railway Company v. Chicago **(1897)** This case effectively overruled *Barron* by affirming that the due process clause of the Fourteenth Amendment did prohibit states from taking property for a public use without just compensation.

Citizens to Preserve Overton Park, Inc. v. Volpe **(1971)** Beginning with the Supreme Court's decision in this case, the federal courts allowed countless challenges to federal agency actions, under the National Environmental Policy Act (NEPA), brought by public interest groups asserting that the agencies had failed to consider the adverse effects of their actions upon the environment as required by NEPA.

City of Boerne v. Flores **(1997)** In this decision the Court supported a Texas federal district court's ruling that the Religious Freedom Restoration Act of 1993 is unconstitutional as a violation of the separation of powers.

City of Richmond v. J. A. Croson Co. **(1989)** In this case the Supreme Court held that minority set-aside programs would have to redress specific instances of identified discrimination in order to avoid violating the rights of whites.

The Civil Rights Cases **(1883)** The Court struck down the Civil Rights Act of 1875, which attempted to protect blacks from discriminatory treatment by proprietors of public facilities. It ruled that the Fourteenth Amendment applied only to discriminatory actions by state officials and did not apply to discrimination against blacks by private individuals.

Cooper v. Aaron **(1958)** In this historic case, the Supreme Court required that Little Rock, Arkansas, desegregate its public schools by immediately complying with a lower court's order, and warned that it is "emphatically the province and duty of the judicial department to say what the law is."

Craig v. Boren **(1976)**   In this decision, the Court made it easier for plaintiffs to file and win suits on the basis of gender discrimination.

Doe v. Bolton **(1973)**   Decided along with *Roe*, this case extended the decision in *Roe* by striking down state requirements that abortions be performed in licensed hospitals; that abortions be approved beforehand by a hospital committee; and that two physicians concur in the abortion decision.

Dolan v. City of Tigard **(1994)**   This case overturned an Oregon building permit law that required a portion of property being developed to be set aside for public use. The Court established stricter guidelines to be followed in order for state and local governments to avoid violating the Fifth Amendment by taking property "without just compensation."

Dred Scott v. Sandford **(1857)**   This was the infamous case in which Chief Justice Roger Taney wrote that blacks were not citizens; that they "were never thought of or spoken of except as property." In a vain attempt to settle the slavery issue, which was threatening to tear the country apart, the Court went further to rule that the Missouri Compromise was unconstitutional, and Congress could not bar slavery from the territories. This ruling probably hastened the onset of the Civil War.

Duke Power Co. v. Carolina Environmental Study Group **(1978)**   The Supreme Court dealt anti–nuclear power activists a significant blow by upholding a federal statute limiting liability for damages accruing from accidents at nuclear power plants.

Duncan v. Louisiana **(1968)**   The Court established the right to trial by jury in state criminal cases where the accused faces a serious charge and sentencing.

Eisenstadt v. Baird **(1972)**   The Court struck down state laws prohibiting the use of contraceptives by unmarried persons.

Engel v. Vitale **(1962)**   In interpreting the separation of church and state doctrine, the Court ruled that organized prayer in the public schools was unconstitutional.

Escobedo v. Illinois **(1964)**   The Supreme Court expanded the rights of the accused in this case by giving suspects the right to remain silent and the right to have counsel present during questioning.

Felker v. Turpin **(1996)**   The Court unanimously upheld provisions of the Anti-Terrorism and Effective Death Penalty Act of 1996, which imposes tight time limits on appeals and restrictions on federal courts' review of death sentences among other things.

Flast v. Cohen **(1968)**   The Court ruled that a taxpayer has standing to file suit in federal court if alleging that Congress has breached restrictions placed on its taxing and spending powers by the Constitution.

Frontiero v. Richardson **(1973)**   The Court rendered an important decision relating to the economic status of women when it held that the armed services could not deny married women fringe benefits, such as housing allowances and health care, that were automatically granted to married men.

Fullilove v. Klutznick **(1980)**   The Court upheld the Public Works Employment Act of 1977, which required that at least 10 percent of federal funds for federal public works contracts be awarded to minority-owned businesses to remedy past discriminatory barriers, even if there was no evidence of deliberate discrimination by individual contractors.

Garcia v. San Antonio Metropolitan Transit Authority **(1985)**   The question of whether the national government had the right to regulate state and local businesses was again raised in this case. The Court ruled that the national government had the right to apply minimum-wage and overtime standards to state and local government employees. This case overturned *National League of Cities v. Usery* (1976).

Gibbons v. Ogden **(1824)**   An early, major case establishing the supremacy of the national government in all matters affecting interstate commerce, in which John Marshall broadly defined what Article I, Section 8, meant by "commerce among the several states." He affirmed that the federal government alone could regulate trade, travel, and navigation between the states.

Gideon v. Wainwright **(1963)**   The Warren Court overruled an earlier case (*Betts* 1942) and established that "any person haled into court, who is too poor to hire a lawyer, cannot be assured a fair trial unless counsel is provided for him."

Gitlow v. New York **(1925)**   The Court ruled that the freedom of speech is "among the fundamental personal rights and 'liberties' protected by the due process clause of the Fourteenth Amendment from impairment by the states."

Griffin v. Prince Edward County School Board **(1964)**
The Supreme Court forced all the schools in Prince
Edward County, Virginia, to reopen after they had
been closed for five years to avoid desegregation.

Griggs v. Duke Power Company **(1971)**   The Court held
that although the statistical evidence did not prove intentional discrimination, and although an employer's
hiring requirements were race-neutral in appearance,
their effects were sufficient to shift the burden of justification to the employer to show that the requirements
were a "business necessity" that bore "a demonstrable
relationship to successful performance."

Griswold v. Connecticut **(1965)**   The Court ruled that
the right to privacy included the right to marital privacy and struck down state laws restricting married
persons' use of contraceptives and the circulation of
birth control information.

Hague v. Committee for Industrial Organization (CIO)
(1937)   The Court extended the concept of a public
forum to include public streets and meeting halls and
incorporated the freedom of assembly into the list of
rights held to be fundamental and therefore binding
on the states as well as on the national government.

Harris v. New York **(1971)**   In a ruling that limited the
Miranda ruling, the Burger Court held that although
a statement was inadmissable because of failure to
give the Miranda warning, it could be used to impeach the defendant's testimony if the defendant took
the stand.

Herring v. State **(1904)**   In this perjury case, the Georgia Supreme Court declared that if the Fourth Amendment right to privacy means anything, it means that
"before Georgia can prosecute its citizens for making
choices about the most intimate aspects of their lives,
it must do more than assert that the choice they have
made is an 'abominable crime not fit to be named
among Christians.' "

Hodgson v. Minnesota **(1990)**   In this case the Supreme
Court upheld a Minnesota statute requiring parental
notification before an abortion could be performed on
a woman under the age of eighteen.

Holder v. Hall **(1994)**   The Court ruled that a single-
commissioner form of government in a Georgia
county did not violate the 1965 Voting Rights Act.

Humphrey's Executor v. United States **(1935)**   The
Court in this case made a distinction between
"purely executive" officials—whom the president
could remove at his discretion—and officials with

"quasi-judicial and quasi-legislative" duties—who
could be removed only for reasons specified by Congress. This decision limited the president's removal
powers.

*Immigration and Naturalization Service (INS) v.
Chadha* **(1983)**   This was the first of two cases since
1937 in which the Court invalidated an act of Congress on constitutional grounds. In this case the Court
declared the legislative veto unconstitutional.

In re Agent Orange Product Liability Litigation **(1983)**
In this case, a federal judge in New York certified Vietnam War veterans as a class with standing to sue a
manufacturer of herbicides for damages allegedly incurred from exposure to the defendant's product
while they were in Vietnam.

In re Debs **(1895)**   The Supreme Court upheld President Cleveland's power to obtain an injunction
against the Pullman Strike, even in the absence of any
statutory warrant, on the grounds that "the wrongs
complained of by the President were such . . . as affect
the public at large."

In re Neagle **(1890)**   The Supreme Court held that the
protection of a federal judge was a reasonable extension of the president's constitutional power to "take
care that the laws be faithfully executed."

In re Oliver **(1948)**   The Court incorporated the right to
a public trial in the Fourteenth Amendment as a restriction on the states.

Johnson v. DeGrandy **(1994)**   In a unanimous decision,
the Court ruled that the 1965 Voting Rights Act did not
require a state legislature to create the maximum possible number of congressional districts in which minority groups would constitute an electoral majority.

Katz v. United States **(1967)**   In repudiation of the
Olmstead doctrine, the Supreme Court declared that
the Fourth Amendment "protects people, not places,"
and held that electronic surveillance conducted outside the judicial process, whether or not it involves
trespass, is *per se* unreasonable.

Katzenbach v. McClung **(1964)**   The Court gave an extremely broad definition to "interstate commerce" so
as to allow Congress the constitutional authority to
cover discrimination by virtually any local employer.
Although the Court agreed that this case involved a
strictly intrastate restaurant, they found a sufficient
connection to interstate commerce resulting from the
restaurant's acquisition of food and supplies so as to
hold that racial discrimination at such an establish-

ment would "impose commercial burdens of national magnitude upon interstate commerce."

Korematsu v. United States (1944) The Court held that it was not unconstitutional to impose legal restrictions on a single racial group, in this case wartime measures prohibiting persons of Japanese ancestry from living in certain areas.

Lochner v. New York (1905) Seeking to protect business from government regulation, the Court invalidated a New York State law regulating the sanitary conditions and hours of labor of bakers on the grounds that the law interfered with liberty of contract.

Loving v. Virginia (1967) The Court invalidated a Virginia statute prohibiting interracial marriages, on the grounds that the statute violated guarantees of due process and equal protection contained in the Fourteenth Amendment of the Constitution.

Lucas v. South Carolina Coastal Council (1992) The Court remanded this case to the state courts to determine whether the owner of a beachfront property had suffered economic loss by a zoning restriction aimed at preserving the beach and sand dunes. The Court's ruling recognized that a property owner is entitled to just compensation when a government's regulations diminish the value of private property, just as in an eminent domain proceeding.

Lujan v. Defenders of Wildlife (1992) The Court restricted the concept of standing by requiring that a party bringing suit against a government policy show that the policy is likely to cause them direct and imminent injury.

McCleskey v. Zant (1991) This ruling redefined the "abuse of writ" doctrine, thereby limiting the number of writs of *habeas corpus* appeals a death-row inmate can make.

McCulloch v. Maryland (1819) This was the first and most important case favoring national control of the economy over state control. In his ruling, John Marshall established the "implied powers" doctrine enabling Congress to use the "necessary and proper" clause of Article I, Section 8, to interpret its delegated powers. This case also concluded that, when state law and federal law were in conflict, national law took precedence.

Mack v. United States (1997) Filed with *Printz v. United States*.

Madsen v. Women's Health Center (1994) The Court upheld the decision of a Florida judge to enjoin (issue an order prohibiting) peaceful picketing by protesters outside abortion clinics, ruling that such injunctions do not necessarily constitute "prior restraint" in violation of the First Amendment.

Malloy v. Hogan (1964) The Court ruled that the right of a person to remain silent and avoid self-incrimination applied to the states as well as to the federal government. This decision incorporated the Fifth Amendment into the Fourteenth Amendment.

Mapp v. Ohio (1961) The Court held that evidence obtained in violation of the Fourth Amendment ban on unreasonable searches and seizures would be excluded from trial.

Marbury v. Madison (1803) This was the landmark case in which Chief Justice Marshall established that the Court had the right to rule on the constitutionality of federal and state laws, although judicial review was not explicitly granted by the Constitution.

Martin v. Hunter's Lessee (1816) In this case, the Supreme Court confirmed its congressionally conferred power to review and reverse state constitutions and laws whenever they are clearly in conflict with the U.S. Constitution, federal laws, or treaties.

Martin v. Wilks (1989) The Supreme Court further eased the way for employers to prefer white males when it held that any affirmative action program already approved by federal courts could be subsequently challenged by white males who alleged that the program discriminated against them.

Masson v. New Yorker (1991) The Supreme Court held that a successful libel claim must prove that an allegedly libelous author and/or publisher acted with requisite knowledge of falsity or reckless disregard as to truth or falsity in publishing the allegedly libelous material.

Metro Broadcasting v. FCC (1990) In one of its few efforts to continue some affirmative action programs, the Rehnquist Court upheld two federal programs aimed at increasing minority ownership of broadcast licenses on the grounds that they serve the important governmental objective of broadcast diversity, and they are substantially related to the achievement of that objective.

Miller v. Johnson (1995) This decision struck down a congressional redistricting plan in the state of Georgia that had purposely created black-majority electoral districts. The Court found that the creation of electoral districts solely or predominantly on the basis of race violated the equal protection rights of non-black voters in those districts.

Milliken v. Bradley **(1974)** The Supreme Court severely restricted the *Swann* ruling when it determined in this case that only cities found guilty of deliberate and *de jure* segregation (segregation in law) would have to desegregate their schools. This ruling exempted most Northern states and cities from busing because school segregation in Northern cities is generally *de facto* segregation (segregation in fact) that follows from segregated housing and other forms of private discrimination.

Miranda v. Arizona **(1966)** The Warren Court ruled that anyone placed under arrest must be informed of the right to remain silent and to have counsel present during interrogation.

Mississippi University for Women v. Hogan **(1982)** The Court, in a 5-to-4 decision, upheld the use of the Fourteenth Amendment in declaring gender discrimination illegal.

Missouri v. Jenkins **(1990)** The Court upheld the authority of a federal judge to order the Kansas City, Missouri, school board to raise taxes to pay for a school plan to achieve racial integration.

Missouri ex rel. Gaines v. Canada **(1938)** Rather than question the "separate but equal" doctrine, the Court in this case ruled that Missouri had violated the equal protection clause of the Fourteenth Amendment by not providing a law school for blacks. The ruling reiterated that states must furnish "equal facilities in separate schools."

Missouri v. Jenkins **(1995)** In this decision, part of an ongoing lower-court involvement in the desegregation efforts of the Kansas City, Missouri, school district, the Court found that a federal district court had exceeded its remedial powers in its efforts to eliminate the vestiges of past discrimination. While it did not overturn its previous decision in *Missouri v. Jenkins* (1990), the Court's opinion encouraged lower courts to withdraw from supervision of school districts when the requirements of the Constitution have been met.

Moran v. McDonough **(1976)** In an effort to retain jurisdiction of the case until the court's mandated school-desegregation plan had been satisfactorily implemented, District Court Judge Arthur Garrity issued fourteen decisions relating to different aspects of the Boston school plan that had been developed under his authority and put into effect under his supervision.

Morrison v. Olson **(1988)** The Supreme Court upheld the constitutionality of the special prosecutor law, which allows the attorney general to recommend that a panel of federal judges appoint an independent counsel to investigate alleged wrongdoing by officials of the executive branch.

Myers v. United States **(1926)** The Court upheld a broad interpretation of the president's power to remove executive officers whom he had appointed, despite restrictions imposed by Congress. (Later limited by *Humphrey's* [1935]).

NAACP v. Alabama **(1958)** The Court recognized the right to "privacy in one's association" in its ruling protecting the NAACP from the state of Alabama using its membership list.

National Labor Relations Board v. Jones & Laughlin Steel Corporation **(1937)** In a case involving New Deal legislation, the Court reversed its earlier rulings on "interstate commerce" and redefined it to permit the national government to regulate local economic and social conditions.

National League of Cities v. Usery **(1976)** Although in this case the Court invalidated a congressional act applying wage and hour regulations to state and local governments, it reversed its decision nine years later in *Garcia v. San Antonio Metropolitan Transit Authority* (1985).

Near v. Minnesota **(1931)** In this landmark case, which established the doctrine of "no prior restraint," the Court held that, except under extraordinary circumstances, the First Amendment prohibits government agencies from seeking to prevent newspapers or magazines from printing whatever they wish.

New York Times v. Sullivan **(1964)** In this case, the Supreme Court held that to be deemed libelous, a story about a public official not only had to be untrue, but had to result from "actual malice" or "reckless disregard" for the truth. In practice, this standard of proof is nearly impossible to reach.

New York Times v. United States **(1971)** In this case, the so-called *Pentagon Papers* case, the Supreme Court ruled that the government could not block publication of secret Defense Department documents that had been furnished to the *New York Times* by a liberal opponent of the Vietnam War who had obtained the documents illegally.

New York v. Quarles **(1984)** The Supreme Court made a significant cutback in the area of criminal procedure when it ruled that statements obtained in violation of the *Miranda* requirements are admissible when those statements are responses to police questions asked out of concern for public safety.

Ohio v. Akron Center for Reproductive Health (1990) The Supreme Court upheld a state law requiring parental notification before an abortion could be performed on a woman under the age of eighteen.

Olmstead v. United States (1928) The Supreme Court first confronted the issue of electronic surveillance in this case, which involved the wiretapping of a gang of rum-runners. The Court concluded that the Fourth Amendment was not applicable, because there had been no trespass of a constitutionally protected area nor a seizure of a physical object.

Palko v. Connecticut (1937) The Court decided that double jeopardy was not a provision of the Bill of Rights protected at the state level. This was not reversed until 1969 in *Benton v. Maryland.*

Panama Refining Company v. Ryan (1935) The Court ruled against a section of the National Industrial Recovery Act, a New Deal statute, as being an invalid delegation of legislative power to the executive branch.

Penry v. Lynaugh (1989) In this case the Supreme Court eased restrictions on the use of capital punishment by allowing states to execute mentally retarded murderers.

Planned Parenthood of Southeastern Pennsylvania v. Casey (1992) Abandoning *Roe*'s assertion of a woman's "fundamental right" to choose abortion, a bare majority of the Court redefined it as a "limited or qualified" right subject to regulation by the states, so long as the states do not impose an "undue burden" on women. Specifically, the Court upheld portions of Pennsylvania's strict abortion law that included the requirement of parental notification for minors and a twenty-four-hour waiting period.

Plessy v. Ferguson (1896) The Court, in this now infamous case, held that the Fourteenth Amendment's "equal protection of the laws" was not violated by racial distinction as long as the "separate" facilities were "equal."

Plyler v. Doe (1982) The Supreme Court invalidated on equal-protection grounds a Texas statute that withheld state funds from local school districts for the education of children who were illegal aliens and that further authorized the local school districts to deny enrollment to such children.

Pollock v. Farmers' Loan and Trust Company (1895) In this case involving the unconstitutionality of an income tax of 2 percent on all incomes over $4,000, the Supreme Court declared that any direct tax as such must be apportioned in order to be valid.

Printz v. United States (1997) With this ruling, the Court struck down the provision of the Brady Handgun Violence Prevention Act of 1993 that required state and local law enforcement officials to run background checks on gun purchasers. The Court found that it was unconstitutional for Congress to require state and local officials to enforce a federal law.

Red Lion Broadcasting Co. v. FCC (1969) In upholding the fairness doctrine in this case, the Court differentiated between the broadcast media and the print media with regard to the First Amendment. The Court ruled that "a license permits broadcasting, but the licensee has no constitutional right to be the one who holds the license or to monopolize a radio frequency to the exclusion of his fellow citizens."

Reed v. Reed (1971) In this case, which made gender lines in the law illegitimate for the first time, the Supreme Court invalidated an Idaho probate statute that required courts to give preference to males over females as administrators of estates.

Regents of the University of California v. Bakke (1978) This case addressed the issue of qualification versus minority preference. The Court held that universities could continue to take minority status into consideration because a "diverse student body" contributing to a "robust exchange of ideas" is a "constitutionally permissible goal" on which a race-conscious university admissions program may be predicated.

Reno v. A.C.L.U. (1997) With this ruling, the Court repealed parts of the Communications Decency Act of 1996, extending First Amendment free speech principles to the internet.

Roe v. Wade (1973) This is the famous case that rendered unconstitutional all state laws making abortion a crime, ruling that the states could not interfere in a woman's "right to privacy" and her right to choose to terminate a pregnancy.

Rust v. Sullivan (1991) In this case, the Court upheld regulations of the Department of Health and Human Services that prohibited the use of Title X family planning funds for abortion counseling, referral, or activities advocating abortion as a method of family planning.

Romer v. Evans (1996) The Court upheld the ruling of the Colorado State Supreme Court, which invalidated an amendment to the Colorado state constitution that forbid the enactment of ordinances outlawing discrimination against homosexuals.

Rosenberger v. University of Virginia (1995) This case was brought by a group of students who published a

Christian newspaper but who were refused funding for their publication by the University of Virginia's Student Activities Fund. The university argued that it excludes funding for religious activities because such funding would violate the principle of separation between church and state. A bare majority of the Court found that the university's policy violated the First Amendment guarantees of free speech and religious exercise and was not in itself a violation of the First Amendment's establishment clause.

St. Mary's Honor Center v. Hicks (1993)   Hicks accused his former employer (St. Mary's Honor Center) of discharging him for racially motivated reasons, but ultimately failed to prove, as the law requires in such cases, that the adverse actions were racially motivated. A court of appeals then held that Hicks was entitled to judgment as a matter of law because he was able to prove that all of St. Mary's proffered reasons for firing him were pretextual. The Supreme Court reversed the decision, arguing that a court may not so rule in favor of judgment for the plaintiff just because it has rejected the employer's explanation of its actions.

Schechter Poultry Co. v. United States (1935)   The Court declared the National Industrial Recovery Act of 1933 unconstitutional on the grounds that Congress had delegated legislative power to the executive branch without sufficient standards or guidelines for presidential discretion.

Shaw v. Hunt (1996)   The Court reversed the ruling of the federal district court in North Carolina, finding that the creation of a majority black electoral district in the state was unconstitutional. Race was the primary factor considered in creating the district, which was not acceptable in this case under a proper reading of the Voting Rights Act.

Shaw v. Reno (1993)   The Court ruled that a North Carolina congressional district was so irregular in its shape and clearly drawn only to ensure the election of a minority representative that it violated the Fourteenth Amendment rights of white voters.

Shelley v. Kraemer (1948)   In this case, the Supreme Court ruled against the widespread practice of "restrictive covenants," declaring that although private persons could sign such covenants, they could not be judicially enforced, since the Fourteenth Amendment prohibits any organ of the state, including the courts, from denying equal protection of its laws.

Shuttlesworth v. Birmingham Board of Education (1958)   This decision upheld a "pupil placement" plan purporting to assign pupils on various bases, with no mention of race. This case interpreted *Brown v. Board of Education* to mean that school districts must stop explicit racial discrimination but were under no obligation to take positive steps to desegregate.

The Slaughter-House Cases (1873)   The Court ruled that the federal government was under no obligation to protect the "privileges and immunities" of citizens of a particular state against arbitrary action by that state's government. This was similar to the *Barron* case, except it was thought that the Fourteenth Amendment would now incorporate the Bill of Rights, applying it to the states. The Court, however, ruled that the Fourteenth Amendment was meant to "protect Negroes as a class" and had nothing to do with individual liberties.

Smith v. Allwright (1944)   The Supreme Court struck down the Southern practice of "white primaries," which legally excluded blacks from participation in the nominating process. The Court recognized that primaries could no longer be regarded as the private affairs of parties because parties were an integral aspect of the electoral process, and thus became an "agency of the State" prohibited from discriminating against blacks within the meaning of the Fifteenth Amendment.

Stanford v. Kentucky (1989)   The Supreme Court again eased restrictions on capital punishment by allowing states to execute murderers who were as young as sixteen at the time of the crime.

Stanley v. Georgia (1969)   In reversing a conviction based on a Georgia statute, the Supreme Court held that mere private possession of obscene materials could not be made a crime even if the actual material itself was unprotected by the First and Fourteenth amendments.

Steward Machine Co. v. Davis (1937)   A case, resulting from New Deal legislation, in which the Court upheld the Social Security Act of 1935.

Swann v. Charlotte-Mecklenburg Board of Education (1971)   This case involved the most important judicial extension of civil rights in education after 1954. The Court held that state-imposed desegregation could be brought about by "busing," and under certain limited circumstances even racial quotas could be used as the "starting point in shaping a remedy to correct past constitutional violations."

Sweatt v. Painter **(1950)**   The Court ruled in favor of a black student who refused to go to the Texas law school for blacks, arguing that it was inferior to the state school for whites. Although the Court still did not confront the "separate but equal" rule in this case, it did question whether any segregated facility could be equal.

Turner Broadcasting, Inc. v. FCC **(1994)**   The Court upheld the 1992 Cable Television Act's "must carry" provision, which requires cable television systems to carry some local commercial and public broadcast stations, on the grounds that the act was not a violation of the First Amendment.

United States v. Curtiss-Wright Export Co. **(1936)**   In this case the Court held that Congress may delegate a degree of discretion to the president in foreign affairs that might violate the separation of powers if it were in a domestic arena.

United States v. Lopez **(1995)**   In this 5-to-4 decision, the Court struck down a federal law banning the possession of a gun near a school. This was the first limitation in almost sixty years on Congress's "interstate commerce" authority.

United States v. Nixon **(1974)**   The Court declared unconstitutional President Nixon's refusal to surrender subpoenaed tapes as evidence in a criminal prosecution. The Court argued that executive privilege did not extend to data in presidential files or tapes bearing upon criminal prosecution.

United States v. Pink **(1942)**   The Court ruled that executive agreements have the same legal status as treaties, despite the fact that they do not require the "advice and consent" of the Senate.

United States v. Robertson **(1995)**   This unanimous decision upheld the use of a federal racketeering law against the owner of an Alaskan gold mine. Handed down only a week after *U.S. v. Lopez*, this case signaled that the Court was not prepared to narrow significantly the broad interpretation of "interstate commerce" that gives Congress wide regulatory power.

United Steelworkers v. Weber **(1979)**   In rejecting the claim of a white employee who had been denied a place in a training program in which half the spots were reserved for black employees, the Supreme Court claimed that Title VII of the Civil Rights Act of 1964 did not apply to affirmative action programs voluntarily established by private companies.

Virginia v. United States **(1996)**   In this case, the state of Virginia challenged the 1992 ruling of the Fourth Circuit Court, which found that the Virginia Military Institute's exclusion of women was not substantially related to an important governmental interest and therefore violated the Fourteenth Amendment's equal protection guarantee. At the same time the United States requested review of the Fourth Circuit's ruling that the creation of the Virginia Women's Institute for Leadership (VWIL) was a satisfactory alternative for women. The Court reviewed the cross petition and upheld the lower court's decision regarding the violation of the equal protection guarantee, but reversed the ruling that VWIL was an acceptable remedial plan.

Wabash, St. Louis and Pacific Railway Company v. Illinois **(1886)**   The Supreme Court struck down a state law prohibiting rate discrimination by a railroad, arguing that the route of an interstate railroad could not be subdivided into its separate state segments for purposes of regulation. In response to the need for some form of regulation, Congress passed the Interstate Commerce Act of 1887, creating the Interstate Commerce Commission (ICC), the first federal administrative agency.

Wards Cove Packing, Inc. v. Atonio **(1989)**   The Court held that the burden of proof of unlawful discrimination should be shifted from the defendant (the employer) to the plaintiff (the person claiming to be the victim of discrimination).

Webster v. Reproductive Health Services **(1989)**   In upholding a Missouri law that restricted the use of public medical facilities for abortion, the Court opened the way for states to again limit the availability of abortions.

Wickard v. Filburn **(1942)**   In this case, the Supreme Court established the "cumulative effect" principle. The Court held that Congress could control a farmer's production of wheat for home consumption because the cumulative effect of home consumption of wheat by many farmers might reasonably be thought to alter the supply-and-demand relationships of the interstate commodity market.

Worcester v. Georgia **(1832)**   The Court ruled that states could not pass laws affecting federally recognized Indian nations, and therefore Georgia had no right to trespass on the Cherokee's lands without their assent. To which President Andrew Jackson is reported to have replied, "John Marshall has made his decision, now let him enforce it."

Youngstown Sheet and Tube Co. v. Sawyer **(1952)**   This case is also known as the *Steel Seizure* case. During the Korean War, when the United Steelworkers threat-ened to go on strike, President Truman seized the mills and placed them under military operation. He argued he had inherent power to prevent a strike that would interfere with the war. The Court ruled against him, however, saying that presidential powers must be authorized by statute and did not come from anything inherent in the presidency.

Acknowledgments

CHAPTER 1

Page 1 Corbis-Bettman.

CHAPTER 2

Pages 36 and 37 Corbis-Bettman.

CHAPTER 3

Pages 54 and 55 AP/Wide World Photos.

CHAPTER 4

Page 80 Reuters/Bettman; **page 81** UPI/Bettman; **page 86** Warder Collection; **page 87** AP/Wide World Photos.

CHAPTER 5

Page 101 Copyright Smithsonian Institution; **page 108** AP/Wide World Photos; **page 109** Stadt—und Universitatsbibliothek Bern.

CHAPTER 6

Pages 146 and 147 AP/Wide World Photos.

CHAPTER 7

Page 192 Warder Collection; **page 193** UPI/Bettman Newsphotos.

CHAPTER 8

Page 207 AP/Wide World Photos; **page 218** UPI/Bettman Newsphotos; **page 219** AP/Wide World Photos.

CHAPTER 9

Page 258 Courtesy of Carol Moseley-Braun; **page 259** Courtesy of Newt Gingrich.

CHAPTER 10

Pages 277 and 278 Copyright 1993 Joe Dator and the Cartoon Bank Inc.; **page 291** Courtesy of the Lyndon Baines Johnson Presidential Library.

CHAPTER 11

Pages 318 and 319 AP/Wide World Photos.

CHAPTER 12

Pages 352 and 353 Warder Collection.

CHAPTER 13

Pages 372 and 373 AP/Wide World Photos.

CHAPTER 14

Pages 412 and 413 Courtesy of the White House.

Index